D1462768

THIS BOOK BELONGS TO
John Mark Trent

PERSONALITY
SEARCHING FOR THE SOURCES OF HUMAN BEHAVIOR

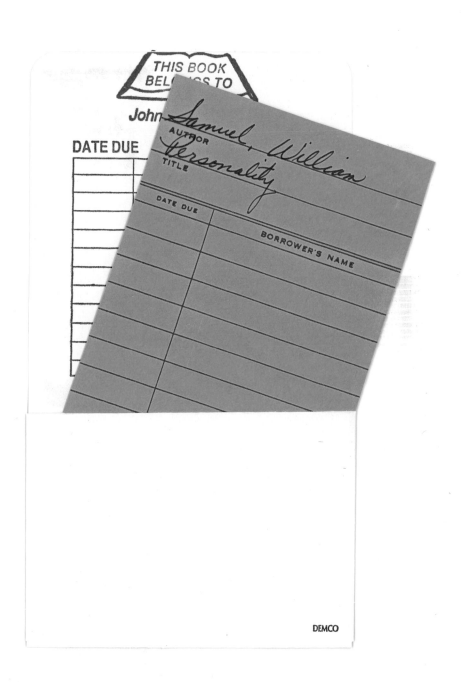

PERSONALITY
SEARCHING FOR THE SOURCES OF HUMAN BEHAVIOR

WILLIAM SAMUEL
California State University

McGRAW-HILL BOOK COMPANY

New York   St. Louis   San Francisco   Auckland   Bogotá   Hamburg
Johannesburg   London   Madrid   Mexico   Montreal   New Delhi
Panama   Paris   São Paulo   Singapore   Sydney   Tokyo   Toronto

This book was set in Trump Medieval by Black Dot, Inc. (ECU).
The editors were Patricia S. Nave, Janis M. Yates, and David Dunham;
the designer was Joan E. O'Connor;
the production supervisor was Dominick Petrellese.
The photo editor was Linda Gutierrez;
cover photo by United Press International Inc.
The drawings were done by Fine Line Illustrations, Inc.
R. R. Donnelley & Sons Company was printer and binder.

PERSONALITY
Searching for the Sources of Human Behavior

1234567890 DODO 8987654321

Library of Congress Cataloging in Publication Data

Samuel, William, date
    Personality, searching for the sources of human
behavior.

    Bibliography: p.
    Includes index.
    1. Personality. I. Title.
BF698.S229   155.2   80-19791
ISBN 0-07-054520-0

CONTENTS

PREFACE

Most of us, when we are speaking in general terms, would probably agree that no single point of view can capture all the facets of so complex a gem as human personality. When the discussion gets down to specifics, though, we often find that psychologists, as well as the general public, begin to speak from fairly polarized positions. Is there an unconscious portion of the mind? Do human beings possess a capacity for free will? Do biologically based motivations influence our behavior? These are just a few issues that continue to be vigorously debated.

Psychoanalytic, trait-dispositional, and behavioral approaches to the study of personality have each enjoyed their heyday of dominance over the field. After an initial burst of enthusiasm, each approach has been greeted with increasing skepticism as its early claims of all-inclusiveness proved to be somewhat overstated. Humanistic psychology, an approach that gained widespread acceptance during the 1960s, was originally conceived as a challenge to the psychoanalytic and behavioral schools of psychological thought. Like its predecessors, however, it has so far not persuaded most professionals that it offers a comprehensive model of human thought and action. Today, personality psychology is viewed from a variety of frequently conflicting perspectives by professionals clustered in somewhat competitive and even occasionally hostile camps.

Behaviorism has been the most recently ascendant approach in American psychology. A leading textbook on personality for the past decade reflects a clear behavioral preference in its selection of topics and discussion of issues. There appears to be mounting dissatisfaction with such a restricted focus, however, as can be seen in the resurgence of the "person-situation controversy" (which is given detailed consideration in Chapter 1). As a result, there is a need for a book which takes a more balanced or "eclectic" approach to the study of personality—a book which will critically evaluate all major traditions in this field but which will point out the strengths as well as the weaknesses in each and will *not* end up pronouncing just one theory, one assessment technique, or one method of research as being most "correct."

Other books have attempted to give an equal share of attention to each of the major theoretical traditions by grouping them along with their associated assessment techniques and research findings into separate, self-contained chapters or units. A serious problem with this procedure is that it makes it difficult to compare and contrast the psychoanalytic, trait-dispositional, humanistic, and behavioral viewpoints within the context of a single content area. The origins and implications of self-concept, for example, can be interpreted from each of the foregoing perspectives. The organization of the present text permits these approaches to be presented side-by-side in Chapter 10, "Emergence of the Self-Concept and the Growth of Competence," which provides a more meaningful opportunity for comparative evaluation than can be offered by a book in which the coverage of a specific topic is broken up into separate units.

The sequence of topics in this text is as follows: a general overview of the field and a discussion of statistical methods in Chapter 1, followed by theories in Unit One, assessment techniques in Unit Two, and research findings in Unit Three. For instructors who prefer to postpone statistics, Chapter 1 is conveniently divided into two self-contained parts, the second of which deals with statistics and research design. Thus, the first part of Chapter 1 could be assigned at the beginning of the course and the second part could be assigned before the class begins Unit Two. For those who like to cover a theoretical approach and its associated assessment techniques together before moving on to the next theory, each chapter in Unit One has a corresponding chapter in Unit Two. Thus, psychoanalytic theory, presented in Chapter 2, is closely associated with projective techniques of assessment, discussed in Chapter 5. Similarly, consideration of trait-dispositional theories (Chapter 3) could be followed by the chapters on objective tests and biological approaches to assessment (Chapters 6 and 7); behavioral theories (Chapter 4) could be followed by behavioral approaches to assessment (Chapter 8). Within each chapter in Unit Three, research studies relevant to a particular theoretical tradition are grouped together under a main heading. A table inside the book's front and back endpapers will assist students and instructors in tracing the continuity of a given tradition.

The broad range of areas covered in this book gives instructors great freedom to design their own courses. Regardless of the issues selected for lectures, students will find the book to be a valuable source of background information. Despite its breadth, the text, moreover, has depth and has been extensively researched and documented with many classic as well as post-1975 references. An accompanying Instructor's Manual discusses the book's coverage of various topics within each chapter, suggests alternative ways in which instructors might approach this material, and provides multiple-choice and essay examination questions.

Usually, the area of application of personality psychology has been clinical diagnosis and treatment. This has tended to focus attention on the "unhealthy" rather than the "healthy" aspects of personality. Because of my background as a social psychologist and the orientation of the journals from which much of the research evidence in Unit Three was drawn, this text is relevant for social as well as clinical applications. A good example of these features is Chapter 11, "Moral Reasoning and the Emergence of Prosocial Behavior."

In addition to neither overemphasizing or underemphasizing any major theoretical and research traditions, the book makes interesting reading. In a way, it is a kind of detective story. Where did these traditions originate, how have they been applied, and to what extent has each been supported by subsequent experience and research? The case study of Ernest Hemingway, which is introduced after Chapter 1 and continued after Chapter 14, focuses the reader's attention on a possible real-world application of issues long debated among psychiatrists and psychologists. The Hemingway case study serves to heighten suspense and interest value. It could be that this book is one which students will want to read from cover to cover without much prodding by their instructors.

Acknowledgments seem to be a natural endpoint for all prefaces, and like other authors I have many people to thank. First and foremost, I must express appreciation to Professor Norman Garmezy (University of Minnesota) who recommended that this project be pursued by the publisher and who provided detailed guidance and much-needed encouragement as the ideas on the prospectus were translated into several thousand words on paper. Academic reviewers who provided feedback on all or nearly all the manuscript included Reuben Baron (University of Connecticut), Robin Di Matteo (University of California, Riverside), Susan Filskov (University of South Florida), Lawrence Pervin (Rutgers University), and Robert Zucker (Michigan State University). Other colleagues who reviewed portions of the text in early final form were Michael Coles (University of Illinois), Ellen Dickstein (Southern Methodist University), Jeffrey Goldstein (Temple University), Robert Kaplan (University of California, Riverside), Elizabeth Kirkley-Best (Florida State University), Martha Mednick (Howard University), David Russell (Ohio University), Lee Sechrest (Florida State University), and Walter Vernon (Illinois State University). Of particular help were William Froming of the University of Florida and Susan Filskov of the University of South Florida, who permitted a preliminary version of the manuscript to be tested in their classes during Spring 1979 semester. If there is anything about this book that still stands in need of improvement, it is only because I was unable to assimilate all the good advice offered by these excellent commentators.

Richard Wright originally signed the contract for the book, but Janis Yates was the McGraw-Hill editor who saw it most of the way through to its completion. She was quite perceptive in calling attention to crucial points raised by the reviewers, very creative in finding ways of testing and improving the manuscript, and an important source of enthusiastic support. Linda Gutierrez worked diligently to provide the book with genuinely interesting photographs. David Dunham, the development editor, and Patricia Nave, the marketing manager at McGraw-Hill, have also been most helpful. The main burden of typing the final draft was borne by Connie Chiechi, who is affiliated with California State University, Sacramento; vital assistance was also provided by Verda La Rue of the University of California, Davis campus.

I should also express appreciation to my wife, Marylynn Samuel Barkley, Assistant Professor in the Department of Animal Physiology at the University of California, Davis, who served as an informal consultant on the text's physiologically related material. Equally appreciated was the patience and support of the children of our household, Donald and Janelle, who have grown up considerably during the time it took to complete this project.

Last but by no means least in this list of thanks comes you the reader. Without the time and attention that you will devote to it, the efforts of all those who contributed directly or indirectly to the making of this book would have served no purpose.

William Samuel

TO THE STUDENT

Though it may not appear to be so, the book you have in your hands is an adventure story. Somewhat like explorers of unmapped continents, the main characters in this adventure have for the past century been charting various tributaries of the stream of human consciousness and behavior in a determined search for the sources of our ideas, feelings, and actions. The mind is the dark continent about which they have sought to become more enlightened. As in the days of geographical exploration, different parties have set off from different starting points and have competed with one another in their efforts to be recognized as the "first discoverers." Each of these parties has its own view of the landscape and, consequently, its own idea of what it expects to find at the end of its journey.

Speaking in less metaphorical terms, the exploring parties I am referring to are rival schools of psychological thought. One of these is probably already familiar to you as the *psychoanalytic* orientation begun by Sigmund Freud. Another familiar grouping of psychologists, actually the dominant one in the United States, adheres to a *behaviorist* viewpoint. Psychoanalytically oriented psychologists emphasize instincts and emotional conflicts occurring within the mind of the *person* as the primary determinants of his or her thoughts and actions. Behaviorally oriented psychologists emphasize features of the social or physical *situation* in which a person is placed as the primary causes of his or her covert or overt behavior.

Still another approach to the study of human personality is taken by *trait-dispositional* psychologists, who believe that enduring aspects of one's character are formed early in life either through experiences occurring in infancy and childhood or through the action of biologically based dispositions which differ in their nature and intensity between individuals. Trait-dispositional theorists believe that it is possible for a person to make changes in his or her character as an adult, but that alterations in long-enduring traits can usually be accomplished only through special efforts. Finally, *humanistic* psychologists believe that the built-in aspects of human nature are fundamentally cooperative, kindly, and prosocial. It is only when the individual is prevented by others from expressing his or her "true self" that personality and behavior take on negative or antisocial features.

These four major approaches to the study of personality—psychoanalytic, behavioral, trait-dispositional, and humanistic—place varying degrees of emphasis on processes inside the person or forces impinging on the individual in the external situation as the mainsprings of thought and action. Such differences in emphasis have fueled a long-standing *person-situation contro-versy* among psychologists which is given a great deal of attention in the opening chapter of this book. Throughout the book, you will find that the point of view held by each major theoretical tradition receives some degree of consideration on each of the topics we will cover. My underlying premise is that each of the major traditions in personality psychology has its strengths as well as weaknesses and that a unified view is not only possible and desirable but also necessary if psychology is to advance beyond its present stage of bickering among rival schools and move on to its next major stage as a science of behavior and mental life.

Now that you know the direction I propose to take, I hope you will join with me in this quest. In the end, it will be readers like yourself who will decide whether or not we have arrived at the intended destination.

William Samuel

PERSONALITY
SEARCHING FOR THE SOURCES OF HUMAN BEHAVIOR

1.

PERSONALITY
COMPETING CONCEPTIONS
AND METHODS
OF RESEARCH

ISSUES TO CONSIDER

1 Do we decide what we are going to do on the basis of internal plans, needs, and wishes, or is our behavior entirely shaped and controlled by the external environment?
2 Are people consistent in their character traits and patterns of behavior across different time periods in their lives and across different situational settings?
3 What are the various methods by which psychologists have studied human personality, and what are the advantages and disadvantages of each?

In 1978, in Boulder, Colorado, a young man brought suit against his parents for willful negligence in their childrearing practices (Goodman, 1978). Finding himself unable to hold a steady job and a frequent inmate of mental hospitals, this 24-year-old decided that it was his parents' "intentional infliction of emotional distress" which had caused his inability to cope with life. He estimated his damages at $350,000.

This precedent-setting lawsuit was not expected to be successful, but the fact that it was brought to court at all calls attention to a fundamental conflict in our conceptions of human personality. Are we the creations of our social and physical environment, or are there forces inside us which shape our response to environmental events? If internal forces shape our behavior, do these forces consist of habits that are learned relatively early in life and carried along with us as we develop into adults, or do they consist of biological predispositions with which we come equipped at birth? Or, is there any internal force that has the capacity to over-rule environmental pressure, past habits, *and* biological predisposition and so generate behavior that is independent of any of these sources? Is there, in short, a capacity for free will which carries with it the potential for holding individuals personally responsible for the acts they choose to commit?

If human personality and behavior are entirely determined by the social and physical environment to which the individual is exposed from birth, then the young man from Colorado has some logical basis for his lawsuit. Our parents, after all, are usually the major figures in our social lives as children, and they control the physical environment in which our early development occurs. The behavior patterns we learn in childhood may be modified by later experience, but they may also persist unmodified into adulthood. If the patterns that persist turn out to be ones which hamper our efforts to cope successfully with life's problems, it follows that our early caretakers must bear the primary responsibility

for these handicaps. Consequently, a psychologically handicapped adult should be able to collect compensation from his or her parents for the damage they have done.

Of course, it could be said that there are many environmental forces which shape a child's behavior aside from those which are controlled by the parents. Untangling all these threads of influence is virtually impossible, so it is unfair to hold parents directly accountable for the actions of their adult offspring. Furthermore, as was suggested earlier, there may be internal forces which shape behavior more or less independently from environmental experience. To the extent that such internal forces are outside parental control, it would be unfair to hold parents responsible for their effects on a child's behavior.

What we are considering here is one possible implication of what has come to be known as the *person-situation controversy* in the field of personality psychology. The issue being debated in this controversy is whether the primary causes of our behavior lie inside of us—in our desires, habits, expectations, biological processes, and so forth—or outside of us—in the pressures and learning experiences provided by our physical and social environment. The former, internal causes are called *person variables*; the latter, external ones are called *situation variables*.

A PREVIEW OF SOME ISSUES AND CONTROVERSIES IN PERSONALITY

Before becoming too wrapped up in the person-situation controversy, it would be useful for us to take a preliminary look at the topics which will be covered in this personality textbook. The most logical place for us to begin is with a definition of the term *personality*.

What Do We Mean by "Personality"?

Madame de Pompadour, an old song tells us, had a "well-developed personality." In this lyric, the word "personality" has a humorous double meaning and refers, simultaneously, to Madame de Pompadour's shapely figure and to her alluring charm and social grace. When we say someone "has personality," we are usually referring to socially desirable characteristics which set that individual apart from others and cause him or her to be attractively and distinctively "different." Although psychologists prefer to use less value-laden terms when defining personality, there are still some areas of agreement between their descriptions and popular usage.

The first definition I will present is one which you are almost certain to perceive as overly detailed and complicated: "Personality is the dynamic organization within the individual of those psychophysical systems that determine his characteristic behavior and thought."

The late Gordon Allport, who wrote this definition (1961, p. 28), was a very influential theorist whose ideas are presented in Chapter 3 of this book. What, exactly, does his definition mean? By placing personality "within the individual," Allport reveals himself as having a "person" orientation in the person-situation controversy. In referring to "dynamic organization," he wishes to convey his belief that someone's diverse behaviors and thoughts are perceived by that individual as being patterned into a coherent, purposeful whole. *Personality disorder*, by implication, refers to a breakdown of this patterning so that the individual's thoughts and behavior seem disorganized, incoherent, and purposeless. The "dynamic" aspect of personality organization implies that we are always open to change as a result of new experiences and new goals, but a well-ordered personality will maintain its coherence even as it undergoes such changes. By "psychophysical," Allport means that personality is neither an exclusively mental nor an exclusively physiological phenomenon. The physical body influences the mind, the mind influences the physical body, and personality organization includes the operation of both body and mind. This process determines behavior and thought in such

a way as to shape these activities into a pattern *characteristic* of a particular individual.

Another definition of personality is proposed by a spokesman for the "situation" side of the person-situation controversy. Walter Mischel (1976, p. 2) describes personality as "the distinctive patterns of behavior (including thoughts and emotions) that characterize each individual's adaptation to the situations of his or her life." Here, the emphasis is on the environmental conditions which cause a person to experience certain thoughts and to exhibit certain behavior. The dynamic, organizational, physiological, and goal-striving features of Allport's definition are all conspicuously absent in Mischel's definition.

Both definitions use the words "characteristic" or "characterize," and there appears to be agreement that personality implies some degree of individual uniqueness. This aspect of these psychologists' definitions of personality is also reflected in the popular usage with which we began our discussion. Psychologists, though, do not apply the term "personality" solely to someone's socially desirable characteristics. They would, for example, distinguish between a hostile or antisocial personality and a friendly or prosocial one, but they would not deny that a person of either type possesses a "personality." One other implication of using the word "characteristic" in defining personality is that this must be a fairly stable feature of a given individual. In referring to someone's "personality" at all, we are implying that we expect that individual's style of thinking and behaving to be fairly consistent across time and in different circumstances. As we will see below however, psychologists with a person orientation place a much stronger emphasis on the consistency of personality than do psychologists with a situation orientation.

When we speak of a *theory of personality*, we are referring to a set of basic principles intended to organize and explain a large body of evidence concerning human behavior and thought. An illustration of the importance of theories is provided by the fact that the origins of the person-situation controversy are traceable to a rivalry between two well-known and somewhat incompatible theoretical positions.

HISTORICAL BEGINNINGS OF THE PERSON-SITUATION CONTROVERSY

Around 1900, the Austrian founder of psychoanalysis, Sigmund Freud, essentially began the person tradition in modern psychology. He maintained that instinctual desires and the interaction of conscious and unconscious mental processes were the primary determinants of behavior. He recognized that the physical and social environment (particularly the environment provided by one's parents) also influences behavior, but even here his emphasis was on how events in the external world are translated into mental processes. Mental illness, he said, is caused by unusually intense emotional conflict and can, in many cases, be cured by achieving insight into the origins of such disturbances. Freud's theory of personality was based on the principle that social customs cause us to become afraid of many of our instinctual motives and to relegate them to the unconscious portions of the mind. All behavior, Freud believed, was either the direct expression of instinctive impulses or an indirect expression of such impulses resulting from an effort of the conscious mind to exert control over its unconscious portions. Many theorists who do not accept all of Freud's ideas nonetheless follow along in the Freudian tradition of describing personality in terms of internal events, or *person variables*.

Also around the turn of the century, two American psychologists, E. L. Thorndike and John B. Watson, and a Russian physiologist named Ivan P. Pavlov began the situation tradition in psychology. By demonstrating that animals learn to respond in a predictable way to previously neutral stimuli if a particular pattern of response is consistently rewarded, these investigators called attention to the powerful effect of the environment on behavior.

Later, B. F. Skinner expounded his theory of *radical behaviorism*, which maintains that events occurring inside the person are of little importance as causes of behavior. The goal of psychology, he said, is not to understand the interplay between unconscious and conscious portions of the mind but to discover the laws by which environmental *stimuli* (S) become capable of evoking particular *responses* (R). This approach, called *S-R psychology*, regards all behavior as determined by situational constraints and represents events occurring inside the person only by a hyphen between the S and the R. Many theorists who do not wholeheartedly endorse radical behaviorism nonetheless follow along in the Skinnerian tradition of attributing behavioral differences between individuals to differences in their learning histories or differences in the immediate situations to which each is responding. These theorists believe that person variables, if they exist at all, are simply the product of past experiences with environmentally administered rewards and punishments.

Allport, author of the person-oriented definition of personality we examined in the preceding section, himself called attention to certain broad philosophical differences between European and American theories of personality (1957). Though he recognized the considerable extent to which the European and American traditions have influenced one another, he felt that they had somewhat distinct, and occasionally antagonistic, orientations toward the field of psychology. The Europeans, he said, shared a belief derived from the eighteenth-century German philosopher Immanuel Kant that every human being has an active mind which interprets environmental events and (consciously or unconsciously) initiates behavior directed toward the satisfaction of personally important desires. The Europeans were also, Allport believed, more inclined to attribute instincts or innate components of temperament to human character, and he noted that in continental Europe the term *characterology* is widely used as a synonym for the study of personality.

In America, we almost never hear the word "characterology," and it appears that American theorists place a much greater emphasis than do their European counterparts on the role of social environment in the shaping of personality. The American tradition, according to Allport, has its roots in the British philosophers John Locke and David Hume, who regarded the mind at birth as a *tabula rasa* (blank slate) which learned about itself and its environment through the association of simple ideas and experiences. In fact, Allport grouped British and American theorists into a common Anglo-American environmentalist tradition, which he contrasted with the characterological leanings of the continental Europeans.

In this book, however, a further distinction is drawn between thoroughgoing behaviorist analyses of personality within the American (as well as Soviet) tradition in psychology and the more wide-ranging, eclectic bunch of theories grouped under the heading of *personology*. Like behaviorism, personology acknowledges the influence of the social environment on individual behavior. In addition, though, personologists emphasize the importance of forces which work inside the individual to instigate behavior. Consequently, personologists call attention to the individual needs and traits which motivate a person and bring about a certain consistency or "style," in his or her actions in different situations and during different time periods. Some of these needs and traits may have a biological basis and could even be, to some extent, inherited. Others may be simply habits and emotional reactions developed within the early social environment provided mainly by the individual's parents.

Personologists, in contrast to their behaviorist counterparts, wholeheartedly accept the existence of a *self* (conscious identity), which is capable of initiating, reflecting upon, and altering personal behavior. There is a general consensus among personologists that the self, while affected both by biological processes and by the social environment, is capable of breaking, or at least modifying, the constraints on behavior which

come from these sources. Though personologists borrow ideas from both the characterological and the behaviorist traditions, personology tends to reject the view that on individual's personality and behavior are determined in any fixed or final way by either internal biology or the external environment. Perhaps the distinction between characterological, behaviorist, and personological approaches will be clearer if we explain them in terms of a real-life situation.

A Case Study in the Person-Situation Controversy

Patty Hearst, daughter of the wealthy newspaper publisher William Randolph Hearst, was kidnapped by self-styled revolutionaries from her Berkeley, California, apartment on February 4, 1974. Two months later, the captive heiress announced, by means of a tape-recorded message, that she had joined the Symbionese Liberation Army (SLA) and taken the name of "Tania." Accompanying the tape was a photograph of Miss Hearst wearing military fatigues and brandishing a weapon in front of the group's symbol—a seven-headed cobra. Within two weeks, the SLA, accompanied by "Tania," robbed a bank in San Francisco. In another tape-recorded message, "Tania" boasted that she had willingly participated in the robbery, denounced her "pig" father, and called her fiancé, with whom she had been living prior to the kidnapping, a "clown." Three weeks later, she reportedly fired an automatic rifle in order to cover the escape of two SLA members caught shoplifting in a sporting goods store. She and the remaining members of the group eluded police until September 18, 1975, when they were arrested at two locations in San Francisco.

What accounts for the transformation of Patty Hearst into "Tania" the revolutionary? Were her tape-recorded statements and illegal acts made solely in an effort at saving herself from being murdered by her captors (who had openly admitted murdering the Oakland, California, superintendent of schools)? If so, then Miss Hearst's

If you were kidnapped, held hostage, threatened with death, and exposed only to the ideas and information communicated by your captors, would your personality begin to change? These pictures of Patty Hearst, the newspaper heiress who was kidnapped in February, 1974, by a radical terrorist group called the SLA, may document such a change. At the top left, we see her as a happy teenager probably occupied more with romance than with politics. The photo above right was released by the SLA after her kidnapping, when she assumed the "revolutionary" name of "Tania" and perhaps also began to accept much of the group's antiestablishment ideology. The picture at the left was taken after her arrest in San Francisco following more than a year of eluding the police. Here she has the appearance of a cynical, hardened criminal. Finally, in the picture on the facing page, her happiness restored by a pardon from President Carter, she seems ready to resume the life she led before the kidnapping (she was, in fact, married shortly after this photo was taken).

The saga of Patty Hearst could be taken as proof of the power of the situation in determining one's personality. On the other hand, there are indications

that Miss Hearst's character traits prior to the kidnapping may have left her susceptible to being genuinely won over by the SLA ideology once she was under the group's control and all other sources of information had been cut off. (United Press International)

behavior is attributable to the traumatic circumstances of her kidnapping and the coercive situational pressures subsequently exerted upon her. Or, alternatively, did something in Patty Hearst's personality cause her to be genuinely won over by the SLA's political ideology and revolutionary program? Boulton (1975) saw the seeds of Miss Hearst's conversion in an adolescent longing for love and affection combined with a stubborn rebelliousness toward her parents and other traditional figures of authority. Much against her parents' wishes, she had become romantically involved with Steven Weed, a young philosophy teacher at her private boarding school. Upon her graduation, she and Weed moved into a Berkeley apartment and enrolled in classes at the University of California. By this and other actions, Patty Hearst placed herself in conflict with her parents and in a geographical center of revolutionary political activism some time before she was kidnapped.

Once again, then, we may ask whether the illegal acts subsequently committed by Miss Hearst were an outcome of the irresistible coercive pressures exerted on her by her captors or whether she willingly joined forces with them, as she claimed in the tape recordings. Does the situation of being held captive or the psychology of Patty Hearst as a person offer a better explanation of her behavior as "Tania"? How would the different theoretical traditions in the study of personality interpret her actions?

A characterologist would probably explain her behavior as an expression of deep-seated desires and conflicts of a personal nature. A behaviorist would emphasize the constraints placed on Miss Hearst by the situation into which her kidnappers placed her. A personologist would tend to take the middle ground, arguing that certain aspects of Patty Hearst as a person interacted with the pressures exerted by the environment in which she found herself to influence her decisions as to how she should behave.

Apparently, our institutions of government were unable to resolve these different viewpoints in a clear-cut way. Tried and convicted of her crimes in 1976, Miss Hearst exhausted her appeals in 1978 and began serving a seven-year prison term. She was pardoned by President Carter on January 29, 1979.

In the meantime, in the pages of academic journals, far removed from the drama of the Patty Hearst episode, psychologists have continued to debate the many implications of the person-situation controversy.

The Person and the Situation as Determinants of Behavior

When we describe the personalities of others, we tend to speak in terms of the beliefs, values, and behavior patterns they exhibit across situations and across time. These perceived consistencies are called *traits*. Thus if we say that a person possesses the trait of honesty, we are speaking not only of that person's internal value system but also of the behavior which he or she exhibits consistently from one situation to the next (behavior such as never telling lies or trying to cheat other people). In addition to regarding others as "honest" vs. "dishonest," we often find ourselves perceiving them as "polite" vs. "blunt," "friendly" vs. "hostile," "bright" vs. "dull," "warm" vs. "cold," and so forth.

Sometimes, especially when we are trying to form a first impression of another's personality, we may categorize that person's traits in an either-or fashion. We may perceive the individual as *either* honest *or* dishonest, bright *or* dull, warm *or* cold, and so on. Such all-or-none categorizations are called *types* rather than *traits*. When we have time to think more carefully about our perceptions, however, we are likely to become aware of the inadequacy of type categorization. Only rarely do people exhibit traits to the extreme and uncontaminated degree that would justify use of a type category to describe them. Instead, traits are generally distributed along personality dimensions such that most people exhibit them to a moderate degree, with fewer and fewer representatives being found as one moves toward the more extreme forms in which a trait may be expressed. Even on a socially valued trait like honesty, extreme forms of expression are rare and regarded as somewhat peculiar by most people. The seventeenth-century French playwright, Molière, wrote a very insightful comedy called *The Misanthrope* about a man who resolved always to tell the truth as he saw it. He quickly made enemies of his casual acquaintances because his bluntly stated opinions of their ideas, clothing styles, manners, and so on were usually not what they wanted to hear. Eventually not even his formerly close friends could stand much more of his unrelenting honesty, and at the end of the play the misanthrope decides to moderate his stand on truth-telling.

When psychologists attempt to "size up" someone's personality for the purpose of individual counseling, the interview is, and has been since the time of Freud, the preferred approach. The impressions and biographical information gathered in interviews are, however, frequently supplemented by information gathered from tests designed to expose hidden emotional conflicts or measure an individual's expression of personality traits. The inferences drawn from interviews and tests regarding the nature of someone's character and how it relates to that individual's overt behavior fall within the person tradition of psychology.

Advocates of the situation tradition have been highly critical of this approach to the study of personality. Mischel (1968, 1973), a prominent spokesman for the situational point of view, claims that scores on personality tests have been found to be only very weakly related to actual behavior. This, he says, implies that the probability of reward or punishment in an immediate situation is a much more powerful determinant of behavior than are any internal personality traits of the individual. Furthermore, he sees little evidence that either traits *or* actual behavior are as consistent across time and different situations as the person tradition holds them to be.

To return to our example of "honesty" vs. "dishonesty," a study often cited as supporting the situational viewpoint explored the consistency of children's resistance to temptations to cheat in a wide variety of social situations (Hartshorne & May, 1928). One such situation consisted of allowing children to score their own true-false tests; another provided them with an opportunity to cheat in an athletic contest. The investigators found little evidence of consistency in dishonest behavior from one situation to the next. It seemed that there was no strong personality trait of "honesty" vs. "dishonesty" which guided individual behavior in different environmental settings. A child who cheated in one situation might very well refrain from cheating in another. Burton (1963) reanalyzed this study and did find some evidence of individual consistency across situations. The relationships were not strong, however, and did not substantially alter the earlier conclusion that resistance to temptation is more situation-specific than it is a basic personality trait.

Other traits besides honesty have been found to be unstable across time and situational contexts. Such disappointing findings led one psychologist to abandon ten years' research on personality traits and conclude that "traditional conceptions of personality as internal behavior dispositions were inadequate and insufficient" (Peterson, 1968, p. 23).

Replying to the criticism and pessimism, Rabin (1977) reviewed evidence gathered in investigations by himself and others which indicated that feelings, beliefs, values, and behavior did show considerable consistency from childhood through adolescence to adulthood. In one of these investigations, Tuddenham (1959) reported that ratings of personality derived from interviewers' impressions of seventy-two individuals examined in adolescence and again at the age of 33 were generally consistent. The traits which showed the most stability were aggressive motivation (in the men) and desire for social prestige (in the women). Kagan and Moss (1962) examined the results of repeated observations of a sample of forty-four males and forty-five females made from birth through about 25 years of age. Observers' ratings were supplemented by scores on various personality tests. Passivity and aggression against peers were stable traits in both sexes at all stages of maturity. Dominance, competitiveness, recognition-seeking, and actual displays of achievement in childhood were significantly related to adult achievement-striving in both sexes. Childhood anxiety in the presence of strangers and in unfamiliar situations was related to social anxiety in adulthood, especially among the males in the study. Hyperactive behavior had high stability from childhood to adulthood for boys but only moderate stability for girls.

Block (1971) used a procedure for standardizing interviewers' impressionistic ratings of the personalities of 170 young men and women at three different time periods: junior high school, senior high school, and adulthood. His results agreed with those of Kagan and Moss in that they showed consistency in four tendencies: (1) to withdraw from failure, (2) to become angry at others, (3) to become anxious in social encounters, and (4) to strive for achievement. He also noted, however, that some traits were not at all consistent from one time period to the next, and he suggested that these traits might be somewhat situation-specific. In addition, despite the overall evidence for consistency of personality, there were some individuals in this study who showed great changes in personality from adolescence to adulthood—perhaps because of changes in their physical and social environments.

The Usefulness of Research Findings for Understanding Personality

The work described in the preceding paragraphs suggests that one way to resolve the person-

Social anxiety and a tendency to withdraw from others appears to be a fairly stable trait from childhood onward. (Sybil Sheldon/Monkmeyer)

situation controversy might be to examine the individual personality traits and overt behavior of a group of people across time and across different situations. Evidence of consistency in personality would support the person viewpoint; evidence for inconsistency in personality would support the situation viewpoint. Unfortunately, research seldom provides a clear-cut answer to complex questions like the ones we have been asking.

Psychological research is sometimes ridiculed for alleged triviality. Senator William Proxmire has publicly bestowed "Golden Fleece Awards" symbolic of a waste of the taxpayer's money on federally funded investigations into the origins of romantic love and the tendency to clench one's jaw when angry. In a more humorous vein, newspaper columnist Art Buchwald (1979) lampooned personality research by describing the differences between persons owning odd- and even-numbered license plates which had supposedly been revealed in a study conducted by a renowned "auto-psychologist." Among other things, he wrote, it was discovered that male owners of cars bearing odd-numbered plates "have strong convictions about the price of gasoline and need constant soothing and sympathy to calm them down. . . . They make good companions and get depressed only on even-numbered days when they become unstable and self-pitying." Female owners of odd-numbered plates, "while excellent bed companions, had trouble staying on the right side of the road." Even-numbered women, on the other hand, "are bored with their lives and have fantasies about being married to a man with an odd-numbered license plate." Meanwhile, even-numbered men "usually had strong mothers and are afraid of women gas station attendants."

Despite its limitations and the serious or light-hearted criticisms which have been made of its value and validity, research (the gathering of evidence in a systematic way) remains a powerful tool. As research evidence accumulates, an informed consensus is likely to emerge regarding the most plausible solution to a problem. While research may never be able to provide a firm and final answer to the person-situation controversy, it can help to organize our thinking on this and other important topics. Consequently, it is useful for students to gain an appreciation of the manner in which evidence is gathered and evaluated by personality psychologists. The second major division of this chapter (starting with "Methods of Research") examines the various approaches taken toward personality research. This section need not be read prior to beginning Unit One, which deals with personality theories. It should, however, be read before beginning Units Two and Three. If you want to postpone your close encounter with research methods and statistical analysis, you should skip to Chapter 2 after reading the next two sections, which suggest a tentative resolution of the person-situation controversy and provide a preview of the organization of the many topics to be covered in this book.

Can the Person-Situation Controversy Be Resolved?

What do psychologists conclude regarding the person-situation dilemma with which we are so often confronted? Do the internal characteristics of persons or the external features of the situations in which they find themselves offer a better explanation for their behavior? The question cannot really be answered, nor should it ever have been posed in either-or terms. *Both* person variables *and* situational constraints have important effects on our social and psychological lives, and our behavior usually reflects both sources of influence. This is the position taken by Bowers (1973, p. 307), who felt compelled to publish a critique of the extreme situationist viewpoint only because it "has gone too far in the direction of rejecting the role of organismic or intrapsychic determinants of behavior." The notion that person and situation variables interact with one another in determining behavior is apparently shared by other, more recent reviewers of the literature relating to this controversy (Runyan, 1978). Even Mischel, who is generally regarded as the foremost proponent of a situationist position in the person-situation controversy, has, since 1968, moved toward a greater acceptance of an emphasis on person variables: "To understand the interaction of person and environment we must consider *person variables* as well as environmental variables" (Mischel, 1977, p. 251).

Was Patty Hearst's cooperation with the Symbionese Liberation Army an outcome of her willing acceptance of the group's goals, or was it behavior compelled by threat of punishment? Were her actions a reflection of Miss Hearst as a person or of the constraints of the extreme situation in which she was placed? Both sources of influence probably had a part in determining her behavior. Such a conclusion is somewhat frustrating because it leaves us in a state of uncertainty regarding the mainsprings of human action. Despite the discomfort it causes, however, this interactionist resolution of the person-situation dilemma in the Hearst case represents an effort at confronting, rather than avoiding, a very important issue. A writer who carefully researched the history of the SLA, the biography of Patty Hearst, and the events which occurred subsequent to her kidnapping also arrived at an interactionist conclusion regarding the reasons for her collaboration with the revolutionary group (Boulton, 1975).

One person variable we have not considered here is the existence of a capacity for personal choice, or spontaneous free will. Without this capacity, all personality traits and internal physiological processes are ultimately reducible to situation variables of one sort or another. If person variables consist solely of the residues of habits learned in childhood or temperamental factors produced by inherited physiological characteristics, we need only specify how these environmental and physical forces constrain us in order to have a completely situationist model of human personality and behavior. Without a capacity for free choice, neither Patty Hearst nor anyone else can ultimately be held personally accountable for his or her behavior. We will postpone further consideration of this age-old philosophical question until Chapter 3, where we will examine humanistic and phenomenological personality theories.

A LOOK AHEAD AND A CONNECTION WITH SOCIAL PSYCHOLOGY

This book is divided into three units. The first presents theories of personality which were developed from (1) the European psychoanalytic tradition, (2) the American trait and humanistic tradition, and (3) American and Soviet behaviorism. The first two traditions have a person orientation, though they recognize that environment influences thought and action. Behaviorism has a definite situation orientation, though it has, since 1960, included more person variables in its analysis. Throughout Unit One, we will repeatedly consider the implications of one's theory of personality for the manner in which one would diagnose personality disorder and the recommendations one would make for therapeutic intervention.

Unit Two describes techniques for the assessment of personality which were derived from each of the theoretical orientations presented in Unit One. These techniques include the well-known Rorschach inkblot test, the highly sophisticated paper-and-pencil inventories, psychobiological approaches, and the functional analysis of behavior. Each technique of assessment is associated with a different style of therapeutic intervention, and Unit Two will explore these relationships.

Research in various areas of personality psychology is set forth in Unit Three. The chapters in this unit are arranged to parallel the stages of social and intellectual development through which an individual passes while growing from infancy to adulthood. Here we examine studies of the origins of temperament, language, moral reasoning, prosocial and antisocial behavior, methods of coping with stress, and sex differences. We also examine the evidence for both stability and change in personality through middle and late adulthood. Within each chapter, specific attention is called to evidence which tends to support or refute one or another of the theoretical orientations described in Unit One.

At the end of each chapter in all units is a summary, which should help you review what you have just read. You might even want to look over the summary before beginning a chapter so as to get a preview of the material to be covered and the way in which it is organized.

Those of you who have taken a course in social psychology are sure to run across much material that is familiar, particularly in Unit Three. That is no accident, since virtually all theorists believe that one's personality is mainly revealed by one's behavior in social encounters and that personality is significantly shaped by one's experiences in and emotional reactions to those encounters. The title of a leading professional publication, the *Journal of Personality and Social Psychology*, reflects the close involvement of social psychologists in the study of personality. So if the content of Unit Three appears to constitute a miniature course in social psychology as well as personality, this is to be expected given the past and present interdependence of these two fields. Even though my own professional background is primarily in social psychology, I have made a conscious effort to take the perspective of the personality side of the social-personality discipline in selecting and organizing the material for this book.

What should you get out of all the theorizing, evidence-gathering, and discussion with which you will be confronted in the next thirteen chapters? I hope that you will gain an appreciation for the complexity of the person-situation interaction in human personality and, beyond that, a sense of emerging order in what at first appears to be a jumble of conflicting theoretical positions and research findings. While human personality cannot be reduced to simple terms, its structure can be approached and, to some extent, understood by means of thoughtful theorizing, careful assessment, and patient research. Personality psychology stands at the junction of all the major areas and subareas of the field—clinical, experimental, developmental, humanistic, physiological, social, and so on. For this reason, it is encouraging to see that new techniques, new findings, and new conceptual advances have breathed life into a topic that was once, like Latin, thought to have died along with its early theorists.

METHODS OF RESEARCH

When we think about doing research in personality, two closely related methods immediately come to mind: the interview and the questionnaire. The questionnaire is no more than a self-administered interview in which specific questions are answered by selecting from among a limited number of response alternatives (usually "true-false" or "agree-disagree"). The interview techniques employed by psychologists and psychiatrists will be discussed at several points throughout this book.

Interviews and questionnaires are not the only methods employed by psychologists who study personality, however. The major alternative to these methods is the experiment, which will be discussed further on in this chapter. Another important research technique is the naturalistic observation of behavior. Sometimes, especially since the 1950s, psychologists have attempted to assess personality by examining the internal biological process which are assumed to underlie overt behavior. The latter approaches will be briefly considered once we have described the manner in which questionnaires and experiments are used in personality research.

The Questionnaire Approach

Suppose we were interested in measuring the personality trait of "assertive-aggressiveness" and studying the way it is expressed in a person's behavior. To do this, we might design a questionnaire like the hypothetical one shown in Table 1-1. As you can see, it contains ten statements. For each statement, the response that would

TABLE 1-1   Hypothetical assertion-aggression questionnaire

Circle "T" if you feel that the statement applies to you.
Circle "F" if you disagree with the statement.

T	<u>F</u>	1.	Before I act, I make sure that anything I say or do will not offend anyone else.
<u>T</u>	F	2.	When I see a person doing something I can't do, it annoys me so much that I will often say something critical just so he or she will not get too big headed.
<u>T</u>	F	3.	You often have to tell other people where to get off so they won't try to take advantage of you.
<u>T</u>	F	4.	I believe in the old saying, "Someday the meek will inherit the earth."
<u>T</u>	F	5.	It's funny, but when I meet a person who owns something that I really would like to have but can't afford to buy, I get an urge to do some kind of damage to their property.
<u>T</u>	F	6.	If you want to get anywhere in life, you have to beat other people to the best deals, even if it means hurting their feelings a lot of the time.
T	<u>F</u>	7.	In a group, I always have the best time when I let someone else hassle with all the decisions about where to go and what to do.
T	<u>F</u>	8.	If someone cuts ahead of me in line, I generally ignore it; nothing you're waiting for is worth arguing over.
<u>T</u>	F	9.	The best way to handle people is to learn how to convince them that what you want them to do is really what they want to do.
T	<u>F</u>	10.	I get anxious when I find myself standing too far out from the crowd, so I often find myself concealing my true opinions and abilities.

Note: The underlined responses are those which would reflect the trait of assertive-aggressiveness.

reflect the trait of assertive-aggressiveness is underlined. The score on this test could range from 0 to 10.

The next step in designing a questionnaire that will measure a trait is to confirm that the questionnaire is _reliable_. Most important, we want to be sure that if a person is given the same test on two occasions, he or she will obtain the same score both times. If the scores are very different from one another, it means either that there is no stable personality trait of assertive-aggressiveness or that there is some defect in the questionnaire. This technique of giving the same test twice measures _test-retest reliability._

Another type of reliability, called _split-half,_ is measured by comparing scores on different parts of the same test. We would arbitrarily divide the questionnaire in half, perhaps by taking every second item, and then look to see whether a person's score on one half matches the score on the other half. Inconsistency among the items selected for measuring a trait could be one factor contributing to low split-half reliability.

Any technique for assessing the reliability of a test involves a search for _correlations._ Since correlations play a crucial role in personality research, we must devote a few paragraphs to considering what they mean.

The Meaning of a Correlation   We can search for correlations whenever we have scores on at least two measures taken from each member of a group of research participants. Suppose, for example, that we measure the length of the right arm of each person in a group of thirty people who range in age from infants to adults. Next, we stand each person sideways against a wall and measure how far each can reach out horizontally along the wall using the right arm. We now have two scores for everyone—arm length and horizontal reach. A graph, or _scatterplot,_ showing the placement of our hypothetical thirty subjects on these dimensions is shown in Figure 1-1.

An infant whose arm is only 8 inches long will have a horizontal reach of exactly 8 inches (point A), a child whose arm is 16 inches long will have

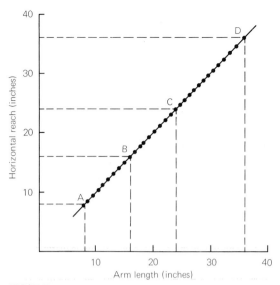

FIGURE 1-1

Measurements of horizontal reach and arm length for an imaginary sample of thirty people. The correlation between these two measurements would be $r = 1.0$.

a horizontal reach of exactly 16 inches (point B), an average adult whose arm is 24 inches long will have a horizontal reach of 24 inches (point C), while a professional basketball player whose arm is 36 inches long will have a horizontal reach of 36 inches (point D). Obviously, all 30 points will lie on a straight line pointing in a northeasterly direction. In this case the correlation, which is calculated using a formula you can find in any statistics book, will be 1. This means that we can exactly predict a person's score on one dimension, or *variable*, when we know his or her score on another variable. In other words, if I know the length of your right arm I can exactly predict your horizontal reach using that arm, and if I know your horizontal reach I can exactly predict the length of your arm. Furthermore, the orientation of the line in a northeasterly direction tells me that in a large group of people, those with long arms will have greater, and those with short arms will have smaller, horizontal reaches.

My example probably seems trivial. Of course the length of someone's right arm exactly equals that person's right-handed horizontal reach. How

could it be otherwise? One small change in the example will show us how.

Suppose we measure how high up on the wall (from the floor) people can reach using their right arms. Now we are measuring vertical rather than horizontal distance, and the distribution of scores should look something like Figure 1-2.

In general, it will still be true that people with long arms have the greatest, and those with short arms the smallest, reach. As before, the distribution of points will be oriented in a northeasterly direction, and our infant may reach only 24 inches up from the floor while the basketball player may attain 108 inches. However, the length of people's torsos and legs is not always proportionate to the length of their arms. Consequently, there will be individual *variability*

FIGURE 1-2

Measurements of vertical reach and arm length for the same group of thirty people whose data were shown in Figure 1-1. The correlation between these two measures would be about $r = .8$.

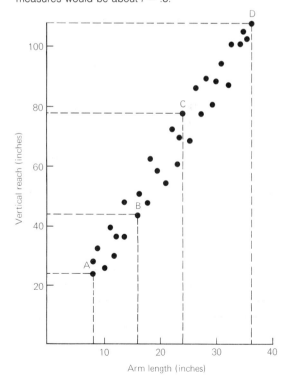

around the general tendency for short, medium, or long arms to be associated with small, moderate, or great vertical reach. Instead of a neat, straight line of points, we may get a cigar-shaped distribution which reflects individual variability in body proportions. This variability will cause the correlation to drop from 1 in Figure 1-1 to about 0.80 in Figure 1-2. A correlation of 0.80 means that there is a fairly strong relationship between arm length and vertical reach but that we can no longer make exact predictions from one variable to the other. Instead, we must make statements such as, "If a person's right arm is 24 inches long, the odds are 95 out of 100 that he or she will have a right-handed vertical reach of between 82 and 86 inches."

Now let us consider an example of a 0 correlation. Suppose we measure the lengths of the right arms of apartment dwellers in a high-rise building and then relate these measurements to their apartment numbers. The resulting scatterplot of points would probably resemble Figure 1-3. Some people living on upper floors will have long arms, but others on these floors will have short arms. Similarly, some people living on lower floors will have short arms, while others on these floors will have long arms. Knowing the length of someone's arm tells us nothing about his or her apartment number. In other words, there is no correlation between arm length and apartment number. A 0 correlation is graphically represented as a *blob* of points, like the one shown in Figure 1-3.

A correlation, then, ranges from 0 (meaning there is no relationship between the variables) to 1 (meaning that scores on one variable are perfectly predictable from scores on another variable). When you see a correlation reported in a textbook, it is usually represented by the letter *r*. Weak relationships between variables are on the order of *r* = 0.20, moderate relationships would be *r* = 0.40, and fairly strong relationships would be *r* = 0.80. Correlations increase geometrically rather than linearly in their predictive power. This means that an *r* of 0.40 is four times as powerful as an *r* of 0.20, and an *r* of 0.80 is four times as powerful as an *r* of 0.40.

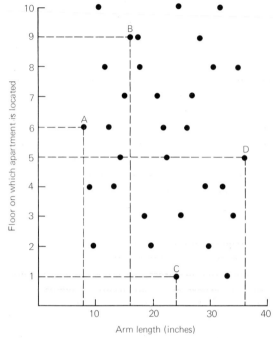

FIGURE 1-3
The floor on which a person lives in a ten-story apartment building plotted against the length of his or her right arm. The correlation between these two scores would be *r* = 0.

Correlations can be *negative* as well as positive. A negative correlation means that as scores on one variable *increase*, scores on the other *decrease*. A scatterplot of points would be oriented in a northwesterly rather than a northeasterly direction. For example, if a group of thirty people completed our assertive-aggressiveness questionnaire plus another test designed to measure the trait of shyness and introversion, we would expect to find a negative correlation. Because highly assertive-aggressive people tend to be low in shyness, while those low in assertiveness tend to be high in shyness, we might find that the *r* between assertiveness and shyness is -0.50.

Uses of Correlations As was mentioned earlier, we would use correlations to check on the reliability of our assertive-aggressiveness questionnaire. To assess test-retest reliability, we could administer a questionnaire to a group of thirty people in September and then repeat the process with the same group one year later. The correlation between the two sets of scores would be our numerical index of test-retest reliability. Usually, this r must be at least 0.70 for a test to be accepted as reliable.

Another use of correlations would be to verify the *validity* of scores on a questionnaire. Here, the question we are asking is not whether the scores are stable but whether they relate to scores on other measures of belief or behavior in a way we would expect. The concept of validity can be illustrated by a study which investigated the same trait we have been considering here (assertive-aggressiveness).

Gormly and Edelberg (1974) asked fifty-two members of one fraternity to type themselves and other members as either assertive-aggressive or not particularly assertive-aggressive in their social interactions. Each person was also asked to rate his own aggressiveness by marking one alternative on the following trait dimension:

———I am more aggressive than most people.

———I am more aggressive than average.

———I am as aggressive as many other people—average.

———I am less aggressive than average.

———I am less aggressive than most people.

This dimension can be thought of as one-item personality scale, and the validity of the scale can be checked by correlating each individual's self-rating with the number of peer nominations he or she received for being an assertive-aggressive type. When this was done, the resulting r was 0.40, indicating that people who rated themselves most aggressive on the personality scale also tended to be perceived by most of their fellow fraternity members as behaving in an assertive-aggressive manner. While the correlation does show the personality scale to have some validity, the r is only moderate in size. One interpretation of this result could be that people are only moderately accurate when they attempt to describe their own personalities.

Gormly and Edelberg also investigated another method of checking the validity of the foregoing procedures for assessing an individual's assertiveness. They selected from among the group of fraternity members the eight people most often nominated as assertive-aggressive and the eight most often nominated as not assertive-aggressive. Randomly chosen pairs, consisting of one of the former and one of the latter types, were then asked to interact in several social situations while being observed by judges drawn from an undergraduate course in the psychology of personality. The judges, seated behind a one-way window, indicated which member of a pair was probably more assertive-aggressive in his interactions with people in general. If a judge rated as assertive-aggressive a person whose fellow fraternity members had also rated him assertive-aggressive, or if a judge rated as not assertive-aggressive a person who had been typed as such by other fraternity members, this was scored as a *hit*. If, on the other hand, a judge placed a person in a category different from that to which he had been assigned by his fellow fraternity members, it was scored a *miss*.

Four different groups of judges were used to observe the interaction of the eight pairs of subjects, and the total number of judges was fifty. Judges made their ratings after observing an initial interaction (with the sound off) involving an experimenter entering the room with the two subjects and seating them on opposite sides of a table. Judges repeated their ratings (1) after observing attempts by each subject to convince the other of his position on a social issue (the sound was now on) and (2) after watching the two participate in a game which evoked assertive behavior. On the ratings made after this game, the judges scored 72 percent hits and only 28 percent misses. That is, they agreed with the assessments made by fraternity members (who were well-acquainted with the subjects) 72 percent of the time. The results are shown in Table 1-2.

People having an assertive-aggressive personality tend to behave aggressively in many types of situations. (de Sazo/Photo Researchers)

Note that totally random guessing should produce 50 percent hits. If all fifty observers simply flipped a coin to decide which member of a given pair was to be labeled *assertive* and which was to be labeled *nonassertive*, we would expect to see twenty-five hits and twenty-five misses in identifying subjects of either type. Statistics are applied to tell us how far the results Gormly and Edelberg actually obtained deviate from random guessing. This probability is shown as p in textbooks, and for the data in Table 1-2, p is less than 0.001. That is, the odds are less than one in a thousand that chance alone could produce observations that deviate as far from twenty-five hits or misses per cell as do those in Table 1-2. Usually, psychological journals require that a study show at least p less than 0.05 in its results, which means less than a 5 percent probability that the results could have been produced by chance alone. In print, this is shown as $(p < .05)$. Another way of expressing this would be to say that we must have 95 percent confidence that our results are not due to a random association between variables before we can claim to have discovered a "true" phenomenon. When the term *statistically significant* is used in textbooks, it refers to the 95 percent level of confidence.

Returning to the Gormly and Edelberg study, an even more intriguing finding than that shown in Table 1-2 is that on the very first judgment made by the observers, 65 percent hits were scored. This, too, differs significantly $(p < .01)$ from the 50 percent hits that would be expected by chance alone. Since the first judgment was based solely on behavior exhibited in a soundless social interaction, the result implies that people are fairly accurate even in their first impressions regarding the trait of assertive-aggressiveness. The authors of the study concluded that assertive-aggressiveness must be a personality trait of some stability across time and different situations if acquaintances', strangers', and subjects' ratings show this degree of agreement in their assessment of it.

TABLE 1-2 Agreement of observers and fellow fraternity members in perceiving the trait of assertiveness-aggressiveness

Observers' Perception	FRATERNITY MEMBERS' PERCEPTION	
	Assertive	Nonassertive
Assertive	36 (Hits)	14 (Misses)
Nonassertive	14 (Misses)	36 (Hits)

Source: Gormly & Edelberg (1974, p. 191).

We have seen that correlational statistics are useful for evaluating the reliability and validity of scores on a questionnaire and for investigating the stability of traits across different situations. In the next section, we will examine an approach toward research in personality psychology which is very different from the correlational one described so far.

The Experimental Approach

If we examine the statements in our assertion-aggression questionnaire (see Table 1-1), it appears that many relate to fears of appearing inadequate in comparison or competition with others and experiences of being treated unfairly by others. This observation suggests a hypothesis which can be tested experimentally: namely, perhaps the personality trait of assertive-aggressiveness develops as a kind of self-defensive reaction to life events. If this hypothesis is correct, we should be able to cause a temporary increase in practically anyone's aggressive behavior by exposure to a dose of disrespectful, unfair treatment.

Suppose we recruit a group of 20 college undergraduates for an experiment and schedule their appointments so that each will arrive at the laboratory individually. As each subject is walking down a hallway leading to the laboratory, a student accomplice of the experimenter suddenly emerges from a side corridor and bumps into the

subject, dropping a load of books in the process. For one-half of the subjects, an "insult" condition is set up. The accomplice says, "Why don't you look where you're going?" He then picks up his books and walks off muttering hostile comments about "clumsy people" who "shouldn't be allowed to walk the hallways." For the other half of the subjects, a "no-insult" condition is set up. The accomplice profusely apologizes for bumping into the subject, picks up his or her books, expresses concern over perhaps startling or hurting the subject, and departs with a cheery "Have a nice day." In other words, half the subjects are exposed to an insulting accomplice and half to a noninsulting accomplice on the way to the laboratory.

Upon arrival at the laboratory, the subject is met by the experimenter and asked to complete the questionnaire shown in Table 1-1. Suppose that ten subjects were exposed to the "insult" and ten to the "no-insult" treatment and that the results were as shown in Table 1-3. According to this table, all of the subjects in the "insult" condition scored 7 points on the assertion-

TABLE 1-3 A set of variance-free results for the hypothetical Insult-Aggression experiment

Subject Number	NO. OF ASSERTIVE-AGGRESSIVE RESPONSES	
	Insult	No Insult
1	7	3
2	7	3
3	7	3
4	7	3
5	7	3
6	7	3
7	7	3
8	7	3
9	7	3
10	7	3
Sum of scores =	70	30
Average = $\dfrac{\text{Sum of scores}}{\text{No. of subjects}}$	7	3

aggression questionnaire, while all of those in the "no-insult" condition scored 3 points. In experimental research, it is customary to use the average score (often called the *mean*) for a given condition to represent the behavior of all subjects in that condition. The average is computed by adding up the scores for all participants and dividing by the total number of subjects. Here, the average for the "insult" condition is 70 divided by 10, which equals 7; the average for the "no-insult" condition is 30 divided by 10, which equals 3. These findings would appear to support our hypothesis that aggressiveness occurs in response to disrespectful, unfair treatment. Subjects in the "insult" condition scored more than twice as high on the questionnaire as did their counterparts in the "no-insult" condition.

If you suspect that experiments do not turn out as neatly as this table in real life, you are correct. A set of more realistic-looking results for our experiment is shown in Table 1-4. Here, the *mean* for the "insult" condition is still 7, but not all subjects scored *exactly* 7. In fact only one did; the others' scores ranged from 4 to 10. Similarly, the mean for the "no-insult" group is still 3, but only two subjects actually scored exactly 3. What

TABLE 1-4 A set of more realistic results for the hypothetical Insult-Aggression experiment

| Subject Number | NO. OF ASSERTIVE-AGGRESSIVE RESPONSES | |
	Insult	No Insult
1	5	3
2	9	1
3	4	4
4	4	5
5	10	2
6	8	2
7	9	2
8	7	3
9	6	7
10	8	1
Sum of scores =	70	30
Average = $\dfrac{\text{Sum of scores}}{\text{No. of subjects}}$ =	7	3

has happened here is that subjects in both conditions are showing individual variability around the mean for their group. *Variance* is the term for this phenomenon. In specific statistical terms, variance is the sum of the squared differences of each score from the group mean divided by the total number of subjects in the group. Another very important statistical quantity is the *standard deviation*, which is simply the square root of the variance. The *standard deviation* is, literally, the average absolute difference between the subjects' individual scores and the mean score for the group as a whole.

In Table 1-3, there was no variance because all the scores in each condition exactly equaled the mean for their respective conditions. In Table 1-4, on the other hand, we see that two people in the "insult" group scored rather low (4) in assertive-aggressiveness, even though they had been provoked in the hallway only a few moments earlier. One subject in the "no-insult" group was rather aggressive (scored a 7), even though he had *not* been treated disrespectfully in the hallway. In real life, the scores in different experimental conditions usually do show this kind of overlap due to individual variability, and it poses problems when it comes to interpreting a difference in average score between conditions. Table 1-4, like Table 1-3, shows that the average score in the "insult" group was more than twice as great as the average in the "no-insult" group. The question is, how confident can we be that this difference represents a real effect of the "insult" treatment on aggressiveness and is not a result that might have arisen merely through random variation among the scores in each condition?

To answer the above question, psychologists turn, once again, to statistics. The tests used to evaluate experimental data like those shown in Table 1-4 look first at the size of the difference in average score between groups. If there is *no* difference, then we know right away that the experimental treatment had no overall effect. If there *is* a difference in average score, it must then be discounted by the amount of variability in scores within each condition. If there is no variability, even a small difference in average score may be statistically significant. If variability is high, then a very large difference in average score will be required to achieve statistical significance. As always, we must attain a 95 percent level of confidence ($p < .05$) that the effect we have observed is genuine and not the result of random variation. The statistics most often used to make this evaluation for a set of experimental data are called the t test and the F test. For the results in Table 1-4, you might see in a textbook a statement such as the following: "Subjects exposed to the "insult" treatment scored significantly higher in assertive-aggressiveness than did subjects in the "no-insult" group ($F = 5.10$, $p < .05$)."

Sampling and Other Sources of Bias

In both correlational and experimental approaches to research, the manner in which participants are selected has important implications for the believability of the results. For correlational studies, the sample must be as *representative* as possible of the population to which results will be applied. For experimental studies, representativeness is also a worthy goal, but a far more important requirement is that the sampling be *random*.

If, in our experiment, placement of subjects into conditions was accomplished by a random process (tossing a coin as a subject is walking down the hall and initiating the "insult" procedure if it comes up heads or the "no-insult" procedure if it comes up tails, for example), the results of the study would permit us to draw very strong inferences regarding cause and effect. Recall that participants in the study were subjected to identical treatment with one exception: one group was insulted after being bumped into by the accomplice in the hallway while the other group was not insulted. Consequently, if the two groups differed in their subsequent aggressiveness, this must be due to the action of the "insult-no insult" variable. If the "insult" group had not been treated disrespectfully in the hall-

In polls and surveys which use the questionnaire approach, it is absolutely essential that sampling be as representative as possible if the results are to accurately reflect public opinion. (Charles Gatewood/Magnum)

way, they would, it can be assumed, have scored as low on the questionnaire as did their counterparts in the "no-insult" group. We may infer that being insulted caused subjects to become temporarily more aggressive than they would otherwise have been.

A questionnaire, or correlational, study, on the other hand, has a more difficult time specifying what is cause and what is effect in a statistically significant association between variables. Suppose we found a correlation of $r = 0.60$ between scores on our aggression questionnaire and the frequency with which subjects in our sample reported having hostile social interactions with others. This finding could be interpreted as meaning that people with aggressive personalities are likely to engage in provocative behavior which evokes hostile reactions from others. Alternatively, it could mean that people who have been picked on and antagonized by others are likely to develop aggressive personalities as a means of protecting themselves from being bullied. Furthermore, a "hidden" factor, associated both with an aggressive personality *and* with the frequency of one's hostile interactions, could be the true source of the correlation between these variables. For instance, people who perceive themselves as members of a social out-group may feel they are treated in a disrespectful, hostile manner by others and may have developed aggressive personalities as psychological overcompensation for their out-group status. In this case, self-perceived membership in a social out-group could be the true causal factor underlying a relationship between aggression-questionnaire responses and the frequency of hostile encounters.

Whatever problems are posed by the sampling of subjects and inferences regarding cause and effect, a potentially greater source of difficulty in interpreting research results is the possibility of bias. Subject bias occurs when participants attempt to figure out what the researcher's hypothesis is and then distort their questionnaire responses or behavior so as to either support or contradict the hypothesis as they perceive it. Experimenter bias occurs when the researcher, who knows the hypothesis, unwittingly influences subjects' behavior so as to generate results which will confirm the researcher's expectations. Rosenthal (1966, 1969) has written extensively on the problems posed by bias in interpreting research results and on procedures which may be employed to minimize these problems.

Other Research Approaches

Some methods of personality research—particularly those with an "applied" orientation—call for one-to-one interaction between interviewer and interviewee, therapist and client,

or any two participants in an "encounter" group. As was mentioned earlier, however, these methods have much in common with the questionnaire approach, and the same problems that must be considered in interpreting correlations apply here as well.

For instance, if we observe that an encounter-group participant became somewhat assertive and aggressive following an insulting comment by another participant, we might interpret the "correlational" association between the comment and the hostile reaction as meaning that the former caused the latter. However, it could be that the aggressive participant had been directing hostile looks toward other participants and it was these looks that provoked the insult. Finally, maybe everyone in the encounter group is feeling hostile and thin-skinned because of some "hidden" factor, such as the room's being too hot or too crowded.

Naturalistic observation is also basically a correlational strategy. We might, for example, observe the behavior of children in a school playground and make note of the degree to which each engages in aggressive behavior (picking fights, taking away another's toys without asking, calling names, and so forth). We might then administer our assertion-aggression questionnaire to each child's parents and correlate the child's behavior with parental attitudes. A positive correlation might imply that children imitate the aggressive traits exhibited by their parents. Other methods of researching the origins of children's aggressiveness could involve making a change in an individual's life—rewarding a child with candies for punching a Bobo-the-clown doll, for example—and then looking for a change in the individual's behavior, such as an increase in the child's aggressive behavior in social interaction. This would essentially amount to applying an experimental treatment to a single subject and then comparing that subject's pretreatment behavior with his or her posttreatment behavior. Such single-subject experiments are vulnerable to many of the same problems of interpretation as are the more elaborate types of experiments described in the preceding pages of this chapter.

The number of ways in which one can conduct research in personality is limited only by the ingenuity of the investigator. When it comes to evaluating and interpreting the results of this research, however, practically all approaches can be classified as either basically *correlational* or basically *experimental*. If you are familiar with the conceptual, procedural, and statistical distinctions between correlational and experimental research, you will be well-equipped to understand the sorts of findings reported in this and other books in psychology.

Perhaps one other approach to personality research should be briefly introduced: the *biological*. Here, the emphasis is not upon the internal beliefs or environmental events which influence our behavior but upon the physiological processes which underlie our mental processing of internal and external stimuli and which activate the muscles by which we execute behavior. In the area of aggressive behavior, in particular, a great deal is known about its biological components, as will be explained in Chapter 12. Investigators who take the biological approach to research must still design studies and evaluate results, however, and two fundamental methods can again be distinguished: correlational and experimental.

ETHICAL ISSUES

Regardless of the approach to personality research selected by a particular investigator, there are certain ethical guidelines which must be followed if the work involves human participants. These guidelines are contained in a publication of the American Psychological Association (1973) and are *also* enforced by the Department of Health, Education, and Welfare of the United States government. The guidelines call for the "informed consent" of all participants prior to commencement of a research project. Partici-pants need not be told the specific hypothesis under investigation, but they must be told of any risks that might influence their willingness to participate. Physical or psychological stress which goes beyond what one might experience in everyday life is an example of the type of risk that would need to be mentioned. Even after informed consent is obtained, the subject must be told that he or she is free to withdraw from the research at any time without penalty (except, perhaps, the loss of any payment contingent upon completion of the study).

At the conclusion of the research, each participant has a right to a full explanation of its purposes and procedures. Any deceptions must be revealed, and an opportunity for asking questions must be provided. Campuses around the country have standing committees whose purpose is to review research proposals; determine the potential risks, if any, to participants; and consider requests for modification of the guidelines to fit the needs of a particular study.

There are many other ethical issues surrounding research in personality that we do not have space to deal with here. For example, many people have protested the use of personality questionnaires in personnel selection. Because of the involvement of personality psychology with the clinical notions of "health" and "illness," there is some concern that these tests may be insensitively applied for the purpose of "labeling" people and then unfairly restricting the opportunities or civil rights of those defined as *deviant*. These issues will be examined in some detail in Chapters 5, 6, 7, and 8.

THE PERSON-SITUATION CONTROVERSY REVISITED

Recall the debate with which this chapter began: Is what we do and say the result of motivations, thoughts, and impulses occurring inside of us (*person variables*), or is it a response to the constraints of the immediate situation in which we find ourselves? Do individuals show the behavioral consistency across time and situations that is implied by the term *personality trait*, or is there very little consistency in individual behavior from one situation to the next?

Mischel (1968) summarized the results of many studies bearing on this issue by commenting that correlations between a score on a personality questionnaire and actual behavior or between a person's behavior in one situation and his or her behavior in another seemed to have a maximum size of $r = 0.30$. He called this relatively weak correlation the *personality coefficient* and argued that its weakness was due not to difficulties in making precise measurements of personality and behavior but to the fact that people are simply not very consistent. Mischel concluded that the situations in which people find themselves are much stronger determinants of their behavior than are any internal person variables.

In a critique of Mischel's situationist position, Bowers (1973) noted that the impact of person variables is obscured when one adopts the experimental-research strategy preferred by Mischel and others who work within the behaviorist tradition in psychology. In an experiment, you will recall, subjects are randomly assigned to conditions regardless of their individual personality characteristics. The goal is to demonstrate that some environmentally manipulated variable (such as exposure to "insult" vs. "no insult") has a net effect on the *average* behavior of subjects in a given condition. Individual differences in responsiveness to the manipulation, which could plausibly be argued to be due to individual differences in personality, are viewed as troublesome sources of variance that may undermine the significance of a difference in average scores between conditions. By contrast, a correlational-research strategy is, according to Bowers, much more sensitive to individual differences in beliefs, feelings, and other person variables.

Bem and Allen (1974) agree that correlational methods can yield evidence of greater stability in personality traits than Mischel allowed for. They report on a study in which a group of thirty-two male and thirty-two female students completed a questionnaire designed to measure the degree to which they expressed the traits of friendliness and conscientiousness. They were also asked to indicate how *consistent* they felt themselves to be in expressing each of these traits from one situation to the next. Ratings of each participant on each of these dimensions were also obtained from parents and a close friend. Finally, behavioral measures were taken. Friendliness was rated according to the quality of the subject's participation in a group discussion and the amount of time it took for the subject to strike up a conversation when left alone in a room with a stranger. Conscientiousness was rated according to promptness in returning course-evaluation forms and the number of reading assignments completed on time. Among students who perceived themselves as being fairly consistent in expressing friendliness and conscientiousness, these various sources of information regarding their expression of the trait showed a remarkably high degree of agreement (correlations averaged about 0.50). As Bem and Allen (1974, p. 514) put it, "[Mischel's] magic + 0.30 barrier appears to have been penetrated." Among students who did *not* perceive themselves as consistently friendly or conscientious, however, the correlation between questionnaire and behavioral measures averaged only about 0.20.

Bem's research demonstrates that agreement among self-rating, peer-rating, and behavioral measures of personality will be increased if we take the individual's self-perceived consistency into account. The studies discussed earlier in this chapter, though, did not categorize subjects into groups with high and low self-perceived consistency but were nonetheless able to demonstrate a reasonable degree of stability in personality traits from childhood to adulthood and across different situational contexts. The safest conclusion, as was mentioned earlier, seems to be that personality is the product of a complex *interaction* between person and situation variables.

Students are sometimes discouraged when they learn that different researchers of the same problem often turn up different findings and arrive at divergent conclusions. Generalizing from our experiences as grade-school children learning "the three R's," we tend to assume that higher education, too, consists in learning the "facts" about some subject. Consequently, we are confused and even dismayed to discover that the closer we get to the heart of any discipline—including, incidentally, the so-called hard sciences—the more disagreement we encounter over what facts are the "true" ones. In the end, what is important for students of higher education to learn is not a collection of facts but a given discipline's procedures for generating information and evaluating its significance. Once students have learned these procedures, they are prepared to decide for themselves which facts are *most likely* to be true (we can never be certain of truth) and which theories do the best job of accounting for the available evidence.

As we will see in the chapters which follow, different theoretical approaches to the study of personality frequently employ different procedures for gathering information and place different values on various sources of evidence. The social sciences do appear to have more fundamental disagreements in these areas than do the hard sciences. Rather than becoming dismayed by such disorderliness, though, we should be challenged by the difficulty of understanding something as complex as human personality. Unlike physical objects, human personality can change even as we are attempting to observe and describe it. In the course of reading this book, you will encounter a diverse array of theories and a mountain of not-always-consistent research evidence. Your task is not to learn which theories and which evidence are "right" and which "wrong" but to give each viewpoint and each finding a share of your attention and, ultimately, to draw your own conclusions based on a reasoned evaluation of all you have encountered. At times you are bound to feel overwhelmed, but I think that by the end of the book you will feel that we have made real progress in our search for the origins of human personality and behavior.

SUMMARY

1 We often find ourselves wondering whether someone can be held personally responsible for the actions he or she commits or whether the environmental pressures to which that person was exposed compelled him or her to behave in a certain way. Before attempting to resolve this person-situation dilemma, we should define what we mean by "personality." Most definitions use words like "characteristic" or "characterize," words which suggest that the notion of personality includes the idea of individual uniqueness. Another implication of these words is that personality must be a fairly stable feature of a given individual across different situations and time periods. A *theory* of personality attempts to organize evidence pertaining to human behavior and thought according to a basic set of explanatory principles.

2 Sigmund Freud's psychoanalysis can be regarded as the source of the person tradition in modern psychology, whereas B. F. Skinner's radical

behaviorism represents an extreme statement of the situation view-point. Allport drew a similar distinction between European character-ology and American environmentalism. The present textbook makes a further distinction between American _personology_—which combines characterological and environmentalist viewpoints—and a thoroughgoing American behaviorism. The case of Patty Hearst, a kidnapped newspaper heiress who subsequently cooperated with her kidnappers, offers a real-life example of the person-situation dilemma and suggests the different interpretations of her behavior which might be made by a characterologist, a behaviorist, and a personologist.

3   When we try to form an impression of someone else's personality, we often find ourselves using type categories: "shy" vs. "outgoing," "neat" vs. "sloppy," "bright" vs. "dull," and so on. When we think more carefully about what we are doing, however, we realize that trait dimensions are more realistic than all-or-none types and that most people, in fact, represent a blend of contrasting personality characteristics. Psychologists have traditionally attempted to gather information about an individual's most prominent traits by means of interviews and tests. Critics of this approach have pointed to studies demonstrating that supposedly stable characteristics, such as honesty, actually show very little consistency across situations. Other studies, however, have examined the personalities of individuals at different time periods from infancy through adulthood and have found evidence for the stability of at least some traits.

4   Returning to the person-situation controversy with which it began, the first section of the chapter concludes that there is evidence supporting both sides of this debate. The emerging consensus is that person variables _interact with the constraints_ of the immediate situation in determining our behavior. While such a conclusion may appear to avoid the issue rather than confront it, optimism is expressed regarding the ability of theory and research to clarify the role of person-situation interactions in shaping human personality. Much of this work has been completed by researchers in the closely related field of social psychology.

5   Interviews and questionnaires are the most widely known methods by which information is gathered regarding human personality. Questionnaire measures of personality must be demonstrated to be both reliable and valid, and the main statistical technique employed in making these evaluations is called a _correlation_ (symbolized as _r_).

6   The experimental approach to the study of personality involves the creation of two standardized social settings, identical except for one crucial condition that is anticipated to have an effect on the behavior of those exposed to it. Participants are randomly assigned to the two conditions. If the experimental group, which is exposed to the crucial factor, is found to differ in its behavior from the control group, which

is treated identically except for the absence of the crucial factor, we can claim to have found support for our hypothesis. The behavior of participants in the experimental and control groups is represented by the average score for each group. The main statistical techniques used to evaluate the strength of a difference in average score between groups are called the *F test* and the *t test*.

7   A correlation between variables usually does not tell us whether or not we have observed a cause-effect relationship. An experimental procedure, provided it is not contaminated by biasing factors, is much more capable of identifying which variable caused an observed effect on behavior. While there are many different specific strategies for conducting research in personality, all these approaches can, in the end, be classified as either basically correlational or basically experimental. This is true even in research which seeks to discover the biological processes underlying human personality.

8   All research involving human participants must follow certain ethical guidelines. Obtaining informed consent and providing a complete explanation of purposes and procedures at the conclusion of a study are among such guidelines. University campuses have standing committees which review proposals for their adherence to these rules.

9   Faced with what appears to be a mountain of often conflicting data on on human personality and the divergent interpretations that are made of it, students sometimes become confused and discouraged. This reaction is unwarranted, however, since the goal of higher education in all research-oriented disciplines is not simply to learn the "facts" but to learn how to evaluate evidence and the theories which attempt to organize it.

TERMS TO KNOW

person variables	validity
situation variables	correlational research
traits	experimental research
types	experimenter bias
reliability	person-situation interaction

UNIT ONE

THEORIES OF PERSONALITY

High up on anyone's list of the greatest works of fiction produced in the twentieth century would be the writings of Ernest Hemingway. Starting in the 1920s and continuing through the 1950s, this remarkable author published a succession of novels and stories whose very titles throb with strong emotions and the drama of events in distant places *The Torrents of Spring, The Sun Also Rises, A Farewell to Arms, Death in the Afternoon, Green Hills of Africa, To Have and Have Not, For Whom the Bell Tolls,* and *The Old Man and the Sea* are a few of his best-known works. He was awarded the Nobel Prize for Literature in 1954. ▣ Often when we hear about someone like Hemingway, we find ourselves wondering, "What kind of *person* was he?" A good part of what we mean by this question consists of wanting to understand why he did the things he did and wrote the things he wrote. Learning the biographical facts of his life is a necessary first step toward achieving this understanding, but the facts alone will not tell us why his life followed a particular course. In order to answer our question, we must _interpret_ these facts, and it is here that we all become personality psychologists. As we begin this task of interpretation, we are likely to realize that the same body of evidence can be interpreted in a variety of ways. My purpose in discussing the life of Ernest Hemingway in this introduction to Unit One is to show how different theories of personality can lead to entirely different conclusions regarding the origins of an individual's actions and ideas. The theories of personality to be considered in this unit include psychoanalysis and European characterology (Chapter 2), the dispositional and humanistic approaches within the American personological tradition (Chapter 3), and American and Soviet behaviorism (Chapter 4). Hemingway was born on July 21, 1899. His father was a well-known physician in Oak Park, Illinois (a suburb of Chicago) and chief obstetrician at the hospital there. Dr. Hemingway's hobbies (he liked to be called _Papa_) included hunting, taxidermy, and cooking the family meals. His wife, Grace, was a would-be opera singer whose hopes of a career had been thwarted by eye problems. She retained her artistic interests, however, and insisted that the family's Oak Park home include a spacious music room complete with a concert stage from which she could sing to invited audiences. Besides Ernest, the offspring of this contrasting pair included four daughters and, finally, another son who was sixteen years younger than Ernest. Papa and Grace Hemingway did share one important trait: a devout Christian religiosity. Papa punished misbehavior by applying the razor strap and hairbrush liberally and by requiring that the wayward child pray on his or her knees for God's forgiveness. Despite his sternness and outdoorsman's image, Dr. Hemingway was perceived by young Ernest as somewhat cowardly and dominated by his wife (Aronowitz & Hamill, 1961; C. Baker, 1969). At the same time, Ernest strongly identified with his father's interest in the outdoors. He received his first fishing rod at age 3 and owned a shotgun by age 10. When angry with his father Ernest would hide with his shotgun in a gardening shed and take aim at Papa's head while the unsuspecting Dr. Hemingway worked in the yard. Meanwhile, Mrs. Hemingway tried to interest her son in artistic pursuits such as playing the cello. Ernest was not motivated to do well at music, and after several years of diligent pressure his mother abandoned her efforts. Ernest took up boxing lessons instead and was pulverized by a succession of professional fighters against whom he recklessly allowed himself to be matched. Hemingway's life and writings were closely interwoven with the themes of fighting and death. His very first published work, appearing in 1916 in the literary magazine of his Oak Park high school and titled "Judgment of Manitou," described a French hunter caught in his own bear trap after murdering a companion wrongfully accused of theft. The hunter shot himself rather than face the imminent attack of ravenous wolves (S. Baker, 1967). During World War I, Hemingway eagerly volunteered for military service but was rejected because of impaired vision in his left eye resulting from injuries sustained in his short-lived boxing career. He then enlisted in the Red Cross ambulance service, was sent to Italy, insisted on front-line duty, and was promptly blown up by an Austrian mortar shell. Hundreds of steel fragments were imbedded in his legs, and he had to be fitted with an aluminum kneecap, but Hemingway miraculously came through the incident with no worse permanent damage than a slight limp. Three other men standing near him were all killed by the explosion. ▨ In 1928, "Papa" Hemingway, then 67 years old and suffering from two incurable, life-threatening diseases, told his wife he was going upstairs to take a nap, calmly walked to his bedroom, and shot himself in the head with a treasured antique revolver. Shocked by his father's suicide, Ernest became even more firmly convinced that Papa was a coward and said so through one of his characters in *For Whom the Bell Tolls* (Aronowitz & Hamill, 1961, p. 25). ▨ Hemingway seems to have fought a life-long battle, literally as well as figuratively, to avoid being called a coward himself. Impulsive and quick to anger, like his father, he would answer insults or even, sometimes, mild criticisms with challenges to duels and fistfights. ▨ In addition to the wounds and broken bones received in these encounters, he experienced a long series of accidents that frequently involved damage to his head. He was gored by a bull while practicing bullfighting, badly gashed about the left eye in a taxi accident in London during World War II, and badly battered in two plane crashes while hunting for big game in Africa in 1954. (In the latter episode, his skull was fractured, and he suffered internal injuries to his spleen, liver, kidney, and vertebrae.) In an automobile accident in Cuba in 1945, a rear-view mirror support broke through the front of his skull. In 1949, a mild case of skin cancer spread across his face. ▨ It is not unlikely that these many injuries, combined with high blood pressure and a lifetime of eating and drinking to excess, adversely affected Hemingway's mind; he had always complained of tendencies toward mental disturbance (S. Baker, 1967). After World War II, he began to experience severe headaches, ringing in the ears, slowness of thought and speech, a tendency to write syllables backwards, and a hearing impairment. He also was depressed by the death of his mother, a former wife, and several close friends. During the late 1950s he was forced by civil war in Cuba to leave his home near Havana. He feared that the FBI was following him because of his support for Fidel Castro, and his periods of depression became more frequent and more prolonged. ▨ For seven months, beginning in late 1960, Hemingway underwent psychiatric treatment and was given electroconvulsive therapy, which involves passing about 100 volts of electricity across the brain from one temple to another for a fraction of a second and which is often successful in lifting severe depression. One side effect of electroshock therapy is memory loss, and Hemingway objected to a friend that the treatment was erasing the store of memories which were crucial to his success as a writer. On the morning of July 2, 1961, subject to physical and mental ailments he felt unable to resist, Hemingway accepted the "judgment of Manitou" and reenacted his father's final defeat by shooting himself in the forehead with his favorite double-barreled shotgun. How would a psychoanalytically oriented theorist account for the events in Hemingway's career? The instincts of life and death are fundamental to this theoretical approach. The death instinct is an urge to die which, when deflected away from the self by opposing life instincts, produces a desire to aggress against others. The aggressive impulse is first expressed in the male child when he falls in love with his nurturant mother, seeks to possess her sexually, and grows to hate his father as a rival. Around the age of 5, the male child, fearing castration by the father, abandons his sexual attraction to the mother, identifies with his father, and internalizes his father's moral code. The more strongly the child fears castration, the more strongly will he imitate his father's masculine traits. A psychoanalytic theorist, therefore, might say that Hemingway achieved only a partial identification with his father due to his belief that "Papa" was overly submissive to the strong-willed Grace Hemingway. Ernest adopted the superficial aspects of his father's outdoorsman image but also identified partially with his mother's artistic interests. Sensing, at an unconscious level, that his choice of a literary career represented an "acting out" of the "feminine" component of his personality, Hemingway attempted to hide the truth from himself and others by a process called *reaction formation*. In other words, he tried to be supermasculine and supertough. That this was a defensive process rather than a direct expression of the aggressive instinct is demonstrated by Hemingway's many accidents. *Masochism* (aggression against oneself) is a "feminine" characteristic in psychoanalytic theory. Hemingway had an unconscious wish to suffer and even to die, a wish which was expressed whenever his displays of masculine courage ended in "accidental" injury. Threatened as an adult by the "feminine" cowardice of his father's suicide, Hemingway resolved to be even more of a man than he already was. This false front began to collapse as his accumulating injuries and deteriorating health made it increasingly difficult for him to sustain athletic vigor. As Hemingway's psychological defenses weakened, the "feminine" side of his character intruded more and more into his conscious awareness. Unable to accept this aspect of himself or his increasing dependency on others, he first drifted into depression and then was overwhelmed by the self-destructive impulse which had waited sixty years for the opportunity to express itself directly. Behaviorally oriented theorists would regard the foregoing interpretation of Hemingway's personality as somewhat fanciful. Children, they would say, are motivated to engage in behavior and adopt beliefs that are rewarded by their parents. It is no surprise that Grace Hemingway was able to interest her son in artistic pursuits since a child's mother can dispense important rewards for any interests she seeks to encourage. Both mothers and fathers usually impose culturally accepted sex-typing on their children, however, which means that it is also no surprise that young Ernest "acted out" more of his father's than his mother's behaviors and interests. In later life he even wore a full beard, as his father had, and preferred that wives and friends alike refer to him as *Papa*. The themes of death, aggression, and the individual fighting against hopeless odds in an incomprehensible world, all of which appear in Hemingway's stories, reflect the forces at work in a society trapped between two world wars, and society provided ample rewards to authors who said what it was ready to hear. Having been rewarded for describing men of action, Hemingway incorporated the traits of his fictional characters into his own personality. As the social climate began to change after World War II, Hemingway's style of writing and behaving was no longer so enthusiastically received. The death of close friends and relatives and his accumulating physical ailments probably also made life seem less rewarding than it had been. Death might have seemed a welcome relief from intolerable discomfort, and in committing suicide Hemingway imitated yet another behavior of a valued parent. What would personologists have to say about Hemingway? On the dispositional side, they might point out that aggressiveness and depression are traits with biological and perhaps even hereditary components. Hemingway's disposition toward aggressiveness could have had a biological relationship to whatever caused his father to exhibit this trait, while his susceptibility to depression could have been a characteristic inherited from the brooding, frequently unhappy Grace Hemingway. Early experiences, such as receiving painful spankings from a parent who demanded praying on one's knees before love could be restored, might have laid the foundation for his masochistic self-destructiveness. Furthermore, Hemingway's experience of being severely wounded in World War I produced recurrent nightmares and insomnia and perhaps contributed to the personality disturbances which appeared to escalate in intensity during his later years. Finally, one might consider the possibility that damage to the brain from alcohol or external injury may have interacted with Hemingway's dispositions and traits in a manner that left him incapable of coping with the stresses which accompany advancing age. On the humanistic or phenomenological side, one can see in Hemingway's writings that his vision of the purpose of life was not to accumulate creature comforts and self-indulgently withdraw from the battles of the real world but to "fight the good fight" for causes which one intuitively feels to be the "right" ones. At the same time, one realizes that all such individual struggles are waged against very long, almost hopeless odds in a world that says it respects abstract principles of justice but is very inconsistent in living up to them. The best and cleanest fights are those waged on an individual level between man and man or, better still, between man and beast, fights in which abstract principles are involved only minimally. At the end of the struggle, one celebrates a victory or resigns oneself to defeat. Those are the ideals in which Hemingway believed, those are the themes of the books that he wrote, and that is the way he lived, and ended, his own life. Which interpretation of Ernest Hemingway's biography seems to you to be most correct? Is it necessary that one theoretical approach toward understanding his personality be right and the others wrong? Can each of the foregoing approaches provide us with valuable insights into the character of this unique human being? You will be better prepared to answer such questions after you have examined the contents of Unit One.

2.

PSYCHOANALYSIS AND THE EUROPEAN CHARACTEROLOGICAL TRADITION

ISSUES TO CONSIDER

1 How did different theorists in the psychoanalytic tradition describe the unconscious mind and its influence on personality development and function?
2 What are the implications of childhood experiences for the nature of adult personality?
3 What was a theme common to the theorists who came after Freud and who dissented from psychoanalytic principles?

Not even the most independent thinkers remain totally isolated from the social and physical environments into which they are born and in which they live as adults. The ideas of Freud and others in the European characterological tradition are most easily understood when placed in the context of the nineteenth-century society in which they developed.

As Hall (1954) observed, science in the nineteenth-century was beginning a period of rapid progress on all fronts which continues to the present day. Phenomena which had previously seemed unfathomably mysterious or even supernatural were yielding to systematic analysis and naturalistic explanation. Darwin's *Origin of Species,* published in 1859, demonstrated how the diversity of life forms on earth could be explained by the processes of evolution and natural selection, processes which might move too slowly to be directly observable but whose existence might be inferred from the fossil record. As Freud's ideas were some years later, Darwin's ideas were met with skepticism and sometimes even hostility and ridicule from a populace unwilling to accept their implications.

The second half of the nineteenth-century was, after all, the Victorian age, an era in which books on etiquette were best-sellers and biological processes were not discussed in polite conversation. Anyone who suggested that humans might be descended from lower animals or might have instincts in common with such creatures was regarded as a shockingly indecent person.

Advances in physics, chemistry, and engineering did not pose so great a threat to moral sensibilities as did work in the life sciences, and it was in the former fields that nineteenth-century science made its most spectacular progress. Electrical, magnetic, and electromagnetic energy powered new devices like incandescent lamps, the telegraph, and the telephone. Hermann von Helmholtz, a many-sided genius who formulated the law of conservation of energy, also founded a school of medicine based on the assumption that the body is a mechanical and chemical system to which the laws of physics apply. It followed that there was nothing about the human organism that could not eventually be understood by means of careful observation and the accumulation of empirical data. Ernst Brücke, who became director of the physiology laboratory at the University of Vienna in 1874 (the year after Freud entered medical school there), was a leading figure in the Helmholtz school. Brücke had a strong influence on Freud's thinking (Amacher, 1965).

This chapter will begin with and concentrate most heavily on the theories of Sigmund Freud, the man who must be regarded as the originator of what we call *the European characterological tradition.* Next, we will examine the slightly different views of two early Freudian disciples who became rivals of their teacher: Alfred Adler and Carl Gustav Jung. After a briefer presentation of the views of Erik Erikson and Karen Horney, the chapter will conclude with a discussion of *existentialism,* a unique variation on the European tradition.

The effect which social forces as well as personal life experiences have on the models of human personality constructed by these theorists will be a constantly recurring theme. Though they have all been grouped together here as characterologists, one can detect, in their successive elaborations on and revisions of Freud's original theory, a continuous movement away from the notion that personality is firmly fixed by one's biological inheritance acting in combination with one's childhood environment. The possibilities for major personality change in adulthood were first pointed out by Adler and Jung and increasingly emphasized by Horney and Erikson. The latter theorists, because they moved from Europe to the United States, form a convenient bridge to the material on American personology presented in Chapter 3. Finally, the existentialists in the European tradition raised an issue that was to become a central concern of adherents to a phenomenological position within the American tradition: namely, to what extent do individuals have a capacity for free choice which is independent of biological or environmental determinism?

FREUD:PSYCHOANALYSIS

According to an extremely thorough biography written by Ernest Jones (1961), an early follower who later became a prominent British psychoanalyst, Sigmund Freud was born of Jewish parents on May 6, 1856, in what is today a province of Czechoslovakia. His father, Jakob, already had two sons by his first marriage; Freud was the first offspring of Jakob's second marriage, at age 40, to Amalie Nathanson, who was barely 20. Jakob Freud was a wool merchant of modest means, means which were stretched even thinner by the birth of two more sons and five daughters. Through it all, it is reported, he maintained a gentle disposition and was loved and respected by his family. Nonetheless, Jakob was the disciplinarian in the household: Amalie was inclined to indulge her children. Jones (1961, p. 7) comments that during his self-analysis, Freud was able to recall several childhood interactions with his parents that may shed some light on the reasons why his theorizing took the direction it did. He recalled that, at age 2, he had felt sexually attracted to his mother when he saw her naked and that around this time he was still wetting his bed, which brought him several reprimands from his father. On one occasion, Jakob Freud became irate when young Sigmund crept into his parents' bedroom to satisfy his (sexual) curiosity.

Upon reaching young adulthood, Freud rejected a career in business as incompatible with his intellectual interests and entered the medical school at the University of Vienna in 1873. At first he occupied himself with pure research in the laboratory of the well-known physiologist, Ernst Brücke. By 1881, however, he was eager to begin a career so that he and his fiancée, Martha Bernays, could be married. On Brücke's advice,

Sigmund Freud, the founder of psychoanalysis, explored socially tabooed feelings in his patients, for example, sexual attraction or hate between a child and a parent. Two views of Freud: (top) at age 8, standing next to his father; (bottom) as an adult. (New York Public Library Picture Collection: The Bettmann Archive)

Freud took his M.D. degree and prepared himself for private practice.

Around 1883, Freud learned of the work of a German physician who had used cocaine as a stimulant to restore the vigor of soldiers exhausted from a day of hiking in the mountains (see Snyder, 1974, pp. 173-178). Trying it out on himself, Freud found that cocaine relieved his frequent fits of depression. Since psychiatrists, up to that time, had known only about drugs which suppressed, rather than stimulated, nervous activity, Freud was quick to see the career and economic benefits that could occur to him from this discovery. He wrote enthusiastically to Martha to say that they might be able to set up housekeeping sooner than they thought and also to let her know that cocaine aroused his sexual appetite. Freud prescribed cocaine to friends and patients for a wide variety of ailments, and in an article which appeared in a medical journal in 1885 he pronounced the drug totally free of addictive potential (Freud, 1885). Unfortunately, while some (like Freud) are immune to cocaine addiction, others are not. As a result of Freud's article, physicians all over Europe began prescribing cocaine for their patients, and there followed an epidemic of addiction which took more than two decades to run its course. Fortunately for Freud, he received a grant in 1885 that permitted him to leave Vienna and spend half a year in Paris studying with the famed French physician Charcot.

Charcot specialized in the use of hypnosis to treat hysterical disorders, thought at that time to be exclusively women's ailments. The hysteric typically developed her symptoms following a traumatic emotional shock. These symptoms could include partial paralysis, blindness, loss of hearing, uncontrollable shaking, or other maladies. Under hypnosis, the hysteric might remit the symptoms if ordered to do so by the hypnotist, or she might recall the original traumatic episode, which also sometimes resulted in a _remission_ (disappearance) of symptoms when the trance was lifted. Freud described Charcot's

methods to his Viennese colleagues when he returned from Paris and also noted that Charcot had discovered several cases of _male_ hysteria. Many doctors ridiculed Freud for accepting hypnosis as a therapeutic technique (it had a rather disreputable past) and for believing in the existence of male hysteria. Freud may already have lost some credibility with his colleagues as a result of the cocaine episode.

Freud nonetheless settled into private practice, using hypnosis to treat nervous disorders. He also married his fiancée, Martha, and began raising a family that eventually included six children. He was 30 years old.

Development of a Therapy for Nervous Disorder

Despite its ability to cure some of his patients, hypnosis was a troublesome technique for Freud. Many people could not be hypnotized at all, and for many others the "cures" were only temporary. Around this time Freud heard of a new method devised by a fellow Viennese physician, Joseph Breuer. Breuer simply listened while his hypnotized patients (the first was a young woman with a seemingly endless variety of symptoms of nervous disorder) talked about the emotional experiences which appeared to be related to their symptoms. Breuer found that in many cases this "talking-out" therapy effected a cure. Freud tried the technique on several of his own patients, and in 1895 he and Breuer collaborated on a volume of case studies describing their clinical successes (Breuer & Freud, 1895). Breuer, however, had developed strong feelings of attraction for his original patient (and, apparently, she for him); recollections of his painful emotional involvement in this case finally led him to conclude that it was professionally impossible for him to continue to use either hypnosis or the "talking cure." Moreover, the technique, and particularly its sexual undertones, was rapidly becoming a focus of controversy in the medical community. Despite Breuer's misgivings and eventual withdrawal from further collaboration, Freud persisted with the "talking-cure." He discovered that patients frequently expressed strong feelings of love (or, occasionally, hate) for their therapist, but he felt that the <u>therapist</u> was really only a <u>symbol</u>, or <u>substitute, for the true objects of their emotions.</u> To this symbolic expression of strong emotions Freud gave the name <u>transference</u>.

Freud also began developing a standardized therapeutic procedure. His patients reclined on a couch while he sat out of sight behind them. He encouraged the patient to relax and allow ideas to float into consciousness spontaneously; the patient was instructed to verbalize these spontaneous ideas, regardless of any embarrassment it might cause them. Freud called this method <u>free association.</u> Dreams recalled by the patient were exceptionally rich sources of associational material, and Freud found that often both he and the patient realized that dreams had a hidden, symbolic meaning in addition to their manifest content. He also found that when he, the therapist, offered his interpretation of dream symbols, his suggestions were usually rejected by the patient.

Freud decided that the origins of nervous disorders usually lay in emotional traumas experienced in childhood and that patients developed strong resistances and defense mechanisms which blocked conscious awareness of these traumas. Accordingly, his treatment became an intricate, long-term affair. The therapist could not confront the patient with his interpretation but had to exercise a subtle guidance over the course of the dialogue so that the patient would arrive at a similar interpretation after talking through and abandoning his or her resistances (Freud, 1922). Once this stage was reached, the therapist's interpretation might be expressed openly and provide the final push toward achieving insight into the origins of the patient's problem.

Since an analysis which delved only into recent memories tended to effect only a temporary remission of symptoms, Freud recommended that a thorough analysis consist of no fewer than five sessions a week for a period of months or years and that it push memories as far back as possible into childhood. The transference process might be used by the therapist to draw out

Freud's office and couch. During psychoanalysis Freud's patients would relax on the couch and verbalize whatever they became aware of. Freud and his patient would thereby uncover the patient's unconscious feelings. (Historical Picture Services, Chicago)

socially tabooed feelings of love (of a daughter for a father, for example) or hate (of a son for a father).

Because in so many of his patients hidden desires of a sexual nature were revealed to be at the core of the neurosis, Freud made the frustration of sexual impulses a cornerstone of his early theorizing. He even expounded a theory of infantile sexuality and maintained that children have both erotic and hostile feelings for their parents.

Social Reactions

If you can imagine the rigid rules of etiquette according to which Victorian Viennese society functioned, you can imagine the uproar Freud created. He was not able to publish much of his work. When *The Interpretation of Dreams* appeared, in 1900, it was ignored by professionals, and it took eight years to sell the first printing of 600 copies. Many of Freud's colleagues did not consider his views worthy of presentation at scientific meetings. In general, Freud and his followers "were regarded not only as sexual perverts but also as either obsessional or paranoic psychopaths, and the combination was felt to be a real danger to the community" (Jones, 1961, p. 299). As the word spread, Freud's private practice dwindled. In January, 1900, he wrote that he had seen no new patients in the preceding eight months and that he was in straitened financial circumstances. Despite his plight, Freud persisted with his work.

In 1902, Freud began weekly meetings in his home with a discussion group that included Alfred Adler and, by 1907 or 1908, Carl Jung and Ernest Jones. Despite his active recruitment of new adherents, Freud felt that he alone should decide what could or could not be called *psychoanalysis* because he had devised the technique and given it its name. Others were welcome to make changes, but they could not then call their methods *psychoanalysis*. It was this characteristically uncompromising stance on the part of Freud that led to the later breaks with Adler and Jung.

This, then, was the personal and social context within which Freud's theories developed. What were the specific ideas which created all the controversy that surrounded his life?

The Three Components of Personality

Since the nineteenth-century was the age of energy, Freud was careful to give the mind a source of power. The *dynamo* (generator) of personality he called the *id;* its energy supposedly comes prepackaged with each infant in the form of instincts. Each of the instincts motivates behavior that promotes individual pleasure or survival. The needs for food and water are the most obvious of these instincts, but Freud assigned paramount importance to the sexual urge. All of these instincts Freud grouped under the heading of *life instincts* (or libido). As will be explained further on, after World War I Freud gave greater emphasis to the aggressive urges and assigned as much status to the destructive impulses, or *death instincts,* as he assigned to the instincts which promote life.

Each instinct produces a need state, which disappears when the need is satisfied. For example, we get hungry, which means that energy is being accumulated in a state of internal tension. We then release that stored energy in the course of finding and eating food. We eat until we are "full" and do not think again about eating until several hours later, when our body once more requires fueling. Thus, instincts are conservative energy systems; they are also *regressive* in that they act to return the organism to an earlier state, and they are cyclically *repetitive.* The id operates on the basis of the *pleasure principle;* that is, if something feels good, the id will want to have it.

When the id directs energy toward the fulfillment of some need, this is called a *cathexis.* Not every cathexis meets with success, of course. The young man looking for love may be unable to find a willing partner and so may resort to masturbation. Freud calls such substitute activities *displacement.* Alternatively, the young man may form an image of the desired object by looking at pictures in *Playboy* magazine; this would reflect _wish fulfillment._ He might even dream about making love to his ideal partner, which would involve a special form of wish-fulfillment called *primary process.* *Primary process* means that an image of the desired goal which has been established by experience can be perceived as being the same as the goal itself and so can reduce (or stimulate) tension. Freud believed that some primary-process images could even be inborn along with the other instincts. Some modern research on the imagery and physiological processes involved in dreams is described in Box 2-1.

The ego develops after birth, Freud theorized, apparently because the evolutionary goals of survival and reproduction are not adequately served by the id. The blind operation of the pleasure principle in disregard of the competing desires of others or of environmental dangers can easily result in disaster for the individual. The ego, therefore, operates on the basis of the *reality principle* and the *secondary process.* This means that the ego postpones the discharge of tension generated by the id until it has used its special powers of reasoning and creativity to devise a plan by which the actual object (not the image) being cathected by the id can be obtained. Freud believed that the ego might even have a physiological basis in the evolutionary development of conscious control over sensory and mechanical systems by the brain's cerebral cortex (Freud, 1940, p. 104). The means by which the ego evaluates the practicality of its plans for satisfying the needs of the id is called *reality testing.*

The third structure of personality is the superego. It develops as the child assimilates and internalizes the moral judgments of parents, teachers, and peers, and so it is the last of the basic structures to be activated. The superego rewards or punishes the thoughts and deeds of the ego, just as a parent rewards or punishes a child. Excessive self-reward produces *narcissism* (overweening pride); excessive self-punishment can lead to masochism.

If the id desires something which the ego can easily devise a superego-approved plan for procuring, energy ebbs and flows easily through the psychic system and there is no personality disorder. For instance, we usually have little trouble locating food when we are hungry at noon-time, and eating lunch is not usually an emotionally disturbing experience. If, however, our id generates a cathexis for food but there is some obstacle (such as a large crowd at the cafeteria) which frustrates the ego's strategy for obtaining the food, we can easily become upset. On the other hand, if we obtain food at the cafeteria by cutting to the head of the line, our superego may punish our ego for taking unfair advantage, and feelings of guilt and anxiety may ruin our meal.

Freud believed that many personality disorders were rooted in situations which had been highly frustrating to the individual or which had evoked strong feelings of anxiety or guilt. Given the Victorianism of the middle- and upper-class Viennese society to which most of Freud's patients belonged, it is not surprising that many of their most frustrating and guilt-ridden experiences were sexual in nature. The development of personality disorders can best be explained by using an illustrative example.

The case of Anna O "Anna O" was the fictitious name given by Joseph Breuer to the patient with whom he originated his "talking-out" therapy. Jones (1961) revealed that Anna's true name was Bertha Pappenheim and that she deserved personal recognition as the discoverer of the cathartic method described below.

In 1880, Anna was an attractive, intelligent young woman of 21 who had exceptionally strong feelings of affection for her father. Anna's father was stricken with a serious, incapacitating illness during the summer of that year, and she cared for him day and night, rarely leaving his bedside. By December, Anna herself had developed a variety of ailments and hysterical symptoms. These included full or partial paralysis of three limbs, inability to take food, severe disturbances of sight

BOX 2-1

For Freud, sleep was not a period of mental relaxation from the troubles of one's waking life, and dreams were not a form of recreation for the idle mind. While some dreams are fairly simple repetitions of humdrum events of the day, many are active attempts to express a repressed desire in symbolic form. To understand the purposes of the latter dreams, it is necessary to look beneath their superficial, *manifest content* so as to discern their unconscious meanings, or *latent content.* Freud believed that dreams serve the additional purpose of protecting the dreamer from being awakened by stimuli in the external environment. Lights, sounds, odors, or tactile sensations might even be incorporated into the manifest content of the dream so that they will not disturb the sleeper.

Laboratory research on dreams began in the early 1950s, when a group at the University of Chicago discovered that at various times during the night, sleeping subjects enter periods of muscular rigidity combined with rapid eye movements called *REMs* (Aserinsky & Kleitman, 1953). The coordinated, up-and-down, back-and-forth oscillations of the eyes appear to be associated with dreaming; if sleepers are awakened during a REM period, they almost always report having been engrossed in a vivid dream. Summarizing results obtained at several sleep laboratories, Dement (1972, p. 38) noted that in 2240 instances of REM awakenings, vivid dream recall was elicited in 83 percent of the cases. If sleepers were awakened during periods when REM was absent (called *NREM periods*), vivid dreams were recalled in only 14 percent of the cases.

The striking difference between REM and NREM sleep is not so clear, however, if one defines a "dream" as any short series of thoughts or scenes which contain relatively little sensory imagery and a minimum of emotional involvement. If one applies such a definition, up to 74 percent of NREM periods may be said to contain dreams. If, instead, a dream is required to have a coherent story line, vivid imagery, and emotionally evocative content, less than 20 percent of NREM awakenings result in dream reports. These complications have led dream researchers to draw a distinction between true REM dreams and NREM *mentation* (mental activity), the latter consisting of a relatively routine replay of disconnected events and concerns from one's day-to-day waking life.

The transmission of nervous impulses in the brain is partly an electrical and partly a chemical process. The changes in electrical potential associated with this process can be measured at the surface of the scalp (using a highly sensitive recording instrument called an *electroencephalograph*) and translated into the deflection of a pen on a piece of moving chart paper. The record is called an *electroencephalogram*, or EEG. On the EEG, the brain's electrical activity appears as a line of waves. Different types of activity are distinguished by wave patterns that differ in *frequency* (the number of up-and-down deflections of the pen that occur within a given time interval) and *amplitude* (the deflections of the pen in tracing the high and low points of each wave cycle).

When the mind is awake and alert, its EEG shows beta waves of high frequency (15 to 30 cycles per second) and moderate amplitude. As sleep commences (stage 1), the amplitude of brain waves is dramatically reduced but the frequency remains fairly high. The sleeper then passes through stages 2 and 3 to 4, which is characterized by delta waves with a frequency of less than 8 cycles per second but a very high amplitude. It takes about twenty minutes for a sleeper to enter the deep sleep of stage 4, but after ten to twenty minutes of stage 4, the pattern of brain activity begins to reverse itself through the sequence of stages until it has returned to stage 1. At this point, approximately seventy to eighty minutes after the onset of sleep, the first REM period begins: it lasts for about ten minutes, after which the sleeper descends again to stage 4. Between seventy and one hundred ten minutes later, the sleeper is back in stage 1 for a somewhat longer REM period. As the night progresses, REM periods increase in length—though always spaced about ninety minutes apart—until, near morning, a REM dream may last as long as an hour.

It is during the deep sleep of stage 4 that sleepwalking or bed-wetting are most likely to occur. REM periods are reserved for vivid dreaming, and it occurs even more frequently in infants and young children than it does in adults. Interestingly, much as Freud would have predicted, among infant as well as adult males, penile erections regularly occur during REM periods (Fisher, Gross, & Zuch, 1965; Dement, 1972, p. 26). Furthermore, subjects who are selectively deprived of dreaming by being awakened during REM periods show a *rebound* effect once the awakenings are terminated; that is, they show a considerable increase in the number of REM periods they experience in a night. Control subjects awakened the same number of times during NREM periods show no such rebound effect (Dement, 1972, p. 91). It is as though the mind has a "need" to dream, a conclusion with which Freud would have been quite satisfied.

On the other hand, there is no strong evidence that REM deprivation results in any severe psychological disturbance, even when it is carried out over as many as sixteen consecutive nights (Webb, 1975), so Freud's notion that the wish-fulfilling function of dreams is important for maintaining psychological health has not been verified by dream research. Even so, it might be noted that Singer (1975) has observed several similarities between daydreams and "night" dreams, including the possibility that there are REM-like periods, spaced about ninety minutes apart, during the daytime waking state (Kripke & Sonneschein, 1973). Subjects deprived of REM sleep at night, then, could conceivably be avoiding mental disturbance by showing a compensatory increase in their daydreams. This is just a speculative idea, but it is one which could be explored in future research.

As for the erotic or aggressive content that Freud believed was latent in most dreams, the results are even less clear-cut. Dement (1972, p. 71) maintains that the greater the time since the onset of sleep, the more likely it is that the dream's content will be related to childhood experiences rather than day-to-day affairs. Dement and others have also found, though, that dreams are often put to the task of thinking through the dreamer's unsolved problems and making plans for the future. In a study by Grieser, Greenberg, and Harrison (1972), college students had been unable to solve a set of difficult anagram problems presented to them as a highly reliable test of their intelligence and scholastic ability. The subjects then went to sleep, and their brain waves were monitored. Half of the students were REM-deprived; the others were awakened an equal number of times during NREM periods. The following morning, the REM-deprived subjects were not able to recall as many of the failed anagrams as were those who had been permitted to dream about their ego-threatening experience.

To sum up, it appears that several of Freud's hypotheses regarding dreams do find support in the results from laboratory research. The content of a dream, though, may be based on any of a number of concerns or events in a person's life. It can even be influenced by such transient stimuli as a fine spray of water on the dreamer's face during the REM period (Dement, 1972, p. 67). If a person happens to be troubled with problems of a sexual or aggressive nature—as all of us are at one time or another in our lives—these problems are likely to be reflected in dream content. Research has by no means demonstrated that dreams always—or even usually—incorporate latent erotic or hostile themes. It is even conceivable that some dreams serve no purpose beyond providing entertainment during an otherwise rather boring eight-hour period of repose.

---

and speech, and fits of coughing (the latter being the immediate reason for Breuer's being called in on the case). The patient also had a double personality—one being fairly normal and the other embodying the naughtiness of a troublesome child. Transition from the former state to the latter was associated with a self-induced trance, from which Anna emerged refreshed and once again relatively normal. When Anna's father died, in the spring of 1881, her symptoms worsened. She was beset by terrifying hallucinations and nightmares and was able to communicate only in English, having suddenly forgotten her native German. Once, when she was in her trance, she related to Breuer the circumstances under which one of her symptoms first appeared; when she awakened, the symptom vanished. Anna herself labeled this procedure *the talking cure*; Breuer called it *catharsis*. To speed up the process, Breuer himself began placing the patient into a hypnotic trance and thereby successfully alleviated one symptom after another. Treatment continued until June of 1882.

A psychoanalytic interpretation of the origin of

A still from the motion picture *Freud*. Freud listens while Anna O. verbalizes the traumas of which partial paralysis was a symptom. Through the "talking cure," as she called it, her symptoms decreased. (Culver Pictures)

Anna's neurosis might be that she had a repressed desire to possess her father sexually. For a time, socially acceptable displays of affection for her father sufficed as a substitute for this desire, but his fatal illness threatened this psychic compromise and caused the eruption of full-blown neurotic symptoms. Anna transferred her love for her lost father to her therapist, and when he attempted to terminate the therapy she went into labor with a hysterical pregnancy which scandalized the community and caused Breuer to embark on a second honeymoon with his wife in order to save his marriage (Jones, 1961, pp. 148–149).

Putting Anna's case into more general terms, let us consider the various psychological possibilities for any young woman experiencing a libidinous desire to have sexual relations with her father. Not only is this desire forbidden by strong social taboos, it is also likely to meet with outright rejection by the father. Moreover, the young woman herself will probably feel guilty over having such desires in the first place (Freud called this fear of punishment by the superego *moral anxiety*). Her ego might therefore *repress* the id's cathexis for the father and confine its energy to an unconscious part of the mind. A less restrained young woman, on the other hand, might actually consider approaching her father, despite her feelings of inhibition and her fear of rejection. In this case, the girl's desire for her father might at various times be repressed and at other times allowed into her consciousness; such vacillation would be characteristic of a state of *inner conflict*. Fortunately for those who find themselves in this sort of predicament, it is also possible to achieve a satisfactory *synthesis* of the opposing forces of desire for the father and moral anxiety by developing strong feelings of *affection*, or nonsexual love, for the father. This kind of love for one's parents meets with social approval, and the young woman in this case would be said to have *sublimated* her original, incestuous desire into a motive that could be overtly acted upon without fear of punishment. To the degree that the original desire remained latent, however, the young woman might resort to *displacement* of it by marrying another man.

Note that in *sublimation*, the original love object (the father) can be retained, but the tension-reducing fulfillment of the original cathexis (sexual relations) cannot. In *displacement*, the original love object is abandoned, but sexual fulfillment is permitted. Probably the most stable synthesis would involve both sublimation *and* displacement. In some cases, the young woman might achieve a synthesis by marrying an older man who bears a strong physical resemblance to her father.

The above processes are schematically outlined in Figure 2-1. In the event that neither sublimation *nor* a satisfying displacement can be brought about, our young woman will probably be forced to repress her desire, running the risk of personality disorder as a result. What Freud called *neurotic anxiety* is the fear on the part of the ego that it will be unable to maintain the barriers it has erected to prevent conscious awareness and expression of socially unacceptable impulses. Since the vigilance of the ego is lower when we are sleeping, these impulses often emerge as wish fulfillment in our dreams. The young woman in our example might actually dream of being embraced by her father, or the wish might be cast in symbolic form (she might imagine herself galloping along on a large, powerful stallion, for example). If she remembers the dream on awakening and is able to perceive its wish-fulfilling motivation, the young woman will experience still greater neurotic and moral anxiety (Freud, 1900).

Our young woman is also likely to exhibit minor or major neurotic symptoms. The minor ones include the sometimes humorous, sometimes embarrassing "Freudian slips" that Freud made famous with his book *The Psychopathology of Everyday Life* (1901). Our young woman might lose things that her father gives her because her ego's repression of the forbidden desire

FIGURE 2-1

A Freudian analysis of the psychodynamics of a young women's sexual desire for her father. The arrows point to possible outcomes of a given psychic event.

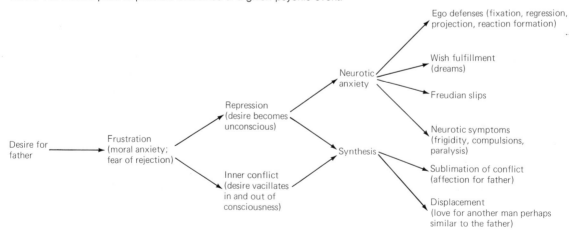

causes her to avoid thinking about him; or she may, on an evening out, call her escort by her father's name. A more serious possibility is that she may develop hysterical symptoms, including sexual frigidity, compulsive rituals such as washing her father's clothing over and over again (like the instincts which energize them, such compulsions are cyclically repetitive), uncontrollable spasms of shaking, or even full or partial paralysis.

Alternatively (or in addition), the young woman is likely to have a few defense mechanisms other than simple repression by which she can remain unconscious of her incestuous desire. She may fixate at her present stage of maturation and find ways of avoiding the step of leaving home and establishing an independent career; by remaining at home she keeps herself in the closest possible contact with her desired father. She may go further and *regress* to an earlier stage of development, becoming more childlike, or perhaps even chronically ill, so that she will be able to demand greater care and attention from her parents. Alternatively, she may *project* her desire for her father outward and begin to believe that *he* desires *her*. According to Freud, anxiety arising from internal tension is relieved by attributing its cause to some menace in the external world; in other words, it is psychologically easier to cope with objective danger (*reality anxiety*) than with neurotic fear of one's own repressed instincts. Finally, the young woman may actually come to hate her father through a process called *reaction formation*. Freud argued that since instincts form opposing pairs (life-death, love-hate, dominance-submission, action-passivity, and so on), the ego may try to disguise the anxiety aroused by one instinct by allowing its opposite to become conscious. Reactive hate or love may be recognized by its extravagant, "show-off" quality; it is generally manifested in unreasonably excessive amounts.

I should at this point reemphasize that I am using the case of Anna O as an example around which to build a discussion of neurotic symptoms and defense mechanisms. It happens that Anna developed many neurotic symptoms and simultaneously appears to have employed various defense mechanisms in her unconscious attempt to cope with her neurotic conflict, but Freud believed that practically everyone employs ego defenses of one sort or another and that use of such defenses may or may not be associated with neurotic symptoms. Similarly, the appearance of neurotic symptoms need not necessarily be associated with overuse of defense mechanisms. All these phenomena are presumably the result of greater or lesser neurotic conflict, and any or all of them may be exhibited by a particular person at one time or another.

Furthermore, let me make it clear that the example of a young woman's incestuous love for her father could be recast as a young man's desire for his mother or as the desire of one sibling for another. There is no implication here that neurosis is an exclusively feminine affliction. The dynamic mechanisms of personality are the same in everyone though a person's gender does, according to Freud, matter a great deal when it comes to personality development.

Finally, the real-life case which inspired my example, that of Bertha Pappenheim (Anna), provides considerable encouragement to women or men who might be similarly disabled. According to Jones (1961), Bertha temporarily lapsed into morphine addiction and was placed in a sanatorium after Breuer discontinued her treatment, but she successfully overcame her dependency and moved to Germany, where she became a social worker. She founded a journal and several schools, where she trained students in this profession. She worked for women's emancipation and the care of orphans. Deeply religious, she never married, and she died in 1936 at the age of 77.

Freud's revised theory The idea that instincts are matched in opposing pairs is one which occurred to Freud during the First World War. Prior to the war, he had believed that the energy of the *libido, or life instincts*, alone fueled the personality, but he came to feel that these instincts alone were inadequate to account for the destructiveness and cruelty of war. This led him to theorize that the instincts which promote life are offset by an equally powerful death instinct (*Thanatos*) which seeks to return life to an inorganic state; paramount among these instincts is an instinct for aggression. Within each of us, there is a (usually unconscious) wish to die, which may have a physiological basis in the gradual loss of cells and the breakdown of metabolic processes which accompanies advancing age.

Freud believed that anything a person does is either a direct expression of an instinct or a combination of instincts, a compromise between cathexes and anti-cathexes, or the product of an ego defense. All behavior—even mistakes, accidents, and "Freudian slips"—is thus determined by psychic conditions and activated either by present needs or by experiences occurring in the more-or-less distant past. Since civilized existence demands the suppression or concealment of so many instinctive, primary-process motivations, it follows that syntheses, sublimations, displacements, and ego defenses will be the most frequent determinants of our behavior. Since we strive to keep the instinctive forces which motivate our behavior a closely guarded secret (especially from ourselves), it follows that most of what goes on in our minds is at the level of the unconscious. The unconscious cannot be directly observed, but its dynamics can be indirectly assessed and understood by paying attention to dreams, slips, neurotic symptoms, and the free associations generated in therapy. In this respect, Freud's theory of psychodynamics was analogous to Darwin's theory of evolution, which held that the course of evolution could not be directly observed but had to be inferred from the fossil record and from the adaptive characteristics of existing organisms. Both men endured a great deal of skepticism before their theories met with any sort of general acceptance.

Freud's Five Stages of Personality Development

Three major sequential stages in childhood (oral, anal, and phallic) were believed by Freud to have a powerful influence on the adult personality (Freud, 1905). These stages are *psychosexual* in that each is identified with a different *erotogenic zone* in the infant and young child—that is, it is identified with an area of the body which, when stimulated, produces feelings of sexual pleasure.

One of the first sources of pleasure for the infant is the stimulation of its lips and mouth by the milk-giving nipple. All babies, sooner or later, experience frustration when this pleasurable stimulation is withdrawn at the time of weaning. The intensity with which the frustration is felt may have permanent effects on the child's personality. For example, a baby who is weaned early or very abruptly may develop a strong desire to hold on to things in order to avoid a symbolic repetition of the traumatic weaning experience. Traits of selfishness, competitiveness, and insecurity would tend to follow from this early experience, as well as susceptibility to depression and "giving up" when some important goal, possession, or relationship has been lost or ended. A baby who is nursed liberally and weaned late, on the other hand, is likely to develop an *oral incorporative* character, which includes traits like sociability, conformity, gullibility, openmindedness, and optimism.

The next stage, which commences with the initiation of toilet training around the second year of life, Freud called the *anal stage*. It generally provides the child's first experience with regulation of its behavior by a demanding and sometimes punitive external authority. Training which relies heavily on either punishment or praise can create problems for character formation. Severe punishment for inappropriate bowel movements may cause the child to fear these events and to try to "hold it in" for as long as possible. Alternatively, if the child receives extreme praise for a bowel movement at the appropriate time and place, the feces themselves may be perceived as having great value, and the child may hold onto them for as long as possible before giving them up. Whether it arises through excessive punishment or praise, this *anal-retentive* mode could become the prototype for obstinacy, thrift, orderliness, or an interest in collecting things.

It should be noted that Freud believed an adult may exhibit the *opposite* of the traits toward which he or she has been disposed by experiences at the oral or anal stages of development if the ego defense of reaction formation was utilized. Thus the person who was weaned early may, through reaction formation, display a very giving, nurturing style of behavior (perhaps choosing nursing as an occupation), while a reaction formation against anal retentiveness could produce wanton generosity, carelessness, or the recklessness of the compulsive gambler.

The third, or phallic, stage begins as the child experiences the sensual pleasure aroused by stimulation of the genitalia and becomes aware of differences in the appearance of male and female genitalia. Freud (1933) maintained that the boy begins to imagine himself as his mother's lover and his father's rival at this stage. He tries to seduce his mother "by showing her the male organ which he is proud to own." At the same time, he is fearful of castration by his more powerful opponent; he sees his father as thwarting his desires and would like to be rid of him. Freud called this the *Oedipus complex*, after the Greek myth of Oedipus, who killed his father and married his mother when he became king of Thebes. The boy may fear castration by his father because he has seen that his sister has no penis and so assumes that castration has already occurred once in his family. For the girl, this awareness of genitalia is all the more frightening because she is the one who has been "mutilated." For some reason (Freud never clearly stated exactly why), the girl is likely to blame her mother for her castrated condition and to develop *penis envy* for the organ she is lacking. Accordingly, she is attracted to her father and regards her mother as a rival. This female counterpart of the Oedipus complex is sometimes called the *Electra complex*, after the Greek myth of Electra, who persuaded her brother to kill her mother and her mother's lover (who had previously killed her beloved father). Freud believed that it is the hygienic activities of the child's parental caretaker (traditionally, the mother) in changing diapers, bathing, and so forth which first stimulates the child's genitalia and so awakens the sexual impulse.

The Oedipus complex is generally resolved by the age of 5, when the boy realizes that it is impossible for him to possess his mother and that the continuation of his rivalry with his father is not worth the risk of castration. Consequently, he chooses the course of *identification with the aggressor* (a term coined by Anna Freud) and tries to become as much like his father as possible. It is through this sequence of events that the male child develops a strong, sometimes excessively strong, superego. Freud believed that the development of a superego was somewhat more complicated in girls but that they eventually identify with their mothers and internalize a "feminine" value system. More will be said about sex-typing and Freudian identification theory in Chapter 13.

Once the Oedipus and Electra complexes have been resolved, the boy and the girl enter the *latency period* of middle childhood. Sexual urges do not reappear as major determinants of personality until the onset of puberty. Freud felt that the identification of each child with its same-sexed parent is always to some extent ambivalent; some hostility, as well as some desire to possess the opposite-sexed parent, remains. It is the relative strength of the identification that determines the degree of "masculinity" or "femininity" that will be manifested by the children when they become adults. All persons are to some extent bisexual in that they possess some traits of the opposite sex, owing to the (supposed) impossibility of a total identification with one parent only.

If an adequate identification has been made,

the adolescent will experience the "appropriate" feelings and be able to develop satisfying sexual relationships with the opposite sex. If no extraordinary emotional traumas occur during childhood, and if none occur during the *genital stage of adolescence,* the adult will be able to get through life by making a healthy and appropriate use of ego defenses and will probably never develop a neurosis. Freud's definition of a happy life was a combination of an intimate love relationship and a productive career through which any residual tensions might be sublimated.

Psychoanalytic Theory: A Final Overview

Freudian psychology was controversial from the very beginning and remains so today. Psychoanalysis and related formulations within the European tradition tend to cast the analyst in the role of ultimate interpreter of the true meaning of the speech, dreams, and life experiences of those around him. As the psychoanalytic viewpoint gained greater acceptance and influence, it and its most favored analytic interpretations moved in the direction of rigidity and conservatism. Catalogues specifying the meanings of a wide variety of dream images were published. This, in the minds of many observers, was carrying the process of interpretation to implausible extremes. On a social level, women who abandoned skirts for trousers and aspired to attain a level of personal freedom and economic self-sufficiency equal to that of men might, from a psychoanalytic perspective, be regarded as manifesting symptoms of psychopathology. Similarly, young people engaged in political dissent could be dismissed as acting out unresolved Oedipal conflicts arising from the breakdown of family authority and the absence of a strong father in the home (Markowitz, 1972).

Psychoanalytic theory had a tremendous influence on fields outside psychology, including the fields of sociology, art, literature, and social philosophy (see Hall and Lindzey, 1970, pp.

61–72). Consequently, to the extent that its viewpoint became institutionalized and somewhat conservative and inflexible, there were far-reaching effects. Inevitably, the theory lost popularity among those who sought a conception of human personality which was more optimistic regarding the possibilities for individual growth and social change. Freud's commitment to the idea that personality was determined by biological instincts interacting with psychosexual conflicts in childhood was regarded by many as placing excessive constraints on the goal-setting and decision-making powers of the individual. Within the European tradition, these sources of dissatisfaction with psychoanalytic theory stimulated the growth of existentialism. Within the American tradition, both humanistic and behavioral psychology developed partly in reaction to Freudian psychodynamics.

While Freud sought verification of his theoretical ideas in the clinical cases encountered by himself and his associates, more research-minded investigators attempted to test empirically various hypotheses derived from the theory. Some reviewers of this literature have found it to be generally supportive of the theory (Hilgard, 1968; Kline, 1972); others believe that it tends to refute the psychoanalytic viewpoint (Eysenck & Wilson, 1973). We will examine the evidence on which these reviewers based their conclusions in Unit Three, along with the revisions of classical psychoanalytic theory which have been suggested by this material. Thinking in this area by no means stopped with the death of Freud in 1939.

One example of Freud's creativity in applying concepts like the unconscious mind to everyday experience is his analysis of humor. While our appreciation of some jokes may be due to their ability to tease the brain with novel or incongruous combinations of words or events, he said, other jokes are funny because they relieve inner tensions created by repressed sexual or aggressive impulses (Freud, 1905a). For instance, a Caucasian American woman about to enjoy a romantic interlude with a well-known Oriental comedian said, "I never made love to a Korean guy before."

The comedian replied, "Neither have I." The set-up to the joke might be interpreted as arousing repressed antagonisms regarding interracial sexual contacts; the punch-line relieves this tension by deflecting our imaginations toward a very different type of sexual encounter between two members of the same ethnic group. Empirical investigation has verified that the more anxiety over the possible threatening outcome of a situation has been aroused, the more fully a humorous outcome is enjoyed (Shurcliff, 1968). Given the sexual or aggressive content of so much of what passes for comedy or humor in human affairs, it is difficult to dismiss Freud's explanation of these phenomena as mere speculation. While Freud has frequently been criticized for his narrow-minded focus on sexual or aggressive instincts as determinants of behavior, one must also admire the cleverness of many of his insights into human foibles.

Perhaps surprisingly, two of the earliest and most intense controversies regarding the adequacy of psychoanalytic theory occurred, not between Freud and his critics outside the psychoanalytic movement, but between Freud and two of his most loyal followers, Alfred Adler and Carl Jung. We will briefly examine the ideas of each of these men.

Alfred Adler, an early follower of Freud who later founded the rival school of individual psychology (The Bettmann Archive)

ADLER: INDIVIDUAL PSYCHOLOGY

Alfred Adler was born in Vienna in 1870, the third child (and second son) in a family which ultimately included five boys and two girls (Furtmuller, 1973). He was a frail child who suffered from rickets and other ailments and was envious of the good health and privileged status of his older brother (Bottome, 1957). By age 5, he had already been run over by carriages, twice, had witnessed the death of a younger brother, and had survived a severe case of pneumonia from which he was not expected to recover. Later in life, he was to trace his interest in medicine to these childhood brushes with death (Ansbacher & Ansbacher, 1956, p. 199).

After receiving his M.D. degree from the University of Vienna in 1895, Adler opened an office in a working-class neighborhood near the Prater amusement park. Many of Adler's early medical patients were performers at the park. These people, who displayed their athletic physiques and prowess to the general public, came to Adler for treatment of their physical disabilities and ailments (Furtmuller, 1973). The heroic efforts of these performers to overcome their deficiencies caused Adler to develop the concept of _overcompensation_, which was later to become a cornerstone of his theory of personality.

During this period, Adler encountered Freud's book *The Interpretation of Dreams*. When a Vienna newspaper ridiculed the book, Adler is reputed to have come to Freud's defense in a vigorously worded letter to the editor, though documentary proof of this has never been found (Furtmuller, 1973, p. 336). Shortly afterward, however, in the autumn of 1902, Adler and four other physicians received invitations from Freud to meet for regular discussions of psychoanalytic theory at Freud's residence on Wednesday afternoons. The "Wednesday Society" was renamed the Vienna Psychoanalytical Society in 1908, and Adler and Freud became close friends. For a while, their views were so compatible that Adler succeeded Freud as president of the society in 1910. By 1911, however, they were in open and bitter disagreement, and Adler resigned the presidency of the society to establish a rival school of individual psychology.

Adler's Components of Personality

A *drive for aggression* was the core of Adler's early model of personality, and he assumed that the drive was as innately biological as was the sexual urge. Interestingly, even though Freud rejected this idea in 1911, he later included it in his own theory as a derivative of the death instincts.

For Adler, one element of the *drive for aggression*—a term for which he later substituted *striving for superiority*—is the desire to overcome feelings of inferiority. As a physician, he had noted how an individual who was handicapped in some way would seek to compensate for the defect by, say, exercising a partially paralyzed limb or becoming especially visually attentive following an impairment to the eye. He also observed that some feelings of inferiority stem from social, rather than biological, conditions (conditions such as underprivileged status, the dependency of childhood, or the inequality of privileges extended to the oldest, middle, and youngest child in a family, for example). Researchers in recent years have, in fact, found that birth order has a significant influence on personality, though not all of Adler's ideas on this

subject have been supported by research. Some of this work will be presented in Chapter 10.

Adler took it for granted that everyone experiences some feelings of inferiority, as a result of either real or imagined defects in their bodies, their place in the family, or their experiences in social interaction with others. Only in some individuals, however, will the sum total of these feelings of physical or social inferiority develop into an *inferiority complex* (Ansbacher & Ansbacher, 1956, pp. 256-261). Sometimes, this will result in the individual's becoming depressed and apathetic, or perhaps even so overwhelmed by feelings of worthlessness that suicide seems the only way out. Other times, an inferiority complex will activate an overcompensatory *superiority complex*, which in turn leads to aggressiveness rather than withdrawal and competition with others rather than suicide.

The superiority strivings which are energized by normal feelings of inferiority may express themselves in socially useful ways, such as the choice of a career which involves a productive or helpful domination of others (a career in business, law, teaching, preaching, or medicine, for example). When motivated by an overcompensatory superiority complex, however, these strivings may also (or simultaneously) be expressed in antisocial ways, such as bullying, selfishness, conceit, and disregard for the rights of others. Thus, some striving for superiority is healthy and to be expected, but extreme striving and overcompensation are symptoms of neurosis (Adler, 1929, chap. 9).

Adler proposed *social interest* as a personality characteristic which promotes a *pro*social rather than an *anti*social expression of superiority strivings. He believed that childrearing practices had a strong influence on an individual's characteristic way of dealing with human relationships, or the individual's *style of life*. In particular, he felt that both pampering and neglect are likely to stunt a child's development of social interest and so orient him or her toward antisocial behavior. While it is possible for new experiences to increase social interest in adulthood, and while encouragement of such an openness to change is a primary goal of therapy, "the whole burden of the guidance of our psychological life rests on proper childhood guidance" (Adler, 1929, chap. 13).

Individual Psychology: A Final Overview

Adler disputed Freud on several major points. First, he assigned sexual urges a secondary role in the dynamics of personality and instead emphasized superiority strivings. Second, he viewed behavior as primarily goal-directed and consciously chosen rather than driven and predetermined by biological urges or the unconscious mind. Third, he called attention to the influence that an individual's immediate social environment had on his or her behavior.

In his therapy, Adler asked patients for their earliest childhood recollections, not because he hoped to achieve insight into their psychosexual conflicts but because he believed that these memories contained clues as to the client's present style of life. Some individuals will strive to overcome their childhood feelings of inferiority in a productive, goal-oriented manner, while others will seek to make people feel sorry for them and so drift over to apathy, dependency, and the "useless" side of life. Dreams he regarded as either "productive" attempts to solve life's problems or "useless" efforts to withdraw from them. Even a person's posture while sleeping (stretched out full length or hunched up in a ball, for example) could reveal something about his or her style of life. Adler took an active, interventionist approach with his clients, urging them to replace their "useless" behavior patterns with a healthy striving for self-improvement and an increase in social interest (Ansbacher & Ansbacher, 1956).

So Adler differed from Freud in that he de-emphasized sexuality as a determinant of character and, instead, concentrated on goal-directed behavior in a social environment as the mainspring of mental life. In these respects, his views resemble those of another early dissenter in the Freudian camp, Carl Jung. There were many differences between Adler's and Jung's philosophies, however. One of these differences lay in Jung's tendency to downplay the importance of childhood experiences in shaping adult personality while placing great emphasis on the possibilities for dramatic personality growth and change throughout one's life.

JUNG: ANALYTICAL PSYCHOLOGY

Somewhat younger than either Freud or Adler, Carl Gustav Jung was born in 1875 near Basel, Switzerland. In his autobiography (Jung, 1961), he recalled that his parents had a strained marital relationship which caused him to feel somewhat unhappy and lonely as a child. Jung's father regarded himself a failure because he had been compelled to accept the position of country parson instead of fulfilling his boyhood dream of becoming a university professor; he also doubted the sincerity of his religious beliefs and worried continually about his physical health. Jung's mother, by contrast, had a strong-willed, dominating personality. Though she had the appearance of an ordinary, plump Swiss housewife, she seemed to young Carl to harbor an uncanny, witchlike character that was concealed from everyone but her son.

During his boyhood, Jung also perceived several distinct personalities within himself. At times he believed he was a large, cold, unchanging stone in his parents' garden. On other occasions, he saw himself as the reincarnated spirit of a powerful, wise old man who had lived in the eighteenth century. At the age of 10, Jung carved a small wooden figure and dressed it in a tiny frock coat and boots, perhaps as a representation of his "old man" personality. This doll was provided with its own special stone and tucked away in a bed made out of a pencil case. The case

Carl Gustav Jung, another famous dissenter from Freudian theory, who founded the school of analytical psychology. (The Bettmann Archive)

was then carefully hidden in the rafters of the attic where no one else would ever find it. Sometimes Carl would deliver messages to the doll in his own secret code. Later in life, Jung interpreted the psychological purpose of these multiple personalities and secret pastimes as protecting him from strong feelings of loneliness, inferiority, and persecution. Whenever he felt anxious, he would think about the stone or the doll and regain a sense of calm. Whenever he was scolded as a child, he would brush off the criticism by imagining himself to be the powerful, wise old man.

After passing through a childhood and adolescence filled with vivid and often frightening dreams, visions, and *deja vu experiences* (the feeling of having previously lived through an ongoing situation), Jung obtained his M.D. degree from the University of Basel. He then went to the Burgholzli Hospital in Zurich to work with Eugen Bleuler, a prominent psychiatrist who specialized in treating *schizophrenia,* a mental

disorder which up to that time had been called *dementia praecox.* Bleuler was highly interested in Freud's theory of personality and therefore required his associates to become familiar with it.

At Zurich, Jung devised a word-association test which permitted a fairly scientific approach toward Freud's technique of free association (see Chapter 5). Jung and Freud began to correspond concerning this research, and in 1909 Jung traveled to Vienna. In 1910, he became the first president of the newly founded International Psychoanalytic Association. Like Adler, however, he was to develop some strong differences of opinion with Freud. One of his dissenting opinions was rather similar to a view held by Adler: namely, that life is goal-directed rather than strictly determined by biology or the unconscious. The main bone of contention between Jung and Freud, though, was the nature of the libido. Jung denied that the libido consists mostly of sexual energy and described it as a general *life force* that promotes growth and development in all aspects of one's existence. Jung also deemphasized childhood sexuality and the importance of the Oedipus complex. Freud objected to Jung's attempt to "clean up" the libido, so Jung resigned his presidency of the International Psychoanalytic Association in 1913 and set up his own school of analytical psychology the following year (Freud, 1914). Ironically, as happened with Adler, Freud later revised his own thinking so as to include within the libido some of the elements of Jung's life force.

An examination of the 360 letters which passed between Freud and Jung between April, 1906, and January, 1913, reveals that though theoretical disagreements were the origins of the cooling of their friendship, feelings became especially bitter when the two began psychoanalyzing one another's motives (see McGuire, 1974). In any event, the rupture was apparently so traumatic for Jung that he lapsed into a prolonged period of schizophreniclike mental derangement in the years 1913–1917. He emerged from this stormy period with his sanity intact and was able to continue a productive career as a psychiatrist.

Jung's Components of Personality

Probably the most distinctive feature of Jung's theorizing was his insistence on the inheritance of cultural symbols, or *archetypes,* as a result of frequent and consistent use extending across many generations. He studied religions, myths, and literature from around the world for evidence of this accumulation of symbols in a *collective unconscious* and found recurrent themes of the "mother image," the "magician or trickster," the "hero," the "old wise man," and "birth and rebirth" (often in a flood or other creation epic). The theme of darkness (or the "shadow") was interpreted as representing the inherent evil in human beings.

Within the individual, Jung theorized, the libido is compelled by social pressures and conventions to adopt certain behaviors and beliefs; i.e., to assume a role. This role eventually becomes a mask, a *persona,* behind which the libido conceals those individual qualities and desires that would not meet with social approval. These hidden qualities may be repressed into a *personal unconscious,* which exists alongside the collective unconscious discussed above. Males, for example, are compelled to adopt a "masculine" persona and to supress the *anima,* or feminine component of their personalities. For females, it is the *animus,* or masculine component, that must be suppressed.

Ironically, the more extreme an individual's persona appears, the more energy she or he is probably expending in order to suppress his or her hidden qualities. The more "masculine" a man appears to be, the stronger must be his anima. The more energetic someone appears to be in his or her moralizing, the stronger that person's "shadow" must be. Jung agreed with Freud in assuming that these repressions could produce neurosis (Jung, 1951). Indeed, Jung distinguished between the *ego,* or conscious mind, and the *self,* which comprises both conscious *and* unconscious aspects of the mind. The self, displaced from the ego in the direction of the unconscious, he theorized, is the true center of the personality, even though the individual may falsely perceive the ego to be the center. It is this estrangement of the conscious mind from the true self that produces minor or severe neurotic symptoms. Those aspects of the self that are denied expression by the persona (e.g., the feminine side of a man's personality or the capacity for evil instinctive in human beings) may be revealed in fantasies, "Freudian slips," or, more seriously, full-blown neuroses or psychoses like hysteria or schizophrenia.

According to Jung (1923, pp. 611-612), the ego has two modalities (thinking and feeling) which generate four separate *functions,* each of which may be the basis for an individual temperament. The thinking modality may be either active or passive. When active, it is engaged in rationally coping with problems or events and is called *intellect* or, simply, *thinking.* When passive, the thinking modality becomes irrational because it is guided by unconscious processes: in this case, it is called *intuition.* The feeling modality may also be either *rational* (engaged in making subjective evaluational judgments) or *irrational* (merely perceiving). In the first case, the function is called *feeling;* in the second case, it is called *sensation.* If these four functions are placed at the corners of a square, the center of the pattern would represent an ideal synthesis of the four, and the geometric pattern would resemble a *mandala,* the symbol of unity in Eastern philosophy (symbols were very important to Jung, as we will see below). In nearly everyone, unfortunately, this unity is lacking. One of the four functions is almost always more highly developed than are the other three and thus becomes the *superior* one, which then dominates the persona. The *least* developed of the four is the *inferior* function; this function is so thoroughly suppressed that it is able to find expression only in dreams and fantasies.

In addition to the four functions, the ego orients itself toward the world by means of one or another of two *attitudes*. *Extraversion* is an interest in events and objects in the world *outside* oneself; extraverts are likely to be unhesitating in initiating action in the world. *Introversion* is in an interest in events *within* oneself; introverts are likely to be withdrawn and passive in their interactions with the world. As happens with the four functions, the attitude which is denied expression in the individual's persona becomes an unconscious force in his or her personality. Every extravert has a suppressed desire to be an introvert, and every introvert has a secret yearning to be an extravert. The extraversion-introversion dimension of Jung's character typology has excited the interest of many psychologists, most notably Eysenck (1947). Active investigation of this dimension of personality has continued to the present day. Some of this research is considered in Box 2-2.

Jung regarded personality as both *caused by its past* (particularly by its inherited archetypes) and *directed* toward its goals for future development. The primary goal of personality is *self-realization*, a concept that can be more easily understood if we look at a diagram illustrating Jung's components of personality (see Figure 2-2). The diagram shows the unconscious aspects of personality to the left and the conscious aspects to the right. Near the center of the diagram is the *self*, which comprises both the unconscious and conscious elements of the mind and which Jung regards as the true center of personality.

Self-realization consists of (1) incorporating the unconscious aspects of personality into the ego, (2) achieving an *equipotentiality* (equal strength) of the four functions of the ego, and (3) achieving a similar equipotential flexibility in adopting an extraverted or introverted attitude toward life. One practical result of self-realization should be an openness to a wide variety of ways of living and experiencing one's life, but self-realization

has other implications, too, as will be seen below.

One pressure toward self-realization which acts on both a cultural and a personal level is our use of symbols. *Symbols* are abstractions of things that are unconsciously desired; as a result, symbols can never be totally satisfying. The desire to create more satisfying symbols inspires art, knowledge, and *self*-knowledge to progress to more sophisticated levels of understanding (Jung, 1917, p. 468). We can become more consciously aware of the repressed elements in our personal and cultural libidos if we attend to our dreams, word associations, fantasies, accidents, and coincidences and if we strive to interpret the meanings of universal symbols. Within the individual, this process is helped by the fact that an energy system (as Jung supposed the mind to be) has a natural tendency to move toward equilibrium, according to the laws of thermodynamics. Thus there is an inherent motivation to progress toward a state of *unity*, or self-realization, in which all of the unconscious elements, each of the four functions, and both of the attitudes have an equal opportunity for expression in the persona.

Analytical Psychology: A Final Overview

Jung's theory of personality has had a definite impact on the thinking of psychologists, historians, writers, and artists. Indeed, a spectacularly successful motion picture based on a science-fiction novel titled *Star Wars* (Lucas, 1976) literally abounds in Jungian themes. In this film, one sees the young hero (Luke Skywalker) being made aware of the existence of a *universal life force* ("the Force") by an old wise man (Obi-Wan Kenobi). A state of open-minded acceptance must precede effective use of the Force to accomplish important goals such as battling the foremost champion of the despotic Empire, a formerly honorable knight (Darth Vader) whose personality succumbed to the *dark* (or "shadow") side of the Force. The evil dark lord appears to slay the

BOX 2-2 THE EXTRAVERSION-INTROVERSION DIMENSION OF PERSONALITY

After Jung's description of extraverted and introverted personality types had been translated into English, there were many attempts to put together questionnaires for the purpose of measuring this trait and relating it to other aspects of individual character. Eysenck (1973), reviewing the history of these efforts, noted that they were generally unsuccessful because the selection of questionnaire items was statistically unsophisticated and was not guided by a clear definition of the trait being measured. Eysenck (1947) moved to correct both of these faults by constructing the Maudsley Personality Inventory. He considers Jung's contribution to this area of research in personality to be primarily a stimulation of popular interest in the concept; otherwise, he believes Jung's connection of extraversion-introversion to rational and irrational functions of the conscious and unconscious minds served mainly to confuse and impede psychological research.

Eysenck uses the terms *extraversion* and *introversion* in much the same way Jung did. The former refers to an orientation toward, and seeking of, stimulation from outside sources: the latter consists of an orientation toward *internal* stimuli, such as moods or thoughts. Extraverts, therefore, are expected to be sociable, carefree, and impulsive, while introverts should be shy, self-concerned, and controlled. Eysenck (1964) added the dimension of emotional "stability" vs. "instability" to extraversion-introversion so as to categorize personalities as falling into four basic types. These types correspond fairly closely to a 2000-year-old formulation by the Roman physician, Galen, who in turn drew upon the earlier work of the Greek founder of medical science, Hippocrates. They are *choleric* (impetuous), *sanguine* (lively), *phlegmatic* (quiet), and *melancholic* (depressed). On the next page is a diagram of this typology, including adjectives which Eysenck has found to be associated with each character type.

It should be noted that Eysenck himself regards the four character types as merely a convenient way of distinguishing broad categories of human personality. Extraversion-introversion and stability-instability are really *dimensions* rather than *typologies* (see Chapter 1 for a discussion of this point). Most individuals will find themselves near the center of the diagram but, say, leaning just a bit more toward introversion than extraversion or toward stability rather than instability. Fewer and fewer personalities will be represented as one moves out from the center of the diagram toward any of the poles, and a "pure" psychological type would be rare.

The following paraphrases of some questions included in the Eysenck Personality Inventory are intended to measure extraversion-introversion:

UNSTABLE

Moody | Touchy
Anxious | Restless
Rigid | Aggressive
Sober | Excitable
Pessimistic | Changeable
Reserved | Impulsive
Unsociable / Melancholic | Choleric | Optimistic
Quiet | Active

INTROVERTED | EXTRAVERTED

Passive | Sociable
Careful | Phlegmatic | Sanguine | Outgoing
Thoughtful | Talkative
Peaceful | Responsive
Controlled | Easygoing
Reliable | Lively
Even-tempered | Carefree
Calm | Leadership

STABLE

The answer which would indicate extraversion is underlined for each.

1 Are you always ready for adventure?   <u>Yes</u>   No
2 Do you tend to be a "wallflower" when out with other people   Yes   <u>No</u>
3 Do you enjoy tasks and games that call for quick reflexes?   <u>Yes</u>   No
4 Are you "put off" by loud and rowdy parties?   Yes   <u>No</u>

Below are some questions intended to measure emotional "stability" vs. "instability." The stable choice in each case is "No".

1 Do you often wish you could take back something you have   Yes   <u>No</u>
   done or said?
2 Do you think so much about past events and future plans   Yes   <u>No</u>
   that you cannot sleep?
3 Are you sometimes eager and enthusiastic about life while   Yes   <u>No</u>
   other times you couldn't care less?
4 Are you touchy about being criticized?   Yes   <u>No</u>

Eysenck (1973) has brought together, in a single volume, many studies of extraversion-introversion. One of these studies noted that business executives tend to be somewhat extraverted while those involved in research and development lean slightly toward introversion. Extraverts are tough-minded in their political philosophies relative to the more tenderhearted introverts. Among unmarried male or female college students, sensation-seeking extraverts have sexual intercourse about twice as often as do introverts, whereas the latter are more likely than the former to engage in masturbation. The impulsive aspects of extraversion appear to lead extraverts more than introverts into conflict with the law; the former also have a greater tolerance for painful stimulation. Eysenck also reports on evidence indicating that introverts have higher levels of arousal in the brain and central nervous system than do extraverts. One method of measuring this level of arousal is by means of an electroencephalogram, as mentioned in Box 2-1. As a result of their high level of internal arousal, introverts are likely to find any additional stimulation from outside themselves to be *overstimulating* and even somewhat unpleasant. Extraverts, on the other hand, are chronically understimulated and seek external stimulation as a means of raising the arousal level to a more optimally stimulating moderate level. An ingenious way to demonstrate the greater reactivity of introverts to external stimuli is to place a few drops of lemon juice on the tongue and then measure the amount of saliva secreted. Extreme introverts show an increase in salivation of about one gram following such a procedure; extreme extraverts show almost no increase in salivation.

Cattell (1957) also found evidence for more than two basic dimensions of personality, using his Sixteen Personality Factor Questionnaire, but first among these, he found, was an "outgoing" vs. "reserved" factor, which he felt closely resembled extraversion-introversion (see Chapter 6). A combination of several factors, called "exvia-invia" by Cattell, has a somewhat stronger relationship to extraversion-introversion. Introversion was found to be relatively high among researchers, artists, and executives engaged in creative work. Extraversion was more prevalent among mechanical workers and people in occupations requiring alertness (such as cooks or fire fighters). Introversion was related to the presence of certain clinical symptoms (especially depression), and women were more likely to be introverted than were men.

---

old wise man, but there is a strong implication that Obi-Wan Kenobi has not really been destroyed and will reappear to fight again in some new and even more powerful form (the theme of death and rebirth).

Despite the popularization of many of Jung's concepts, those who read his works frequently found his somewhat obscure writing style an obstacle to understanding. Consequently, with the exception of a few, generally rather isolated, converts, analytical psychology did not, for many years, pose an effective challenge either to psychoanalysis or to individual psychology.

Jung's ideas were able to gain a greater measure of popular acceptance during the 1960s, when—particularly in the United States—there developed a social and political counterculture interested in experiencing the alterations in consciousness which can be achieved through the use of drugs, meditation, or a simple alteration in one's outlook on life (Roszack, 1969). Members of the counterculture were seeking something comparable to the self-realization Jung had talked about, and so here, at last, was a fertile field in which even the most exotic Jungian notions could take root and thrive.

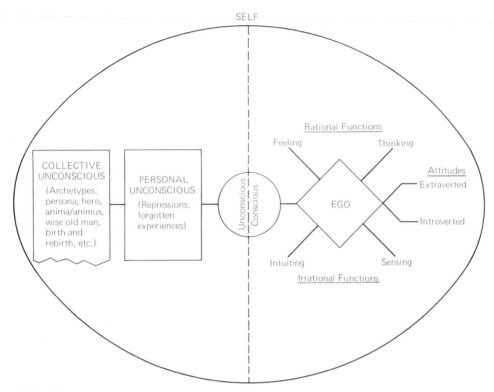

FIGURE 2-2

A diagram of Jung's model of personality. In the unconscious mind are the inherited archetypes as well as the Freudian unconscious of individual repressions. The ego, or conscious mind, has four possible functions and two possible attitudes toward perceiving and acting in the world. The self comprises both the unconscious and conscious aspects of the mind, and its center is, therefore, displaced from the ego in the direction of the unconscious.

Ironically, Jung himself doubted that full self-realization was possible, mainly because of our strong resistance to awareness of the personal capacity for evil. At a certain stage of life, though—mainly after the age of 40—an individual is likely to become aware of the futility of striving to uphold a false persona. There may be a turning inward of the ego toward the unconscious processes that it has so long repressed. Religious feelings and a concern for one's heritage are likely to emerge. It is this stage of life that is ripest for self-realization, and Jung had considerable success as a therapist in treating middle-aged patients (Jung, 1931). This emphasis on the possibility of dramatic changes in personality in adulthood distinguished Jung's theory from both Freud's and Adler's, and it may account for Jung's

relative lack of interest in the childhood stages of development.

Jung leaves for the most part unspecified the superficial traits the self-realized individual is likely to possess. He says they "cannot be indicated in the form of a recipe," but he is willing to make the following general statement:

Conscious and unconscious do not make a whole when one of them is suppressed and injured by the other. If they must contend, let it at least be a fair fight with equal rights on both sides. Both are aspects of life. Consciousness should defend its reason and protect itself, and the chaotic life of the unconscious should be given the chance of having its way too—as much of it as we can stand. This means open conflict and open collaboration at once. That, evidently, is the way human life should be. It is the old game of the hammer and anvil: between them the patient iron is forged into an indestructible whole, an "individual." (Jung, 1959, p. 289)

Apparently we, as individuals, must be willing to accept imperfections in ourselves and in the world in which we live. Presumably (and this is my own reading-between-the-lines of Jung's complicated prose), it is only by tolerating a little evil and a little injustice in ourselves as well as others that we will ever be able to form the honest, accepting sort of human relationships based on mutual recognition of individuality which can prevent far greater evils and injustices from occurring. Jung was highly suspicious of appeals to idealism and mass movements as pathways toward social reform because they usually serve as a camouflage for the "shadow" motives of their leaders (Jung, 1958, p. 115). In this respect, his ideas were in conflict with the desire of many in the counterculture to achieve social change by just such means. Despite these areas of incompatibility, the countercultural attraction to Jungian concepts must be credited with stimulating a resurgence of interest in Jung's theory within the field of psychology as well as within society as a whole.

At this point, we will briefly consider the ideas of two other theorists who began their careers as Freudian adherents and then modified their thinking so as to place greater emphasis on cultural forces and goal-directed strivings as determinants of personality and behavior. These theorists, then, moved somewhat further along the trail of dissent from orthodox psychoanalysis blazed by Adler and Jung.

ERIKSON: THE EIGHT STAGES OF DEVELOPMENT

Erik Erikson's mother was divorced by her Danish husband before her son was born in Copenhagen in 1902. When Erik was 3 years old, his mother married a Jewish pediatrician, Theodor Homberger, who lived in Karlsruhe, Germany. Homberger tried to raise Erik as though he was his own biological offspring, but this illusion proved impossible to sustain as Erik grew taller, remaining fair-haired, and blue-eyed. Erikson (1975, pp. 26–28) reports that he was considered a Gentile by the Jewish community and a Jew by his Gentile schoolmates. These circumstances provided the first of many *identity crises* in Erikson's life—crises which he himself felt had a direct bearing on the content of his theories.

During the 1930s, Erikson studied at the Vienna Psychoanalytic Institute and underwent his personal psychoanalysis with Freud's daughter, Anna. Following completion of his training, he left Vienna because of the unstable political atmosphere there in the years preceding World War II and went to Denmark; from Denmark he traveled to Boston, accepting an appointment at Henry Murray's psychological clinic at Harvard University, and, later, a position at the University of California. In the United States, Erikson experienced yet another identity problem when he tried to learn English and assimilate into the American culture. This experience was repeated in the 1950s, when a number of professors were fired by the Unviersity of California during the loyalty-oath controversy of the McCarthy era; Erikson and other foreign-born professors who refused to take the oath were urged by some newspapers to "go back to where they came from" (Erikson, 1975, pp 42–43). Following this unpleasant experience, he returned to Boston and joined the faculty at Harvard.

Erikson did not dispute the Freudian model of the mind as being divided into id, ego, and superego. He also accepted Freud's notion of the psychosexual stages of personality development. His major innovation was to reinterpret the conflicts being resolved in these stages as being psycho*social* rather than merely sexual in content. In addition, he extended the number of stages past late adolescence (Freud's genital stage), through adulthood, and on into old age.

The first of Erikson's stages corresponds to

Freud's oral stage, the stage at which the child resolves conflicts related to the availability of the tension-reducing, milk-giving nipple. According to Erikson (1959), though, the most important aspect of this stage is not the fact that the infant experiences stimulation of an erotogenic zone but that it develops a sense of either *trust* or *mistrust*, depending upon whether the mother is responsive or unresponsive to its cries. Erikson's second stage of personality development matches Freud's anal stage and begins with the initiation of toilet training, but psychosexual urges are, for Erikson, once again less important than is the psychosocial development which occurs here. The child at this stage is experimenting, in many aspects of its behavior, with holding on to and letting go of things, and this experimentation will naturally extend to its bowel movements. Firm parental insistence upon self-control, combined with expressions of confidence in the child's ability to accomplish this goal, should instill in the child a sense of *autonomy*. On the other hand, a child who is made to feel unworthy of parental confidence because of occasional accidents and one who has been toilet trained by means of enforced compliance to parental demands and threats may develop a self-concept strongly tinged with *shame and doubt*.

The child enters the third stage of development at about the age of 4 or 5, a stage when Freud felt that Oedipal conflicts were being resolved. For the male child, the crisis of Erikson's third stage is due only partly to his desire to possess his mother sexually; more broadly, the crisis arises from the competing demands of the boy and his father for the time and nurturant attention of the mother. The child eventually realizes that his father is an overwhelmingly powerful rival, and so he uses a developing capacity for planning to work out strategies by which he can maximize the time he spends with his mother while minimizing the risk of confronting his father. One fairly effective plan is simply to internalize and impose on himself the same sort of restrictions that his father would enforce. If the superego emerges through such a planning process in the mind of the child, he gains a sense of *initiative*. If, instead, he simply abandons his forbidden goals because of his fear of punishment and is unable to work out any satisfactory alternative strategy for goal-attainment, he will always be inhibited in his purposeful, goal-directed behavior by a lingering sense of *guilt*. For the female child, there is, as Freud suggested, some degree of psychosexual attraction to the father, but attempts to "act out" her desire to "catch" or (as Erikson puts it) "make" her father bring her into conflict with her mother and thus threaten the loss of mother's nuturant attention. Like the boy, then, the girl finds it prudent to internalize the self-controlling prohibitions which the same-sexed parent is likely to enforce.

Erikson's fourth stage, entered when the child leaves home for school, corresponds to Freud's latency period. In this stage, the child comes to value recognition and approval from those outside the immediate family. The psychosocial possibilities here are that the child will gain a sense of competence and *industry* in such settings *or* be impaired by a sense of *inferiority*.

The fifth stage begins at puberty, around the same time as Freud's early genital stage. Erikson describes the basic conflict to be resolved here as that of "identity" vs. "role diffusion." Either the adolescent senses that the development of his (or her) interests is moving in a direction congruous with some viable social role or he feels that he has no place in society. Role diffusion is likely to produce anxiety over the prospect of becoming a social outcast and results in the adoption of faddish styles, the formation of cliques, and overidentification with youth heroes. The conflict to be resolved in the sixth stage, which is associated with the end of adolescence, is that between needs for *intimacy* (i.e., a mutually satisfying compromise of self-interests within a love relationship) and the complexity of modern society, which exerts pressures toward impersonal *isolation*.

Finally, quite unlike Freud, Erikson proceeds to delineate two further stages of development in adulthood, both emphasizing the individual's capacity to make intelligent choices between alternative strategies for living. The *generative* choice of the seventh stage involves deciding whether to contribute to the lives of succeeding generations, either by having offspring or by engaging in some creative work. The last stage consists of establishing *ego integrity,* or accepting personal responsibility for the pleasures and disappointments of one's life. After passing through this final stage, people are prepared to die with dignity, secure in the knowledge that whatever the content of their life experiences, they played a part in human history (Erikson, 1950). A summary of Erikson's eight stages of development is shown in Table 2-1.

Erikson himself said his major theoretical innovation was the concept of the identity crisis. In his later writings (1968), he attempted to correct a possible source of misunderstanding in his earlier work. Particularly in the first four stages of development, he wrote, a healthy resolution of a conflict does not involve an either-or choice between two mutually exclusive alternatives. In infancy, for example, achieving a sense of basic trust would appear to be the socially desirable choice, the one which contributes to psychological health. Erikson points out, however, that trust can be carried to excess. The overly trusting individual is likely to be taken advantage of by others and, later in life, to experience

TABLE 2-1 Erikson's stages of the life cycle and a description of the major psychosocial conflict to be resolved at each stage. The corresponding Freudian psychosexual stages are shown in parentheses.

Stage in the Life Cycle	DEVELOPMENT WITHIN STAGE	
	Early	Late
Infancy	Trust vs. Mistrust regarding the reliability and helpfulness of others in times of distress (Freud's Oral stage)	Autonomy vs. Shame and Doubt in controlling one's own, sometimes socially unacceptable, impulses (Freud's Anal stage)
Childhood	Initiative vs. Guilt, stemming from one's ability to find solutions to difficult social conflicts (Freud's Phallic stage)	Industry vs. Inferiority as a result of striving to meet the expectations of others in the social world outside the home (Freud's Latency period)
Adolescence	Identity vs. Role Confusion in one's efforts at setting a course toward self-sufficiency (Freud's Early Genital stage)	Intimacy vs. Isolation, resulting from success or failure in attaining an intimate sexual relationship based on mutual affection and respect (Freud's Genital stage)
Adulthood	Generativity vs. Stagnation in seeking to make some contribution to the lives of future human beings	Ego Identity vs. Despair in coming to terms with the meaning of one's life and the inevitability of death

difficulty in establishing intimate relationships based on mutual respect for the legitimate interests of each party and in achieving a sense of ego integrity. Some mistrust (along with a basic sense of trust), then, is an important component of a healthy personality. The most productive resolution of a conflict such as "trust" vs. "mistrust" is a *blend* of the two alternatives which leans more toward the *positive* (trusting) pole. At other stages of development also, psychosocial conflicts are most satisfactorily resolved by some compromise of alternatives.

Erikson is often grouped with Heinz Hartmann and the *ego psychologists*. These theorists were basically Freudian in orientation, but they believed that certain portions of the ego had their own sources of energy which were independent of the id. In this *conflict-free ego sphere* are the processes of rational thought and accurate perception that are employed by the adult in setting and accomplishing life goals (Hartmann, Kris, & Loewenstein, 1947). This notion of an adult personality capable of rational choice and self-insight seems, in fact, to have constituted a widespread basis for disagreement between Freud and those who carried forward the European characterological tradition. Freud (1923, 1926) had, himself, modified his early theory so as to endow the ego with a greater capacity for autonomous functioning in its relations with the id. He also commented that the whole purpose of psychotherapy was to enhance the ego's understanding of, and control over, the id (Freud, 1933). These revisions were further elaborated on by Freud's daughter, Anna (A. Freud, 1936), but they still did not go far enough to satisfy many of the ego psychologists, one of whom was Karen Horney.

HORNEY

Karen Horney was born in Hamburg, Germany, in 1885. Her father was a Norwegian sea captain, which caused the family to move frequently and which probably gave young Karen a lasting appreciation for the great differences in social customs and role expectations between one culture and another. Horney received her M.D. degree from the University of Berlin in 1913 and was graduated from the Berlin Psychiatric Institute in 1917. She practiced as an orthodox Freudian analyst for the next fifteen years, but she finally rejected the instinctivist and determinist theories of Freud because in her experience, almost every patient had some problems which did not fit these theories (Horney, 1939).

She did, however, ascribe at least one innate component to personality: *basic anxiety*, or a "terrible feeling of being isolated and helpless in a potentially hostile world" (Horney, 1945, p. 41). In response to this anxiety, she theorized, a child may learn habitual modes of interaction with other people. In *moving toward* others, the child complies with their wishes to gain affection; in *moving against* others, the child combats them because of a resentment at feeling isolated; in *moving away* from others, the child withdraws from them out of fear of being isolated or disliked. All three modes of interaction are exhibited by the healthy person at one time or another, but the neurotic makes habitual use of only one mode.

Horney believed that humans also, fortunately, come equipped with a tendency to search for positive emotional response patterns that will reduce conflicting feelings toward others and so reduce insecurity. This tendency, combined with a *central inner force* toward *self-realization*, the expression of genuine feelings, and the experience of *inner freedom*, can break through the *vicious circles* that negative response patterns so often create in people's interpersonal relationships. The achievement of such a breakthrough, she felt, should be the primary goal of therapy (Horney, 1950).

Horney (1939) strongly objected to Freud's account of the resolution of the Oedipus complex and the origin of *penis envy* in women. The Oedipus complex, she said, occurs only in cultures which require that children be excessively dependent upon their parents and which, as a result, arouse strong anxieties in them. The response of "moving against" the opposite-sexed parent and "moving toward" the same-sexed parent is not sexually motivated but is, rather, an attempt to cope with culturally imposed feelings of insecurity. Penis envy, when it occurs, is also culturally determined and does not involve a literal desire on the part of the female child either to have sexual relations with her father or to grow a male sex organ. Rather, it represents a rational, and by no means neurotic, resentment on the part of the girl for the special privileges and prerogatives assigned to males in Western societies.

To conclude the present chapter, we will consider yet another offshoot of the psychoanalytic tradition, one which also emphasizes the individual's capacity for making ego-based, rational choices and downplays the importance of instinctual forces in human personality. This approach has its own unique variations on the foregoing themes, however.

EXISTENTIAL PSYCHOLOGY

Existentialism began as a philosophical system vigorously advocated by Søren Kierkegaard, a Dane who died, in 1855, deeply troubled by his personal adjustment to the social system in which he lived. Heidegger (1927) extracted the essence of this philosophy, which is that the individual exists simply by virtue of acting in the world and the world exists because there are individual minds which perceive its existence. The perceptual world and the world of "real" things are ultimately indistinguishable from one another, and the special capacity of human beings is the ability to *choose* how they will perceive themselves and the world of which they are aware. Since each invividual's perception is unique, it is inappropriate for one person to attempt to impose his or her world view on

another. Heidegger's reformulation of Kierkegaard's philosophy appealed to Ludwig Binswanger, a Swiss psychiatrist who had studied under Jung's early mentor, Eugen Bleuler, and, as a consequence, had become a close friend of Freud's. Binswanger, like Jung and Adler, moved away from psychoanalysis in his theorizing, but there was never any bitterness between him and Freud; their personal relations remained cordial (Jones, 1961, p. 311). Another Swiss psychiatrist, Medard Boss, who also worked with Bleuler, was a later convert to existentialism.

Immediately following World War I, existentialist analysts started to notice new types of disorders, disorders that were not sexual in nature but involved strong feelings of loneliness, anxiety, and depersonalization. These symptoms seemed to reflect a fear of *nonbeing*, or nothingness, that had been activated by the devastation of a world war. Later, the threat of an ultimate holocaust, implicit in the cold war of the atomic age, activated the same fear. They called this fear *ontological dread*.

The existentialists described three levels of being: the *Umwelt* or, literally, "surrounding world," the *Mitwelt* (or "with-world"), and the *Eigenwelt* (or "own-world"). Everyone begins in the Umwelt, in which experience is shaped primarily by biological urges and innate sensory responses. In the Mitwelt, the individual expands his or her personal urges and sensations to include the feelings of others. This is accomplished through a process called *encounter*, a process by which the individual notices the impact that his or her actions have upon the environment and other people.

Rollo May (1958), a contemporary American existentialist, describes four modes in which these encounters can take place: (1) in the *anonymous mode*, the person avoids developing a sense of personal identity in order to avoid being held responsible for his or her acts (slavish conformity is in the anonymous mode); (2) in the *singular mode*, the person is preoccupied with self-evaluation in comparison with others; (3) in the *plural mode*, others are regarded as *its*, to be exploited for the attainment of one's own ends; and (4) in the *dual mode* (the most satisfying mode of existential existence), oneself and others are perceived as *we*, and mutually satisfying cooperative relationships can be established.

Finally, the individual may arrive at the third level of being, the *Eigenwelt*, a level at which the greater self-awareness achieved in the *Mitwelt* permits the establishment of a secure sense of identity.

The existentialists emphasize that one can understand behavior only by understanding the social situation in which it occurs and the intentions of the person who demonstrates it. They disagree with Freud in accepting immediate behavior as existence in and of itself, for which there is no need of further analysis or interpretation (in the words of Kierkegaard, "to be is to do"). All behavior constitutes an attempt to cope successfully with present events, and personality disorder consists of learned behavior which interferes with the natural desire either to establish mutually significant relationships with others or to achieve "the realization of one's inherent potentialities" (Ruitenbeek, 1962). As a result of this belief, the existentialists took a *phenomenological* approach toward therapy, listening carefully to the patient's description of his or her ongoing problems in living without probing for repressions or childhood traumas.

The primary goal of existentialist therapy is to lead the patient out of the anonymous mode of the *Mitwelt* and to encourage the acceptance of responsibility for one's actions. The patient is therefore urged to make conscious choices in the selection of goals and to expand his or her sense of identity by encountering others in significant relationships (May, 1961; Keen, 1970). Binswanger (1958) applied these principles to an analysis of the case of Ellen West, a woman born into a family with an extraordinarily high rate of mental distress and suicide. The woman herself had a lifelong fascination with death. Feeling that she was unattractive to men, she worried from adolescence onward about her weight and, paradoxically, developed an eating compulsion. She also had a strong desire to make a "name" for herself as a poet, a name that would outlive her. She was finally hospitalized at Binswanger's sanatorium, and Bleuler himself was brought in as a consultant on the case. Treatment was ineffective in altering Ellen's sense of being overwhelmed by fate, and she made the "existential choice" of suicide three days after leaving the hospital.

Fundamental to existential philosophy is the notion that we are all free to decide the course of

Jean Paul Sartre, French essayist, playwright, and existential philosopher, who believed that freedom is found in self-conscious choice.
(Cartier-Bresson/Magnum)

our lives, or at least the psychological orientation we take toward the good or bad fortune which befalls us (Boss, 1963). The famed French essayist and existential philosopher Jean Paul Sartre set the scene of his play *No Exit* in hell; the punishment being meted out to the three characters in this play is to relive the events of their past unhappy lives with the understanding that they could have made different choices. The existential perspective on evil is that it is an unpleasant but inevitable consequence of the human failure to exercise individuality and to choose constructive alternatives. Strong echoes of these themes can be heard in the writings of phenomenologically oriented theorists within the American personological tradition, theorists who will be encountered in Chapter 3.

CONCLUSION

It was stated at the outset of this chapter that the primary distinguishing feature of the European tradition in personality theory is a belief in the inherent quality of certain traits in an individual's character. For many of the theorists, these inherent qualities were the product of instincts directed toward satisfaction of one's sexual needs (Freud and, to a lesser extent, Erikson), one's superiority strivings (Adler), or one's sense of security (Horney). In Jung's theorizing, character was strongly influenced by inherited archetypes. Superficially, it might appear that the existentialists were disinclined to accept this emphasis on inborn predispositions as a determinant of character. Much like Jung, however, the existentialists insisted that we had to understand and accept the inevitability of all aspects of human nature, particularly those of which we would prefer to remain unaware (e.g., our capacity for evil).

A close cousin of the European tradition is the American personological tradition, to be discussed in the next chapter. Like their European counterparts, these American theorists paid a certain amount of attention to the shaping of individual character by internal disposition and needs, but they also examined the degree to which individuals shared certain traits because they had been reared in similar social environments. The personologists considered human behavior to be purposeful and future-oriented rather than entirely determined by past experiences or inherited instincts. Social influences on personality and the goal-striving aspects of human behavior also received greater emphasis in the European tradition as successive generations of theorists deviated ever more widely from Freud.

While we are on the subject of social issues, it might be mentioned that the European tradition in general, and psychoanalysis in particular, have been sharply criticized in recent years for the manner in which they described the psychology of women. It has been alleged that these theories justify a second-class, inferior social status for women by arguing that they are psychologically best suited for dependent roles. It must be remembered, however, that Freud did not seek to describe the social and psychological world as he thought it *should* be but rather as he *found* it. He felt that the many restrictions placed on women were detrimental to their psychological health, and he deplored this outcome. On a personal level, he encouraged the professional career of his daughter, Anna, who became a leading theoretician and psychoanalyst. Adler, too, promoted the education of his daughter, Alexandra. She became a neurologist, a psychiatrist, and head of the Individual Psychology Association. While it may be true that some psychoanalysts have interpreted Freud's theory in a manner that justifies or even advocates a subordinate role for women, this does not appear to be the conclusion reached by Freud himself or by any other theorist considered in Chapter 2. There is a lengthier discussion of this social issue in Chapter 13, which deals with sex differences in personality.

SUMMARY

1   The European characterological tradition developed within a social context strongly influenced by nineteenth century Victorianism. First in association with Charcot, and later in collaboration with Breuer, Freud used hypnosis to treat nervous disorders like hysteria. Freud and his hypnotic technique became somewhat controversial in the Viennese medical community, partly because hypnosis had had a disreputable past.

2   Freud abandoned hypnosis in favor of free association, a method which required the patient to verbalize every thought that came to mind while in a relaxed state. From evidence gathered by means of this free association, Freud concluded that hidden desires of a sexual nature were the origin of most neuroses and that children have both erotic and hostile feelings toward their parents. These conclusions scandalized many of his contemporaries.

3   The id is the source of energy for the entire personality, and the energy comes prepackaged with each infant in the form of instincts. Foremost among the instincts which promote life is the sexual urge; foremost among those which draw the individual toward death is the aggressive instinct. When the id desires some object, it may form an image called a *wish fulfillment*; dreams are a type of wish fulfillment called *primary process.* The ego seeks to formulate reality-based plans (the secondary process) to satisfy id impluses, while the superego acts as the conscience in judging the moral acceptability of such plans.

4   When a *desire,* or cathexis, from the id cannot be consciously expressed, it is repressed into the unconscious mind, resulting in neurotic anxiety. Unless an effective sublimation of the repressed. impulse can be achieved, neurotic symptoms such as hysteria, compulsions, or "Freudian slips" may develop. In addition, the neurotic is likely to employ a variety of defense mechanisms such as fixation, regression, projection, or reaction formation so as to maintain his or her repressions.

5   Freud believed that conflicts arising at four psychosexual stages of child development were the primary determinants of individual differences in adult personality. In the oral stage, conflicts revolve around the weaning experience; in the anal stage, it is the initiation of toilet training which provokes anxiety; and in the phallic stage, it is the child's awakening erotic interest in the opposite-sexed parent that produces conflict. Resolution of the Oedipal conflict in the phallic stage causes the child to identify with the parent of the same sex, thus initiating sex-typing and the development of the superego. In the genital stage of adolescence, the emerging adult seeks to

establish a satisfying sexual relationship with a loved partner and to sublimate any residual tensions through productive work.

6 Psychoanalytic theory has been criticized for being excessive in its interpretations of the unconscious causes of human behavior and for becoming somewhat antifeminist and socially conservative in its outlook. Dissenters from Freud emphasized the goal-setting and decision-making powers of the individual, powers which allow for dramatic changes in personality in adulthood.

7 Adler's struggles to overcome childhood diseases and his feelings of inferiority in comparison with his older brother were probably the origins of his theories of overcompensation for physical and social inferiority and striving for superiority. A person's style of life was established in childhood, Adler said, and childhood feelings of inferiority could lead to apathy and a need for pampering from others. Alternatively, these feelings could stimulate a productive striving to overcome one's inferiorities. Such strivings, if regulated by genuine social interest, should not go so far as to develop into an overcompensatory superiority complex.

8 During an unhappy and somewhat lonely childhood, Jung found some relief from anxiety in imagining that he had other personalities besides that of a small boy, and he experienced many vivid dreams and visions. His theory of personality emphasizes the inheritance of archetypes which are the accumulated residues of universal themes in human evolutionary history. An individual's true self is composed of unconscious archetypes, the personal unconscious of Freudian repressions, and the conscious ego. Self-realization consists of developing a conscious awareness and acceptance of the unconscious elements in one's personality and exploring each of the various aspects of consciousness—rational, irrational, introverted, extra-verted. Self-realization can be encouraged by attending to cultural symbols, such as works of art or the symbolism of dreams.

9 Erikson experienced many identity crises in his own personal life, and he himself identified his major theoretical innovation as being the concept of the adolescent identity crisis. He accepted Freud's division of personality into id, ego, and superego and his notion of stages in child development. In disagreement with Freud, however, he argued that the basic conflict to be resolved at each stage is psycho*social* rather than psycho*sexual*. Erikson described eight stages of development, two of them in adulthood and middle age.

10 Erikson, Horney, and other ego psychologists believed that certain portions of the ego have their own sources of energy independent of the id and that this gives the adult a capacity for rational goal-setting and self-insight. Horney considered basic anxiety, rather than sexuality, to be the primary motivating force in a child's personality. The Oedipus complex she considered a childhood response to

anxieties induced by excessive dependency on parents and felt that it would not emerge in cultures which did not create such strong dependencies. Penis envy in women is not a biological fact of life but a rational expression of resentment for the special prerogatives assigned to males in Western societies.

11 Existentialism takes a phenomenological approach to psychology in arguing that the only reality is the world as perceived by the individual. Since each individual's perception is unique, it is inappropriate for one person to attempt to impose his or her world view on another. Because human beings are able to choose how they will perceive themselves and the world of which they are aware, each person is responsible for the choices he or she makes. Movement toward greater self-awareness of one's options and responsibilities is accomplished through a process called *encounter,* a process by which the individual notices the impact that his or her actions have upon the environment and other people.

TERMS TO KNOW

free association	inferiority complex
insight	overcompensation
instincts of life and death	collective unconscious
unconscious mind	introversion-extraversion
reality testing	psychosocial stages
neurotic anxiety	identity crisis
repression	basic anxiety
ego defense	existentialism
Oedipus complex	

3.

TRAITS, PHENOMENOLOGY, AND THE AMERICAN PERSONOLOGICAL TRADITION

ISSUES TO CONSIDER

1 Why have American personologists emphasized the "healthy" rather than the "disturbed" personality in their theorizing?
2 Where do traits originate, how are they organized so as to activate patterns of behavior, and to what extent can they account for individual differences in character?
3 What is meant by the term self-actualization?

There are several historical reasons why American psychology deviated in its development from the lines laid down by the European psychoanalytic tradition. For one thing, as was mentioned in Chapter 2, many of the European dissenters from Freud—a group which included Adler, Erikson, and Horney—emigrated to the United States, bringing with them their optimistic vision of a self-determining, goal-striving conscious mind. These well-known theorists, however, were only part of a great mass of immigrants who traveled from the Old World to the New World.

Europe is made up of national groups who have occupied separate geographical spaces for long periods of time and have developed distinctive languages, traditions, and characteristics as a result. In America, on the other hand, the historical emphasis has been on the extent to which newcomers could discard their previous national characteristics and conform to American styles of dress, speech, and behavior. If the psychological price paid for such assimilation into the melting pot was sometimes high, the compensation that was promised was the American dream of economic advancement in the land of opportunity. Given these differences in outlook, it is hardly surprising that European theorists chose to focus on the enduring elements of individual character while their American counterparts preferred to concentrate on the possibilities for individual change and growth.

Perhaps because personality change is so commonplace here, American psychologists have shown a greater interest in the healthy personality than have the Europeans, who are more inclined to study the symptoms of personality disturbance. In Chapter 1, it was noted that the psychoanalytic tradition provides us with a *medical model* of mental illness, in which bizarre and inappropriate behavior is regarded as the external symptom of internal psychological disease. In contrast to the European characterologists, American personologists have devoted greater attention to the extent to which "normal" as well as "abnormal" behavior can be influenced by the social forces at work in day-to-day interactions.

An American theorist who represents a blend of the European and American viewpoints is Harry Stack Sullivan. Born in 1892, Sullivan was, as a medically trained, practicing psychiatrist rather than an academically oriented psychologist, the closest American counterpart to Freud. After a decade spent treating schizophrenic patients at various hospitals in the vicinity of Washington, D. C., Sullivan opened a private practice in New York City in 1929. He felt that knowledge of the means by which neurotic office patients had learned to cope with life crises would provide insight into the reasons for the failure of these means in individuals who contracted schizophrenia.

Throughout his career, Sullivan argued that individual personalities could not be understood apart from the social environments in which they developed. This conviction brought him into contact with members of the Chicago School of Sociology. This group of academics at the University of Chicago had, for some time, maintained an association with Jane Addams' Hull House, a private institution of social welfare founded in 1889 and dedicated to improving the lot of immigrants in transition. Besides the social philosopher George Herbert Mead, the Chicago school included, among others, noted sociologists W. I. Thomas and Robert E. Park (who coined the term *marginal man*), cultural anthropologist Edward Sapir, and political scientists Charles E. Merriam and Harold Lasswell.

Sapir and Lasswell collaborated with Sullivan on the establishment of the William Alanson White Psychiatric Foundation, which was to be dedicated to promoting a fusion of psychiatry and social science. White was a leading figure in the movement toward a medical model of mental illness and, as president of the American Psychiatric Association, facilitated, in 1928 and 1929, the convening of the first and second Colloquium on Personality Investigation. Psychiatrists, members of the Chicago school, and psychologists (including Gordon Allport) were encouraged in convention proceedings to "survey the field of interrelations of psychiatry and the social sciences, with view to greater cooperation among those concerned in studying *the nature and influence of cultural environments*" (Perry, 1964, p. xviii).

Sullivan (1947, p. xi) defined personality as "the relatively enduring pattern of recurrent interpersonal situations which characterize a human life." Taken literally, this would suggest that one need go no further in studying personality than the mere observation of the content of social interaction. Sullivan cautioned, however, that observation of the superficial aspects of any interpersonal situation might mislead one as to its psychological meaning for the participants. Therefore, it is important to understand the dynamics of the mind before one can properly interpret the impact that experiences in the social environment have on personality.

Sullivan's view of personality as the product of an interaction between internal psychological dynamics and the external sociocultural environment is a theme which runs throughout the American personological tradition. Another trend in American (and Soviet) psychology went much further than the personologists in calling attention to the effects of environmental conditions on individual behavior and, in fact, denied that internal dispositions needed to be considered at all in analyzing human action. This behaviorist orientation is considered in Chapter 4. For now, our attention will be focused on the personologists, who included both internal and external forces in their model of human personality.

Henry Murray coined the term *personology*, and so his theoretical position will be examined first. A colleague and friend of Murray's, Gordon Allport, comes next, followed by three theorists not normally considered *personologists*: George Kelly, Abraham Maslow, and Carl Rogers. The labels usually applied to the three latter psychologists are *cognitive*, *phenomenological*, or *humanistic*.

Regardless of how they are customarily catego-

rized, however, it will be seen that Kelly, Maslow, and Rogers all believed that human beings had certain inherent needs and potentialities which motivated their interactions with their social and physical environments. All believed that the outcome of this process was a unique personality for every individual. Taking a somewhat existential or phenomenological stance, they maintained that reality for a particular person was that person's subjective experience of the world. Any attempt to impose a definition of reality on an individual would be detrimental to the psychological health of that individual. None of these theorists regarded himself as a *behaviorist*.

My confidence in grouping all these psychologists together is bolstered somewhat by Maddi and Costa (1972), who perceived enough common ground among Murray, Allport, and Maslow to describe them as coequal contributors to *humanism in personology*. With this support for the basic thrust of the chapter, I have been encouraged to go a step further and include a box describing Asian approaches to personality psychology. Asian conceptions of personality are somewhat similar to the phenomenological and humanistic positions within the American personological tradition.

Just what are the theories that make up the personological perspective?

MURRAY'S COMPONENTS OF PERSONALITY

The middle child of a wealthy New York family, Henry Murray, born in 1893, led a comfortable childhood of summer vacations on Long Island, trips to Europe, and attendance at private schools, culminating in a B.A. from Harvard College, a medical degree from Columbia University (in 1919), and, later, a Ph.D. degree in biochemistry from Cambridge University (in 1927). A practicing surgeon, his conversion to psychology occurred partly because of an exhilarating three

Henry Murray, the theorist who coined the term personology. It refers to a distinctively American tradition of psychology that emphasizes the importance of social interactions on the personality. (Harvard University)

weeks spent in the company of Carl Jung (Murray, 1967, pp. 288–290).

Murray suffered from two physical defects: an *external strabismus* (a turning outward of one eye) and a severe stutter. He tried to compensate for the first by working to excel at sports which required a great deal of eye-hand coordination and for the second by aspiring to professional attainments which others would admire. Despite his lack of formal education in psychology, then, Murray's background and persuasive talents convinced Morton Prince, founder of the Harvard Psychological Clinic, that he would make a good assistant. In 1928, Murray became director of this clinic and commenced his research and theorizing in personality.

Murray accepted the psychoanalytic position that behavior is motivated by internal needs which crave satisfaction. In place of just two major psychodynamic needs (sex and aggression), however, Murray compiled a long list of needs (which he abbreviated *n*). This list included *n* Abasement, *n* Achievement, *n* Affiliation, *n* Aggression, *n* Autonomy, *n* Deference, *n* Dominance, *n* Exhibition, *n* Nurturance, *n* Order, *n* Play, *n* Sentience, *n* Sex, and so on. (The *n* should be read, in each case, as "a need for.") These needs can be activated not only by internal biological or temperamental processes but also by environmental events, which he called *press* (Murray, 1938). For example, the press of a frustrating opponent (*p* Opposition) might activate *n* Aggression, the presence of a higher-status person (*p* Superior person) might evoke *n* Deference, or the presence of a physically attractive person might arouse *n* Sex.

Needs may *fuse* with one another to produce the unique temperament of a particular human being. Thus, *n* Sex fused with *n* Affiliation would probably describe an individual who seeks a mutually satisfying intimate relationship with a partner, while *n* Sex fused with *n* Aggression would represent people who seek to degrade their romantic partners.

Murray believed that one's overall orientation toward sensual expression developed from a clustering of *n* Exhibition, *n* Play, *n* Sentience, and *n* Sex. This entire cluster of needs might be satisfied simultaneously, as when a couple dresses in their finest clothes (*n* Exhibition) to go dancing at a dazzlingly lit disco (*n* Play and *n* Sentience), following which they share a romantic interlude (*n* Sex). On other occasions, only some aspects of the cluster might be satisfied, as when one experiences the excitement of participation in a competitive sports activity or is thrilled by the beauty of a sunset.

Another important clustering of needs forms the trait of *ascendance*. This cluster consists of *n* Aggression, *n* Dominance, and *n* Exhibition. Note that satisfying the trait of ascendance requires the presence of other individuals who are willing to be deferent (p Deference). It is in this way that needs within a person interact with the social environment to produce a particular character structure. Two additional clusters identified by Murray were (1) the needs for organization, stability, and sameness and (2) the needs for nurturance, abasement, and a desire to be dominated or even abused by other people.

Thema is the term used by Murray to describe one need being both activated and fulfilled by one press. For example, a child in the presence of a doting mother (p Nurturance) may experience activation of a desire to be hugged (n Affiliation) and is also likely to have that need satisfied. People tend to seek out other persons and situations which are likely to activate and satisfy their most important needs and fusions of needs. Murray calls these tendencies thematic dispositions and regards them as the fundamental components of individual character (Murray, 1959). He devised a famous personality test, called the Thematic Apperception Test, or TAT, which permitted him to assess the strength of such thematic dispositions in an individual's character (Morgan and Murray, 1935). The TAT presents the client with a pictorial scene and asks him or her to make up a story which includes the scene. The TAT and some of the research derived from it are described in Chapter 5. The greatest success of the TAT has been encountered in efforts to measure n Achievement.

Two paper-and-pencil personality inventories have also been derived from Murray's theory of needs. The Edwards Personal Preference Schedule, or EPPS, requires the client to choose the most preferred alternatives from among 210 pairs of items matched for their general social desirability (Edwards, 1959). A sample pair would be "I like to say what I think about things" vs. "I like to forgive my friends who may sometimes hurt me." Using this scale, Milton and Lipetz (1968) confirmed the existence of Murray's clusters of ascendance, deference, and orderliness. The EPPS appears to have adequate test-retest reliability,

but evidence for the validity of the scoring procedure has been inconclusive (Stricker, 1965). See Chapter 1 if you cannot remember what is meant by the terms reliability and validity. Need for achievement, as measured on the EPPS, has been found to be correlated with grade-point averages in high school and college.

Jackson (1967) has devised a Personality Research Form which does not employ the paired-item format of the EPPS. Instead, each item describes a personal characteristic, and the examinee simply indicates the extent to which the statement applies to himself or herself. Both Edwards (1959) and Jackson (1967, 1974) have reported that men score higher than women on this test in each of the three needs in the ascendance group (n Aggression, n Dominance, and n Exhibition).

Murray's description of personality development during childhood follows Freud's quite closely, but Murray adds a claustral ("return-to-the-womb") and a urethral stage to Freud's oral, anal, and phallic stages. As for personality development in adulthood, Murray simply drew a further distinction between middle age and old age (which he calls senescence). He accepted the Freudian notion of repression and the possibility that unconscious needs and impulses can exert a strong influence on human behavior.

ALLPORT'S COMPONENTS OF PERSONALITY

A colleague of Murray's at Harvard, Gordon W. Allport, shared his belief in the fundamental uniqueness of each individual's internal needs and dispositions, but he disputed the importance of unconscious determinants of behavior. Allport also rejected Freud's psychosexual stages and offered his own alternative model of the growth of personality from birth to maturity.

Allport was born in Indiana in 1897, but his father, a physician, soon moved the family to Cleveland, where Allport spent most of his childhood. With the encouragement of his elder brother, Floyd, Gordon entered Harvard University in 1915. Floyd was, at the time, a graduate student in psychology. Upon completing his doctorate, he went on to become a well-known psychologist. This no doubt had an influence on Gordon's choice of a career.

Like Sullivan, Allport had a keen interest in fusing psychological thought with a concern for social issues. He was also something of an activist; even as an undergraduate, he devoted his spare time to "conducting a boy's club in Boston's West End, visiting for the Family Society, serving as a volunteer probation officer, registering homes for war workers, and assisting foreign students" (Pettigrew, 1970, p. xvi).

Upon receiving his doctorate in psychology in 1922, Allport was awarded a fellowship which funded a year's study in Europe. During this period, he visited Freud and was surprised and slightly offended when the famed psychoanalyst suggested that an anecdote which Allport told—about a small boy on a bus who was excessively fearful of getting dirty—might have an unconscious, personal significance.

Allport was, throughout his life, an academic, and he never practiced psychotherapy. Even so, his studies in Europe gave him an enduring appreciation for the uniqueness of each individual's perception and interpretation of life experiences. He rebelled against what he called the *nomothetic* approach of the behaviorally oriented psychologists whom, he believed, were overlooking individual variations in experience and style of expression in their search for universal laws of behavior. Allport (1961, pp. 8-9) stressed the importance of taking an *idiographic* approach to psychology, an approach in which the individual is viewed as "a system of patterned uniqueness."

Allport substituted the word "proprium" for what other theorists had called the *self* or the *ego*. He did this primarily because he considered personality to be composed of several different *aspects* of selfhood, each incorporated at a different stage of development. The first aspect to evolve, he believed, is a sense of the *bodily self*, or an awareness of the body as an entity distinct from its surrounding environment. Allport believed that this sense of bodily self emerged mainly as a result of recurrent muscular sensations. He cites research on sensory deprivation as evidence of the disorientation and loss of selfhood that occurs when these sensations are drastically reduced (see the discussion of this topic in Chapter 10).

In learning to speak, a child experiences a growing awareness of self-identity. He or she is given a personal name and is taught that evaluations ("good" vs. "bad") or feeling states ("happy," "angry," and "sick," for example) can be attached to that name. Along with this devel-

Gordon Allport, a personologist who placed great emphasis on the development of the self and the uniqueness of each individual's collection of traits. (Harvard University)

opment of self-identity comes a sense of *self-esteem*, an outgrowth of a (possibly inborn) *need for autonomy*. At this stage, the child wants to manipulate the environment and do things independently. In succeeding, the child experiences a feeling of mastery and pride; in failing, or when its activities are interfered with, the child experiences a loss of confidence and may erupt in anger. Allport's need for autonomy resembles Adler's drive for power (see Chapter 2).

By the age of 3, then, Allport believes the child has developed a sense of *early self*, which includes the bodily self, self-identity, and self-esteem. Between the ages of 4 and 6, the child begins to engage in *self-extension*. Other persons (e.g., siblings, friends) or objects (favorite toys, for example) are perceived as important components of one's own identity. A rudimentary *self-image*, or conscience, also emerges at this time, as the child internalizes his or her parents' expectations for behavior and so begins to establish personal standards of "goodness" and "naughtiness."

In the years 6 to 12, self-identity, self-esteem, self-image, and the capacity for self-extension continue to develop, and the child also gains an awareness of the *self as rational coper*. Previously, although the child has been capable of solving simple mental problems, he or she has done so almost reflexively. Now, suddenly, the child becomes consciously aware of his or her capacity for abstract thought and the opportunity it offers to work through complex problems in a planned sequence of logical steps.

Allport agrees with Erikson (see Chapter 2) that the chief characteristic of adolescence is an increasingly urgent search for self-identity. The adolescent ". . . seeks popularity and is fearful of ostracism. . . . Seldom does the adolescent defy teen-age mores. His self-image and sense of identity are not firm enough to stand the strain" (Allport, 1961, p. 125). The major cause of this identity problem is the necessity for choosing a career and establishing an independent life. The attainment of independence requires the selection and pursuit of long-term goals and calls forth

one additional aspect of selfhood: *propriate striving*. Through successful attempts to achieve self-defined goals, the adult finally attains a durable sense of self-esteem and a stable self-identity and self-image.

The fully formed adult personality, or *proprium*, consists of all the foregoing aspects of selfhood. Allport believed the nature of the individual proprium was revealed by certain consistencies in thought and action, consistencies which he called *traits:*

> In everyday life, no one, not even a psychologist, doubts that underlying the conduct of a mature person there are characteristic dispositions or traits. His enthusiasms, interests, and styles of expression are far too self-consistent and plainly patterned to be accounted for in terms of specific habits or identical elements. (Allport, 1937, p. 339)

Traits, according to Allport, can be *cardinal*, *central*, or *secondary*. A *cardinal trait* is one so dominant in an individual's personality that it is expressed in nearly every aspect of his or her behavior (the preoccupation with sexuality which is manifested in the erotic life-style of a Casanova, for instance). The personalities of most of us, however, are characterized by five to ten central traits rather than a single cardinal trait. In addition, each of us generally possesses a number of secondary traits which are relatively weak and inconsistent determinants of our life-style and, hence, provide little insight into our true personalities. Box 3-1 describes some research which has shown the effect of traits on our perception of another's personality.

As part of their study of traits, Allport and Vernon (1933) looked for evidence of individual patterning by taking repeated measurements of traits such as speed of walking, strength of handshake, drawing of geometric figures, and so forth. These tended to be consistent for each subject, even though there were wide variations between individuals. Subjects were consistent

BOX 3-1

TRAIT CENTRALITY IN PERSON PERCEPTION

Solomon Asch (1946) reversed the focus of Allport's concept of trait centrality when he proposed that there are certain characteristics of other people which play a dominant role in shaping our impressions of their personalities. Asch gave subjects lists of adjectives and asked them to write a description of the type of person to whom the adjectives would apply. Two of these lists read as follows:

1 Intelligent, skillful, industrious, warm, determined, practical, cautious
2 Intelligent, skillful, industrious, cold, determined, practical, cautious

The only difference between these lists was the substitution of the adjective "cold" for the adjective "warm." Yet the first was found to describe someone like a competent, socially dedicated scientist trying to do some good for humanity; the second was found to describe a selfish snob whose success had made him or her a manipulative and unsympathetic elitist. Asch tried substituting other evaluative adjective pairs in the lists (e.g., "polite" vs. "blunt"), but none of them had the same dramatic effect. When asked to attribute other traits to these hypothetical persons, 91 percent of subjects given the "warm" list described the person as "sociable," 86 percent said he was "humane," 84 percent "popular," and 77 percent "humorous." The corresponding percentages for subjects reading the "cold" list were 38 percent, 31 percent, 28 percent, and 13 percent, respectively. Asch concluded that warmth or coldness was a central trait in person perception.

Inspired by Asch's study, Kelley (1950) told students in one of his classes that a guest lecturer would be coming in to give a brief talk and to preside over a class discussion. The department faculty were allegedly interested in the students' reaction to the instructor, and this mimeographed sheet describing his background was handed out:

Mr.———is a graduate student in the Department of Economics and Social Science here at M.I.T. He has had three semesters of teaching experience in psychology at another college. This is his first semester teaching Ec. 70. He is 26 years old, a veteran, and married. People who know him consider him to be a rather warm person, industrious, critical, practical, and determined.

Half the students received the above description; the other half received a description which was identical except for the substitution of "cold" for "warm." The "lecturer" then gave his talk, and students were asked for their reactions. Sure enough, students in the "warm" group gave the instructor a more favorable evaluation than did those in the "cold" group, even though all of the students had heard the same talk. Students in the former group were also more likely than those in the latter to initiate interaction with the instructor during the class discussion. In terms of the specific trait attributions studied by Asch, the students given the "warm" description rated the instructor significantly more sociable, humane, popular, and generous than did their counterparts in the "cold" group.

Wishner (1960) argued that many traits besides the "warm" vs. "cold" dimension could become central if placed in the proper context. Asch, he said, had selected adjectives for his list that, with the exception of warmth-coldness, correlate fairly highly among themselves when people give their impressions of others. This meant that inclusion of "warm" or "cold" on the list added *new* information not already supplied by the other adjectives, all of which clustered around the general characteristic of competence. In addition, the warm-cold dimension correlates rather strongly with the traits (sociable, humane, popular, and so forth) on Asch's dependent measure, while the competence cluster does not. If the context created by the adjectives on Asch's list were different, Wishner predicted, other dimensions, such as humane-ruthless, could become central traits. He obtained experimental results which supported his conclusion.

For anyone wanting to do their own experiments, Anderson (1968) has provided *likableness* ratings of 555 common personality traits. The most liked were "sincere," "honest," "understanding," "intelligent," and "dependable." The least liked were "malicious," "dishonest," "mean," "phony," and "liar." In the middle were "quiet," "ordinary," and "critical."

---

even to the point of activating the same muscle groups each time they confronted a given task. The authors reported additional research by a professional handwriting analyst which indicated that handwriting samples can, with an accuracy greater than chance, be matched by untrained judges with brief personality sketches describing the writers. Allport and Cantril (1934) found that untrained judges were also somewhat successful in identifying a speaker's occupation, political orientation, extraversion, and dominance, merely by listening to voice cues.

Interested in finding out how many personality traits there were, Allport and Odbert (1936) consulted an unabridged dictionary and compiled a list of 4541 psychological trait names. Given the large number of traits and the varying intensi-

ty with which each trait might be present in a given person, Allport concluded that it was highly unlikely that any two individuals would have identical personalities.

Before bringing to a close our treatment of Allport, we should comment on his views of human motivation and the mature personality. Allport agreed that simple conditioning (doing what is rewarded and not doing or avoiding what is unrewarded or punished) can account for behavior at a very elemental level. Once a given behavior has been repeated several times, however, it remains in a person's repertory only if it is congruous with that individual's developing propriate organization. The principle of *propriate learning* states, therefore, that it is extremely difficult to teach someone something that one

Professional graphologists believe they can accurately discern an individual's personality traits from a sample of his or her handwriting. (United Press International)

does not perceive as being of value to him- or herself. The motivations which endure become *functionally autonomous*, which means that goals are selected and pursued on the basis of their congruity with the person's self-image, self-identity, propriate strivings, and desire for growth and self-extension. As Allport (1961, p. 138) puts it, "Quasi-mechanical principles account for the emergence of the proprium; but once established, the proprium becomes the principal source of subsequent learning." Thus, one often observes that the perfectionist who goes to extra effort to put on all of the finishing touches is not paid anything more for the extra trouble; one does one's work well for its own sake because that is the type of character one has developed. An implication of this reasoning, for Allport, was that adult motivation could only be

understood in terms of its present purposes. It would be debasing and misleading to attempt to explain perfectionism, for example, by delving (as psychoanalysts are prone to do) into the perfectionists receiving parental praise for making bowel movements at appropriate times and places during toilet training.

Allport was led from these considerations into the study of values, which he and Vernon (1931) designated as *theoretical, economic, aesthetic, social, political,* and *religious.* A personality inventory was designed to measure the strength of each of these values in an individual's character. Groups tested usually showed the differences in value orientation one would expect to find; for example, medical students had a strong commitment to theoretical values and theology students to religious ones (Allport, Vernon, & Lindzey,

1951). As one of the few available measures of such traits, the scale of values has withstood the test of time and continues to be used today.

Allport believed, finally, that the mature personality possesses a fairly stable *self-image* (emotional security) and *self-identity* (acceptance of oneself) based on its orientation toward each of the foregoing value areas; these, plus propriate strivings, produce a unifying philosophy of life. The mature individual, or *whole man*, should also have a capacity to relate warmly to others, to extend his or her life beyond the bounds of immediate needs and duties, and to regard his or her personal foibles with humor and insight.

KELLY'S COMPONENTS OF PERSONALITY

George A. Kelly was born in 1905 in Kansas. He grew up there and attended, first, a local college and, later, Park College in Missouri, where he received his B.A. degree. He sampled graduate education at the University of Kansas, the University of Minnesota, and the University of Edinburgh before finally completing his doctorate at the State University of Iowa in 1931.

Kelly then organized a mobile psychological clinic which provided treatment both for troublesome students referred by the public schools and adults suffering from the stress and social dislocation caused by the Great Depression. Though he initially experienced success in offering his clients standard Freudian insights into the origins of their psychological problems, Kelly (1963, p. 52) soon discovered that almost *any* interpretation of their problems, no matter how preposterous, achieved similar results. Individuals troubled by recurrent indigestion, for example, might be told that they were "rebelling against nourishment of all kinds—parental, educational, and nutritional," and digestion would improve. The success of such treatment, Kelly decided, was due to the patients' acceptance of his status as a professional

adviser and their willingness to try out a new way of perceiving themselves and the manner in which they interacted with others. Psychological distress, he concluded, was caused by some inadequacy in an individual's current outlook on life and could be reduced by trying out an alternative viewpoint which would break the person free of his or her former belief system and permit some adaptive modifications in it.

Kelly gave his theorizing a formal structure during the years he was director of the Psychological Clinic at Ohio State University. He later became professor of psychology at Brandeis University, a position he held until his death in 1966.

The scientific method of formulating hypotheses and checking them against empirical data is, according to Kelly, analogous to the manner in which the human personality copes with the physical and social environment. Like a scientist, each of us in our everyday life retains those hypotheses which are confirmed by experiential evidence and discards or revises those which are denied or contradicted; our ultimate goal is to arrive at a set of hypotheses which will allow us to predict and so control our environment. Kelly (1955, p. 9) calls these hypotheses *personal constructs:*

Man looks at his world through transparent patterns or templets which he creates and then attempts to fit over the realities of which the world is composed. The fit is not always very good. Yet without such patterns the world appears to be such an undifferentiated homogeneity that man is unable to make any sense out of it. Even a poor fit is more helpful to him than nothing at all.

One very challenging implication of this proposition—which Kelly himself pointed out (pp. 6–12)—is that we can never be certain of perceiving absolute reality; we can only distinguish between constructs in terms of the degree to which they are able to account for past events and provide an accurate forecast of future ones. One reason why it is often difficult for people to communicate is that persons generally "differ from one another in their construction of events" (p. 55). Moreover, "Each person characteristically evolves for his convenience in anticipating events, a construction system embracing ordinal relationships between constructs" (p. 56). This means, for example, that someone may have a "good" vs. "bad" construct which is superordinate to other evaluative dimensions, such that goodness includes attributes like honesty, helpfulness, friendliness, and so on. If this person experiences a contradiction in the evidence provided by subordinate constructs, as in the case of a politician who has always appeared helpful and friendly but who is now indicted for dishonesty, the dominant impression of "goodness" may nonetheless be regarded as validated by most of the available evidence, and the contradictory data may be suppressed.

Because we experience *anxiety* whenever we perceive that our construction system cannot account for all the available data, we suppress contradictory subordinate constructs as one means to avoid making psychologically painful, large-scale alterations. Anxiety must be a fairly common feeling since, according to Kelly, most people construe their world in a rigidly dichotomous, "either-or" manner. These dichotomies are revealed by asking someone to describe a way in which two individuals, say a father and a liked teacher, are similar (e.g., quiet and easygoing) and a way in which they both differ from a third party, say a *pitied person* (nervous and hypertensive). Usually, within twenty to thirty presentations of such role triads, someone's construction system has been adequately elaborated. The formal procedures to be followed in administering the triads and subjecting the construct system to mathematical analysis have been known as the Role Construct Repertory (or Rep) Test. A great deal of empirical research has been conducted using the Rep test; some of this work and the test itself are described in Box 3-2.

Identifying the construct system is crucial to understanding an individual's behavior since, according to Kelly's *fundamental postulate*, "A person's processes are psychologically channelized by the ways in which he anticipates events" (1955, p. 46). In other words, the way in which we construe ourselves and our physical and social environments will determine our behavior.

Kelly did not specify any sequence of stages in the development of the construct system from birth to maturity. Neither did he feel it was necessary to explain why human beings are motivated to create these systems; he had no use for psychoanalytic dynamisms, believing that every person is motivated "for no other reason that that he is alive" (Kelly, 1958, p. 49).

He did, however, include a definition of mental disorder: "From the standpoint of the psychology of personal constructs, we may define a disorder as any personal construction which is used repeatedly in spite of consistent invalidation" (Kelly, 1955, p. 831). He maintained that in a sense, "all disorders of communication are disorders involving anxiety" (p. 895). He felt that the neurotic is frantically searching for ways of construing his or her world that will achieve sufficient validation to reduce anxiety, while the psychotic has already found at least a temporary constructive system which receives validation through his or her fantasies.

When treating a mental disorder, Kelly first tried to create an *atmosphere of experimentation*, in which the patient felt free to reveal his or her constructions of reality in a protected environment. If the client attempted to cast him in a role defined by the client's constructs (as a father figure, a medical doctor with a magic prescription for cure, a priestly absolver of guilt, and so on) he would gently disassociate himself from this role and ask the client to view him differently. The client will persistently seek validation of old constructs ("Don't you agree my spouse is impossible?"), but the therapist will respond by adding new elements to the construct and asking the patient to react to them. In this way, the patient

BOX 3-2
THE ROLE CONSTRUCT REPERTORY (REP) TEST

Although Kelly's Rep test may appear very formal and structured, it actually permits the examinee to describe the social world in his or her own terms. The first task for the test-taker, or client, is to list, on the right, the names of people in his or her life who correspond to descriptions on the left. Here is an example of items on the test:

1	Self (yourself)	1	____
2	Mother (or the person who has played the part of mother in your life)	2	____
3	Father (or the person who has played the part of father in your life)	3	____
4	Brother (or, if you have no brother, the person who is most like one)	4	____
5	Girl cousin (or other female relative close to you in age)	5	____
6	Boyfriend (if you are male, your closest male pal; if female, the male with whom you have a close dating relationship)	6	____
7	Girlfriend (if you are female, your closest female pal; if male, the female with whom you have a close dating relationship)	7	____
8	Disliked person	8	____
9	Unhappy person	9	____
10	Successful person	10	____

Kelly (1955) suggested twenty-two persons who might be described in the list, but the ten descriptions shown above should be sufficient to illustrate the procedures of the Rep test. These are the ten that Kelly himself felt were most relevant to understanding the constructs of a particular client.

Next, three names are drawn from this list, and the client is asked to indicate which two of the three seem in some way to be similar and in what respect these two differ from the third. The characteristic which two of the three share is called the *construct*, and the client is asked to write out a phrase describing this dimension. The characteristic which causes the third person to be perceived as different from the other two is called the *contrast*.

The Rep test is traditionally presented in a *grid*, or graph-paper, format. Circles are drawn under the names of the three people who are to be compared and contrasted on a given trial, or *sort*. The examinee places X marks in the circles of the two people who appear to be similar and leaves the circle of the contrasting person blank. Then X marks are placed under the names of people who share the characteristic which defines the perceived similarity between the two people getting the X's. This process is repeated across several sorts. As in deciding which persons will be described, Kelly would make some selection of the most diagnostically interesting from among the large number of possible sorts.

An example of a Rep grid, completed by a young woman named "Sue B.," is provided by Sechrest (1977, p. 224); see the accompanying illustration.

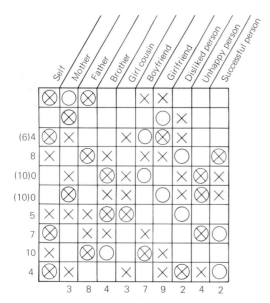

Name	Sue B

Sex   M   (F)   Age   19

	Construct	Contrast
1	easy-going	tense
2	artistic	not artistic
3	females	males
4	outgoing	introverted
5	nervous	calm
6	tense	easy-going
7	my family	not my family
8	down to earth	sort of pretentious
9	fun loving	serious
10	females	males

In Sue's first sort, "Self" and "Father" were perceived as similar (X's within the circles), and the construct was described as "easygoing." Mother was assigned the contrasting trait of "tense." "Boyfriend" and "Girlfriend" were perceived as sharing the characteristic of easygoingness with "Self" and "Father." In addition, it might be noted that "Brother," "Girl cousin," "Disliked person," "Unhappy person," and "Successful person" were *not* given an X for easygoingness.

On her second sort, Sue described "Mother" and "Girl cousin" as alike in terms of artistic interests and different from "Girlfriend," who was not artistic. "Disliked person" shared artistic interests with Sue's mother and cousin. The third sort simply discriminated females from males, but it is noteworthy that "Disliked person" and "Unhappy person" received checks for having feminine attributes.

Additional interesting information can be obtained from the constructs Sue used on Sorts 4–10, but it is also helpful to look down the columns as well as across the rows. From this perspective, it can be seen that the people Sue liked best ("Father," "Boyfriend," and "Girlfriend") she described as *easygoing, not artistic, outgoing, calm,* and *fun-loving.* The people Sue liked least ("Mother," "Girl cousin," and "Disliked person") were perceived as tense, artistic, female, introverted, nervous, pretentious, and serious. "Brother" seems to have been viewed ambivalently, as outgoing and down to earth but, at the same time, nervous, tense, and serious. "Successful person" was regarded with similar ambivalence.

The most important construct dimension in Sue's categorization of people appears to have been the cluster of adjectives comprising sociability ("easygoing," "calm," "outgoing," "fun-loving") versus those describing a tendency to withdraw from others ("tense," "nervous," "introverted," "serious"). Another important construct might be called *"snobbish"* (artistic, pretentious) vs. *"genuine"* (not artistic, down-to-earth). If these constructs were causing Sue to experience anxiety in her interpersonal relationships, Kelly might ask her to play the role of a serious, introverted person who appreciates art. This role-playing could perhaps reveal to Sue that the negative cluster of traits she attributed to such people was an overly simplistic stereotype and so might lead her to make some adaptive changes in her construct system (e.g., people of this sort qualify as "Disliked persons" only if they are also inconsiderate and pretentious).

Research using the Rep test has shown that commune members who participate in close interpersonal interaction over an extended time period become progressively more alike in their constructs (Karst & Groutt, 1977). People who possess an embarrassing personal characteristic, such as stuttering or alcoholism, tend to place others sharing this characteristic at the negative pole of their construct system, while, at the same time describing themselves in very different terms from those they use to describe the afflicted "others" (Fransella, 1977). Fransella speculates that this failure to categorize one's self in a realistic manner may contribute to the maintenance of problem behavior.

These and other intriguing findings are contained in a collection of articles (mostly authored by British psychologists) on personal-constructs theory which was edited by Bannister (1977).

---

will get feedback on the validity of his or her constructs in an environment which minimizes anxiety reactions.

Eventually, the patient will be asked to participate in *fixed-role therapy.* Here, the client submits a detailed self-description, and a panel of psychologists familiar with the case writes up a personality sketch describing an individual who has selected alternatives on the whole contradictory to choices that the client has made on his or her construct dimensions. The patient is then asked to read the sketch and act out the contradictory role. The client's first attempts will, of course, be rather clumsy, but they will be acted out within the security of the clinical setting, with the therapist taking part in the make-believe by assuming the role of "significant others" in the patient's life. Then the therapist asks the client to "play the role continuously— eat it, sleep it, feel it"—for a period of about two weeks (1955, p. 388). It is hoped that the client will find validation for at least some aspects of this new role and so learn new ways of behaving and of constructing himself and others, ways that will provide better predictions of events than did his or her old constructs.

Kelly's role-playing technique has been adapted for use in more recent attitude-change experiments. Mann (1967), for example, found that smokers who played the role of someone who has been diagnosed as suffering from lung cancer, and who underwent preparations for exploratory surgery at the direction of their "physician," were significantly more likely to reduce or give up smoking than were counterparts who were exposed to rational arguments designed to arouse a sense of shame and fear. The popular technique of _psycho-drama_ represents an extension of fixed-role therapy into the field of theatrics, though its proponents are sometimes unaware of the connection. Unfortunately, Kelly himself probably felt that his theory had not been sufficiently understood and appreciated by his contemporaries, since many of these validating developments occurred subsequent to his death.

In 1976, the annual Symposium on Motivation at the University of Nebraska was devoted to a discussion of personal-construct psychology. Pa-

In psychodrama, people act out the roles of significant others in their lives. The technique has much in common with Kelly's fixed-role therapy. (Editorial Photocolor Archives)

pers by Sarbin (1976) and Mancuso (1976) described Kelly's theory as a bold anticipation of the growing interest in "contextualism" and the declining authority of psychoanalytic or behavioral concepts among psychologists. By *contextualism*, they meant the study of the quality of interpersonal relationships as the basic unit of analysis rather than unconscious repressions or stimulus-response sequences. The metaphor of actors wearing masks and attempting to interpret the meaning of the masks worn by others in social encounters has been used increasingly in recent years to describe the working of human personality (Bateson, 1972; Goffman, 1959, 1974; Jourard, 1971). This aspect of contextualism has a clear historical relationship to the concepts on which Kelly based his technique of fixed-role therapy. Personal-constructs theory has been particularly popular among British psychologists (Bannister, 1977), who have done a great deal of research using the Rep test and have sought to improve on Kelly's original design and procedures (Bannister & Mair, 1968).

MASLOW'S COMPONENTS OF PERSONALITY

Born to a Russian immigrant couple in New York City in 1908, Abraham Maslow recalled his childhood as being for the most part an unhappy time (Wilson, 1972, pp. 130–131). As his family became more prosperous and moved from a Jewish ghetto to more middle-class neighborhoods, young Abe found himself the target of abuse by gangs of Irish and Italian children.

As an undergraduate, Maslow majored in psychology at the University of Wisconsin and remained there for his postgraduate studies. Two of his professors in the small psychology department—Harry Harlow and William Sheldon—offered their protection and guidance to this brilliant but shy and socially awkward student.

Maslow's doctoral dissertation was an observation of the sexual and aggressive behavior of primates housed in a zoo in Madison, Wisconsin, and in Harlow's laboratory at the university (Maslow, 1936; Maslow & Flanzbaum, 1936). He concluded that the social and sexual dominance of some animals over others was customarily maintained not by means of overt physical aggression but through a feeling of self-confidence which the dominant animal was able to communicate to subordinates. Maslow (1937, 1939, 1942) extended this concept of *dominance feeling* to human beings in a series of interview studies and found that highly dominant people tend to have strong feelings of competence and self-esteem and to be lacking in timidity, self-consciousness, or embarrassment.

It was in the course of these early investigations that Maslow developed the notion that people have certain internal needs (e.g., the need for self-esteem) which must be satisfied before they can progress to higher levels of character development (e.g., dominance feeling). From this point onward, he abandoned the observation and interview techniques acceptable to scientifically oriented psychologists and took a more intuitive approach toward putting together a theory of personality. After a decade on the faculty of Brooklyn College in New York City, Maslow became professor and chairman of the psychology department of Brandeis University in 1951, a position he held until a year before his death in 1970.

The fulfillment of certain needs is at the core of Maslow's (1943) conception of personality functioning. Foremost among such needs is the need for the substances necessary to maintain the body's physiological functioning—water, oxygen, proteins, minerals, and so forth. When these physiological needs have been satisfied, the individual looks to his or her safety and security. Maslow's special contribution to theories of human motivation was the idea that needs are hierarchically ordered so that those lower in the hierarchy must be satisfied before the needs of the next higher stage are evoked. For example, a

THE THIRD FORCE IN PSYCHOLOGY

Abraham Maslow, on the top, and Carl Rogers below, were prominent figures in the development of the humanistic offshoot of the American personological tradition. Humanistic psychology shares with psychoanalytic theory the belief that humans are endowed with innate needs and desires, but it differs from psychoanalysis in its assumption that the core of human nature is kindly, cooperative, and prosocial. Humanistic psychology shares with behaviorism the belief that humans can expand their interests and activities in an almost infinite variety of directions, but it differs from behaviorism in its assumption that an inner self freely initiates many of these choices. To emphasize the distinctions between his approach and the psychoanalytic and behaviorist viewpoints, Maslow applied the term *third force* to humanistic psychology. (*Top:* Brandeis University; *bottom:* Bettman Archives)

The picture opposite illustrates a peak experience which, according to Maslow, may be very helpful in assisting the individual to become more aware of his or her inner core of selfhood and to translate this increased awareness into behavior which reflects greater spontaneity, genuineness, and pursuit of personally meaningful goals. In this way, says Maslow, peak experiences promote the self-actualization of the person whose mind is open to them. They often occur when one is awed by the beauty of some scene or impressed by the wisdom of some great truth. (Burk Uzzle/Magnum)

man gasping for air does not worry about his financial security; all he wants is one breath of air.

According to Maslow, a person must have the physiological and safety needs fairly well met before a need for love and a sense of belonging is strongly activated. Then, when a sense of belonging has been attained, the person becomes more aware than ever before of his or her desire to be esteemed by others. This need for esteem is likely to instigate a striving for competence at some task or recognition for having achieved some goal.

Physiological needs, safety needs, love needs, and esteem needs are called *D-needs* by Maslow, with the "D" standing for *deficiency*. By this he means that whenever there is a failure to fulfill one of these needs, the individual perceives it as a deficiency and is motivated to eliminate it.

Satisfaction of all the D-needs will still not produce a completely contented person, however. Such individuals are likely to look beyond their past concerns with meeting their D-needs toward some higher goals in life. It is here that the need for *self-actualization* emerges, by which Maslow means the desire to "become everything that one is capable of becoming." Self-actualization is achieved by exploring one or more of the B-values, with the "B" standing for *being*. The B-values are divided by Maslow (1970) into those concerned with the *need to know* (e.g., Truth, Justice, Meaningfulness) and those involving *aesthetic appreciation* (e.g., Beauty, Perfection, Order, Simplicity). Some B-values, such as Effortlessness, Playfulness, and Self-sufficiency, are not easily placed in either of the foregoing categories. Maslow (1971) finally settled on a list of fifteen B-values, plus a few subsidiary ones. A diagram of his complete hierarchy of needs is shown in Figure 3-1.

Actualization of a B-value is often associated with an event called a *peak experience*. Peak experiences produce a mystical or spiritual state in which a person feels he or she has attained insight into a great truth. "Peakers" come away from these experiences feeling more unified and whole within themselves and within their relationships with their fellow human beings. They also feel more spontaneous, creative, playful, good-humored, and self-confident. While nearly all people have peak experiences, some—called *nonpeakers* by Maslow—actively strive to close their minds to these phenomena. Nonpeakers supposedly seek to defend themselves against an awareness of their own imperfections and unfulfilled human needs by objectifying and so suppressing their emotional involvement with the world around them. Maslow offers the tough-minded, hard-nosed, rigorous scientist as one example of a nonpeaker. At the same time, he argues that a full appreciation of peak experiences

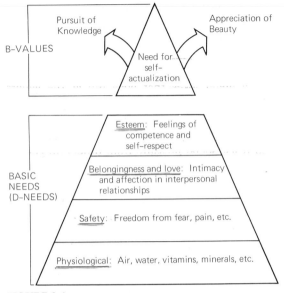

FIGURE 3-1

Maslow's hierarchy of needs. The ones lower in the hierarchy must be satisfied before any of the needs above them are activated.

requires a self-disciplined mind; and he criticizes members of the youth counterculture who try to induce peak experiences artificially through drugs, meditation, or a general overeagerness and so cheapen these phenomena (Maslow, 1971, p. 345).

Feeling that he should explain what he meant by the *self-actualized person*, Maslow (1950) undertook a detailed study of thirty-eight historical and contemporary persons whom he felt were examples of this type of individual. Among the historical figures he chose were Thomas Jefferson and Abraham Lincoln; the contemporaries included Albert Einstein and Eleanor Roosevelt. Self-actualizers, Maslow felt, have several traits in common, most especially an "efficient perception of reality" which permits them to see through complex issues more rapidly and accurately than do other people. In a problematic situation, they quickly grasp the most crucial ends to be pursued and thus are more likely to find an effective means of achieving these ends.

They accept what cannot be changed in their own and others' characters and are basically democratic in their approach to social relationships. They have a philosophical rather than a hostile sense of humor, by which Maslow means that they prefer jokes that poke fun at the general human condition to those exploiting the weaknesses of a particular individual. They have a need for privacy which sometimes causes them to resist social pressure from others. In general, their values are autonomous ones, maintained for reasons that are independent of the cultural norms. While autonomous and self-directed in their decision making, they are usually quite conventional in their outward appearances and behavior; it is the *reasons* for doing things which make the self-actualized different from other people.

On the negative side, the self-actualized can be ruthless in pursuing their chosen ends when they feel they have been betrayed or seriously misunderstood by others. On the other hand, they can be too kind, even to the point of allowing exploiters to impose upon them. Anxiety and guilt stemming from philosophical concerns can cause them to lose their sense of humor. They are relatively uninterested in superficial social conversation of the type that goes on among people "out for a good time," even though they have a spontaneous and inexhaustible enjoyment of the genuinely good things in life (nature, travel, sex, sports, food, and so on). They also suffer, to some extent, from absentmindedness.

Maslow believed that people differ from one another in the degree to which they have satisfied their D-needs and in the extent to which they have actualized one more of their B-values. These individual differences in need fulfillment produce different personality types or *syndromes*. He felt that the various needs were instinctive (and therefore innate) but that they could be distorted or overridden by adverse environmental influences. Consequently, an ideal society would be one in which children are provided with a protected physical and psychological environment that satisfies their basic needs and encourages attentiveness to the types of internal events that promote self-actualization.

It is interesting to contrast Maslow's belief that psychological health requires the nurturance and expression of instinctual needs with both the psychoanalytic position, which argues that instincts must be suppressed, and the behaviorist position, which holds that motivation is the product of rewards and punishments arising outside the organism. To distinguish his approach from the latter two traditions, Maslow (1971, pp. 3–4) called it *"third-force,"* or humanistic, psychology. Partly through his efforts, an Association of Humanistic Psychology was founded in 1962. This association provided both a professional organization and a publishing outlet for psychologists with a "third-force" orientation. Another major contributor to this orientation was Carl Rogers.

ROGERS' COMPONENTS OF PERSONALITY

Carl R. Rogers was born in Oak Park, a suburb of Chicago, on January 8, 1902. He was the fourth of six children in a home organized along strict religious and ethical lines. Alcoholic beverages, dancing, theatre, and even card games were forbidden.

After majoring in agriculture as an undergraduate at the University of Wisconsin, Rogers attended Union Theological Seminary in New York City. He soon discovered that while interested in involving himself in the improvement of the human condition, "I could not work in a field where I would be required to believe in some specified religious doctrine" (Rogers, 1961, pp. 8–9). Consequently, he became a graduate student in clinical psychology at Teachers College, Columbia University. He received his doctorate in 1931, having previously accepted a position as a psychologist in the Child Study Department of the Society for the Prevention of Cruelty to Children at Rochester, New York.

Following publication of *Clinical Treatment of the Problem Child* (Rogers, 1939), he began a new career as an academic when he was appointed to a full professorship in psychology at Ohio State University. In 1945, Rogers moved to the University of Chicago, where he developed his client-centered approach to therapy into a theory of personality. Here he ran into open conflict with the department of psychiatry, which had asked the university administration to close a counseling center directed by Rogers on the grounds that its staff were practicing medicine (i.e., psychotherapy) without a license. In a "blistering counterattack," Rogers persuaded the administration to ignore this demand (Rogers, 1973, p. 130).

From 1957 to 1963, a period during which he held a joint professorship in psychology and psychiatry at the University of Wisconsin, Rogers tried to encourage greater cooperation between these two often antagonistic fields. In 1964, he became affiliated with the Western Behavioral Sciences Institute in La Jolla, California.

To speak of Rogers' *components of personality* is actually somewhat misleading because Rogers is mainly concerned with just one, rather monolithic element: the self. This preoccupation with the self was a direct outgrowth of his experiences with clients in psychotherapy.

Speaking personally, I began my work with the settled notion that the "self" was a vague, ambiguous, scientifically meaningless term which had gone out of the psychologist's vocabulary with the departure of the introspectionists. Consequently I was slow in recognizing that when clients were given the opportunity to express their problems and their attitudes in their own terms, without any guidance or interpretation, they tended to talk in terms of the self. Characteristic expressions were attitudes such as these: "I feel I'm not being my real self." "I wonder who I am, really" . . . "I never had a chance to be myself" . . . "I think if I chip off all the plaster facade I've got a pretty

solid self—a good substantial brick building, underneath." It seemed clear from such expressions that the self was an important element in the experience of the client, and that in some odd sense his goal was to become his "real self." (Rogers, 1959, pp. 200–201)

Rogers took it for granted that reality for the infant is entirely defined by its subjective experience, or *internal frame of reference*. The infant comes equipped with an inherent motivation to expand its frame of reference. This motivation is called the *actualizing tendency* and is expressed not only in a drive to satisfy the basic needs for food, water, and so forth, but also in "development toward the differentiation of organs and of functions, expansion in terms of growth, expansion of effectiveness through the use of tools, expansion and enhancement through reproduction" (Rogers 1959, p. 196). Like Allport, Rogers believed that the human organism has an inborn need to learn how to gain mastery over its environment and avoid being controlled by forces external to itself. We can speak of *self-actualization* to the extent that a person's *self* (that aspect of the phenomenal field which is designated *I* or *me*) is in harmony or congruent with the person's experiences during the course of actualization.

These self-experiences may or may not be associated with expressions of *positive regard* by others (attitudes such as warmth, liking, respect, sympathy, and acceptance). Rogers believed that each of us has an actual *need* for positive regard. Although at one point he was inclined to treat this need as socially learned (p. 223), he later decided that "the need for love and affection seems to me to be innate" (Frick, 1971, p. 90).

If self-experiences are judged by others to be more or less worthy of their expressions of positive regard, then the individual's self-regard is likely also to become selectively judgmental. The individual is said to have acquired a *condition of worth* and will seek out or avoid self-experiences to the degree that they are congruous or incongruous with feelings of self-regard. If they are incongruous with feelings of self-regard, self-experiences may be denied access to conscious awareness or they may be perceived in a distorted fashion so as to make them congruous.

It is through the acquisition of conditions of worth and the selective choice and perception of self-experiences that mental illness may develop. Sometimes conditions of worth are congruous with self-actualizing behaviors, but on other occasions the individual is aware of an incongruousness. Tension and anxiety then develop, and the individual's behavior may fluctuate erratically between expressions of true feelings and desires and efforts to win the approval of others. The traditional neurotic defenses (rationalization, compensation, fantasy, projection, compulsions, phobias, and so forth) are manifestations of such incongruousness. In extreme cases of incongruousness, the individual may feel compelled to create actualizing experiences by retreating into the florid fantasy life of the psychotic.

Therapy, according to Rogers, should be *client-centered*, meaning that the therapist should view the patient with an unconditional positive regard and strive for an empathic understanding of what the client is thinking and feeling. To the extent that the client is aware of this orientation (the accurate communication of this orientation is another duty of the therapist), the client's own internal drive toward self-actualization will, in most cases, lead to a cure.

It is neither necessary nor desirable for the therapist to direct the course of the interview (i.e., therapy should be *nondirective*). The therapist's empathy for the client, however, may help the client to articulate his or her self-experiences. Mainly, though, what happens during the interview is that the client begins to realize that it is possible to express feelings, *all* feelings, openly without fear of losing the positive regard of the therapist. As was noted earlier, Rogers found that most of these expressions concerned the *self* and the lack of congruousness between one's self and one's experiences. As this incongruousness is

articulated, with the encouragement of the therapist, anxiety is aroused which motivates the patient to consider possible ways of reorganizing his or her self-structure. If the anxiety becomes too intense, of course, it motivates denial and distortion rather than constructive change, but the unconditional positive regard of the therapist should keep anxiety at a moderate level.

The pressure exerted by the actualizing tendency causes the client to strive to achieve greater congruousness between self and experience. There is an increase in positive *self-regard*—or a feeling that one's self, as it is presently felt to exist, has become closer to one's *ideal self* (the kind of person one would most like to be). The ideal self may also come to be viewed more realistically and thus more capable of attainment than before.

These predictions have been empirically tested by Rogers and his students using a standardized technique, called a *Q-sort*, for eliciting self-descriptions of personality (Rogers & Dymond, 1954). The client distributes around seventy cards, each of which contains a self-referent statement, into nine piles arranged along a dimension ranging from "least characteristic of me" to "most characteristic of me." The statements might read, "I express my emotions freely," "I put on a false front," "I understand myself," and so forth. To satisfy the requirements for a statistical analysis of these data, the client must place most of the statements in the central categories (Piles 4, 5, and 6) with progressively fewer statements going into the categories closest to the extremes of "least" or "most" characteristic of oneself (Piles 1 and 9). This requirement has been criticized for placing artificial constraints on clients' self-descriptions, but most people seem to experience little difficulty in completing the task.

Butler and Haigh (1954) asked clients to do two sortings: one for how they perceived themselves at that time and another for how they would ideally like to be. A control group of people who had no desire to participate in nondirective therapy also did both sortings. Before counseling, there was no relationship between the self sorting and the ideal-self sorting done by the clients (the average correlation was virtually 0), but in the control group the two sortings *were* related (the average correlation was 0.58). In other words, the control group experienced substantial congruousness between their real and ideal selves while the clients did not. Following an average of thirty-one therapy sessions, the clients repeated the Q-sorts, and the control group repeated its sortings after an equivalent passage of time. The correlation between the self sortings and the ideal-self sortings remained the same for the controls, but for the clients it increased significantly (the average correlation was now 0.34). Follow-up studies demonstrated that this change persisted among the clients for periods of at least six months following the termination of therapy.

As Rogers had supposed, then, one effect of nondirective therapy is to produce a change in self-concept so that the client begins to perceive himself or herself as somewhat more congruous with the kind of person he or she would ideally like to become. As a result of such changes in self-concept, the client becomes less defensive, more open in expressing true feelings, and more accepting of self and others. This, in turn, leads to more positive regard from others, and the client is perceived by them as better adjusted and more mature. In these respects, Rogers' and Maslow's notions of self-actualization have a great deal in common with Asian concepts of personality, as is explained in Box 3-3.

BOX 3-3
ASIAN CONCEPTS OF PERSONALITY

Until the decade of the 1960s, Eastern views of personality were almost entirely ignored by Western theorists. Even today, the religious affiliations of Asian psychologists have caused them to be regarded with suspicion by scientifically oriented Western psychologists, who take some pride in the hard-won independence of their field from its domination by religion and philosophy as recently as a century ago.

"Third-force" and humanistic approaches to personality theory, however, have several themes in common with Eastern concepts. One of these is *phenomenology, the position that reality is defined by the subjective experience of the perceiver.* Related to this philosophical belief is the recommendation that people must look inside themselves rather than outward toward the material world in order to achieve self-actualization, inner peace, or general mental health. As "third-force" and humanistic approaches have gained greater acceptance with Western psychology, professional interest in Asian concepts of personality has increased.

One cannot, in a few paragraphs, do more than sketch the broad outlines of Eastern thought, and I cannot claim much familiarity with the source materials from which this ancient tradition derives. Consequently, this box will attempt to present a creative synthesis of the contents of two excellent reviews of the literature on Eastern concepts of psychology (Pedersen, 1977; Hall & Lindzey, 1978, Chap. 10).

Pedersen cautions that Asia is a very big continent containing many diverse cultures and that any attempt to describe Asian personality theory must necessarily gloss over numerous regional and cultural differences in viewpoint. Even so, he believes at least one broad distinction can be drawn between Eastern and Western viewpoints. Western psychologies encourage the individual to resolve emotional conflicts and overcome dependence on others so as to achieve personally important, self-gratifying goals. Eastern psychologies, on the other hand, promote interdependence, particularly within clans, castes, and other social groups, and advocate attainment of insight into emotional conflict rather than efforts to resolve it.

Insight is attained, according to Asian psychology, through techniques of meditation. Yoga is the technique used in the Indian Hindu tradition; the Indian, Chinese, and Japanese Buddhist traditions make use of techniques variously called *transcendental meditation, I Ching, Zen,* and so forth. The goal of meditation is to place the individual into a physically relaxed state in which the mind will be free to concentrate. During meditation—which usually requires sitting in a cross-legged position, regulating one's breathing, and, perhaps, repeating a sound (the *mantra)* over and over again—there are measurable decreases in oxygen consumption, heart and breathing rates, blood pressure, muscle tension, and other indices of arousal. The *electroencephalogram,* or EEG (see Box 2-1), shows the increase in alpha waves which researchers have associated with a relaxed but alert state of consciousness (see Benson, Beary, & Carol, 1974; Wallace, 1973).

The mental state produced by meditation has been compared by Sato (1968) to the mental state produced by the accepting and permissive attitude advocated by Rogerian theory in client-centered therapy. In Zen Buddhism, the goal of meditation is a sudden burst of enlightenment (*satori*) regarding the true nature of reality within and without oneself. The meditator becomes "awakened to his true . . . self" and becomes truer in his relations with the physical and social worlds around him (Mills & Campbell, 1974, p. 192). This sounds somewhat similar to Maslow's notion of the peak experience as the gateway to self-actualization.

Hall and Lindzey (1978, Chap. 10) maintain that the foregoing Eastern concepts are most clearly articulated into a theory of personality in the classical Buddhist philosophy called *Abhidharma.* Buddhism was founded by Gautama Buddha, who lived around 500 B.C. in what is today called *India.* Buddha taught that the essence of one's psychological being is *atta,* or self, but the self is not an unchanging core of personality around which more transient characteristics are added or removed. Instead, all of one's traits are in a continual state of change from one moment to the next. The atta is likened to a river which maintains its shape within its banks but is, at the same time, continuously changing.

The stream of consciousness is composed of sensations from each of the five major senses as well as memories, plans, and other thoughts, which are counted as a sixth sense. A mental state is made up of various *factors* of sensations or thoughts. In Abhidharma, there are fifty-three categories of mental factors, but the most important division is that between the unhealthy and healthy ones. *Unhealthy factors* are those which, in the experience of ancient Buddhist meditators, interfered with one's ability to maintain concentration. *Healthy factors* are those which were found to facilitate concentration.

The most dominant of the unhealthy factors is delusion (*moha*), which prevents the individual from perceiving things clearly without prejudice or distortion. Other unhealthy factors are *perplexity* (inability to make correct judgments because of excessive self-doubt), agitation, worry, shamelessness, remorselessness, egoism, greed, avarice, envy, inflexibility, and lethargy. Each has a corresponding healthy factor which, when present in consciousness, drives out its unhealthy counterpart. Foremost among these are insight (*panna*) and mindfulness (*sati*), which permit sustained clear perceptions of objects and so counteract delusion and perplexity. Other healthy factors are composure, easygoingness, modesty, discretion, confidence, nonattachment, buoyancy, impartiality, adaptability, and proficiency.

The purpose of meditation is to bring into consciousness as many of the healthy factors as possible and so drive out the unhealthy ones. One major meditational technique, called _one-pointedness_, involves focusing attention on a single thought or sensation. After sufficient experience and effort, the meditator achieves a rapturous break with normal consciousness in which the mind seems to fuse with the object of attention and is totally dominated by healthy factors. This state is called *jhana*, and there are seven progressively more blissful levels of it.

The second major meditational technique, called _mindfulness_, requires the mind to become highly aware of all objects, sensations, and thoughts in the steam of consciousness. Each event is given equal attention and then dropped from awareness as the next comes along. Eventually, the meditator becomes aware of the discontinuities and irrationalities in what normally appears to be a continuous and rational process of sensing and thinking. This perception leads to a desire to abandon the incoherent world of experience by shutting down all mental processes and entering the state of *nirvana*.

Certain unhealthy factors, called *anusayas*, always lie latent in the mind, waiting for an opportunity to enter consciousness. Hall and Lindzey comment that the anusayas are the closest counterpart in Abhidharma to Freud's notion of the unconscious. The lasting benefit to the individual of entering the state of nirvana is that some or all of the anusayas may be perpetually obliterated. The ecstatic state of jhana only temporarily suppresses the anusayas; nirvana, while providing no feelings of ecstasy, leaves the individual permanently changed in the direction of greater psychological health.

The healthy person is characterized by openness and impartiality in interactions with others and a ready responsiveness to their needs. He or she does not suffer from anxieties, resentments, embarrassment, lust, or anger and maintains his or her mental composure even under trying conditions. There is a notable absence of desire for any personal possessions beyond the bare necessities. On the whole, these traits do seem to bear some resemblance to those which Maslow attributed to the self-actualized person. Indeed, Maslow (1971) described an even higher level of human existence which transcends the ecstatic peak experiences of the self-actualized. He called it the *plateau experience* and apparently believed that when one had developed one's capacity for and understanding of peak experiences to the point where even the most commonplace events of one's life became peak experiences, one had reached this level. All of one's activities would then take place at this higher level of consciousness.

Individual differences in personality are, in Buddhist philosophy, explained in part by differences in the relative strength of healthy and unhealthy factors in consciousness. This mix of forces is in turn influenced by the religious training available in one's social environment and the extent to which the individual accepts such guidance and strives to achieve higher consciousness. As basic guidelines for this effort, Buddhist teaching supplied "four noble truths" and the "eightfold path" to the cessation of suffering.

> The four noble truths were: 1) all life is subject to suffering, 2) desire to live is the cause of repeated existences, 3) only the annihilation of desire gives release from suffering, and 4) the way of escape is through the eightfold path. The eightfold path was: right belief, right thought, right speech, right action, right livelihood, right effort, right mindfulness, and right concentration to escape from desire. (Pedersen, 1977, p. 370)

In addition, the Eastern belief in reincarnation decrees that each person possesses certain personality traits as a result of previous lives. The quality of behavior and development of consciousness in one's present life will have some bearing on the pleasurable or unpleasurable existence encountered in the next incarnation. Even the noblest behavior and devoted study in the present, however, may not erase the "badness" of some past life. Thus, we are predisposed toward one type of existence or another by an unavoidable fate, or *Karma*, which can be modified only slightly within a single lifetime. Only those who have achieved nirvana can transcend their Karma.

On a practical level, Eastern religious psychologies deny the importance of individual desires and achievement and, instead, emphasize the participation of the individual within a cultural stream of consciousness that is reflected in the quality of interpersonal relationships. Children are socialized into a dependency on such relationships by being treated very permissively and indulgently for the first few years of life. Then, however, the child is reminded that how he or she behaves will reflect upon the group—family, clan, village, or caste—which is responsible for his or her upbringing. A strong sense of obligation is therefore imposed on the child to seek guidance from parents and teachers regarding the correct way to live, and strong feelings of shame and remorse are invoked as the penalty for failure to live up to social obligations. High achievement is encouraged, but not for its worth to the individual. Instead, success is valued only to the extent to which it fulfills one's duties to the group.

From a Western point of view, Eastern psychologies give too much encouragement to conformity and a passive acceptance of social injustice and authoritarian control. Hall and Lindzey (1978, p. 354) paraphrased Murphy and Murphy (1968) in concluding that these fatalistic belief systems—which have, as their highest goal, a state of *nonexistence*, or nothingness—are "essentially a reaction to life viewed as full of suffering and frustration." In this respect, Eastern psychologies have a very different orientation from those of Maslow and Rogers, whose notion of self-actualization explicitly encourages resistance to group pressure and the attainment of personally important goals and self-satisfaction.

On the other hand, to Westerners who are continually driven to perform well in competition with others and who are taught to measure their worth by the material possessions they have acquired, the communal and spiritual emphases of Asian psychologies look very appealing indeed. Advocates of "third-force" and humanistic positions within American personology have denounced psychoanalysis and behaviorism for their alleged failure to give sufficient positive emphasis to communal and spiritual values. In this sense, then, Asian psychologies have much in common with the perspective of Maslow and Rogers. In present-day historical terms, what seems to be happening is that Western values are penetrating Eastern cultures along with Western technology. At the same time, partly because of this increased contact, and partly because of a spiritual hunger in Western cultures, Eastern values are finding a receptive audience here (see Pedersen, 1977). Each cultural tradition is influencing the other, and perhaps a fusion of the best elements of both will be the ultimate result.

If no conditions of worth had ever been applied to an individual, his or her self would not be incongruous with his or her experiences and there would therefore be no need for therapy. It is at this point that Rogers' theory of personality touches upon some practical aspects of child-raising as well as some age-old questions regarding fundamental nature of human beings. He believes that society would have nothing to fear and everything to gain from removing all evaluations of or restrictions upon the expression of individual impulses because "the innermost core of man's nature, the deepest layers of his personality, the base of his 'animal nature,' is positive in nature—is basically socialized, forward-moving, rational and idealistic" (Rogers, 1961, p. 91). He also emphatically disagrees with the psychoanalytic viewpoint that "man is basically irrational, and that his impulses, if not controlled, will lead to destruction of others and self."

> The experience of extreme satisfaction of one need (for aggression, or sex, etc.) in such a way as to do violence to the satisfaction of other needs (for companionship, tender relationship, etc.)—an experience very common in the defensively organized person—would be greatly decreased. He would participate in the vastly complex self-regulatory activities of his organism—the psychological as well as physiological thermostatic controls—in such a fashion as to live in increasing harmony with himself and others. (Rogers, 1961, pp. 194–195)

By this he means that the "natural balancing of one need against another" would provide all the control necessary to maintain peace and order within a society of self-actualized persons. Moreover, "when an individual discriminates himself as satisfying another's need for *positive regard*, he necessarily experiences satisfaction of his own need for positive regard" (Rogers, 1959, p. 223). Thus the encouragement of "actualization" is a reciprocal and mutually satisfying process.

Rogers did have some apprehension that certain behavior—especially in children—might need more explicit regulation than is provided by natural balancing, but he stressed that in such cases, it must be made clear that only the behavior, not the *feelings*, of the child are meeting with disapproval. He illustrates this concept by suggesting that an "actualizing" mother might say the following to her misbehaving offspring:

> "I can understand how satisfying it feels to you to hit your baby brother (or to defecate when and where you please, or to destroy things) and I love you and am quite willing for you to have those feelings. But I am quite willing for me to have my feelings, too, and I feel very distressed when your brother is hurt (or annoyed or sad at other behaviors), and so I do not let you hit him. Both your feelings and my feelings are important, and each of us can freely have his own." If the child were thus able to retain his own organismic evaluation of each experience, then his life would become a balancing of these satisfactions. Schematically he might feel, "I enjoy hitting baby brother. It feels good. I do not enjoy mother's distress. That feels dissatisfying to me. I enjoy pleasing her." Thus his behavior would sometimes involve the satisfaction of hitting his brother, sometimes the satisfaction of pleasing mother. But he would never have to disown the feelings of satisfaction or dissatisfaction which he experienced in this differential way. (pp. 225–226)

Skeptics might complain that such an elaborate explanation would be more likely to confuse a child than to "actualize" him. They might also be inclined to ask what physical or psychological harm would befall the occasionally battered baby brother. Concern for feelings has its place, they might say, but we also need to be concerned about the broader social consequences of self-satisfying behavior. Furthermore, if the mother has consistently behaved in an "actualizing" manner, and if human nature is fundamentally positive and socialized, why is it so satisfying for the child to hit baby brother in the first place?

On an adult level, Rogers has endorsed the growth of encounter groups and other techniques of increasing interpersonal sensitivity and awareness. Encounter groups ideally involve a candid exchange of feelings among participants, who are encouraged by a permissive setting to reveal thoughts and desires that they would normally conceal from others in their daily lives. One form of encounter group, called a *T-group*, has a professionally experienced leader, or *trainer*, who tries to remain in the background as much as possible but who will intervene if a participant is abusively attacked. The leader attempts to keep members of the group focused on expressing their feelings honestly and trying to understand *why* they said certain things. Like non-directive therapy, the process of self-examination, release of repressed feelings, and exposure to the feelings of others in the nonjudgmental atmosphere of a T-group should be conducive to self-actualization. In fact, many participants do report feeling more joyful, caring, genuine, and generally happier with themselves following a group experience.

From a peak of interest attained in the early 1970s, encounter groups have declined in popularity in recent years. One reason for the decline may be the fact that the group is a very temporary collection of strangers who go back to their separate lives once the session is finished. To the extent that a participant's good feelings are related to the group setting and the companionship of the particular people who shared it, there is bound to be a letdown when the group is disbanded.

Anthropologist James Fernandez (1978) has commented that there are many parallels to encounter groups in the ceremonies of tradition-bound cultures and primitive tribes. These ceremonies also produce feelings of exhilaration among the participants, but the feelings are more enduring than the feelings produced in encounter groups because the group itself endures after the ceremony is completed. Furthermore, while the purpose of these ceremonies is to integrate the individual more solidly into the society, an encounter group has the opposite, somewhat paradoxical goal of promoting individualism and so undermining group cohesion.

Smith (1978), a humanistic psychologist, also perceives a fundamental inconsistency between the hunger of the encounter-group participant for a sense of belonging and the individualistic goal of self-actualization, or *"doing one's own thing."*

Furthermore, says Smith, these groups may have declined in popularity because the leaders were, in some cases, unable or unwilling to maintain a nonjudgmental atmosphere and tolerated verbal and even physical abuse of the participants. Some investigators estimate that a fifth to a third of encounter-group members show *negative changes* (decreased self-esteem, decreased ability to cope with problems and human relationships, and decreased trust in others) as a result of the experience. (Rosenthal, 1978)

People sometimes become addicted to the latest popular trends in group experience, wandering from one technique to another in search of the sense of community they feel is missing from their lives. These nomads are vulnerable to exploitation by promoters of popularized psychology and instant "actualization." Rogers' recommended procedures for encouraging self-actualization may be dramatically effective under ideal conditions, but, due to problems of application in a less-than-ideal world, they do not always have the intended beneficial effects.

CONCLUSION

A distinctively American tradition is discernible among the theorists whose views have been discussed in this chapter. This tradition includes an agreement that a person's social interactions have a powerful (and often negative) effect on his or her personality. According to these theorists, interaction with others may generate debilitating tensions (Sullivan), frustrate the development of an integrated sense of selfhood (Allport), compel adoption of a distorted frame of reference (Kelly), prevent the satisfaction of basic needs (Maslow), or establish conditions of worth that thwart one's drive toward self-actualization (Rogers).

Each of these theorists believed that there is some core of identity within the individual. Social pressures can cause us to misrepresent this identity or relegate it to the unconscious, but despite all pressure, it will continue to struggle for recognition and self-expression. This is like the dilemma of the immigrant undergoing the process of assimilation into a new culture, and it is not inconceivable that the American immigrant experience contributed to the emphasis which these personologists placed on keeping in touch with one's self in the face of social forces exerting powerful pressures toward self-distortion.

Maddi and Costa (1972, pp. 49–50) have pointed out that Allport, Murray, and Maslow all believed that personality has a neurophysiological basis, which is in turn related to innate needs. Kelly was not clear as to the possible physiological origins of his need to anticipate future events, but Rogers clearly believed that the "actualization" tendency and the need for positive regard are inherent characteristics. In their acceptance of unconscious mental processes and innate determinants of personality, the personologists echoed certain aspects of the European psychoanalytic tradition, but they did not regard the self as being shaped and energized primarily by powerful instincts.

The Americans did view the satisfaction of basic needs as an important character-forming experience, but they were convinced that as an adult, each individual is able to choose which needs will be met and when, how, or where they are to be met. Adults have the capacity to reflect upon themselves and make changes if they decide they are not happy with what they see. For Allport, it is never too late to become a "whole man"; for Kelly, old frames of reference can be replaced with new, better-fitting ones at any time in a person's life; and for Maslow and Rogers, even if the drive for self-actualization is "nipped in the bud," it will always have the potential to blossom forth and achieve fruition. These theorists, in other words, shared a trait which has long been held to be a vital component of the so-called American character: a boundless optimism regarding the capacity of people to change themselves and the social and physical environments in which they live. As was noted at the end of Chapter 2, this outlook seems to have been infectious because the European theorists who emigrated to America became somewhat more socially and optimistically oriented than did their colleagues who stayed behind.

There is, however, a distinct variation on this theme which incorporates two basic ingredients of the American tradition: (1) an emphasis on the social environment as a determinant of individual behavior and (2) a utopian optimism regarding the possibilities for behavior change. But it dispenses with the notion of self. In taking the latter step, this *behaviorist* variant incurred the displeasure of both the European characterologists *and* the American personologists. Interestingly, a very similar behaviorist approach to psychology developed concurrently in the Soviet Union, a European country which has, in many aspects of its history, always been somewhat outside the continental mainstream. We will consider this development in Chapter 4.

SUMMARY

1 The immigrant experience, which required the abandonment of an Old World identity and assimilation into American culture, may account for the difference in orientation between European characterology and American personology. Personologists often included instincts or the unconscious mind in their theorizing, but they also believed that human beings make conscious choices regarding person-

ality development. They perceived many of these choices as being directed toward the goal of achieving a sense of unity among the physiological, cognitive, and social aspects of one's personality. Individual personalities were regarded as unique combinations of needs, traits, and choices. Several personologists adopted the phenomenological position that reality, for a particular person, consists entirely of that person's subjective experience of the world. Sullivan was a psychiatrically trained personologist who believed that all the foregoing aspects of personality were revealed in one's pattern of interpersonal relationships.

2   Murray believed that human behavior is motivated by a variety of internal needs—for achievement, affiliation, dominance, exhibition, play, sex, and so forth. Needs may also be activated by environmental forces, called *press*, and may fuse with one another to produce the temperament of a particular human being. Two important clusters of needs identified by Murray are ascendance and sensual expression. The fundamental units of character he called *thematic dispositions*. Murray's Thematic Apperception Test and other personality scales were designed to measure needs and dispositions.

3   Allport identified seven aspects of selfhood, each of which emerged at a different stage of a child's development from birth to maturity. He held that each individual could be described fairly well using only five to ten central traits, but he argued that the number of possible traits was so large as to make each person unique. While some behavior patterns are established in childhood through externally applied rewards and punishments, the behavior of the mature adult is characterized by functionally autonomous motives and values.

4   According to Kelly, the fundamental motivating force in personality is the desire to predict future events. People create their own models (called *constructs*) of the way the world works so as to make it seem more coherent and predictable. They then experience anxiety if their constructs fail to predict or explain events. Kelly's main therapeutic innovation was to present his clients with a personality sketch describing someone with a very different construction system. Clients are then asked to act out the contradictory role for a certain period of time. Presumably, the "acting out" breaks them free of their old, anxiety-arousing constructs and permits modifications in them, modifications that will provide better predictions of events.

5   Maslow's early studies of monkeys convinced him that feelings of self-confidence *inside* these animals, rather than physical size or strength, were the main determinants of their dominant or subordinate status. While searching for the origins of this dominance feeling in humans, Maslow concluded that certain basic needs must be satisfied before it can be fully developed. Needs, he said, are hierarchically organized, beginning with physiological needs and going on to

the needs for security, sense of belonging, self-esteem, and, finally, self-actualization. _Self-actualization_ means becoming everything that one is capable of becoming. It is achieved by exploring what Maslow calls _B-values_. Actualization of a B-value is often associated with an event he called a _peak experience._ Self-actualized persons have a more efficient perception of reality than do most people and are different in other respects as well. In contrast to both psychoanalytic and behaviorist psychologists, Maslow felt that a healthy personality requires the nurturance and expression of instinctual needs.

6   Like Allport, Rogers believed that people have an inborn need—called the _actualizing tendency_—to learn how to gain mastery over their environment and avoid being controlled by external forces. They also, however, have a need for positive regard from others, a need which may cause them to suppress aspects of their true selves when pressured to do so by the social environment. Rogers' therapeutic approach is nondirective and relies on the actualizing tendency to push the individual toward greater self-awareness in a permissive social setting. Research using the Q-sort technique has verified the progress toward greater self-congruousness that Rogers predicted would occur during nondirective therapy. Asian conceptions of personality have a great deal in common with Rogers' and Maslow's notions of self-actualization. Rogers recommends permissiveness in childrearing and in social organization so as to promote a self-actualized community in which the basically good impulses of human beings will predominate.

TERMS TO KNOW

thematic dispositions	fixed-role therapy
early self	self-actualization
central traits	peak experience
functional autonomy	client-centered therapy
personal constructs	encounter group

4

BEHAVIORISM AND THE AMERICAN AND SOVIET ENVIRONMENTALIST TRADITION

1   It has been said that behavioral approaches to the study of personality are based on a *materialist* philosophy. What is materialism, and in what way is it expressed in behavioral psychology?

2   What are the similarities and differences between the radical behaviorist and social learning viewpoints within the environmentalist tradition?

3   In what ways do radical behaviorism, social learning theory, and contemporary Soviet psychology agree and disagree regarding the issue of free will versus determinism?

round the turn of the century, a new trend in psychological research developed independently in the United States and Russia. This new approach was strongly opposed to the assumptions of European characterology and carried to extremes the belief in environmental determinants of personality which was a principal component of American personology. It came to be called *behaviorism*, though many of those who contributed to the new approach did not think of themselves as behaviorists. One who did not mind being referred to as a *behaviorist*—and who, in fact, coined the term *behaviorism*—was John B. Watson. It is with his work and the slightly earlier but somewhat parallel research of Edward L. Thorndike and the Russian Ivan P. Pavlov that this chapter begins.

The focus on environment shared by American and Soviet behaviorism meant that each individual could develop in practically an infinite variety of psychological directions, depending upon the culture within which he or she was raised. It meant that a change in someone's social environment could bring about great changes in personality at any time in that person's life. It rejected the Freudian view that personality was fixed for life by instinctual forces interacting with traumatic events experienced during childhood. Somewhat analogously, it also rejected the "social Darwinist" notion that the cultural status quo had evolved by some natural process of selection among alternatives and so represented the best of all possible socioeconomic arrangements. Behaviorism was, therefore, highly compatible with the spirit of political reform and social change that stimulated a revolution in Russia and energized American idealism and the goal of becoming a self-made man.

Early behaviorism was, to a considerable extent, stimulated by a bold nineteenth-century conception of biology known as *materialism*. Materialists believed that biological phenomena were entirely explainable in terms of the laws of physics and chemistry by which inorganic matter was organized. Four eminent nineteenth-century physiologists—Herman von Helmholtz, Ernst Brücke, Emil DuBois-Reymond, and Carl Ludwig—formed, in Berlin, a private club of materialists dedicated to the eradication of *vitalism* from biological science (Miller, 1962, p. 174). Materialists regarded the body as an electrical-chemical-mechanical system, whereas vitalists believed in the existence of properties (such as consciousness) that were unique to living systems. Psychologists with a materialist orientation therefore focus on conditioned (i.e., learned) or unconditioned reflexes as the basic units of behavior.

After examining some of the origins of materialist concepts in psychology, we will proceed to the *radical-behaviorist* position of B. F. Skinner and the compromises with materialist principles which were made by (1) the more psychodynamically oriented John Dollard and Neal Miller and (2) the more cognitively oriented social-learning theorists. The chapter concludes with a consideration of historical developments in Soviet psychology and of the place which the study of personality presently occupies in this tradition.

THE FIRST BEHAVIORISTS

Pavlov

It will be recalled from Chapter 2 that one person who had a profound influence on Sigmund Freud was his physiology professor, Ernst Brücke. Brücke was a charter member of the Berlin club of materialists, as was Carl Ludwig, the professor under whom Ivan Petrovich Pavlov studied. Freud attempted to found his psychoanalytic concepts on materialist principles but was compelled to drift further and further away from these concepts in his efforts to account for the complex thoughts and actions of human beings. Pavlov concentrated his research on simple reflexes in animal subjects and, perhaps for this reason, was more convincingly able to maintain throughout

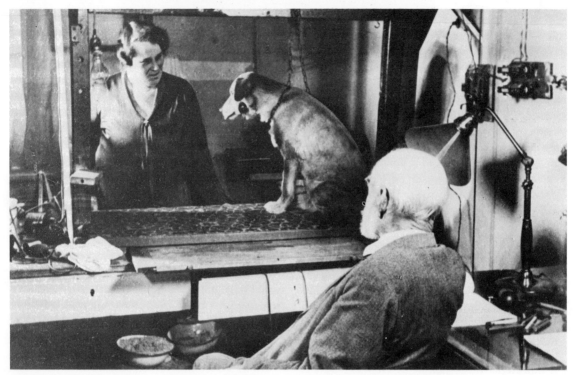

Ivan P. Pavlov in his laboratory with a dog in the conditioning apparatus. Pavlov studied the simple reflexes, such as salivation, in animal subjects. (Sovfoto)

his life that he was a physiologist rather than a psychologist (see Miller, 1962, pp. 174–175).

Much of Pavlov's work was in fact physiological and concerned with the functioning of the digestive system. In the course of these investigations, he developed surgical procedures for connecting various digestive glands to the exterior of an animal's body (the secreting orifice is called a _fistula_). He discovered that the animal's digestive juices began to be secreted upon the mere sight of its caretaker and before any food was presented. This led him to conclude that the unconditioned reflex of secreting juices in response to food had been transferred to the sight of the caretaker through frequent association of the caretaker with the delivery of food. It was Pavlov's research into this phenomenon, beginning in 1902, which is most relevant for the field of psychology.

In a typical Pavlov study (Anrep, 1920), a hungry dog fitted with a salivary fistula is harnessed to a stand which holds it in an upright posture facing a small window. It had been observed previously that when a dish of food was swung into the dog's sight and held beneath its nose, saliva was secreted though the fistula, but no salivation occurred when a tone (say of 700 cycles per second) was sounded in the absence of food. Now, at intervals of five to thirty-five minutes, the tone was sounded for five seconds, followed by presentation of the food. A total of fifty such pairings were made over a period of sixteen days. After the first pairing, and after every tenth pairing thereafter, a test trial was made in which the tone was presented by itself and a count was made of the number of drops of saliva secreted in response to the tone itself. No saliva was secreted to the tone after the first test trial, but with increasing numbers of pairings, more and more secretion occurred at each test trial, reaching a maximum of about sixty drops at the test trial after the thirtieth pairing. Also, the latency of appearance of the first drop decreased from eighteen seconds after the first pairing to about two seconds after the thirtieth. A representation of Pavlov's apparatus and a schematic of the conditioning procedure are shown in Figure 4-1.

In other investigations, Pavlov demonstrated that once conditioning has occurred, other stimuli which are similar to the conditioned one will also elicit the salivary response, though to a lesser degree. In the above example, tones of 500 cycles per second, 600 cycles per second, 800 cycles per second, and 900 cycles per second would all produce some secretion of saliva once the 700 cycle-per-second tone had been conditioned, and the 600 cycle-per-second and 800 cycle-per-second tones—being more similar to the conditioned stimulus—would elicit more saliva than would the 500 cycle-per-second and 900 cycle-per-second ones; this phenomenon is called _stimulus generalization_. Pavlov also discovered that if the conditioned stimulus was presented for a number of trials without any further association with food, it would lose its power to elicit salivation; this loss is called _extinction_. Finally, combining several of these processes in one experiment, Pavlov created what he termed an _experimental neurosis_. A circle was paired with food and an ellipse was shown when no food was present. On successive trials, the ellipse was made more and more circular until the dog could no longer distinguish between the two forms. The animal then became emotionally upset. It squealed, squirmed in its harness, bit and tore the equipment, and barked violently when it entered the laboratory.

Pavlov also discovered, however, that individual animals differ widely in their conditionability and in their emotional reactions to the experimental situation. Behavioral psychologists sel-

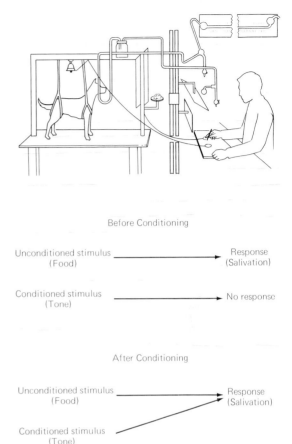

Before Conditioning

Unconditioned stimulus ———————————→ Response
  (Food)   (Salivation)

Conditioned stimulus ———————————→ No response
  (Tone)

After Conditioning

Unconditioned stimulus ———————————→ Response
  (Food)   (Salivation)

Conditioned stimulus
  (Tone)

FIGURE 4-1
Diagram of Pavlov's apparatus and a schematic of his conditioning procedure. Initially, the sight of food automatically elicits a dog's salivation, but a tone does not. After several pairings of a tone with the sight of food, however, the tone itself will elicit salivation. (Diagram from Dashiell, 1949)

dom call attention to Pavlov's suggestion that innate, temperamental factors may be the source of such differences (Williams, 1967). Pavlov attempted to relate his observations of conditioning to the occurrence of excitatory or inhibitory neurochemical events in the cerebral cortex as well as to the irradiation of these processes over the entire surface of the cortex versus their concentration in a particular spot. He in turn related various combinations of these events to the appearance of pathological states such as neurosis, catatonia, or schizophrenia.

Accepting the fourfold classification of the ancient Roman and Greek physicians, Galen and Hippocrates, Pavlov (1955, p. 260) argued that there are four basic temperaments, based on the relative strengths of excitatory and inhibitory impulses: sanguine (lively), phlegmatic (quiet), choleric (impetuous), and melancholic (depressed). In Chapter 2, you will recall, it was mentioned that Eysenck adopted the same basic categories of personality in his interpretation of scores from his scale for assessment of extraversion-introversion (see Box 2-2). Pavlov believed these temperaments might have an innate, biological origin, but he also recognized that they were influenced to a great extent by learning. While attempting to apply his findings to human behavior, Pavlov realized that language adds many complexities that are not resolvable by means of animal data alone. He therefore distinguished between the *first signaling system* (the conditioned reflex) and a second signaling system of verbal symbols.

Pavlov was engaged in studying the second signaling system when he died in 1936 at the age of 87. During his long lifetime, Russia experienced a political revolution and was transformed into the Union of Soviet Socialist Republics. Pavlov's status as a psychologist has had its ups and downs under the new government. This and other aspects of Soviet psychology are discussed near the end of the present chapter.

Thorndike

Edward L. Thorndike (1874–1949) was somewhat younger than Pavlov but made his discoveries in behavioral psychology at a slightly earlier date. Thorndike studied under William James at Harvard. "Under" is a very appropriate word here because Thorndike's first research, on the behavior of animals placed in mazes and puzzle boxes, was actually conducted in the basement of James' home. Thorndike continued this work after join-

ing the faculty of Columbia University in 1896. Years later, Rogers and Maslow were, respectively, doctoral and postdoctoral students of Thorndike's before they redirected their interests from experimental to clinical and then humanistic psychology.

Thorndike's most widely known studies employed cats as subjects (Thorndike, 1898). Typically, a hungry, young, active cat was placed in a box from which escape was possible only by pulling a loop attached to a string (or, in other studies, by pressing a button or deflecting a lever). The cat would initially explore all corners and small openings in the box, apparently in an effort to squeeze its way through. Eventually, it would accidentally claw at the loop, and the door would open, permitting the cat to leave the box and obtain a bit of food placed outside as a reward. On successive trials, the cat would pull the string sooner and sooner after entering the box until finally it would run immediately to the loop to obtain release.

Thorndike (1905, p. 203) argued that a given behavioral act would be *stamped in* by satisfying results (results which the organism will work to repeat) and *stamped out* by unsatisfying results (results whose repetition will not be worked for and which may actively be avoided). These propositions were termed the *law of effect.* Nearly thirty years later, Thorndike (1932, p. 58) modified this law because additional research had convinced him that "Rewarding a connection always strengthened it substantially; punishing it weakened it little or not at all." A behavioral act is stamped in by satisfying results; unsatisfying results do very little to stamp it out. Thorndike proposed other laws and corollaries, but the law of effect was his single most important contribution to behavioral psychology.

Watson

John B. Watson (1878–1958), holder of the first Ph.D. in psychology granted by the University of Chicago, was first to define *psychology* as the science of behavior. Appeals to subjective mental processes like *consciousness* and *will* were, he said, to be avoided along with phenomenologically oriented theories and methods. All behavior was to be analyzed in terms of observable stimuli which produced or regulated observable responses (Watson, 1914).

Watson preferred Pavlov's conditioning process to Thorndike's law of effect as a way of accounting for human behavior. In a classic study (Watson & Rayner, 1920; Watson & Watson, 1921), he exposed a human infant named Albert to a frighteningly loud sound (a hammer striking a steel bar behind the child's head) in association with the presence of a white rat. Although Albert had previously enjoyed playing with the rat, he soon acquired a fear reaction to the presence of the animal, even when the noise was discontinued. Stimulus generalization then occurred to the extent that Albert cried, cringed, or both in the presence of other furry objects such as a dog, a rabbit, a Santa Claus mask and beard, or Watson's hair.

Although this study has been cited in subsequent psychology textbooks as a clear-cut demonstration of stimulus generalization of a conditioned fear response in a human being, Harris (1979) has revealed that a great deal of inaccurate information crept into the story in the course of retelling it. For example, the rabbit became a *white* rabbit (which it was not) in order to become consistent in coloration with the white rat. More seriously, no texts mention that Watson banged the bar in association with the rabbit and the dog on several occasions or that once, the dog barked loudly at Albert, scaring him. Furthermore, Albert's reaction to the test stimuli of the Santa Claus mask and Watson's hair was described as "negative" rather than as a full-blown fear response. The infant showed no fear of the hair of an observer (probably Albert's mother) or of Watson's female assistant. Even Albert's fear of the white rat, established over a total of nine conditioning trials, was not so strong as to constitute a phobia. On his very last encounter with this animal, Albert permitted it to crawl on his chest, but he seemed clearly uncomfortable.

Harris concluded that Watson's study demonstrated the conditioning of a weak emotional response and suggested a generalization of this response to other furry animate objects, though evidence for the latter was somewhat inconsistent.

Mary Cover Jones (1924) assisted Watson in a more benign experiment aimed at *removing* previously established fears from another child named Peter, who was somewhat older than Albert (2 years 10 months at the start of the procedure). Peter was as naturally fearful of a white rat and rabbit as Albert had been of the hammer striking the steel bar. Jones' first procedure in deconditioning Peter's fears was to expose him to other children playing happily with a rabbit and then, over successive sessions, to bring the animal closer and closer to Peter. After the child happened to be frightened by a large dog on the street during this period, which reinstated his former fears, Jones tried a different procedure. Now a cage containing the rabbit was placed about 12 feet away from Peter while he was sitting and eating in his high chair. At successive meals, the cage was brought closer and closer. Peter also witnessed another child clamber down from his high chair to play with the rabbit. Eventually, Peter held the rabbit in his lap while eating. The deconditioning also generalized to the extent that Peter was less afraid than he had originally been of a white rat and a fur rug. Jones' deconditioning procedures anticipated by nearly half a century techniques developed by *cognitively* oriented behavioral psychologists, whose ideas will be examined further on in this chapter.

Watson (1924, p. 76) was so firmly convinced of the dominance of behavioral conditioning over any inborn traits or abilities that he issued the following famous challenge:

Give me a dozen healthy infants, well-formed, and my own specified world to bring them up in and I'll guarantee to take any one at random and train him to become any type of specialist I might select—doctor, lawyer, artist, merchant-chief and, yes, even into beggar-man and thief, regardless of his talents, penchants, tendencies, abilities, vocations, and race of his ancestors.

The individual who has come closest to realizing this *radical behaviorist* vision for psychology was, however, not Watson but B. F. Skinner. Skinner integrated Thorndike's law of effect as well as Pavlov's conditioned reflex into his system and extended both concepts further than they had been by their originators.

SKINNER'S RADICAL BEHAVIORISM

Burrhus Frederic Skinner was born in 1904 in a small Pennsylvania town. As a child, he spent a great deal of time designing and constructing an amazing variety of mechanical contraptions, but as a college undergraduate he majored in English with the intention of becoming a fiction writer. When this career choice proved unfruitful, he returned to academia and completed his doctorate in psychology at Harvard University in 1931. After teaching at the Universities of Minnesota and Indiana and publishing his text *The Behavior of Organisms* (Skinner, 1938), he returned to Harvard in 1948 and has remained on the faculty there ever since.

Skinner referred to the Pavlovian conditioned reflex as *Type S,* or respondent, conditioning and to Thorndike's law of effect as *Type R,* or operant, conditioning. His research concentrated almost entirely on the latter, probably because it offered a more flexible approach to learning. In respondent conditioning, the researcher can attach new stimuli only to a previously established relationship between an unconditioned stimulus and an unconditioned response. In operant conditioning, the researcher can use a reward such as food or water to increase the probability of occurrence of responses that have never before been exhibited by the organism.

An Example of Operant Conditioning

Consider the situation of a thirsty rat in a typical conditioning apparatus called the *Skinner box.* There is a slot in the wall of the box through which a tiny dipper protrudes and, near the dipper, a wide lever, or pedal, about an inch up from the floor. Activation of an electrical mechanism causes the dipper to leave the box and reach backwards to pick up a sip of water from a tank, after which it returns to the interior of the box.

Suppose the researcher connects the circuit activating the dipper mechanism to a switch which is closed whenever the lever inside the box is depressed. The rat will initially show little

B. F. Skinner, the inventor of the Skinner box, is training a rat to press a bar by rewarding this behavior with delivery of a food pellet. (Nina Leen/Time-LIFE)

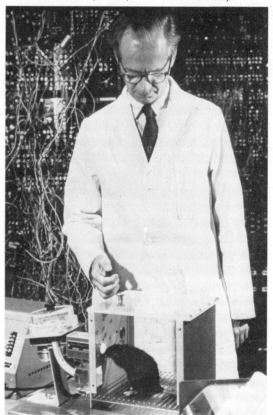

interest in the lever, since it has never seen or operated one before, but its natural curiosity will cause it to explore the walls and corners of the box. In the course of these movements, it will, at some point, depress the lever, which will in turn activate the dipper. After taking its drink, or *reinforcement*, the rat will resume exploring and will sooner or later depress the bar again, which will provide it with another dipper full of water. As time goes on, the lever presses will come more and more frequently until a stable, high rate of perhaps four presses a minute is reached. Obviously, the rat is responding to the lever very differently from the way it was when first put into the box. This change in behavior is apparently due to the fact that reinforcement was made contingent upon lever-pressing. As a result, a response that has a very low probability of occurring in the rat's natural repertory is now its most dominant behavior when placed in the chamber. A drawing of the apparatus, and a graph showing the *cumulative record* of the rat's responses as a function of time, are set forth in Figure 4-2.

If the dipper mechanism is, at some point, disconnected from the lever, the rat's rate of lever-pressing will gradually decline until it returns to its initial, relatively infrequent baseline level; this decline is called *extinction*. Alternatively, the mechanism may be adjusted so that it provides reinforcement on a *schedule* rather than following each individual lever press. On a *fixed-ratio* schedule, for example, the rat may be required to press the lever five, ten, or even twenty times before it gets a drink; on a *fixed-interval* schedule, the rat might be reinforced for the first bar press to occur after passage of a five-minute interval since the last reinforcement. Variable-ratio and variable-interval schedules are also sometimes used. The common feature of these schedules is that they maintain higher rates of response than can be achieved by continuous reinforcement delivered after each lever press.

If the rat is exposed to a variable-interval

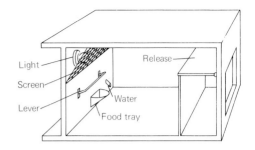

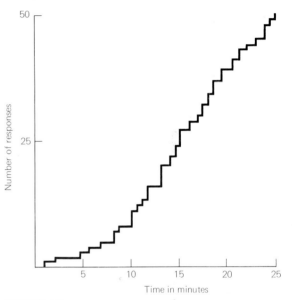

FIGURE 4-2
Diagram of Skinner's original operant-conditioning apparatus. The graph shows the number of bar presses made as a function of time after a rat has been reinforced for emitting this response. (Diagram from Skinner, 1938)

schedule of *non-contingent reinforcement* (i.e., the dipper is activated at random times) on the first occasion of its being placed in the box, *superstitious behavior* may result. Since whatever the rat happens to be doing when the dipper is activated is reinforced, its behavior is likely to develop stylized *quirks*. If the rat is scratching its ear when the first reinforcement is given, for example, the probability of ear-scratching will increase, and so will the likelihood that the rat will be scratching its ear on the occasion of the next reinforcement. Skinner believes that the faith many people have in good-luck charms and other superstitious beliefs are the result of this sort of accidental conditioning.

The rat can also be trained to press the lever for reinforcement when a tone of one frequency is sounded and to refrain from pressing the lever when a different tone is sounded. This is an example of _stimulus discrimination_. Stimulus generalization can also be observed, in that tones which are similar in frequency to the one which signals the availability of reinforcement will also elicit lever-pressing, though at a less rapid rate.

Somewhat like Thorndike, Skinner (1938) concluded that reward has a much more significant effect on behavior than does punishment. Punishment may cause short-term suppression of a response, he said, but when punishment is discontinued, responding will resume its prepunishment rate. Estes (1944), a student of Skinner's, discovered that punishment has the same suppressive effect on responding whether it was made contingent upon the response or whether it occurred independently. This suggested that the temporary suppressive effect of punishment was not due to a weakening of the conditioned response per se but rather to the occurrence of distracting _emotional responses_ due to being placed in an aversive environment. It appeared, therefore, that only reward had a lasting influence on the strength of a response. Skinner was subsequently forced to modify this view as a result of evidence gathered by Solomon (1964) and others which indicated that severe punishment of a response could result in its permanent disappearance from an animal's repertory. His present position appears to be that severe punishment may permanently suppress behavior but that it is, nonetheless, a poor method of modifying behavior because of its negative emotional side effects (Evans, 1969, p. 33).

Social and Psychological Implications

Adopting an uncompromising _radical behaviorist_ stance, Skinner has attempted to account for the origins and ongoing dynamics of human personality in terms of operant and respondent conditioning, schedules of reinforcement, response extinction, and phenomena such as stimulus generalization and emotional reactions to punishment. The fact that human behavior is obviously very complex is not perceived by Skinner to pose a significant problem for a behaviorist analysis. In a process called _shaping_, rats, pigeons, and other animals have been taught a series of simple operant responses that were then chained together in marvelously intricate sequences of seemingly _purposive_ behavior. For example, a rat might jump on an elevator, throw a switch to raise the car 2 feet off the ground, then walk across a tightrope, open a door, and climb down a ladder in order to reach a lever which it can depress in order to obtain a food pellet. According to Skinner, there is nothing more mysterious about the origins of complex human behavior than there is about the origins of this sequence in the rat. Furthermore, stimuli which have been associated with primary reinforcers like food and water may, through respondent conditioning, acquire _secondary reinforcing_ properties of their own. Thus human behavior which appears to be engaged in for its own sake may actually be maintained by powerful secondary reinforcers such as money or social approval.

Skinner (1957) even attempts to account for development of the most human of all behaviors—language and _thinking_ (i.e., talking to oneself)—in terms of behaviorist principles of conditioning. In general, his position has been that all, or nearly all, behavior can be explained in terms of the stimuli and response contingencies to which an organism has been exposed, with the effect of these contingencies being regulated by empirically derived laws of learning. This _stimulus-response_ (S-R) psychology is not concerned with mental or even physiological events going on inside the organism. Rather, it attempts to discover the functional relationships between stimulus conditions in the environment and the organism's observable responses to them; the organism itself appears to be represented only by the intervening hyphen.

Obviously, the assumptions and methodology of Skinner's radical behaviorism sharply conflict with the European and American traditions considered in Chapters 2 and 3. These traditions took for granted the existence of an ego, identity, or self, and their proponents have accused Skinner of treating humans and other organisms as though they were internally empty. Skinner (in Evans, 1969, p. 23) has denied this accusation, though he admits that radical behaviorism's functional approach does at least pretend that the organism is a *black box.* The inner mechanisms of this box are not at present fully understood, but, understood or not, they are, for the most part, irrelevant to a functional analysis of the box's behavior. In a novel, *Walden Two* (1962), and in a more recent work of nonfiction, *Beyond Freedom and Dignity* (1971), Skinner has argued for the extension of a behaviorist viewpoint to the design of human societies. In these popularized writings, he maintains that human nature does not exist, or that it may at least be ignored for most practical purposes. The environment, not the individual, must be given credit for the occurrence of good behavior or the development of bad behavior. If we wish to eliminate bad behavior, the most efficient way to accomplish our goal is to see to it that no one is ever reinforced for being bad and that everyone experiences some scheduled reinforcement for being good. Recall that Skinner does not believe that punishment is an effective means of changing behavior; he also has little faith in appeals to reason or exhortations to change one's identity. Since future behavior is determined by its past consequences, he says, change the reinforcement contingencies if you wish to reform society.

In a novel entitled *Walden Two*, B. F. Skinner proposed that a utopian community be established and organized according to strict behavioral principles of shaping and reinforcement. Only behaviors which served the good of the community were to be rewarded, thus making unnecessary any punishment for "bad" behavior. Shown here are members of a commune in Virginia which was originally intended as a working model of Walden Two. Called Twin Oaks, it later deemphasized behavior principles and became more typical of other groups seeking an alternative life-style. (Twin Oaks)

The most widely known therapeutic application of behaviorist psychology, called *behavior modification,* is discussed in some detail in Chapter 8. Two case studies illustrating the application of these techniques are contained in Box 4-1. Behavior modification also has historical

BOX 4-1

Bijou (1965) described the successful treatment of psychotic symptoms with behavior-modification techniques. The case-history material was gathered by M. M. Wolf, T. R. Risley, and H. I. Mees in the course of their treatment of a 3-year-old named Dicky. Dicky had had cataracts removed from his eyes at the age of 2 and, following the operation, was supposed to wear glasses. He had experienced temper tantrums before the operation, but the tantrums increased markedly in severity afterwards. He began banging his head and scratching and mutilating himself. Judged by specialists to be retarded, brain-damaged, and psychotic, he was diagnosed as a *childhood schizophrenic* and admitted to a state hospital at the age of 3.

Dicky might well have spent the rest of his life at the hospital if he had not been found by the team of behavior modifiers. They reacted to his tantrums by taking him immediately to his room, closing the door, and leaving him alone until some interval after the cessation of the tantrum (a procedure they called *"time out"*). At mealtimes, Dicky would habitually grab food off other children's plates and throw it around the room. When he did this, he was immediately removed from the dining room and left alone for awhile.

By these and other behavior-contingent techniques, tantrums and food-throwing were removed from Dicky's behavior repertory. Then he was taught to wear glasses. First he was rewarded with food for just touching a pair of lensless frames, then he was rewarded for putting them on, for keeping them on for a few minutes, for wearing them with nonmagnifying lenses, and so on. Besides food, the reinforcements included going for a walk, taking automobile rides, and playing outdoors. Finally, his tantrums replaced with socially adaptive behavior, Dicky returned home. Six months later, his mother reported to the psychologists that "he continues to wear his glasses, does not have tantrums, has no sleeping problems, is becoming increasingly verbal, and is a new source of joy to members of his family."

The therapeutic techniques used with Dicky were derived fairly straightforwardly from operant-conditioning procedures found to be effective in changing the behavior of rats in a Skinner box. In the years since these early efforts, however, behavior-modifying interventions have been used with individuals experiencing far less maladjustment than Dicky and living in everyday social environments. In cases like this, the contemporary behavior modifier is unable to control all the reinforcement contingencies to which the client will be exposed, and applications of conditioning principles are therefore somewhat less straightforward than in Dicky's case.

McCullough, Huntsinger, and Nay (1977) offer an example of the type of case which might come to the attention of an applied behavioral psychologist practicing in the community. The client was a 16-year-old boy named Larry whose public school records showed a consistent pattern of temper tantrums, physical assaults, and other emotional outbursts from first grade onward. Larry had recently been expelled from the football team for fighting with a teammate and then having to be physically restrained from attacking the head coach. At home, he took the family car without permission and was verbally abusive in response to any reprimand or frustration. Five weeks after his parents brought him to see the psychologist, on December 12, 1973, Larry was suspended from school after a violent argument with his physical education teacher over being late for class, followed by an equally violent argument with the school principal.

Larry reported that whenever others frustrated him or evaluated him negatively, he began to mutter curses under his breath and felt his body tense up, culminating in great tension in his right arm and hand just before he lashed out verbally or physically.

Larry was taught to stop thinking and stop muttering to himself in the early stages of stressful interactions so as to suppress the generation of curses which might goad him or others to greater anger. He was also taught how to keep his muscles in a relaxed state, and told that if he felt his right arm becoming tense despite these efforts, he was to walk away from the interaction immediately until he could regain a state of relaxation. Larry's parents and teachers agreed to allow him to walk away from such encounters and to refrain from pursuing the conversation until Larry was in a calmer psychological state. He was to receive praise and congratulations as a reward for each successful completion of this sequence. At school, special permission was obtained for Larry to leave the classroom when under stress and to stand outside the door in the hallway for a few minutes. A school counselor agreed to compile weekly detailed reports from Larry's teachers and to send these reports to the psychologist.

The records indicated that while Larry did have three emotional outbursts over the next 2½ months, none of these outbursts was severe. One involved swearing at a female student who took his notebook without permission, another involved threatening to hit a male student who had taken his seat, and a third involved refusing to complete an examination on which he was doing poorly. After the end of February, there were no additional outbursts through the end of the spring semester in June. Furthermore, Larry managed to get through one or more highly stressful encounters on at least nine days during this period without having even a mild outburst. At home, too, Larry's behavior became much less volatile and more reasonable.

Continued follow-ups indicated that Larry lost his temper only twice during the 1974–75 academic year—once when he fought with a fellow student and once when he refused to complete an examination. As of 1976, Larry was continuing to exhibit progress toward greater self-control of his emotions, though he was having chronic difficulties in completing homework assignments and maintaining average grades.

roots, however, in a less radical approach first taken by Clark L. Hull and later expanded into a theory of personality by John Dollard and Neal Miller.

DOLLARD AND MILLER'S SYSTEMATIC BEHAVIORISM

John Dollard, a sociologist, and Neal Miller, a psychologist, together combined an elaborate theory of behavioral psychology developed by Clark L. Hull with theoretical ideas derived from European characterology. Hull (1884–1952) described the sequence of events in learning as S-O-R rather than S-R. In other words, he recognized events going on within the organism (O) as important factors which have an influence on the organism's response to environmental stimuli. While carefully avoiding any reference to consciousness, Hull was, with his inclusion of internal factors, better able than Skinner to account for phenomena such as foresight and planning. He called his approach systematic behaviorism.

The Institute of Human Relations at Yale University, of which Hull was a member for some twenty years, was dedicated to interdisciplinary cooperation and included on its faculty anthropologists, political scientists, psychiatrists, and sociologists. After a period of exposure to Hull's ideas at the Institute, Dollard and Miller each received training in psychoanalysis at European institutes and so were quite familiar with this tradition when they published their now-classic work, *Personality and Psychotherapy* (1950).

Experimental Models of Neurotic Conflict

The manner in which Dollard and Miller reinterpreted psychoanalytic theory within the framework of behavioral psychology can best be understood by means of an example. Suppose a hungry rat is trained to run down an alley to a black goal box illuminated by a distinctive light; the reinforcement for this behavior is a bit of food in the box. Now suppose the rat is placed in a white goal box and given a painful electric shock through the grid floor; here, the rat will soon learn to run out of the "goal box" to the opposite end of the alley. Finally, the rat is placed in the alley facing a white goal box (signaling shock) which contains the distinctive light (signaling food). What will the rat do? Most likely, it will exhibit conflict. On the one hand, it will be motivated to approach the box because it desires food, but it will, at the same time, be motivated to avoid the box because it fears the shock. Behaviorally, it should oscillate back and forth around some *equilibrium point* where the motivation to approach the box is exactly canceled out by the motivation to avoid it. Dollard and Miller argue that this type of approach-avoidance conflict is similar to Freud's notion of neurotic anxiety.

Suppose, for instance, that a young man experiences difficulty in making the acquaintance of young women and establishing heterosexual relationships. This could be due to anxiety over the expression of heterosexual interests, anxiety which developed from fears of rejection and punishment that occurred or were perceived to have occurred during the Oedipal period. On the one hand, the young man is motivated by sexual impulses to try to establish such relationships; on the other hand, he is fearful of rejection, punishment, or *moral anxiety* should he act on these impulses. This young man's neurotic conflict is essentially the same as the approach-avoidance conflict faced by the rat in the above example. On a behavioral level, his symptoms of conflict may involve first attending a dance for the purpose of meeting a young woman and then spending the evening in a corner. He might even go so far as to try to strike up a conversation with a young woman and then develop a stammer or have his mind go blank so that he is unable to communicate effectively.

Implications for Personality Theory and Therapy

Dollard and Miller went much further than did their more radical contemporaries, Skinner and Watson, toward including events inside the organism within the domain of behavioral psychology. These events, to be sure, were regarded as arising from past conditioning experiences and were emphatically *not* attributed to some special inner consciousness. Dollard and Miller cite the example of someone learning to drive a stick-shift automobile. Initially, each of the separate responses of putting in the clutch, selecting the proper gear, releasing the clutch while slightly depressing the gas pedal, and so forth will be grossly exaggerated and associated with verbal instructions overtly expressed by the driver or the driver's teacher. With a little more practice, however, the driver will recite the verbal instructions silently, to himself or herself, and the sequence of responses will become more smoothly executed as the muscular sensations associated with each response become more reliable in eliciting stimuli for the next response in the sequence. These implicit S-R connections are reinforced by an occasional congratulations from the teacher and by the successful operation of the vehicle. Eventually, the chained sequence will occur *automatically*, meaning that the driver's behavior will, in most circumstances, be controlled by subtle internal cues rather than by cues in the external environment.

Thinking, for Dollard and Miller, amounts to the attachment of verbal labels to stimuli and responses occurring in the environment or within the individual. Consequently, Freud's concept of repression is, for them, simply the response of *not thinking*. According to Dollard and Miller (1950, pp. 203–214), fear-producing stimuli elicit this reaction, which effectively terminates the drive sequence that led up to it. A boy who desires to possess his mother sexually, for instance, may be made so fearful by the threat of punishment from the father that his desires will never be overtly acted upon. This would be Dollard and Miller's explanation of the resolution of the Oedipus complex.

If the fear of punishment is reduced, however, the response of not thinking may fail to occur, which would permit previously tabooed drives to be correctly labeled and freely discussed. This, according to Dollard and Miller, is the function of therapy:

> In addition to permitting free speech, the therapist commands the patient to say everything that comes to mind. By the free-association technique the therapist sets the patient free from the restraint of logic. The therapist avoids arousing additional anxiety by not cross-questioning. By encouraging the patient to talk and consistently failing to punish him, the therapist creates a social situation that is the exact opposite of the one originally responsible for attaching strong fears to talking and thinking. The patient talks about frightening topics. Since he is not punished, his fears are extinguished. This extinction generalizes and weakens the motivation to repress other related topics that were originally too frightening for the patient to discuss or even to contemplate. Where the patient cannot say things

for himself, the therapist helps by attaching a verbal label to the emotions that are being felt and expressed mutely in the transference situation. (Dollard & Miller, 1950, p. 230)

More recent developments in behavioral psychology have placed an even stronger emphasis on internal feelings, thoughts, and expectations than did Dollard and Miller. These contemporary approaches are firmly rooted in the importance of studying the "O" in Hull's S-O-R model of learning and behavior.

SOCIAL-LEARNING THEORY

The social-learning approach to the study of personality is most closely associated with the work of Albert Bandura and Richard Walters, and a bit of biographical material may be helpful in gaining some perspective on their theoretical orientation.

Bandura was born in 1925 in Canada. After spending his undergraduate years at the University of British Columbia, he received his Ph.D. degree from the University of Iowa, a well-known center of behavioral psychology, in 1952. He then joined the psychology faculty at Stanford University and has remained there since. In 1974, he served as president of the American Psychological Association.

Richard Walters was born in the British province of Wales and educated at Oxford University. After a few years of lecturing in philosophy in New Zealand, he entered the graduate program in psychology at Stanford and, as a student of Bandura's, received his doctorate in 1957. He was a professor at the University of Toronto when he died, unexpectedly and at a young age, in 1968.

Though both of these men were well versed in behavioral psychology, each received his early education outside the United States. Perhaps this made it easier for them subsequently to deviate from the mainstream of American environmentalism.

An Alternative Conception of Reinforcement and Learning

Bandura and Walters' first major statement of social-learning theory was contained in a book titled *Social Learning and Personality Development* (1963). They acknowledged that any behavior which is followed by presentation of a positive reinforcer (reward) or withdrawal of a negative reinforcer (termination of punishment) becomes strengthened in an animal's repertory. In humans, such learning experiences have an additional consequence: the human forms hypotheses regarding the probable consequences of future actions. Humans are also able to imagine future events in symbolic form and thus, through anticipation of the rewarding or punishing consequences, "teach" themselves patterns of behavior they have not yet overtly performed. This means that they are able to make plans and achieve insightful solutions to problems.

One interesting implication of this approach is that an observer can symbolically represent the actions of another individual as well as the consequences that those actions had for that individual. Rather than learn new behaviors in a step-by-step, trial-and-error sequence, we can simply imitate an entire sequence that we have witnessed someone else perform successfully. Alternatively, we may protect ourselves from wasting effort or making mistakes by learning not to initiate behaviors which others have found to be unrewarding or even punishing. To take Dollard and Miller's example of learning to drive a stick-shift automobile, it is entirely possible for a teenager to know this complicated sequence of behaviors without ever having actually performed it. Mere observation and symbolic representation of successful performances by adult drivers is apparently the source of this *vicarious learning*. Trial-and-error plays an important role in refining the sequence of behaviors into a smoothly executed chain once the novice driver is placed behind the steering wheel. Many teenagers are certain that they know how to drive a stick-shift automobile, but unless their vicarious learning has been exceptionally observant and precise, their first attempt to operate a vehicle will probably be rather clumsy. Even so, the novice driver who is able to model his or her behavior on the successful actions of accomplished drivers will learn much more rapidly than will a novice who proceeds exclusively on the basis of trial-and-error.

Vicarious learning provides an individual with a variety of internal self-reinforcements which can be used to guide that individual's future behaviors, regardless of the presence or absence of reinforcing consequences in the immediate environment. Thus, children who observe an aggressive model being praised may learn that violence is "good" and show an increase in their own aggressive behavior, partly because they are congratulating themselves for engaging in it. Conversely, children who observe an aggressive model being punished may learn that violence is "bad" and show a subsequent decrease in aggressive behavior due to self-administered punishment for engaging in such acts (Bandura, Ross, & Ross, 1963; Bandura, 1965). These processes, according to Bandura and Walters, are essentially what Freud and other theorists are referring to when they speak of a superego or conscience.

Bandura (1965) demonstrated that a distinction can be drawn between the acquisition and performance of behavior. Even children who have witnessed an aggressive model being punished for his or her deeds and who are, as a result, inhibited from imitating the model's actions can accurately reproduce the sequence of aggressive behaviors if offered attractive rewards for doing so. Thus acquisition, in the form of information storage, can occur simply as a result of observation, in the absence of either direct or vicarious reinforcement. Whether or not acquired behavior patterns are acted upon, however, depends on the expectations of reward or punishment which the individual attaches to their performance.

The description of conditioning provided by social-learning theory is somewhat more complex than that derived from the behavior of a rat in a Skinner box. Bandura (1971) divides the learning process into subcomponents titled attention, retention, motor reproduction, and motivation. For learning to occur, the individual must first attend to a stimulus, and the likelihood of attention is increased by the value or distinctiveness of the stimulus or by past experience with direct or vicarious reinforcement in association with similar stimuli. Stimuli that are attended to may still not be remembered or retained, however, unless there is a cognitive or behavioral rehearsal of their content and probable consequences. Motor reproduction of modeled behavior is the observable outcome of the processes of attention and retention. If this attempt at imitation is successful, the actor may provide himself or herself with self-administered congratulations, or reinforcement may be provided by access to material or social rewards (e.g., money or praise) in the external environment. Either way, successful reproduction of a modeled stimulus behavior is likely to motivate the individual to repeat this sequence in the future.

Implications for Therapy

Applications of social-learning theory to the treatment of problem behaviors differ in many ways from the techniques derived from Skinnerian and Hullian behaviorism described in Box 4-1. Most notably, therapists with a social-learning orientation are less inclined to employ direct delivery of rewards or punishments in attempting to modify behavior, preferring instead to rely upon vicarious processes. The uniqueness of the social-learning approach can best be illustrated by an example.

Bandura (1967) sought to reduce an unreasonable fear of dogs among a number of phobic nursery school children. Those placed in a modeling-plus-reinforcement group participated in a party, during which they saw a child displaying no fear interact more and more closely with a dog across eight short sessions. A modeling-only group saw the child model perform the same acts, but this time the atmosphere was *neutral* (i.e., it lacked the reinforcing aspects of a "party"). A third group saw the dog in the party setting but without any child model, and a fourth group participated in the party with neither a model nor a dog being present. Two tests of fear of dogs were administered, one immediately after this treatment and one a month later. In these tests, the children were encouraged to pet, feed, and remain alone in a room with a dog. The children in the two modeling groups were found to be much less fearful than were those in the groups which saw no model, both immediately after the treatment session as well as one month later. The modeling-plus-reinforcement group was found to be less fearful than the modeling-only group in the one month follow-up. These results were replicated using films which presented children with the appropriate behavior to be modeled.

In this study, simply rewarding a child (with a party) for being in the presence of a dog seemed to have much less of a therapeutic effect than did exposing the child to a peer model who interacted fearlessly with the animal. There is some indication that reinforcement did serve to increase the impact of the modeled behavior, however, in that the modeling-plus-reinforcement group showed the greatest long-term reduction of fear.

Bandura himself noted a similarity between his techniques and George Kelly's *role-playing therapy*, in which clients are provided with behavioral models and encouraged to practice new action patterns in a protected setting before trying them out in real life (see Chapter 3). In addition, there are striking parallels between Bandura's procedures and those employed by Mary Cover Jones over four decades earlier to cure "Little Peter's" fear of furry animals. What Bandura added to Jones's previous demonstration, though, was a theory which could account for the vicarious-learning processes involved in the removal of such phobias. In fact, Bandura has speculated that *all* viable psychological therapies, whether they intend it or not, have, as their common outcome, an increased sense of self-efficacy within the client (Rosenthal & Bandura, 1978). That is, the client develops a strengthened expectation of success in overcoming fears, coping with life's problems, and expanding his or her behavioral repertory. Bandura believes that behavior therapies—particularly those with a social-learning orientation—provide the most direct and effective means of increasing feelings of self-efficacy.

More recent applications of social-learning theory have become even more cognitive and less behavioral in that clients may be asked to *imagine* various types of anxiety-arousing situations and how they might be successfully confronted rather than observe a real-life model in such a setting. Clients are sometimes taught to recite self-controlling statements to themselves so as to "talk through" a problem-solving sequence or an anxiety-arousing social encounter. They are also taught to congratulate or criticize themselves when they make right or wrong choices. These and other behaviorally based therapeutic techniques are described in some detail in Chapter 8.

Current Controversies in Behavioral Psychology

Social-learning theorists agree that direct delivery of reward or punishment serves to encourage or inhibit a target behavior. Conflict between social-learning and radical behaviorism emerges only when the proponents of the former look beyond observable behaviors to inferred changes in the subject's cognitions regarding the probable outcomes of future events as well as his or her deservedness of self-reward or self-punishment. Skinner, in an article entitled "Why I Am Not a Cognitive Psychologist" (1977), argued that this acceptance of inner processes as causes of behavior can only hinder the development of a true (i.e., materialist) science of psychology. He said he was also concerned with the potentially misdirected consequences of practical applications of the social-learning viewpoint.

> The appeal to cognitive states and processes is a diversion which could well be responsible for much of our failure to solve our problems. We need to change our behavior and we can do so only by changing our physical and social environments. (Skinner, 1977, p. 10)

For his part, Bandura (1974, 1977) maintains that only social-learning theory provides a plausible, behaviorally based account of creativity and planning. Conditioned or vicariously learned response sequences can be rehearsed mentally and combined with one another in unique ways so as to produce an overtly enacted behavior pattern that the individual has never before displayed. Without such a capacity for cognitive restructuring of learning experiences, says Bandura, human beings would be incapable of innovative behavior and would, instead, be locked into an endless repetition of actions directly reinforced by the physical or social environment. Since the survival of human beings as a species has depended in large part on our capacity for rapid innovation, it seems unlikely that trial-and-error learning can completely account for our behavior. Bandura goes so far as to maintain that even in the case of direct reinforcement for trial-and-error learning, there is evidence of the importance of cognitive processes. People, he says, do not learn from the pairing of rewards with specific behavioral acts unless they become cognitively aware that the rewards are contingent upon the acts. As he puts it: "Behavior is not much affected by its consequences without awareness of what is being reinforced" (Bandura, 1974, p. 860).

The foregoing debate between the radical and social-learning wings of the environmentalist tradition bears upon an ageless psychological quandary that has been a central element in the behaviorist model of human personality. Do human beings have a capacity for free will and spontaneous behavior, or are their decisions and actions determined by past environmental experience? The American personologists, you will recall, rejected both psychoanalysis and behaviorism because of the determinist philosophy underlying these traditions and put forward the alternative view that a human being possesses a conscious mind which strives toward self-chosen goals. What is particularly interesting about the debate described in the preceding paragraphs, however, is that it has arisen within the behaviorist tradition itself rather than between behaviorists and their humanistic critics. This controversy is given further consideration in Box 4-2.

Soviet behaviorism, like its American counterpart, also moved in the direction of showing increasing interest in cognitive processes as mediators of behavior. The reasons for this development were somewhat different, however, as will be explained below.

LATER DEVELOPMENTS IN THE SOVIET BEHAVIORIST TRADITION

Bauer (1952) traced the progress of Soviet behaviorism from the Revolution of 1917 through the rule of Josef Stalin, which ended with the latter's death in 1953. Pavlov's theory that conditioned reflexes and physiological processes determine all behavior was initially accepted wholeheartedly by the Communist government because it was felt to be compatible with the materialist, mechanist, and determinist emphases of Marxist political theory:

> . . . materialist in that it holds for the reality of matter independent of the perceiver and stresses the importance of material factors over ideas in life; mechanist in that the basic model for all theories is that of a machine which is essentially a system of levers and is moved by the

BOX 4-2 THE ISSUE OF CONSCIOUSNESS AND FREE WILL IN THE ENVIRONMENTALIST TRADITION

Bandura (1974) dropped a theoretical bombshell on behavioral psychologists when he appeared to abandon the principle of environmental determinism and to endorse the notion of free will. He disputed the application of the concept of the conditioned reflex to human learning and insisted that reinforcement changes behavior only "through the intervening influence of thought" (Bandura, 1974, p. 860). In other words, he assumed human behavior to be preceded and guided by expectations, images, self-instructions, or other conscious cognitive activity. Bandura (p. 867) further declared that "People may be considered partially free insofar as they can influence future conditions by managing their own behavior." He did not doubt the importance of environmental contingencies, but he insisted that impulses arising from within an individual could produce actions which altered those contingencies. Thus there is a reciprocal relationship between internal person variables and external situation variables. In 1977, he repeated and elaborated upon these contentions.

A direct attack on Bandura'a position was published by Wolpe (1978), who argued that cognitions are the product of physiological events in the central nervous system and that those events are, in turn, the product of environmental conditioning. The only other sources of activity in the central nervous system are, according to Wolpe, inherent biological processes such as breathing or digestion. Wolpe was an originator of behavior-modification therapy, and his reciprocal inhibition technique is discussed in Chapter 8. Briefly, the technique requires a phobic client to visualize an anxiety-arousing scene while maintaining a state of muscular relaxation. Presumably a state of relaxation is incompatible with a state of anxiety, so the former inhibits the latter, which enables previously phobic situations to be encountered without the subjective experience of anxiety. Wolpe differs from Bandura in that he considers the cognitive components of his procedure to be mere physiological responses to environmental conditioning, just as muscular relaxation is a physiological response. Wolpe (p. 441) refuses to accept the notion that cognitive activity can be generated independently from environmental conditioning so as to be a first cause of behavior.

> Thoughts are responses, whether they are perceptions or imaginings. Like other responses, they are evoked when the relevant neural excitations occur. They are a subset of learnable responses and, inasmuch as they have stimulus aspects, may be conditioned to other thoughts and to responses in other categories. They are not part of a separate *mechanism* of learning that only human beings possess.

He goes on to say that our subjective impression of cognitive freedom is only an illusion and that "our thinking is behavior and is as unfree as any other behavior."

In somewhat the same vein, Skinner (1977, p. 4) criticized cognitively oriented psychologists who, he said, felt compelled to invent terms such as *intentions, purpose,* or *will* to account for behavior whose conditioning history was obscure. The generation of innovative behavior is due not to some spontaneous mental process but to past learning of chained sequences of verbal or other behaviors which may be internalized as subvocally spoken rules capable of being elicited by a widely generalized class of stimulus situations. It is not necessary, Skinner argues, to hypothesize stored mental representations of the environment which combine spontaneously with one another in order to explain the appearance of seemingly creative or planned behavior.

It is not at all clear, however—to return to the article which precipitated this controversy—just how free Bandura believed one's cognitive life to be. Immediately after declaring people to be "partially free," Bandura (p. 867) made the following, somewhat paradoxical statement: "Granted that selection of particular courses of action from available alternatives is itself determined, individuals can nonetheless exert some control over the factors that govern their choices."

What he seems to be suggesting here is that the expectations, memories, and motives that guide behavior can only have gotten inside the organism through past environmental conditioning. The reinforcement value attached to each of these conditions would itself be a product of environmental conditioning. Hence the extent to which one cognitively represented behavior pattern is evoked ahead of another in response to stimuli present in a given situation depends upon the cumulative impact of prior conditioning, and the individual's choice is no more freely determined in Bandura's cognitive model than it is in Skinner's radical-behaviorist one. Bandura's use of the word "free" appears to refer to the capacity of an organism to select behaviors which are anticipated to change the environment so as to provide the organism with increased access to rewarding consequences in the changed setting. Bandura does not commit himself to the position that the selection process is guided by a spontaneous inner will. Quite the contrary, he says it "is itself determined."

What is the present status of the controversy, then? Is it merely a dispute over semantics, or does it represent a genuine philosophical cleavage within the environmentalist tradition? These questions cannot yet be answered, but future exchanges between radical and cognitive behavioral psychologists may bring into sharper focus the fundamental lines of disagreement.

application of external force; deterministic in that it considers all events of the universe to be subject to rigid causality, but most especially in that it places a strong emphasis on the inevitability and predictability of future events. (Bauer, 1952, p. 6)

The materialist orientation in psychological theory denies the existence of personal, subjective interpretations of reality and asserts that the material (environmental) conditions of existence dominate individual ideas and are the mainsprings of personal and societal behavior. Consequently, Soviet psychologists in the 1920s denounced subjectivism, voluntarism, and idealism and rejected phenomenology and introspection, with their associated concepts of consciousness and free will.

Beginning with the First All-Union Congress on Human Behavior in January 1930, however, psychologists were compelled to abandon the concept of strict environmental and physiological determinism. In particular, it was decided at the higher levels of Soviet government that psychologists must accept two principles: (1) mental events cannot be explained *entirely* in terms of the less complex phenomena observed by physicists, physiologists, biologists, or chemists, and (2) human behavior is directed toward goals consciously chosen by the actor.

According to Bauer, several political considerations motivated these directives to psychologists. By 1930, the Communist government had been in power for more than a decade, and continuing problems with education, the economy, class differences, and dissension were occurring within an environment largely created and maintained by that government. Thus, to blame the environment for the existence of chronic problems was essentially to fault the government. Furthermore, strict physiological or environmental determinism clearly suggested that individuals could not be held personally accountable for their behavior. The first Soviet criminal code, promulgated in 1919, in fact had stated that "crime in a class society is a result of the latter's social structure, not of the 'guilt' of the criminal" (Bauer, 1952, p. 32). Implied in this code was the belief that as a Marxist government eliminated social classes, crime would disappear. By the early 1930s, though, Stalin was consolidating his control over the government and was eager to hold certain political opponents personally responsible for alleged crimes against the state which, Stalin claimed, had created many of the social and economic problems facing Soviet society.

The conscious purposiveness with which human nature was now endowed did not, though, include free will. According to S. L. Rubinshtein, one of the leading *dialectical* psychologists of this period who served as a spokesman for the party line, "Freedom is the recognition of necessity" (Bauer, 1952, p. 133). While behavior in the immediate present is directed toward consciously chosen goals, the goals that an individual will choose have been *determined* by the individual's prior experience and the structure of his or her society. Thus the normal person will "freely" choose those goals which the state has decided are most conducive to the general welfare. Personality was thus regarded as shaped to some extent by inherited physiological processes and immediate environmental conditions but also heavily influenced by *training* (p. 126). Training occurred not only in the schools and at the work place but also in the course of an individual's interactions with friends and family; the individual also had a responsibility for *self-training*, which involved a conscious understanding and acceptance of the ideals of society and of his or her duty to uphold them. Any individual failure to perform as expected could thus be blamed on improper training by educators, friends, or family or on a willful lack of attention to self-training (pp. 148–149).

After 1930, psychologists who had previously emphasized physiological or environmental determinism were explicitly advised to change their views. In a thinly disguised attack on Pavlov, for example, a play entitled *Fear* was conceived and officially promoted in 1930. The play described the influence that various counterrevolutionaries and "class enemies" had over the misguided director of the "Institute of Physiological Stimuli." The director, a distinguished scholar named Ivan Illitch Borodin, deliberately samples only dissident elements in the Soviet population so as to draw biased conclusions regarding people's social motivation. The counterrevolutionary nature of this research is exposed by an old Bolshevik woman in a public meeting, and Borodin recognizes the error of his ways. His institute is, for a time, taken over by a young woman activist, who rids it of "class enemies." Finally, repentant and reformed, Borodin is welcomed back to his former position of honor (see Bauer, 1952, p. 106;

Miller, 1962, p. 186). Pavlov was, in fact, often in bitter conflict with the Stalinist government between 1930 and 1933. After 1933, however, and until his death in 1936, he and the government had something of a reconciliation as Pavlov's work shifted toward the *second signal system* (i.e., language) and higher, more conscious mental processes.

The new official line in Soviet psychology also rejected the major trends in Western European and American psychology, which were perceived to be *Freudianism* and *radical behaviorism*, respectively. This stance has persisted to the present, as is revealed in a relatively recent monograph by Bluma V. Zeigarnik, a professor at the University of Moscow whose early work on memory is well-known among Western psychologists.

An application of Soviet psychology for the purpose of relieving stress among workers at an industrial plant. Here, workers relax in an air-conditioned room while viewing outdoor scenes, accompanied by appropriate sounds of nature. (Sovfoto)

In contemporary American and West European psychology we encounter a different concept of the content of consciousness and its role in human activity. One school tries to prove that the leading forces to which consciousness is subordinate are biological instincts primordially buried in the depths of the mind (Freudianism). Another school basically denies the existence of consciousness, viewing the human being as an automaton blindly reacting to environmental stimuli (behaviorism).

Thus, from different angles both theories seek to minimize the role of consciousness. (Zeigarnik, 1972–73, p. 8)

Zeigarnik also endorses the line laid down in the 1930s by approvingly quoting a colleague, L. S. Vygotsky, to the effect that conscious thought in no way implies free will. "We know," Vygotsky said, "that freedom of the will is nothing other than a recognition of necessity" (p. 19). A continuing concern of Soviet psychologists is with dissident behavior or "a pathology of thinking, described in the psychiatric clinic as 'disputativeness' " (p. 80).

Partly because of these practical concerns and because of the role played by the central government in defining "correct" and "incorrect" theoretical positions, Soviet psychology became predominantly an applied science. The questions that were researched consisted of such things as how to improve the training and productivity of workers or how to design equipment so that it would suit the perceptual and physical capabilities of human operators. Most theorizing and research in personality psychology came to a halt.

After 1950, however, there was an effort to reorganize psychology along "correct Pavlovian lines"—i.e., emphasizing Pavlov's later work on the second signal system and higher mental processes (Bauer, 1952, p. 171). Pavlov's four temperaments—choleric, sanguine, melancholic, and phlegmatic—are still thought to underlie personality and to be due to differences in the activity of individual nervous systems, though there remains a firm insistence that training is the main determinant of character and that "Great abilities may be found just as often in connection with any type of temperament" (p. 166). While Pavlov has been restored to a place of honor among Soviet psychologists, then, there has been no tendency to accept the physiological reductionism and environmental determinism which guided much of his research and writing. Studies of the relationship of neurochemical events to behavior and of the conditioning of animals are classified as physiology rather than psychology (Brožek, 1969).

Besides according a greater acceptability to Pavlov's theories (a step probably facilitated by the de-Stalinization of the 1950s), few changes seem to have been made in the basic line pursued by Soviet psychology since the 1930s; namely, that environmental determinism is mediated by the conscious choices of the individual. This line appears to be an exceedingly narrow one, since the Soviets reject free will (the errors of idealism or voluntarism), on the one hand, and the determination of behavior by unconscious reflexes, instincts, or neurochemical events, on the other. A 1967 paper by A. N. Leont'yev (Brožek & Slobin, 1972, p. 146) suggests that "the role of the unconscious in the mind" as well as other "questions that in past years have been ignored in our country" are being given more serious consideration. Leont'yev is a prominent psychologist at Moscow University, but whether his paper foreshadows a genuine interest in developing general theories of personality based on psychological data rather than political expediency remains to be seen.

Bieliauskas (1977) reported that therapy in Soviet mental hospitals relies primarily on the administration of psychoactive drugs. There is also an active interest in applying neurological techniques to the treatment of psychological problems. Psychology has only recently emerged as an independent discipline, however; psychologists tend to be kept apart from what are regarded as "medical" applications and to be focused on basic research. Recently, psychotherapeutic-interview techniques of the type familiar to Western psychologists have become more acceptable in the Soviet Union. There has also been an increasing interest in the diagnostic techniques and tests utilized in the West, such as the Rorschach inkblots, the Minnesota Multiphasic Personality Inventory, the Wechsler Intelligence Scales, and so forth (see Chapters 5 and 6). Group therapy, particularly involving families with psychologically troubled members, is also being tried in innovative centers such as the psychology department at the University of Leningrad.

Because of its belief that "correct" behavior signifies the mental capacity to make healthy choices, Soviet psychology views "incorrect" behavior as an indication of mental illness. People who express more than a mild degree of dissatisfaction with Soviet society may be diagnosed as suffering from "anti-Soviet delusions." Segal (1976) notes that no distinction is drawn in the treatment of political dissidents, psychotics, and mentally disturbed common criminals. He therefore doubts that the routine administration of psychoactive drugs to political as well as other patient groups represents a deliberate effort to drive the former into a genuine state of madness. Ziferstein (1976) observed that Soviet psychiatrists are very active in their treatment methods and are likely to employ drugs, EEG, and intensive counseling simultaneously when working with a given client, regardless of the nature of the presenting complaint. Segal concludes that what appears to Western eyes to be exceptionally harsh treatment of political dissidents in the Soviet Union must be viewed in the context of a society which, both under the czar and under communism, has never placed much emphasis on the rights of the individual. In the past as well as in the present, deviance of any sort has been regarded as a manifestation of psychological imbalance,

a threat to social stability, and grounds for the imposition of punitive countermeasures.

CONCLUSION

There are several intriguing parallels between the American and Soviet behaviorist traditions. For one thing, both began with a strong emphasis on environmental determinism, in that each assumed the conditioned reflex to be the basic unit of behavior. Unlike his American counterparts, though, Pavlov also assigned a central role to physiological processes as determinants of behavior. Pavlov's theories were thus somewhat closer to nineteenth-century materialist philosophy than were those of the American radical behaviorists, though both Russian and American behaviorism were consistent with a materialist viewpoint.

Later developments in American as well as Soviet behaviorism gave more emphasis to internal mental events as mediators of action. For American theorists—such as Dollard and Miller and, especially, Bandura and Walters—an interest in cognitive mediators of behavior was provoked by the observation that complex human learning often occurs so rapidly that it is difficult to explain in terms of the trial-and-error learning of conditioned reflexes. Even Bandura and Walters, though, seem to hold fast to the fundamental principle of behaviorism, which is that all action is determined by direct experience with, or vicarious observation of, past or present contingencies of reinforcement. The Soviets have gone some uncertain distance beyond this principle in allowing for the existence of consciousness and purposiveness. They agree with the principle to the extent that they perceive an individual's goals to be determined by past experience (especially training) and to the extent that they deny the capacity for free will. They disagree with the principle to the extent that they believe an individual is ultimately personally responsible for choosing "correct" goals. The free-will issue has been raised among American behaviorists, too, as was explained in Box 3-2, but here there is no central authority which can resolve the debate by defining a "correct" position.

It should be clear by now that the environmentalist tradition is, in many respects, no more unified in its philosophical viewpoint than are the psychoanalytic and personological traditions. All theoretical models of human personality still have considerable ground to cover before they can be knitted into a comprehensive model of the mind. In subsequent chapters we will be examining assessment techniques and research evidence which bear upon each of the foregoing traditions. Interestingly, most of the theorizing in personality occurred before there was sufficient research evidence available to permit an objective evaluation of the theorists' claims. While evidence has still not accumulated to the point where a definitive choice among theories can be made, we will attempt to explore the future possibilities for making such comparative judgments in the units which follow.

SUMMARY

1 Early behaviorism was based on the nineteenth-century philosophy of materialism. Materialists believed that biological systems were entirely explainable in terms of the laws of physics and chemistry by which inorganic matter was organized. Vitalists, by contrast, believed in the existence of properties that were unique to living systems. Pavlov and Freud both studied under prominent materialist physiologists.

2 In a procedure called *classical conditioning,* Pavlov demonstrated that a previously psychologically neutral tone could be made to elicit salivation in a dog if the tone was repeatedly paired with the sight of food. In other investigations, he found that tones similar to the conditioned one would also elicit salivation, but to a lesser degree. This phenomenon is called *stimulus generalization.* Pavlov maintained that there are four basic psychological temperaments—based on excitative and inhibitory processes in the central nervous system—which influence an organism's conditionability. He also believed that language adds a capacity for higher-order learning to the lower-order conditioned reflex.

3 Thorndike discovered a different type of conditioning from that observed by Pavlov. Here, an animal would learn to initiate behaviors it had never before displayed by being rewarded with a bit of food. He named this observation the *law of effect;* it was later termed *operant conditioning* by B. F. Skinner.

4 Watson was the first to define psychology as the science of behavior. He apparently successfully conditioned a fear of a white rat in an infant called Little Albert by pairing the presence of the animal with a frighteningly loud noise. In subsequent research, Watson and his

associates sought to decondition previously learned fears in other infants.

5   Skinner invented the standardized operant conditioning chamber, known as the *Skinner box*. He demonstrated that operantly conditioned behavior will increase in frequency and become more resistant to extinction if reinforcement is delivered on a schedule rather than continuously. Skinner has used scheduled reinforcement and a procedure known as *shaping* to create laboratory analogues of superstitious and purposive behavior. In applying his findings to the organization of human society or to individual therapy (a technique called *behavior modification*) Skinner has consistently advocated that the environmental contingencies of reinforcement must be altered if "good" behavior is to be encouraged and "bad" behavior extinguished. Appeals to reason or to some nonexistent inner identity are relatively ineffective techniques of inducing behavior change.

6   Hull's version of behaviorism, unlike Skinner's explicitly regarded events inside the organism as mediating between environmental stimuli and the organism's observed response. Dollard and Miller showed how incompatible internal drives (such as simultaneous tendencies to approach and to avoid a stimulus) could produce neurotic behavior in a rat. The approach-avoidance conflict was, in fact, their laboratory analogue of a Freudian neurosis. Dollard and Miller believed that the function of psychotherapy is to reduce the fear of punishment for the expression of certain internal drives.

7   Bandura and Walters proposed that reward and punishment do much more than simply increase or decrease the frequency of the behavior which preceded them. Their most important effect is to stimulate the individual to generate hypotheses regarding the probable outcome of future behavior. Such hypotheses may even develop as a result of simply witnessing the pleasurable or unpleasurable outcomes which another individual has received from a given course of action—a process called *vicarious learning*. Bandura distinguishes between the acquisition and performance of behavior and notes that only those actions for which rewarding outcomes are anticipated will actually be performed, even though they may nonetheless have been acquired and stored in memory. The approach to therapy which is based on Bandura's social-learning theory differs from behavior modification in that it is more cognitive. Clients are often asked to watch a model act out adaptive behavior rather than experience direct reinforcement for personally attempting the sequence in a trial-and-error fashion. Bandura has gone so far in his emphasis on cognitive processes as to suggest that human behavior is consciously motivated and, to some extent, free of environmental contingencies. Such statements have created a controversy within the environmentalist tradition.

8   Though the post-Revolutionary Soviet government initially endorsed

the materialist and determinist implications of Pavlov's work on the conditioned reflex, it was later decided that psychology must adhere to a new official line. Human beings have free will to the extent that they can be held responsible for failing to discover and adhere to those goals which are most conducive to the general welfare of their society. After a period of uncertainty, Pavlov's work has been restored to a place of honor in Soviet society, but it is his later work on language and higher mental processes which is most emphasized. Soviet therapy is heavily oriented toward psychoactive drugs, neurology, and other medical techniques, though Western-type interviews, personality tests, and group therapies are making inroads. Because of its ideological belief that mental health is exhibited in "correct" behavior, Soviet society perceives "incorrect," or dissident, behavior as a manifestation of mental illness. This has sometimes resulted in the use of psychological techniques of intervention to "cure" the politically dissatisfied along with the genuinely mentally disturbed.

TERMS TO KNOW

stimulus generalization
experimental neurosis
respondent conditioning
operant conditioning
shaping

approach-avoidance conflict
vicarious learning
radical behaviorism
cognitive behaviorism
consciousness

UNIT TWO

TECHNIQUES OF ASSESSMENT AND INTERVENTION

Unit One set forth three theoretical approaches toward understanding personality: the psychoanalytic approach, the dispositional approach, and the environmentalist approach. These approaches were described as representing, respectively, European characterology, American personology, and American and Soviet behaviorism. In Unit Two, we will examine the techniques for assessment of personality associated with the foregoing traditions. ▣ Projective techniques, a main topic of Chapter 5, are historically related to the European tradition. Clinicians using these assessment devices typically present the client with an ambiguous stimulus, such as an inkblot, and ask for a description of what objects, events, or persons are suggested by the stimulus. These descriptions are then studied for evidence of the client's inner conflicts and motivations. ▣ Chapters 6 and 7 examine the two distinct ap-

131

proaches toward assessment associated with different aspects of the American personological tradition. This tradition, it will be recalled from Chapter 3, stresses the importance of the individual patterning of personality and regards each person as a unique combination of psychological and physical traits. On the psychological side, the personological approach generated a variety of objective tests which continue to be widely used and which are easier to administer and score than are projective tests. These tests are the topic of Chapter 6. On the physical side, there is a very old belief in psychology and folklore that a person's biological characteristics play a part in shaping his or her personality. Some of these biological hypotheses have been discredited by subsequent research, but others have found some support. Biological approaches to assessment are considered in Chapter 7. Psychologists in the behaviorist tradition have, as was noted in Chapter 4, a theoretical commitment to searching for the observable environmental stimuli which influence overt behavior. Consequently, the behavioral perspective on assessment has relatively little interest in the unconscious motivations supposedly revealed by projective tests. Behaviorists also doubt that the individual traits and predispositions which are major concerns of theorists taking a personological approach really represent enduring mental structures which compel the individual to behave in a characteristic way regardless of short-term environmental reinforcement contingencies. The behavioral perspective is presented in Chapter 8. In each of the chapters in Unit Two, there is a section describing the implications for therapy and personality change which are offered by a particular approach toward assessment. In addition, each chapter contains a section detailing what seem to be the major shortcomings of a given assessment strategy. As we shall see, all strategies have some liabilities, but these weaknesses tend to be concentrated in different areas. Consequently, a combination of several different approaches would seem to offer the best hope of providing a fairly complete assessment of an individual's personality. Often the goal of assessment is the accurate diagnosis of a personality disorder so that an appropriate therapeutic strategy can be selected. Just as often, however, the goal is the description of a perfectly healthy personality for the purpose of counseling an individual attempting to decide which of several alternative courses of action might be most conducive to his or her future happiness. Another frequent use of these devices is in academic research on the structure of personality and its relationship with behavior. Occasionally, companies will use these measures to decide who should or should not be employed, and this application has aroused considerable ethical concern, as will be seen in Chapter 6. Although there is a parallel between the sequence of chapters in Unit Two and the organization of Unit One, the analogy is not as close as it appears. Interviews, discussed in Chapter 5, are conducted not just by psychoanalytic and other theorists in the European tradition but by trait, phenomenological, and behavioral psychologists within the American tradition as well. Some of the concern with diagnosis of personality disorder which is discussed within the European-oriented Chapter 5 can also be seen in the American-oriented Chapters 6 and 7. A well-known projective test was developed by the American personologist Henry Murray and is described in Chapter 5, while the first reliable measure of the trait known as *intelligence* was devised by two Europeans named Binet and Simon. In short, the order in which techniques of assessment are presented in Unit Two roughly parallels the organization of theories in Unit One, but this overall similarity should not be taken too literally.

5
INTERVIEWS AND PROJECTIVE ASSESSMENT

ISSUES TO CONSIDER

1 What is meant by the term *projective* as it is applied to certain techniques of clinical assessment?
2 There is a historical connection between projective techniques and the European psychoanalytic tradition. Can you describe it?
3 What are the major diagnostic categories employed by clinicians who adhere to a medical model of mental illness?

It was explained in Chapter 2 that Freud devised an interview technique which became the mainstay of his psychoanalytic approach to therapy. For Freud, the most important aspect of this technique was the method of free association, which consisted of the patient's agreeing to verbalize every thought which came to mind, regardless of how embarrassing or irrelevant it might seem to be. In addition, Freud tried to interpret the symbolic meanings of dreams, slips of the tongue, peculiar behavior, and so forth in an effort to discover a client's unconscious motivations. Projective techniques for assessment of personality may be thought of as formal methods of stimulating the process of free association and encouraging the client to create a story, or "dream," while fully conscious and able to respond to questions from the therapist.

Because of its fundamental importance to psychoanalysis, the *interview* has a special relationship to the European tradition. It should be kept in mind, however, that physicians have been taking case histories from their patients since the time of Hippocrates. Freud did not invent this procedure; he simply adapted it to his particular purposes. Furthermore, as we shall see in Chapter 8, even psychologists doing personality assessments and therapy within the behavioral tradition typically gather case histories from their clients before beginning treatment. An interview is commonly initiated by all types of professionals (including lawyers and the clergy) who want to understand the nature of a client's case. It is by no means a technique employed exclusively by psychoanalysts.

Following its discussion of interviews, this chapter considers five specific devices frequently used for projective assessment: (1) the word association test, (2) the Rorschach inkblot test, (3) the Thematic Apperception Test, (4) the sentence-completion technique, and (5) the picture-drawing technique. There is then a description of the diagnostic categories to which projective and other types of psychological assessment refer when there is reason to believe a client is suffering from some sort of mental disorder. The chapter concludes with a discussion of the difficulties and dangers posed by the diagnosis and treatment of mental illness and a critical examination of the reliability and validity of projective techniques of personality assessment.

THE DIAGNOSTIC INTERVIEW

Especially since the advent of psychoanalysis, it has been generally accepted among mental health professionals that there should be a series of interviews between therapist and client in order to assist the former in his or her assessment of the latter. Not all interview techniques are the same, however.

Freud's method of *free association* represents an extreme form of what Sundberg (1977, Chap. 3) called an *open interview*, in which the patient defines the content and direction of the dialogue, except for an occasional probing question by the therapist. In a totally *closed interview*, the patient responds with a short answer or choice to a series of questions such as: At what times do you feel most anxious? or How old were you when your parents were divorced? *Clinical interviews* fall somewhere between these two extremes, but they are generally oriented more toward openness.

Another way in which interview techniques can vary is in the degree of social distance maintained between therapist and patient. Freud felt that the therapist should sit behind the patient and remain both physically and psychologically aloof. Adler, on the other hand, preferred to face his patients and often took an active role in calling attention to what appeared to him to be aspects of the patient's style of life which were causing him or her to experience distress. Adler overtly recommended alternative ways of solving life's problems and encouraged his patients to develop greater social interest. Rogers went still

Left, the traditional technique for conducting a clinical interview: The therapist sits out of sight of the client, who relaxes and engages in free association, that is, verbalizes all the thoughts which spontaneously float into the consciousness. *Right,* a more relaxed, informal interview technique. The therapist and client sit facing one another, as though they are engaged in an everyday conversation. (John Briggs; Dr. Ann Kaiser Sterns)

further in decreasing social distance in the therapeutic interview. His *nondirective technique* stressed the importance of creating an atmosphere of friendship and acceptance. The interviewer and patient remained in full view of one another, as though engaged in an everyday conversation. The interviewer consciously avoided giving advice or offering criticism, and confined himself or herself to recognizing and clarifying the patient's own feelings and paraphrasing the patient's own statements. So Freud's technique maintained the greatest social distance between therapist and client and Rogers' the least. Sundberg (1977, p. 64) believes that in general, "it is not desirable to be either overly friendly or overly distant. The interviewee should feel well-received and relaxed, but still be in a 'working' frame of mind."

Much of the communication between therapist and client is at a nonverbal—as opposed to a verbal—level. Freud (1905, pp. 77–78) once described this aspect of the assessment process as follows: "He that has eyes to see and ears to hear may convince himself that no mortal can keep a secret. If his lips are silent, he chatters with his finger-tips; betrayal oozes out of him at every

pore." Clinicians differ as widely among one another in their sensitivity to such cues as they do in the types of questions they ask or the degree of social distance they maintain. People in general differ in this ability, so there is little reason to doubt that clinicians are similarly variable. Interestingly, women have generally been found to be more accurate than men both as transmitters and receivers of nonverbal communication (Hall, 1978). Clinical judgment consists of a subjective evaluation by the therapist of the verbal *and* the nonverbal content of an interview. In making this assessment, the therapist attends to what is left unsaid by the client as well as to what is said and makes use of such clues to inner feelings as eye contact, tone of voice, gestures, repetitive movements, and so forth.

Clinicians generally have confidence in their ability to make reasonably accurate assessments by means of one or more of these interview techniques, particularly when the information provided by the interview is supplemented by knowledge of the client's performance on one or more tests of personality. The accuracy of clinical judgment has, however, been called into serious question by empirical studies of the validity of these assessment techniques. Discussion of the latter studies is contained in the concluding section of this chapter. For now, we will consider several projective assessment devices often used as supplements to the clinical interview.

DEVICES FOR PROBING THE UNCONSCIOUS

The best-known projective devices used for personality assessment are word association tests, the Rorschach inkblot test, the Thematic Apperception Test, sentence-completion techniques, and picture-drawing techniques.

Word Association Tests

Someone taking a word association test is typically presented with a verbal or pictorial stimulus to which an unlimited number of responses can be made. He or she is then asked to complete the thought suggested by the verbal stimulus or describe the images or the stories suggested by the pictorial stimulus. On such open-ended tasks, the subject has ample opportunity to express what he or she *wants* to say in response to the ambiguous stimulus provided by the clinician or experimenter. Frank (1939) was the first to call these methods *projective* in the sense in which Freud used the word "projection" to describe a type of ego defense. What we may not be consciously aware of in our own personalities we may, nonetheless, *project* outward onto environmental stimuli.

You may recall from Chapter 2 that the word association test as a device for revealing unconscious motivations and conflicts was originally used by Jung (1909). Jung might ask the subject to say the first word which came to mind in response to the word "mother," for instance. An unusually long reaction time, an increase in breathing rate, blushing, stammering, or a failure to respond altogether might indicate that the

subject had conflicting feelings regarding his or her mother. Jung compiled a standardized list of words which he felt to be useful in disclosing such conflicts, words like "bride," "sin," "death," "abuse," "angry," "head," and so forth. He successfully used the technique to discover which of a group of nurses had committed a petty theft in the hospital at which he worked. He also (1968, pp. 59–61) inferred from the long reaction times of a woman diagnosed as a depressed schizophrenic that her symptoms were caused by guilt over her inattentiveness to a child who had reminded her of a former lover. The inattentiveness resulted in the death of the child. Upon gaining insight into the origins of her disturbance, the woman was reported by Jung to have been cured of her symptoms and to have remained so for at least fifteen years.

Lanyon and Goodstein (1971, p. 9) report that Jung's methods are mainly of historical interest as early models of today's assessment techniques. The *word association test* is not often used in clinical practice. Jung, however, must also be credited with anticipating the use of the polygraph to monitor changes in a person's internal state. The role of the polygraph in the therapeutic technique called *biofeedback* will be discussed in Chapter 8.

The Rorschach Inkblot Test

Probably the most famous of all psychological tests is the inkblot test devised by Hermann von Rorschach around the turn of the century. Rorschach was a psychotherapist who thought that showing patients pictorial stimuli might elicit projective associations which would be as useful to the therapist as those obtained by Jung's word association test. He began by showing clients simple geometric forms, but he soon abandoned these forms for the more complex and suggestive shapes formed by blots of ink. He finally settled on a set of ten blots—five of them black (or gray) and white and five of them colored. These blots were described, along with his system of interpreting them, in a 1921 monograph (Rorschach, 1921). Rorschach died soon after publishing this report, so he was unable to make any further refinements in his choice of stimuli or his technique of evaluating subject responses. Even though Rorschach himself regarded his methods as preliminary and in need of additional testing and validation, all the blots in his original set and many of his scoring techniques are still used in clinical assessment.

What are these techniques? The basic procedure is to have the subject go through each of the ten cards, freely giving associations to the blots. Then the examiner runs through the set again, asking the subject (1) to specify exactly where in the blot he or she saw the associations reported and (2) to explain what features of the blot suggested these associations. The information obtained from the subject's associations and responses to the two questions (called the *inquiry stage*) allows the following criteria to be scored:

Location　How much of the total blot is utilized in the subject's percept? If it is the whole blot rather than a part or a small detail, the examiner records this as *W*.

Determinant　Which attributes of the blot evoked the percept? Some possibilities are form (F), color (C), or texture (K).

Content　What was the subject matter of the response? Possibilities here are animal (A) or human (H).

Originality　How typical is the response? If the percept is a novel one for a particular card, the examiner may write down a key word describing this percept as a shorthand reminder.

Klopfer, who has done considerable research on the inkblot test, suggested an additional scoring category; namely, *form level*, or a rating of how appropriate the percept is to the actual shape of the blot (Klopfer et al., 1954).

As for interpretation, Rorschach was impressed by Jung's distinction between introverted and extraverted personality types and felt that the inkblot test provided a means of assessing these traits. He felt that an attentiveness to color is indicative of an emotional, impulsive, extraverted personality, while perception of a great deal of human movement in the blots is associated with a reflective, imaginative, introverted style. Consequently, a high ratio of color to movement responses suggests extraversion whereas a low ratio suggests introversion. Other traditional systems of interpretation have assumed that seeing animal rather than human figures is a sign of immaturity and that a persistent tendency to respond to parts rather than to the whole configurations of the blots may reflect a general orientation toward the trivial aspects of problems or of life in general—a desire to avoid thinking about abstract principles or larger issues. Predominantly popular rather than original responses to the cards may indicate an overly conforming personality, but responses that are highly inappropriate to the images on the cards implies a peculiar and egocentric style of thinking which could, in extreme cases, suggest an imminent psychotic break with reality.

Shown in Figure 5-1 are approximate reproductions of Cards IV and VI from the Rorschach inkblot test. Common percepts of these blots are bats or other winged creatures. Card IV might also suggest boots pointed in opposite directions or something with big feet; the narrow appendages off the sides at the top are often described as snakes, a response associated with sexual themes. Klopfer and Davidson (1962, p. 10) noted that many clinicians refer to this as the "father card" because they believe responses to it reveal attitudes toward paternal authority, masculine aggression, and needs for dependency.

An example of the use of the Rorschach in clinical assessment is provided by Lockhart and

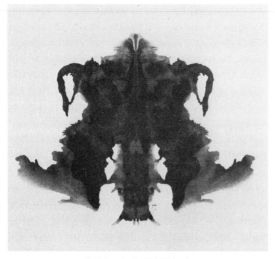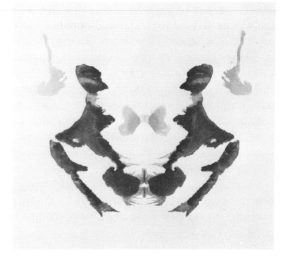

FIGURE 5-1
Approximate reproductions of cards IV and VI from the Rorschach inkblot test.

Siegel (1976), who obtained the following responses to Cards IV and VI from a 15-year-old male inmate of a mental hospital:

Card IV

1 Looks like you're down on the ground, you're looking up at a real big person, having feet and hands out and the face way up high. When a dog is on its back you know you are looking from the bottom seeing his face and legs up.

2 Looks something like a monster. Something someone might dream of.

Card VI

1 Some kind of animal looking into a pond and it's got that little reflection.

2 Without the top that kind of looks like a gun.

3 Looks like two faces, like with the nose and mouth and everything.

These responses were shown to an expert in interpreting Rorschach *protocols* (individual responses). The first response to Card IV was scored as WM+H, which means that the location of the image was the whole blot (W), that the determinant was action, or movement (M), that the form perceived was appropriate to the shape of the blot (+), and that the content was *human* (H). The expert's overall interpretation of the Card IV material was that it "shows how enormous his (the inmate's) masculine aspiration is, and how frightening and deflating his pathetic little speck of it is to him." The following interpretation was made of the inmate's response to Card VI:

It would be important to know what kind of animal is looking at its reflection. . . . here we have something destructive, a gun. "Gun" is the way he would impose his masculine energy outwardly. He is so unrelated and socially dangerous, he is at the mercy of impulse and has no idea who he is.

The expert concluded that the inmate suffered from intense feelings of inadequacy and had not achieved a stable masculine identity. He was likely to be assaultive, crude, and impulsive as a result of his efforts to conceal his sense of inferiority. In fact, an independent investigation of the biography of the inmate by another psychologist unfamiliar with the Rorschach data revealed a long history of violent acts which often involved the use of weapons (an indication of insecurity and weakness). As a young child, the inmate had been abandoned by his mother and was raised by his father. The expert was pessimistic regarding the possibilities for psychological rehabilitation of this inmate, and in an apparent confirmation of this pessimistic diagnosis, the inmate's period of hospitalization was punctuated by frequent fights with other patients and staff and by an unsuccessful suicide attempt.

Despite evidence of occasional diagnostic accuracy, interpretations of responses to the Rorschach inkblots must be treated with caution. Even if some images are produced by unconscious motivations, it is unlikely that all of them are. Sundberg (1977, pp. 206–207) observed, for example, that a person who has recently gone for a hike in the woods is more likely to see boots in the inkblots, while someone living near an airport is more inclined to see a plane. An examiner who looks for any deeper symbolic significance in these responses is probably guilty of "overpsychologizing."

While the Rorschach remains the single most popular assessment device among clinicians (aside from the interview itself), serious and long-standing questions remain regarding the reliability and validity of the interpretations customarily derived from it (Wade et al., 1978). The apparent shortcomings of the Rorschach (and other projective techniques) are discussed in the concluding section of this chapter. For the present, we will examine two of the more important innovations in the extensive literature on the technique.

The Comprehensive System   Exner (1974) tried to increase the reliability of the scoring system for the original Rorschach inkblots by redefining the dimensions on which the examiner was to make evaluations. He refers to his overall approach as the *comprehensive system*.

Weiner and Exner (1978) identified five specific scoring categories on which it was possible for independent raters to achieve reliabilities of better than 0.80 (see Chapter 1 if you need to be reminded of what is meant by *interrater reliability*). These categories are:

Deviant verbalization   Using distorted language or words with a personalized meaning that prevents clear communication.

Autistic logic   Using arbitrary or illogical reasoning in formulating a response.

Incongruous combination   Unifying two or more details of a blot into a single incongruous percept ("A person with the head of a bat").

Fabulized combination   Describing an implausible relationship between two or more blot details ("Two chickens holding basketballs").

Contamination   Fusing two or more distinct impressions of a single blot into a percept that violates reality ("The front of a bug-ox").

Weiner and Exner compared the Rorschach responses of a group of adolescent and adult psychiatric patients with those of appropriate nonpatient controls. They found that the patients were much more likely to give responses falling into all of the above categories except the contamination category (which was a very rare type of response in both groups). Interestingly, nonpatient adolescents were significantly more likely than were their adult counterparts to make use of autistic logic, incongruous combination, and fabulized combination. Many parents who have difficulty communicating with their adolescent offspring may find reassurance in Exner's findings, which can be taken as evidence of their sanity in comparison to the teenagers in their households.

The Holtzman Inkblot Technique Holtzman (1975) took a somewhat different route from the one chosen by Exner in trying to improve on the reliability of the Rorschach inkblot test as an assessment device. Reasoning that allowing subjects to give multiple responses to a given card decreased the reliability of the test, Holtzman and his associates (Holtzman et al., 1961) substituted a large number of new blots of ink for Rorschach's original set and restricted subjects to one response per card.

The *Holtzman Inkblot Technique,* or HIT, uses two parallel sets of forty-five cards which reliably evoke similar patterns of response in the same subject. In addition to this parallel-form reliability, scores on the HIT correlate fairly highly with comparable scores obtained from the original Rorschach test. Responses to the HIT, however, are scored on twenty-two well-defined variables on which acceptably high levels of interrater reliability have been demonstrated. These variables include Reaction Time, Form Definiteness, Shading, Movement, Pathognomic Verbalization, Hostility, Popularity, and so forth. Despite methodological improvements over the Rorschach and generally impressive reliabilities, though, few strong relationships have been found between the HIT and other personality inventories. Holtzman (1975) suggested there was clear evidence relating a high "Movement" score to imaginative capacity. He also maintained that the HIT could reliably discriminate between clinical populations such as schizophrenics and depressives.

The Thematic Apperception Test

While the psychoanalytic rationale for the Thematic Apperception Test, or TAT, is the same as that for the Rorschach inkblot test, TAT stimuli are pictures of people in real-life settings rather than totally ambiguous shapes. The TAT, first introduced by Morgan and Murray (1935) and subsequently elaborated upon by Murray (1943), asks the subject to make up a story appropriate to

FIGURE 5-2
A picture from the Thematic Apperception Test.

a picture like the one shown in Figure 5-2. The subject is told that his or her story should describe what the people in the picture are currently thinking and doing, what led up to the scene depicted, and what the outcome will be. There are thirty-one cards available to the examiner, but typically only twenty—selected for their appropriateness to the subject's sex and age level (child or adult)—are used.

Murray assumed that the main characters (heroes) of the stories would be described in terms that reflected attributes of the subject's own personality. He also felt that the environment inhabited by the hero would have features in common with the subject's own environment. The pictures represent a wide range of scenes: a young boy contemplating a violin, a young woman leaning against a doorway with downcast head, a surgical operation, a rowboat drawn up on the bank of a woodland stream, a dragon lurking among high cliffs adjoining a road, and so on.

The examiner may ask the subject to write out the stories or may arrange to transcribe or tape-record them. Murray's suggestions for scoring the content were that the following elements of each story be specifically attended to by the examiner or therapist: (1) identification of the hero and the hero's most *salient traits,* such as leadership, passivity, cooperativeness, or quarrelsomeness, (2) the *needs* of the hero (abbreviated *n*), broken down into *primary survival needs* (*n*-Food, *n*-Water, and so on) and *secondary social needs* (*n*-Affiliation, *n*-Dominance, *n*-Nurturance, *n*-Abasement, *n*-Acquisition, and so on), (3) the *environmental forces,* or *presses* (abbreviated *p*), *on the hero* (*p*-Aggression, *p*-Nurturance, *p*-Rejection, and so forth), (4) *outcomes,* in terms of the relative satisfaction or dissatisfaction of the hero, and (5) *themas,* or the overall plot line created by description of the hero's needs, the presses experienced by him or her, and the outcomes that he or she encounters. The examiner is also instructed to look for clues in the story which might reveal the interests and sentiments of the teller. Kleinmuntz (1967, p. 305) notes that "there are numerous other non-quantitative scoring systems available . . . but it is generally agreed that none of these will replace Murray's needs-press approach."

An example of TAT responses and interpretation is provided by Lanyon and Goodstein's (1971, pp. 57–58) transcription of a story told in response to the picture shown in Figure 5-2. The woman telling the story is a 23-year-old psychiatric outpatient.

> Well, there's a young woman in the foreground and an older woman in the background, and the older woman looks as though she has planned something that will be harmful to the younger woman, who looks very naive. And in fact the older woman has planned to keep the younger woman captive, and to make her serve her, for the rest of the older woman's life. But although the girl is naive, she's also rebellious; and by asserting herself with other people and getting a group of friends she's able to move out of the—not exactly spell, but she's able to break

the bond that the older woman has round her. Right now, she's just beginning to realize that she is being put in a position like this, but she's still very much under the control of the older woman, because these two have lived together for a long time. In fact, the younger woman was raised by the older woman. She's still very much under her control as I said, and she has strong feelings of guilt and fear of facing the world on her own. But fortunately she is able to make friends. At this point, though, she hasn't broken the bonds and she feels very confused, like she's being drawn between two poles. Ultimately, she's able to go out and make friends, and getting to know people and the different ways they have from the ways the old woman had taught her, she's able successfully to face the older woman, and defy her control, and go out and live a life of her own.

According to Henry (1956, pp. 254–256) this woman's response to the picture would be regarded as fairly typical. Younger women often perceive the old woman in the background as a controlling mother figure. Sometimes the old woman is regarded as a symbolic representation of a particular facet of the young woman's character (her "evil self," or herself when she is older, for example). The latter symbolism is most usually expressed by women of middle age.

In this story, the old woman is perceived as exerting a repressive influence (*p*-Dominance), on the heroine who wants to make new acquaintances and establish a separate life (*n*-Affiliation and *n*-Independence). The client's use of the words "guilt" and "fear" to describe the feelings associated with her heroine's drive for independence suggests that the older woman has partially persuaded the younger one that she is being held captive partly out of love and a concern for her safety in a threatening social world. The client appears to be reassuring herself that the external world is not as menacing as it appears to be; her heroine breaks free of the old woman's control, learns that other people can be "friends" even though they have "different ways," and successfully establishes a life of her own.

In a caution which should be attached to any example of projective techniques of personality assessment, Lanyon and Goodstein warn the reader not to read too much into a patient's reaction to a single card. Clinicians should draw inferences from the overall patterning of responses across several such stimuli and only after listening to the client's own explanation of his or her responses during the course of the interview.

One pattern that is sometimes looked for is a tendency to follow a dramatically vivid story which supposedly projects a genuine repressed motive with a dull, evasive, or superficial one. Bellak (1971, p. 122), for instance, observed that the TAT responses of a young male adolescent were not particularly indicative of psychopathology except for a few striking stories that, intriguingly, also contained slips of the tongue. The card to which the following story was a response depicts an adolescent boy staring straight at the viewer. The barrel of a rifle is visible at one side of the picture, and in the background is a dim scene of a surgical operation.

These two boys have gone out hunting. They shot a lot of boys—I mean animals, and decided to split up to get more pheasants. They agreed to meet at 8:30 at night to count the game and to go home. This boy was standing in the bushes. Twenty feet from him he heard something move. He goes to look at what he caught and finds his friend and rushes him to the doctor. The doctor says the boy will be all right, and in the end the boy gets OK and forgives him for what he did.

Bellak notes that "An inquiry into the small detail of 8:30 at night revealed that this was the time for lights out at the institution and strongly suggested that it was at this time that his fantasies were permitted to emerge." The subject

had been placed in a mental institution after murdering a small child, possibly while in a state of sexual excitement (though his exact motives were unclear). He had been a model inmate after being institutionalized. Even though he was cooperative, however, his emotionally bland demeanor made him inaccessible to psychotherapy. Bellak was asked to assist in determining whether or not this boy should be released.

Bellak (1954, 1971) pioneered the use of a Children's Apperception Test in which cartoon-like pictures of animals were substituted for the stimuli in the adult version. Blum (1950) devised a similar test, called the Blacky Pictures, which portray scenes in the life of a puppy named Blacky (sex unspecified), its parents, and a sibling. The Blacky Pictures are specially designed to evoke Freudian themes. For example, a picture on the theme of castration anxiety shows Blacky watching as a knife falls on the tail of its sibling. Oral themes may be elicited by a picture of Blacky nursing, and so forth.

The TAT and its derivatives share a problem with the Rorschach inkblot test: the subject responses are so open-ended and variable that reliable scoring systems are difficult if not, indeed, impossible to develop. One system devised by Eron and his associates scores such attributes as *emotional tone* and *interpersonal theme*, but it has not been found to be very effective in diagnosing psychiatric disorders (Eron, 1950; Zubin et al., 1965).

An alternative quantitative scoring method that has been widely used in research is McClelland's measure of *need for achievement*. McClelland and Atkinson began their program of research at Wesleyan University in the mid-1950s (Atkinson, 1958). They wanted to use the TAT to search for evidence of a generalized motive to achieve.

Male undergraduates were given a battery of tests under either relaxed and casual or stressful and competitive conditions. Subjects in the latter group were also led to believe that they had failed the tests (in order to arouse their need to achieve). Upon completion of the tests, all subjects were asked to write stories in response to the TAT pictures.

Several categories of response were found to distinguish between the relaxed and the stressed groups. These categories are shown in Table 5-1. McClelland made the theoretical assumption that the themes which appeared in stories written under stressful, competitive conditions would also appear in stories written under ordinary conditions by people whose personalities included a strong motivation to achieve. Consequently, the procedure for scoring the need for achievement expressed in a TAT story, or in any other written work, involves searching for themes which can be classified in each of the categories shown in the table. In the case of a story told in response to a TAT picture, the first item to be scored would be Achievement Imagery (AI). If the TAT story contained only *task imagery* (i.e., tasks are approached as a matter of routine rather than as means to attain some goal) or *unrelated imagery*, the story would not be scored for AI and all further scoring would cease. Assuming AI is present, the fact that goal attainment and goal affect are scored separately means that the highest possible score a story could receive is 11, one point being allotted to each of the categories listed in Table 5-1: AI, N, GA+, GA−, I, G+, G−, Bp, Bw, Nup, and AchTh.

McClelland used only four cards out of the complete TAT set to score need for achievement (*n*-Ach). This restriction on stimulus content probably contributed to his success in attaining high interrater reliabilities. Test-retest reliabilities were only low to moderate, which would seem to indicate that *n*-Ach is not a trait with long-term stability in an individual's character. McClelland et al. (1953) concluded, however, that

TABLE 5-1   McClelland's components for scoring need achievement (nAch)

Component	Meaning	Description
AI	Achievement imagery	A character in the story shows concern with competing sucessfully with some standard of excellence
N	Need	The story contains a statement indicating that someone wants to reach an achievement goal
GA±	Goal attainment	A character anticipates success (+) or failure (−) in attaining the goal (scored separately)
I	Instrumental activity	A character engages in activity that is instrumental for attaining the goal
G±	Goal affect	Positive (+) or negative (−) affective states are connected with goal attainment (scored separately)
B$_p$	Personal block	There is a block to goal attainment due to some characteristic of the individual
B$_w$	World block	There is a block to goal attainment due to some obstacle in the external world
Nup	Nurturant press	Someone either helps the individual attain the goal or indicates sympathy for the individual's goal-directed strivings
AchTh	Achievement thema	Achievement imagery is elaborated into the central plot or theme of the story

Need for achievement helps win a bronze medal at the 1976 Olympic Games. The runner at the right either fell or, very possibly, threw himself across the finish line, thus coming across a fraction of a second ahead of the runner at the far left and so captured third place. (United Press International)

In support of the validity of McClelland's measure are results indicating that parental expectations of independence and competence at young ages tend to increase a child's need for achievement. High n-Ach has, in turn, been associated with relatively high (but at the same time realistic) levels of aspiration for task performance and with better grades in school. These findings are based primarily on male rather than female subjects, an aspect of the achievement literature which will be discussed more fully in Chapter 13.

McClelland (1961) also arranged to have raters code achievement imagery in randomly selected children's stories published in thirty nations in the year 1925. Reasonably objective measures of economic growth in each of these countries during the period from 1925 to 1950 were then derived from figures for per capita income and consumption of electricity in the country. Results for both of the latter measures were in the same direction, so they were combined into a single index of economic growth. The correlation between 1925 achievement imagery in children's stories and economic growth over the succeeding twenty-five years was 0.43, which was interpreted to mean that societies which developed high n-Ach in their children showed the greatest economic advances. Using a similar procedure, de Charms and Moeller (1962) discovered that increases and declines in n-Ach imagery in children's stories in the United States were paralleled by rises and falls in the number of patents issued to inventors by the U.S. Patent Office (the index represented the frequency of patents per million individuals in the population). What was especially interesting about their findings was that the patent index lagged behind changes in n-Ach by about twenty years, which is approximately the time it takes for a generation of children to grow up.

Aronson (Atkinson, 1958) discovered that the doodles scrawled by people high in n-Ach differed from the scribbles of low-n-Ach people in several consistent ways. High scorers made discrete

even though test-retest reliabilities were low, the placement of an individual above or below the median for his or her group did have a long-term stability which was sufficient for most research purposes and even for certain types of individual assessment.

rather than fuzzy overlaid lines, made more diagonal than horizontal or vertical configurations, produced more S-shaped but fewer multi-wave lines, and left a smaller margin at the bottom of a page.

Aronson's criteria were also used to score the *n*-Ach of designs on ancient Peruvian pottery. The pottery had been dated by carbon-14 methods, so *n*-Ach scores could be related to an index of economic prosperity (measured by the volume of public buildings at various time periods). Once again, *n*-Ach was found to be positively correlated with prosperity, and the two periods of lowest *n*-Ach were associated with the conquest of Peru by foreign civilizations.

McClelland (1971) has reported successful attempts at modifying achievement motivation in individuals by teaching them the *n*-Ach scoring system and then training them to write stories in response to the TAT pictures that are high in achievement imagery. Presumably, this role-playing technique of encouraging people to start thinking in achievement terms will ultimately generalize to their style of thinking about life in general—not just TAT pictures. While the method seems peculiar, McClelland believes that an iron foundry in India and a development company in Curaçao owe their existence (in part, at least) to his techniques of enhancing *n*-Ach.

Needs for *affiliation* (*n*-Aff) and for *power* (*n*Power) have been assessed by McClelland and his associates using scoring techniques similar to those developed in the achievement research. One of the more intriguing findings in this area has been that the relative strengths of affiliation and power themes in popular literature has a historical relationship to periods of social reform or war. When the former themes were dominant, American society typically entered reformist periods. When, instead, themes of power predominated and there was a sudden drop in affiliation imagery, a war occurred in about fifteen years. In recent years, this time lag has been decreasing, so McClelland (1975) predicted, on the basis of an increase in *n*-Power and a drop in *n*-Aff in the early 1970s, that a war involving the United States would occur before 1980. Fortunately, this prediction did not come true.

Sentence-Completion Techniques

Sentence-completion methods gather projective information by providing the subject with a sentence fragment and then asking him or her to finish it. Some sample fragments are:

My father always _____
The happiest time _____
My mother and I _____
I worry a great deal about _____
When I am angry or upset _____

The most widely used scoring system for such items was proposed by Rotter and Rafferty (1950). In their system, each completion is scored as representing either a *high-conflict* (6), *neutral* (3), or *positive* (0) reaction to the material in the fragment. To the first item above, for instance, a completion like "frightened me" might be scored 6, whereas "worked very hard" might be a neutral 3, and "loved me and made me laugh" would be a zero. A net-maladjustment index is provided by adding the scores on forty such items. Norms provided by Rotter and Rafferty indicate where a given total score places an individual in terms of relative maladjustment or conflict. The index provided by Rotter and Rafferty's Incomplete Sentences Blank has been found to differentiate among adults with varying degrees of psychiatric disturbance (Goldberg, 1965) and between college students who make frequent visits versus those who make infrequent visits to the campus infirmary (Getter & Weiss, 1968). Interrater reliabilities are also reasonably good.

Another scoring procedure for responses to incomplete sentences has been devised by Loevinger (1976). Her test employs thirty-six fragments, and each completion is assigned to one of nine categories of ego development. The distribution of a subject's responses among these categories is used to derive his or her *stage of ego development*. These stages range from *impulsive* through *opportunistic, conforming, conscientious, autonomous,* and *individual.* The sequence is developmental in that children predominate at the impulsive and opportunistic stages, whereas more and more representatives of the autonomous and individualistic stages are found as children grow into adults. There is some similarity between Loevinger's categories and Kohlberg's stages of moral development, which will be discussed in Chapter 11. Loevinger has demonstrated that once raters are trained in her scoring procedure, a high degree of split-half and interrater reliability can be attained (Loevinger & Wessler, 1970).

Picture-drawing Techniques

The last major technique to be discussed in this chapter continues to be a popular one among clinicians despite meager evidence for its reliability and validity as an assessment device. Typically, the client is asked to draw a person, sex unspecified. Then he or she is instructed to draw a person of the opposite sex.

The best known of these methods is the Draw-A-Person (DAP) test by Machover (1948, 1951). Machover recommends that the drawings be followed by an inquiry in which the client is asked to describe the physical features, personal history, ambitions, and fears of the figures drawn. He also recommends numerous specific interpretations of such drawings. He believes, for example, that (1) the first figure drawn represents the subject's psychosexual identity, so a first drawing of the opposite sex indicates homosexuality, (2) the sex given the larger head is the sex accorded more intellectual and social authority, (3) highlighting the eyes indicates paranoia, (4) erasing and redrawing the nose reveals castration anxiety, and so forth. The evidence supporting such sweeping generalizations has been criticized by Anastasi (1961) and others as being woefully inadequate. Regarding the first generalization, for example, Roback and associates reported that heterosexuals and homosexuals showed no significant differences in the sex of the first figure drawn (Roback, Langevin, & Zajac, 1974). Cressen (1975) has noted that interpretations of drawings on the DAP are considerably influenced by the level of the subject's artistic skill.

THE PURPOSES OF PSYCHIATRIC ASSESSMENT

Freud and his early followers were all medical doctors in addition to being psychoanalysts. Consequently, they worked within what has come to be called a *medical model* of mental illness, which regarded such maladies as analogous to infections and other physical ailments. This orientation caused them to devise and implement a set of "categories" for mental disorder comparable to the system of diagnostic classification of symptoms which had proved to be extremely useful in other areas of medical science. To the present day, a major concern of mental-health professionals who adopt the medical model has been to refine and sometimes to supplement the diagnostic categories established by early theorists in the European tradition.

Kraepelin, a German psychiatrist and contemporary of Freud, is generally credited with originating the first reasonably comprehensive system for diagnosing clinical symptoms of mental disorder. His system was developed and elaborated upon in successive editions of his textbook, *Clinical Psychiatry*, which appeared around the turn of the century (Kraepelin, 1923). The most basic distinction he perceived between varieties of mental illness was that some people, even though they might be temporarily severely disorganized in their thoughts and behavior, eventually improved with the passage of time; others simply became psychotic and continued to deteriorate until they reached incurable states of dementia. Kraepelin believed that the former, curable illness was probably caused by environmental conditions, while the latter was caused by hereditary and biological factors. The American Psychiatric Association (1968, 1978) publishes a *Diagnostic and Statistical Manual of Mental Disorders*, often referred to as *DSM,* which employs many of Kraepelin's original categories in its attempt to standardize clinical diagnosis.

Psychiatrists, unlike psychologists, must complete medical school and hold M.D. degrees; they may or may not also have doctorates in psychology (most, in fact, do not). Consequently, psychiatrists are somewhat more likely than are psychologists to adhere to a medical model of mental illness.

Shown in Table 5-2 are some of the major diagnostic classifications contained in the most recent revision of the DSM. The first few headings, down through "Affective Disorders," refer to *psychoses,* the most severe forms of mental disturbance for which the prognosis is relatively poor. The remaining headings describe less severe problems for which the prognosis is more optimistic. These headings appear both in the 1968 edition of the manual *(DSM II)* and in the revised version *(DSM III),* which is currently coming into use. They are also found in the *Manual of the International Statistical Classification of Diseases, Injuries, and Causes of Death,* abbreviated ICD, which is published by the World Health Organization (1977).

A major change in DSM III as compared with DSM II is the adoption of a *multiaxial* method of classification. The first axis calls for matching a client's presenting complaint with the manual's description of a formal psychiatric syndrome, wherever this is possible. The second axis describes symptoms which appear less clear-cut, less disabling, or more transient—in particular, personality disorders or disorders related to developmental changes in childhood and adolescence. The third axis asks the clinician to indicate any physical ailments which may be relevant to an understanding of the client's mental state or which may have to be considered in prescribing treatment. The fourth axis calls for a subjective evaluation of the intensity of stress in the client's life for a year prior to his or her presentation for treatment. Severe but temporary life stresses—the death of a close friend or relative, for example—may precipitate a *reactive* personality disorder from which the client may be expected to recover as the stress diminishes. People who develop a personality disorder in the *absence* of any significant life stress may be suffering from a *chronic* condition, for which improvement is less likely. On the fifth, and last, axis, the clinician rates the highest level of adaptive functioning attained by the client during the preceding year in the areas of social relations, occupation, and use of leisure time. By encouraging clinicians to evaluate a patient on five axes, DSM III is advocating greater attention to the physical and social conditions that can contribute to mental disorder. In addition, it is attempting to provide more specific behavioral descriptions of the symptoms of various disorders. While psychologists have generally applauded these social and behavioral emphases, they have expressed concern that DSM III will foster the impression that holders of an M.D. degree are more legitimate and knowledgeable practitioners in the field of mental health (Schacht & Nathan, 1977).

The primary goal of assessment of personality disorder using a medical model is accurate diagnosis, achieved through interviews and the application of projective (as well as other) techniques. Once a particular patient's symptoms have been matched with a diagnostic category, certain forms of treatment may be prescribed which have in the past been successful in alleviating that type of disorder. These treatments may range from a series of therapeutic interviews for the milder *(neurotic)* cases to administration of electroconvulsive shock for the more extreme ones. Procedures for monitoring and modifying maladaptive behaviors may be implemented, or patients may be given drugs to reduce their anxieties or stimulate euphoria. Some of the theoretical and ethical issues surrounding the latter

TABLE 5-2 Selected major headings in the diagnostic and statistical manual of mental disorders

Heading	Description or example
Organic mental disorders	Senility, for example, in cases which are caused by atrophy of the cerebral cortex due to aging
Substance use disorders	Alcoholic psychosis, for example, which results from the chemical action of alcohol on the brain and which, in extreme cases, may produce vivid visual, auditory, and tactile hallucinations of a terrifying nature
Schizophrenic disorders	A broad category of psychotic disorders characterized by emotional detachment from others (autism), inappropriate and occasionally extreme emotional reactions, illogical thinking, delusions, and hallucinations
Paranoid disorders	Characterized by extreme sensitivity to presumed ill-treatment by others and irrational suspicions concerning their supposed plots against one's own well-being
Affective disorders	Mania, in which moods are excessively euphoric or hostile and speech and motor activity are accelerated; depression, in which apprehension, confusion, and unhappiness are associated with mental and motor retardation. Sometimes manic and depressive episodes alternate with one another
Anxiety disorders	Characterized by anxious overconcern extending to panic but which is not restricted to any specific situations or objects and which is obviously unrealistic in its intensity
Somatoform disorders	Hypochondriacal complaints, feelings of estrangement from one's body, or even loss of function of some bodily processes with no physical cause
Dissociative disorders	Alterations in one's consciousness or in one's sense of identity which produce symptoms such as somnambulism, fugue, or even multiple personality
Personality disorders	Characterized by behavior patterns which, even though they are clearly maladaptive, are generally less severely debilitating than those described above. These patterns include paranoid, schizoid, obsessive-compulsive, hysterical, passive-aggressive, and antisocial personalities
Psychosexual disorders	Characterized by problems in establishing gender identity, by chronic sexual dysfunction, and so on
Disorders usually arising in childhood or adolescence	For example, mental retardation, attention deficits, stereotyped movements, speech disorders, eating disorders, or disorders characteristic of late adolescence
Sleep disorders	For example, chronic insomnia

treatment approaches will be discussed in Chapters 7 and 8.

CRITICISMS OF PROJECTIVE TESTS AND PSYCHIATRIC ASSESSMENT

Rickers-Ovsiankina (1960) once commented that projective tests originated within a philosophical tradition which valued insight into the mental life of an individual patient more than it did statistical verification of reliability and validity. This being the case, it is hardly surprising that these tests appear inadequate to the more psychometrically oriented contemporary psychologist.

Even allowing for such special considerations, though, one is likely to be troubled if two independent raters of the same set of Rorschach or TAT responses arrive at entirely different conclusions regarding the patient. One might even begin to wonder whether these devices result in assessments which reflect the personality characteristics of the examiners more than they do the psychodynamics of the examinees. Furthermore, when a retest of the same examinee produces responses very different from his or her responses on a previous test using the same assessment device, both qualitative as well as strictly quantitative questions must be raised as to the reliability of the measuring instrument. Finally, reliability aside, when it cannot be convincingly demonstrated that responses to the assessment device permit one to distinguish between subjects who are and those who are not psychologically disturbed (that is, when validity cannot be demonstrated), one must surely begin to doubt the usefulness of the instrument. Each of the foregoing criticisms has been leveled at the Rorschach, TAT, and other projective techniques (Kleinmuntz, 1967, Chap. 9).

The Case of the Nazi Rorschachs

An example of the validity problems of projective tests is provided by a rather dramatic episode in the annals of inkblot-test research. In 1946, a psychiatrist named Douglas Kelley was appointed by the Nuremberg international tribunal for war crimes to examine the personalities of wartime Nazi leaders. Kelley (1946) administered the Rorschach test to seventeen of these leaders, including Hermann Göring, Rudolph Hess, and Joachim von Ribbentrop, among others. Kelley concluded that the Nazis did not appear to be pathologically deviant on the basis of their responses to the inkblot and other tests, and the tribunal did not take much further interest in his findings. Then, Miale and Selzer (1975) reanalyzed the Rorschach protocols and emphatically asserted that the results showed the Nazis to be clearly pathologically abnormal and mentally unhealthy. Harrower (1976) tested this conclusion by sending the records of eight Nazis and eight "normal" adult male controls to fifteen Rorschach specialists, ten of whom provided analyses. The experts were not told anything about the identities of the people whose protocols they were examining but were asked to look for common themes in the records and to group them. There was no tendency to group the Nazis separately from the "normals," but there was a tendency to categorize the protocols in terms of *presence or absence of psychopathology*. The Nazis, though, were not perceived as being any more pathological than were the controls. Ritzler (1978) compared the Rorschach-test responses of the Nazis with the responses of a *contemporary* control group of Kansas state troopers which had been studied in the late 1930s by another investigator. He also compared the Nazis with a *modern* control group of medical students and technicians at the University of Rochester. Relative to the controls, the Nazis showed more concern with status, mentioned human figures (especially females) less often, and mentioned dead and mounted animals more often. Ritzler suggested that the Nazis might have been more status-conscious and opportunistic and, hence, somewhat depressed over losing the war. There was no clear indication that the Nazis were different from the "normals" in a pathological sense.

Is the Rorschach inkblot test capable of dis-

Wartime Nazi leaders on trial in Nuremberg, Germany, in 1945. In the front row, from left to right, are Hermann Göring, Rudolf Hess, Joachim von Ribbentrop, and General Wilhelm Keitel. (United Press International)

criminating between "normal" adult males and Nazi war criminals who are known to have been perpetrators of or accomplices to acts of almost unspeakable cruelty? The answer seems to depend on whose Rorschach analysis one attends to. The contradictions contained in the foregoing interpretations of a historically dramatic set of protocols reflect the general validity problems faced by the Rorschach inkblot test and the Thematic Apperception Test. As was explained earlier, however, recent innovations in scoring and administering the inkblot test offer grounds for hope that the reliability and validity of this test can be improved. Exner's comprehensive system for scoring the original Rorschach stimuli seems to achieve acceptably high levels of inter-rater reliability, and data so far gathered indicate that the scores do discriminate between patient and nonpatient groups. The new and larger set of stimuli employed in the Holtzman Inkblot Technique also appears to be reliably scorable and to have some predictive validity in identifying psychopathology. As regards the TAT, it appears that reliabilities and validities high enough for research purposes (though not, perhaps, for individual assessment) can be attained by using well-defined scoring systems which focus on a single personality component (n-Ach, n-Aff, n-Power, and so forth).

Tests or Techniques?

The contemporary view of projective methods of personality assessment is that they are most properly regarded as *techniques* available to therapists for the purpose of gaining insight into their clients' personalities. They are not "tests" in the formal psychometric sense and cannot, therefore, be evaluated in terms of strictly statistical criteria, such as reliability and validity.

Meehl (1959) noted that the correlational statistics employed to evaluate reliability and validity search for a linear relationship between variables (see Chapter 1 if you need to be reminded of the meaning of a *correlation*). Variables can, however, be related to one another in a complex, curvilinear fashion, and such complexity is very likely to emerge in a clinician's diagnoses. Moreover, when multiple sources of information are available to a clinician (and they usually are), these sources can be combined in some simple, additive manner or in a nonadditive, *configural* way to arrive at an overall assessment of personality. Meehl argued that clinicians take a configural approach to assessment that is inadequately represented by such mathematical oversimplifications as correlational statistics and additive decision rules.

Applying Meehl's argument to projective techniques in particular, it might be said that their purpose is not to provide some score which, by itself, permits reliable and valid assessment but rather to provide alternative sources of information to the clinician which, when combined in a complex, insightful way with the information obtained from interviews and other tests, will allow him or her to form an accurate overall impression of the client's personality structure and dynamics. The clinician will thereby be able to diagnose the origin of the client's symptoms of distress, prescribe a course of treatment, and offer a prognosis regarding the likelihood of cure.

Accuracy of Clinical Judgment

The accuracy of clinicians' configural insights has been studied in a variety of ways. In one study, thirty-two professional clinicians observed the extensive diagnostic testing of a hospital patient who was a chronic alcoholic. Ignorant of the patient's alcoholism, the professionals were asked to submit diagnostic write-ups at the conclusion of the examination. Fourteen different diagnoses were obtained, including temporal-lobe epilepsy and paranoid schizophrenia. Needless to say, the professionals in this study were neither unanimous nor very accurate in their clinical insights (Nathan et al, 1969).

Some who have carefully examined the evidence on the accuracy of clinical judgments believe the clinician makes a productive contribution to the diagnostic process which is above and beyond any input derived from formal tests and measurements (Sawyer, 1966). It is also likely that some clinicians are consistently more accurate in their insights than are others. Perhaps, in the last analysis, the judgmental components which produce highly accurate clinical insights cannot be studied by means of conventional research techniques. It may be an area in which science blends into art. Even if the latter is true, however, clinical judgment remains an art form with important consequences for the lives of individual clients, and sometimes even for their personal freedom. Consequently, when accuracy cannot be demonstrated with a high degree of statistical reliability, the implications are disturbing.

In a highly controversial study of these implications, Rosenhan (1973) arranged for eight "pseudopatients" (one of whom was himself) to present themselves at the admissions offices of twelve hospitals in five different states on the East and West coasts. The "pseudopatients" gave false names and occupations but otherwise provided accurate biographical information to the intake officer. They all complained of hearing voices which were unfamiliar to them and which repeated the words "empty," "hollow," and "thud." Rosenhan commented that these particular hallucinations were chosen because they had a superficial similarity to existential symptoms relating to concern over the meaninglessness of one's life (as though the voices were saying, "My life is empty and hollow"). Rosenhan also noted that no cases of existential psychoses had ever been reported in the clinical literature.

All of the pseudopatients were admitted to the psychiatric ward, and the diagnosis in all cases (with one exception) was schizophrenia. The exception occurred at the one private hospital in the study, where the pseudopatient was diagnosed as manic depressive. Upon admission, each pseudopatient set about trying to convince the hospital staff that he was now sane and should be released. If asked by the staff how he was feeling, the patient replied that he was fine and no longer experienced any symptoms. The pseudopatients cooperated with the staff at all times, though they secretly disposed of their drug medications.

The length of hospitalization ranged from seven to fifty-two days, with an average stay of nineteen days. The pseudopatients, when released, were labeled *schizophrenic in remission*. For real mental patients, of course, such labels have profoundly negative social, legal, and vocational consequences, and the ease with which they were attached to the pseudopatients is disturbing, to say the least. Within the hospital environment, Rosenhan found that behavior and biographical details that would be regarded as commonplace anywhere else were interpreted in such a way as to justify the diagnostic label. Worse yet, patients were often treated in a dehumanizing manner which, if they were not insane when admitted, might have been sufficient to drive them insane. For example, out of 185 attempts to initiate polite conversation with psychiatrists, the pseudopatients were able to get meaningful verbal replies only 6 percent of the time. They fared still worse with the nurses and attendants. Rosenhan (p. 255) even has "records of patients who were beaten by staff for the sin of having initiated verbal contact."

Rosenhan gave a talk on his findings at a research and teaching hospital, where the staff insisted that *they* could never have made the diagnostic mistakes he described. He told them he would send one or more pseudopatients to *their* admissions office during the next three months and asked them to rate their degree of confidence that each new patient was, in fact, one of his pseudopatients. Of the 193 patients admitted to the hospital during the next three months, nineteen were judged with "high confidence" by

at least one psychiatrist and one staff member to be pseudopatients. In fact, Rosenhan sent no pseudopatients at all to the admissions office. He (p. 252) commented that this finding "indicates that the tendency to designate sane people as insane can be reversed when the stakes (in this case, prestige and diagnostic acumen) are high."

Several letters critical of Rosenhan's research were published in *Science* magazine (the journal in which Rosenhan's original report had appeared) on April 27, 1973. Most of these letters came from psychiatrists and emphasized several main points: (1) Rosenhan's sample of institutions was not large enough to draw any general conclusions, (2) the symptoms reported by the pseudopatients were not severe enough to warrant admission to most hospitals, which suggests that they may have said more to the admitting officers than Rosenhan described in his report, (3) contrary to Rosenhan's assertions, the pseudopatients did at least one very unusual thing that could reasonably be assumed to indicate severe mental distress—they volunteered to be admitted to a mental hospital, and (4) since all of the pseudopatients were eventually diagnosed as *recovered* and released, the ultimate diagnosis should be regarded as 100 percent accurate.

CONCLUSION

A major difficulty with the psychoanalytic approach to the study of personality is that it has traditionally been founded on assumptions that were tested using *correlational* rather than *experimental* methods. Freud would see a set of neurotic symptoms in a patient (paranoid fears of being attacked, for example) and try to relate these symptoms to events in the patient's childhood (e.g., hostility toward the parent of the opposite sex). These events would, in turn, be related to some presumed psychodynamic cause, such as an Oedipal state of tension between sexual desires emanating from the id and repressions established by the ego out of fear of parental punishment. The hypothesized causal connections between these observations and theoretical constructs can neither be directly observed nor experimentally manipulated.

A danger in such correlational inferences is that they may create an impression of causality which is, in fact, an illusion. Chapman and Chapman (1967) found that when college undergraduates were shown word pairs arranged so that all possible pairings appeared equally often, they nonetheless perceived certain pairings to occur more often than was actually the case. Pairs with high associative strength (e.g., salt-pepper, table-chair, hungry-food, and so on) were mistakenly perceived to occur with a greater-than-chance frequency, while pairs with low associative strength were perceived as having a frequency which was less than chance. Chapman and Chapman (1969) further discovered that observers will perceive statistical links between certain types of figure drawings or descriptions of ink blots and various symptoms of personality disorder when there is, in fact, only a random association between test responses and symptoms.

How much of clinical insight, projective assessment, and psychiatric diagnosis is reliable, how much is derived from illusory correlations, and how much is based on guesswork? At this point, no one can say for sure. Eysenck (1952) estimated that about two-thirds of people diagnosed as neurotic will eventually recover whether they are treated by general practitioners, treated by psychoanalysts, given custodial care, or

simply left untreated. Debates over the validity and usefulness of psychiatric diagnosis and therapy were intensified by the appearance of Eysenck's article, and practitioners and researchers have often been bitterly divided on this and other issues (Bergin, 1971; Rachman, 1973). Lambert (1976) did a careful evaluation of the evidence and concluded that although some neurotics *do* recover in the absence of any treatment, Eysenck had probably overstated the rate of such *spontaneous remission* of symptoms. Instead of two-thirds, an estimate of two-*fifths* seemed to him to be a more accurate reflection of the available data. Lambert cautioned against an uncritical acceptance of even his estimate, however, since different studies report remission rates ranging from 0 percent to 90 percent. One reason for this variability in results is differences in the definition of *psychological improvement*. Another problem lies in the fact that supposedly untreated neurotics often do receive some minimal therapy, which casts doubt on the truly spontaneous origins of some of their reported remissions.

Since 1965, when a subcommittee on invasion of privacy of the U.S. House of Representatives conducted hearings on the uses and abuses of psychological testing, all approaches toward assessment and treatment, not just those associated with projective techniques or psychiatric diagnosis, have been subjected to searching criticism. These questions will be given additional, detailed examination in Chapters 6, 7, and 8.

SUMMARY

1 Because of its fundamental importance to psychoanalysis, the *interview* has a special relationship to the European tradition. Even so, psychologists working within all theoretical traditions typically regard interviews as an important part of psychological assessment. Interviews may be *open*, in which the client defines the content and direction of the dialogue, or *closed*, in which these features are

structured by the interviewer. Clinical judgment consists of a subjective evaluation by the therapist of the verbal *and* the nonverbal content of an interview.

2 On word association tests, the client is asked to complete the thought suggested by a verbal or pictorial stimulus. In addition to the content of the client's replies, long reaction times, increases in breathing rate, or blushing and stammering may indicate a *complex* of conflicting emotions. On the Rorschach inkblot test, the client describes images and scenes suggested by an inkblot. Perceiving human movement is presumably associated with introversion whereas attention to color indicates extraversion. There is little evidence to support the reliability and validity of such traditional approaches to scoring and interpretation. A *comprehensive system* devised by Exner retains the original blots but changes the scoring criteria. The Holtzman Inkblot Technique, by contrast, changes the original blots but retains many of the traditional criteria for scoring.

3 The stimuli on the Thematic Apperception Test (TAT) are pictures of people in real-life settings rather than ambiguous shapes. Stories told in response to these pictures are scored for *needs* attributed to the main characters and environmental forces which *press* upon them. These are assumed to reflect the needs and presses in the life of the person taking the TAT. McClelland devised a specialized scoring system for stories told to four of the TAT pictures which permits him to measure the strength of a person's need for achievement. Scoring procedures have also been devised for the measurement of needs for affiliation and power.

4 Sentence-completion techniques provide the client with a sentence fragment and then ask him or her to complete it. Completions have been scored for level of maladjustment and conflict or stage of ego development. Picture-drawing techniques typically ask the client to draw a person, sex unspecified, and then to draw a person of the opposite sex. Various features of these drawings are interpreted as revealing unconscious motivations of the client, but this technique probably has the lowest reliability and validity of any discussed in Chapter 5.

5 The medical model of mental illness refers clients' symptoms to a system of diagnostic classification for the purpose of prescribing the most appropriate type of treatment. The latest edition of the *Diagnostic and Statistical Manual of Mental Disorders*, published by the American Psychiatric Association, specifically asks clinicians to attend to environmental factors, such as stress, which may have precipitated psychological disturbance.

6 Criticisms of projective tests have been that interrater and test-retest reliabilities are low. In addition, it has not been clearly demonstrated that scores are valid indicators of the types of conflicts and disturbanc-

es they are supposed to be measuring. One reply to such criticism is that projective devices, interviews, and so forth provide diverse sources of information about a client to the clinician, who is not concerned with formal scoring procedures so much as gaining insight into the origins of a client's problem. The accuracy of such clinical judgments has itself been called into question.

TERMS TO KNOW

open and closed interviews	Thematic Apperception Test
word association test	Need for Achievement
clinical judgment	medical model
comprehensive system	illusory correlation
Holtzman Inkblot Technique	

6

OBJECTIVE MEASURES OF PERSONALITY TRAITS

ISSUES TO CONSIDER

1 How is an "objective" test of personality different from a projective one?
2 What distinguishes "face validity" from "empirical validity" in the selection of test items?
3 Various professional and social criticisms (and defenses) have been made for tests like the MMPI and IQ. Can you summarize these?

A fundamental premise of the personological tradition in personality theory is that each individual is a unique combination of psychological and physical traits. While acknowledging individual variability, however, most theorists in this tradition also believe that personality consists of traits with a *patterned uniqueness*. Even though the pattern of traits in one individual may never exactly match that in another, the two patterns may be similar enough so that the two individuals' personalities share certain common characteristics. Individual differences can, therefore, be regarded as variations on a finite number of basic themes in human personality. Identifying these basic themes and trying to measure their relative strengths in an individual's character became important goals for those engaged in personality assessment within the personological tradition.

These researchers tried consciously to avoid the more obvious shortcomings of the projective techniques described in Chapter 5. Most notably, they altered the procedure for administering their assessment devices so as to allow only a limited number of possible responses to each item. That is, they designed tests that were *structured* and objectively scorable rather than unstructured and subject to interpretation. Even on the more objective measures, some interpretation of scores is possible, but these tests clearly improved upon projective devices in terms of reliability and validity and greatly reduced the degree to which the preconceptions of the examiner could influence an examinee's responses.

Some theorists in the personological tradition, most prominently Rogers (1942), objected to nearly all psychological testing on the grounds that it reinforces the therapist's role as evaluator and diagnostician and so hinders rather than assists the patient in taking personal responsibility for his or her life. We saw in Chapter 3 that Rogers himself used an objective assessment device called a *Q-sort* in research on the effectiveness of his nondirective approach to therapy.

On the Q-sort, though, the examinee describes his or her conception of the "ideal" personality, and therapeutic progress is evaluated in terms of the subject's self-perceived movement toward this self-imposed standard. When the therapeutic goal is defined by the client rather than by the therapist's conception of "normality," Rogers believed, the Q-sort assessment device will not interfere with self-actualization. Another device of this type is Kelley's Rep Test, which was also discussed in Chapter 3 (see Box 3-2).

The most widely used and best known of the objective tests, however, have some set of normative standards against which the scores of a given individual can be judged. This aspect of psychological testing is what provoked Rogers' concern, since such normative comparisons are frequently used in clinical diagnoses of *deviance* and psychopathology. Some employers also use scores on psychological inventories to make personnel decisions. These uses (and, occasionally, abuses) of personality tests are of concern to many lay people as well as professionals and have provoked a continuing controversy over the potential of psychological testing for invading one's privacy and endangering civil liberties.

This chapter will begin with a brief consideration of two paper-and-pencil tests that were forerunners of the many objective tests in use today. These early inventories were the Woodworth Personal Data Sheet and the Strong Vocational Interest Blank (which, in revised and updated form, is still being used). Next, we will take an extended look at the best known of the objective tests, the Minnesota Multiphasic Personality Inventory, and at its close relative, the California Psychological Inventory.

Factor-analytic techniques provide a method of test construction which differs somewhat from that employed in the development of the Minnesota and California inventories. The factor-analytic approach will be illustrated using Cattell's Sixteen Personality Factor Questionnaire. This chapter's presentation of objective assessment devices will then turn to the well-known and somewhat controversial measures of IQ. The design and validation of these measures incorporated features from all of the major approaches which have historically been taken in the development of objective tests of personality.

Finally, the chapter will conclude with a discussion of the limitations of objective personality assessment and the many controversies stimulated by this *applied* area of psychological theory and research.

WOODWORTH PERSONAL DATA SHEET

The origin of self-administered personality inventories can be dated fairly precisely. During World War I, the commander of the American forces in Europe, General Pershing, discovered that many recruits were unfit for military service due to *mental disorders*. A screening device

which would disqualify such recruits at the time of induction was needed, and a psychoanalytic approach to the problem would obviously have been too cumbersome and time-consuming.

Personal Data Sheet

Robert S. Woodworth and his associates responded to this need by creating the first questionnaire for personality assessment, a questionnaire they called the Personal Data Sheet.

Woodworth (1920) reported that items were selected for the data sheet by searching through psychiatric textbooks and case histories for the symptoms of personality disturbance. This straightforward, commonsense approach to test construction produced items said to have a high degree of *face validity*—that is, items whose content has an obvious relationship to the trait being measured.

In its final form, the Personal Data Sheet

Recruits who were inducted in the Army during World War I were required to answer a questionnaire to assess mental fitness. (Bettmann Archive)

contained 116 questions which were answered yes or no. Some examples are listed below, along with the response that would be scored as indicating maladjustment.

Do you suffer from headaches or dizziness? (Yes)

Is your speech free from stutter or stammer? (No)

Do you often feel miserable and blue? (Yes)

Do you find that people understand and sympathize with you? (No)

This device permitted assessment of large numbers of recruits both quickly and inexpensively. The more time-consuming and costly interview procedures could then be reserved for those who reported an unusually large number of symptoms. This approach was actually quite successful in identifying the more disturbed of the recruits. Looking back from the vantage point of our more psychologically sophisticated era, the success of the data sheet may seem somewhat surprising, since item content was so obviously diagnostically oriented that many people would be expected to see through the test's intent and so *"fake good."*

As the public became more familiar with paper-and-pencil tests and the kinds of questions that were likely to be asked, the designers of personality inventories realized that they would have to increase the subtlety of their techniques. Consequently, items with a high degree of face validity began to be replaced with items which had a less obvious relationship to the trait being tested.

STRONG VOCATIONAL INTEREST BLANK (SVIB)

During the 1920s, Edward K. Strong, a psychologist at Stanford University, noticed that people working in different professions and trades had different sorts of hobbies, interests, and preferred activities. Some of these differences were obviously related to the different requirements of their occupations. For instance, engineers liked working with numbers, while forest rangers liked working outdoors. Other traits which characterized different occupational groups, however, had no apparent relationship to the nature of the jobs they performed. Strong concluded that people in a particular profession or trade are distinguished by their style of life as well as by their method of making ends meet.

In a bold departure from the method of test construction used by R. S. Woodworth, Strong administered questionnaires designed to measure a wide variety of interests and activities to employees in various occupational groups. He compared their responses with the responses of "persons in general" and retained, for his final inventory, only those items which distinguished people in a given profession or trade from the general public. Each occupational group, then, had its own distinctive *profile* of interests and activities. Strong's procedure is said to select for items with <u>empirical</u> rather than face <u>validity</u>. The content of a given item may have <u>no clear</u> <u>relationship</u> to the job requirements of a given criterion group, <u>but</u> so long as responses to the item <u>can be shown to discriminate between</u> <u>members of this and other groups,</u> it is included on the inventory. Such a procedure is also sometimes called *criterion keying.*

Strong published the first version of his inventory in 1927, but he revised it and refined the scoring system in 1938. The revised version is the one which became widely used by organizational psychologists and vocational counselors (Strong, 1943). It is referred to as the Strong Vocational Interest Blank, or SVIB. Because differences in sex as well as occupation seemed to influence a person's interests, the original SVIB had separate forms for male and female examinees. (At one point, the publishers of the SVIB even bound the male version in a blue booklet and the female version in a pink one.) Later, with the resurgence during the 1960s of the women's rights move-

It is important for high school students to be exposed to a variety of sources of information about possible career choices. One of these sources could be a test like the Strong Vocational Interest Blank which identifies personal interests that have been shown to be compatible with the demands of certain professions. (United Press International)

ment, objections were raised that the separate female form of the SVIB contributed to the perpetuation of sex differences in occupational status. Consequently, yet another revision was made, culminating in the Strong-Campbell Interest Inventory, a single test with separate scoring keys for men and women (Campbell, 1972; 1974). Clients are cautioned that many other factors besides the interest inventory should be considered when choosing an occupation, especially individual *skills* (which are different from *interests*) and first-hand experience working in an area. Even so, they are urged to consider seriously any occupations with which they show a strong compatibility of interests and to examine criti-

cally those occupations for which their interests seem unsuited.

MINNESOTA MULTIPHASIC PERSONALITY INVENTORY (MMPI)

Starting around 1937, J. C. McKinley, a neuropsychiatrist, and Starke R. Hathaway, a clinical psychologist, both at the University of Minnesota Medical School, applied Strong's technique of criterion validation to the construction of a questionnaire designed to measure the degree of psychological disturbance in an individual's character. Hathaway (1964) later described one of their purposes as an effort to standardize psychiatric diagnosis. This was regarded as a desirable goal because it was widely known that the patients placed in a given diagnostic category by one clinic might be placed in a completely different category by another due to differences in the experience, training, and theoretical orientation of the staff. Furthermore, the unreliability of diagnosis can carry with it certain treatment risks to the patient, since the diagnosis influences the clinic's decisions as to whether the patient should be exposed to potentially hazardous forms of therapy, such as electroconvulsive shock or insulin injections.

Hathaway and McKinley (1940) reported that more than 1000 potential questionnaire items were collected from textbooks of psychiatry, intake forms used by psychiatrists, neurologists, and general practitioners, and published scales of personal and social attitudes. This procedure resulted in the inclusion of many items with an obvious relationship to personality disorder (e.g., "Most of the time I wish I were dead"), but it also resulted in the inclusion of statements which had no clear connection with disorders ("I am against giving money to street beggars"). For some items, a response of "True" is scored as signifying a stronger tendency toward psychopathology, while for other items (like the one about street beggars), a response of "False" is scored in this direction.

Regardless of their verbal content or the direction in which they were ultimately scored, the only items which were retained for the final version of the Minnesota Multiphasic Personality Inventory, or MMPI, were those for which the responses of mental patients and "normal" people differed significantly. The criterion against which the MMPI was validated, then, was its ability to distinguish the responses of the mentally disturbed from those made by people who appeared relatively well-adjusted. In addition to meeting the foregoing overall criterion, the items selected for inclusion in the MMPI were grouped according to their ability to discriminate between patients diagnosed by clinicians as falling into one category of mental illness (such as depression) from patients in another diagnostic category (such as schizophrenia).

The original patient group on which the MMPI was validated consisted of patients hospitalized in the psychopathic unit as well as those in the outpatient clinic of the University Hospital at Minnesota (a total of 221 individuals). The "normal" group consisted mainly of visitors to the hospital (724 individuals) and hospitalized nonpsychiatric medical patients (254 cases). Additional groups of psychiatric patients and "normals" were added later as validation of the scales progressed.

In its final form, the MMPI had 550 different items grouped on ten clinical scales. The raw score of number of items answered in the direction of psychopathology on a given scale (for the "normal" group) was converted to standardized format so that "normality" would always be represented by a value (called a *T score*) of 50, the average for the "normal" group. Since most psychologically "healthy" people do not land exactly at 50 on each scale but, instead, deviate from the average to some extent, only scores above 70 are regarded as sufficiently different from the average to be a fairly clear sign of psychopathology. Because the raw scores for each scale are standardized, each has a standard deviation of 10 units around the average of 50; consequently, a score of 70 is two standard deviations from the average. (Refer to Chapter 1 if you have forgotten what is meant by terms like *average* and *standard deviation*). On the various scales of the MMPI, the distributions of scores are skewed toward high values, so it is more likely that someone will score *above* rather than *below* 50. It is very rare to see a score as low as 30, two standard deviations below the average.

The ten clinical scales measure tendencies toward hypochondriasis (Hs), depression (D), hysteria (Hy), psychopathic deviance (Pd), masculinity or femininity (Mf), paranoia (Pa), psychasthenia (Pt), schizophrenia (Sc), hypomania (Ma), and social introversion (Si). They are listed in Table 6-1, along with brief descriptions of the traits

TABLE 6-1 The ten clinical and four validity scales of the MMPI and paraphrases of obvious and subtle items from each

Scale no. as symbol	Scale name	Item type	Item content	Characteristics of high scorers
1	Hypochondriasis (Hs)	Obvious	I feel "butterflies" in my stomach several times a day or oftener. (True)	Overconcern about health; exaggeration of the extent and importance of any real or imagined physical ailments
		Subtle	My skin is usually very sensitive to even the slightest touch. (True)	
2	Depression (D)	Obvious	I have had several days in a row where I could not get over feeling "blue." (True)	Feelings of hopelessness, worthlessness, and pessimism regarding future prospects
		Subtle	I consider myself to be a very active, energetic person. (False)	
3	Hysteria (Hy)	Obvious	I frequently notice trembling or shaking in various limbs of my body. (True)	Overenthusiasm suggestive of immaturity; tendencies toward complaints of physical ailments when under stress
		Subtle	I get pretty annoyed when someone outsmarts me with a practical joke. (False)	
4	Psychopathic deviance (Pd)	Obvious	I would never take anything that wasn't mine, even if I was sure I couldn't be caught. (False)	Frequent manifestations of delinquency; inability to empathize with the feelings of others, to establish satisfying emotional relationships, or to anticipate consequences of one's own behavior
		Subtle	I win just about every argument I get into. (False)	
5	Masculinity or femininity (Mf)	Obvious	The best movies are those with lots of action and no romance. (False)	Feminine interest in men; masculine interest in women
		Subtle	I'm no gambler; games are most enjoyable when no betting is involved. (True)	
6	Paranoia (Pa)	Obvious	It is hard for me to think of anyone I could call an enemy. (False)	Marked degree of defensiveness, suspiciousness, jealousy, and so forth

	Scale	Type	Item	Description
7	Psychasthenia (Pt)	Subtle	I hear bells ringing a lot of the time. (True)	
		Obvious	I always wipe my feet two or three times before entering a building, even if no doormat is available. (True)	Obsessive-compulsiveness; excessive introspection which dwells at length on fears and self-doubts
8	Schizophrenia (Sc)	Subtle	Dreams are very rare occurrences for me. (False)	
		Obvious	I often find myself frightened by my own thoughts. (True)	Bizarre thinking and distortions of reality; withdrawal from interpersonal contacts and inappropriate expressions of emotion
9	Hypomania (Ma)	Subtle	I do not play any games that I think I can't win. (True)	
		Obvious	I feel I am rushing around all the time, even though I have no good reason to be so busy. (True)	Hyperactivity, excessive irritability, and a pronounced lack of realism in setting goals that one will be able to achieve
		Subtle	When I eat at home I am a lot less polite than when I go out for dinner. (False)	
0	Social introversion (Si)	Obvious	I really enjoy talking things over with a group of people. (False)	Tendencies toward excessive shyness and modesty; easily embarrassed or hurt
		Subtle	Few people stand up for others' rights as strongly as they stand up for their own. (True)	
?	Cannot say	Validity indicator	No items—count of "cannot say" responses or items left blank.	Evasiveness or uncooperativeness
L	Lie	Validity indicator	Once in a while I poke fun at others' mistakes.	Denial of common personal faults
F	Frequency	Validity indicator	My nose often swells up so it is larger than normal size.	Highly unusual thoughts symptoms, or perceptions
K	Correction	Validity indicator	I often wish I could be 5 years old again.	Excessive defensiveness (very low score suggests excessive "revealingness")

associated with each diagnostic category. Also shown are examples of obvious and subtle items, which I have written to approximate the MMPI questions assigned to each scale. The obvious items would be said to have face as well as empirical validity, and the subtle items would be said to have empirical validity only.

Validity Scales

A highly innovative feature of the MMPI was the inclusion of four scales (also shown in Table 6-1) which provide a check on the accuracy of an examinee's responses on the ten clinical scales. The first of these *validity scales* is the *Cannot Say*, or ?, scale. Since the MMPI allows for a response of "cannot say" to any item, the ? score is simply the number of "cannot say" responses or totally blank items on an examinee's sheet. Since most examinees are able (with a little prodding from the examiner) to answer "True" or "False" to all 550 items on the MMPI, an elevated ? score may indicate evasiveness in responding, which casts doubt on the accuracy of the profile obtained from the ten clinical scales.

The *Lie* (L) scale is the second validity indicator. It is made up of fifteen items which attest to common personal faults readily admitted by most people but likely to be denied by the defensively organized individual. The third validity indicator is the *frequency* (or *infrequency*) *scale.* It is abbreviated "F," but it should not be confused with the F scale for identifying authoritarian personalities discussed in Chapter 12. The sixty-four items on this F scale attest to highly unusual thoughts and symptoms or denial of common experiences and perceptions. While any single item might be endorsed by "normal" people, highly elevated scores on the F scale may suggest psychotically disorganized thinking or medical conditions such as brain tumors.

Finally, a *Correction* (K) scale was added to the MMPI in an attempt to improve the instrument's accuracy in discriminating between the mentally disturbed and individuals who are just exception-

ally frank in revealing personal information. For example, a "revealing" person might endorse the statement, "I often wish I could be 5 years old again," while a defensive person might perceive the item as an admission of regressive fantasies and so reject it. A high K score suggests a pathological sort of defensiveness, while a very low score suggests excessive "self-revealingness." To correct for these tendencies, empirically derived proportions of the K score are customarily added to an examinee's scores on scales 1, 4, 5, 8, and 9. K-correction of the other scales was not found to improve diagnostic accuracy.

Interpretation of MMPI Profiles

One of the first interpretational problems to become apparent as MMPI profiles became available for different populations of examinees was, as in the case of the SVIB, that "normal" males often differed from "normal" females in their raw scores on various scales. Hathaway and McKinley reported that females typically score higher than males on scales 1 (hypochondriasis) and 2 (depression), whereas responses to scale 5 (masculinity or femininity) must be scored in opposite directions for examinees of different sexes. Consequently, there are separate norms for male and female examinees, whose profiles are plotted on score sheets prominently labeled *male* or *female*.

It is not possible here to describe in detail the many diagnostic signs which experienced MMPI interpreters perceive in various profiles of scores. Two common patterns can, however, serve as examples of the interpretational process. The first three scales of the MMPI—Hs, D, and Hy—have become known as the *neurotic triad* because high scores on scales 1 and 3 (hypochondriasis and hysteria) combined with a low score on scale 2 (depression) are often associated with neurotic anxieties, indecisiveness, and frequent somatic complaints and illnesses. The pattern, also known as *conversion V*, is illustrated by the profile for a female examinee shown in Figure 6-1. While this person's T-scores on Pa, Pt, and Si

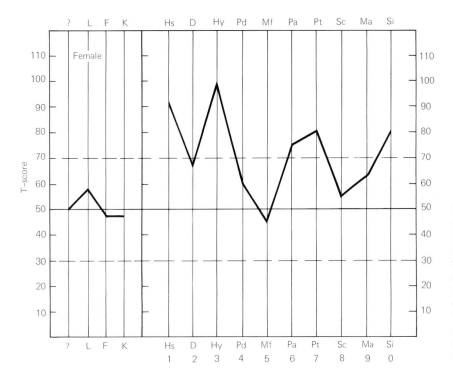

FIGURE 6-1
Example of an MMPI profile for a female examinee which shows the "conversion V" pattern often associated with neurotic anxiety. That is, elevated scores on scales 1 and 3 (hypochrondriasis and hysteria) and a lower score on scale 2 (depression).

were also above 70, the upper boundary of the "normal" range, it is the scores on the first three scales which would be of greatest interest here. They form the V-shaped pattern said to be characteristic of the anxiety neurotic.

A second cluster of scales is said to be useful in identifying more serious mental disorders, the psychoses. This *psychotic tetrad* comprises scales 6, 7, 8, and 9—*Pa, Pt, Sc, and Ma*. One pattern illustrated in Figure 6-2 is often referred to as *paranoid valley* because it consists of high scores for scales 6 and 8 (paranoia and schizophrenia) combined with low scores on scales 7 and 9 (psychasthenia and hypomania). For this male examinee, scores higher than 70 were also observed for D and Pd, but the portion of the profile which would probably be of greatest interest would be the "valley" between the "peaks" on scales 6 and 8. Dahlstrom and Welsh (1960) associated this pattern with paranoid schizophrenia, but more recently they seem to have deem-

phasized the strength of this association and indicated that milder forms of mental disturbance may also produce the "paranoid-valley" configuration (Dahlstrom, Welsh, & Dahlstrom, 1970, pp. 277–278).

Among themselves, MMPI interpreters often describe a profile by referring to the numbers of the scales which contribute to its most salient features. Thus, a profile exhibiting the "neurotic triad" may be referred to as a "13" or a "31", depending on whether the peak at scale 1 is higher or lower than the peak at scale 3. A "paranoid valley" may be called a "68" or an "86". In an analysis of group profiles, Lanyon (1968) summarized the results of many independent research investigations as indicating that neurotics tend to score highest on the Hs, D, Hy, and Pt scales (1, 2, 3, and 7) while psychotics tend to score highest on the D, Pd, Pa, and Sc scales (2, 4, 6, and 8). Apparently depression (scale 2) is a trait that can be associated with either neurosis

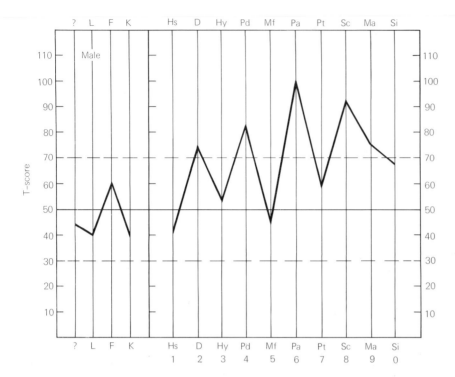

FIGURE 6-2
Example of an MMPI
profile for a male
examinee which shows
the "paranoid valley"
configuration sometimes
associated with paranoid
schizophrenia. That is,
elevated scores on scales
6 and 8 (paranoia and
schizophrenia) combined
with lower scores on
scales 7 and 9
(psychasthenia and
hypomania).

or psychosis. Groups of adult prisoners and juvenile delinquents tend to score highest on the Pd, Sc, and Ma scales (4, 8, and 9). Among the prisoner groups included in Lanyon's review, the Pd score (psychopathic deviance) seemed consistently to be the highest one in the profile. Among adolescent delinquents, a high Pd score was usually accompanied by a peak on the Ma scale.

The advent of computer technology has led to standardization of the answer sheets for the MMPI so as to permit machine scoring and computer analysis. A nonprofit corporation, the Roche Psychiatric Service Institute, will, for a fee, provide a computerized interpretation of the profiles derived from machine-scorable MMPI answer sheets. The computer's decision rules for arriving at a given interpretation are, of course, programmed into it by scientists familiar with the results of empirical research using the MMPI (Newmark et al., 1978).

The easy availability of rapid machine scoring

and computer interpretation is one reason for the popularity of the MMPI among clinicians. After the Rorschach inkblot test, it is their favorite assessment device.

However, the proliferation of the MMPI has led to its use in personnel selection by some corporations and government agencies. In other words, the MMPI is being used to discriminate between individuals in "normal" (nonpatient) populations rather than exclusively for its original purpose of making diagnostic classifications within clinical (or at least potentially clinical) populations. The Roche service interprets at least 1600 MMPI profiles weekly, and the growth of personality testing into a major industry has aroused concern among professionals as well as the general public (Butcher, 1972). Some of these issues—and controversies—will be examined in the conclusion of this chapter.

There are several factors which limit the extent to which MMPI interpretations can be accepted at face value. For one thing, the MMPI in use today is the same MMPI that was validated on patient and nonpatient groups around 1950. Times and, one suspects, "normal" personalities have changed a great deal since then. Furthermore, the criterion groups of patients were usually not larger than fifty and included only thirteen homosexual males in the case of the Mf scale. This raises questions concerning the validity of the MMPI even in the 1950s, when it was a brand-new instrument. As Sundberg (1977, p. 196) and others have pointed out, scores on different scales have often been found to be highly correlated with one another, indicating that the criterion groups were not necessarily exhibiting different types of pathology. Finally, test-retest reliabilities near zero, or even slightly negative, have occasionally been reported, and this must surely raise doubts as to the stability of the personality characteristics inferred from an MMPI profile that reflects someone's mental state at a particular point in time. These and other limitations of the MMPI will receive additional consideration further on in this chapter.

CALIFORNIA PSYCHOLOGICAL INVENTORY (CPI)

The primary goal of Harrison Gough in designing the California Psychological Inventory, or CPI, was to assess the degree to which various personality characteristics differ among "normal" individuals who are not members of psychiatric populations and not necessarily manifesting any obvious symptoms of psychopathology. Megargee (1972, Chap. 1) noted that Gough's selection of personality dimensions was based on common-sense abstractions from "what people everywhere appeal to when they talk about themselves and others." He believed that the eighteen scales finally included on the CPI are based on widely shared "folk concepts" regarding the components of human character.

The scales of the CPI are grouped in clusters by

Gough, partly on the basis of his intuitions regarding shared themes but partly also on the basis of results from factor analyses (see the next section of this chapter for an explanation of this statistical technique). The first grouping, or *class*, consists of six scales measuring traits in the area of interpersonal relations and self-assurance. The names of the scales are Dominance (Do), Capacity for Status (Cs), Sociability (Sy), Social Presence (Sp), Self-Acceptance (Sa), and Sense of Well-Being (Wb). Unlike the MMPI, the CPI uses names for its scales which convey, even to the nonpsychologist, a fairly clear idea of what personality dimensions are being measured.

Gough's procedure for constructing, scoring, and validating his scales can be illustrated by using "Do" as an example. First, members of fraternities and sororities (fifty in each group) at the University of Minnesota were provided with a hypothetical description of a dominant individual which emphasized the capacity to initiate courses of action, influence others to follow along, and exercise leadership. Then the participants rated their own dominance and nominated ten other participants whom they considered to be high in dominance and ten whom they considered to be low in dominance. On the basis of these data, Gough selected sixteen high-dominance and sixteen low-dominance individuals, equally divided by sex. These people were then given the MMPI, along with about one hundred additional items specifically written to measure dominance. Responses to sixty of these items (twenty-eight from the MMPI) discriminated between high-dominance and low-dominance individuals, but only forty-six were actually used for the CPI's Do scale. Since the selection of items was ultimately determined by the empirical criterion of ability to distinguish individuals perceived by their peers to be highly dominant from those perceived as low in dominance, the content of the items often had an obvious relationship to the trait being measured. An example of such an item might be "I feel happiest in a group when I am the person in charge." Other items, though, are more subtle. Here is a close paraphrase of a subtle item: "If people send their children to private schools, they should not have to pay taxes to support the public ones" (for a similar statement on the CPI, a reply of "False" contributes to a high Do score).

Scoring is done in a manner similar to that used for the MMPI. The average raw score for "people in general" on a given scale is set at 50, and one standard deviation is 10 units above or below the average. Validating studies have shown that high school students nominated by their principals as most dominant do, in fact, score higher on "Do" than do students described as least dominant (Gough, 1969a, b). Similarly, successful and effective executives and managers have been found to be higher in "Do" than their unsuccessful and ineffective counterparts (Rawls & Rawls, 1968; Mahoney, Jerdee, & Nash, 1961). These supportive findings should be qualified, however, by noting that the mean score differences between groups were sometimes rather small, despite their statistical significance.

The second class of scales (Class II) on the CPI consists of measures of Responsibility (Re), Socialization (So), Self-Control (Sc), Tolerance (To), Good Impression (Gi), and Communality (Cm). This cluster seems to represent various aspects of reliability, trustworthiness, and other socially valued characteristics that parents around the world generally strive to inculcate in their children.

The last two scales—"Gi" and "Cm"—were originally designed as *validity scales* for the CPI. Like their counterparts on the MMPI, these indices measure the extent to which one attempts to present oneself in an overly favorable light ("Gi") or the extent to which one agrees with the views expressed by other people ("Cm"). The second scale ("So") is particularly interesting. It was originally validated by comparing the questionnaire responses of delinquent and nondelinquent adolescents in Minnesota. In subsequent tests, So scores were found to be consistently higher in nondelinquent/noncriminal groups than in delinquent/criminal groups. Fur-

thermore, So scores show a steady decline as one moves from high school disciplinary problems to juvenile offenders to prison inmates (Gough, 1969b). In one series of studies, Ohio teachers were asked to nominate 101 sixth-grade boys whom they felt were "likely to get into trouble" and a socioeconomically matched group of 125 "good" boys. When tested, the "good" boys were found to have higher So scores than the "bad" ones. Four years later, 39 percent of the seventy "bad" boys who could be traced had police records indicating chronic delinquency; only 4 percent of the 101 "good" boys who could be traced had police records (Reckless, Dinitz, & Kay, 1957; Dinitz, Reckless, & Kay, 1958; Dinitz, Scarpitti, & Reckless, 1962; Scarpitti, Murray, Dinitz, & Reckless, 1960). In translated form, the So scale has reliably discriminated between adjudicated criminal offenders and nonoffenders in countries as diverse as Austria, Costa Rica, India, Israel, Italy, Japan, Switzerland, and Taiwan (Megargee, 1972, p. 62).

The third class of scales (Class III) on the CPI consists of measures of intelligence and achievement. Items on the Intellectual Efficiency (Ie) scale attest to enjoyment of activities such as reading in academic-content areas and also to feelings of self-confidence uncontaminated by worry or anxiety. Items on the Achievement via Conformance (Ac) scale reflect ability to accomplish goals (usually academic ones) in a structured environment and in a self-disciplined, organized way. Items on the Achievement via Independence (Ai) scale reflect ability to accomplish goals within a looser, less structured environment that encourages independent thinking, creativity, and self-actualization. Both achievement measures have low to moderate positive correlations with grades in high school and college. "Ie" has been shown to correlate with standardized tests of scholastic aptitude and other indirect measures of IQ.

Finally, a fourth class of scales (Class IV) consists of measures that did not seem to fit into the other categories. A high score on Psychological-Mindedness (Py) indicates a capacity for insight into the feelings, motivations, and logical processes of other people. The Flexibility (Fx) scale tries to identify people who can adapt their thinking and behavior to incorporate new information or changes in the external environment; the contrasting trait is rigidity in one's ideas and actions. The Femininity (Fe) scale discriminates stereotypically feminine traits, at the high end, from those that are culturally defined as *masculine* (a low score implies masculine sex-typing). Some items on the Fe measures are obviously sex-typed (e.g., "I love to hug and feed babies"), but others are more subtle, particularly when embedded in the context of hundreds of CPI items measuring diverse personality characteristics. Some of the more subtle items deal with feelings of anxiety in social situations, tendencies toward boastfulness or pranksterism, and interest in current political events.

Kleinmuntz (1967, pp. 239–240), summarizing the available evidence on the CPI, finds high test-retest reliabilities and an impressive string of validating studies for the instrument. Because of the care Gough took in developing the CPI and his use of a geographically diverse sample of thousands of psychologically "normal" individuals in keying its component scales, Kleinmuntz regards it as "one of the best, if not the best, personality measuring instrument of its kind." More recent replications of earlier validating studies have found that people's subjective perceptions of the personalities of individuals whom they know fairly well do, indeed, correlate with the CPI profiles of those individuals (Gregory & Morris, 1978). These accomplishments notwithstanding, the CPI, like other objective tests, has received its share of criticism. The latter will be dealt with further on in this chapter

FACTOR-ANALYTIC TECHNIQUES

Before one can fully appreciate the difference between the techniques used by the developers of the MMPI and those used in factor analysis, one must know something about the statistical meaning of a factor analysis. A brief and necessarily oversimplified account is offered here; readers interested in learning more details of the procedure are referred to Comrey (1973).

Statistical Meaning of a Factor Analysis

Suppose that a large group of government students is shown a documentary film portraying the political career of former President Lyndon Johnson. After the film, the students are asked to rate various aspects of Johnson's personality on ten-unit scales running from *"not at all"* (0) to *"extremely"* (10). The specific traits on which Johnson will be rated are, in alphabetical order: boisterous, capable, creative, domineering, modest, organized, and self-confident.

Now suppose the students' ratings of Johnson on each of the foregoing trait dimensions are correlated with their ratings of him on all other dimensions, yielding the *correlation matrix* shown in Table 6-2. (If you have forgotten what a *correlation* is, look back at Chapter 1 for a quick review.) Assuming you recall the statistical meaning of a *correlation*, take a close look at the information in Table 6-2.

Note that the trait labels are not listed in alphabetical order. This is done so that the pattern of their interrelationships will be more apparent. Each number in the table represents the correlation between the variable shown for the row in which the number is located and the variable shown for the column in which the number is placed. Thus, to find the correlation between Domineering and Modest, one would place one's finger at the row labeled Domineering and move it to the right until reaching the column labeled Modest; the number shown at that point is −0.6. Dashes are drawn at the points on the diagonal of the table, because these points represent the correlation of each variable with itself, which is of course always 1. No numbers appear below the diagonal because they would be the same as the numbers above the diagonal. The diagonal, in other words, splits the table into two identical halves, one the mirror image of the

TABLE 6-2   Correlation matrix of traits attributed to Lyndon Johnson

	Domin- eering	Boist- erous	Modest	Organ- ized	Self- confident	Cap- able	Crea- tive
Domineering	—	+0.9	−0.6	+0.1	0.0	+0.1	−0.1
Boisterous		—	−0.7	0.0	−0.1	−0.1	+0.1
Modest			—	+0.1	+0.1	+0.1	0.0
Organized				—	0.0	+0.1	−0.1
Self-confident					—	+0.8	+0.6
Capable						—	+0.9
Creative							—

other; consequently, the correlations below the diagonal are customarily not shown.

There seem to be two clusters of moderate to strong correlations between variables in Table 6-2. Domineering and Boisterous are very positively correlated with each other (+0.9), and each is negatively correlated with "Modest" (−0.6 and −0.7, respectively). Perhaps these three traits are all aspects of a single personality characteristic we might call *flamboyance*. The second cluster of strong correlations is between Self-confident and Capable (+0.8), Self-confident and Creative (+0.6), and Capable and Creative (+0.9). Perhaps these three are all part of a single personality dimension of perceived Ability. Most importantly, the three traits which constitute the Flamboyance dimension are only very weakly correlated with those which constitute the Ability dimension (*r*'s range from −0.1 to +0.1). Consequently, it appears that Flamboyance and Ability are relatively independent *factors* in the students' perception of Lyndon Johnson. In other words, someone who perceives Johnson as high in Flamboyance might regard him as either low or high in Ability, and the same could be true of someone who perceives Johnson as low in Flamboyance. Since the trait labeled *Organized* is essentially uncorrelated with any of the others in Table 6-2, it probably represents a personality dimension which is somewhat independent of both of those just described. That is, one might regard Johnson as organized or disorganized independently of whether one perceives him as flamboyant or competent.

The main advantage of a factor analysis of a matrix of correlations like the one in Table 6-2 is that it provides a mathematical technique for simplifying a complex array of information about a person. Instead of inspecting students' ratings of Johnson on seven separate traits, we can adequately represent their perception of him by summing up their net rating on each of two or three factors: Flamboyance, Ability, and Organization. Usually, of course, factors are not as clear-cut as they are in Table 6-2; furthermore, the personality researcher is generally trying to find relationships among many more than seven traits. Precise, objective mathematical procedures can be and have been established for the extraction of factors from correlation matrices. These procedures include weighting each component variable of different factors so as to maximize the extent to which the factors are independent of one another; the weighting technique is called *rotation* and can be accomplished in any of several popular ways. Obviously, a factor analysis of even a small correlation matrix like that in Table 6-2 would take a long time to do by hand. Consequently, the factor-analytic approach to personality measurement virtually requires access to a high-speed computer.

While the procedures for extracting and rotating factors are established mathematically and without regard to the particular hypotheses being pursued by a given researcher, a great deal of subjective judgment enters into the process at the point at which factors are to be named. What we have called Flamboyance as a dimension of

Lyndon Johnson's personality someone else might call Vanity or even Popularity. What we have labeled Ability might be perceived by someone else as Stubbornness or Independence. Furthermore, individual traits sometimes correlate equally highly with more than one factor. In this case, the researcher must decide which factor is to be assigned the trait. Because of the inevitable entry of subjective judgment into the final stages of factor analysis, the technique is not as mathematically pure and value-free as it first appears. This aspect of the procedure is the weakest link in the factor-analytic chain, particularly when these methods are applied to the study of human personality.

Cattell's Sixteen Personality Factor Questionnaire

You may recall from Chapter 3 that Gordon Allport, the foremost "trait" theorist in the American personological tradition, concluded that no fewer than 4541 trait labels existed in the English language. This list could be reduced to 200 if closely related terms were grouped together and if very rare characteristics were eliminated. Raymond Cattell and others demonstrated that intercorrelations of subjects' ratings of the presence or absence of the latter traits in someone's personality revealed an even smaller number of basic dimensions—thirty-five or fewer—which could account for most of the variability in perception of personality. Further research convinced Cattell (1965, 1973) that the number of independent factors in personality can be reduced still further.

Cattell believes it is useful to distinguish three types of data concerning personality.

1   The *life record* (L data) of an individual includes actual observations of and reports concerning a person's behavior in society. In practice, Cattell's L data consist of ratings of people by others who know them well on traits like "emotional" vs. "calm," "conventional" vs. "unconventional," "considerate"

vs. "inconsiderate," "quitting" vs. "persevering," and so forth.

2   *Self-descriptive questionnaires* (Q data) provide information regarding personality from the inside rather than from the perspective of outside observers.

3   Finally, apart from questionnaires, *formal objective tests* (T data) provide yet another source of information regarding personality. What Cattell views as an objective test may involve the administration of a paper-and-pencil questionnaire, but the thing which distinguishes T data from Q data is the subtlety of the items. For a test to be objective, according to Cattell (1965, p. 104), the examinee must "not know on what aspect of his behavior he is really being evaluated." Cattell and Warburton (1967) have listed more than 400 tests which appear to them to meet this criterion.

When factor-analyzed, L data and Q data have generally been found to agree with one another in identifying the major components of personality. Cattell then proceeded to rank the components in order of their importance (i.e., the percentage of the total variability in trait ratings that each factor explains or accounts for). The results of this ranking are shown in Table 6-3. Cattell (1965) explained that his assignment of letters to these factors was similar to the procedure followed by early researchers of vitamins, who could identify the effects of the substances they were studying long before complete chemical descriptions were available. Partly to prevent the statistical meaning of his factors from being distorted by popularizers, Cattell invented names for them that do not readily evoke any commonplace associations. His name for factor I, for instance—*Premsia*—is a contraction of "protected emotional sensitivity." Cattell designed a paper-and-pencil test whose specific purpose is to measure the degree to which each of the sixteen attributes in Table 6-3 is expressed in an individual's character; the test is called the Sixteen Personality Factor Questionnaire, or 16 PF. In

TABLE 6-3 Traits measured by Cattell's Sixteen Personality Factor Questionnaire

Factor	INTERPRETATION OF SCORES	
	High (+)	Low (− pole)
A	Affectothymia—outgoing	Sizothymia—reserved
B	High "g"—more intelligent	Low "g"—less intelligent
C	High ego strength—stable	Low ego strength—emotional
E	Dominance—assertive	Submissiveness—humble
F	Surgency—happy-go-lucky	Desurgency—sober
G	High superego—conscientious	Low superego—expedient
H	Parmia—venturesome	Threctia—shy
I	Premsia—tender-minded	Harria—tough-minded
L	Protension—suspicious	Alaxia—trusting
M	Autia—imaginative	Praxernia—practical
N	Shrewdness—shrewd	Artlessness—forthright
O	Guilt-proneness—apprehensive	Assurance—placid
Q_1	Radicalism—experimenting	Conservatism—conservative
Q_2	Self-sufficiency—self-sufficient	Group adherence—group dependent
Q_3	High self-concept—controlled	Low integration—undisciplined
Q_4	Ergic tension—tense	Low ergic tension—relaxed

Source: Cattell, 1965.

addition to these sixteen, Cattell strongly suspects the existence of the missing alphabetical factors D, J, K, and P. The four factors labeled Q in Table 6-3 are derived mainly from Q data rather than L data, and Cattell has found evidence for factors Q_5, Q_6, and Q_7 in addition to the four listed in the table.

The traits which carry most weight in accounting for personality are, according to Cattell, the first three in the list: Affectothymia ("A"), High "g" ("B"), and High ego strength ("C"). L data associated with the positive pole of factor A consist in trait attributions like good-natured, cooperative, attentive to people, and adaptable. The negative pole of factor A is associated with traits like critical, obstructive, aloof, and rigid. "Normality," defined as always by the traits exhibited by "people in general," falls between these two extremes. In terms of Q data, a response of "False" to the item, "I could stand being a hermit," on the 16 PF would be scored in the direction of the positive pole of factor A. In response to an item asking what type of person one would like to marry, selection of a response

reading "a thoughtful companion" would be scored toward the negative pole, while "effective in a social group" would be scored toward the positive.

Factor B is regarded by Cattell as a measure of ability rather than temperament, and his assessment of intelligence as a personality trait correlates fairly highly with performance on standardized intelligence tests. People scoring toward the positive pole of factor C are described by others as steady, calm, realistic, and mature, while those scoring toward the negative pole are regarded as changeable, impulsive, evasively procrastinating, and low in frustration tolerance. On the 16 PF, high scorers on factor C indicate that they have the willpower to change old habits when it is important to do so but that they can also accept frustration when some goal is obviously unattainable. Low scorers report that their moods often drive them to the point of being unreasonable or that they frequently have "really disturbing dreams."

The sixteen factors in Table 6-3 (plus, perhaps, a few others, as was explained earlier) are, according to Cattell, *source traits*. He regards some source traits as determined mainly by heredity and others as shaped mainly by the environment, but he believes that all of them constitute the basic building blocks of personality out of which the more complex and familiar *surface traits* are formed. Surface traits are most generally tapped by *objective tests* (T data), and the factors derived from T data do not agree very closely with the more elemental factors extracted from L data and Q data. However, the scale scores for examinees taking the 16 PF can themselves be intercorrelated with one another and a factor analysis performed on the sixteen source traits. Since this is essentially a factor analysis of a factor analysis, the dimensions which emerge are called *second-order factors*. Cattell has found that these second-order factors sometimes show a close correspondence with T data. For example, what he calls Exvia-Invia combines "outgoing" ("A"), "happy-go-lucky" ("F"), and "venturesome" ("H"); it correlates well with Eysenck's measure of extraversion-introversion (see Box 2-2).

Personality profiles can be plotted for the 16PF in much the same manner as for the MMPI. Theoretically, these could be used for individual personality assessment, but the 16PF has been criticized for the arbitrariness with which its source traits were extracted and named, their lack of statistical independence from one another, and a disappointingly small number of validating studies showing that the scales predict behavior in the anticipated manner (Kleinmuntz, 1967, pp. 199–201; Lanyon & Goodstein, 1971, p. 88). Despite these limitations, the factor-analytic approach remains a unique and highly valuable one, and Cattell remains a prolific writer and researcher who is constantly refining the technique.

The Basic Dimensions of Personality—Factor Analysis of the MMPI and CPI

Armed with the factor-analytic techniques pioneered by Cattell and others, investigators have searched for the basic personality components underlying the profiles obtained for the MMPI and CPI. On the MMPI, though the results vary to some extent depending upon whether clinical or "normal" populations are studied, at least two major factors have been found: (1) "expressiveness" vs. "self-control" and (2) "anxiety/maladjustment" vs. "ego strength/adjustment" (Dahlstrom et al., 1975, pp. 122–124). On the CPI, the two strongest factors seem to be: (1) "outgoingness" vs. "shyness" and (2) "ego strength" vs. "ineffectiveness" (Megargee, 1972, Chap. 8).

Lanyon and Goodstein (1971, pp. 88–89) have commented that there is general agreement among researchers, derived from factor-analytic studies of many different personality scales, on the existence of two major dimensions: (1) "*extraversion*" vs. "*introversion*" and "*emotional stability*" vs. "*emotional instability.*" These factors correspond very closely to the two basic dimensions underlying Eysenck's personality typology, discussed in Box 2-2.

INTELLIGENCE TESTS

Around the turn of the century, the French Minister of Public Information commissioned two psychologists, Alfred Binet and Theodore Simon, to devise measures which would identify children who were likely to fail in a traditional academic curriculum and might find the training available in a trade school of greater value. Intrigued by the apparent success of the Binet-Simon scale, an American psychologist named Lewis Terman had the test translated and made a few revisions. Since Terman was at Stanford University, the new version was called the Stanford-Binet test, and what it was alleged to measure became known as the *intelligence quotient*, or IQ.

Actually, it is inappropriate to refer to the Stanford-Binet as an IQ test since the score it yields represents an individual's overall performance on a number of diverse subtests. From the very beginning, *intelligence* was conceived to be a highly complex personality trait combining

A child performing a task similar to subtests of the Wechsler Intelligence Scale for Children, Revised. Tests such as these provide data by which personality can be measured. (Wayne Miller/Magnum)

differences, the WISC-R includes more members of racial minorities in its pictorial subtests; for the most part, however, it is similar to the original WISC. The subtests of the WISC-R are listed in Table 6-4, along with sample items or descriptions of their contents. The first six subtests, through Digit Span, are called *verbal subtests* because presentation of the items and subjects' responses to them involve a considerable amount of verbal interaction with the examiner. The second six are called *performance subtests* because subjects' responses consist almost entirely of physical manipulation of materials presented by the examiner and involve a minimum of verbal interaction. The performance subtests are often regarded as less culturally biased than their verbal counterparts and therefore more appropriate for use with socioeconomically disadvantaged groups.

Originally, IQ was scored by age-grading the Stanford-Binet test so that for children of various chronological ages (month and year being specified), the average performance on each subscale was determined. The performance of an individual child could then be translated into a mental age (MA). For the average child, the MA should equal his or her chronological age (CA). Often, however, a child's MA is either advanced or retarded from his or her CA, and this is the basis on which IQs are distinguished from one another. Traditionally, IQ is defined as the MA divided by the CA and multiplied by 100. For instance, an 8-year-old child with a mental age of 8 years would have an IQ of 8/8 × 100 = 100; an 8-year-old with an MA of 6 years would have an IQ of 75 and one with an MA of 10 years would have an IQ of 125.

Calculation of IQs using the Wechsler scales is more complex than the traditional MA/CA ratio. Here, each individual's performance is compared with that of others within his or her own age group. If the examinee scores at the average for the group, the IQ is 100, but if the examinee's score deviates from the average in a positive or negative direction, the IQ will be above or below

many different cognitive abilities and perceptual-motor skills. In his original battery of tests, Binet included measures of reaction time along with accuracy in defining words or following directions.

The Wechsler Adult Intelligence Scales (abbreviated WAIS) or Wechsler Intelligence Scale for Children (abbreviated WISC) were the next major advances in the measurement of intelligence (Wechsler, 1949, 1955). Devised by psychologist David Wechsler, they incorporated eleven and twelve subtests, respectively. In the early 1970s, partly in response to charges that IQ tests were culturally biased, the scales for children (5 to 16 years of age) were revised, and the new version is called the *WISC-R* (Wechsler, 1974). Among other

TABLE 6-4   Subscales of the Wechsler Intelligence Scale for Children

Subscale name	Sample item or description
VERBAL SUBTESTS	
General information	What is celebrated on Thanksgiving?
General comprehension	What should you do if you see a house on fire?
Arithmetic	Three boys had twenty-four pennies and divided them equally among themselves. How many pennies did each receive?
Similarities	In what way are a turkey and a chicken alike?
Vocabulary	What are "scissors"?
Digit span (alternate—may be substituted for others)	Listen carefully to the following numbers, and when I am through repeat them just as I said them: 7-3-9-1-4.
PERFORMANCE SUBTESTS	
Picture completion	Pictures of persons, animals, or common objects have parts that are missing; child is asked to point to or verbally identify the missing part.
Picture arrangement	Comic strip-like panels are presented in mixed-up order, and the child is asked to rearrange them in a meaningful story sequence.
Block design	Four or nine colored blocks must be arranged so as to reproduce a pattern shown on a card.
Object assembly	Cut-up figures resembling jigsaw puzzles must be reassembled from jumbled pieces.
Coding	Geometric symbols are matched with numbers; then the child is shown a row of numbered boxes and asked to write in the appropriate symbol below each number.
Mazes (alternate—may be substituted for others)	Child places a pencil in the center of a printed maze and is asked to trace a path out of the maze which does not cross any of the printed lines.

Source: Wechsler, 1974.

100, respectively. While the MA/CA ratio is probably the easiest way to remember what is meant by IQ, Wechsler's "deviation IQ" is generally regarded as more accurate mathematically.

Regardless of the scoring method, the theoretically predicted result is a "normal," or bell-shaped, curve distributed evenly around a mean of 100 (see Figure 6-3). Percentages of the population which should fall within 10-unit intervals of this theoretical distribution of IQs are also shown in Figure 6-3. Half the population is expected to score within 10 points of 100, and about 84 percent is expected to score within 20 points of 100. Only a bit more than 2 percent should score below 70 or above 130. The actual distribution has been reported by Jensen (1969, pp. 23–25), based primarily on Stanford-Binet IQs gathered by Cyril Burt (1963). Similar data were reported by Wechsler (1958, p. 107), based on more than 2000 cases in a national sample to which the

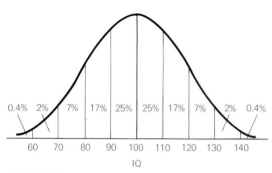

FIGURE 6-3
The theoretical "normal" distribution for IQs, showing the percentage of the population expected to fall into 10-unit intervals.

Wechsler IQ scales had been administered. The actual distributions approximate the theoretical one quite closely, though they are not perfect bell-shaped curves. Dorfman (1978) noted that statistically significant departures from perfectly bell-shaped distributions are frequently observed for IQ and achievement tests, and he therefore questioned the theoretical assumption that IQ is "normally" distributed in the general population. Referring to the Burt data in particular, Dorfman offered what appeared to be compelling statistical evidence that Burt may have knowingly adjusted or even invented some of his IQ data so that the actual distribution of IQs would closely approximate the theoretically derived normal curve. This issue will be considered more thoroughly in Chapter 7, since it bears on the controversy over the heritability of intelligence.

Assessment of so important a personal characteristic as intelligence naturally tends to provoke controversy, since this term is used in everyday language and is a trait that people usually regard as highly desirable. What, however, is meant by the word "intelligence"? According to purists in the environmentalist tradition in psychology, intelligence is simply the cumulative effect of a lifetime of learning experience. Thus, people become more intelligent as they grow older and learn more things, and practically any two people would become equally intelligent if they were exposed to identical learning experiences during their lifetimes.

Contradicting this position are researchers in the area of *differential psychology*, who believe that a person's level of intelligence is a relatively stable personality characteristic which can, only to a limited degree, be influenced by environmental experience. These researchers point to the fact that when people complete a diverse battery of tasks requiring mental effort, the scores on different tasks tend to be positively and significantly correlated with one another. For example, in a group of 100 male and 100 female fifth-graders in Wechsler's (1949) standardization sample for the WISC, scores on the Vocabulary subtest correlated 0.54 and 0.47 with scores on the Block Design and Picture Completion subtests, respectively. The General Information subtest correlated 0.69 with Arithmetic, 0.48 with Block Design, and 0.41 with Mazes. When the matrix of correlations between individuals' scores on these and other cognitive tasks was factor-analyzed, the first factor to emerge was called g, for general mental ability.

The extent to which scores on a given subtest correlate with the overall *g* factor is called the *loading of that subtest on g*. The tests loading most highly on *g* are those which require the most conceptual manipulation of a problem, such as finding the missing piece to increasingly complex geometric designs or finding a picture which correctly completes a concept begun by another set of pictures (Cattell, 1940). Tasks such as remembering and repeating a string of digits or removing one's finger from a key as quickly as possible following a light flash are only weakly loaded on *g*. However, if the digits must be repeated in backwards order or if the observer is faced with two lights and is required to lift a finger when either (but not the other) is flashed, the *g* loadings on the digit-recall and reaction-time tasks will be found to increase. Apparently, increasing the amount of mental manipulation required or introducing more complexity and uncertainty into a stimulus array serves to boost a task's g loading. The g factor can be interpreted in a variety of ways. Some regard it as nothing more than skill at test-taking or as an index of the range of someone's social experience.

Psychologists who study individual differences regard abstract reasoning as the essence of g and note that the tests which are most highly loaded on g are those which combine scores on a variety of moderately to highly g-loaded subtests—in other words, the Stanford-Binet and Wechsler IQs. These IQ scores came to have great educational and social significance because they correlated strongly with scholastic achievement in elementary and high school (but not so strongly with achievement in college). A representative study of this relationship examined IQ and achievement scores (the latter being assessed using the Iowa Test of Basic Skills) obtained from more than 5000 schoolchildren when they were in the fourth grade and again when the same children were in the sixth grade. In terms of specific skills, IQ was correlated 0.65 with reading comprehension, 0.55 with spelling, 0.57 with map reading, 0.63 with grasp of arithmetic concepts, and so forth; it was correlated 0.73 with a child's overall percentile rank on the Iowa tests. These relationships all became somewhat stronger at the sixth-grade level. IQ in the fourth grade was correlated 0.83 with IQ in the sixth grade, indicating a high test-retest reliability. Finally, IQ in the fourth grade was more strongly related to achievement in the sixth grade than achievement in the fourth grade was related to IQ in the sixth grade. While the difference between these correlations was small in an absolute sense, the fact that it was statistically significant indicated that IQ was a stronger predictor of scholastic achievement than the latter was of the former. Consequently, it seemed that abstract-reasoning ability had a greater impact on school achievement than achievement had on IQ (Crano et al., 1972).

With such evidence of their validity as predictors of school achievement and with high test-retest and split-half reliabilities, IQ tests met all the desired statistical criteria for individual assessment. Partly because of this, they became widely accepted for counseling students in the nation's schools. Academic institutions and some industries use IQ and IQ-related tests as criteria for selecting students and employees. Ironically, it was the very success of IQ tests in winning such widespread acceptance that caused them to become the subjects of controversy.

CRITICISMS OF OBJECTIVE TESTS

During the past two decades, the tests employed in dispositional assessment have often been the targets of scathing criticism. One type of criticism has dealt primarily with the psychometric accuracy of the tests in assessing personality for the purpose of guidance counseling or clinical diagnosis. These concerns, generally expressed by psychological researchers and practitioners, might be categorized as *professional criticisms*. A second type of criticism, however, has often come from outside the profession. The issues raised here usually revolve around the potential for personality assessment to infringe upon civil liberties; these issues might be called *social criticisms*.

Professional Criticisms of Testing

As always, the major source of professional dissatisfaction with objective tests has been in the areas of reliability and validity. We saw earlier that some of the subscales on the MMPI have disappointingly low test-retest reliabilities. Although other personality scales may do somewhat better than the MMPI in this regard, reliability must be considered in the broad context of measurement precision as well as in the narrow one of repeatability of a numerical score. There is evidence that people's answers on an assessment device may be influenced by consistent tendencies toward (1) being either agreeable or contrary ("yea-saying" vs. "nay-saying"), (2) portraying oneself in an unrealistically favorable or unfavorable light ("social desirability" vs. "faking bad"), or (3) outright falsification (Edwards, 1964; Husek, 1961; Kaplan & Eron, 1965). More recent investigations have indicated that examinees can shift their MMPI scores in a socially desirable direction when asked to "fake good" and in an undesirable direction when asked to "fake bad." Items whose diagnostic content was obvious were found to be significantly more "fakable" than were subtle items (Burkhart et al., 1978; Harvey & Sipprelle, 1976).

Faking, social desirability, acquiescence, and other such response sets aside, a person's emotional state at the time a test is administered can influence his or her response to it. Motivation, or the lack of it, can significantly influence task performance and IQ score, for example. Research evidence relating to this topic will be presented in Chapter 10. Sundberg (1977, p. 198) has argued that performance on all objective tests can be affected by temporary mood *states* as well as the personality *traits* they are supposed to be measuring.

As the foregoing material has indicated, reliability of scoring is an important concern for psychologists interested in the use of objective tests for personality assessment. A problem with these tests which relates more to validity than to reliability is the complex issue of base rates for mental illness. Suppose that 60 percent of schizophrenic patients versus only 2 percent of "normal" people score above 70 on the Sc subscale of the MMPI. Now suppose that half of all people who present themselves for treatment at a psychological clinic are schizophrenic while the remainder are just temporarily distressed and essentially "normal." If we randomly diagnose patients as schizophrenic or "normal," we should correctly identify half of the schizophrenics and half of the normals. If we instead administer the MMPI and call any patient with a T score of 70 or higher on the Sc scale a schizophrenic, 30 percent

(= 0.60 × 0.5) of the population will be correctly identified as schizophrenic while 49 percent (= 0.98 × 0.5) will be correctly identified as "normal." Thus, our diagnoses derived from the MMPI will be accurate in 79 percent of cases, much better than the 50 percent accuracy obtainable from the base rate alone. Furthermore, only 1 percent of all patients will be "normal" but incorrectly diagnosed as schizophrenic, whereas 25 percent would fall into this category under random diagnosis.

When base rates are at or near 50 percent, a test with moderately high validity, such as the MMPI, will be very helpful as a diagnostic instrument. When attempting to predict relatively rare events, however, use of a test of this sort may actually work against accurate assessment (Meehl & Rosen, 1955). In the foregoing example, if the population administered the MMPI consisted of nonpatient college students, only 1 percent of whom were schizophrenic, it can be shown that 0.6 percent (= 0.60 × 0.01) would be correctly identified as schizophrenic and 97 percent (= 0.98 × 0.99) correctly identified as "normal." Here, 97.6 percent of the population would be accurately diagnosed using the test, which is *less* than the 99 percent accuracy which could be obtained simply by calling everyone normal. What is worse, employing the MMPI would result in 2 percent of the population's being labeled as schizophrenic when they are, in fact, "normal." Rosen (1954) has demonstrated that in attempting to predict a very rare behavior, such as suicide, use of a test which correctly identifies 75 percent of potential suicides will actually include far more "normal" people than self-destructive types in the suicide category.

Part of the problem posed by base rates lies in the fact that examinees as well as administrators will often accept test results at face value and fail to give adequate consideration to the possibility of misdiagnosis. Forer (1949) administered a self-devised test he called the Diagnostic Interest Blank to a group of thirty-nine undergraduates who, at a later date, were given a diagnostic "sketch" of their individual personalities. Unknown to the students, each sketch was identical and included such statements as "You have a great need for other people to like and admire you," "You have a great deal of unused capacity which you have not turned to your advantage," "You prefer a certain amount of change and variety and become dissatisfied when hemmed in by restrictions and limitations," and "Your sexual adjustment has presented some problems for you." The students were overwhelmingly enthusiastic in their endorsement of the accuracy of the test in revealing their basic personality characteristics. They burst into laughter when it was explained that the sketches were standardized creations not at all related to their answers on the interest blank and that their behavior exemplified the *Barnum effect* in personality testing. (It was P. T. Barnum who said, "There's a sucker born every minute.") The Barnum effect has been replicated many times since Forer first reported it (Ulrich, Stachnik, & Stainton, 1963; Glenn & Janda, 1977). The effect may also explain the success of such enterprises as astrology in inducing some members of the public to accept rather broadly written personality descriptions. Forer, in fact, gathered most of the statements for his bogus personality sketch "from a newsstand astrology book."

Related to the Barnum effect is the tendency toward perceiving illusory correlation between test scores and stereotyped patterns of behavior. As explained in Chapter 5, *illusory correlation* refers to the perception of statistical links between test data and symptoms of personality disorder when there is, in fact, only a random association between the two. Dowling and Graham (1976) found that illusory correlations between MMPI scale names and brief behavioral descriptions were evoked more strongly among psychology graduate students trained in the background and use of the MMPI than they were among inexperienced undergraduates. In the worst of all possible diagnostic situations, then, the clinician could derive an erroneous diagnosis

from a moderately valid personality test which the clinician would, nonetheless, perceive as accurate because of theoretical preconceptions, social stereotypes, or other sources of illusory correlations. The misdiagnosis could then be "sold" to the client by means of the Barnum effect.

Mindful of the dangers of misdiagnosis posed by the somewhat less-than-perfect reliabilities and validities of objective tests, Sechrest (1963) proposed that clinicians attend to what he called *incremental validity*. That is, before a test is administered, it must be demonstrable that the addition of these data will produce a better clinical prediction than will biographical and interview information obtainable independently of the test.

Despite their limitations and the cautions that must be exercised in interpreting them, Meehl believes that the major objective tests reviewed in this chapter—the Strong, the MMPI, and the CPI—do offer enough incremental validity to justify their use. His feeling is that "A device that takes a negligible amount of time for the skilled clinician to administer or interpret is often worth using even when the inferences it permits are of only moderate validity" (Meehl, 1972, p. 146).

Social Criticisms of Testing

Probably the primary source of public dissatisfaction with personality testing is the application of these instruments to personnel selection and school counseling. We will consider the complaints raised against personality tests in a separate subsection from the issues being debated in what has become known as the *IQ controversy*.

The ethics of testing It did not take many years before the MMPI was applied outside the clinical settings for which it was originally intended. As use of this test expanded, one of its developers published a lengthy reply to a letter from a concerned citizen who objected to the religious content of some items and questioned the constitutionality of using this test for the screening of job applicants. Hathaway (1964) admitted that the MMPI had "manifest weaknesses" which called for a revision and updating of items. but he noted that a thorough revision would cost more than $100,000 and would be so different from its predecessor that years of research with the present MMPI would be essentially wasted. Hathaway defended the rationale and methodology underlying construction of the existing instrument, however, and insisted that despite its faults, the MMPI was still a useful device in personnel selection. He maintained that only psychologically "healthy" types should be placed in positions of social influence and power over others and that the MMPI could assist in screening out the "unhealthy" ones. Furthermore, he

said, personality testing could provide a means by which unhappy employees might find job placements for which they were psychologically more suited.

A year after Hathaway's letter was published, subcommittees of the House and Senate of the U.S. Congress opened hearings for the purpose of examining "serious questions" concerning "psychological or personality testing of government employees and job applicants by federal agencies" in the course of which examinees had been asked to reveal information about their "sex life, family situations, religion, personal habits, childhood, and many other matters" (Gallagher, 1965, p. 955). The author of a popularized attack on personality testing, called *The Brain Watchers* (Gross, 1962), testified that the tests obviously

Personality tests are sometimes administered by companies seeking to screen prospective employees. This application of personality testing has raised serious questions concerning invasions of privacy, interpretation of scores, and confidentiality of results. (Sam Pierson/Photo Researchers)

represented an unwarranted invasion of privacy but were made especially inappropriate and immoral by the fact that they were inaccurate. In his words, "The results of many careful experiments that have attempted to validate personality testing have all proven the tests to be worthless" (1965, p. 959).

People from different racial groups tend to have different-appearing profiles on the MMPI, CPI, and other projective and objective tests of personality (Kardiner & Ovesey, 1951; McDonald & Gynther, 1963; Mason, 1969). This phenomenon has been investigated most extensively in comparisons of whites with blacks. The differences are in a direction that suggests greater manifestations of psychopathology among blacks than among whites. More recent investigators have maintained that racial differences on the MMPI and CPI are due to differences in cultural background which only *appear* to be related to psychopathology because the tests were standardized and validated on white populations (Cross et al., 1978; Gynther, 1972). If this is, in fact, the case, use of objective tests in personnel selection would discriminate unfairly against members of minority groups.

Controversies in IQ testing Many of the same issues have arisen in respect to IQ testing. Despite their overall reliability, individual IQ scores must always be thought of as being surrounded by an *error of measurement*—that is, a range through which an individual's score might be expected to vary on a retest due to random fluctuation. Too often, this possibility for measurement error is overlooked as school counselors and teachers scrutinize a child's numerical score for evidence of "superior," "average," or "inferior" ability. To mention but a few sources, error may result from (1) long-term motivational and emotional traits of the examinee which can either facilitate or undermine performance, (2) short-term positive or negative reactions to the immediate test environment, (3) the degree of past experience with the types of tasks found on

various subtests, and (4) lucky or unlucky guesses.

Rosenthal and Jacobsen (1968) investigated the possibility that naive labeling of children's ability levels on the basis of IQ scores, without due consideration to the foregoing sources of error, could cause teachers to give greater attention to "superior" students and to write off "inferior" ones. These researchers informed teachers in a San Francisco grade school that several students in their classes had been identified as "late bloomers" and could be expected to show dramatic gains in scholastic achievement during the coming year. Actually, the students named were chosen arbitrarily by the researchers and had no known tendencies toward "blooming." Nonetheless, these children *did* show significant gains in reading, mathematics, and IQ scores during the school year. Rosenthal and Jacobsen concluded that the teachers must have communicated their high expectations to the "bloomers" by calling on them more often, giving them more praise, and so forth. The increased attention presumably *caused* the "bloomers" to blossom. The researchers did not directly observe the classroom behavior of the teachers, however, so alternative explanations of the results cannot be ruled out. Furthermore, there have been serious criticisms of the methodology and statistics employed in this study, and difficulty has been encountered in replicating the main findings (Brody & Brody, 1976, p. 163). These problems notwithstanding, we cannot afford to overlook the possibility that test scores may inadvertently create self-fulfilling prophecies by influencing the positive or negative expectations of the persons who have control over important aspects of the examinee's life.

The self-fulfilling prophecy has been invoked as an explanation for the racial differences in mean score routinely found on IQ tests. In particular, black and Chicano populations in the United States generally average 11 to 15 points lower than the white average of 100. If teachers, who are for the most part members of the white majority population, harbor prejudicial attitudes regarding the low abilities of minority students, they may fail to motivate these students to do their best either in the classroom or on standardized tests. Furthermore, Garcia (1972) and others claim that IQ tests were standardized on white populations in such a manner as to cause them to be inevitably culturally biased against blacks, Chicanos, and other minorities.

Early-childhood intervention programs designed to boost scholastic achievement were judged by Jensen (1969) to have failed because they were unable to produce enduring gains in IQ scores among minority populations. Zigler and Trickett (1978) replied, however, that the focus on IQ gain as the criterion against which such efforts are evaluated distracts us from paying attention to more important goals, like the acquisition of vital social skills, increased school attendance and achievement, and decreased delinquency. In other words, the very existence of a test which measures IQ quickly and cheaply may inadvertently obscure the success of social programs whose objectives are broader than the mere increase of this one numerical score.

At the same time, it should be acknowledged that scores on standardized tests of ability and achievement do provide information which merits one's attention. When these scores show a dramatic overall decline, as has the national average on the Iowa Tests of Basic Skills and the Scholastic Aptitude Test since the mid-1960s, there are justifiable grounds for concern. Various explanations—ranging from television to the breakup of the nuclear family to the drift away from the basics in education—have been offered for this nationwide phenomenon (Lipsitz, 1977). Whatever the explanation, it is embarrassing for an affluent, technologically advanced society to be failing in this regard. At the lower end of the achievement distribution, it has been estimated that as much as a fifth of our adult population has not acquired a minimum competence in reading, writing, and arithmetic.

CONCLUSION

Partly in response to the congressional hearings of 1965, the American Psychological Association (1966) published the first edition of its *Standards for Educational and Psychological Tests and Manuals*. While the ethical issues raised by the social critics have not been ignored by professionals, then, the controversy has not disappeared. It would be presumptuous for a book to try to resolve these issues in an absolute, final way because most of them rest ultimately on a consensus as to how much individual privacy and liberty must be surrendered to the common good. Any society requires some balancing of these two values. Some societies place a strong emphasis on the rights of the individual; others place more emphasis on the needs of the community. One consensus which seems to be emerging in our society is a concern for the confidentiality of private information. If it is not important that personal data be identified with a particular individual, the data should be anonymously coded. If it is important that personal identification be retained, then the examinee has a right to expect that the information provided will be shared only among those who have a legitimate professional interest. Lovell (1967) proposed that examinees and examiners enter into *test contracts* specifying to whom and for what purposes data might be released, thus providing grounds for a lawsuit against the agency sponsoring the test in the event of a breach of contract.

Looking at the issue from a more general psychological viewpoint, it appears that objective tests are more likely to avoid controversy if they are restricted to the purposes for which they were originally intended: clinical diagnosis in the case of the MMPI; counseling in the case of Strong, the CPI, and the 16 PF; and determining the reasons for scholastic failure in the case of the IQ test. Giving a test to a client who is clearly in need of psychological assessment because he or she is suffering from mental distress, dissatisfaction with a job, disrupted interpersonal relationships, or excessively low achievement in school is one situation. Applying a test in blanket fashion to a large group of job applicants or schoolchildren—most of whom are showing none of the foregoing symptoms of social pathology—and then using the obtained scores to make fine distinctions among individuals is an entirely different situation.

Even when personality tests are restricted to their original areas of application, however, caution must be exercised in interpreting an individual's profile of scores. The limitations on reliability and validity that have been repeatedly discussed in this chapter suggest that while tests can provide useful information, the indications they provide must be corroborated by interview and biographical information before any real confidence can be placed in even tentative interpretations. If personality testing was always conducted in such a prudent manner by trained professionals who were motivated primarily by a desire to help the examinee, much of the controversy over testing would probably dissipate. For the present, it seems clear that the controversy which erupted in the mid-1960s has served to heighten the awareness of psychologists to the dangers posed by misapplication and misinterpretation of the measuring instruments they have created.

SUMMARY

1 The devisers of structured and objectively scorable personality tests tried consciously to avoid the reliability and validity problems associated with projective techniques. The first self-administered personality inventory was Woodworth's Personal Data Sheet, devised for the purpose of screening out mentally unfit recruits during World War I. Despite the fact that the items had an obvious *face validity*, the test was fairly effective in identifying those for whom adjustment to Army life would be particularly difficult.

2 Items selected for inclusion on the Strong Vocational Interest Blank (SVIB) had *empirical* rather than *face* validity. This meant that the content of a given item might have no clear relationship to the job requirements of a given occupational category, but so long as responses to the item could be shown to discriminate between members of this and other occupations, it was included on the inventory.

3 Statements included on the Minnesota Multiphasic Personality Inventory, or MMPI, were also selected on the basis of their empirical validity in distinguishing clinical from psychologically "normal" populations. Scores are statistically standardized so that a value (called a *T score*) of 50 represents "normality" on each scale; scores above 70 are customarily regarded as indicators of potential psychological disturbance. Various scales of the MMPI are also designed to measure tendencies toward hypochondriasis (Hs), depression (D),

hysteria (Hy), psychopathic deviance (Pd), masculinity or femininity (Mf), paranoia (Pa), psychasthenia (Pt), schizophrenia (Sc), hypomania (Ma), and social introversion (Si). In addition, there are four *validity scales* which provide a check on the accuracy of an examinee's responses on the ten clinical scales. Interpretation of an examinee's profile involves looking for particular patterns of relationships between scores. Two well-known patterns are *conversion V* and *paranoid valley*. Diagnostic decision making can, to some extent, be based on statistical associations between such patterns and particular forms of mental disorder.

4   The California Psychological Inventory, or CPI, was designed to assess the degree to which various personality characteristics differ among "normal" individuals not known to be suffering from any sort of mental disorder. Items were selected which distinguished persons known to possess a particular trait from those who expressed the trait to a lesser degree. The traits included were such things as dominance, sociability, self-acceptance, socialization, self-control, tolerance, intellectual efficiency, achievement, and femininity.

5   Cattell's procedure for constructing his Sixteen Personality Factor Questionnaire (16 PF) was to place on a single dimension those items which factor analysis had shown to be highly correlated with one another. The three factors which seemed to carry the most weight in accounting for people's impressions of others' personalities are, according to Cattell, Affectothymia (which resembles introversion-extraversion), High "g" (intelligence), and High ego-strength (which resembles "emotional stability" vs. "emotional instability"). Factor analyses of the MMPI and CPI generally agree on the existence of at least two major dimensions of personality: (1) "introversion" vs. "extraversion" and (2) "emotional stability" vs. "emotional instability."

6   Tests of intelligence were originally devised for the purpose of identifying children who were likely to fail in a traditional academic curriculum and might find the training available in a trade school of greater value. The Stanford-Binet and Wechsler intelligence (IQ) tests each contain a variety of subtests with diverse content ranging from general information, vocabulary, and arithmetic to matching a pictured pattern using a set of colored blocks and wending one's way out of a printed maze with a pencil. The *intelligence quotient*, or IQ, traditionally refers to the extent to which a person's *mental age* (MA) matches his or her *chronological age* (CA). Researchers in the area of *differential psychology* point to the existence of significant and positive correlations among scores on the diverse subjects of the Stanford-Binet and Wechsler tests as evidence of an underlying "g factor" of general mental ability which is a relatively fixed personality characteristic for a given individual. The test-retest and split-half

reliabilities of IQ tests are high, and their validity is supported by strong correlations with measures of school achievement.

7   Professional criticisms of objective tests have pointed to the relatively low test-retest reliabilities of measures of "character" like the MMPI and the possibility that people may influence their scores by either "faking good" or "faking bad." A test such as the MMPI, which is designed to place examinees into clinical diagnostic categories, is likely to have an acceptably high level of validity only when applied to clinical populations in which the base rate of true mental disorder is near 50 percent. There is a danger that erroneous diagnoses derived by unsophisticated interpreters of tests like the MMPI and CPI can be "sold" to naive clients by means of the "Barnum effect."

8   Social criticisms of objective tests have emphasized the potentially harmful consequences of invasion of privacy and labeling of people as healthy or sick, bright or dull, and so forth. Differences between racial groups in the average scores achieved on these tests have brought charges that they are culturally biased against minority groups and, to the extent that they are used in personnel selection, may contribute to discriminatory practices. It is concluded that objective tests may have sufficient reliability and validity to make a positive contribution to a broad-based effort at personality assessment which is open to information from a variety of sources. At the same time, these tests are more likely to avoid controversy if they are restricted to the purposes for which they were originally intended: clinical diagnosis, counseling, and determining the reasons for scholastic failure.

TERMS TO KNOW

face validity
criterion keying
Strong Vocational Interest Blank
MMPI
neurotic triad
CPI

factor analysis
Sixteen Personality Factor Question-
    naire
IQ
mental age
Barnum effect

7.

BIOLOGICAL APPROACHES TO PERSONALITY ASSESSMENT

ISSUES TO CONSIDER

1 In what way are biological approaches to personality assessment an offshoot of the American personological tradition?
2 Can you describe the procedures used in twin studies and how they permit one to draw inferences regarding the heritability of traits like IQ and extraversion?
3 What types of evidence suggest that the electrical and chemical aspects of brain function are related to personality and behavior?

In Chapter 3 it was explained that one off-shoot of the American personological tradition was the construction of assessment instruments which would permit identification of the major traits in an individual's character. Some of these instruments were projective, such as Murray's Thematic Apperception Test, but most were objective tests like the Minnesota and California personality inventories discussed in Chapter 6. A second offshoot of the personological tradition, however, was an interest in the biological basis of human personality and the role of biological processes in producing or altering the many habits and dispositions that together make up what we call an individual's *temperament.*

The history of biological approaches to personality assessment is strewn with misunderstandings and controversies among researchers as well as between researchers and the general public.

Consider, for example, the once highly regarded but now disgraced science of phrenology. An eighteenth-century German physician named Franz Joseph Gall proposed that the cerebral cortex of the human brain was the place in which personality resided and so was the center from which behavior was controlled. He argued that each specialized aspect of personality (including abilities) was associated with a particular area of the cortex. A bump on the surface of the head supposedly indicated an especially well-developed trait in the area of the cortex which corresponded to the location of the bump. A bump in the area which controlled the trait of avarice, for instance, would indicate a somewhat greedy individual.

Gall devised a formal system for measuring the size and shape of the human head, and he set about trying to relate these measurements to the types of personality characteristics predicted by his theory. Sometimes he was even able to autopsy individuals whose personalities he had described while they were living to see whether their brains showed any anatomical features that might confirm phrenological predictions.

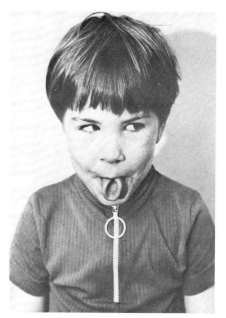

How many of your relatives can curl their tongue? Can you relate their ability, or lack of it, to dominant and recessive genes? (Anne Feldman)

Gall did find evidence to support his theory. However, later studies of the brain revealed that specific regions of the cerebral cortex were *not*, in general, associated with specific behaviors and abilities. This contradiction between Gall's positive findings and the subsequent refutation of the main premise of phrenology was probably caused by an unconscious bias in Gall's data gathering. That is, he must have paid selectively greater attention to those cases which confirmed his theory or may even have distorted his perception of disconfirming cases so that they appeared to support phrenology after all. Interestingly, it was not the questionable accuracy of Gall's observations that provoked the strongest attacks on phrenology (Davies, 1955). Rather, phrenology was denounced as an "immoral science" because it denied free will and allowed individuals to escape personal responsibility for their actions. Reacting defensively to such charges, phrenologists became increasingly dogmatic, and their

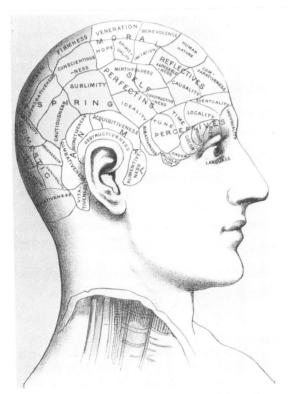

A phrenological chart showing the areas of the brain which were once mistakenly assumed to be associated with various personality traits. (Bettmann Archive)

the very real possibility of experimenter bias in gathering data which appear to support a biologically based theory of personality. Another problem is that personality assessment and therapeutic intervention which rest on biological determinism raise ethical questions similar to those which were leveled at phrenology.

This chapter begins by examining *constitutional psychology*, a scientifically sophisticated extension of the ancient idea that the configuration of various aspects of a person's body is a reliable indication of his or her character. Next we consider the evidence for hereditary factors in personality traits like intelligence and extraversion as well as in personality disorders like schizophrenia. Neuropsychological and neurophysiological approaches to personality assessment will also be examined. As in Chapters 5 and 6, this chapter will conclude with a section describing the limitations of biological assessment and the many ethical dilemmas associated with this approach.

theories became more a doctrine than a set of scientific hypotheses. Like astrology, which began with astronomy, phrenology drifted away from science and into a cultlike insistence on unquestioning faith in its techniques and interpretations.

The history of phrenology is instructive because it illustrates both the promises and problems of all biological approaches to personality assessment. The promise is that by relating personality to some quantifiable biological characteristic, greater precision of measurement will be attained, permitting more reliable assessment and opening the way to more effective therapeutic intervention via medical techniques. One important problem is that the aura of "science" which surrounds such an enterprise may obscure

CONSTITUTIONAL PSYCHOLOGY

Building upon earlier work by a German psychiatrist named Kretschmer (1921), the American psychologist William H. Sheldon developed an elaborate system for measuring the human physique. Kretschmer maintained that people suffering from different types of mental disorder tended to differ in their body builds and that physique, therefore, might be related to temperament. Specifically, he claimed that schizophrenics were usually somewhat slender, while manic-depressives were often overweight. Sheldon sought to make this "constitutional" psychology relevant to the assessment of normal personalities as well as the mentally disturbed individuals who were the focus of Kretschmer's research.

Sheldon arranged for photographs to be taken of several thousand nude males from the front, side, and rear. Various anatomical measurements were taken from the photographs. With the help of other expert judges, Sheldon identified features which would reliably permit all of the photographs to be ranked in ascending or descending series. Eventually, he decided that these features could be grouped in just three basic categories: (1) the narrow-shouldered and thin, (2) the broad-shouldered and athletic, and (3) the rounded and obese. He labeled these categories *ectomorphic*, *mesomorphic*, and *endomorphic*, respectively (Sheldon, 1942).

An innovative feature of Sheldon's typology was that it included a measure of the degree to which an individual fitted into each of his three categories of physique. These measurements determined the individual's overall *somatotype* and could range from 1 (low) to 7 (high) on each component. The "average" physique was presumed to express each component to a moderate degree and would be described numerically as a 4 (ectomorphy) −4 (mesomorphy) −4 (endomorphy). A person with a highly overdeveloped musculature, broad shoulders, and a narrow waist would approach the extreme mesomorph somatotype of 1-7-1, whereas the extreme ectomorph and endomorph somatotypes would be 7-1-1 and 1-1-7, respectively. Theoretically, 343 somatotypes are possible, but Sheldon was originally able to find only 76 distinct patterns among 4000 cases. A change in his scoring system later increased this number to 267 (Sheldon, Lewis, & Tenney, 1969). While Sheldon realized that exercise and diet would affect a person's outward appearance, he also maintained that the somatotype could vary only within a certain range around a "natural" contour which was set by an underlying, inherited *morphogenotype* (Sheldon, 1954).

Sheldon and his colleagues then undertook a series of studies of the primary components of human temperament. In these, hundreds of persons were rated for the extent to which each of fifty to eighty traits were exhibited in their daily activities and in their behavior during clinical interviews. Factor analysis of the ratings (see Chapter 6 for a description of this statistical

procedure) revealed three major clusters of traits, indicating the existence of these three distinct types of temperament:

1 *Cerebrotonia* is indicated by restraint in posture and movement, love of privacy, a mental preoccupation with one's inner feelings and fears, youthful intentness of manner and appearance, and an avoidance of others when troubled.
2 *Somatotonia* incorporates assertiveness of posture and movement, love of risk and physical adventure, competitive aggressiveness, sociability which is oriented toward the goals and activities of youth, and a need of action when troubled.
3 *Viscerotonia* is characterized by relaxed posture and movement, a love of food and physical comfort, sociability, and a need to seek out others when troubled.

In its final form, Sheldon's scale for temperament listed sixty traits, twenty each for viscerotonia, somatotonia, and cerebrotonia.

The culmination of all this work was a study in which 200 white male college students were rated for temperament and somatotyped. Sure enough, each personality style was strongly associated with one and only one body type: cerebrotonia with ectomorphy, somatotonia with mesomorphy, and viscerotonia with endomorphy. Unfortunately, a major problem with Sheldon's data was that they were almost too good to be believable. Humphreys (1957) noted that Sheldon personally made the temperament ratings of the 200 subjects and was actively involved in somatotyping these individuals as well. Consequently, there was considerable potential for experimenter bias to influence the results. Social stereotypes of the skinny intellectual, the action-oriented athlete, and the jolly fat person could have caused Sheldon to perceive a stronger relationship between physique and temperament than actually existed and, incidentally, to find stronger support for his theory than the data in fact offered.

Later research has found evidence of an association between ectomorphy and anxiety (Davidson, McInnes, & Parnell, 1957) and between mesomorphy and delinquency (Glueck & Glueck, 1956). Ectomorphy is positively correlated with IQ (Haronian & Saunders, 1967), while endomorphy is associated with susceptibility to influence by external stimuli (Witkin, 1965). Cortes and Gatti (1972) reported that mesomorphy is associated with the endorsement of traditionally masculine values and a high need for achievement. Rees (1973) reviewed a number of studies indicating an association between physique and psychopathology, but the relationships were not always in a direction predicted by Sheldon's theory.

Though there is some independently gathered evidence to support the hypothesized link between physique and temperament, these relationships never seem to be as strong as the ones originally reported by Sheldon and his associates. This makes somatotyping a procedure of questionable validity for use in individual personality assessment. Moreover, as was suggested above, social stereotypes may cause people to behave (or *appear* to behave) in a manner that confirms our preconceived notions concerning physique and temperament. Because of the potential for bias in Sheldon's observations, many psychologists have tended to disregard his work (Sundberg, 1977, p. 142). Other investigators, however, have been intrigued by Sheldon's main theme of a genetic linkage between human physiology and behavior and have searched more directly for evidence of such a link.

HEREDITARY FACTORS IN PERSONALITY TRAITS AND MENTAL DISORDERS

Virtually all organisms more advanced than single cells engage in sexual reproduction, which means that genetic material from each member of a male and female mating pair is combined to form the biological code by which their offspring will develop. Sexual reproduction is apparently important for the survival of higher plants and animals because it gives them the genetic diversity and behavioral flexibility to adapt to and cope with complex, ever-changing environmental pressures. An extremely intricate chemical molecule known as *deoxyribonucleic acid* (abbreviated DNA) carries the information by which the *genes* and, in turn, each of the individual cells of the body are specified.

The genes are carried on *chromosomes,* and in humans there are forty-six chromosomes, grouped in twenty-three pairs. When a sperm and egg unite during fertilization following mating, the twenty-three chromosomes contributed by the sperm of the father pair up with the corresponding twenty-three chromosomes contributed by the egg of the mother. The fertilized cell now possesses all the genetic material needed to form a new individual. The genes on the father-contributed and mother-contributed chromosomes in each matching pair occupy identical positions. Two genes that are in the same location on a matching pair of chromosomes are called *alleles.* It is the nature of the biochemical information possessed by each member of an allele which determines the degree to which the traits controlled by the genes at that location will be exhibited by an individual. When a gene is *dominant*, the trait it controls is expressed regardless of the traits controlled by its companion gene in the allele. When a gene is *recessive*, the trait it controls is expressed only if it is paired with another recessive gene in the allele. If two parents—each of whom possesses a recessive gene for a trait which neither of them expresses—mate and bear four children, odds are that one of the four will show the recessive characteristic. Figure 7-1 illustrates this process for a fairly unimportant but nonetheless inherited human characteristic: the inability to curl one's tongue inward from the sides.

An example of a genetically related mental disorder is the condition known as *phenyl-*

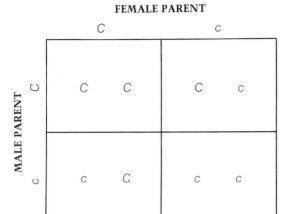

FEMALE PARENT

MALE PARENT

FIGURE 7-1
A tabulation of results of a hypothetical mating of two parents, each of whom has a dominant gene for tongue-curling (C) and a recessive gene for noncurling (c). If these parents have four children, odds are that one should be a purebred curler (CC), two should be curlers but should also carry the recessive gene for noncurling (Cc and cC), and one should receive the recessive gene from each parent, making this child a purebred noncurler (cc).

ketonuria, or PKU. This ailment is caused by a single recessive gene carried by about one out of every hundred persons. Consequently, the odds are only 1/10,000 (1/100 × 1/100) that a male and a female who each carry this gene will mate and have offspring, and if they have four children only one should inherit the pair of recessive genes that causes PKU. Though it is relatively rare, PKU has disastrous consequences for those who inherit it. The disorder results in circulation through the bloodstream of excessive amounts of a normally beneficial amino acid called *phenylalanine.* The excess phenylalanine interferes with brain development and produces severe mental retardation. The IQ of children suffering from PKU is almost always less than 50. Fortunately, knowledge of the genetic basis of the disorder has enabled hospitals to apply tests which detect PKU in newborn infants. Babies having PKU can be

placed on a diet which is low in phenylalanine. This permits their brains to develop normally, and mental retardation is effectively prevented (Vandenberg, 1971).

PKU notwithstanding, it seems to be the case that among organisms high up on the evolutionary scale—such as human beings—control of traits by single genes is very much the exception rather than the rule. More commonly, several genes, called *polygenes,* act together to affect the emergence of a trait. When inheritance is polygenic, the affected traits do not have the all-or-none quality of characteristics like curler vs. non-curler or PKU vs. no PKU, which are controlled by single genes. Instead, individuals manifest polygenic traits in continually varying degrees. Usually, this variation takes the form of a bell-shaped curve, with most of the population exhibiting the trait to a moderate degree and with progressively decreasing numbers of individuals showing it to either a greater or lesser degree. Those who believe that intelligence is largely inherited also accept that it must be polygenic. As you will recall from Chapter 6, IQ scores, which are generally regarded as a rough measure of intelligence, are distributed along a bell-shaped curve in the general population (see Figure 6-3).

The expression of polygenic traits is much more likely to be influenced by environmental factors than is the appearance of traits controlled by single genes. For this reason, as well as because of their sheer complexity, it is difficult to trace the origins of polygenically controlled traits. Furthermore, research on the genetic determinants of human physiology, personality, and behavior is limited by the fact that controlled experiments in this area are socially and ethically unacceptable.

Given these limitations, comparisons between individuals known to have varying degrees of genetic similarity provide nearly all the information available concerning hereditary components of personality. The most valuable information of this sort comes from *twin studies.* Identical twins develop from the splitting of a single

Identical twins, like the pair shown in the left-hand photo, develop from a cleavage of a single fertilized egg and so share all of their genes in common. Fraternal twins, like the pair shown in the right-hand photo, share only about half their genes in common. Since both identical and fraternal twins are born together and usually develop together in the same home environment, there are good grounds for arguing that if the former turn out to be more alike in their personality and behavior than the latter, this must be due primarily to the greater genetic similarity between identicals. (Rita Freed/Nancy Palmer Photo Agency)

fertilized egg and so share all of their genes in common. This is why identical twins are called *monozygotic* (MZ). Fraternal twins, on the other hand, are conceived from fertilization of separate eggs and, though they share a common prenatal environment in the mother's womb, are genetically no more similar than any two siblings would be. Fraternal twins share about half their genes in common and, for this reason, are called *dizygotic* (DZ). It should be noted here that any two people, by virtue of their being human beings and not wolves, birds, or fish, are alike in 99 percent of their genes. It is in the remaining 1 percent that human beings differ from one another in their hereditary characteristics. So when we say that DZ twins share half of their genes in common, we mean half of that 1 percent of genes in which humans show hereditary variability.

Identical twins must always be of the same sex, so the best twin studies include only fraternals who also happen to be in same-sex pairs. Since both MZ and DZ pairs are born together and

usually develop together in the same home environment, there are good grounds for arguing that if the former turn out to be more alike in their personalities and behavior than the latter, this must be due primarily to the greater genetic similarity between identicals. Any traits on which identicals are more alike than fraternals could, therefore, be presumed to be under some measure of genetic control in all human beings. One problem with making such an inference, however, is that parents often take care to treat identical twins more alike than fraternals, even to the point of dressing identical twins in matching outfits. Thus it is important to rule out differential degrees of similarity in parental handling as an alternative explanation for any tendency for identical twins to be more alike than their fraternal counterparts.

The search for hereditary factors which might affect personality has been largely concentrated in the areas of intelligence and extraversion (among psychologically "healthy" individuals) and schizophrenia (among persons suffering from mental disorder). Often, the effect of genes on mental functioning may be assumed to be indirect, as in the case of PKU, where a genetically induced change in the body's physiology results in damage to the brain. For this reason, we will give some consideration toward the end of this chapter to the physiology of the brain and central nervous system.

Hereditary Influences on the Healthy Personality

As was mentioned in Chapter 6, the late Cyril Burt, a British psychologist, conducted a great deal of research on the distribution of IQ scores in the general population and on the heritability of intelligence. Jensen (1969) relied on many of Burt's results in concluding that intelligence is largely inherited and relatively little influenced by the social environment. We will begin this

section with a discussion of the evidence and controversy pertaining to the possibility that intelligence is a polygenic trait.

Heredity and intelligence   The primary evidence for the heritability of IQ is illustrated in Figure 7-2. This figure is taken from a famous article which summarized the results of fifty-two independent studies conducted since 1920 in eight countries on four continents which compared the similarity in IQ of persons with varying degrees of genetic similarity. The column headed "genetic correlation" represents the proportion of common genes shared by two individuals in a given category.

Clearly, there is considerable variability in the results gathered by different investigators. The extent of variability is indicated by the length of the line connecting the correlations obtained within a given category in separate studies. Even so, the *median* correlation in each category

FIGURE 7-2

Correlations in IQ scores for pairs of people who differ in their degree of genetic similarity. The dots show the correlations obtained in fifty-two independent studies, and the lengths of the lines connecting the dots indicate the range of values obtained. The vertical slashes show the median correlation for each type of pairing, and the coefficient above each slash represents its numerical value. The arrows point to correlations reported by Sir Cyril Burt. (Adapted from Erlenmeyer-Kimling and Jarvik, 1963.)

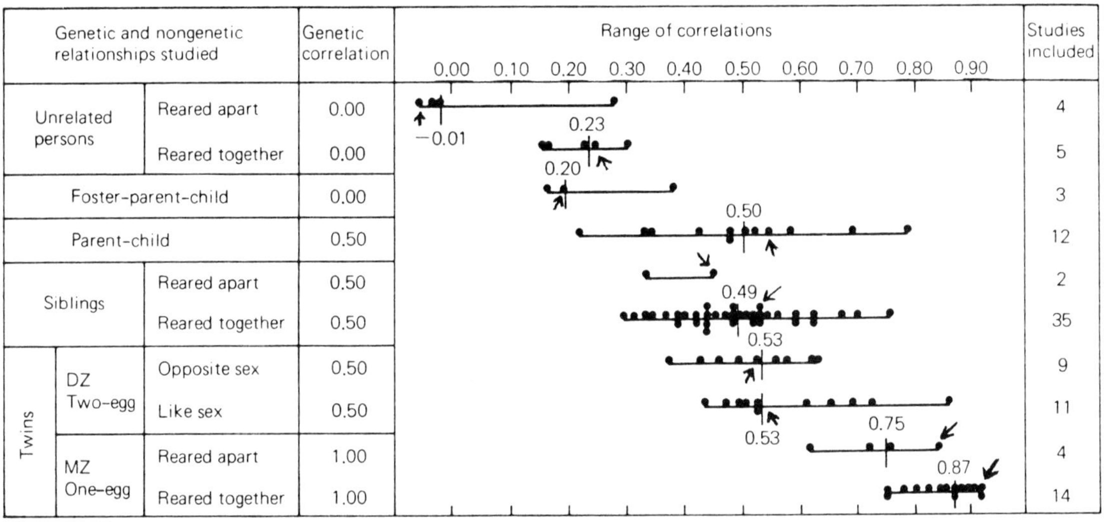

Genetic and nongenetic relationships studied		Genetic correlation	Range of correlations	Studies included
Unrelated persons	Reared apart	0.00	−0.01 ... 0.23	4
	Reared together	0.00	0.20	5
Foster-parent-child		0.00	0.50	3
Parent-child		0.50	0.50	12
Siblings	Reared apart	0.50	0.49	2
	Reared together	0.50	0.53	35
Twins DZ Two-egg	Opposite sex	0.50	0.53	9
	Like sex	0.50	0.75	11
Twins MZ One-egg	Reared apart	1.00	0.87	4
	Reared together	1.00		14

(indicated by the vertical slash and numerical coefficient) shows a strong association with the degree of genetic similarity. The more closely two individuals are related, the higher is the median correlation in their IQ scores. Consider the extremes of the scale. If identical twins, who share 100 percent of their genes in common, are raised together in the same home environment, they correlate about 0.9 in IQ. If unrelated children, who share none of their genes in common and who have been raised in different homes, are randomly paired and correlated with one another for IQ, the result will be about 0. The nature of the rearing environment does show some effect in this figure. Among identical twins and unrelated children, being raised in the same home produces a higher correlation in IQs than being raised in different homes. The figure also reveals, however, that similarity of rearing environment has a much weaker impact on the degree of agreement between two individuals' IQs than does their genetic similarity.

Reduced to somewhat oversimplified terms, the hereditarian argument would be that since identical twins still correlate about 0.75 in IQ even when they are raised in different home environments, 75 percent of their IQ must be contributed by their genetic identity and 25 percent by any differences between the environments. Since unrelated children reared together correlate about 0.25 in IQ even though they share no common genes, 25 percent of their IQs have an environmental basis while 75 percent is produced by their hereditary differences. Thus, by either method of analysis, the proportion of IQ which is contributed by genetic inheritance is estimated to be at least 75 percent. For various reasons too complicated to go into here, Jensen (1969) derived an even higher estimate of 80 percent.

This estimate did not go unchallenged for very long. In an address before the Eastern Psychological Association in 1973 and later in a book titled *The Science and Politics of IQ*, Kamin (1974) argued that Burt's data had been, at best, inaccur-

ately reported and, at worst, deliberately faked, in a manner that caused them to appear more supportive of a hereditarian hypothesis than they actually were. Jensen (1974) himself took note of these statistical inaccuracies but attributed them to carelessness on Burt's part rather than to biased reporting of results. Jensen did agree, though, that the questionable data in Burt's reports were useless for testing hypotheses regarding the heritability of IQ. Finally, Dorfman (1978) published an exhaustive analysis of Burt's data which appeared to establish that Burt must have deliberately fabricated at least some of these results so as to cause the distribution of IQs to fit exactly a bell-shaped curve with a mean of 100 and a standard deviation of 15 points.

If the controversy over the heritability of IQ is beginning to remind you of the history of phrenology with which this chapter began, it must be admitted that there are some similarities. In the case of IQ, though, there remains an important difference. Whatever questionable methods of data gathering and data reporting may be attributed to the major investigator in this field, the results he claimed to find have been, for the most part, replicated by other investigators. Within each of the categories in Figure 7-2, I have drawn an arrow to indicate the correlation reported by Burt and his associates (Burt, 1958; Burt & Howard, 1956). While Burt's data do have a tendency to be above the medians for all studies, they are not widely divergent from the correlations calculated by other researchers. Consequently, the evidence for the heritability of IQ would appear to be alive and well despite the deletion of Burt's results.

Kamin, however, also questioned the validity of some of the independent studies. In particular, he disputed the very important correlation of 0.75 for the IQs of identical twins reared apart in Figure 7-2. He observed that many of these separated twins were raised by close relatives, lived in the same town, attended the same schools, and visited one another frequently. Consequently, their social environments were really very similar, and this could have contributed to the high correlation in their IQs.

Perhaps the clearest suggestion of a hereditary component of IQ is contained in a table provided by Munsinger (1978). The table combines the results of eight independent studies (none of them Burt's) conducted between 1928 and 1975 which investigated the relationship between parents' IQs and those of their biological or adopted offspring. The IQs of parents and their biological offspring living at home were found to correlate 0.48, which closely approximates the parent-child value shown in Figure 7-2. IQs of parents and adoptive children correlated only 0.14, which is even less than the foster-parent–child value shown in Figure 7-2. Most importantly, the IQ of an adopted child correlated 0.43 with that of his or her biological parent with whom the child had not resided since he or she was, at most, 2 years old. Because the relationship between parental IQ and that of biological offspring was reduced only slightly by their inhabiting different environments, while the IQs of a genetically unrelated foster parent and child were only slightly related even though they shared the same environment, these results strongly support the existence of a genetic factor in IQ.

Here again, Kamin (1974, 1978) has some criticisms, but the adoption studies most vulnerable to his critique were done prior to 1935. More recent and methodologically sound studies have continued to find IQ correlations between parents and natural children and foster parents and adopted children which closely approximate the values shown in Figure 7-2 (Scarr & Weinberg, 1977).

To sum up, it seems that IQ, while clearly influenced by the social environment, is also influenced by genetic inheritance. At the same time, it appears doubtful that the heritability of intelligence is as high as the 80 percent figure calculated by Jensen (1969). Computing heritabilities involves making several subjective assump-

tions when applying a polygenic model. Making slightly different assumptions from Jensen's, Jencks et al. (1972) concluded that IQ is 45 percent inherited and 35 percent determined by the environment, with 20 percent arising from an interaction between an individual's genetic endowment and the type of environment he or she is born into. Loehlin, Lindzey, and Spuhler (1975, Appendix I) questioned some of Jencks's assumptions and adjusted them so as to produce a hereditary component of 60 percent, an environmental component of 15 percent, and a heredity-environment interaction of 25 percent. The point to be made here is that the heritability of IQ may be anywhere from 45 to 80 percent but is very unlikely to be as low as 0.

It appears that IQ tests could provide some indication of an individual's genetic potential for abstract-reasoning ability. Let me quickly add, however, that the IQ score cannot be naively interpreted as a direct measure of whatever genetic factors contribute to abstract reasoning. The IQ score only provides us with a rough approximation of these factors, and we know that the score may be considerably influenced both by an individual's social experience and by that person's reactions to the immediate test situation. Furthermore, the subtests which constitute an IQ score call upon many different types of abilities (see Table 6-4). Some subtests emphasize social skills, others numerical or verbal fluency, and still others memory or the manipulation of abstract symbols and designs. People may be strong in some areas and weak in others. Guilford (1967) has devised a Structure of Intellect model which includes five different types of cognitive operations on four possible categories of problem content to produce any of six different kinds of solutions. In Guilford's model, then, there may be as many as 120 ($5 \times 4 \times 6$) separate cognitive abilities. Even Vandenberg (1971, p. 184), who reports data indicating a strong hereditary component in the overall IQ score, also emphasizes that "a model of at least four to eight independent abilities has more pragmatic value." Some of the controversies surrounding the degree to which social experience influences IQ and the degree to which the IQ score influences social policymaking will be discussed in the concluding section to this chapter.

Heredity and extraversion Recall the trait of extraversion-introversion described in Chapter 2 (see Box 2-2). Extraverts are outgoing, action-oriented seekers of external stimulation, while introverts are aloof, contemplative types psychologically oriented toward events occurring within themselves. Using a twin-study approach comparable to that employed in the IQ research, Eysenck (1967) found evidence that this characteristic, too, is to some extent inherited (i.e., about 50 percent).

In Chapter 9, we will encounter several studies which suggest that human infants may be born already possessing certain temperamental characteristics. Some—the "easy" or "happy" babies—like to be held, dressed, and fed and generally respond positively to new experiences. The "difficult" or "colicky" ones tend to respond negatively to new experiences. Given Eysenck's findings, one cannot help but wonder whether such temperamental differences in infants are related to hereditary dispositions toward extraversion or introversion.

Eysenck also sought to specify what physiological systems might be affected by a genetic disposition toward this fundamental dimension of personality. In Box 2-2, it was mentioned that he believes introverts have a higher level of arousal in the brain and central nervous system than do extraverts. The higher level of arousal in the cerebral cortex of introverts presumably exerts an inhibitory control over lower brain centers, which are involved in the sensation and acting-out of emotion. Substances like alcohol, which reduce cortical arousal, tend to make introverts more emotionally uninhibited. It is the generally lower level of arousal in the cerebral cortex of extraverts which presumably allows

them to be more emotionally expressive than introverts in their daily lives.

Space does not permit us to explore in detail the intricacies of Eysenck's theory and research on extraversion-introversion. More will be said further on in this chapter, however, about brain physiology and its implications for behavior.

Hereditary Influences on Personality Disorder

It has long been suspected that susceptibility to mental illness is, to some degree, inherited. Schizophrenia, the most common form of psychosis or severe mental disorder, has been extensively researched with a view to uncovering both hereditary and biochemical factors. Rosenthal (1971) carefully summarized this evidence, and his conclusions have been, for the most part, supported by subsequent research (Wynne et al., 1978).

Schizophrenia, says Rosenthal, occurs in all areas of the world, in primitive societies as well as modern ones. There is evidence of a greater frequency of the disease among socioeconomically deprived groups within modern societies, but it does not seem to be associated solely with exposure to the cultural stresses imposed by technological civilization. Males and females are about equally likely to become schizophrenic, but male first admissions to mental hospitals peak between ages 20–25, while female first admissions peak around 30–35 years of age. The estimated incidence rate for schizophrenia (derived mainly from European studies) ranges from about three per thousand in some countries and subgroups to as high as three per hundred in others. In the United States, the lifetime risk of schizophrenia appears to be about one per hundred.

Shown in Table 7-1 are the concordance rates for schizophrenia among persons with varying degrees of genetic similarity. Concordance refers to the likelihood that a relative of a person diagnosed as schizophrenic will be similarly

TABLE 7-1 Concordance rates for schizophrenia among persons having differing degrees of genetic similarity

Relationship	Concordance, %
Identical twin	45*
Fraternal twin	13*
Sibling (neither parent schizophrenic)	8–10†
Child (one parent schizophrenic)	12–14†
Child (both parents schizophrenic)	36–46†
Grandchild	2–4†
Nephew or niece	2–3†
First cousin	2–4†

*Median estimate from five independent studies.
†The higher figure includes persons diagnosed as "probable" schizophrenics.
Source: Gottesman (1978, pp. 61–62).

diagnosed at some point in his or her lifetime. As in the IQ correlations shown in Fig. 7-2, the closer the genetic relationship between two individuals, the more likely they are to share the same traits (Gottesman, 1978). In a small but nonetheless theoretically very important sample of seventeen identical twins reared separately in which one twin was diagnosed schizophrenic, the other was found to be schizophrenic in 59 percent of cases (Gottesman & Shields, 1972).

An obvious environmentalist explanation can be offered for many of the foregoing findings; namely, people who live in closest association with oddly behaving schizophrenics are themselves most likely to become schizophrenics. The high concordance rate for identical twins reared apart argues against this environmentalist alternative, but the small sample size has caused researchers in this area to seek additional ways to test the genetic hypothesis. If schizophrenia has a hereditary basis, one would expect schizophrenics who were adopted as children to show a higher concordance rate with their biological than with their adoptive relatives. Recent studies do, in fact, indicate that schizophrenic adoptees

are at least four times as likely to share their disorder with their biological than with their adoptive relatives and are four times as likely to have schizophrenic biological relatives than a control group of nonschizophrenic adoptees (Kety et al., 1978).

While the foregoing evidence does imply the existence of hereditary factors in schizophrenia, the percentages are not so high as to suggest a heritability of 100 percent. None of the major researchers in this field seems to doubt that environment plays an important role in precipitating the disease. Their position seems to be that genetic factors may predispose some individuals toward schizophrenia but that it is the nature of the individuals' social environments which determines whether or not they will actually contract it. Like intelligence, schizophrenia is assumed to have a polygenic hereditary component which causes it to be expressed to varying degrees among differentially predisposed individuals rather than developing in the all-or-none fashion that one would expect if it were caused by a single gene. In addition, the complexity of polygenic inheritance causes expression of the trait to be more open to environmental influence than it would be if it were controlled by a single gene. The same type of evidence as that examined for schizophrenia leads Rosenthal (1971, Chap. 6) to conclude that susceptibility to manic-depressive disorders is also to some extent inherited.

What is the advantage of knowing that a mental disorder such as schizophrenia has a hereditary component? For one thing, children who are "at risk" because they have a schizophrenic parent can be given special attention by mental health agencies so that treatment is readily available if or when the disease appears. Garmezy (1978b) noted that high-risk children often experience difficulty in interpersonal relations and academic performance and suggested that these difficulties may create social stresses which serve to activate any inherent susceptibility to schizophrenia. He described several ongoing research programs designed to boost the social and academic competence of such children. Even if schizophrenia appears in full-blown form, about one-quarter of all those stricken will recover entirely and remain recovered, with another 25 percent attaining "nearly full" recoveries punctuated by infrequent relapses of delusional symptoms (Bleuler, 1978). High-risk adults can be taught to recognize and avoid stressful "triggering situations"; to relax following an unavoidable stressful episode; and to locate activities, companions, and employment which maximize feelings of competence and enjoyment without becoming excessively psychologically demanding (Wing, 1978).

Another potential benefit of the research on hereditary factors in schizophrenia lies in the possibility that it may succeed in identifying the physiological processes which are set in motion by the genes contributing to this disorder and which somehow disrupt the normal activity of the brain. As in the case of phenylketonuria, it may then be possible to intervene so as to block these processes and thus counteract the effects of the predisposing genes. Stress from environmental sources also causes changes to occur in the physiology of the brain and central nervous system. Indeed, it has long been proposed that what actually is inherited in a predisposition toward schizophrenia is a diminished capacity of the central nervous system to cope effectively with physically or socially induced stress (Garmezy, 1978a). If a person with this "schizotype" encounters an environment which optimally exercises and strengthens the central nervous system, he or she may never develop the disease. If, instead, the physical and social environment assault the congenitally weak central nervous system with more stress than it can handle, the "schizotype" will develop psychotic symptoms. The amount of stress which is capable of activating psychotic behavior in such individuals might be perceived as quite tolerable by someone with a "normal," more robust nervous sytem. Even among "nonschizotypes," however, extreme levels of stress are capable of overwhelming the central nervous system and so provoking a psychotic break from everyday reality.

MEASURING THE STRENGTH OF THE HUMAN NERVOUS SYSTEM

Every aspect of our behavior is, in the end, controlled by the brain and nervous system of our bodies, and every environmental event which we experience is translated by our sense organs into electrochemical impulses which travel through the nervous system to the brain. Given these facts, the ultimate source of human personality disorder is the brain and the manner in which it processes sensory input and sends out commands to other bodily organs. Consequently, an important area of psychological assessment is that which is concerned with identifying the nature and causes of disruptions of the normal functioning of the brain and nervous system. This field can be divided into two basic approaches:

1 The *neuropsychological approach* requires the clinician to derive inferences regarding the patient's neurological state from the latter's performance on paper-and-pencil tests and simple behavioral tasks.
2 The *neurophysiological approach* seeks to devise and implement fairly direct measures of neurological functioning which minimize the patient's behavioral involvement in the assessment process.

Neuropsychological Approaches to Assessment and Therapy

The most elaborate, sensitive, and widely used behavioral test for making neurological assessments is called the Halstead-Reitan Neuropsychological Test Battery (Reitan & Davidson, 1974). Halstead (1947) originated this battery in an effort to determine the effects on personality of a surgical operation on the brain known as a *lobotomy*. Reitan and his associates later refined Halstead's measures and developed a standardized set of seven tests from which an overall "Impairment Index" could be calculated. Among these tests are: (1) a Category Test, which requires the examinee to state the principle by which objects having a common size, shape, or color have been grouped, (2) a Tactual Performance Test, on which a blindfolded examinee must fit blocks into their appropriate sockets on a board using the right hand, the left hand, or both hands, (3) the Seashore Rhythm Test, which involves listening to two sets of rhythmic musical beats and deciding whether they are the same or different, (4) the Speech Sounds Perception Test, which calls for recognizing a word or syllable that corresponds to a vocalized sound, and (5) a Finger Tapping Test, which simply requires the subject to tap the right or left index finger as rapidly as possible in a series of ten-second trials. In addition to these tests, examinees are usually administered the subtests of the Wechsler intelligence scale, an Aphasia Screening Test, on which they must follow simple spoken directions, and several other measures of perceptual and motor skills.

At this point, we must digress a bit to explain that the brain is divided into two equal halves, or *hemispheres*, connected by a band of tissue known as the *corpus callosum*. As will be discussed more fully in Chapter 9, it appears that for each hemisphere of the brain, there are certain types of specialized abilities. In most people, the left hemisphere is dominant for problems requiring the comprehension of verbal material because the language center of the brain is located on the left side. The right hemisphere, on the other hand, is dominant for problems involving visualization of objects in space. In addition, it is known that the various branches of the nervous system feed into the brain contralaterally. That is, the left half of the brain receives sensory input from and controls the motor behavior of the right side of the body; the right half of the brain connects with the left side of the body. The two halves of the brain share the sensory information they receive and collaborate in the exercise of basic skills by means of the corpus callosum.

While numerous factors—such as age, education, temperament, or symptom severity—may influence a patient's individual performance, and while it is not difficult to find exceptions to the general statements which follow, there are several implications of the material in the preceding paragraph for clinical assessment using the Halstead-Reitan battery. Patients with damage to the right cerebral hemisphere should show deficits on tasks requiring spatial ability (e.g., the Tactual Performance Test), while those with damage to the left hemisphere should show deficits on tasks requiring verbal ability (e.g., the Speech Sounds Perception Test). People with right-hemisphere damage may exhibit problems in using their left hands while people with damaged left hemispheres should show deficits in using their right hands. It will be recalled from Chapter 6 that the subscales of the Wechsler intelligence scales are divided into verbal subtests, which emphasize verbal skills, and performance subtests, which emphasize the spatial manipulation of objects such as colored blocks or jigsaw puzzles. Consequently, a patient's relative achievement on the verbal and performance subtests of the Wechsler intelligence scales may provide an additional indication as to the cerebral location of any brain damage.

As research using the Halstead-Reitan battery progressed, it became possible not only to diagnose the existence and the hemispheric lateralization of damage but also to specify the type of damage most likely to have occurred. It is important to know, for instance, whether the blood supply to certain areas has been restricted by hardening of the arteries, whether the walls of a blood vessel have burst (called a *stroke*), whether portions of the brain's nervous system have degenerated, or whether the patient suffers from epileptic seizures, tumors, and so forth.

Filskov and Goldstein (1974) computed "hit

rates" for the Halstead-Reitan battery and various medical techniques in diagnosing the type of impairment suffered by each person in a sample of eighty-nine brain-damaged patients. The "hit rates" for the Halstead-Reitan were above 80 percent for all types of impairment but epilepsy, where correct diagnoses were obtained in 64 percent of cases. While other techniques might surpass it in diagnosing particular problems, the Neurological Test Battery was the most consistent and most reliable overall.

Reitan (1975) verifies the accuracy of his test battery by making predictions based solely on the Halstead-Reitan results and then checking to see whether they are confirmed by a patient's case history and the outcome of neurological medical examination. In one striking case of a 58-year-old woman who experienced a relatively sudden onset of confusion, memory loss, problems in comprehending spoken instructions, and difficulty in moving her right leg properly when walking, Reitan accurately diagnosed the existence of brain damage in the temporal lobe of the left cerebral hemisphere. A large, malignant tumor was subsequently removed from this location.

Such successes notwithstanding, Heaton, Baade, and Johnson (1978) caution that accurate diagnoses on tests such as these depend heavily on the patient's being motivated to put forth his or her best effort and attending in a realistic manner to the events occurring in the test environment. People with serious motivational deficiencies or thought disorders (e.g., schizophrenia) may easily be misdiagnosed as brain-damaged when, in fact, their problems stem from other causes. Older patients generally do less well on the Halstead-Reitan battery than younger ones; that may yield misleading indications of brain damage among patients sampled from the former group (Prigatano & Parsons, 1976). As in the case of all the other psychological-assessment techniques, the accuracy of this instrument depends greatly upon the care with which it is administered and interpreted by an experienced clinician. Despite the need for such precautions, many psychologists emphatically believe that they can and should play an important role in decision making regarding diagnosis and therapy for disorders arising from damage to the brain and central nervous system (Satz et al., 1970; Saunders, 1975).

Neurophysiological Approaches to Assessment and Therapy

There are several electrical and chemical methods by which the operation of the brain and other organs can be assessed. When individual cells in the nerve networks which connect various organs transmit information to one another (in a process called *firing*), both electrical and chemical events occur. Positively charged sodium and potassium ions on opposite sides of the cell wall flow in and out, changing the cell's electrical polarity. This change can be monitored as a weak electrical current by a highly sensitive recording apparatus, and in this aspect of its functioning the cell behaves similarly to the battery of an automobile.

A child wearing a set of electrodes which monitors electrical activity in various areas of the brain. The resulting pattern, called an EEG, may be compared with that obtained from other children and may be used to diagnose epilepsy, tumors, and other problems in the brain. (Psychology Today)

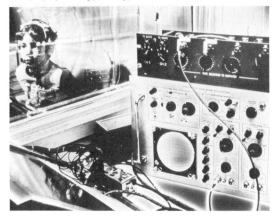

When the wave of depolarization reaches an ending of a nerve cell, it causes a chemical—generally either acetylcholine or norepinephrine—to be released into the space between that cell and the next one in the chain. The junction of two cells is called the *synapse,* and the space between them the *synaptic cleft.* The next cell is equipped with specialized receptors which are activated by one or another of the chemical messengers released into the synaptic cleft. In scientific terms, such a messenger is called a *neurotransmitter.* When activated by a neurotransmitter, this cell will be depolarized and will commence firing, and the message will in this way be carried from cell to cell in the nerve fiber. The chemical activity of the nervous system can be monitored indirectly by analyzing body fluids (blood, urine, spinal fluid, and so on) for the presence or absence of chemical derivatives of neurotransmitters, or directly by means of microscopic examination of nerve tissue. In this section, we will be examining the electrical and chemical aspects of brain functioning and their possible implications for personality.

Electrical observation of the brain The main technique for measuring the electrical aspects of the brain's activity is called *electroencephalography.* Other electronic techniques for monitoring physiological reactions also exist. Some of the more common ones consist of measuring heartbeat, breathing rate, blood pressure, and the ability of the skin to pass a weak electrical current between two closely spaced points (called the *galvanic skin response,* or *GSR*). We will discuss the latter techniques in Chapter 8 in the context of biofeedback research. For now, however, we will restrict our attention to electroencephalography.

When small metal discs called *electrodes* are placed at various spots on the scalp and attached to a device called an *electroencephalograph,* which measures differences in electrical charge (i.e., voltage) between them, a pattern of signals is obtained which can be translated into the movement of a pen over a sheet of recording paper. Several brain-wave patterns have been identified, and these have been useful for investigators studying sleep and dreaming (see Box 2-1). Presumably, the electroencephalogram (called an *EEG*) is picking up at the surface of the scalp the summated activity of thousands of neurons in the human brain.

In an intriguing series of studies, Callaway (1975) and his associates compared the EEG responses of "normals," nonschizophrenic mental patients, and schizophrenic mental patients to two different tones presented in a random order. "Normals" and nonschizophrenic patients were alike in showing very similar EEG reactions to both tones, but schizophrenics showed a markedly weaker reaction to the higher-frequency tone in the pair. This greater variability in the brain's responsiveness to stimulation among schizophrenics has, Callaway says, been observed many times. Variability in EEG reactions is not, though, a very reliable criterion to use in diagnosing schizophrenia. While schizophrenics do seem to suffer from a general difficulty in attending to external stimuli which may be reflected in EEG variability, many nonschizophrenic mental patients or "normal" nonpatients show similar variability in their EEG records (Callaway, p. 71).

The EEG, in combination with IQ tests and the Halstead-Reitan battery, is often used to diagnose children who have learning problems, such as an inability to read or a significant lag in reading ability behind same-age peers. It has been estimated that between 10 and 15 percent of children suffer from emotional or learning disorders which retard their educational development (Gaddes, 1976). Some states, like California, provide special classes in which such children can receive educational training supposedly designed to compensate for their specific impairment. While, as was indicated above, it is difficult to compose a clear definition of an abnormal EEG, some experts in this area have reported that the percentage of abnormal patterns in the EEG is related to the severity of a child's emotional problems. Chronically hyperactive children have the most abnormal EEGs, followed by those with other behavior disorders (such as extremely poor coordination and right-left discrimination), and, finally, those with disabilities specific to learning. One of the EEG patterns that is looked for are high-frequency *spikes*, or bursts of electrical activity, which appear to be more common among children with learning-behavior disabilities than among those without such disabilities (Hughes, 1976). On the other hand, Rourke (1975) reports that while brain-damaged children do seem to be slower to react to visual and auditory signals than their "normal" counterparts, the results of EEG examinations usually reveal no clear differences between groups that would be helpful to a clinician trying to arrive at a diagnosis.

Physical intervention in the brain For many years, neurosurgeons have tried to repair brain damage due to injury, strokes, and tumors and, more recently, have tried to apply these techniques to the alleviation of severe mental disorder. This procedure is called *psychosurgery*. Sweet, Ervin, and Mark (1969) reported the case of a 34-year-old engineer who had fits of uncontrollable violence about once a week during which he physically attacked and injured his wife and children. He had seen three psychiatrists over a period of seven years, but the rages continued. An EEG revealed abnormal electrical activity in the temporal lobes, which are located behind the temples of the head. The patient volunteered for a radical surgical procedure in which holes were drilled on the right and left sides of his skull and fine wires inserted into a structure called the *amygdala*, which is at the base of the brain in the vicinity of the temporal lobes. Extensive research with animals had shown the amygdala to be strongly implicated in the activation and inhibition of aggressive behavior. Some of the wires apparently struck an aggression-activating area of the amygdala because stimulation by a weak electrical current caused the patient to feel one of his fits coming on. Other wires apparently struck an aggression-inhibiting area because stimulation here caused the patient to relax and feel euphoric. Next, a much stronger electrical current was applied to the wires in the aggression-activating area, which destroyed the brain tissue at that spot. Following this, the patient was reported to have "returned to normal life and experienced no further attacks."

The amygdala is part of a set of structures lying beneath the cortex and linked together as the limbic system. "Limbus" means border in Latin, and the limbic system forms the inner border of the cerebral cortex, as can be seen in Figure 7-3. The brain apparently evolved from a swelling (called the *hindbrain*) on the end of the spinal cord which controlled basic functions such as heartbeat, breathing, digestion, sleeping, and so forth. As animals became more behaviorally complex, the midbrain and then the limbic system—which is heavily involved in motivation and emotional states—were added. The cerebral cortex, which provides the capacity for abstract thought and, in humans, language, came last. The cortex reached its greatest development in human beings and is actually folded back over the older parts of the brain. These older structures remain within us, however, as they do in other mammalian species, and they undoubtedly influence our feelings and behavior.

Brain physiology and mental disorder When damage occurs to the brain, epilepsy is likely to develop. In epilepsy, a spontaneous electrical discharge begins at some point (called a *focus*) and spreads until the entire brain is involved in a storm of uncontrolled "firing" of its neurons. Behaviorally, the epileptic has a seizure which may involve thrashing about, gnashing the teeth, crying out in pain, and losing consciousness. According to MacLean (1970), seizures which have their focus on the lower structures of the limbic system—the hippocampus in particular—

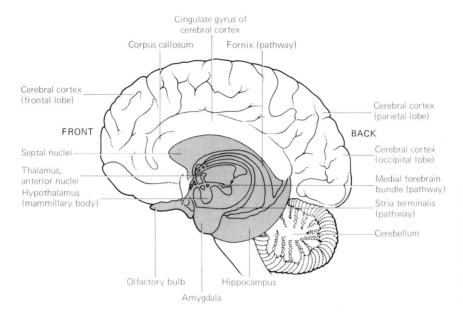

Cingulate gyrus of
cerebral cortex

Corpus callosum   Fornix (pathway)

Cerebral cortex
(frontal lobe)

Cerebral cortex
(parietal lobe)

FRONT   BACK

Cerebral cortex
(occipital lobe)

Septal nuclei

Thalamus,
anterior nuclei
Hypothalamus
(mammillary body)

Medial forebrain
bundle (pathway)

Stria terminalis
(pathway)

Cerebellum

Olfactory bulb   Hippocampus

Amygdala

FIGURE 7-3
Side view of the human
brain and limbic system
(shaded). (Modified from
C. T. Morgan and R. A.
King, *Introduction to
psychology*, 4th ed. New
York: McGraw-Hill, 1971,
p. 601.)

give rise to strong feelings of terror, strangeness, sadness, persecution, and loss of identity. Perceptual distortions and hallucinations associated with any or all of the sensory systems are also very common. All in all, the symptoms of limbic epilepsy are very similar to those exhibited by people having "bad trips" on psychedelic drugs such as *LSD* (lysergic acid diethylamide) or, for that matter, to those exhibited by patients diagnosed as paranoid schizophrenics.

MacLean believes the hippocampus is especially vulnerable to injury from a blow to the head, ingestion of toxic chemicals, or changes in the chemistry of the brain's neural transmission resulting from exposure to prolonged stress. His speculations are particularly intriguing in light of the fact that Ginsburg (1967) has studied specially bred strains of mice which are differentially vulnerable to epilepticlike seizures in response to loud, high-pitched sound. The convulsions associated with these seizures are often fatal to susceptible animals. Mice in a nonsusceptible strain were found to differ genetically from their seizure-prone counterparts. One of the two genes contributing to this difference was found to have

a specific effect on the chemistry of neural transmission in the hippocampus. Ginsburg regarded the genetic and biochemical aspects of susceptibility to audiogenic seizures as but one aspect of the more general phenomenon of vulnerability of the nervous system to stress from any source.

Stress—that is, a physically or psychologically aversive stimulus—has a direct effect on the functioning of many bodily organs, including the brain and central nervous system. Stress causes the autonomic nervous system to activate the secretion into the bloodstream of epinephrine and norepinephrine by the adrenal gland. Circulating epinephrine, as will be explained more fully in Chapter 10, increases heart rate, blood pressure, and breathing rate and, in general, prepares the organism to fight or run away. Norepinephrine, as was mentioned earlier, is an important neurotransmitter.

The concentration and activity of neurotransmitters in the brain appears to have a considerable influence on our psychological state. This can be seen dramatically in studies of the effects of psychoactive drugs, like amphetamine or "speed." Recall that the transmission of a message from one nerve to another requires that a chemical be released into the synaptic cleft separating the two. After this chemical has done its work, the synapse must be rapidly cleared so that firing will not repeat itself uncontrollably and so that the neurons will be prepared to transmit the next message which comes along. This clearing of the synapse is accomplished mainly by the reabsorbtion of the neurotransmitter by the neuron which released it. The phenomenon is called *re-uptake,* and Axelrod (1974) was awarded a Nobel prize for discovering it. The important point to be made here is that the chemical effect of amphetamine on the brain is to stimulate the release and block the reuptake of neurotransmitters, dopamine in particular. Consequently, the transmitters remain highly concentrated in the synapses, provoking the rapid, uncontrolled firing which in extreme cases is characteristic of epilepsy (Snyder, 1974, chap. 12).

Persons who have consumed large amounts of amphetamine over several days may develop amphetamine psychosis. Terrifying visual, auditory, olfactory, and even tactile hallucinations are associated with this malady. Afflicted persons may see approaching monsters, hear threatening voices, smell poison gas, and feel parasites crawling beneath their skin. They are likely to develop obsessive-compulsive behaviors, such as taking objects apart and subjecting them to minute scrutiny. Becoming paranoid, they withdraw from other people, whom they assume to be "out to get" them. Passengers looking out the windows of a bus, for example, may be perceived as a group gathered for the specific purpose of observing and menacing them. Snyder (1974, chap. 10), a professor of psychiatry and pharmacology, maintains that the symptoms of amphetamine psychosis are virtually indistinguishable from those of paranoid schizophrenia.

If amphetamine psychosis is analogous to "naturally" occurring schizophrenia, then the chemical effects of amphetamine may provide a clue as to what "goes wrong" in the brain of someone who develops schizophrenia without ever having taken any drugs. In fact, it appears that schizophrenics may suffer from an overactivity of neurotransmitters in the synapses of the neurons in certain areas of the brain.

Chlorpromazine is a drug which, in the mid-1950s, was found to be dramatically effective in alleviating the symptoms of schizophrenia. It has since been found that what chlorpromazine does is to occupy receptor sites on the neurons so that these receptors cannot be activated by neurotransmitters. Consequently, the "firing" of neurons is considerably moderated, and the schizophrenic patient often experiences relief from his or her hallucinations and delusions. Chlorpromazine is also an effective antidote to amphetamine psychosis. Snyder emphasizes that chlorpromazine does not act simply as a sedative in producing these effects. The common sedatives, such as barbiturates, are either useless for such purposes or may even worsen the symptoms of schizophrenia and amphetamine psychosis. Chlorpromazine, on the other hand, alleviates symptoms apparently because of its specific chemical action of reducing the rate of neural transmission in an "overheated" brain.

Evidence has continued to accumulate that schizophrenia is associated with an overproduction of the neurotransmitter dopamine and an excess number of dopamine receptor sites in the brain's limbic system (Iverson, 1979). Since many psychoactive drugs—such as mescaline, psilocybin, and LSD—are chemically very similar to naturally occurring neurotransmitters, their dramatic and sometimes frightening effects on the mind may be caused by their ability to occupy receptor sites intended for these neurotransmitters. One intriguing discovery has been that the brain naturally manufactures its own morphine-like substances called *endorphins* (a combination of the words "endogenous" and "morphine"). Receptor sites for these opiates exist throughout the brain and in various parts of the body (Guillemin, 1978), suggesting that they may play some role in moderating sensations of pain and so assisting the healing process. Whether or not some disruption in the manufacture or chemical action of endorphins plays a role in the development of mental disorder is a focus of considerable research and speculation.

A neurophysiological approach to psychological assessment, then, would use the EEG and laboratory analysis of body fluids in an effort to identify electrical or chemical evidence of brain malfunction. If such evidence is found, it may be possible to treat the disorder with drugs. Recent studies have even indicated that certain nutrients in the diet may be particularly effective in supplying the body with the chemical building blocks needed for the manufacture of neurotransmitters (Kolata, 1979). Diets rich in lecithin, for example, may facilitate the production of acetylcholine. Control of brain chemistry through diet would be a safer, more natural form of therapy than the administration of drugs, since practically all drugs have some undesirable side effects.

CONTROVERSIAL ISSUES IN BIOLOGICAL APPROACHES TO ASSESSMENT

One psychologist summed up his consideration of biological approaches to personality assessment by stating that "as yet, with possibly a few exceptions, they do not offer practical procedures for the personality assessment of individuals" (Sundberg, 1977, p. 151). Other experts, however, believe that many of the foregoing techniques can make a positive contribution to the accurate diagnosis of a disorder as well as to the selection of the most effective type of therapeutic intervention. This might include (1) concentrated retraining in areas where there is a perceptual or behavioral deficit, (2) the administration of psychoactive drugs, or (3) brain surgery.

As more is learned about the biological structure and chemical activity of the brain as well as the manner in which genes interact with these factors, there is likely to be a dramatic increase in the feasibility, accuracy, and effectiveness of biological approaches to assessment and therapeutic intervention. To some, the key to further progress lies in a finer distinction between diagnostic categories. Schizophrenia, for instance, is a category which includes *hebephrenia*, a reaction characterized by empty-headed giggling and rhyming of words as well as *paranoid schizophrenia*, a psychosis characterized by delusions of persecution which make the patient a real danger to other people. According to Van Pragg (1977), these subtypes of schizophrenia probably have very different underlying biochemical processes.

Ironically, it is the very possibility of attaining the kind of diagnostic and therapeutic precision which would satisfy professional critics that arouses the greatest concern among social critics of a biological approach. At the least, they argue, this theoretical orientation tends to channel our thinking toward fatalistic acceptance of biological determinism, and, at the very worst, it may pave the way toward Aldous Huxley's (1932) *Brave New World.*

Social Issues in the Controversy over the Heritability of IQ

We saw earlier that Kamin (1974) disputed the evidence for the heritability of IQ. In addition, he traced the historical origins of intelligence testing to the eugenics movement of the 1920s— which was concerned that the American Anglo-Saxon genetic heritage would be contaminated by interbreeding with "inferior" groups. Kamin charged that intelligence tests were used to set immigration quotas for and restrict the social mobility of various groups, including southern Europeans and peoples of color. He believes IQ tests continue to be used for these purposes today. One contemporary development which Kamin regards as ideologically linked with the eugenics movement is the interpretation by some academics of interracial differences in average IQ as genetically based. He and other environmentalists point to past and present social and economic disadvantages to which racial minorities have been disproportionately exposed and to which any deficit in IQ-test performance could most plausibly be attributed.

Jensen (1969, 1973) did not disregard this possibility when he put forward his hereditarian explanation for interracial differences in mean IQ, but he maintained that the range of social environments in the United States is not broad enough to account for the size of some group differences that have been observed. It was because of his belief that IQ is 80 percent inherited that Jensen was pessimistic regarding the ability of educational-enrichment programs to eradicate group differences in IQ scores.

On the other hand, if IQ has a much lower heritability, say 40 or 50 percent as suggested by some estimates, then a person's social and educational environment could have a considerable influence on his or her score. Observed IQ would then be the product of equally potent person and situation variables, and environmentalists and hereditarians could perhaps coexist more peacefully.

Jensen has already tried to explain that despite differences in overall group averages, there is substantial overlap in the variation around these averages among individuals in all groups. Thus, he says, his hereditarian hypothesis applies only to groups, and not at all to the IQs of any particular members of groups. He describes his own concept of justice as requiring "that the fact of statistical differences between racial *populations* should not be permitted to influence the treatment accorded to *individuals* of any race—in education, employment, legal justice, and political and civil rights." This, he says, "contradicts the racist philosophy that individuals of different races should be treated differently, one and all, only by reason of their racial differences" (Jensen, 1978, p. 24).

Jensen's comments notwithstanding, it is doubtful that what has become known as the *IQ controversy* will disappear in the near future.

Spokespersons for an environmentalist viewpoint will continue to attack the tests as being insensitive to individual differences in social experience and specific talents. Professional defenders of the tests will point to evidence of their high reliability and validity in predicting school achievement as well as to their usefulness in neuropsychological assessment. The latter application of the tests, however, raises the more general social issue of the dangers of mind manipulation by psychologists, psychiatrists, neurosurgeons, and government agencies.

Controversy Over Mind Manipulation

In the event that we identify a biological defect in the brain of someone with symptoms of disrupted mental functioning—symptoms like retardation, epilepsy, hyperaggressiveness, depression, or schizophrenia—how justified are we in trying to intervene at a neurophysiological level to alleviate the symptoms? The history of such attempts has not been particularly reassuring regarding our ability to make them either prudently or with the welfare of the client uppermost in mind.

In the 1930s, a Portuguese neurologist named Egas Moniz applied results derived from surgery performed primarily on monkeys and dogs to the invention of a new technique for calming highly excitable mental patients. Called *prefrontal lobotomy*, the technique involved surgical detachment of the frontal lobes of the cortex from the rest of the brain. It did calm most patients, but it also had unpleasant side effects, sometimes transforming them into psychologically inert "vegetables" (Valenstein, 1974).

With the advent, in the 1940s, of *electroconvulsive shock therapy* (which involves inducing an epilepticlike seizure by passing a strong electrical current between electrodes placed on either side of the head), lobotomies began to decline in popularity among psychiatrists. Shock treatment often produced the same calming effects on excited patients without inflicting any obvious permanent physical damage to the brain. Electroconvulsive shock (often abbreviated ECT) was also found to be useful in relieving severe depression.

In the 1950s, the discovery of psychoactive drugs resulted in the virtual abandonment of lobotomy *and* the sharp curtailment of ECT (which, it was found, did inflict some physical damage to the brain after all). More recently, efforts have been made to perform extremely delicate operations on specific brain structures in the hope of alleviating mental disorder and maladaptive behavior. This procedure was discussed earlier in this chapter.

Whether or not the foregoing improvements are really any more effective or humane than lobotomy is a matter of some controversy. In a popularized account of what goes on in a mental hospital from the patient's point of view, Kesey (1962) graphically portrayed the horrifying consequences of an insensitive application of all of these techniques within an institution concerned far more about its own efficient functioning than about the mental and physical well-being of its inmates. This book, *One Flew Over the Cuckoo's Nest*, was later made into an Academy-Award–winning motion picture. Other popularized accounts describe individual cases in which ECT had detrimental, identity-destroying effects on personality (Roueche, 1974). Academics have lent support to such criticisms by questioning the quality of the research and theory on which radical techniques like psychosurgery are based (Valenstein, 1974). They have also disputed whether cases in which psychosurgery was actually attempted really had the long-term beneficial effects claimed by the neurosurgeons who performed these operations. In a follow-up of the

A scene from the play *One Flew Over The Cuckoo's Nest*, which presents an unflattering picture of the quality of care offered in mental hospitals. The inmate wheeling the cart has just been horrified by the discovery that a friend, a dangerous troublemaker in the opinion of the staff, has been lobotomized. (Bettmann Archive)

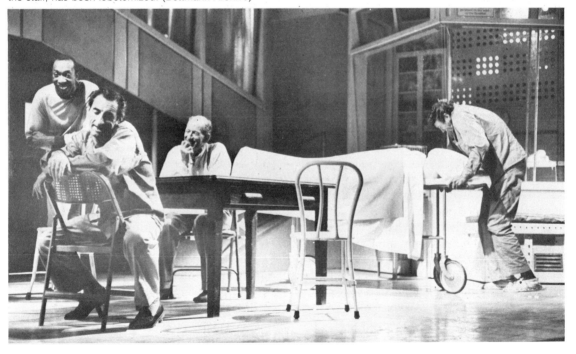

case of the 34-year-old man reported by Sweet, Ervin, and Mark (1969), for instance, Chorover (1974) revealed that the patient was psychologically incapable of resuming work as an engineer, that within a few months he was hallucinating and delusional, and that he was periodically rehospitalized in the years following the operation suffering from paranoid fears that his brain was being destroyed by remote control.

In early 1979, the American Broadcasting Company produced a televised documentary purporting to show how, over two decades, the Central Intelligence Agency recruited psychiatrists, psychologists, and others for the purpose of testing psychoactive drugs and ECT on unsuspecting citizens and mental patients. Allegedly, they wanted to see whether these treatments could induce mental breakdown, susceptibility to persuasion, or forgetting of recent or past memory. At least one person, it was said, died from these experiments. A chemist—married and the father of three children—was given LSD by the CIA's chief psychologist. The victim lapsed into a severe depression and committed suicide by throwing himself from a hotel window (ABC News, 1979).

This documentary urgently raises the question of how much potential for abuse lies in the development of increasingly sophisticated techniques for biological assessment and intervention. As was noted in Chapter 4, the Soviet Union has employed these techniques in an effort to control the "disputative behavior" of dissidents.

CONCLUDING COMMENTS ON BIOLOGICAL ASSESSMENT

In the end, the controversies surrounding contemporary biological approaches to the study of personality are reminiscent of the complaints directed against the science of phrenology nearly two centuries ago. There is a very real difference between these eras, however. Phrenology, because it was based on an erroneous theory of how the brain instigated personality and behavior, was doomed as a science from the very start. The contemporary approaches reviewed in this chapter, on the other hand, have shown considerable promise of being on the right theoretical track in attempting to relate personality to the genetic and biochemical aspects of bodily functioning.

There can be little doubt that biological approaches are capable of contributing significantly to our understanding of the origins and workings of the human personality and to the success of our efforts to relieve mental distress. If we define a "good" outcome in this context as one which permits as many people as possible to live reasonably self-sufficient and productive lives outside of custodial institutions, then biological approaches have a very great potential for accomplishing good things—particularly for the more severely mentally disturbed, who are, for the most part, unapproachable by other therapeutic techniques. As has been cautioned repeatedly in this chapter, however, biological approaches will realize their potential for doing "good" only if they are applied cautiously and with the well-being of the patient uppermost in mind. Cox (1975) urges therapists to prescribe drug medications only when necessary and, in these situations, to do their best to structure the course of therapy so the drugs can be discontinued as soon as possible. Long-term medication may sometimes be necessary, but the overall goal should be to maximize the number of patients regaining complete self-sufficiency.

It must be acknowledged that the major companies which produce and market therapeutic psychoactive drugs have had an inadvertent but, nonetheless, direct involvement in the growth of the worldwide epidemic of drug abuse. A technology, once invented, tends to proliferate. As past world wars have painfully taught us, technologies can be put to destructive, inhumane purposes as well as to productive, life-promoting ones. Consequently, psychosurgery and other techniques for intervening in the functioning of the human brain must be closely monitored in the years ahead. For better or worse, however, these technologies exist today and will continue to increase in sophistication in the future (Snibbe, 1975). What remains to be seen is whether we and the institutions we support have the wisdom and the willpower to enforce their humanistic application.

SUMMARY

1 The promise of all biological approaches to personality assessment is that by relating personality to some quantifiable biological characteristic, greater precision of measurement will be attained, permitting more reliable assessment and opening the way to more effective therapeutic intervention via medical techniques. The problems associated with these approaches are the very real danger of unconscious experimenter bias and the ethical issues raised by techniques which are based on biological determinism.

2 Sheldon reported strong associations between a person's ectomorphic, mesomorphic, or endomorphic physique and his or her cerebrotonic, somatotonic, or viscerotonic personality, respectively. He believed the relationship between physique and temperament was caused by underlying genetic factors. Because of the possibility of unconscious bias in Sheldon's observations, however, psychologists have tended to disregard his work.

3 Genes occur in pairs, with one member of the pair being contributed by the mother and the other by the father. If the genes in a pair control different traits, it will be the trait controlled by the dominant gene which is expressed. The trait controlled by the recessive gene will be suppressed, but it may eventually be expressed if the individual carrying it mates and produces offspring with someone who also carries that recessive gene. Assuming that a single gene pair controls expression of this trait, about one-quarter of the offspring should show the recessive characteristic. Most human characteristics are controlled by an interaction of several genes in different pairs. Because they are polygenic, human traits are seldom exhibited in all-or-none fashion and are, instead, expressed in continuously varying degrees. They are also more susceptible to environmental influence than are traits controlled by single genes.

4 Because human mating behavior cannot be experimentally manipulated, the degree of genetic influence on traits is studied by comparing the degree of concordance among identical versus fraternal twin pairs or by comparing the concordance of adoptive children with their biological or adoptive parents. In the case of IQ, such comparisons

point to the existence of a hereditary factor, though they also indicate that people whose environments are most alike are most similar in IQ. A charge of biased data gathering has been leveled against the principal researcher in this area, but even if his data are disregarded, evidence of a hereditary factor remains. The latter evidence has also been questioned, but it is concluded that *both* heredity and environment appear to have a significant effect on IQ. The trait of extraversion also seems to have some degree of heritability.

5   Using similar research techniques, investigators have found clear indications that schizophrenia is, to some extent, hereditary. Many researchers believe that what is inherited in schizophrenia is a potential for developing the disorder which is activated by environmental stress. Some schizophrenic reactions which appear suddenly following severe stress are thought to be environmentally produced with little or no genetic involvement. The likelihood of recovery is much higher for the latter cases than for the ones in which genetic predisposition is suspected.

6   An important area of psychological assessment is that concerned with identifying the nature and causes of disruptions of the normal functioning of the brain and central nervous system. Neuropsychological tests like the Halstead-Reitan battery require the clinician to derive inferences regarding the patient's neurological state from the latter's performance on paper-and-pencil tests and simple behavioral tasks. Neurophysiological approaches analyze body fluids for the presence or absence of chemical derivatives of neurotransmitters or use x-ray or EEG techniques to observe the brain's structure and functioning. The results of these examinations may be used to recommend medication or special training to the patient in order to overcome deficits. In extreme cases, psychosurgery may be attempted. There is evidence that mental disorders such as epilepsy or schizophrenia may be related to neurochemical changes in brain function.

7   Many controversies surround biological approaches to psychological assessment. Some professionals argue that these techniques are not sufficiently well developed for individual assessment, while others regard them as more than adequate for such purposes. Social critics believe this theoretical orientation channels our thinking toward fatalistic acceptance of biological determinism and may result in unjust, discriminatory, and hurtful applications. Professionals who endorse these techniques maintain that they can be applied humanely and, with further research and development, offer the best long-term hope for treatment of the most severe forms of psychological disturbance.

TERMS TO KNOW

somatotype

genes

monozygotic twins

heritability

schizophrenia

Halstead-Reitan Neuropsychological
    Test Battery

neurotransmitter

electroencephalogram

limbic system

lobotomy

8

BEHAVIORAL APPROACHES TO ASSESSMENT AND INTERVENTION

ISSUES TO CONSIDER

1 What is meant by a "functional analysis" of behavior, and how is it designed to avoid the diagnostic problems associated with a medical model of mental illness?
2 In what ways are behavior therapies based on classical conditioning different from those based on operant conditioning?
3 How are cognitive approaches to behavior modification derived from the ideas of vicarious learning and self-reinforcement put forward by social learning theory?

You will recall that in Chapter 4, the origins of the environmentalist tradition in psychology were traced to materialist philosophy. Materialism asserted that living organisms are regulated by the same physical and chemical processes that control nonliving systems. Materialists, in other words, denied that it is necessary to attribute any special properties—such as consciousness—to living organisms in order to account for their behavior. This philosophical position was compatible with the belief of early behavioral psychologists that with the exception of a few inherited characteristics like fear and other reflexive reactions, behavior is learned in and controlled by an individual's physical and social environment.

John B. Watson's creation and removal of phobic reactions in infants, described in Chapter 4, is an example of a purely behavioral approach to psychology. Little Albert, you may remember, learned to fear a white rat as a result of the animal's presence being associated with a loud, startling noise. Albert's fear then generalized to some extent, so that he came to be frightened of other furry or fuzzy objects, particularly animals. An associate of Watson's, Mary Cover Jones, successfully removed a previously established fear of animals and other furry objects from another infant named Peter. Her primary technique for accomplishing this was to associate the presence of an animal (a rabbit) with a pleasurable stimulus (food), which evoked feelings incompatible with fear. This technique anticipated a modern therapeutic procedure for removing phobias known as *counterconditioning* or *desensitization*.

The point being made here is that the creation and removal of phobias in Little Albert and Peter was accomplished by externally imposed events. It was not necessary to refer to the occurrence of conscious or unconscious conflicts within Albert's mind in order to explain the origins of his phobia, and it was not necessary for Peter to achieve psychoanalytic insight into the origins of his neurosis for the phobia to be removed. All that was needed to understand these processes was the empirically derived knowledge of how environmental events affect learning and, hence, behavior. Jones (1974, p. 582) could still recall, half a century later, the excitement with which she and her fellow students greeted Watson's work: "It shook the foundations of traditional European-bred psychology, and we welcomed it. This was in 1919; it pointed the way from armchair psychology to action and reform and was therefore hailed as a panacea."

As was explained in Chapter 4, there were several social, historical, and scientific reasons why environmentalism achieved widespread acceptance in the United States and the Soviet Union. One of these reasons, in America at least, was a growing discomfort with the medical model of mental illness which was associated with the European tradition in psychology (see Chapter 5). This tradition, and the system of diagnostic classification it fostered, regards disordered behavior as a superficial symptom of some disease acting within the mind of the disturbed individual. Labels like "neurotic" or "psychotic" are attached to the symptoms in an effort to describe the underlying ailment. Many environmentalists objected, however, that it is the individual's disorderly behavior, and not some pathological internal state, which *is* the disease. Szasz (1970) even argued that the placement of diagnostic labels on deviant behavior is analogous to the process by which, in medieval times, social misfits were denounced as witches. Just as the witch was forced (through torture) to "confess" and then burned at the stake to "save" his or her soul, the person labeled *psychologically sick* may be compelled to accept involuntary confinement in a mental hospital and occasionally unpleasant therapeutic treatment such as electroconvulsive shock.

A study by Langer and Abelson (1974) illustrates the possibilities for misdiagnosis of behavior. The subjects were twenty-one clinical psy-

An example of the crude sorts of "treatments" applied to mental patients in the nineteenth century. The idea was to provide a physical shock to the patient's mind and body which might bring him or her back into closer touch with reality. (The Bettmann Archive)

chologists on the faculty of a department which had a strong behaviorist orientation and nineteen psychologists and psychiatrists affiliated with departments having a somewhat psychoanalytic orientation in their clinical programs. All of these clinicians viewed a videotaped interview of a young man conducted by a bearded, professorial-looking older man. The interview contained a great many details of the young man's life, including his conflicts with bureaucratic authorities when he was working with a youth organization and during an unsuccessful attempt to start his own business. To ten of the behaviorally oriented and ten of the analytically oriented clinicians, the young man was identified as a job applicant; to the remaining clinicians in each group, he was identified as a mental patient. All clinicians were asked to evaluate the interviewee for the degree to which he seemed socially and emotionally adjusted.

It was found that the behaviorists regarded the young man as moderately well adjusted regardless of whether he was labeled a *job applicant* or a *mental patient*. Among the analyst types, however, the interviewee was regarded as moderately well adjusted in the former condition but as fairly maladjusted in the latter. Behavioral clinicians in both the "Job Applicant" and "Mental Patient" conditions perceived the young man as realistic and relatively bright, though unassertive. Analytic clinicians viewing a job applicant also perceived him as realistic and fairly bright, but when the young man was labeled a "mental patient" he was seen as tormented by anxieties about his mental and social abilities, sexual adequacy, and repressed aggressive impulses.

Langer and Abelson's preferred interpretation of these results was that the behaviorists ignored the clinical label attached to the mental patient and concentrated on what he was actually doing and saying in the interview setting. The analytical clinicians, on the other hand, were influenced by their acceptance of the medical model of mental illness to perceive certain behavior as a symptom of underlying disease when it was exhibited by a mental patient but interpreted precisely the same behavior as "normal" when displayed by a job applicant.

The authors speculated on the self-fulfilling prophecies which may be set in motion when an individual enters an analytically oriented therapist's office seeking treatment. Having labeled the individual as a *patient*, the therapist expects the client to exhibit symptoms of disturbance and so may interpret behavior—which in any other context would appear "normal"—in a manner which confirms the diagnostic hypothesis.

Behavior therapists, on the other hand, would presumably be less likely to commit such diagnostic errors because they would be concerned only with identifying and treating behavior that was clearly socially maladaptive. They would not be interested in exploring the hidden psychological dynamics which their analytic counterparts assume to underlie all symptoms. If a client exhibited no seriously maladaptive behavior, then he or she would be perceived by behavior therapists as reasonably well adjusted regardless of whether or not this person was labeled a "mental patient."

For theorists in the environmentalist tradition, the terms "personality" and "behavior" are somewhat synonymous. Consequently, personality assessment and therapy are even more closely associated with one another in this field of psychology than they are in the psychoanalytic or dispositional ones. A change in behavior represents, to a greater or lesser degree, a change in an individual's personality, and assessment of personality disorder amounts to identifying those behaviors that are maladaptive sources of frustration and conflict. Therapy consists of implementing a retraining procedure designed to replace the maladaptive behavior with adaptive behavior. Therapy ends when this goal is achieved, and there is no need to interpret behavior as a manifestation of internal psychodynamics or to prolong therapy in an attempt to "cure" some supposed mental disease.

Behaviorally oriented clinicians are not really so mechanistic in their approach to personality assessment and therapy as the preceding paragraph and our earlier discussion of materialist philosophy might seem to imply. In recent years, they have become more and more willing to include mental events—such as expectations, hypotheses, and vicarious learning—in their analysis of human personality. These developments were indicated in Chapter 4 and will be further explored here.

The present chapter begins by showing how clinicians in the behaviorist tradition identify the major environmental contingencies which maintain an individual's behavior. This process may involve interviews, direct observation, and other techniques; it is called a *functional analysis*. Next we will examine procedures for inducing behavior change based on *classical* (Pavlovian)

conditioning, operant conditioning, modeling and imitation, and cognitive self-training. A behavioral alternative to the psychiatric system of diagnostic classification will then be presented. The chapter concludes with a detailed discussion of the limitations of behavioral approaches, including the permanence and generalizability of therapeutic alterations in behavior and various ethical and social criticisms which have been raised against these techniques.

DEVELOPMENT OF A FUNCTIONAL ANALYSIS OF BEHAVIOR

The Behaviorally Oriented Interview

As in the more traditional clinical settings (see Chapter 5), the patient or client typically arrives at a behavior-therapist's office because of some complaint or problem in living. It is the task of the therapist to establish rapport with the client and create an atmosphere of trust in which the complaint can be freely and fully revealed and explored.

For the behavior therapist, complaints can be placed in one of three categories—namely, actions which are excessive, deficient, or inappropriate (Bijou and Peterson, 1971, pp. 64–65). The first category includes actions which have some normal frequency of occurrence but have been carried to extremes by a particular individual; examples would be the hyperactive child or the adult who constantly finds himself or herself embroiled in conflict and hostile interactions with others. The second category refers to behavior that falls *below* a normal frequency of occurrence; examples here would be underachievement in school or shyness and social withdrawal. Finally, inappropriate behavior consists of behavior that is neither excessive nor deficient but is simply exhibited at the wrong time and place; an example would be the public discharge of toilet functions.

The task for the behaviorally oriented interviewer, then, is to make some initial categorization of the complaint and to note areas in which the client's behavior seems appropriate and expressed to a normal degree (these would be called the client's behavioral *assets*). Next, following a procedure recommended by Kanfer and Saslow (1969), the therapist should clarify the specific situations in which problem behavior occurs and who it is in the client's life who objects to this behavior; if the client is a child, the latter individuals are likely to be her or his parents.

Kanfer and Saslow also recommend that a history of the client be taken, with a particular emphasis on biological, sociological, or behavioral changes which may be pertinent to the present complaint. There should be a listing of the major material and social positive and negative reinforcers to which the client is responsive and an analysis of the client's capacity for self-control or self-administration of reward or punishment for appropriate or inappropriate behavior, respectively. The impact on the client of his or her social relationships and the norms upheld by the various social groups to which he or she belongs should also be evaluated. Meyer, Liddell, and Lyons (1978) suggest that inquiries into the history of a client's complaint be divided into those which are concerned with relatively recent events and ongoing conditions and those which are concerned with the client's previous experiences.

A behavior therapist may administer one or more questionnaires for the purpose of describing, in a more structured manner, the client's goals, fears, motivations, and conflicts. Some of the inventories available include a Reinforcement Survey Schedule (Cautela & Kastenbaum, 1967), a Fear Survey Schedule (Wolpe & Lang, 1969), and scales for measuring assertiveness (Rathus, 1973) and marital discord (Stuart & Stuart, 1972).

Often a behavior therapist will want to make some direct observation of the behavior which resulted in the client's complaint. A few techniques for accomplishing this are described below.

Techniques for Observing Behavior

The simplest technique for observing behavior is to have the client make a record of the frequency of occurrence of an undesirable act. Ciminero, Nelson, and Lipinski (1978) comment that this procedure, called *event sampling*, is most useful when the act to be recorded is clearly distinct from other behavior, is of short duration, and is relatively infrequent. Examples are cursing, fingernail biting, smoking, or eating between meals.

The client may wear a mechanical counting device (similar to a golf-stroke counter) on his or her wrist which permits behavior to be recorded at the touch of a button. Alternatively, the client may write the time and day of occurrence of a target behavior on a card known as a *behavior diary*. The events immediately preceding and following the undesirable act may also be entered on the card so as to provide clues as to the stimulus conditions which elicit it and the reinforcing consequences which maintain it. More than two centuries ago, Benjamin Franklin (1840, chap. 6) kept such a diary of his undesirable social behavior, like engaging in malicious gossip or showing a lack of consideration for others. He used the diary as an index by which he could measure his success in eliminating these acts from his repertory.

When the behavior to be observed is less easily defined and recorded than the discrete acts discussed above, the therapist may want to *create* a situation in which the response tendency is likely to be elicited. This technique has been used most extensively in the study of anxiety. People fearful of dogs, for example, can be exposed to an animal placed at varying distances from themselves and asked to indicate how anxious they feel and whether or not they would be able to approach the animal more closely. This type of situation is often called a *Behavioral Avoidance Test*, or BAT (Borkovec & Craighead, 1971).

Especially when the client is a child and unable to make a reliable count or self-report of acts and feelings, the therapist may want to observe behavior in a natural setting. Jones, Reid, and Patterson (1975) have developed a Behavioral Coding System, or BCS, which is an excellent example of this technique. Observers might be present in a child's home environment on several days during the late afternoon, just prior to dinner time. (Jones et al. comment that this is the time of day which seems to reveal most clearly any behavioral problems in a family's pattern of interactions.) Suppose the client is a young boy who has been referred for therapy because of hyperaggressiveness toward girl classmates at school. The behavior of the client and members of his family in the home environment might be classified as follows: playing either alone or with others (PL); performing physical acts with a negative emotional content, such as hitting or inflicting pain (PN); humiliating with the intention of embarrassing (HU); teasing (TE); crying (CR): and issuing a negative command with a threat of aversive consequences if compliance is not immediate (CN).

The observer records the behavior of the client as well as behavior directed toward the client by other family members at six-second intervals during a five-minute period. Two of these observation periods are included on each afternoon of a given week. Imagine that the boy is peacefully playing with some toys (PL) when his sister begins teasing him (TE). He hits his sister (PN), who cries (CR) and attracts the attention of the mother, who threatens the boy with a spanking if he does not leave his sister alone (CN). The mother also tells the boy that he will never amount to any good if he cannot find more constructive ways to spend his time (HU). From a record such as this, we may gain some clues to the way this boy perceives other girls similar to his sister at school and why he behaves aggressively toward them. Perhaps, for instance, he perceives them as aversive stimuli and, by his aggression, is seeking to remove them from his presence.

Jones et al. use twenty-eight categories for coding behavior, and they have developed a standardized form on which observations can be recorded. A copy of this form, which shows the coding categories, is shown in Table 8-1. The authors report that interrater reliabilities are high and that the validity of the coding has been confirmed by independent measures of the same behavior that the coders are supposed to be rating.

Completion of the Functional Analysis and Preparation for Treatment

Goldfried and Sprafkin (1974) describe the goal of assessment as the development of what they called an *SORC model* of a client's maladaptive behavior. That is, the stimulus conditions which usually precede it (S), the cognitive, emotional, or other organismic factors which accompany it (O), what the client does in response to these eliciting conditions (R), and the reinforcing consequences which may serve to maintain the behavior (C). Evans and Nelson (1977) indicated how the SORC model might be applied to the analysis and treatment of excessive social isolation and withdrawal in children.

Before anything else, of course, a therapist in the behaviorist tradition would want to have a clear operational definition of the disorder to be treated. Teachers' nominations might be acceptable as a preliminary indication of which children were the most socially isolated and withdrawn, but direct observation might be undertaken so as to verify this initial categorization. O'Connor (1972), for example, found that in a series of thirty-two randomly chosen observation periods, "normal" children were found to be engaged in an average of 9.1 social interactions. Withdrawn children were then defined as those who were observed to have 5 or fewer interactions with others.

An example of a stimulus condition which might contribute to the social isolation of children in the latter group could be a lack of opportunity for social interaction. Perhaps a child's neighborhood contains no other children her or his age. A therapeutic remedy in this case might consist of the parents inviting a child's

TABLE 8-1 Sample scoring sheet for the behavioral coding system

Family Number_____

ID Number_____

BEHAVIOR CODING SHEET

Phase_____

Subject _____ Observer _____ Date _____ No._____

AP	Approval	HU	Humiliate	PP	Positive physical
AT	Attention	IG	Ignore		contact
CM	Command	LA	Laugh	RC	Receive
CN	Command	NC	Noncompliance	SS	Self-stimulation
	(negative)	NE	Negativism	TA	Talk
CO	Compliance	NO	Normative	TE	Tease
CR	Cry	NR	No response	TH	Touching,
DI	Disapproval	PL	Play		handling
DP	Dependency	PN	Negative physical	WH	Whine
DS	Destructiveness		contact	WK	Work
HR	High rate			YE	Yell

1				
2				
. . .				
10				

Source: Jones, Reid, & Patterson, 1975.

schoolmates to their home and offering to provide transportation. An example of an organismic factor in social isolation might be a child's low reinforcement value to peers because of status-related characteristics such as physical appearance. Therapy for a "fat kid" who was rejected for his or her obesity could involve a weight-reduction program. When status-related characteristics are impossible to change directly, such as membership in an ethnic out-group, teachers or other adult role models may try to increase the reinforcement value of a child by expressing public praise for the child's worthy deeds and abilities or by placing the child in charge of distributing treats or other valued reinforcers.

Alternatively, it could be the child's pattern of responding which is the primary cause of his or her social isolation. If social skills are deficient, children may be shown examples of positive social interaction among peers as a means of teaching them what types of behavior are most likely to lead to mutually reinforcing encounters with others (O'Connor, 1972; Rose, 1972). Then again, the child may find some reinforcing consequence in withdrawing from others—perhaps, for example, a reduction in anxiety aroused by social interaction. In this case, the optimum therapeutic strategy might be to make a teacher's material or social reinforcement of the child contingent upon the initiation of social interaction with peers (Reynolds & Risley, 1968).

In summary, the goal of a functional analysis of behavior such as social withdrawal is to determine the major factors which serve to instigate it. These factors could reside in the stimulus conditions which precede the behavior, the organismic reinforcement value of the individual client, inappropriate responses in the client's repertory, or some reinforcing consequence that serves to maintain a seemingly maladaptive behavior pattern. The outcome of such an analysis should suggest the most effective therapeutic procedure. Since, in a behavioral approach, therapy is closely linked with assessment, we will next examine the therapeutic techniques which are most commonly applied.

METHODS OF BEHAVIOR MODIFICATION

The techniques employed by behavior therapists may conveniently be placed in three broad categories: (1) those conceptually related to classical conditioning, (2) those based on operant conditioning, and (3) those derived from the notion of vicarious learning. We will discuss each category in turn.

Behavior Therapies Based on Classical Conditioning

Sometimes people have an unreasonable fear of certain objects or situations, while on other occasions they are troubled by having too strong an *attraction* toward another object or person. Many of our emotional reactions to objects, situations, or people can be assumed to have arisen through their association with "uncondi-

Social isolation can result from many different causes. A behavior therapist would attempt to identify which cause was the most important and then modify the person's behavior so as to encourage social interaction or to increase the individual's attractiveness to others. (Bob Combs/Photo Researchers)

tioned stimuli," such as food or pain, which evoked pleasurable or unpleasurable feeling-states. If the emotional reactions to which previously neutral stimuli have been conditioned turn out to be undesirable ones, the application of some sort of reconditioning procedure may succeed in modifying them. *Desensitization procedures* seek to reduce debilitating fears, while *aversion therapies* seek to eliminate maladaptive attractions.

Systematic desensitization Joseph Wolpe is a psychiatrist who was trained in traditional Freudian analysis but later became convinced that neurotic behavior is a consequence of learning specific approach-avoidance conflicts in the course of interacting with one's environment. He speculated that successful treatment of such conflicts would, in most cases, involve removal of the internal anxiety or fear reactions which activated the avoidance response. Wolpe's procedure for eliminating such fears, called *reciprocal inhibition*, or *systematic desensitization*, can be described in terms of Pavlov's classical-conditioning paradigm.

Suppose a college student has a fear of speaking in public. Conceivably, such a fear could have originated in childhood, when the individual was spanked for saying "naughty things." Whatever the originating conditions were, the student experiences an intense state of fear whenever he or she is called upon to speak in public, and the emotional reaction invariably disrupts this person's speaking performance.

The initial phase of the therapeutic procedure would consist of establishing with the client a hierarchy of imagined scenes, each of them evoking more anxiety about public speaking than the one preceding it. The first scene might be reading about speeches to be given in a particular course while resting comfortably alone in a quiet room. A more anxiety-arousing vision might be watching while another student gives a speech in the same course a week before the client's scheduled presentation. Walking to the classroom on the day of the speech and actually presenting the speech before an audience would be the most anxiety-arousing scene in the hierarchy.

The client is then trained in a highly detailed procedure for relaxing all the major muscle groups of his or her body. This is generally accomplished while the client is seated comfortably in a deeply cushioned recliner chair. Now the first scene in the anxiety hierarchy is recalled, and the client is asked to visualize it vividly for about fifteen seconds while maintaining the relaxed state. If this is successfully accomplished, the next higher scene in the hierarchy is visualized, then the next, and so on. When the client begins to experience anxiety, he or she signals to

the therapist and the procedure is stopped until relaxation is regained or perhaps even terminated for that session. Eventually, the client will be able to imagine even the most anxiety-provoking scene in the hierarchy while maintaining a relaxed state.

A description of this procedure in classical-conditioning terms can be schematically portrayed as follows. Initially, the objectively neutral stimulus of imagining oneself in a public-speaking situation arouses an emotional reaction of fear. The desensitization procedure associates imagining a public-speaking situation with an internal state incompatible with fear, namely relaxation. After this new association is sufficiently well established through repeated rehearsals, the old association with fear is first weakened, then broken.

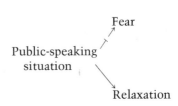

In a classic investigation of the relative effectiveness of different therapeutic approaches, Paul (1966) provided one group of students suffering from public-speaking anxiety with the desensitization treatment described above. A second group received traditional *psychodynamic*, or insight-oriented, treatment from a clinical psychologist. A third group was given an ineffective tranquilizer (*placebo*) and some training which was falsely alleged to have been designed to help them handle stress. A fourth group was left untreated for an equivalent time period. Public-speaking anxiety was assessed before and after training by means of direct observation in a genuine public-speaking situation and by means of physiological measures of arousal. It was found that the desensitization therapy was clearly more effective in reducing scores on behavioral and physiological measures of anxiety than was either insight therapy or the placebo treatment. The latter treatments did not differ in effectiveness, but each produced a significantly greater reduction in anxiety than did the control treatment.

Nay (1976, pp. 262–273) commented that controversy exists regarding whether the relaxation training is really necessary for the success of behavior therapy and whether· a role-playing procedure, involving an "acting out" of phobic behavior, would be therapeutically superior to the anxiety hierarchy of imaginary scenes. Some investigators have even reversed the hierarchy and begun the procedure by asking clients to visualize the most intense anxiety-arousing scenes they can think of. These terminal-presentation techniques are often called *flooding* (Rachman, 1968) or *implosion* (Stampfl & Levis, 1967).

Aversion therapy Unlike desensitization, the goal of aversion therapy is to build in unpleasant emotional reactions rather than remove them. Sometimes people are attracted to things that they or others who know them feel they would be better off without. The alcoholic or the compulsive overeater, for example, would have better prospects for a healthy life if he or she were not so strongly attracted to liquor or food, respectively. The male fetishist who experiences sexual arousal when handling or wearing feminine undergarments, or the person who has strong homosexual impulses, may find these feelings disturbing and a source of difficulty in interpersonal relations. The process by which aversion therapy would seek to remove such inappropriate emotional reactions will be illustrated using a large-scale program for the treatment of alcoholism (Lemere and Voegtlin, 1970).

More than 4000 alcoholics were injected with emetine hydrochloride, a drug which induces nausea and vomiting, shortly before drinking an alcoholic beverage. The drink was first smelled deeply and swished around in the mouth before being swallowed. The drinking procedure was repeated twice; by the second presentation of the beverage, the client was feeling nauseated and preparing to vomit. Generally, six thirty-minute sessions of this sort were conducted on alternate days. The procedure was ended when the mere sight of alcohol (without the drug's being administered) provoked nausea and vomiting in the client. Typically, however, two to four booster treatments were administered at various times following termination of the aversive therapy. Follow-up studies conducted over a thirteen-year period showed that 60 percent remained totally abstinent for ten or more years. The number of booster treatments a client took had a significant effect on abstinence during the first year. Those who took two or more booster treatments were almost unanimously abstinent, while those who took none or only one booster treatment were much less likely to remain abstinent.

A criticism of the foregoing study has been that we do not know what percentage of these apparently highly motivated clients could have remained abstinent from alcohol for a ten-year period *without* having undergone aversion therapy. The absence of an untreated control group in this study leaves us in doubt as to the base rate of spontaneous remission against which the success of the therapeutic intervention ought to be measured (Eysenck, 1970). Even if this comparison could be made and indicated a significantly greater rate of cure among alcoholics given aversion therapy, the possibility of a placebo effect would remain. That is, perhaps any form of special attention given the alcoholics would have helped them to remain steadfast in their resolve to stop drinking.

Such criticisms notwithstanding, reviews by Bandura (1969) and Nay (1976) suggest that aversion therapy does have some genuine psychological impact above and beyond placebo effects. Using procedures similar to those employed with alcoholics, male fetishists have been trained to

Alcoholism is an addiction which has been successfully treated with behavioral methods. In aversion therapy, an unpleasant feeling state is associated with taking a drink, with the goal being to eliminate the urge to consume alcohol. (Charles Gatewood)

al reaction. The therapist now proceeds to associate an unpleasant emotional state, such as nausea, with seeing and tasting the beverage. When the new association becomes well-established through repeated rehearsals, the old emotional reaction of pleasure is either weakened or broken altogether.

develop aversive emotional reactions to women's stockings and girdles (Clark, 1963) and male homosexuals to pictures of nude men (Freund, 1960). Sometimes electric shocks are substituted for the nausea-inducing agents as aversive stimuli (Gelder & Marks, 1969). Techniques of aversion therapy are often employed in clinics designed to help people stop smoking or lose weight.

As in the case of systematic desensitization, the technique of aversion therapy can be represented using classical-conditioning diagrams. Initially, an objectively neutral stimulus, such as an alcoholic beverage, elicits a pleasurable emotion-

Behavior Therapies Based on Operant Conditioning

In addition to techniques involving a simple association of pleasurable or unpleasurable sensations with real or imagined environmental stimuli, behavior therapists have at their disposal a variety of interventions based on operant conditioning. These procedures can be subdivided into those which provide direct material or physical reinforcement for the overt behavior of a client and those which involve a more subtle conditioning of physiological processes in a procedure known as *biofeedback*.

Direct reinforcement Direct reinforcement of behavior may include presenting a positive reinforcer as a reward for desirable acts as well as presenting a negative reinforcer as a punishment for undesirable acts. An example of the latter approach is provided by Merbaum (1973), who taught the mother of a severely self-destructive child how to punish the child's face beating by administering electric shock. Prior to treatment, the boy (named Andy) had a bruised and badly swollen face as a result of self-administered beatings. It should be emphasized that the behavior therapist administered electric shock only as a last resort, in an effort to suppress Andy's self-destructiveness before he inflicted serious injury on himself. Variously diagnosed as autistic, schizophrenic, or brain-damaged, Andy had been treated unsuccessfully using more traditional approaches. The behavior therapy consisted of waiting until Andy began to hit himself and then shocking the boy with an electric cattle prod while shouting "No!" Andy's schoolteacher and mother were equipped with prods and taught to follow this procedure. After receiving seventeen shocks from his teacher and twenty-five from his mother, Andy's masochistic behavior was reduced to a very low frequency of occurrence. When it did occur, his mother reported, a loud "No!" was sufficient to stop it.

The foregoing case was obviously an extreme one which may have necessitated an extremely punitive conditioning procedure. More commonly, the punishment consists of a *time-out*, or placement of the child in a room without toys, other people, or any other source of pleasurable stimulation. You may recall the case study of Dicky from Chapter 4 in which time-outs were used to punish temper tantrums (see Box 4-1). Dicky as well as less disturbed children who throw such fits may be reinforced by the attention they receive from adults as a consequence. Even when the attention takes the form of a spanking, it may be perceived by the child as preferable to being ignored; consequently, tantrum throwing is maintained. Making time-out contingent upon tantrum throwing causes the child to experience even greater deprivation of attention as a consequence of the tantrum than he or she had been experiencing beforehand. If release from the time-out is made contingent on cessation of the tantrum, not only will the objectionable behavior be extinguished, but the learning of prosocial alternatives will be encour-

aged. Lovaas and his associates have found these procedures to be effective in the treatment of autistic children (Lovaas, Freitag, Gold, & Kassorla, 1965).

On the more positive side of the reinforcement spectrum, Allen, Hart, Buell, Harris, and Wolf (1964) described their successful treatment of a 4-year-old girl, named Ann, who suffered from social isolation. A functional analysis indicated that Ann's withdrawal from interaction with other children was inadvertently reinforced by her teachers, who greatly enjoyed talking with this bright, precocious little girl. The modification procedure consisted of the teachers providing attention and toy rewards to Ann only when she was playing with other children. When Ann was seen playing alone or trying to interact only with adults, she was ignored. Before the modification procedure, Ann was seen to interact with adults 40 percent of the time and with other children only 10 percent of the time during a one-week period. Afterwards, she interacted with adults 20 percent of the time and spent 60 percent of her time with other children.

Attempts have also been made to train adults in socially desirable behavior by applying direct reinforcement. The most ambitious efforts of this sort have been the token-economy programs implemented in mental hospitals and prisons. Nay (1976, chap. 4) has outlined numerous criteria for the successful implementation of such programs.

In a token economy, desired behavior is reinforced by the therapist (or the therapist's representatives), while undesired behavior is not. The reinforcement may consist of smiles and verbal approval, access to some desired activity, or a material reward. Sometimes, undesired behavior may be punished rather than simply ignored, but most token economies emphasize positive reinforcement and minimize use of the negative variety. Nay advocates the use of uniform, compact, generalized reinforcers—like coins or poker chips—in such a program. These can be quickly distributed on any occasion when a patient or client has engaged in desired behavior, and the meaning of the reinforcement will be immediately understood by all parties. These generalized reinforcers, or *tokens,* can be exchanged by patients for edible treats, articles of clothing or jewelry, cosmetic and grooming aids, rental of a radio or TV set, or access to a recreational activity. Ruskin and Maley (1972) listed the price of various items available to patients participating in one token-economy program in a mental hospital: penny candy (1 token), pack of chewing gum (5), pack of cigarettes (35), pair of shoes (50), sleeping robe (400), pair of earrings (30), bar of soap (5), toothbrush (10), comb (5), radio rental for one day (10).

In mental hospitals, the major problem addressed by token economies is the tendency for the socially adaptive behavior of patients to disappear over time as they become increasingly dependent on the institution for the regulation of their schedules and the satisfaction of their needs. By requiring them to earn tokens in order to acquire goods, services, and recreational opportunities formerly provided by the institution, the token economy encourages patients to become active participants in the scheduling of their time and reinforces productive behavior that is important for self-sufficiency in society at large. The same procedures have been applied, with similar goals in mind, in institutions for delinquent but otherwise psychologically normal adolescents (Nay, 1974). These techniques have also been used in regular school classrooms, but in these cases the formal token-reinforcement system is often replaced by a less obtrusive procedure of providing social reinforcers for desired behavior, such as social approval or special attention.

In institutional settings, the initiation of a token economy often requires the creation of a large number of jobs that clients can perform in order to earn tokens. These jobs may range in responsibility from filling salt and pepper shakers to ordering and displaying items in the commissary and collecting tokens for goods that are purchased there (Ayllon and Azrin, 1965). Orga-

nizers of these programs argue that the skills learned in token economies should generalize to the patient's life situation outside the institution and offer better hope for rehabilitation and release than the traditional system of institutional dependence.

Critics dispute the effectiveness of token economies in generating self-sufficiency among clients. When a token program is discontinued within an institution, the clients' skills sometimes disappear very rapidly, as though they were maintained only by the immediate rewards being offered. These skills also tend to dissipate when mental patients are discharged into a social world where one does not receive tokens and high praise for brushing one's teeth, making one's bed, or performing the small routines that together constitute a complex job (such as a waitress's filling salt shakers, filling orders, and making change). Of course, the failure of some clients to show durable progress toward self-sufficiency does not mean that it is pointless to make the effort. A more serious complaint based on ethical rather than practical grounds is that token economies often initially deprive institutional clients of goods and services to which they are legitimately entitled and then selectively restore these rights to the individuals most susceptible to being bribed. A practical problem which bears on this ethical issue is that if a group of clients sees through the purposes of the behavior modifiers and organizes a rebellion, the entire program may be undermined. In a token economy designed to reduce the disruptive behavior of nine adolescent boys in a psychiatric hospital school, for example, it was found that disruptive behavior increased when two boys realized the purpose of the program, declared themselves "on strike," and denounced those who cooperated as "fools" (Santogrossi, O'Leary, Romanczyk, & Kaufman, 1973).

Biofeedback The technique of biofeedback uses operant-conditioning procedures for the purpose of teaching individuals how to control their own physiological functioning. Miller (Miller & Banuazizi, 1968) and DiCara (1973) were among the first to demonstrate that rats and humans are able to learn to regulate bodily processes which had long been assumed to be exclusively controlled by automatic internal mechanisms. As was mentioned in Chapter 7, devices can be attached to the body which detect and amplify neural, chemical, and muscular activity associated with such processes. These devices translate the biological activity they are monitoring into electrical signals which can, in turn, be fed back to the individual in the form of a tone or a flashing light. The term for this procedure is, appropriately enough, "biofeedback." Electrical signals can also be translated into the movement of a pen on a piece of paper and so provide a permanent record of an individual's bodily processes during a given time period; such a device is called a *polygraph.*

Miller and associates discovered that thirsty rats rewarded with water for increasing or decreasing their heart rates or the frequency of their intestinal contractions showed changes in these bodily functions in the reinforced direction. Humans, too, have learned to control their heart rates, blood pressure, the volume of blood in the various regions of their bodies, and their brain waves using similar techniques. For humans, the reward generally consists of the pleasure derived from observing a signal which indicates they have succeeded in controlling some internal event. Occasionally, humans may also be rewarded with money, candy, and so forth if it seems important to increase their motivation to persist with the task.

Psychiatrists have long recognized the existence of physical ailments that seem to have some underlying emotional cause. The *Diagnostic and Statistical Manual of Mental Disorders,* described in Chapter 5, lists a number of physical disorders on Axis III for which psychological factors may be implicated (American Psychiatric Association, 1978). Some examples are (1) skin reactions, including excessive itching, sweating, and other neurodermatoses, (2) musculoskeletal reactions, including backache, muscle cramps, muscle pain, and so forth, (3) respiratory reactions, including hiccups, bronchial spasms, asthma, hyperventilation, and so on, (4) cardiovascular reactions, including hypertension, migraine headache, irregular heartbeat, and various vascular problems, (5) gastrointestinal reactions, including peptic ulcer, constipation, or chronic heartburn or gastritis, and (6) genitourinary reactions, including excessive or difficult urination and menstrual disturbances. The involvement of the mind with the appearance or remission of physical ailments has been suggested many times throughout recorded history, from the Greeks—particularly Hippocrates and Aristotle—to the present day (McReynolds, 1975). Falconer (1796) and Tuke (1872), for instance, attributed skin diseases to an emotional inhibition of the activity of the perspiration glands and migraine headache to a constriction of blood vessels in the head and neck. In more contemporary times, there are reports that people in hypnotic trances may develop blisters if they believe they are being touched with a hot iron, while others may show a remission of warts, changes in blood-sugar level, and so forth when given an appropriate hypnotic suggestion.

It would be truly remarkable if operant-conditioning techniques, in conjunction with biofeedback, could provide relief from psychosomatic disorders. There has been some success in treating backache, headache, asthma, and high blood pressure (Engel & Shapiro, 1971). Epileptics have been taught to monitor their brain waves so as to detect when an attack may be imminent and take preventive medication (Schwartz, 1973). Analogously, alcoholics have learned how to monitor the content of alcohol in their bloodstreams and so hold their consumption to a moderate level (Lovibond & Caddy, 1970). While the latter finding has been duplicated, however, it appears that some individuals are not responsive to biofeedback training, while others remain dependent on the biofeedback apparatus to tell

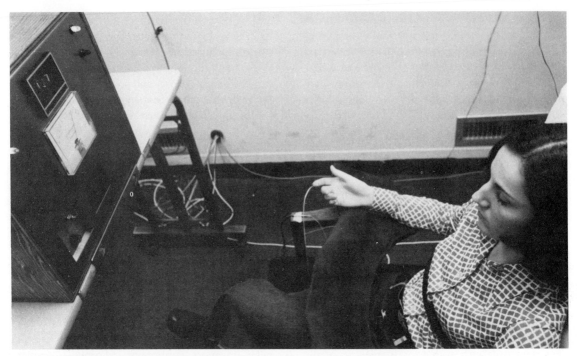

In biofeedback, an electronic device translates biological processes into a signal, such as a tone, light, or movement of a needle on a dial. In learning how to control the signal, the client learns to control his or her biological processes. (John Briggs)

them when they have consumed too much alcohol (Silverstein, Nathan, & Taylor, 1974). Since it is impractical to carry the apparatus around during one's day-to-day activities, the usefulness of the technique remains somewhat limited.

Success has been reported in using biofeedback to help paralyzed patients regain control of various limbs (Andrews, 1964; Johnson & Garton, 1973). The importance of this finding notwithstanding, there is evidence that people can control various physiological and muscular processes simply by making a focused, conscious effort and may not require the assistance of a biofeedback apparatus (Henson & Rubin, 1971; Benson, Kotch, Crassweller, & Greenwood, 1977). While biofeedback remains a promising procedure, the research in this area has often suffered from a lack of adequate controls for the effects of attention, motivation, and other related factors. The appar-

ent inability of some individuals to learn how to use biofeedback to control internal bodily processes also poses problems for the technique. Careful research in this area suffered to some extent from its popularization as a psychological cure-all and pathway to inner peace during the early 1970s.

Techniques Based on Vicarious Learning

You may recall from Chapter 4 that Bandura (1977, p. 21) and other social-learning theorists object to the radical-behaviorist conception of learning, in which reinforcement serves as a "mechanical response strengthener." While not denying that a reward increases the likelihood that the response which preceded it will be repeated, social-learning theorists regard changes in an individual's cognitions as the most significant outcome of such experiences. That is, the individual now anticipates that similar behavior in the future should have similarly rewarding consequences. In fact, merely observing the type of behavior in others that produces a reward for them may have a comparable effect on an individual's cognitions. If, on the other hand, others are observed to be punished rather than rewarded for their behavior, then the individual is likely to anticipate punishment rather than reward for imitating their actions. This type of conditioning, in which an individual need not have direct experience with positive or negative reinforcement in order for his or her future behavior to be affected, is called *vicarious learning*. Because of vicarious learning, we are likely to engage in behavior which others seem to be enjoying and to refrain from behavior which others appear to dislike.

We have, in Chapter 4, already considered one therapeutic technique based on social-learning theory—namely, modeling and imitation. Another example of this approach was provided by Bandura, Blanchard, and Ritter (1969), who treated people having a strong fear of snakes. One group was exposed to the systematic-desensitization technique described earlier in this chapter. A hierarchy of anxiety-arousing scenes involving interaction with snakes was established, and the client imagined each scene vividly while maintaining a state of deep relaxation. A second group watched a film which portrayed fearless models interacting with snakes while the client simultaneously tried to remain in a state of muscular relaxation. A third group was not placed in a state of relaxation but, instead, observed a live fearless model interact with a snake and was then encouraged to imitate the behavior—first with the model's assistance and then on their own.

Clients in all three groups, plus those in an untreated control group, took a behavioral-approach test requiring closer and closer involvement with snakes both before and after the application of the foregoing procedures. It was

A snake handler who apparently does not require any deconditioning of phobic reactions. (United Press International)

found that those in the three treatment groups approached the snake much more closely on the posttest than they had on the pretest, often handling the animal with little apparent fear. The untreated controls showed no such increase in their willingness to interact with the snake. The most effective treatment of all, however, was not systematic desensitization but modeling with guided participation.

Psychoanalytic theorists, of course, would probably interpret a snake phobia as being due to an unresolved Oedipal conflict and would recommend a very different sort of therapy. Alternatively, Seligman (1971) suggested that fear of snakes and other common human phobias may be learned easily because of their survival value in the course of our evolutionary development. Bandura (1977, p. 76) scoffs at such notions and insists that "Snakes acquire threat value through a combination of experiences, involving fearful parental modeling reinforced by frightening personal experiences, grisly folklore, and illustrations of reptiles as menacing animals." To cure such phobias, one need only revise the cognitions which support them. Desensitization of physiologically based fear reactions may also be therapeutic, but it is not a necessary condition for successful treatment. On the other hand, critics of the social-learning viewpoint have expressed doubt that a phobic person induced to handle a snake under controlled laboratory conditions would generalize this fearless behavior to a surprise encounter with a snake while walking in the woods.

An even more cognitively oriented form of treatment than that described above uses language functions rather than modeling and imitation to achieve vicarious learning. Behavioral psychologists have long regarded thinking as inner, or subvocal, speech. How one's mind works, then, has a direct relationship with how one talks. Initially, speech patterns are learned through parental reinforcement for the utterance of certain sounds in association with corresponding objects or persons. As a child is taught how to combine sounds to form meaningful sentences, she or he often thinks out loud by talking to herself or himself. Later, after the sequence of sounds becomes well-rehearsed, thinking becomes a silently enacted pattern of subvocal responses. The overt reinforcements that were initially effective in eliciting and maintaining speech—such as hugs or praise from parents— become internalized self-reinforcers. As internalization progresses, the individual may think of a verbal sequence and then say "That was a bad idea; I'll forget it" or "That was a good idea; I'll act on it."

Vygotsky (1962), Sokolov (1972), and other Soviet psychologists generally agree with this behaviorist view of thinking as the internalization of language training provided by others in an individual's social environment. In addition, many theorists believe that some thinking involves the internal visualization of whole scenes without any necessary involvement of language. Meichenbaum (1977), a Canadian social-learning theorist, would definitely want to add such a capacity for direct imagery to the concept of thinking as inner speech.

A therapeutic application of the foregoing concepts has been made to schizophrenic patients, who have difficulty communicating with others because they are often distracted by imaginary voices and other hallucinations. In addition, schizophrenics tend to ramble aimlessly from one topic to another, rarely pausing to allow others to respond. Meichenbaum and Cameron (1973) trained adult schizophrenics to become aware of their patterns of speaking and behaving and to increase their responsiveness to nonverbal signals from others indicating they were "acting schizophrenic." Next, the patients were taught a series of self-controlling and self-reinforcing statements such as "Go slowly and think this out," "Don't just say the first thing that comes to mind," "Good, I figured it out," "I'm not making myself understood," and "Let me try again." In terms of their performance on tests of memory for digits, perceptual integration on the Holzman Inkblot Technique (see Chapter 5), interpretation of proverbs, and overall frequency of "sick talk," the schizophrenics receiving this training for three weeks performed significantly better than did an untreated control group.

Meyers, Mercatoris, and Sirota (1976) used a similar procedure to train a 47-year-old chronic schizophrenic mental patient and saw so great an improvement that the patient was discharged. At the end of fifteen training sessions in the hospital, the proportion of psychotic speech in the patient's conversation had dropped from a pretreatment level of 65 percent to only 8 percent.

After six months in the community, during which the patient was removed from medication and experienced the death of a parent, the proportion of psychotic speech was estimated as only 16 percent. Impressive as this case study appears to be in demonstrating a long-term therapeutic effect, however, other studies have found that training in self-controlling and self-reinforcing statements does *not* generalize so as to motivate appropriate behavior in situations outside the treatment context (Bellack, Hersen, & Turner, 1976).

Somewhat analogously, Meichenbaum tried to teach hyperactive, impulsive children to slow down and think before they acted. Meichenbaum and Goodman (1971) exposed such children to a model who successfully completed a difficult figure-copying task while verbalizing each step out loud as he did it. Next, each child performed the task under the guidance of the model and then alone while rehearsing the model's verbalizations aloud. Finally, the child repeated the task while whispering the instructions and then while reciting them silently. Shown below is an example of the model's self-instructions that the children were required to imitate:

> Okay, what is it I have to do? You want me to copy the picture with the different lines. I have to go slowly and carefully. Okay, draw the line down, down, good; then to the right, that's it; now down some more and to the left. Good, I'm doing fine so far. Remember, go slowly. Now back up again. No, I was supposed to go down. That's okay. Just erase the line carefully. . . . Good. Even if I make an error I can go on slowly and carefully. I have to go down now. Finished. I did it! (Meichenbaum & Goodman, 1971, p. 117)

In comparison with an untreated control group, it was found that the boys given this training showed significant gains in scores on the Wechsler Intelligence Scale for Children (see Chapter 6)

and on various other pictorial and conceptual tasks. Most studies of this sort have not looked for long-term behavioral effects of self-instructional training, but one by Bornstein and Quevillon (1976) did find a dramatic decrease in the disruptiveness of four hyperactive boys both immediately after the training and over a ninety-day follow-up period. Other studies, however, have *not* found the same long-term behavioral effects of learning self-controlling and self-rewarding statements (Giebink, Stover, & Fahl, 1968; Robin, Armel, & O'Leary, 1975). As with the training procedures applied to schizophrenics, then, there remains some doubt as to the extent to which vicarious learning will generalize so as to maintain adaptive behavior in new situations.

A BEHAVIORAL ALTERNATIVE TO THE PSYCHIATRIC SYSTEM OF DIAGNOSTIC CLASSIFICATION

We saw in Chapter 5 that the traditional system of diagnostic classification of mental disorders is derived from a medical model which assumes the existence of some disease which is causing bizarre or antisocial behavioral symptoms to be exhibited. This system is currently upheld and periodically revised by the American Psychiatric Association. While many psychologists use the traditional diagnostic classifications in their clinical practice or in their textbooks on abnormal psychology, others attack the accuracy and utility of this system.

In a classic investigation of the problems posed by psychiatric diagnostic classification, Zigler and Phillips (1961) listed the percentage of psychiatric patients who exhibited each of thirty-five symptoms, ranging from depression (the most frequent) to emotional outbursts, sexual preoccupation, insomnia, or self-imposed starvation. The patients were grouped into four traditional categories: manic-depressive, psychoneurotic, char-

TABLE 8-2 Frequency of 35 symptoms of psychological disorder among hospitalized mental patients

Symptom	Total hospital (N=793)	Manic depressive (N=75)	Psychoneurotic (N=152)	Character disorder (N=279)	Schizophrenic (N=287)
Depressed	38	64	58	31	28
Tense	37	32	46	33	36
Suspiciousness	35	25	16	17	65
Drinking	19	17	14	32	8
Hallucinations	19	11	4	12	35
Suicidal attempt	16	24	19	15	12
Suicidal ideas	15	29	23	15	8
Bodily complaints	15	21	21	5	19
Emotional outburst	14	17	12	18	9
Withdrawn	14	4	12	7	25
Perplexed	14	9	9	8	24
Assaultive	12	5	6	18	5
Self-depreciatory	12	16	16	8	13
Threatens assault	10	4	11	14	7
Sexual preoccupation	10	9	9	6	14
Maniacal outburst	9	11	6	7	12
Bizarre ideas	9	11	1	2	20
Robbery	8	0	3	18	3
Apathetic	8	8	8	4	11
Irresponsible behavior	7	3	7	9	7
Headaches	6	7	10	4	5
Perversions (except homosexuality)	5	0	5	10	2
Euphoria	5	17	2	2	5
Fears own hostile impulses	5	4	9	5	2
Mood swings	5	9	5	4	4
Insomnia	5	11	7	3	5
Psychosomatic disorders	4	7	6	3	5
Does not eat	4	9	4	2	4
Lying	3	0	1	7	0
Homosexuality	3	3	3	8	2
Rape	3	0	3	8	1
Obsessions	3	8	3	1	4
Depersonalization	3	4	1	0	6
Feels perverted	3	0	3	1	5
Phobias	2	4	5	0	2

Source: Zigler & Phillips, 1961.

acter disorder, and schizophrenic (see Table 8-2). They discovered that there was a great deal of overlap in the behavioral symptoms exhibited by these patient groups. Even so, it might be noted parenthetically that while 64 percent of the manic-depressives appeared depressed, only 28 percent of the schizophrenics did so; and while only 25 percent of the manic-depressives seemed "suspicious," 65 percent of the schizophrenics exhibited this symptom. The psychoneurotics were somewhat more likely than were patients in other categories to appear tense, while those with character disorders were the most likely to have drinking problems. Anyway, the main conclusion derived from this study was that a patient's diagnostic classification does not clearly differentiate his or her behavior from the behavior of patients in other categories.

Zubin (1967) found that two or more clinicians could agree up to 80 percent of the time in trying to place a patient into a broad diagnostic class such as organic brain disorder, psychosis, or neurosis but that agreement fell to less than 50 percent when more specific categories were used. A review by the National Institute of Mental Health (1974) found that the diagnosis of schizophrenia, in particular, has a different frequency of occurrence in different countries, states, hospitals within states, and even wards within hospitals.

In addition to questioning the accuracy of psychiatric diagnosis, behaviorists charge that the category into which a patient is placed is not necessarily related to the type of therapeutic treatment administered (Bannister, Salmon, & Lieberman, 1964). It has also been suggested that one is more likely to be admitted to a psychiatric hospital if one appears on evenings or weekends than if one appears during regular business hours (Mendel & Rapport, 1969) or if one is unrepresented by counsel at a commitment hearing (Wenger & Fletcher, 1969). Finally, as was mentioned in Chapter 5 and at the beginning of the present chapter, many psychiatrists and psychologists object to the negative social and legal

consequences for the individual who is labeled "mentally sick" or "insane" (Laing, 1960; Szasz, 1966; Sarbin, 1967; Ullmann & Krasner, 1969).

Because of the foregoing problems with the medical model of diagnostic classification, Adams, Doster, and Calhoun (1977) proposed an alternative model based entirely on behavioral or physiological criteria. Their main goals were: (1) to define the behavioral and biological aspects of psychological disorder, using clear, operational terms, (2) to create discrete categories for disorders that would avoid the overlapping of symptoms found among psychiatric classifications, and (3) to label categories in a manner that did not stigmatize the patient as a mentally sick person.

The diagnostic approach that Adams et al. recommend first classifies the response system involved in a particular personality disorder. These response systems actually sound somewhat similar to the various divisions of the field of psychology. They are Motor (i.e., behavioral), Perceptual, Biological, Cognitive, Emotional, and Social. Within each response system, the disorder is then placed into a particular response category. Within the Motor system, for example, are the categories of facial, head, limb, and so forth. Within the Biological system there are categories of hunger, elimination, sleep, and so on, while within the Social system there are coercion, submission, nurturance, and succorance.

The authors regard this procedure, called the *Psychological Response Classification System* (PRCS) as a tentative first step toward overcoming the problems they and other behaviorally oriented psychologists see in the diagnostic approach endorsed by the American Psychiatric Association. While admitting that their PRCS model is at present rather sketchy, Adams et al. express the hope that future research and application in clinical settings will serve to expand this preliminary outline and fill in missing details so as to develop a thorough-going behavioral alternative to the *Diagnostic and Statistical Manual of Mental Disorders*.

THE LIMITATIONS OF BEHAVIORAL ASSESSMENT AND THERAPY

As has been observed several times throughout this book, psychologists in the environmentalist tradition have often been severely critical of the adequacy and even, at times, the morality of theories and techniques of assessment or intervention advocated by other traditions in the study of personality. It is only fair, then, that we apply the same evaluative scrutiny to behavioral methods that we directed toward techniques associated with the psychoanalytic or dispositional approaches to personality psychology in Chapters 5, 6, and 7. As in these earlier chapters, criticisms may be conveniently divided into those which are of a professional nature and those which take a broader social perspective.

Professional Criticisms

Behavioral assessment has been taken to task by Sundberg (1977, p. 168) for its failure to evaluate itself according to the traditional psychometric criteria of reliability and validity. The techniques employed by behavior therapists have often been devised for a particular practical purpose without due regard for standardization or the establishment of norms against which performance can be compared. If tests of the projective or objective variety discussed in Chapters 5 and 6 can be called to account for their shortcomings in these areas, then we can surely expect no less of the measures developed by behaviorists.

Direct observation has an obvious face validity as a behavioral-assessment technique, but there is good reason to be skeptical of the accuracy of this procedure. Bijou and Peterson (1971), themselves behavior therapists, have commented that the presence of an observer is likely to alter the behavior of the individuals being scrutinized. The alternative of relying on a client's self-reports regarding the frequency of a target behavior is vulnerable to intentional or unconscious distortion on the part of the client for the

purposes of either "faking good" or "faking bad." One might try to monitor behavior less obtrusively using, for example, remote-controlled television cameras, but this adds to the time, effort, and expense needed to complete a functional analysis. As Bijou and Peterson admit, then, the functional analysis of a behavior disorder can be criticized both for its questionable accuracy and for the amount of effort it involves.

Even if behavioral assessment and the therapeutic techniques derived from it were accepted as fully reliable and valid, it would still be possible to question their generalizability to situations in a client's life which are outside the treatment context. During World War II, long before the term "behavior therapy" was coined by Lazarus (1958), the Office of Strategic Services tried to assess the bravery and leadership qualities of men being considered for dangerous intelligence assignments behind enemy lines (OSS Assessment Staff, 1948). The behavior of these candidates was observed under simulated conditions calling for courage as well as clear thinking and initiative under stress. One test required three men to build a bridge as quickly as possible, using rather skimpy materials, so as to cross a dangerous chasm. Unknown to the real examinee, two of the three were members of the assessment staff, who deliberately ridiculed and frustrated his efforts to complete the assigned task. A second test subjected the examinee to a stressful interrogation to see if he could avoid divulging secrets. Unfortunately, the reliability of these tests was not impressively high—the brave and resourceful leader on one test was easily confused and manipulated on another—and a candidate's performance on the simulations did not predict very accurately the quality of his work on actual missions (Anastasi, 1976). The moral of this story for behavioral assessment seems clear: What a person does under circumstances in which he or she is conscious of being observed and evaluated is not necessarily a valid measure of what that person will do when out of the limelight. Furthermore, behavior in a contrived simulation does not necessarily generalize to real life.

In more recent and more conventional assessment contexts, similar questions have been raised regarding the representativeness of a client's observed behavior and the generalizability of therapist-induced changes to novel situations (Forsyth & Fairweather, 1961; Lazarus, 1971). Generalization is most likely to occur, of course, when clients are ready, willing, and able to become active participants in the rather transparent "contingency games" concocted by their therapists. You may recall the discussion earlier in this chapter of a classroom token-economy program whose effectiveness was seriously undermined by two boys who accurately perceived

its purpose and refused to allow their behavior to be modified in the intended direction. Even when clients *are* highly motivated to learn the routines being taught, however, they may still be unable to generalize their training. Mental patients who develop adaptive behaviors in token-economy programs often experience considerable difficulty in maintaining self-sufficiency when they are discharged into a community which does not provide rewards for each routine involved in grooming oneself or holding down a job.

Sometimes evidence of generalizability *is* found, but even here one can all too easily overlook the limitations of these apparent successes. Fairweather and associates (1964, 1969) initiated a token-economy program to develop

Behavioral psychologists have advocated the removal of mental patients from custodial institutions and their placement in halfway houses like the one shown here. These houses are located in the "normal" community rather than isolated from it and are intended to maintain more normal patterns of behavior among the patients. (Burk Uzzle/Magnum)

self-reliant behavior among a group of chronically hospitalized schizophrenics. As the program continued, the patients were required to assume greater and greater responsibility for administering reinforcement and monitoring one another's performance. As bizarre behavior was replaced by more responsible and self-reliant behavior, the hospital staff withdrew from its direct involvement in maintaining the token economy and simply retained the right to veto any unwise group decisions made by the patients. Ultimately, the patients were removed from the hospital and housed in a "lodge" in the community. Here they were encouraged to become economically self-sufficient in the real world of work. The patients set up a janitorial and gardening service and, after three years, were administering the lodge and the work activities of its members almost entirely independently from hospital staff. Despite the apparent success of this program in developing some degree of self-sufficiency among institutionalized psychotics, however, the patients did not become fully functioning members of the community. Eventually, most experienced a resurgence of psychotic symptoms which necessitated their readmission to the hospital. Relative to a matched group of patients who were simply discharged from the hospital into the outside world though, participants in the lodge program were employed more steadily and able to live in the community much longer.

The view of mental illness fostered by the environmentalist tradition is that it consists of maladaptive behavior which is learned and maintained according to the same principles of reinforcement which regulate normal, adaptive behavior. Consequently, one need only alter reinforcement contingencies to transform the former into the latter, thus "curing" mental illness, which is really not an illness at all but, rather, an individual's socially inappropriate attempt to cope either verbally or behaviorally with the reinforcement schedule offered by his or her environment. Since traditional institutions founded on the medical model of mental illness have been accused of reinforcing the very symptoms they are supposed to be curing (Rosenhan, 1973), behaviorally oriented psychologists have often recommended that patients be "deinstitutionalized" and returned to the community, where their behavior will be shaped by more normal reinforcement contingencies. Since the early 1960s, this strategy has been tried in many states, and the results are not particularly encouraging. Bassuk and Gerson (1978) note that the number of resident patients in mental hospitals has steadily declined since 1960, as has the average number of days of hospitalization experienced by a patient. On the other hand, the rate of *admissions* to these institutions has increased by 129 percent since 1960, with nearly all the increase being accounted for by readmissions of former patients. For most of the so-called deinstitutionalized, mental health care has become a revolving door.

While they are outside that door, the former patients are left to struggle along on funds provided by welfare services—unless they are able to find and hold jobs—and to live either with relatives, on the streets, or in a motley assortment of nursing homes, boardinghouses, halfway houses, or group homes. Typically, they are rejected by the community, which is offended or even sometimes frightened by their frequently disheveled appearance and bizarre behavior (Holden, 1978). In one study of the attitudes of 125 families who experienced a return to their households of a deinstitutionalized patient, it was found that while 75 percent initially welcomed their relative, only 7 percent felt the same after they had witnessed a reappearance of the maladaptive behavior which had caused the relative's hospitalization in the first place (Etzioni, 1978). One could, to be sure, argue that these former patients did not, in many cases, receive the extensive retraining in socially appropriate mannerisms and skills that behavioral psychologists consider a necessary prerequisite to cure. On the other hand, not even the patients in

Fairweather's community-lodge program, who *did* receive extensive training and support from the hospital staff, were able to become fully self-sufficient. As Etzioni (p. 17) cautions:

Let's not kid each other that people who have been institutionalized will quickly flourish (or "normalize") just because they have been deinstitutionalized, and overgeneralize from a few heart-warming successful cases. Most retarded persons, and those suffering from serious mental illness, will need to be sheltered for the rest of their lives, in or out of institutions. It is all right to hope for more, but to base a public policy on more optimistic assumptions is one reason, however well-intentioned, so many helpless souls wander the city's streets.

One last professional criticism of behavioral approaches to assessment and therapy is that the assumptions which are made by its proponents regarding the mainsprings of human personality and the most effective techniques for inducing personality change often appear overly simplistic. These assumptions are customarily derived from the results of contrived laboratory experiments involving animals or people (often children) and are then invoked to account for the behavior of human beings inhabiting environments very different from a psychological laboratory. Hogan, DeSoto, and Solano (1977) remark, for example, that Mischel (1974) conducted an extensive program of research, using experimental designs, which demonstrates that children's self-control is directly related to their ability to divert their attention from distracting stimuli or from desired goal objects such as candy or money. Hogan et al. regard this finding as a verification of common sense and express greater interest in the question of why some children are much less distractible than others. Is self-control a stable personality trait? If so, where does it come from, and what other aspects of an individual's personality might be related to it? How is self-control in an experimental context related to behavior in real life?

In a later study, Patterson and Mischel (1976) compared various techniques for training children in self-control. The children worked at a pegboard task while being tempted by a distracting stimulus called the *Mr. Clown Box.* One group recited temptation-inhibiting instructions to themselves (e.g., "I'm not going to look at Mr. Clown"), another recited task-facilitating instructions (e.g., "I'm going to look at my work"), a third group recited both types of instructions, and a fourth worked at the pegboard with nothing to recite. The study revealed that the first group performed better than any of the others, including the one which recited *both* types of instructions. You will have to decide for yourself whether or not such findings can be generalized to real life. Many critics regard this type of experimental approach as an interesting but highly artificial beginning to the study of human personality which falls far short of being an end.

Social Criticisms

A major source of public as well as professional concern with behavioral techniques of assessment and intervention has been that the model of human thought and action on which they are ultimately based is overly mechanistic. A leading behaviorist, B. F. Skinner (1948, 1971), has, in his popular writings, been largely responsible for the dissemination of the behavioral viewpoint. He has advocated the application of conditioning principles to the design of cultures and the socialization of their members, who are assumed to be lacking any degree of autonomous free will. Many, both within and without the field of psychology, regard this view of personality as a threat to democratic values (Jourard, 1974, pp. 20–21), dehumanizing (Shoben, 1963), or scientifically selective and incomplete (Sperry, 1976).

The techniques employed to change behavior by therapists in the environmentalist tradition have sometimes not been particularly reassuring to those made uneasy by the underlying philosophy. In token-economy programs, as was pointed out earlier in this chapter, patients may initially be denied access to certain goods and services normally available to hospital inmates; in addition, they may be required to complete tasks normally performed by hospital staffs in order to earn back their privileges. Is this procedure exploitative? Is it ethical? Is it even legal? Ennis (1971) has taken the position that it is not.

Further clouding the issue is the fact that participation in token economies initiated in hospitals and prisons has often been involuntary (Stolz, 1977). At the level of individual treatment, Davison and Wilson (1973) reported that as many as 13 percent of behavior therapists said they would apply aversive-conditioning techniques to change a client's homosexuality—with or without the patient's consent. Nay (1976, pp. 320–323) reviewed several court decisions which appear to have established that in most cases, patient participation in programs of behavior modification must, in the future, be voluntary. Even in their treatment of relatively mild disturbances, such as overeating or excessive smoking, behavior therapists have found it morally and legally prudent to enter into contracts with their clients which outline in advance the conditioning procedures to be following during treatment (Thoresen & Mahoney, 1974).

Popular conceptions of behavior therapy have been partly influenced by motion pictures like Stanley Kubrick's *Clockwork Orange.* Here, a young man named Alex—a brutal delinquent and rapist who happens to enjoy Beethoven's Ninth Symphony—is conditioned through aversion therapy to become nauseous whenever he encounters violence, sexuality, or classical music. Later in the film, Alex suffers a mental breakdown when forced to listen to Beethoven's Ninth Symphony, and he is exploited by a political party trying to use public disclosure of his psychological incapacitation as a means of embarrassing the party in power. For those who form many of their opinions in movie houses, however, I would recommend the outcome of the conditioning procedure applied in the *Ipcress File* as more

plausible. In this film, aversive stimuli were applied in an effort to induce a compliant conditioned response in a secret agent. The agent pretends to succumb to the conditioning until his captors become careless and he is able to escape. My point here is that it is highly doubtful that behavioral techniques can produce anything more than superficial and temporary compliance in an adult who is able to discern the purpose of the contingencies being applied and who does not wish to have his or her personality permanently modified in the desired direction.

As long as behavior therapists are careful to enter into contingency contracts with their clients and are scrupulous in obtaining informed consent wherever it is required by law, they should be able to answer the legal and ethical criticisms raised in this section. On a philosophical level, though, they may still be vulnerable to attack for their mechanistic model of personality. One reply to this criticism by social-learning theorists has been that vicarious learning, self-instruction, visualization, and other cognitive processes are now a part of behavioral psychology. This answer would not entirely satisfy many critics, however, since, as was explained in Chapter 4, even social-learning theorists regard cognitive expectations, self-instructions, and so forth to be formed and guided by the same principles of reinforcement which regulate overt behavior. There still does not seem to be much room within the environmentalist tradition for internal forces which influence behavior independently of learning (e.g., biologically based dispositions or autonomous will).

CONCLUSION

The main strengths of the environmentalist tradition in psychology have been its commitment to a clear definition of terms, the minimization of bias in data gathering, and the acceptance or rejection of competing hypotheses on the basis of empirical tests. Behaviorism has acted as a counterweight to the excesses of interpretation sometimes indulged in by psychoanalytically or dispositionally oriented adherents to the medical model of mental health and illness. It has challenged theorists of all persuasions to think more clearly about their conceptions of personality and to suggest ways in which their ideas might be supported or refuted by objective research. Behaviorism and social-learning theory have performed a great service to the fields of psychology and psychiatry and to the formulation of social policy in persistently calling attention to the powerful influence of environmental contingencies on the development of personality and the realization of one's cognitive and behavioral potential. Without behaviorism, the impact of the environment on human character might never have been given its full measure of attention either by professional psychology or by society as a whole.

These accomplishments notwithstanding, behavioral approaches to assessment and therapy may be passing through a period of soul searching and retrenchment. Arnold Lazarus (1977), a founder of behavior therapy, has asked whether it may have "outlived its usefulness." He raised this issue, he said, because of the limitations of behavioral theory and technique and because the term "behavior modification" had come to evoke such unfavorable reactions in many quarters that it was becoming difficult to conduct effective therapy under a behavioral aegis. Accordingly, Lazarus (p. 553) noted that his own work had shifted from a "fairly strict behavioral orientation" toward a "multimodal" approach which might borrow ideas and techniques from any theoretical tradition in psychology or psychiatry. Indeed, he urged therapists of all persuasions to "transcend the constraints of factionalism in which cloistered adherents of rival schools, movements, and systems each cling to their separate illusions." Lazarus expresses the hope that a synthesis of viewpoints will provide the next great advance in psychological knowledge and in the alleviation of human suffering through therapeutic intervention. In the event that such a synthesis is achieved, it will clearly have benefited to a great extent from the past and present discoveries of the environmentalist tradition, but it will not be confined by the assumptions of that tradition alone.

SUMMARY

1 A fundamental assumption of the environmentalist tradition is that behavior is shaped and maintained by environmental contingencies. It is not necessary to hypothesize unconscious psychodynamics to account for behavior, and it is misleading to label behavior by referring to its assumed underlying dynamics. In a study by Langer and Abelson (1974), a person who was identified as a mental patient was perceived as significantly more maladjusted in his speech and actions by psychodynamically trained clinicians than was a person identified as a job applicant. Differential use of a diagnostic label had no such influence on the perception of a person being observed by behaviorally oriented clinicians.

2 Behavior therapists try to develop a functional analysis of a client's excessive, deficient, or inappropriate behavior. This consists of establishing the stimulus conditions which precede the behavior,

cognitive or other organismic factors which accompany it, the specific response patterns which constitute it, and the consequences which maintain it. Interviews, questionnaires, and direct observation are used in the development of a functional analysis.

3   The treatment methods available to behavior therapists may be divided into those based on classical conditioning, operant conditioning, and vicarious learning. The first group includes systematic desensitization and aversion therapy. The second includes direct delivery of negative or positive reinforcement, such as electric shock, time-out, valued "tokens," or social approval, as well as the more intangible rewards associated with learning self-control through biofeedback. The third includes modeling and guided participation along with training in the verbal recitation of self-controlling and self-rewarding statements.

4   In addition to placing socially stigmatizing labels on people, the traditional system of diagnostic classification of mental disorders endorsed by the American Psychiatric Association suffers from its imprecise definition of the symptoms comprising each category of mental illness and a resulting overlap of symptoms across categories. Social factors, such as the time of day one appears at a hospital intake office or the presence or absence of counsel at a commitment hearing, have been shown to influence the diagnoses that are made. In an effort to correct these problems, Adams, Doster, and Calhoun (1977) have proposed an alternative model of diagnostic classification based entirely on behavioral criteria.

5   Behavioral techniques of assessment and intervention have been criticized on several grounds by professional psychologists. First, the traditional psychometric criteria of reliability, validity, and standardization have not been met by many behaviorally oriented questionnaires. Second, the assessment technique of direct observation is susceptible to many sources of bias. Third, behavioral changes induced by conditioning procedures often do not generalize to situations outside the one in which conditioning took place. In the case of patients hospitalized with severe personality disorders, such as schizophrenia, there seems to be only a limited extent to which training in self-sufficient behavior within the hospital will generalize so as to maintain self-sufficiency in the real world when the patient is discharged. Sometimes expectations of the capacity for self-sufficiency of deinstitutionalized mental patients have been overly optimistic, raising doubts as to the wisdom of this procedure as it is currently applied. Finally, some critics charge that behavioral approaches to assessment and therapy and the model of human learning on which they are based are overly simplistic.

6   Social criticisms of behavioral approaches have revolved around a distaste for a mechanistic model of human psychology and ethical

misgivings about the manner in which behavior technology has sometimes been applied. Procedures for obtaining informed consent and entering into contingency contracts with clients have answered many of the ethical and legal complaints, but philosophical disagreements continue to exist. While the environmental tradition has made important and enduring contributions to our conception of the origins and maintaining conditions of human personality, the theory and techniques of behavioral psychology remain a focus of controversy both within and without the profession of psychology. Lazarus (1977) calls for a synthesis of different traditions in the field and the development of a "multimodal" approach.

TERMS TO KNOW

functional analysis
behavior diary
operational definition
systematic desensitization
aversion therapy

token economy
biofeedback
cognitive behavior modification
deinstitutionalization

UNIT THREE

THE GROWTH OF PERSONALITY FROM BIRTH TO MATURITY

Every personality theorist whose views were considered in Unit One accepted the commonsense view that what happens to us as children has a considerable impact on our strengths and weaknesses as adults. It is true that some Europeans (like Jung) and some Americans (like Rogers) preferred to emphasize the changes that can be made in personality in adulthood rather than its initial development during childhood, but even these writers recognized that our experiences as children affect the character traits we exhibit as adults.

243

In tracing the growth of personality from birth to maturity, Unit Three will include evidence on both sides of an issue which has long been debated by psychologists and others: Is someone's personality mainly the reflection of internal cognitive and temperamental factors, or is it the product of an individual's interactions with his or her external environment? Like so many other controversial issues, this one does not appear to have a clear-cut resolution, and exploration of its many facets is a complex and sometimes frustrating exercise. Nearly as complex and frustrating, in fact, as people themselves can be—and every bit as fascinating. As an introduction to the questions being considered in this unit, we will briefly examine some observations made on animals rather than people. These classic investigations, by Harry Harlow and his co-workers at the University of Wisconsin, reveal an intricate interaction of biological and social forces in determining the character of young monkeys and may have implications for the probable influence of similar factors in forming human personality as well. Harlow, his wife, and other members of his research team at Wisconsin accidentally discovered the emergence of peculiar behavior patterns among infant monkeys raised in wire isolation cages as part of controlled studies in which early social experience was to be minimized. These animals spent a great deal of time huddled in balls, clutching themselves, and rocking back and forth. If a piece of cloth was made available, they would cling to it and carry it with them wherever they went. This observation suggested that there might be a need for contact comfort which is independent of the basic needs for food and water (the latter commodities were supplied by the experimental environment). Harlow and Harlow (1962) conducted several studies to explore the importance of tactile stimulation in infancy for the emergence of normal behavior in rhesus monkeys. In the most famous of these studies, infants were taken from their mothers shortly after birth and placed in an environment containing two dummies, or "mother-surrogates." Each surrogate was a wire tube with a wooden block for a head. A milk bottle was attached in the "chest" area of one of these dummies so the monkeys could nurse. The other surrogate provided no milk, but its wire frame was covered with soft toweling. The Harlows discovered that the infants spent nearly all their time clinging to the cloth dummy and remained on the wire surrogate only so long as it took to nurse. When frightened by a fear stimulus (such as a small mechanical bear beating a drum), the infants invariably ran to the cloth surrogate. After being "comforted" by such contact, the monkeys were often emboldened to the point of leaving the mother to confront and attack the fear stimulus. If only a wire mother was present, the infants remained paralyzed by fear and preferred huddling in a corner to clinging to the surrogate. The experiment seemed to demonstrate that the need for tactile stimulation is independent of the need for food and that a mother who dispenses food but not contact comfort does not appear to be

Infant monkeys who are taken from their mothers and raised in social isolation exhibit a need for contact comfort which rivals in its intensity the need for food. The monkeys spent nearly all their time clinging to a cloth-covered dummy and remained on a wire dummy equipped with a milk bottle only until they finished nursing. (Wisconsin Primate Laboratory)

"loved" by, and provides no security for, a baby monkey. In other studies, it was found that animals which had been raised alone in bare wire cages for the first six months of their lives displayed highly abnormal behavior even after spending at least six months in a community of normal monkeys. They were unable to mate or to defend themselves when attacked, and they had trouble learning how to play with others or how to cooperate in mutual grooming. A group of monkeys raised for six months with cloth-covered mother-surrogates and then placed in a social group displayed behavior which more closely approximated normality, but even these animals were noticeably deficient in the areas of sex, defense, and play. In fact, a group raised by their real mothers but not exposed to a play group of other young monkeys showed pronounced deficits in sex and play behavior when placed in such a group at the age of 1, approaching normality only in their defense behavior. Interestingly, the Harlows observed that infant monkeys provided with both a cloth-covered surrogate mother and a peer group showed virtually normal behavior in all categories. This finding suggested that, so long as tactile stimulation was available during the first six months, access to a peer group was more crucial for normal development than interacting with a real, live mother. Summing up the results of these investigations, it is clear that infant monkeys have certain primary needs (e.g., for food) which must be satisfied if they are to survive at all. A mother surrogate which fills these needs will not, however, be "loved" by the infant unless it also satisfies a secondary need for contact comfort. An infant for whom only primary needs are filled will probably survive, but it will display bizarre and maladaptive behavior when placed in a peer group of normal monkeys. If both primary and secondary biological needs are satisfied, the young monkey's behavior will more closely approximate normality, but if the monkey is to become a fully normal animal, it must also have the kinds of early social experiences that only a peer group can provide. Not even a real, living mother is an effective substitute for a peer group. Thus, the emergence of normal behavior in young monkeys is determined by both biological and social forces. As will be explained in the chapters which follow, such forces appear to be at work in shaping human personality as well. Speaking in the broader terms introduced in Chapter 1, biological factors may be regarded as one component of the diverse internal events called _person variables_. Social factors are one component of the external influences we call _situation variables_. There is widespread agreement on the proposition that human personality is the product of an interaction between person and situation variables. As we have already seen in Units One and Two, however, there is also profound disagreement among theorists regarding which class of variable should receive the most emphasis. Unit Three begins by examining the major events in personality formation occurring during infancy (Chapter 9) and ends with a consideration of the pressures toward personality change or stability which are encountered in middle and late adulthood (Chapter 14). Within this more or less developmental sequence of chapters, some specific topics to be covered are emotional expressiveness, language, self-concept, moral reasoning, helping behavior, coping with stress, task performance, creativity, aggressive behavior, sex roles, adult crises in choosing life goals, and the psychological effects of biological changes associated with aging. On many of these topics, different viewpoints are held by adherents to the different theoretical traditions presented in Unit One. Attention will be called to particular areas of disagreement, and research evidence will be cited which might point the way toward a scientific resolution of theoretical disputes.

9.

EARLY DEVELOPMENT AND THE SOURCES OF TEMPERAMENT

ISSUES TO CONSIDER

1 In what ways do psychoanalytic, dispositional, and behavioral theorists agree and disagree in their perceptions of the biological make-up and behavioral potentialities of human infants?
2 What evidence is there that temperamental factors and early social experiences have lasting effects on character?
3 Does the specialization of abilities in the brain's left and right hemispheres have any implications for individual differences in personality?

The personality theorists we encountered in Unit One generally assumed that the people who provide the earliest social experiences for a human infant—usually the parents and especially the mother—have a major influence on the child's personality. An individual's interaction with friends, teachers, and others throughout life either reinforces or modifies the patterns established by early experience. This view of personality as the product of rewarding or punishing experiences associated with behavior in a social environment was most thoroughly elaborated by theorists with a behaviorist orientation.

One can hardly deny the importance of environmental experience for shaping and maintaining the patterns of thinking and behavior which constitute what we call *personality*. Even so, most people who have spent some time around human infants would probably agree that children often have characteristically different ways of expressing themselves even when they are too young to have had very much social experience. Also, as Thomas, Chess, and Birch (1970) pointed out, the family and social backgrounds of children who develop severe psychological problems often do not appear to be very different from the backgrounds of well-adjusted children. Alternatively, subtle environmental differences that are being overlooked by observers may be producing these variations in the behavior of children with seemingly similar backgrounds. In the present chapter, however, we will consider the possibility that there are some aspects of personality which, while partially modifiable by experience, are, for the most part, inherent in the infant at birth. An individual's *temperament* consists of emotional reactions and cognitive and behavioral aptitudes which are, to some extent, the product of that person's biological inheritance. Investigations of human temperament are associated with trait-dispositional and, to a lesser extent, phenomenological approaches to the study of personality.

The psychoanalytic position is that character forms as a result of a head-on clash between biological instincts that are fairly uniform across all individuals and varying degrees of resistance in the social environment. Traits that will last a lifetime are forged in four childhood psychosexual stages, each of which involves some limitation being placed on the gratification of the desire for pleasurable stimulation of a different erotogenic zone.

We will begin this chapter by briefly examining some evidence supportive of this psychoanalytic position, but we will then move on to the more extensive research on dispositional and behavioral determinants of personality formation in childhood. Next, we will focus our attention on the development of basic abilities, such as perceptual and motor skills and the expression of emotion. Finally, we will examine the origins of language, that most uniquely human of abilities, and its relationship with thought processes.

PERSONALITY FORMATION IN CHILDHOOD

There is a surprising area of common ground between psychoanalytic and behavioral conceptions of personality. Both regard physically healthy infants as being very much alike in terms of biological processes and behavioral potentialities at birth. Freud felt that infants came packaged with instincts, but he did not believe that these biological forces differed very much from one child to another. The behaviorists also consider infants to be psychologically identical in that they are all pretty much blank slates who have yet to be inscribed by the chalk of environmental experience. It is dispositional theorists working within the personological tradition who argue that infants may be born with differing temperaments.

Character Types Derived from Psychoanalytic Theory

Kline (1972) reviewed all the studies he could locate which tested hypotheses derived from psychoanalytic theory in a scientifically rigorous manner. This was not an easy task because Freud made no effort to build his theory out of clearly stated hypotheses which could be supported or refuted by objectively quantifiable data. Freud's "data" were the unconfirmed self-reports of patients as recalled after the interview by the therapist. These are not valid results in a modern scientific sense, and Kline felt it was important to search for studies which met contemporary criteria of proof.

More or less specific hypotheses can be derived from Freudian theory in at least two areas of childhood personality development: the effects of weaning and the effects of toilet training. As regards the former, infants who are nursed liberally and weaned late supposedly develop orally gratified personality types distinguished by generosity, sociability, openness to new ideas, and a belief in better days to come (the *oral optimist*). Infants who are nursed minimally and weaned early develop the orally ungratified personality type characterized by depression, withdrawal, passivity, selfishness, insecurity, desire for success combined with feelings of hopelessness, and a belief in harder times ahead (the *oral pessimist*). In the case of toilet training, the anal-retentive character may be produced either by very punitive parental behavior, resulting in a fear of defecation, or by excessive parental praise for bowel movements, resulting in a desire to hold onto the valued feces for as long as possible. Anal retentiveness can be recognized in the personality traits of orderliness, obstinacy, and thrift.

Kline reports that Goldman-Eisler (1951) administered a questionnaire that measured the traits comprising oral "optimism" vs. "pessimism" to a group of 115 young adults, the mothers of whom were asked to indicate the age at which their children had been removed from breast or bottle feeding. It was found that those whose personality leaned toward oral pessimism had been weaned significantly earlier than had those who were oral optimists. In general, however, most studies have failed to find a clear

relationship between age of weaning and oral personality type, Blum and Miller (1952) did find that a child's orality score on a projective test of personality known as the Blacky Pictures was associated with the number of mouth movements made while eating ice cream.

Attempts to relate the severity of toilet training to the emergence of an anal-retentive personality have been similarly inconclusive. Several studies have found that there is a significant tendency for the traits of orderliness, obstinacy, thrift, and all-around compulsiveness to cluster together on personality inventories, much as Freud would have predicted (Beloff, 1957, Cattell, 1957, Kline, 1969). Kline (1968) also found a significant relationship between a questionnaire measure of the foregoing characteristics and a person's anality score on the Blacky Pictures. A more recent review of the literature on the anal character reported that while the traits predicted for it do tend to appear together in adult personalities, there is no statistically significant tendency for this cluster of traits to be related to the severity of toilet training in childhood. Rather, it is the anality of parents' personalities which is most predictive of the orderliness, obstinacy, and thrift of their offspring. This suggests that modeling and imitation may be the factors primarily responsible for the emergence of the so-called anal character (Pollak, 1979).

Freud also proposed a *phallic personality type*, who is supposed to be self-assured, reckless, and proud, but Kline (1972) could find practically no evidence that this collection of traits developed as a result of repressed childhood sexuality. We will postpone until Chapter 11 our discussion of evidence pertaining to the *Oedipus complex*, in which the repression of a child's erotic attachment to the parent of the opposite sex allegedly leads to emergence of the superego.

Treatment of certain other topics with some relevance to psychoanalytic conceptions of childhood determinants of personality will also be postponed. The origins of depressive disorders and the effects of birth order, for example, will be examined in Chapter 10, and Erikson's research on differences in toy preferences between boys and girls is cited in Chapter 13. For the present, it might be said that some suggestive evidence in support of various hypotheses derived from psychoanalytic theory exists, but the results are somewhat inconclusive. We will now compare and contrast the far more extensive results which bear upon the dispositional and environmentalist approaches to the study of early personality development.

Dispositional Approaches to the Origins of Temperament

Thomas, Chess, and Birch (1970) suspected that—independently of weaning, toilet training, and other early encounters with the social and physical environment—children are born with certain emotional and behavioral predispositions which, collectively, constitute what we refer to as *temperament*. To investigate this possibility, Thomas et al. carefully recorded the behavior of 141 children in their home environments.

The information was obtained through structured interviews with each child's parents and sometimes verified through direct observation by the investigators. Each child was evaluated at various ages ranging from birth through 14 years as low, medium, or high on the following nine dimensions: (1) level of motor activity, (2) degree of positive response to a new object or person, (3) degree of regularity of biological functions, (4) adaptability to changes in the environment, (5) threshold of sensitivity to stimuli, (6) customary degree of energy in responding, (7) general friendliness or "good mood," (8) degree of distractibility from ongoing activity, and (9) span of attention. Using these dimensions, the researchers found that two-thirds of the children in their sample displayed sufficient regularity of behavior over time to permit them to be classified in one of three temperament groups:

1 "Easy" infants followed regular rhythms in their biological functions of eating, sleeping,

and eliminating. They quickly adapted to changes in their environment and tended to approach rather than withdraw from new persons or objects (including foods), showed low to moderate levels of energy in responding, and were generally in a good mood.

2 "Difficult" children, on the other hand, tended to be irregular in bodily functions, to withdraw from and be slow to adapt to changes in their environment, to display intense levels of energy in responding, and generally to be in an unhappy mood. One example of a "difficult" child was a boy who wriggled and moved about excessively in his crib at 3 months; "swam like a fish" while being bathed at 6 months; squirmed constantly while being dressed or handled at 12 months; was constantly running, jumping, and climbing at 2 years; and was having difficulty in school at the age of 7 years because he would not sit still long enough to learn anything. Another child of this type screamed intensely upon exposure to even the most minor discomforts, such as bathing or dressing. This reaction was observed from birth onward, and by the age of 7 the child would react to mild frustration by stomping up to his room and screaming for half an hour.

3 There is yet a third temperament group which was described as "slow to warm up." These children differed from both their "easy" and "difficult" counterparts by having relatively low levels of motor activity. Like "difficult" children, they tended to withdraw from and be slow to adapt to new stimuli, and they were somewhat negative in mood. Unlike "difficult" children, they displayed low levels of energy in responding.

The foregoing categorizations were found to be related to subsequent personality development of the infants. For example, 70 percent of the "difficult" children, but only 18 percent of the "easy" ones, presented personality problems that called for professional attention, and the "slow-to-warm-up" group fell between these two extremes. Thomas et al. (1970) note, however, that even an "easy" child can develop a personality disorder if he or she is mishandled, and "difficult" children will develop normally if special care is taken to set and maintain clear, consistent standards for their behavior.

It appears there are grounds for arguing that personality develops from an interaction between social experience and some sort of inherent temperament. To say that a temperament is inherent, though, is not to say that it is necessarily inherited. A mother's experiences during pregnancy may have an influence on her offspring's temperament above and beyond any genetic determinants.

If, for example, a female rat is mated in an environment in which a buzzer is associated with receipt of electric shock, and if the buzzer is then activated at intermittent times during her pregnancy, her pups are more likely to be hyperemotional than are the offspring of mothers who have not had these stressful experiences (Thompson, 1957). Alternatively, gentle handling of a pregnant female rat is likely to reduce the emotionality of her pups (Ader & Conklin, 1963).

Ottinger and Simmons (1964) found evidence suggesting the possibility of similar phenomena in humans, in that women scoring very high on an anxiety questionnaire administered during their pregnancies produced infants who cried more frequently during the first few days of life than did the offspring of low-anxious mothers. It is conceivable, however, that anxious mothers caused the greater frequency of crying in their babies by handling them in a stress-inducing manner *after* the infants were born.

On the other hand, what if temperament *is* to some extent inherited? How would we investigate such a possibility? The twin-study method was described in Chapter 7 as a means of demonstrating the existence of heritable components of schizophrenia and IQ, and it can be applied here as well. Recall that fraternal twins, since they are produced by the fertilization of two separate eggs, are genetically no more alike than any two siblings and share about half of their genes in common. Identical twins are conceived in the splitting of a single fertilized egg and so share all of their genes in common. Since both members of fraternal and identical twin pairs are gestated in the same womb and are usually raised in the same household, these environmental influences on personality are held more or less constant for a given pair. If, on a particular personality trait, identicals turn out to be more alike than fraternals, there are logical grounds for arguing that the result must be due to the greater genetic similarity between identicals. Any traits on which identicals turn out to be more alike than fraternals could be presumed, therefore, to be under some degree of genetic control in all human beings. The only environmental factor which might invalidate this line of logic would be a tendency for parents to make a special effort to handle identical twins more similarly than they do fraternals. As was mentioned in Chapter 7, it is important for researchers to try to rule out this alternative explanation for those genetic factors in personality whose existence has been indicated by twin studies.

In one well-controlled study by Freedman and Keller (1963), expressive behavior and motor abilities were observed in twenty same-sex twin pairs during their first year of life. Neither the researchers nor the parents were certain whether a given twin pair was identical or fraternal until the conclusion of the research, when blood-serum analyses were made. (Even the obstetricians who delivered the babies were correct in their assumptions regarding which pairs were identical and which fraternal in only about half the cases.) Consequently, it is impressive to note that on indices comparable to those used by Thomas et al. (1970), identical twins were found to be significantly more alike than fraternals on dependent measures such as activity level, positive response to objects and persons, reaction to changes in the environment, and so forth.

Wilson (1972) reported standardized scores for tests of mental development administered to approximately eighty identical and ninety-five fraternal twins at 3, 6, 9, 12, 18, and 24 months of age. On these tests, known as the Bayley Scales (Bayley, 1933), the child is presented with a graded sequence of tasks and measured on how far through the sequence he or she can progress before a task becomes too difficult. The earliest tasks are orienting the head toward a dangling ring or, further on, reaching out to grasp it. Later tasks are approaching a mirror image, stacking two or more blocks, saying one or more words, fitting blocks of different shapes into a board with appropriately shaped holes, and so forth. At all ages studied, the scores achieved by identical twins were significantly more alike than were those obtained by fraternals.

Loehlin and Nichols (1976) found comparable results when they compared 514 identical and 336 same-sex fraternal twins who were adolescents rather than babies. Identicals were far more alike than were fraternals on every trait dimension studied. Interestingly, identicals were very similar in their ability to perform various tasks (correlations were 0.7 − 0.8), moderately similar in overall personality and activities (r's = 0.5 − 0.6), and only slightly similar in self-concept, goals, and vocational interest (r's = 0.3 − 0.4). Thus, hereditary factors may play a role in the development of personality traits that persist into adulthood and may contribute more to the expression of some traits than of others. On the other hand, Loehlin and Nichols acknowledged that parents typically report that they deliberately expose identical twins to more similar experiences than they usually require of fraternals (e.g., wearing matching clothing). It is conceivable that such social pressures impinging on the environments of identicals and fraternals could account for the greater similarity of temperament exhibited by subjects in the former group. Consequently, as the authors themselves point out, the data "do not altogether exclude a completely environmentalist position" (Loehlin & Nichols, 1976, p. 94).

Using a somewhat different method of investigating this problem, Grotevant, Scarr, and Weinberg (1977) compared the scores of parents and their biological or adoptive adolescent children on the Strong-Campbell Interest Inventory. The results clearly showed that parents and biological children are much more alike in interests than are parents and adoptive children, even though the mean age of adoption in the study was only 2.6 months. Here again, the evidence points to the existence of hereditary influences on personality development.

A rather remarkable confirmation of the above conclusion seems to be provided by a pair of male identical twins who were separated at birth in 1939 and raised by different adoptive families in the vicinity of Dayton, Ohio (Associated Press, 1979). The families were unaware of one another's existence until both twins became adults. Even so, each twin turned out to have the surname James. Furthermore, on finally meeting one another, they learned that both had married and divorced women named Linda; christened their firstborn sons James Allan (the middle name was spelled "Alan" by one brother); vacationed on the same beach in Florida; taken police training and worked part-time for law-enforcement agencies; and enjoyed carpentry and mechanical drawing as hobbies. Each was also 6 feet tall and weighed about 180 pounds.

Environmentalist Explanations for Early Personality Development

Social-learning theorists like Bijou and Baer (1965) would discount the influence of any inborn temperamental factors on early personality development. They would, instead, point to the many positive reinforcers supplied by the mother (or other caretaker) as the primary, if not the sole, elicitors of infant behavior. It is the conscious or unconscious application of contingencies of reinforcement which shapes the regularly occurring, complex sequences of behavior that we label "temperament" or, later in life, "personality." Thus the hungry infant whose caretakers are responsive to his or her cries for food may develop an "up-and-doing," activist personality, while the baby left to "cry itself out" may become apathetic (Dollard & Miller, 1950, p. 132).

Dollard and Miller (pp. 132–154) believe there are four critical training situations in infancy and childhood which inevitably evoke both the pleasurable internal emotional responses associated with positive reinforcement as well as the unpleasurable emotions associated with negative reinforcement and conflict. These situations are feeding, toilet training, sex training, and the expression of anger.

Two possible implications of feeding practices for personality were described above. Dollard and Miller further suggest that the mother and other caretakers, through their association with food and other reinforcers, become stimuli which signal the occurrence of pleasurable emotions. Through stimulus generalization, the child is likely to view all human beings as beneficent and comforting. While such a child would probably be easily socialized into the community, he or she might also develop an excessive fear of being alone, leading to such childhood problems as fear of quiet or darkness or tendencies toward over-conformity as an adult. Alternatively, the infant who is routinely fed even when not hungry may not attach pleasurable feelings to the presence of others and so may not develop a high degree of concern for the wishes of others (reminiscent of Adler's notion of lack of social interest). Research by Bruner (1967) demonstrates that even so innate a response as sucking for milk can be modified by a feeding system which places an infant on various schedules of reinforcement (see Chapter 4). Sucking behavior can be extinguished if a bottle is designed so that merely "gumming" the nipple supplies milk. Smiling, too, is affected by early reinforcement. The appearance of smiling adult faces accompanied by tickling an infant's tummy will increase the frequency of smiles and vocalizations in the baby, while expressionless adult faces and no tickling will extinguish these behaviors (Rheingold, Gewirtz, & Ross, 1959). Fitzgerald and Brackbill (1976) reviewed more than 100 studies demonstrating

the conditioning of behavior or biological processes in human infants.

Toilet training and sex training are similar in that parents act as the agents of society in imposing cultural restrictions on activities that are inherently pleasurable (e.g., eliminating the bladder when it is full or fondling the genitals). Virtually all societies are absolute in their insistence that this type of behavior be engaged in only at certain times and in certain places. Even the most patient parents are likely, sooner or later, to punish a child's mistakes in these matters. The baby who smears feces over himself or herself and the environment (as nearly all do at least once) is likely to encounter expressions of disapproval on the part of caretakers and to experience some rough handling during the cleanup; the child may even be spanked. Similarly, children who fondle their genitals in public are likely to have their hands slapped. Consequently, approach-avoidance conflicts often develop in the course of early socialization. The child may resist going to bed, for example, out of fear of the consequences of bed-wetting or being caught in the act of masturbating. It is also likely that parents will be viewed somewhat ambivalently by the child. The sometimes-punishing, sometimes-rewarding parents will inevitably generate uncertainty as to the circumstances under which they may safely be approached. The consequences for personality development may range from antisocial rebelliousness to excessive conformity and guilt, depending on the nature and circumstances of these conflicts. Dollard and Miller (1950) go so far as to agree with Freud that Oedipal conflicts may frequently develop in childhood and that their resolution involves learning society's sex-typed role behavior. They also, however, try to account for these events using a behavioral, social-learning terminology and consciously avoid referring to instincts based on the Freudian id.

Animal studies also reveal the importance of early experience for subsequent emotional reactions and other behavior. In one of these studies, rats who had been stressed by being shocked, crowded, or deprived of food during infancy were found to be more emotionally disturbed by a stressful experience as adults than were rats who had been handled gently as infants (Denenberg et al., 1970).

In other studies, an animal's companions during infancy were found to have a strong influence on its social preferences as an adult. Mice reared with rats subsequently chose a rat over a fellow mouse in a social-preference test which consisted of placing a caged representative of each species on opposite arms of a T-maze (Denenberg et al., 1964). For their part, rats exposed to a fondling human hand later showed a stronger desire to be in the presence of a human hand than did a control group of unfondled animals (Werner and Latané, 1974). As young adults, monkeys reared by a human chose a human on a social-preference test, while monkeys reared in the presence of their peers or by a monkey mother chose a monkey on the test. Isolation-reared monkeys chose to sit in the center of the T-maze, moving toward neither a fellow monkey nor a human being (Sackett et al., 1965).

BASIC COMPONENTS OF HUMAN INTERACTION

The foregoing sections provided an overview of the types of evidence which might be cited in support of one or another of the major theoretical approaches presented in Unit One. In the sections which follow, the dispositional and environmentalist approaches are compared and contrasted in the context of several specific abilities which are major components of adult personality.

Perceptual and Motor Skills

Based on reports of the visual experiences of patients born blind but given sight in adulthood by means of surgical operations, it was long assumed that infants could see little beyond a formless haze of color. The newly sighted patients whose reactions were described in von Senden's classic monograph (Hebb, 1949, chap. 2) were at first delighted by a blaze of colors but then became discouraged as they realized they could not distinguish a triangle from a square or even from a circle. This deficit is particularly intriguing when one considers that the patients were socially competent adults who could instantly identify any of the shapes if permitted to touch them. A very difficult problem for the patients was learning how to discriminate one human face from another; it took them a minimum of a month of slow, painstaking learning to begin to see normally. Though Hebb acknowledged that there is probably a primitive, built-in mechanism which permits us to perceive a figure as separate from its background, his main conclusion was that "The course of perceptual learning in man is gradual, proceeding from a dominance of color, through a period of separate attention to each part of a figure, to a gradually arrived at identification of the whole as a whole" (1949, p. 32).

Hebb's essentially environmentalist conclusion has not, however, been entirely supported by subsequent research that studies perceptual processes in infants directly instead of inferring these processes from the behavior of newly sighted adults. In support of Hebb's position, it does seem that infants younger than 1 month cannot adjust the shape of the lenses of their eyes so as to bring objects at varying distances into focus on their retinas; the system seems "set" so as to provide clear images of objects about 8 inches away (which happens to be the approximate distance of a baby's face from its mother's while breast feeding). By the second or third month of life, the infant's ability to focus on objects at varying distances—called *visual accommodation*—approximates that of the average adult (Haynes, White, & Held, 1965). Young infants also have difficulty in converging the eyes so as to bring an object into focus on both retinas simultaneously (Wickelgreen, 1967). Despite this perceptual clumsiness, however, it is remarkable what very young infants can see.

Fantz (1963) presented a series of visual stimuli to eighteen infants ranging from 10 hours to 5 days of age while the subjects were lying on their backs in a crib. The circular targets were a face, a bull's-eye, a section of newsprint, and plain fields of white, yellow, or red. During two days of testing, with the stimuli presented in random order, all infants—even those less than 48 hours old—showed a clear preference for patterned rather than plain targets. Even the youngest infants spent two-thirds of their total gazing time looking at the patterned stimuli, and nearly half of that amount of time was reserved for the human face. Freedman (1974) duplicated Fantz's observations in a better-controlled study that used black and white targets containing eyes, eyebrows, nose, and mouth in either a normal facial configuration or one scrambling these components to a lesser or greater degree. Among 272 infants tested at an average age of 42 hours, there was a much greater willingness to turn the head so as to gaze at a face rather than either of the scrambled configurations. Infants had very little interest in gazing at the blank outline of a head with no facial components. Freedman's facial stimuli are shown in Figure 9-1.

The above studies suggest that while infants learn perceptual skills partly through their environmental experiences, they are also disposed toward attending to the features of that environment which are important for their survival. Foremost among these features are those which make up the human face. Now consider the intriguing observation, reported by Bower (1976), that 6-day-old infants will reliably imitate the facial expressions of an adult (usually the mother) who is holding them and has captured their attention by gazing into their eyes. If the mother sticks her tongue out, the infant is likely to stick his or her tongue out right back—an extremely complex behavior which requires that the infant recognize the unseen object in his or her own mouth as corresponding to the mother's tongue.

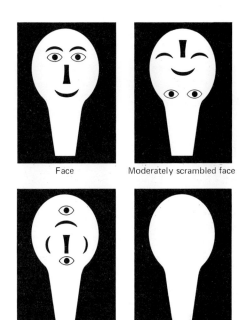

Face   Moderately scrambled face

Scrambled face   Blank

FIGURE 9-1
Some pictorial stimuli used to test infants' preference for gazing at a humanlike face versus alternative patterns. (From Freedman, 1974.)

This imitative ability disappears within a few weeks of birth, however, and does not reappear until the end of the first year.

The newborn child may possess still other remarkable perceptual and motor skills at birth. According to Bower (1974, pp. 83–96) 1-week-old infants will, if seated in an upright position, react defensively to a rapidly approaching object by first widening their eyes and retracting their heads and then interposing their hands between their faces and the object. In a series of well-controlled studies by Bower and other investigators, it was demonstrated that this reaction was produced mainly by the change in apparent size of the approaching object, though the increase in air pressure associated with such an approach in natural situations also played a part in the response. It would seem, then, that there is a capacity for depth perception in the newborn

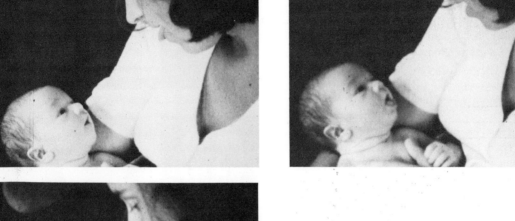

A sequence of pictures showing an infant watching intently and then trying to imitate his mother's gesture of sticking out her tongue. This early capacity for imitation indicates that children have a very complex, built-in perceptual ability which is activated somewhat independently of social experience. (T. G. R. Bower)

because it is unlikely that the infants in these studies could have learned very much about distance cues in just one week of life.

Eye-hand coordination also seems to be present in newborns to the extent that they will, if seated upright, reach out to grasp small objects suspended several inches in front of their faces. This behavior disappears after about age 4 weeks and reappears at around age 20 weeks (Bower, 1974, p. 158). Furthermore, 1-week-old infants will, if held upright, march along a flat surface, putting one foot ahead of another in the complex sequence we call *walking*. This ability typically drops out by age 8 weeks and does not recur until the end of the first year. In the case of both eye-hand coordination and walking, however, practice of the ability during the neonatal stage will hasten its later reappearance and facilitate the growth of competence. Consequently, Bower argues that neonatal abilities are not "lost" but are simply suppressed for different periods of time so that other capabilities may be developed by the rapidly growing brain and body.

There is no doubt, of course, that parents provide their infants and young children with elaborate training in and reinforcement for visual attentiveness, grasping of objects, and walking. Learning (as defined by the environmentalist tradition) is clearly a major factor in the encouragement and refinement of these behaviors. It appears, though, that infants may also come biologically prepared to display such skills and that social learning alone does not completely account for these early developments. There is evidence here which supports the dispositional as well as the environmentalist positions.

Expression of Emotions

It has been suggested that a child's ability to express its feelings—a very basic element of its personality—begins to develop just a few days after birth in the course of its interactions with its mother or other caretaker (Richards, 1974). Through such games as peekaboo, the infant's gaze becomes selectively focused on the caretaker's face—particularly the eyes. Imitation of the caretaker's expression causes the infant to become more expressive (smiling is a behavior highly prized by parents and relatives). Efforts to imitate sounds emitted by the caretaker produce a rudimentary control over pitch, volume, and so on that will be necessary for future speech.

Pleasurable interactions with members of one's own species at an early age are probably important precursors to one's future ability to cooperate and communicate with them. Miller, Caul, and Mirsky (1967) placed isolate-reared and normal monkeys in a situation where they were viewing a televised picture of the face of another monkey. The televised monkey received a series of painful shocks, which caused it to grimace. If the viewing monkey failed to close a switch within a few seconds of this visual cue it, too, received a painful shock. Even though isolates and normals had previously been shown to be equivalent in their ability to learn how to avoid shocks in a nonsocial situation, these groups differed dramatically in their responsiveness to the information provided by the televised mon-

key's face. Normal monkeys quickly learned to avoid shock by throwing the switch when the televised animal grimaced in pain, but isolates showed no such learning. Interestingly, normal monkeys achieved successful avoidance only when viewing another normal monkey; they were unable to learn the avoidance contingency when viewing the grimaces of an isolate-reared animal. Thus, isolates showed deficits in communicating pain cues as well as in reading them.

Human infants who have been deprived of normal social experience also show deficits in communicative as well as other behaviors. Deprived environments are most usually found in institutions such as orphanages and hospitals. Institutionalized infants under 6-8 months of age are likely to show little smiling, to be listless and generally unresponsive to external stimulation, and to have an overall "unhappy" appearance (Spitz & Wolf, 1946; Provence & Lipton, 1962). More recent work relating to the emergence of hospitalism and other emotional disorders in children will be discussed in Chapter 10.

The earliest form of emotional expression in the infant is the cry. Using a device called a *sound spectrograph*, Wolff (1969) obtained voiceprints which permitted him to distinguish cries motivated by hunger from cries motivated by anger or pain. Besides crying, the infant also has a variety of facial expressions which he or she may use to communicate emotion. The one most prized by parents is the smile, which may occur during the first week of life but does not become convincingly social until around 8 weeks of age. The "smiling" of very young infants may be motivated by internal events associated with irregular sleep or gastrointestinal distress (Charlesworth & Kreutzer, 1973, p. 106). In a much-cited study, Ahrens (1953) demonstrated that there are systematic changes over time in the type of visual stimulation required for eliciting smiling in an infant. At around 4 weeks of age, a black dot on a card will be enough to make an infant smile. From the age of 6 weeks to 7 months, the infant becomes more and more selectively responsive to stimuli (e.g., masks) which closely resemble a human face. Freedman (1974) comments that Ahrens's observations have been duplicated many times and disputes the view that smiling in newborn infants is entirely the result of intestinal gas. At very young ages, smiling can be more reliably elicited by a cooing voice and cuddling than by mere exposure to a human face or mask. As was mentioned earlier in this chapter, research by Rheingold et al. (1959) shows that the responsiveness of an adult observer can be an important reinforcement for smiling behavior. Perhaps because of differences in the responsiveness of their caretakers, home-reared and institution-reared children differ in the age of onset as well as the peak frequency of social smiling; the latter were retarded on both these indices (Ambrose, 1959).

Recent research by Ekman and his collaborators (1973) has found support for the thesis advanced by Darwin (1872) that the expression and recognition of emotions is largely a result of innate programming. Ekman's evidence consists of the fact that across diverse cultures (nine literate and one preliterate), adult observers showed a high degree of agreement on the emotional content of a set of still photographs of people portraying happiness, disgust, surprise, sadness, anger, or fear. Ekman argues that this ability of people from geographically and linguistically separate cultures to portray emotions that will be accurately read by one another must be due either to similar practices in the socialization of emotions (which is highly unlikely to have occurred by chance) or to an inherent patterning of emotional expression. Ohman and Dimberg (1978) found further support for the latter possibility in a study which demonstrated that people learn more rapidly that a picture of a human face signals impending shock if the face bears an angry rather than a neutral or happy expression. Subjects in the study also showed physiological evidence (in the form of galvanic skin response—

see Chapter 7) of being more emotionally upset when shock was signaled by an angry rather than a happy face.

Charlesworth and Kreutzer (1973) reviewed many studies on the expression of emotion by infants and young children and concluded that the facial contortions involved in the expression of distress, happiness, anger, surprise, and other feelings probably have biological as well as social determinants. The interrelationship of these factors undoubtedly has an important influence on early personality development. For example, the colicky baby who cries a great deal and resists efforts to establish a regular schedule (the "difficult" baby described by Thomas et al.) will probably induce a great deal of frustration and distress in the caretakers unless they are exceptionally patient and forbearing. If the parents do become tense in their interactions with the infant, it is likely that the child will become anxious about engaging in social interaction (Bell, 1968).

The communication established by eye contact and reciprocal smiling between mother and infant has long been regarded as a mainstay of this earliest of social bonds (Robson, 1967; Bell, 1974). Infants provided with this secure base in their early relationships are likely to be less afraid of strangers and novel stimuli, to cry less, and to be more active in exploring strange environments (Ainsworth, 1964; Rheingold, 1969). The foregoing studies appear to suggest that fully effective mothers and other caretakers are doing more than providing nourishment and protection from physical harm. They are engaging in a social interaction with the infant that lays the foundation for subsequent personality development and successful adjustment. As Reynolds (1976, p. 163) noted, a child's temperament is very likely to influence this communication process.

The infant's level of responsiveness has effects on the mother's ability to cope and her behavior then feeds back to the infant. Thus infantile constitutional factors affect maternal action,

Six people posing the emotions of happiness, fear, and disgust (top row) and anger, surprise, and sadness (bottom row). Ekman argues that the ability of people from different cultures to pose emotions that will be accurately read by one another is probably due to a built-in patterning of emotional expression. (Ekman, Universal and cultural differences in facial expression of emotion. In J. K. Cole (Ed.), *Nebraska Symposium on Motivation.*)

maternal action is itself in part the output of ongoing constitutional factors in the mother, her action affects the development of the infant's action and constitution.

The importance of communication to character formation having been established, we will devote the remainder of this chapter to an examination of that amazing and uniquely human form of communication known as *language.* As in other areas of early development, a clear distinction can be drawn between the environmental and dispositional viewpoints on the acquisition of language and its relationship with thinking.

LANGUAGE DEVELOPMENT

Before the age of 3 months, infants make a great many crying, fussing, gurgling, cooing, and whimpering sounds. These sounds appear to be innately motivated, since they are emitted with approximately the same frequency and patterning even when the infant or the parents (or both) are deaf (Lenneberg, 1964 a, b; Lenneberg, Rebelsky, & Nichols, 1965). The environmental conditions which influence these vocalizations are primarily simple deprivations or discomforts, such as the amount of time since the last feeding or diaper change (Lewis, 1963).

After the age of 3 months, as was noted earlier, infants become increasingly social: they smile, gaze, and appear to be genuinely interested in communicating with others in their environment. It is at about this age also that they begin to babble, emitting long strings of phonemes in a more or less random sequence. A *phoneme* is the smallest single component of speech sounds. These "atoms" of sound may, either individually or combined with one another, constitute *morphemes*, which are the smallest units of meaning in a language. Roughly speaking, phonemes correspond to the individual letters of the English alphabet, while morphemes are the words created by combining these letters (though some morphemes, such as "a" or "I," are composed of only one phoneme). Other languages often contain phonemes that are not represented in the English alphabet. Consequently, linguists have compiled an international phonetic alphabet, which contains all the phonemes used in all known spoken languages and is used by publishers of dictionaries to help us sound out unfamiliar words.

The Progression from Sounds to Speech

How does the infant's babbling get transformed into speech? Surprisingly, this nearly universal aspect of human experience remains somewhat mysterious and even controversial. The environmentalist tradition assumes that the transformation is accomplished through selective reinforcement of certain wordlike sounds by eagerly attentive parents. These sounds then increase in frequency and are further shaped by selective parental attention into recognizable morphemes. (Behavioral psychology's concepts of reinforcement and shaping were defined and discussed in Chapter 4). Probably more important than reinforcement of sounds spontaneously emitted by the infant, however, are the rewards he or she receives for trying to imitate speech samples provided by the parent. As Mowrer (1952) noted, once the infant is motivated to imitate parental speech he or she is able to learn words and sentences at a rapid pace. Deaf children, whose vocalizations during the first three months resemble those of their hearing counterparts, begin to diverge from the latter in their speech development once babbling begins. Without auditory models to imitate, deaf children babble very little and, when they do, tend to repeat the same sounds for long periods of time instead of exploring the full range of phonemes (Lenneberg, 1964b).

Dollard and Miller (1950, p. 227) argued that the parent's voice, through its association with delivery of primary reinforcers such as food, develops secondary reinforcing properties. Roughly speaking, infants learn to associate "feeling good" with parental voice sounds and so they "feel good" again when they can successfully imitate these sounds.

A behavioral-psychologist's account of an infant's acquisition of the word "ball" might run as follows: The mother shows her infant a ball and captures the child's attention by rolling the object and saying "ball." If the infant's babbles at that moment include a "b" sound, the mother will lavish smiles and other secondary reinforcers on this approximate performance. She then repeats the word and pauses, giving the infant time to vocalize. Thus the child is learning not only to emit "b" sounds but also to "take turns" in social communication (Richards, 1974, pp. 91–92). Eventually, the "b," "a," and "l" phonemes will be combined into the morpheme "ball." Next, the child learns that many round objects of different sizes and colors can all be called *ball*. He or she may now be said to have a concept of ball which is independent of the particular object in view and which was formed by the process of reinforcement, imitation, and stimulus generalization. Naturally this concept takes time to unfold. True imitation, which involves accurate recall of something said several minutes before and a faithful reproduction not only of the words and phrases but also of the inflections and intonation, does not emerge until around 9 months of age (Lewis, 1951).

While the foregoing account of language development in terms of social learning and imitation certainly seems plausible, several critics judge it to be incomplete. Mere exposure of children to adult speech will cause them to start talking and, once they get beyond the initial stage of learning names for things, to develop an ability to generate unique grammatical constructions at a very rapid rate—outstripping, it would appear, the explanatory capacity of a social-learning theory. Hymes (Bellugi & Brown, 1964) argued that there must be a "language generator" built into the human brain, and Chomsky (1968) went further to suggest that the child possesses an "innate grammar" which guides its linguistic development. Chomsky argued that an analysis of children's *mistakes* in learning a language across diverse cultures was more informative for the study of linguistic development than was a record of their *successes*. It appeared to him that the emergence of speech in children around the world followed a set of rules that they had never been formally taught and that might or might not be consistent with the rules of their linguistic communities. These and other observations suggested to Chomsky that there must be a universal "deep struc-

ture" common to all human languages and that knowledge of this structure must be somewhat innate. This idea is clearly more compatible with a dispositional than with a behavioral viewpoint.

The Language Capacity of Apes

The notion of a built-in human predisposition for language is supported by the obvious contrast between the rapidity with which human children learn to speak and the slow, painstaking process by which apes, our closest animal relatives, learn the barest rudiments of language. Chimpanzees raised like human children by married teams of psychologists do not learn anything resembling a spoken language (Kellogg & Kellogg, 1933; Hayes & Hayes, 1951). The fact that chimps engage in a great deal of vocal signaling in their natural environment raised false hopes that they could learn to speak. Keleman (1948) and Lieberman (Lieberman, Klatt, & Wilson, 1969) suggested that the main reason for the apes' failure to speak was that their vocal apparatuses can produce only very limited numbers of vowellike sounds. Consequently, different approaches were tried, and better results were obtained. The Gardners (1974) taught a young chimp named Washoe the American Sign Language, which is widely used by deaf persons; the chimp, at last report, had a vocabulary of more than 100 words. The Premacks (1972) taught their chimp, Sarah, to manipulate plastic symbols in order to demonstrate her linguistic capacity. Sarah's vocabulary became at least equal to Washoe's, and both chimps, by this index, achieved a language capability approximately equivalent to that of a 2-year-old child.

The accomplishments of Washoe and Sarah notwithstanding, several prominent linguists express doubt as to the extent to which the chimps' manipulative skills demonstrate mastery of a language. Limber (1977), for example, notes that an organism's repertory of symbolic signs does not necessarily constitute evidence of its linguistic capacity; even dogs can learn to respond differentially to a wide variety of signs. For Limber, the determining characteristics of language are its rules for structural relations between elements and its capacity to generate novel expressions which may be appropriately applied to objects or situations never before encountered. Between 2½ and 3 years of age, children begin to use what linguists call *hierarchically structured complex sentences* (sentences containing subordinate clauses or phrases embedded within them, such as "Do it the way I say" or "I cook it the way Mommy bakes a cake"). In these sentences, the child has placed a subordinate phrase immediately following the word "way." It could plausibly be inferred that the child has developed a concept of ways to do things and can apply this concept to new situations which it has never previously tried to describe. According to Limber, neither Washoe nor Sarah demonstrated the ability to use language as productively as do human children who have gotten past the initial stage of simply learning names for things. Washoe will often spontaneously generate combinations of from two to four signs which appear to have a rudimentary sentence structure. She is not particular as to the order in which she displays the signs, however, so "cat bite" is just as likely to come out "bite cat"—a difference in the sequence of elements which would profoundly affect the interpretation of the sentence by a naive listener (Brown, 1973a, p. 41). Thus, when Washoe emits a sequence of signs, it is not clear that she is doing anything more than spewing forth a series of names for objects and events occurring in a given situation. As for Sarah, the use of plastic symbols as her medium of communication makes it extremely difficult to rule out the possibility that her trainer—who is seated next to her during testing—may unconsciously be transmitting subtle clues as to which choice is the appropriate reply to a "sentence" consisting of an array of symbols on a board (Brown, pp. 49–50).

At an annual meeting of the Western Psychological Association, Savage-Rumbaugh and Rumbaugh (1979) reported on their efforts to teach chimps to use a simplified form of English by pressing keys which caused the symbols for words to be displayed on a television screen. The Rumbaughs concluded that much of the chimps' use of "language" was simply the attachment of labels to various objects and actions. At these same meetings, Premack (1979) also shifted his position and became rather pessimistic about the language ability of chimps. These reports were echoed in print by yet another researcher who had unsuccessfully tried to develop genuine linguistic ability in a chimp (Terrace et al., 1979).

Even if future research does demonstrate a true capacity for language in apes, there remains a striking contrast between the laborious procedures by which this ability must be developed in them and the relative ease with which children learn to speak (Fouts, 1974). Consequently, one must continue to entertain the hypothesis that there is a special, built-in human predisposition to learn and use language. Geschwind (1969) linked one important component of language—the ability to form associations between such things as abstract verbal symbols on the one hand and overt actions on the other—with a structure unique to the human brain, the angular gyrus. This structure presumably gives humans the capacity to disengage their emotions from the representation of an action or object. Apes and other animals, by contrast, have methods of communication which are closely linked with the brain's limbic system (a set of structures heavily involved in the expression of emotion).

Consequently, it seems reasonable to conclude, on the basis of present knowledge, that humans have a unique capacity for language and a motivation to learn it which set them clearly apart from other species and which, in the almost infinite forms of linguistic expression of which human beings are capable, constitutes a considerable part of what we call *human nature* and *individual personality*. It has been argued (Reynolds, 1976, pp. 58–61) that the capacity for language was the single most important feature which distinguished human precursors like the australopithecines from the ancestors of modern apes. Exactly how our ancestors came to evolve this capacity will probably never be known, but it has been speculated that it was related to leaving the protection of the trees, journeying out into the open grasslands, forming strong social organizations for mutual protection, and standing erect so as to free the hands for tool use (including the use of weapons). However it evolved, language provided humans with the means to benefit from the accumulated experience of others in their group so that they did not have to relearn the discoveries of past and present generations every time a given problem recurred. It was this feature of language, subsequently greatly enhanced by the invention of writing in Mesopotamia around 3500 b.c., that permitted the emergence of civilization as we know it today.

Stages of Language Development in Children

Brown (1973a) reported the most extensive available analysis of stages of language acquisition in American children. He notes that his major findings have been replicated in a larger sample of American children studied by de Villiers and de Villiers (1973a, 1973b) and in cross-cultural studies by Slobin (1971). What follows is a summary of Brown's review of this material.

Brown devised a statistic, which he called *mean length of utterance* (MLU), that permitted him to compare the linguistic performance of any two children, even if they differed in chronological age. An MLU is the number of morphemes contained in a distinct grouping (i.e., an "utterance"), with the average number of morphemes per utterance being computed for a given observation period. Brown found that children's MLU scores rise as a direct function of their linguistic sophistication and, hence, of their chronological ages.

Brown distinguished five stages of linguistic development, based on his MLU. Stage 1 begins when the MLU passes 1; that is, when combina-

tions of two or more words are observed for the very first time in the child's utterances. Stage 1 ends and stage 2 begins when the MLU passes 2, at which time the child's utterances will occasionally be as long as seven morphemes. (Remember that the MLU is the *average* length of all of the child's utterances in a given time period, so some will be shorter and some longer than average.) At the beginning of stage 1, the child is approximately 18 months old (though there is considerable individual variation around this average age) and is saying things like "Daddy hit" or "Hit ball" or "Daddy ball." It seems as though he or she can, at one time, deal with just two out of the three major sentence elements we call subject, verb, and object. Toward the end of stage 1, at around 2 years of age, the three sentence elements are much more likely to appear together, as in "Daddy hit ball."

During stage 2, which covers the progression from 2 to 2.5 MLU, the child shows a steady increase in the usage of fourteen functional morphemes, including the articles "a" and "the" and the prepositions "in" and "on." Fully formed, adultlike sentences now appear more and more frequently in the child's repertory; e.g., "Daddy hit the ball." Brown believes it is useful to distinguish three additional stages above stage 2, each representing an increase of 0.5 MLU. He has not, however, characterized these stages in the same detail as he has stages 1 and 2.

Interestingly, Brown (1973a, 1973b) argues that selective reinforcement by parents seems to have little to do with the improvement in grammatical complexity and accuracy shown by their offspring. Parents, he says, provide corrective feedback for mispronunciation, "naughty" words, and highly irregular words like "digged" or "goed," but they seldom correct a child's grammar. Therefore, Brown suggests, one is compelled to consider the possibility that the motivation to learn a language and master its grammatical rules may be inherent in the child. Chomsky (1968), as was noted earlier, would go further to argue that the rules themselves—the "deep structure" common to all languages—must be somewhat innate in the human species.

The position of social-learning theorists, on the other hand, would be that selective parental reinforcement of verbal behavior is indeed the mechanism by which a child learns to speak. Of prime importance is rewarding the child for successfully imitating whatever the parent says or does. Bruner (1975) takes something of a middle ground between Chomsky's position and that of the social-learning theorists. He believes that we may, in fact, be predisposed to learn language easily but that the rules by which such learning proceeds are by no means self-evident to the child. Bruner maintains that the recognition process consists of fruitful interaction between an innately curious and verbally active child, who is motivated to communicate his or her needs and experiences, and others who provide training in the particular rules by which effective communication can be established.

Language and Thought

Beginning with Watson's paper "Psychology as a Behaviorist Views It" (1913) and extending through Skinner's *Verbal Behavior* (1957), the traditional-behaviorist interpretation of thought processes has been that they represent subvocal, internalized speech patterns which were initially conditioned on an overt, vocal level. What human beings call thinking, then, is closely related to their mastery of language, and thought consists of silently talking to oneself. The Soviet behaviorist tradition, too, accepts the notion that thinking begins as internalized speech (see Chapters 4 and 8). They also assume, however, that adult thinking employs movielike sequences of images that go far beyond the internalized speech of childhood.

Jean Piaget and his associates in Geneva, Switzerland, have a dramatically different point of view. They maintain that the capacity for progressively more complex modes of thinking develops independently in the maturing child and

that language is one of the many effects (rather than the cause) of cognitive development. Piaget's classic work on this topic, *The Language and Thought of the Child* (1923), described four major periods of cognitive development: (1) sensory motor (0-18 months), (2) preoperational (18 months-7 years), (3) concretely operational (7-12 years), and (4) formal operations (12 years and up). The ages indicated are approximations; Piaget's main point is that cognitive development follows a constant sequence in all individuals, even though people may differ in the exact age at which they enter a given period.

It is clear from our earlier discussion of language development that most children will have passed through Piaget's sensory-motor stage and entered the preoperational stage before they can be said to have learned to speak. What sort of thinking, then, can be attributed to children in the prelinguistic, sensory-motor period? Much of what children are doing at this time, according to Piaget, consists of learning how their actions influence their environment and how certain features of the environment remain essentially constant even though they may be out of view or viewed from a new perspective. In the course of observing his own infant children, Piaget (1936) noticed his daughter, at 11 months of age, sitting in a swing and viewing her dangling foot from a variety of different angles. It seemed as though she wanted to assure herself that this object, whose shape was very much altered when viewed from different perspectives, was indeed a single foot which she was able to kick back and forth.

As the sensory-motor stage ends and the preoperational stage begins, the child increasingly behaves as though objects outside his or her immediate sphere of action do continue to exist and may be found and retrieved when needed. To test this hypothesis, Piaget (1937) exposed a number of infants to a situation in which a favorite toy was slowly moved out from behind a screen. At first the toy was not recognized; when enough of it had appeared, the child smiled with delight but did not try to move the screen or grasp the toy. Piaget (p. 31) inferred that, "When the child sees a part of the object, he does not yet consider this totality as being formed 'behind' the screen; he simply admits that it is in the process of being formed at the moment of leaving the screen." As the sensory-motor period ends, however, a child begins to remove the barriers which he or she knows conceal the desired object.

The primary characteristics of entry into the preoperational stage are, for Piaget (1976b), the emergence of delayed imitation and representational play. *Delayed imitation* consists of witnessing behavior on the part of someone else and then, in the absence of the model, repeating the behavior for one's own amusement or to achieve the same result obtained by the "model." *Representational play* consists of using one object to stand for another (e.g., a child might move a small shell along the edge of a wooden block and say "meow" in order to represent a cat walking along a fence). Piaget believes these activities mean that the child has developed the ability to form mental images of objects and actions and that the subsequent development of language is the outcome rather than the cause of the child's general cognitive growth.

The cognitive style of a preoperational child, though it includes a certain degree of linguistic skill, can be clearly distinguished from the cognitive style of a concretely operational child who is approximately 7 years of age or older.

In a famous experiment by Piaget, two identical balls of clay were shown to a 5-year-old and placed in balance so that it was clear that they were of equal weight. Then, with the child looking on, the experimenter rolled one of the balls into a long "snake." The child was asked how the amount of clay in the snake compared with the amount of clay in the remaining ball.

Some children asked this question focus on the long length of the snake and decide it must contain more clay; others focus on its skinniness and decide it has less. Very few say that the snake and ball contain equal amounts of clay. Suppose, on the other hand, that an 8-year-old child is run

Piaget discovered that children pass through stages in their reasoning ability as they grow into adults. This child has witnessed a beaker containing exactly the same amount of liquid as the one on his right poured into a tall cylinder at his left. If he is younger than about 7 years of age, he will probably decide that the cylinder contains more liquid than the beaker. (Mimi Forsyth/Monkmeyer)

through the same procedure. Without much hesitation or inspection of the ball and snake, the 8-year-old will respond that the two objects contain the same amount of clay. He or she knows that only the shape (and not the quantity) of clay is altered when it is rolled into a snake. We say that the 8-year-old has the concept of the conservation of matter, a concept which is lacking in preoperational intelligence.

Piaget (1976a) believes that the cognitive development of a child is the outcome of biological changes associated with maturation. Consequently, it is difficult to change a child's stage of development by providing special training; he or she cannot generally advance to the next stage until the brain and nervous system are appropriately mature. If children are close to the age at which they will move naturally from one stage of thought to another, special training can hasten the transition; but if children are not at all close to making a natural transition, intensive training will have little effect. Even the former children, moreover, are vulnerable to regressing to their pretraining stage if new and unusual conservation problems are posed to them.

Here again, Bruner takes a middle position between Piaget's notion that cognitive (and linguistic) development are regulated almost exclusively by biologically based maturational processes and the behavioral-psychologists' notion that language represents a collection of conditioned responses much like any other such collection in an organism's repertory and that cognition, for the most part, consists of internalized speech. Bruner, Oliver, and Greenfield (1966) agreed with Piaget that children's cognition begins at a sensory-motor, or "action," level and then progresses to a more visually oriented style that attends closely to the perceptual qualities of objects and events and is able to use some capacity for imagery to group and classify these phenomena. Bruner disagreed with Piaget, however, in asserting that increasing linguistic sophistication must precede further cognitive growth.

In Bruner's research, children of around 6 years

According to Bruner, the function of schools in diverse cultures is to provide formal instruction in the use of abstract reasoning to form concepts which are independent of one's immediate perceptual experience. Instruction in the use of language is a key element in this process. (Reed/Monkmeyer)

of age were found to sort objects into categories primarily on the basis of their visual features. For example, candles, rulers, and taxis might all be grouped together "because they are yellow." Children of around 8 years of age were more likely to group things on the basis of functional criteria. For example, rulers, hammers, and nails might go together because "they can all be used for tools." Bruner believes that formal instruction is necessary to encourage this progression from highly perception-bound groupings to ones based on an abstraction of common features to create broader, more meaningful categories. Formal instruction compels children to use language to describe objects, events, or feelings independently of the particular context in which they appear. As a result, it breaks the bond between language and direct perception which is characteristic of Piaget's preoperational stage. Bruner maintains that this is the common function of schools in diverse cultures and that the school-children of Mexico City or of Dakar closely resemble those of the Boston suburbs in their creation of abstract, superordinate linguistic groupings for objects or events. He further notes that "the village child of rural Mexico and the unschooled Wolof of Senegal seem very different . . . much more perceptually oriented" and that the shift from dependence upon immediate perception to abstract thought "is *not* a universal property of growing up" (Bruner et al., 1966, p. 85).

So the debate continues between those who argue that language, cognitive development, or both are based on biological processes inherent in the maturing organism and those who believe that training and environmental experience, to a greater or lesser degree, are important contributors to the growth of linguistic and intellectual skills. It is significant to note, however, that none of the points of view examined here—from the radical behaviorists' view to Piaget's view—denies that language is related to thought and, hence, to reasoning and intelligence. Even for Piaget, when one arrives at his most advanced stage of cognitive development—formal oper-

ations—there is an explicit recognition that maturation alone is not sufficient to bring it about and that training and social experience play a vital role in realizing it. The problems designed by Inhelder and Piaget (1958) to test for formal operations involve taking a set of known propositions or quantities and arriving at a logical conclusion or the general principle which guides their combination. It is difficult to imagine that such problems could be either posed or solved without a sophisticated use of linguistic skills. It is hardly an accident, therefore, that when the first efforts were made to measure intelligence, the scales which were devised heavily emphasized verbal ability. As a young man, Piaget himself worked with Binet and Simon, the French investigators who originated the IQ test (see Chapter 6).

Cerebral Lateralization of Language and Other Mental Abilities

Recent advances in brain research have hinted at the possibility that many of the cognitive abilities we have been speaking of are associated with particular regions of the cerebral cortex. You will recall from Chapter 7 that the cortex is divided into two equal halves, or *hemispheres;* the right and left hemispheres are able to communicate through a band of connecting tissue known as the *corpus callosum.*

Sometimes individuals suffering from epilepsy experience seizures of such severity that radical surgery is required in order to save the patient's life. In this operation, the corpus callosum is severed, resulting in a split brain. People who undergo this procedure show surprisingly little evidence of abnormality in their daily lives. A patient holding the left hand out of sight and then having a pencil placed in it, however, will be unable to name the object or even describe it. If the pencil is placed on a tray alongside a can opener, a key, and a book, the patient will be able to pick it out as the object that he or she was holding a moment before. If the pencil is placed out of sight in the patient's *right* hand, he or she will have no trouble naming and describing it verbally. The explanation for these peculiar results is apparently that sensation in the left hand is transmitted to the right hemisphere. Language ability, however, is localized in the left hemisphere (this is true for nearly all right-handed and for most left-handed patients studied). Sensations from the right hand go to the verbal left hemisphere, thus enabling the patient to name the object in the right hand. The abilities of the right, nonverbal hemisphere are concentrated in the areas of form perception and pattern recognition. Hence, the pencil held in the left hand could be recognized and picked out of an array of objects even though it could not be named. Though this hemispheric specialization of abilities is most easily observable in *commissurotomized* (split-brain) patients, it presumably operates in the rest of us as well.

The foregoing findings were originally reported by Roger Sperry and his associates (Gazzaniga, Bogen, & Sperry, 1962, 1963). In an early burst of enthusiasm over their possible implications, the left hemisphere was identified as the seat of logical, analytic, objective thinking while intuitive, holistic, subjective thinking was alleged to predominate in the right. It was even suggested that the mind is divided between reason on the left and emotion on the right (Ornstein, 1973). Subsequent research has shown, however, that the right hemisphere does have some linguistic capability after all and that the hemispheres are not as specialized in their abilities as had initially been supposed (Nebes, 1974; Searleman, 1977).

Such reservations notwithstanding, it does seem reasonable to conclude that the left hemisphere is more heavily involved in the processing of linguistic input and the production of speech than is the right. For its part, the right hemisphere appears to have more highly developed spatial abilities than the left, one aspect of which is the recognition of pictorial stimuli, including faces (Moscovitch et al., 1976). In one intriguing study, Sackheim et al. (1978) took full frontal photographs of the faces of models portraying emotions like happiness, anger, or disgust and then cut the photographs in half and pieced together new frontal views composed of either two left sides or two right sides (see Figure 9-2). In judgments of the intensity of the emotions being

FIGURE 9-2
Three pictures used to demonstrate that emotions are expressed more intensely on the left side of the face. The center photo is the original full-face view of a person expressing disgust. The left photo is a composite of two left halves of the full-face view, while the right photo is a composite of the two right halves. (From Sackheim, Gur, and Saucy, 1978.)

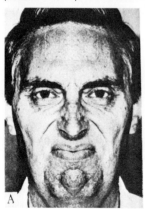  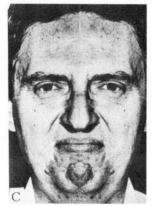

expressed by the models, groups of male and female college students rated the left-left combinations as significantly more intense than the right-right combinations. Thus, emotions seem to be expressed more strongly by the left side of the face, whose muscles are activated by the right cerebral hemisphere.

While the more dramatic early conclusions drawn from split-brain research seem to have been somewhat overstated, it does remain conceivable that some individual differences in personality style may reflect differences in the degree to which each hemisphere is habitually used in situations requiring problem solving or self-expression. Animal data exist which suggest that exposure to handling in infancy may cause right-hemisphere lateralization of certain abilities in rats which affect their activity level in an open-field test situation (Denenberg, Garbanati, Sherman, Yutzey, & Kaplan, 1978). Perhaps certain types of early experience affect the cerebral lateralization of abilities in human beings as well.

CONCLUSION

Chapter 9 has presented evidence concerning the development of personality in infancy and early childhood which bears upon each of the major theoretical traditions—psychoanalytic, dispositional, and environmentalist—discussed in Unit One. While support for Freud's psychoanalytic hypotheses regarding the psychosexual determinants of character is rather skimpy, that for the dispositional and environmentalist viewpoints is fairly extensive. As Kline (1972) observed, psychoanalytic theorists would not necessarily be dismayed by the inconclusive results obtained from empirical tests of their hypotheses. The foundations of this tradition rest upon clinical case studies rather than upon formal hypothesis testing; and while supportive evidence derived from such procedures would be welcomed by its adherents, a failure to find such support would not, in itself, cause them to abandon their theoretical position.

In comparing and contrasting evidence relevant to the dispositional and environmentalist traditions, the chapter has worked its way toward a conclusion that early personality development appears to involve an interaction between biological potentialities (or possibly even predispositions), on the one hand, and a tremendous capacity for learning from environmental experience on the other.

It is perhaps in the area of biological predispositions to patterns of behavior that an interactional perspective finds itself on shakiest ground. We have here paid particular attention to the possibility of such predisposing factors in temperament, perceptual and motor skills, emotional expressiveness, and language acquisition. It is easy to see how social learning shapes human behavior in each of these areas, but it is fairly difficult to demonstrate conclusively the existence of a biological component. Consequently, given the imperfect state of our knowledge of these matters, any suggestion that there are biological determinants of human behavior patterns and, hence, of personality must be regarded as somewhat speculative. Biological factors are much easier to identify in animal research, where it is possible to do controlled experiments. For this reason, animal studies which have examined mechanisms which appear to be analogous to those regulating human behavior have been discussed at various points in this chapter. Reasoning by analogy is not the same as direct proof, however, and generalizing too freely from one species to another can sometimes be extremely misleading.

This chapter must therefore conclude, as have so many others before it, by expressing the hope that future investigation will increase our understanding of the ways in which social and biological forces interact to shape human personality. At the very least, the research reported here suggests that both types of factors probably play some part in early development and that humans are, as a result, "biosocial" beings. This issue will be explored further in subsequent chapters.

SUMMARY

1 Temperament is composed of the emotional reactions and cognitive and behavioral aptitudes which are, to some extent, the product of an individual's biological inheritance. The concept of temperament is associated with the trait-dispositional approach to the study of personality. It is here contrasted with the psychoanalytic and environmentalist approaches, each of which assumes that newborn infants cannot, for the most part, be distinguished from one another in terms of temperament and that it is exposure to frustrations, gratifications, and other experiences in the social environment which causes individual differences in personality.

2 Studies of the personality types predicted by psychoanalytic theory have turned up inconclusive results. Some evidence suggests that early weaning may produce the oral-pessimist type. The all-around compulsive traits which Freud predicted for the anal-retentive personality do seem to cluster together on personality inventories, but there is little evidence that these traits are caused by especially punitive toilet training.

3 Evidence exists to support the dispositional view that infants differ in temperament at the time of birth. Thomas et al. (1970) typed infants as "easy," "difficult," or "slow to warm up," and Freedman and Keller (1963) found evidence for the heritability of such characteristics using the twin-study method. Other twin and adoption studies have also suggested that abilities, personality traits, vocational interests, and so forth are, to some degree, inherited.

4 Theorists in the environmentalist tradition regard learning experiences as practically the sole source of personality development in childhood. Feeding on demand, for example, may produce an activist character, and feeding on a strict schedule an apathetic one. Punishment delivered during toilet or sex training may produce approach-avoidance conflicts in a child's relationship with his or her parents. Many studies have shown that sucking, smiling, and other behavior can be reliably conditioned in infants. Animal studies also reveal the importance of early experience to subsequent emotional and social behavior.

5 In perceptual and motor skills—such as depth perception, smiling, and walking—there are indications of inborn abilities and predispositions as well as the influence of social learning. The same can be said about the expression and recognition of emotions.

6 The environmentalist tradition accounts for language acquisition by the progressive shaping of random sounds into words by means of both direct reinforcement and the secondary reinforcement provided

by successful imitation of the parents. This explanation is challenged by advocates of the dispositional approach, who point to evidence of a uniquely human motivation to learn and use a language according to certain built-in structural rules. Generally unsuccessful efforts to teach apes to use language have frustrated the environmentalists and provided support for the dispositional viewpoint. Further support for the latter position has been provided by studies of language development.

7 Behaviorists have historically regarded thinking as subvocal speech, but Piaget's theory of cognitive development regards thinking as linked to internal maturational processes which are independent of language. Thinking begins at a sensory-motor level and progresses to an abstract, symbolic level. It is when this transition is made that the child is "ready" to learn a language. Recent advances in brain research suggest that language ability as well as (perhaps) other logical, analytic processes are mainly localized in the left hemisphere of the cerebral cortex. The right hemisphere seems to specialize in spatial abilities, including recognition of faces, the expression of emotion, and (perhaps) intuitive modes of thinking. It is conceivable that some individual differences in personality style may reflect differences in the degree to which each hemisphere is habitually used in situations requiring problem solving or self-expression.

TERMS TO KNOW

temperament	morpheme
oral optimist	Mean Length of Utterance
anal retentive character	subvocal speech
four critical training situations	preoperational reasoning
neonatal abilities	split brain

10
EMERGENCE OF THE SELF-CONCEPT AND THE GROWTH OF COMPETENCE

ISSUES TO CONSIDER

1   Is a child's character permanently influenced by his or her order of birth?
2   What is the *self*, and when do children first attain self-recognition?
3   How do the mind and body interact to produce the internal sensation that we call emotion?

For the most part, Chapter 9 was concerned with events that occur before the age of 2. The present and subsequent chapters will extend our coverage to events occurring throughout an individual's life. As a child leaves infancy and develops the personal and social skills that lay the foundation for the emergence of an independent character, his or her sense of identity, competence, and ability to cope with stress become increasingly important determinants of future personality growth. Chapter 10 concerns itself with the development of these aspects of personality.

In this chapter, we devote a great deal of attention to a concept associated with several different approaches to the study of personality. Many theorists—beginning with Adler and Jung and extending through Erikson, Horney, the existentialists, and those in the American personological tradition—assumed that an individual's sense of self was a crucial component of his or her character. In fact, for all these theorists, *neurosis* is an outgrowth of societal pressure on the individual to conform to the expectations of others and to deny his or her own "true" self, or *identity*.

Just what is this sense of identity? Is it something inherent in a human being at birth, or is it a characteristic that appears as a result of learning? What implications does one's sense of self have for other aspects of one's temperament and behavior? In particular, how does it relate to one's feelings of competence and ability to cope with stress? These are questions for which Chapter 10 seeks to suggest some answers.

THE SELF IN EUROPEAN CHARACTEROLOGY

Freud, you will recall from Chapter 2, originally believed that sexual instincts provide most of the energy which powers the operation of the mind. It is when these instincts are denied expression that personality disturbance and symptoms of neurotic anxiety are likely to occur.

Adler, on the other hand, believed that the drive for aggression is the primary motive force in personality and that it is the frustration of the aggressive impulse which causes mental distress and neurotic symptoms. Later on in his theorizing, Adler substituted the term "striving for superiority" for his original aggressive drive. Implicit in this new term is the idea that a child is motivated to develop skills, expand areas of competence, and attain a sense of usefulness and purpose. At this stage in his thinking, Adler would probably have preferred the word "self-assertion" to the word "aggression." He now viewed physical aggression, along with apathy and other maladaptive behavior, as overcompensation for a frustration of superiority strivings which had pushed the individual to the neurotic extremes of the superiority or inferiority complexes. According to Adler, the earliest opportunities for superiority strivings to be either thwarted or encouraged occur within the family and particularly in the differing experiences of children having different positions in order of birth.

Birth Order and Personality

Adler (1929) maintained that the firstborn child, who is initially the center of his or her parents' attention, will be dethroned and made anxious by the appearance of siblings born later. As a result, the firstborn's style of life is likely to be characterized by striving to get ahead through winning the approval of authority figures and by defending any hard-won gains from the encroachments of younger rivals. The second-born (or *middle*) child is faced with both a more powerful and more knowledgeable sibling ahead of him (or her) and with the possibility of competition from children born later. The second child will probably develop strong feelings of incompetence or inadequacy and may try to compensate for these by becoming highly competitive in his or her relations with

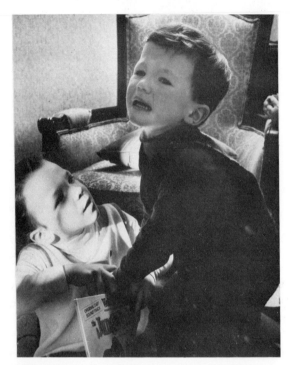

Alfred Adler emphasized the importance of rivalries between siblings for the development of feelings of self-confidence, independence, and the motivation to achieve. (Burk Uzzle/Magnum)

peers. Adler believed that parents were generally less stringent in socializing their second, as compared to their first, child. Consequently, the middle child's style of life is likely to be characterized by rebelliousness or nonconformity (or perhaps cynicism and apathy if rebellious tactics do not produce the desired outcomes). Next we have the youngest child, who tends to be indulged as the baby of the family, who is never threatened by the arrival of a later sibling, and who is likely to compensate for his or her lack of genuine achievements by developing a superiority complex. The youngest child is likely to internalize the family's attitude and remain a self-indulgent "baby" all of his or her life. Finally, an only child is likely to develop a style of life which represents a blend of the stringent sociali-

zation applied to the firstborn with the attention and pampering lavished on the youngest.

Schachter (1959) obtained experimental results indicating that behavior in a stressful situation is, indeed, influenced by the order of birth. In Schachter's study, female undergraduates were led to expect that they would be receiving either very painful or very mild electric shocks. The women were told that while walking down a hallway to find a room where they could wait while the experimenter set up the equipment, they would discover that there were two rooms to choose from. One of these rooms was empty, while the other contained a few students. Two-thirds of the females in the high-fear condition chose to wait with others, while two-thirds in the low-fear condition chose to wait alone. Examining the birth order of his subjects, Schachter was surprised to find that only firstborn or only children showed the fear-affiliation relationship; later-born children tended to prefer to be alone, even in the high-fear condition. It appeared that the affiliative tendencies of the firstborns might have been due to a belief on their part that the presence of others would be reassuring. In a later study, Schachter (1964) found that, indeed, first-borns and only children are more dependent on the approval of others and more easily influenced than are later-born children (Sampson & Hancock, 1967).

As for the achievement strivings that Adler attributed to firstborns, Schachter (1963) reported that eldest children are vastly overrepresented in college populations and tend to have higher grades than later-born children. There could, of course, be socioeconomic factors involved in such differences. It may be that families often strain their resources by sending their firstborn child to college, thereby making it more difficult for later-born children to attend. Despite such complications, Sampson (1965) concluded that the evidence for the greater social eminence of firstborns and only children is "overwhelming"; he offered the higher need for achievement which some studies have found to exist within this group as a possible explanation. Later-born children tend to score higher on measures of aggressiveness and lower on impulse control than firstborn or only children. Later-born children are also overrepresented among alcoholics. Perhaps the latter findings reflect the rebelliousness and apathy which Adler said might characterize the later-born child's style of life.

As a possible explanation for the affiliative tendency of firstborns and only children, Schachter (1959) suggested that parents may provide more attention and emotional comforting to their first child than to their later-born children. Unfamiliar with how durable children really are, parents may respond solicitously to every indication of distress from their firstborn. After gaining this experience, however, they may be less responsive to the demands for attention of their later-born offspring. Consequently, the firstborn is more likely to perceive others as a source of comfort in times of distress. Ring, Lipinski, and Braginsky (1965) proposed, instead, that firstborn children are more likely than are their later-born siblings to receive inconsistent treatment from their novice parents. This produces a confused self-concept and an especially strong desire to affiliate with others for the purpose of self-evaluation through comparison of beliefs and emotional reactions.

One aspect of superiority striving in European and American society is a person's IQ score, which is, in turn, related to scholastic achievement. Zajonc et al. (1979) summarized the results of large-scale studies in Europe and America which indicated that children's IQs decrease with increasing family size, which would suggest that a later-born sibling is likely to be less intelligent than the firstborn. Paradoxically, though, when the effects of birth order on IQ were examined independently from the effects of family size, the results were inconsistent. Often, later-born children were found to have higher IQs, on the average, than the firstborn.

To account for this inconsistency, Zajonc et al. proposed that opposing forces act on a child's intellectual development at the time that a new sibling is added to the family. The positive forces consist of losing the "handicap" to intellectual growth which is associated with being the most dependent, last-born member of the family and, at the same time, acquiring the intelligence-facilitating responsibility of taking care of a younger sibling. The negative force is the "dilution" of the family's intellectual environment brought about by the addition of an infant member; this decrease in intellectual stimulation acts to diminish the IQs of older siblings. Zajonc believes that the interaction of these positive and negative forces can account for the seemingly inconsistent finding that family size is negatively related to IQ while birth order is sometimes negatively and sometimes positively related to IQ.

While the foregoing results provide some support for Adler's propositions, many of the studies showing stronger affiliative tendencies among firstborns have been criticized on statistical grounds (Schooler, 1972). In addition, affiliativeness appears to be a trait shared by only children as well as firstborns. It would seem, therefore, that these phenomena are more the result of the special pressures (e.g., higher parental expectations) experienced by first and only children than (as Adler would argue) the firstborn's dethronement by later siblings. Despite this qualification, the evidence for an effect of birth order on affiliativeness and superiority strivings remains impressive and very intriguing. Now we will examine the possible effect of other events in childhood on an individual's ability to cope with anxiety and stress.

Psychoanalysis and Perceptual Defense

It will be recalled from Chapter 2 that Freud drew a distinction between realistic anxiety, neurotic anxiety, and moral anxiety. *Realistic anxiety* refers to anxiety arising from a genuine threat to one's well-being in the external world, while both of the latter refer to anxiety arising from internal sources. In *neurotic anxiety,* the ego fears that acting out or even thinking about some repressed desire of the id's will result in punishment either from a social community outraged by the expression of such impulses or from the superego. *Moral anxiety* refers specifically to the ego's fear of punishment by a disapproving superego or conscience. The superego is itself an internalization of the admonishments of parents, teachers, peers, and others who have had the power to reward or punish a child. The nature of an individual's repressions and of the strength and contents of his or her superego essentially defines that person's character and accounts for regularities in beliefs and behavior.

Evidence for repression and neurotic anxiety has been obtained in the context of research on a phenomenon called *perceptual defense.*

McGinnies (1949) opened this area of investigation with a study of the relative ease with which we recognize taboo and neutral words. McGin-

nies used a *tachistoscope,* a device that permits the illumination of words or pictures at varying intensities and for varying durations of time. One at a time, subjects were exposed to sets of words, some of which were neutral (for example, "apple") and some taboo (for example, "penis"). McGinnie's measure of ease of recognition was the duration of exposure required for a given word to be readable. Subjects were to report the words out loud as soon as they could read them. Since the perception and report of taboo words was expected to be anxiety arousing, subjects were wired to a meter that monitored their galvanic skin responses (GSR), a measure of emotional arousal described in Chapter 7. McGinnies found that taboo words had to be presented for much longer periods of time before subjects were able to "see" them; neutral words were recognized much earlier in the series of presentations (see Figure 10-1). Yet on the preidentification trials, before the subjects reported recognition of the taboo words, a GSR reaction was recorded whenever one of them appeared in the tachistoscope. Apparently there was subliminal perception of the

FIGURE 10-1

Mean recognition thresholds for the neutral and taboo words used in the perceptual defense experiment. A higher threshold indicates that a word was more difficult to recognize. (From McGinnies, 1949, p. 247.)

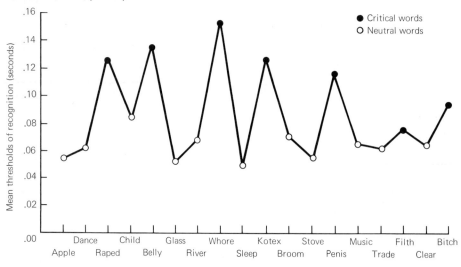

words. The nervous system recognized the taboo, anxiety-arousing material and repressed it some time before the conscious mind was forced by the constraints of the experimental situation to allow it into awareness.

Other researchers have used a sophisticated procedure for continuously tracking a subject's visual-recognition threshold while emotionally disturbing or neutral words are displayed at subliminal intensities to one eye using a tachistoscope. Higher thresholds were recorded when emotional rather than neutral words were being shown. One emotional word which produced a strong perceptual-defense reaction and which was clearly disturbing to subjects was "cancer" (Dixon, 1958; Dixon & Haider, 1961).

Not all participants in such studies show perceptual avoidance of disturbing material. Some show the opposite phenomenon—called perceptual vigilance—of being quicker to respond to emotional than to neutral stimuli. We are all likely to be perceptually vigilant for material in which we we are personally interested (Postman et al., 1948), but people also show consistent differences in perception depending upon whether they are predominantly repressors, who are more likely to employ perceptual defense, or sensitizers, who are more likely to show perceptual vigilance in the presence of emotionally laden material. Eriksen and Pierce (1968) noted that high scores on the hysteria subscale of the MMPI (see Chapter 6) are, as would be predicted by psychoanalytic theory, associated with the repressor personality style. High scores on the MMPI's psychasthenia subscale, on the other hand, indicate the sensitizer type. Byrne (1964) devised his own repression-sensitization scale and reported that repressors, as expected, tend to be perceptually defensive while sensitizers tend to be vigilant. Repressors seem to have a strong need to think highly of themselves and avoid unpleasant thoughts, while extreme sensitizers are often anxious and maladjusted.

Silverman (1976) summarized the results of a program of research in which pictures presumably evoking erotic or aggressive impulses were shown at subliminal speeds using a tachistoscope. Examples of the stimuli employed were pictures of a nude female or of one man stabbing another, respectively. Erotic pictures were moderately successful in evoking sexual themes in response to the Rorschach inkblot test among male college students, and Silverman found aggressive pictures to be highly successful in evoking pathological thinking among institutionalized schizophrenics. Freudian theory would also predict that the activation of repressed impulses would interfere with the ego's competence at problem solving. It was, in fact, found that subliminal presentation of erotic or aggressive scenes was more disruptive of the performance of male schizophrenics on subtests of the Wechsler Adult Intelligence Scale than was presentation of an emotionally neutral picture of a man reading a newspaper. Interestingly, Silverman reported that subliminal presentation of a reassuring statement such as "Mommy and I are one" served to reduce pathological thinking among schizophrenics, while a statement like "I am losing mommy" acted to increase it.

The ego defense of projection was demonstrated by Bramel (1962) by exposing clearly visible pictures of nude males to psychologically well-adjusted male college students. Students high in self-esteem who received (bogus) indications on a GSR meter that they were becoming sexually aroused by the pictures attributed greater arousal to an experimental partner than their own meter had indicated for themselves. In other words, they had projected the threatening trait of homosexuality outward onto their partners, presumably to assure themselves that their partners were more disturbed than they and to make their own apparent homosexuality seem more "normal." Students low in self-esteem, on the other hand, attributed less homosexuality to their partners than they had seen indicated for themselves.

While the foregoing material is compatible with the concepts of neurotic anxiety and ego defense in psychoanalytic theory, there have been strong criticisms of the procedures used and the conclusions drawn from studies demonstrating perceptual defense (Eriksen & Pierce, 1968; Eriksen & Eriksen, 1972; Howes & Solomon, 1950). Some of these criticisms have been answered by studies which included appropriate controls in their designs and still found evidence of perceptual defense (Cowan & Beier, 1954; Lazarus & McCleary, 1951). A major issue in this debate has been whether subliminal perception is even possible, much less the activation of neurotic anxiety by whatever has been shown. That is, can we "see" and respond to something that we are unaware of seeing? The behaviorist position has been that we can be conditioned only to stimuli of which we are aware. If we are unaware of a visual stimulus, then, from the standpoint of behavioral psychology, we cannot have "seen" it. Eriksen and his associates have argued that the results of perceptual-defense studies can be wholly accounted for by conscious learning processes. Such criticisms notwithstanding, psychoanalytically oriented theorists believe that early childhood experiences relating to the unconscious stimulation and frustration of sexual and aggressive impulses can, in certain cases, precipitate emotional disturbance, distort an individual's self-concept, and seriously impair his or her social competence.

Psychoanalytic Explanations for Affective Disorders

Affective disorders are disorders which involve extremes in the expression of emotions and an inability to control them. Depression is the most common of these maladies. Depressives make up the single largest category of patients both among those presenting themselves for psychological therapy or counseling and among those who are actually institutionalized for mental distress. *Depression* is characterized by lethargy, dejection, a sense of hopelessness, self-contempt, suicidal preoccupation, insomnia, loss of sexual interest, loss of appetite, digestive difficulties, and constipation. Work and other activities require tremendous effort for the depressive and, somehow, do not seem worth the effort.

Freud (1917) maintained that depression results from the loss of a loved object. This could include the loss of possessions toward which one has developed a symbolic or sublimated sexual attachment (e.g., one's home), but most often it refers to a traumatic separation from a loved person. *Anaclitic* (a term derived from the Latin verb meaning "to lean on") depression emerges when the relationship that is broken provided narcissistic gratification to one party only, with little or no demand for reciprocity. In this type of relationship, the frustration of *narcissistic* (self-indulgent) impulses causes the aggressive component of all love relationships to be turned inward, producing the immobilization and self-contempt which are characteristic of depression.

Young children enjoy this type of narcissistic relationship with their mothers, and, as was noted in Chapter 9, Spitz and Wolf (1946) have found a high incidence of anaclitic depression among human infants separated from their mothers during their first year of life and placed in orphanages. Bowlby (1952) maintained that these ill effects are caused by maternal deprivation and noted that the depression can be lifted if the institution provides a substitute mother in the form of a caretaker who spends a great deal of time interacting with the infant or, better still, if the child is adopted into a normal home environment. Failure to provide such nurturant caretaking has long-term effects on personality. In their later years, children who were institutionalized until the age of 3 before being placed in foster homes tended to differ in several respects from members of a control group who went right from their mothers into foster homes (Goldfarb, 1945). Institutionalized children scored lower in IQ, reading and speaking ability, and social maturity; they were also more likely to be hyperactive, unable to concentrate, craving of affection, and unable to keep rules (and lacking in guilt over breaking them). According to Bowlby, they were also prone to become juvenile delinquents.

You will recall that somewhat similar reactions to social isolation were observed among infant and juvenile monkeys by Harlow and Harlow (1962) in research described in the overview to this unit. Subsequent research confirmed that the response of monkeys to maternal separation is strikingly similar to that of human children experiencing object loss: angry protest followed by deep depression (Bowlby, 1960; Mineka & Suomi, 1978). Bowlby (1969, 1973) concluded from such studies that human infants have a built-in need to be physically and psychologically attached to parental caretakers. Disruption of these bonds produces extreme stress which initially activates *resistance* (the protest phase) but which, when separation is prolonged, leads to *despair* (the depression phase). A childhood experience with object loss allegedly predisposes an individual to depressive disorders in adulthood and increases his or her susceptibility to neurosis.

Bettelheim (1967), another psychoanalytically oriented investigator, speculated that childhood *autism*—a severe personality disorder characterized by complete withdrawal from involvement with others and a failure to develop normal speech—has its origins in a disruption of the emotional bond between infant and caretaker. Here, the "mothering one" remains physically present but somehow communicates to the child—perhaps at a subliminal level of behavioral signals—a desire that the child not exist. This desire could stem from lingering parental unhappiness over an unwanted pregnancy or a tendency for preautistic babies to be especially difficult to care for. Either way, Bettelheim believes that the child's response to this psychological object loss is massive withdrawal from social interaction. In many cases, autistic children act as though they perceive themselves as inanimate objects or machines—that is, as unfeeling automatons who cannot be hurt by others. While it seems doubtful

that all childhood autism arises from physical or psychological object loss, it is clear that this is an event which can have important implications for an individual's self-concept and social competence.

THE SELF IN AMERICAN PERSONOLOGY

Many theorists in the European as well as the American tradition assumed that an individual's sense of self is a crucial component of his or her personality. For all these theorists, neurosis or maladjustment is often the result of societal pressure on the individual to conform to the expectations of others and to deny his or her own "true" self, or *identity*. One spokesman for this viewpoint was the foremost advocate of trait psychology, Gordon Allport.

Trait-Dispositional Approaches to Understanding the Self

Allport, you will recall from Chapter 3, believed that the "early self" is formed by the age of 3 and that its subcomponents are (1) a sense of bodily self, (2) a sense of personal identity (which is related to the emergence of language), and (3) a feeling of self-esteem (which develops as the child experiences success in manipulating the environment and exercising a need for autonomy). This early self forms a core of identity which strongly influences all subsequent personality development. Individuals differ in the degree to which they develop each of these three components of selfhood. Such differences, as well as differences in the expression of the four remaining aspects of selfhood in Allport's chronological sequence, produce the wide variations in traits which we observe in adult personalities. Research involving both animals and human children has turned up evidence of something similar to what Allport meant by the early self.

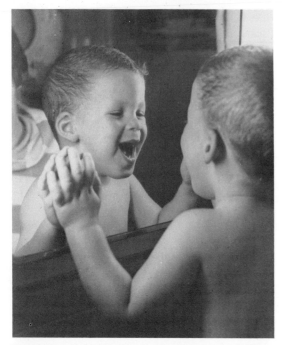

The ability to recognize a mirror image as being oneself is assumed to be related to the emergence of a sense of personal identity in human beings as well as other higher primates. Young children respond very positively to their mirror images as young as 6 months of age, but self-recognition is not reliably observable until about 2 years of age. (George Zimbel/Monkmeyer)

Self-recognition   The behaviorists, starting with Watson, argued that the sense of identity is learned and that, in particular, it is associated with the emergence of language ability. What we call the *self* is simply people talking *to* themselves *about* themselves in words reinforced by their linguistic communities. The importance of the research designed to teach chimpanzees how to use sign language and symbols to express ideas (see Chapter 9) was that if the effort was successful, these animals could be assumed to think in much the same way we do and to have learned a sense of identity.

Now it seems that even among chimps who have never been taught a language, there is at least a rudimentary self-concept. Gallup (1970)

placed normal adult chimps in a cage which had a mirror on one wall. Initially, like nearly all other species in this situation, the chimps responded to the mirror as though it was another animal—menacing it, vocalizing toward it, and so forth. After a few days, however, these responses waned, and the animals began to use the mirror as a source of information about visually inaccessible areas of their bodies; the mirror was especially useful in helping them groom their backs. To be certain that the chimps recognized that the mirror images were themselves, Gallup anesthetized them and placed a spot of odorless red dye above one eyebrow and at the top of the opposite ear. After they had regained consciousness, the animals were returned to their home cages, from which the mirrors had been removed. A count was kept of the number of times the animal touched either of the two spots (this was very infrequent). Then the mirrors were reintroduced to the cages, and it was discovered that the number of mark-directed responses increased by a factor of 25. Each animal seemed to know that the image in the mirror was itself and that there was an unfamiliar red mark on its forehead. As a control, Gallup marked a group of chimps who had never seen a mirror before and then placed them in cages with mirrors. These animals made virtually no mark-directed responses and treated the image as though it were a strange chimp with a red mark over one eye.

Gallup (1977) reports that these findings have been duplicated by German researchers and that while orangutans respond much the same way as chimps in the marking experiment, baboons and monkeys seem unable to develop self-recognition even after ten to twenty-one days of exposure to mirrors. He argues that the self-concept preexists among the chimps he has studied and that the mirror situation is just a means by which a human observer can verify this aspect of a chimpanzee's mental life. He feels that the evolutionary growth of the brain has provided great apes and humans with the capacity for representational thought necessary for self-recognition.

It therefore appears that a sense of self is not an exclusively human attribute and that it may emerge even in the absence of language. Learning probably plays some role in developing selfhood, though, since mirror recognition does not become reliably observable in human children until they are almost 2 years old (Amsterdam, 1972; Schulman & Kaplowitz, 1977).

Gallup, McClure, Hill, and Bundy (1971) reported that early social interaction is an important contributor to the development of a sense of selfhood among chimps. Unlike chimps raised in a peer group, isolate-reared animals show no evidence of self-recognition after ten days of exposure to a mirror. Thus, someone's perception that he or she has a personal identity or "self" appears to be an inherent biological potentiality to the extent that humans may share this capacity with other species. Even if the foregoing statement is verified by subsequent research, however, it also seems to be true that the development of this potentiality depends on a certain amount of social experience with other members of one's species.

Lewis and Brooks-Gunn (1972) found evidence of such a biosocial interaction in the response of human infants (7–19 months old) to several stimuli placed at varying distances. The stimuli included a mirror, the infant's mother, and three strangers (a female child 4 years of age and two male or female adults). An extreme positive reaction to a given stimulus was a broad smile; an extreme negative reaction was the facial contortions that precede crying. The infants responded neutrally to all stimuli placed at a distance of 15 feet, but they became increasingly enthusiastically positive as they drew closer to their images in the mirror or to their mothers. They remained somewhat neutral as a child approached them, but they became decidedly negative when approached by a strange adult of either sex. Lewis and Brooks-Gunn argued that the mirror was positively responded to because even at this young, preverbal age, the infant has a self-concept. The authors accounted for the emergence of the self by means of perceptual and motor learning occurring after the time of birth, but the possibility remains that human beings and great apes are biologically predisposed toward the development of a self-concept.

Research on sensory deprivation indicates that even for adults, there is a close connection between social and perceptual-motor experience and self-concept. Heron (1957) paid student volunteers a sizable hourly fee for resting in bed in a totally quiet room. Most subjects initially went to sleep, but after twenty-four hours of sensory deprivation, they became motorically restless and reported frequent episodes of daydreaming (perhaps in an attempt to increase stimulation). Eventually, nearly all reported visual hallucinations, ranging from simple patterns of dots and lines to complete scenes, like the passage of a herd of pink and black elephants. A few reported feeling that their "self" had floated out of their body. These experiences were so disturbing to the subjects that nearly all underwent the embarrassment (and loss of wages) involved in pushing a "panic button" to demand release.

Play behavior   My dictionary defines *play* as activity which is engaged in "by way of amusement or recreation" and is often "undirected, spontaneous, or random." Bruner (1972) treats *play* as a non-goal-directed exploration of various patterns of activity, tool use, or vocalization. Applying these definitions, it is intuitively clear that playfulness is most often exhibited by the young of any species—including our own—and that it is generally the young of the most recently and highly evolved species who play the most. Bruner argues that the greater immaturity of the young of these species at birth requires a relatively long period of learning and physical growth before they become fully functioning individuals; hence, their early behavior patterns are somewhat flexible and much less likely to be fixed by genetic programming. This flexibility permits the most highly evolved species to adapt themselves to diverse environments; humans, for example, can learn to survive in the extremes of climate found in both the Arctic regions and the Sahara desert region. Because of its evolutionary survival value, it is conceivable that the motivation to play arises somewhat spontaneously in the young organism.

Thus, while playfulness is related to a plasticity in behavior which maximizes the impact of environmental learning experiences, the initial motivation to exercise one's limbs, explore the uses of objects, and vocalize even when others are absent may have a biological origin. Weisler and McCall (1976) distinguish between exploration and play and conclude that the former precedes the latter when the organism encounters new or unusual objects or situations. It is only when exploration has provided reassurance that the novel stimulus is not threatening that playfulness begins. The motivation to explore such a stimulus appears to be an inverted U-shaped function of its strangeness. This means that while familiar stimuli do not arouse much interest, moderately unusual ones excite a great amount of curiosity, but extremely unusual and bizarre stimuli are likely to motivate fear and withdrawal rather than exploration. More will be said about inverted U-shaped functions further on in this chapter.

Aside from its evolutionary value for species survival, play—when it occurs in interaction with other species members—serves to allow the individual to practice behavior and social skills that will be helpful for making the transition to adult status. Animal species who live in groups have need of similar skills (e.g., learning when to cooperate and when to express or inhibit aggression), so it is not surprising that McCrew (1972) and others have noted similarities in the play behavior of young monkeys and apes on the one hand and children in nursery school on the other. Vandenberg (1978) reviewed the literature on this topic and noted that among chimpanzees as well as among human children, there are specific behavior patterns which signal the commencement of play. The "play face," which typically includes contortions resembling a smile, is supposed to communicate to other members of the group that the action sequence which follows is not to be taken seriously. It is interesting to recall at this point that Harlow and Harlow (1962) found that young monkeys who had been isolated from a playful peer group were disastrously deficient in the social skills required for mutual cooperation, the timing of aggressive displays, and appropriate sexual behavior. Other studies showed that isolation-reared monkeys had difficulty interpreting and transmitting facial cues signaling emotion (Miller, Caul, & Mirsky, 1967), and forming a self-concept (Gallup et al., 1971).

Competence   You will recall from Unit One that various theorists in the European and American traditions believed human beings were endowed with a motivation to exercise their abilities and attain self-chosen goals. R. W. White (1959), a well-known personologist, called this motivation *drive for competence*. He maintained that it is inherently pleasurable for a human infant to attain mastery over some aspect of the body or the environment—as can be seen, for example, in the cackle of joy often heard when a toddler succeeds, for the first time, in pulling himself or herself upright. It is the drive for competence which motivates the child to repeat behavior over and over again for no reward other than the refinement and mastery of some skill.

B. L. White (1971, 1975, 1976) is less convinced that the growth of competence is an inevitable aspect of human maturation. He believes that the natural unfolding of processes of cognitive development, in particular, may not, by itself, be sufficient to insure that a child will achieve his or her full intellectual potential. White, concentrating on the first three years of life. discovered that providing young infants with perceptually stimulating toys (such as mobiles hung over the crib) and older infants with open spaces containing sofas to climb on and safe objects to manipulate (e.g., plastic refrigerator jars) had a positive relationship to the child's intellectual competence at the age of 3. Another very positive influence was the amount of live language (i.e., *not* television or radio) directed toward the child. While White's research would agree with Piaget's in pointing to the importance of the sensory and motor apparatus for the cognitive development of the child, White gives less emphasis to maturational processes and notes that a child's physical and social environment can be structured so as to retard or promote intellectual growth.

Self-esteem Based on his studies of a large sample of boys and their parents in Connecticut, Coopersmith (1967, 1968) concluded that the environmental sources of high self-esteem are early experiences of success in setting and accomplishing one's goals, which in turn produce recognition and praise by parents and others and thereby instill feelings of competence and pride. Coopersmith found that the boys in his sample who were highest in self-esteem set more ambitious (but, at the same time, more realistically attainable) goals for themselves in a bean-bag game which required them to choose between tossing bags into nearby boxes for a small potential reward or into faraway boxes for a larger reward. An absence of esteem-building experiences seemed to have widespread negative effects on character formation. Coopersmith discovered that a majority of the boys low in self-esteem were described by their mothers as having marked, frequent "problems"—destructiveness in particular—whereas less than a fifth of the high self-esteem group was reported to have such problems. Other traits associated with low self-esteem were feelings of discouragement and of being unloved, as well as tendencies toward shyness and insecurity in social interaction.

What, exactly, is meant by the term "self-esteem"? On a scale devised by Bachman and O'Malley (1977), a person agreeing that "I am able to do things as well as most other people" would be indicating relatively high self-esteem, while one who endorsed the statement, "I feel that I can't do anything right," would be low in self-esteem. Bachman and O'Malley observed that self-esteem was positively related to a child's academic ability and scholastic achievement through the end of high school and, later, to his or her occupational status.

Crowne and Marlowe (1960) published a personality scale measuring self-perceived social desirability which has been widely used ever since. People scoring high on social desirability tend to agree with items like "I have never deliberately said something that hurt someone's feelings" and "I never hesitate to go out of my way to help someone in trouble." They are likely to disagree with statements like "On occasion I have had doubts about my ability to succeed in life." Arlin (1976) reported a significant positive correlation between scores on the social-desirability scale and a scale measuring favorability of self-concept among children. The correlation between social desirability and self-esteem might be even more positive but for the fact that extremely high scores on the social-desirability scale may indicate defensiveness rather than honest self-appraisal. Many individuals with extremely high scores seem actually to feel they are socially *un*desirable, but they answer all the items in the desirable direction in an attempt to make a good impression on the interviewer.

Phenomenological Approaches to Self-Understanding

It appears that events which Allport believed contribute to development of the "early self" can, indeed, have a significant and lasting impact on personality. Humanistic psychologists like Rogers have long maintained that when an individual is dissatisfied with certain aspects of his or her self, it "feels good" to reveal these worries and preoccupations to others (Jourard, 1964). This need for self-disclosure obviously contributes to the success of traditional as well as humanistic techniques of psychological assessment and therapy. In day-to-day interpersonal interactions, according to Jourard, disclosure of personal de-

(Marion Bernstein/Editorial Photocolor Archives)

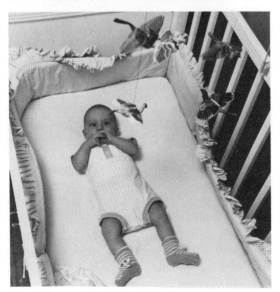

(Lew Merrim/Monkmeyer)

Self-Esteem and Self-Disclosure: Keys to Mental Health?

Concentrating his research on the first three years of life, B. L. White has discovered that providing young infants with perceptually stimulating toys (such as mobiles hung over the crib) and older infants with open spaces containing soft furniture to climb on and safe objects to manipulate had a positive relationship with the child's intellectual competence at 3 years of age.

Allport believed that such early experiences of attaining mastery over one's motor skills and the objects in one's environment lay the foundation for a child's lifelong sense of self-esteem. Coopersmith has found that high self-esteem is developed and maintained by experiences of success in setting and accomplishing goals, which in turn produces recognition and praise from others and thereby instills feelings of competence and pride. An absence of esteem-building experiences may lead to self-defeating behaviors, including underachievement, antisocial destructiveness, or excessive shyness and insecurity. According to humanistically oriented psychologists, these and other unhealthy personality characteristics may be alleviated or avoided altogether if one routinely engages in honest self-disclosure. Self-disclosure consists in revealing one's problems, interests, feelings, and other private information to a partner who reciprocates with disclosures at a comparable level of intimacy.

sires, fears, embarrassments, and so forth to at least one "intimate other"—supplemented by more moderate levels of disclosure to a few close friends—is necessary for maintaining mental health.

There seem to be social norms by which mutual self-disclosure progresses among strangers who are in the process of becoming better acquainted. One rule is that a disclosure by one party must be reciprocated by a disclosure from the other if the interaction is to continue. People tend not to stay in one-sided disclosure situations. Another informal rule is that reciprocal disclosures should be at a comparable level of intimacy. For example, if person A says "I am worried that my new car will cost me more than I can afford," it would be inappropriate for person B to reply "I worry a lot myself; I worry that my hallucinations and fear of being persecuted may put me into a mental hospital." Reciprocity and level matching have been verified as norms of self-disclosure by several different investigators (Cozby, 1973; Altman & Taylor, 1973). It has also been found that as people encounter reciprocity and approval for their self-disclosures the frequency of these expressions increases, but if they encounter disapproval they are likely to stop making such disclosures (Taylor et al., 1969).

Some individuals, though, are unable to engage in much social interaction or mutual self-disclosure with others any any level. These people possess, to an extreme degree, the trait called *shyness*. Pilkonis (1977) reported data indicating that around 40 percent of high school and college students regard themselves as shy. Shyness is manifested by such symptoms as a state of internal arousal during or while anticipating social interaction, a fear of negative evaluation by others, and inappropriate or clumsy behavior when in the presence of others. It is associated with other personality traits like introversion, self-consciousness, and social anxiety. Most people are able to master their shyness to a degree sufficient to permit normal social interaction, and Pilkonis even noted the existence of some "shy, but extraverted" types who managed to conceal their social insecurities behind a mask of false bravado. For a few, though, shyness so debilitates their capacity for social interaction that the shyness becomes, to quote Pilkonis and his associates, a "silent prison."

Emotions: A Combination of Dispositions and Phenomenology

What are the "states of internal arousal" which cause the shy person to avoid social interaction or, to return to an earlier topic, fail to perceive a taboo word or picture on a test of perceptual defense? What, in short, are emotions, and how do they contribute to our self-concept, our competence, and our ability to cope with stress?

Throughout recorded history, people have pondered the origins of emotions. We will introduce this section by tracing the development of a famous psychological theory which began by assuming that emotions are largely physiological events and progressed to the idea that our subjective experience of emotion depends on an interaction between physiological and cognitive factors.

A theory of emotion   William James (1884) speculated that the body initially responds to an external source of excitement almost reflexively, with little emotional involvement. Once the body has begun to respond, however, physiological changes occur that lead to an internal state of arousal known to us as an emotion. Suppose, for instance, you are driving down a city street and another car suddenly darts into your path from a cross street; reflexively, you swerve to avoid a collision and brake to a stop. Only after you have stopped do you become aware that your heart is palpitating, your breathing is fast, your palms are sweaty, and there is a queasy feeling in your stomach. It is then that you say to yourself, "I'm scared," and begin to tremble with fright. James supposed that there must be a different physiological state specific to each of the emotions: anger, fear, joy, and the rest.

W. B. Cannon (1927) criticized James's theory on several grounds, one of the more important of which was that the response of the viscera (the most plausible location of a state of internal arousal) to emotion-inducing situations is rather undifferentiated. Thus it appeared impossible that there could be different physiological states associated with various emotions. This and other features of Cannon's critique appeared to be rather compelling, and there matters rested for more than thirty years, until Schachter's famous research.

Schachter (1964) acknowledged the essential validity of Cannon's point concerning the undif-ferentiated nature of arousal states. On the whole, internal arousal is characterized by the same symptoms, regardless of the emotion being expressed. In research by Ax (1953) and Schachter (1957), the emotions of fear and anger were distinguishable on only a handful out of many physiological indicators, and the arousal symptoms of subjects experiencing one or another of these emotions were far more alike than they were different. Schachter reviewed a large number of studies which attempted to find physiological differentiations of the emotions and concluded that the vast majority found no differences in the internal state of people experiencing a wide variety of feelings. Here is a puzzle, then. How can emotions that we *feel* to be very different from one another, such as joy and anger, be associated with nearly identical states of internal arousal? Schachter believes that the interpretation that the mind places on a state of arousal determines the emotional response.

Activation of the sympathetic nervous system brings about the state of internal arousal that we have been discussing. Epinephrine, also called *adrenaline,* is a substance naturally secreted by the adrenal medulla whose effects on the body (when it is artificially injected) are nearly identical with those produced by activation of the sympathetic nervous system. Its effects are an increase in heart rate, blood flow, and concentrations of blood sugar and lactic acid. For the recipient of an injection, the subjective symptoms are heart palpitations, hand tremors, and (sometimes) flushing and more rapid breathing. By Schachter's theory, if someone were injected with epinephrine and experienced a state of internal arousal as a result, his or her emotions would be extremely malleable. If placed in a joyous party situation, he or she might interpret the arousal as an emotion of great happiness and respond with gaiety. If placed in an angry crowd, he or she might, instead, conclude that the arousal represented an emotion of outrage and respond with pugnacity.

Reduced to a mathematical oversimplification, Schachter's theory is that

$$\text{Emotion} = \text{Cognition} \times \text{Arousal}$$

In other words, an undifferentiated state of internal arousal is a necessary prerequisite for an emotion but is not, in itself, sufficient to produce one. Only when an individual is aroused *and* finds that he or she is in a situation perceived as calling for the expression of an emotion will that individual experience a full-blown emotional state. Arousal which lacks an appropriate cognition merely causes people to become confused by their apparent "excitement over nothing." A cognition in the absence of arousal may cause the individual to try to act out an appropriate emotion, but the emotion will not be truly "felt." An emotion is also unlikely to occur if the arousal state is attached to a nonemotional cognition. In our earlier example, for instance, a subject, knowing he or she has been injected with epinephrine, will probably interpret his or her aroused state as being a side effect of the drug and so will not be influenced by the party or the angry crowd, respectively.

As a test of this reasoning, Schachter and Singer (1962) recruited male students at the University of Minnesota for a research project. Some subjects were injected with what was alleged to be a vitamin compound (actually, epinephrine) and either told nothing about its side effects or given misinformation such that they anticipated numb feet, itching sensations, and a slight headache. The emotions of subjects in these two groups, who experienced an epinephrine-induced state of arousal for which they had no explanation, were expected to be highly influenceable. A third group received the epinephrine injection but was correctly informed as to its side effects (i.e., a nonemotional cognition was supplied for their arousal state). A fourth group was injected with saline solution, a placebo which does not produce the arousal state neces-

sary for the experience of an emotion. After receiving their injections, subjects in all groups spent twenty minutes in a waiting room with another participant who was actually Schachter's accomplice. The accomplice behaved in a happy, joyful manner for half the subjects (culminating in hula hooping with a circular piece of tubing) and in an angry, irritated manner for the rest (culminating with tearing up a questionnaire they had been given by the experimenter and stomping out the door).

As expected, subjects in the two groups which were either kept ignorant of or misinformed as to the side effects of epinephrine were very much influenced by the behavior of the accomplice. Both in terms of the degree to which they imitated the happy or angry behavior of the accomplice during the waiting period and in terms of a subsequent self-rating of their mood, these subjects showed more imitation of the accomplice's emotions than did their counterparts who had been correctly informed as to the side effects of the epinphrine injection or who had been injected with saline. Minor complications appeared in the results, apparently due to the fact that some of the subjects in the saline control group were frightened by the injection and so received a dose of their own, naturally secreted epinephrine. These "self-aroused" individuals tended to become somewhat emotional in the presence of the accomplice, since they, like the subjects in the epinephrine-injected but uninformed group, were experiencing an arousal state for which they had no readily available explanation. Schachter and Singer (1962) identified the "self-aroused" among the saline controls as those whose heart rates increased following the injection. Among the remaining, truly unaroused controls, there was, as predicted, little tendency for emotions to be influenced by the happy or angry accomplice.

Our emotions appear to function much like a jukebox (Mandler, 1962). The dose of epinephrine is like the coin that turns the jukebox on, but our interpretation of which emotion is appropriate to the situation is like our selection of a particular record. Turning the machine on is a necessary precondition for hearing any music at all; but a record must be selected in order to complete the process, and an activated machine can play a happy tune as well as an angry or sad one. Analogously, "activated" people without a readily available nonemotional cognition to explain their aroused state will be strongly influenced by the emotional "selections" provided by the environment.

Marshall and Zimbardo (1979) conducted a replication of Schachter and Singer's euphoria conditions whose results appeared to challenge the accuracy of the "jukebox" model. They found that epinephrine-injected but misinformed subjects were no more (and even slightly *less*) likely than were placebo controls to become happy in the presence of a euphoric accomplice. The value of their results is unfortunately clouded by a change in the instructions given to the misinformed group, as Schachter and Singer (1979) emphatically pointed out. Yet another partial duplication of the original study, using a different drug which has similar arousing effects on the body, was, for the most part, supportive of Schachter and Singer's (1962) results (Erdmann & Janke, 1978). Indeed, Schachter (1964) believes that the experiences of first-time users of drugs like marijuana generally confirm his theory. Marijuana produces symptoms—such as dry mouth, elevated heart and breathing rates, and stomach queasiness—which are comparable to the symptoms of epinephrine-induced arousal. Whether the first-time user of marijuana interprets these symptoms as a euphoric "high," as emotionally neutral, or as an unpleasant "bad trip" depends on his or her interpretation of the social setting in which the drug is taken (Becker, 1953).

Two of Cannon's (1927) criticisms of James's (1884) theory that could apply to Schachter's theory of emotion as well were that (1) visceral changes are too slow to serve as mediators of emotion and (2) when visceral sensation is cut off

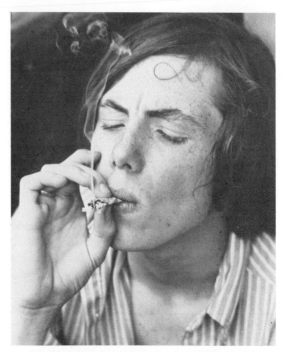

Marijuana produces changes in the physiological state of the user which are in many ways similar to the effects of an epinephrine injection. Whether these symptoms of arousal produce a euphoric "high," a "bad trip," or an emotionally neutral experience depends heavily on the pleasurable or unpleasurable aspects of the setting in which the user takes the drug. (Paul Conklin/Monkmeyer)

from the central nervous system (in an operation called *sympathectomy*), emotional behavior remains unaltered. Schachter (1964) agrees with Mandler (1962), however, in noting that sympathectomized animals and humans who are paralyzed by damage to the spinal cord have had an opportunity to learn the association between situational cues and internal states before sensation of the latter is cut off. As a result of prior learning, then, presentation of the cues alone may be sufficient to activate emotional behavior. Schachter maintains that awareness of internal arousal is a necessary condition for the acquisition of true emotional behavior but that arousal may not be crucial for its maintenance. He also argues that sympathectomized individuals probably do not experience full-blown emotions but, instead, tend to act them out.

Especially in humans, emotions are likely to be highly flexible. Because of our unique capacity for language, we can talk ourselves into and out of cognitive labels for our internal states that would be much more directly and rigidly applied by even the most evolutionarily advanced animal species. Anyone who has witnessed the rapid changes which may occur in human emotion cannot fail to be impressed by the extent to which cognition influences our feelings. For example, people can become infuriated if they believe someone has misplaced an important possession which they desperately need. In the midst of this towering rage, the angry person may discover that the possession was, in fact, misplaced by none other than himself or herself. Very quickly, anger gives way to embarrassment and then, perhaps, humor at the absurdity of the situation. Theories of emotion developed subsequently to Schachter's (Lazarus et al., 1970; Valins, 1970) placed an even heavier emphasis on interpretive processes (called *appraisal*) as determinants of emotional state. The human capacity for interpretation is apparently what gives us a far more flexible and differentiated emotional system than that possessed by animals.

Emotionality and task performance Anxiety is the emotion which has most frequently been related to task performance, and the relationship which has generally been found is a negative one. High levels of anxiety have been found to undermine performance. Sarason (1957), for example, reported that scores on a paper-and-pencil measure of test anxiety were significantly negatively correlated with scores on college-entrance examinations and four-year grade-point averages. In an extensive review of this literature, Wine (1971) noted that highly anxious people describe themselves in more negative terms than do their less anxious counterparts. Sarason (1975) suggested that this preoccupation with oneself in terms of worries about one's competence and personal worth, on the one hand, or feelings of ambivalence about striving to attain externally imposed standards of achievement, on the other, may interfere with one's concentration on the task and consequently undermine one's performance.

Early studies of anxiety and performance assumed that the former was a personality trait that the subject brought to the task environment. To measure this trait, Taylor (1953) constructed a Manifest-Anxiety Scale by first selecting 200 likely appearing items from the MMPI (see Chapter 6) and then asking five clinical psychologists to select the items which seemed to measure anxiety most directly. The resulting inventory contained some items specifically concerned with task performance (e.g., inability to concentrate or stick to one's work), while other items were more global in content (e.g., feelings of worry and worthlessness or tendencies to blush or cry a lot). Low scorers on the Manifest-Anxiety Scale were found to do better than their highly anxious counterparts on complex tasks requiring a great deal of mental effort. On simple tasks, however, highly anxious persons performed best. One explanation for these results, derived from behavioral psychology, is that "high-drive" states (like hunger or anxiety) increase the probability of well-learned habits. On simple tasks, such habits are likely to be correct, so highly anxious people outperform low scorers. On complex tasks, well-learned habits are likely to be incorrect, so highly anxious people become especially prone to make mistakes (Spence & Spence, 1966).

There is an alternative to the behavioral interpretation of the foregoing findings, however. This alternative is based on the observation by several investigators that performance on a task appears to be an inverted U-shaped function of *activation*, or arousal, so that low arousal is insufficient to energize peak performance while, at the other extreme, excessively high arousal is disruptively distracting (Duffy, 1957; Malmo, 1959; Yerkes & Dodson, 1908). Peak performance should be achieved when arousal is at some optimal, moderate level.

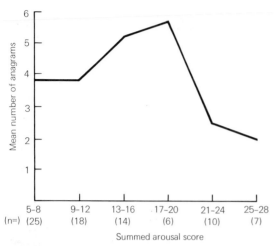

FIGURE 10-2
Mean number of anagrams solved as a function of subjects' combined self-ratings for five bodily symptoms indicative of internal arousal. (From Samuel et al., 1978, p. 211.)

The inverted-U hypothesis has become known as the *Yerkes-Dodson law* and is illustrated by the results shown in Figure 10-2. In this study by Samuel, Baynes, and Sabeh (1978), subjects worked on a set of anagram problems in one of four experimental settings ranging from very threatening to very reassuring. Following work on the anagrams, subjects rated the degree to which they were experiencing each of five symptoms of autonomic arousal. They were grouped according to their scores on this "summed-arousal" index, and the mean number of anagrams solved by each group was calculated. Anagram performance was then related to arousal, and the resulting function was an inverted U.

Samuel, Soto, Parks, Ngissah, and Jones (1976) and Samuel (1977) administered the Wechsler Intelligence Scale for Children (see Chapter 6) to 832 junior high school students in four experimental settings comparable to those employed by Samuel et al. (1978). As predicted by the Yerkes-Dodson law, they observed that both highly threatening and highly reassuring settings under-

mined performance relative to those in which a moderate degree of arousal was maintained. Samuel (1980) found evidence of an *upset,* or arousal, factor in these students' self-ratings of their emotional states. When IQ for all 832 students was plotted as a function of arousal, the curve had the appearance of an inverted U and bore a marked resemblance to that shown in Figure 10-2. Samuel (1980) as well as Fisher and Kotses (1973) found evidence that blacks were more disposed than whites to becoming physiologically aroused while working at such tasks. A disproportionate number of blacks in higher, overly stressed levels of arousal could be a factor contributing to the interracial differences in average IQ discussed in Chapter 6.

From what initially appeared to be a straightforward negative relationship between anxiety and task performance, then, we have arrived at a relationship that is somewhat more involved. When anxiety (or, more generally, emotional arousal) is at a very high level it may indeed disrupt performance, but when it is at a very low level it may be insufficient to motivate peak performance. It is when anxiety or arousal is at a moderate level that performance is optimal. To return to the earlier discussion of anxiety and achievement on simple versus complex tasks, chronically anxious people may outperform their low-anxious counterparts on simple tasks because the ease with which they find solutions prevents the former from becoming excessively aroused but holds the arousal of the latter at an insufficiently motivating level. On frustrating, complex tasks, however, highly anxious subjects quickly become overaroused, causing their performance to deteriorate, while low-anxious scorers are aroused to a moderate, optimally motivating level, causing their performance to improve.

It has long been suspected that the stress produced by a fear of failing at problem-solving tasks or at coping with life's problems in general may, if it becomes extreme, undermine an individual's health and increase susceptibility to disease (Selye, 1976; Holmes & Masuda, 1972). A

Air traffic controllers must work in a high-stress environment in which the slightest mistake can have disastrous consequences. They have a high rate of ulcers and other psychosomatic disorders. (United Nations)

paper-and-pencil scale devised by Jenkins, Zyzanski, and Rosenman (1971) tried to identify individuals with coronary-prone personalities. These people, called *Type A's*, were extremely "time-urgent" and competitive and had very strong needs for environmental control. When compared with persons expressing such traits to a more moderate degree (called *Type B's*), the Type A's were found to be twice as likely to suffer from coronary heart disease, even when statistical techniques were used to control for the effects of predisposing physiological factors such as

serum-cholesterol levels and high blood pressure. Snow (1978) suggested that the Type A's set unrealistically high goals for themselves and so experience excessive stress in the face of life's occasional setbacks.

Dispositional Explanations for Affective Disorders

Dispositional theorists would regard stress as the underlying cause of affective disorders and refrain from psychoanalytic speculation regarding the disruption of narcissistic bonds between an infant and its mother. To be sure, maternal separation or rejection is almost always stressful and may, therefore, precipitate depression, but other stressors could also have the same effect.

Stress causes a depletion in the central nervous system of neurotransmitters concentrated in areas of the brain which are involved in arousal, sleep, appetite, sex drive, and perceptual-motor activity (see Chapter 7 if you need a review of brain physiology). Reserpine is a drug which, when injected, will also cause these *neurotransmitters* (dopamine or norepinephrine) to be depleted. Reserpine is used as a tranquilizer for hypertensive humans whose lives are endangered by the risk of heart failure. When given in doses above 0.5 milligrams per day, reserpine precipitates depression in about a fifth of these patients, and in a third of such cases the depression is severe enough to necessitate psychiatric hospitalization. When reserpine was tested on monkeys for eighty-one days, the animals exhibited significant decreases in locomotion and visual exploration and an increase in huddling behavior. Pictures of them look very similar to pictures of the mother-deprived monkeys in the studies described earlier (Akiskal & McKinney, 1973).

Using twin-study data comparable to those used to demonstrate the possibility of a hereditary component in schizophrenia, Rosenthal (1971) concluded that evidence also exists of an inherited predisposition toward manic-depressive psychosis. What would presumably be inherited here would be a susceptibility to stress. Whybrow and Mendels (1969) reviewed numerous studies comparing depressives and "normals" on muscle tension, EEG, sleep disturbance, excretion of substances important for neural activity, and physiological response to various drugs. They decided that an unstable, easily excitable central nervous system is a personal characteristic which contributes to depression. Consequently, they regard depression as "a generalized response of the organism to stress." The *anti*depressant drugs which are given to people suffering from this

disorder have the physiological effect of raising concentrations in the central nervous system of the neurotransmitters which are known to be depleted by stress (Akiskal & McKinney).

THE SELF IN THE BEHAVIORIST TRADITION

It was mentioned in Chapter 4 that Soviet behaviorism has, since the 1930s, emphasized the existence of consciousness and treated it as a legitimate object of study. In recent years, American behaviorism has also moved in this direction, though it prefers to call its investigations *cognitive psychology* rather than the *study of consciousness.*

One behavioral approach toward understanding the self-concept is the theory of objective self-awareness, developed by Duval and Wicklund (1972). It states that how we perceive ourselves is directly related to the feedback we receive regarding how others view our appearance and behavior. In research on self-awareness, this feedback is typically provided by a mirror, but in real life it could also be provided by others' comments regarding how we look and act. Duval and Wicklund assume that this feedback almost always puts us in an unpleasant emotional state because we have internalized images of "ideal" standards of appearance and action which are never matched by social reality. Consequently, external feedback generally leads us to do one of three things: (1) revise our appearance and behavior so as to more closely approximate the "ideal," (2) revise our self-concept so as to recognize a greater difference between ourselves and the "ideal" standard than we have previously accepted, or (3) escape the feedback situation.

Carver (1979), however, argues that objective self-awareness need not be unpleasant if the person receiving the feedback feels capable of matching the "ideal" through step 1, above. It is only when the person feels incapable of initiating behavior changes which will permit matching the "ideal" that external feedback leads to a loss of self-esteem or an effort to escape from the situation. Brockner (1979) found that a person's self-esteem influences his or her selection of a method for coping with objective feedback regarding a failure to complete a problem-solving task. Among low self-esteem subjects, those who viewed themselves in a mirror during the failure experience showed more impaired performance on a subsequent task than did those who had no mirror available during the failure experience. For subjects high in self-esteem, objective feedback during a failure experience led to *improved* performance on a subsequent task.

Self-Esteem, Attribution of Ability, and Belief in Internal Control

An area of social psychology known as *attribution theory* emphasizes that it is not just an individual's successes or failures that determine his or her self-concept and self-esteem but rather the interpretations which are placed on such events. In an extensive program of research, Weiner et al. (1971) obtained data suggesting that failure may not lower self-esteem if the failure can be attributed to some external cause such as "bad luck" or to an impossibly difficult task. Specifically, Weiner's results indicate that failure may not produce a lowered motivation to achieve if it can be attributed to one of the foregoing causes rather than to internal causes such as lack of ability or effort. These investigators found that people tend to protect their motivational systems and self-esteem by selectively attributing their personal successes to internal causes and their failures to external ones.

Weiner et al. also observed that success at one task tends to generate at least a short-term expectation of success at other tasks, whereas failure is likely to produce an expectation of other failures to come. If these expectancies become long-term rather than temporary, they may result in what Rotter (1966) called a *generalized expectancy* regarding internal versus external

control of reinforcement. According to Rotter, *internals* are people who believe that they have control over the major events in their lives; *externals* believe that their fates are decided by powerful deliberate or circumstantial forces beyond their control. On Rotter's *internal-external* (I-E) scale, an internal would tend to agree with items like, "Promotions are earned through hard work and persistence"; an external would be more likely to agree that "Making a lot of money is largely a matter of getting the right breaks." Children are not born with these generalized expectancies; they learn them as they successfully or unsuccessfully interact with their cultures. Presumably, internals, through generally successful encounters with others, develop a belief that they are able to influence the world to get things done and so fashion a life for themselves with which they will be somewhat satisfied. Internals are optimistic achievers. Externals, on the other hand, may have encountered failure more often than success as they were growing up and so gravitate toward discouragement and pessimism. An association between externality and self-esteem appears to be suggested by the finding that externals are more attentive to negative information about themselves than are internals (Phares, Ritchie, & Davis, 1968). Intriguingly, Rotter himself believes that mental health on the I-E dimension consists of a *blend* of internality and externality. An extreme internal is probably *too* optimistic regarding his or her control over life events, while an extreme external is overly pessimistic.

Behavioral psychologists with a social-learning orientation also called attention to the possibility that providing a tangible reward like food or money to someone for completing a task may serve to reduce that person's intrinsic motivation or future interest in performing a task when a tangible reward is absent (Deci, 1975; Lepper, Greene, & Nisbett, 1973). This paradoxical outcome presumably occurs because the individual continues to perceive himself or herself as motivated by *extrinsic* (external) reinforcement and so fails to learn the internalized self-reinforcements (e.g., self-congratulatory statements) which underlie the perception of being intrinsically motivated. It has even been suggested that in extreme cases, life experiences which contribute to the development of the perception of being externally rather than internally controlled, or extrinsically rather than intrinsically motivated, may lead to severe emotional disturbance.

Behavioral Explanations for Affective Disorders

Seligman (1975) believes he found the origins of depressive disorders in a conditioning procedure which he applied to dogs. One group of animals was given the experience of unavoidable shock by being suspended in hammocks with their legs sticking through holes and electrodes attached to the pads of their rear feet. When later placed in a shuttle box in which shock could be avoided by jumping over a shoulder-high barrier, these "helpless" animals failed to learn the avoidance response and simply endured the pain until it stopped. By contrast, a control group of dogs not previously exposed to the experience of unavoidable shock quickly learned to escape pain by leaping over the shuttle-box barrier. The "helpless" dogs could not be enticed into making the simple avoidance response by calls from the experimenter or even by the smell of fresh meat on the "safe" side of the shuttle box. If the barrier was removed and they were tugged across the line with a leash, they eventually learned to escape by themselves. In their home cages, the "helpless" dogs were lethargic; they ate less, lost weight, and became sexually and socially deficient. Seligman felt that the behavior of the "helpless" animals was due to their having learned during pretreatment in the hammock that (negative) reinforcement occurs independently of any responses; this experience left them in a state of _learned helplessness_ (unmotivated to respond in a situation where escape is, in fact, possible).

Hiroto and Seligman (1975) observed similar behavior in research involving human participants. One group was exposed to an aversive noise which some could and some could not control by means of a sequence of button pushes. Another set of subjects received a series of concept-formation problems. The problems received by some were soluble; the problems received by others were not. Those who experienced the noise (_instrumental_) or the problem (_cognitive_) pretreatment were then presented with either an instrumental shock-avoidance task or with a series of cognitively oriented anagram problems (both of these posttreatment tasks were soluble). The results showed evidence of learned helplessness in that those who had undergone inescapable noise or inescapable failure during the pretreatment session were less successful in coping with the instrumental or cognitive tasks, respectively, in the posttreatment than were those who felt that they had previously been successful in avoiding many noises or solving several discrimination problems. Furthermore, the sense of helplessness arising from experience with one type of aversive stimulation was found to undermine performance in a new situation involving a different task altogether. Thus, people exposed to inescapable noise subsequently showed poor performance on an anagrams task, and people who had failed to solve the discrimination problems subsequently had trouble learning the appropriate escape response on the shock-avoidance task.

People oriented toward externality on Rotter's (1966) I-E scale seem to be more susceptible to learned helplessness than are people oriented toward internality (Hiroto, 1974), and the Type A coronary-prone personality may be more vulnerable to becoming helpless than is the Type B when faced with a highly stressful and insoluble avoidance task (Krantz et al., 1974). Some business executives who must solve problems in a high-stress atmosphere on a daily basis become ill and vulnerable to depression, while others seem to thrive on stress. Kobasa (1979) found that a major difference between these executives is that the vulnerable group perceive their jobs as less personally satisfying and socially worthwhile and are more oriented toward externality on the I-E scale.

It should be noted that Seligman's early behavioral model for the origins of learned helplessness and depressive symptoms, particularly as it applies to human beings, was subjected to searching criticism in the February 1978 issue of the *Journal of Abnormal Psychology* (Abramson, Seligman, & Teasdale, 1978). Partly because of these criticisms, Seligman revised his model to make it more cognitive and less strictly behavioral. Now he says it is the individual's self-perception or *expectation* of being unable to control his or her environment so as to gain access to pleasurable experiences or relief from unpleasurable ones which brings about the helpless state. While this expectation of an inability to control must have been created by certain types of life experiences (often very stressful ones), it is usually not an accurate description of the contingencies which actually exist in the individual's environment. The "helpless" or depressed person does have the ability to control certain aspects of his or her environment but, for some reason, *perceives* himself or herself to be helpless. Seligman cites as an example the case of a middle-aged woman who requested psychotherapy.

Every day, she says, is a struggle just to keep going. On her bad days she cannot even bring herself to get out of bed, and her husband comes home at night to find her still in her pajamas, with dinner unprepared. She cries a great deal; even her lighter moods are continually interrupted with thoughts of failure and worthlessness. Small chores such as shopping or dressing seem very difficult and every minor obstacle seems like an impassable barrier. When I reminded her that she is a good-looking woman and suggested that she go out and buy a new dress, she replied, "That's just too hard for me. I'd have to take the bus across town and I'd probably get lost. . . . What would be the use anyway, since I'm really so unattractive?"

Her gait and her speech are slow and her face looks very sad. Up until last fall she had been vivacious and active, the president of her suburban PTA, a charming social hostess, a tennis player, and a spare-time poet. Then two things happened: her twin boys went away to college for the first time, and her husband was promoted to a position of much greater responsibility in his company, a position that took him away from home more often. She now broods about whether her life is worth living, and has toyed with the idea of taking the whole bottle of her antidepressant pills all at once. (Seligman, 1975, pp. 1–2)

Seligman believes that helplessness is also a factor in the prisoner-of-war syndrome in which seemingly healthy men "give up" and die simply because they are confined without hope of release.

CONCLUSIONS

To a greater or a lesser extent, each of the major theoretical approaches to the study of personality relates the development of the self-concept to the individual's experiences of success or failure in coping with problem situations that arouse strong emotions. Within the European tradition, we find Adler arguing that the firstborn child must cope with feelings of threat accompanying his or her dethronement by the birth of a younger sibling. Later-born children must deal with the feelings of inferiority generated by the existence of a more powerful and more knowledgeable older sibling. How each child handles his or her superiority strivings determines much of his or her self-concept and style of life forever after.

Within American personology, theorists like Allport emphasize the importance of the emerging sense of self-recognition during childhood and the attachment of feelings of self-esteem to this core of identity through early experience with gaining mastery over certain aspects of one's environment. Humanistically oriented personologists believe that the self-concept is never firmly and finally established and that we have a continuing need to reveal our feelings and self-perceptions to others. This process is called *self-disclosure,* and if it is conducted in an atmosphere of nonevaluative openness at a level of intimacy appropriate to the situation in which two people find themselves, it renews one's awareness of the genuine core of one's identity and relieves the tensions created by the pressures toward self-distortion which are so often felt in our lives as social animals. Schachter's theory that *emotion* is a combination of a state of physiological arousal and an individual's subjective interpretation of the emotional significance of the arousal is a blend of the trait-dispositional and humanistic-phenomenological viewpoints.

Finally, the behaviorist tradition maintains that the self-concept is created, maintained, or altered through feedback from the external environment that tells us how well or poorly our appearance or behavior matches some socially defined standard (which may be internalized as a personal standard). To the extent that we perceive ourselves as capable of matching this standard, we are likely to develop a self-perception of internal control and high self-esteem. Otherwise, we are likely to develop a self-concept oriented toward externality and low self-esteem.

Which of these traditions is correct? Probably all are correct to the extent that each can explain certain types of findings that are not so easily handled by the others. At the same time, all are, to a greater or lesser extent, incorrect in that no theory is ever supported by research 100 percent of the time. Competing theories may also have areas of overlap, as in the case of dispositional and behavioral explanations for motivation and task performance or for the origins of affective disorders.

It may be unsatisfying to arrive at a conclusion which does not name one theoretical viewpoint as the winner in the contest for research support. This is really as it should be, however, since all traditions contribute their own valuable insights to our understanding of the origins of the self-concept and the growth of competence.

SUMMARY

1   As a child leaves infancy, his or her feelings of competence and ability to cope with stress become increasingly important determinants of future personality growth. Adler, a theorist in the European tradition, believed that a child's birth order has a great impact on these attributes and that, in particular, the firstborn will be approval seeking and achievement oriented while the second-born child will be either rebellious or apathetic. Some support for these predictions has been found in subsequent research.
2   The psychoanalytic concept of repression holds that neurotic anxiety unconsciously refuses to accept those stimuli that are disturbing. Evidence for this idea has been found in a long series of studies on perceptual defense, although the role of unconscious processes in this

phenomenon remains somewhat controversial. Repressor and sensitizer personality types have also been distinguished. The former are more likely to employ perceptual defense, while the latter are likely to be perceptually vigilant for emotionally laden stimulus material.

3 *Affective disorders* are disorders which involve extremes in the expression of emotions and an inability to control them. Depression is the most common of these disorders, and theorists in the psychoanalytic tradition maintained that depression results from the loss of a loved object. The most extreme form of object loss is early separation from one's mother, and research with both monkeys and human orphans indicates that severe depression is often the outcome of this experience.

4 Allport, an American personologist, believed that the "early self" is composed of a sense of bodily self, a sense of personal identity, and a feeling of self-esteem. Formed by the age of 3, it lays the foundation for subsequent personality development. Some of Allport's ideas have been supported by studies indicating that great apes share with humans the capacity to develop a sense of *identity*, or self-concept, even though these animals do not use a language. This suggests that the motivation and ability to form a self-concept may be somewhat inherent in higher primates, much as play behavior or efforts to gain mastery over one's environment appear to be inherently motivated. Enriched rather than deprived social and physical environments factilitate the emergence of these behaviors, however. The trait of self-esteem appears to be a result of early successes in setting and accomplishing goals, an accomplishment which elicits recognition and praise from parents and others. Humanistic psychologists believe that a positive, genuine self-concept is maintained through reciprocal self-disclosure with trusted others.

5 The leading theory of emotion, proposed by Schachter (1964), represents a blend of the dispositional and phenomenological viewpoints. The theory holds that both an internal state of physiological arousal *and* an emotional label for that arousal are necessary to produce a genuinely felt emotion. Because of the uniquely human capacity for language and interpretation, we have a far more flexible and differentiated emotional system than that possessed by animals. *Anxiety* is an emotion which is associated with excessive worry about competence and self-worth and which generally interferes with concentration and performance on a task. More specifically, though, it appears that arousal (one component of which is anxiety) has an inverted-U relationship with performance. This means that up to a point, increasing anxiety can improve performance; it is excessive anxiety and overarousal which reliably undermine performance. Chronic overarousal can be damaging to one's health, as is indicated by studies of the coronary-prone personality. Dispositional theorists regard

depression as one of several possible psychological responses to severe stress. Biochemical evidence suggests that depression is associated with stress-induced depletion of important neurotransmitters from the central nervous system.

6 Behavioral psychologists with a cognitive orientation believe that the self-concept is directly related to the feedback we receive regarding how others view our appearance and behavior. Consistently favorable feedback may cause one to develop a generalized belief that environmental reinforcement is under one's control, whereas consistently unfavorable experiences may create the perception that reinforcement is outside one's control. A belief in internal control of reinforcement is an important component of one's motivation to achieve. One's intrinsic motivation also appears to be weakened by excessive use of tangible rewards rather than internalized self-reinforcers.

7 Behaviorally oriented researchers see the phenomenon of learned helplessness as a laboratory analogue of clinical depression. *Learned helplessness* is a state in which an animal that has been unable to control its receipt of aversive stimulation is later found to be incapable of learning how to avoid such stimulation when escape is possible. The personality traits of externality and coronary-proneness may be related to human susceptibility to learned helplessness.

TERMS TO KNOW

birth order	epinephrine
subliminal perception	Yerkes-Dodson law
anaclitic depression	internal control
self-concept	learned helplessness
self-esteem	coronary-prone personality
self-disclosure	

11

MORAL REASONING AND THE EMERGENCE OF PROSOCIAL BEHAVIOR

INTERNALIZATION OF MORAL NORMS
Psychoanalytic Explanations for Moral Norms
Dispositional Explanations for Moral Norms
Research on Environmentalist Explanations for Moral Norms

DETERMINANTS OF PROSOCIAL BEHAVIOR
Dispositional Explanations for Prosocial Behavior
Environmentalist Explanations for Prosocial Behavior

CONCLUSION

ISSUES TO CONSIDER

1   What are moral norms, and how do children learn and internalize them?
2   Do humans possess any biologically based predispositions toward helping one another?
3   Which is the stronger determinant of a person's motivation to help: his or her personality traits or the stimulus characteristics of the immediate situation?

In Richmond, Virginia, a married, 51-year-old postal worker, who earns $13,000 a year and lives in a decrepit tenement, reads a newspaper article about a high school student who, even though he is himself impoverished and lacks enough money for lunch, turned in $40 he found on the floor of his school bus. The article notes that the student was ridiculed for this helpful act by many of his classmates, and the postal worker decides to demonstrate to all concerned that honesty is, in fact, the best policy. He rewards the student with a check for $1000. Actually, the postal worker is something of a ghetto philanthropist who lives cheaply so as to use his salary to subsidize a $1000-per-year college scholarship, $1000 toward prisoner rehabilitation in the state penal system, and $1000 to an Egyptian boy in need of expensive surgery (Associated Press, November 26, 1976).

Though the actions of the ghetto philanthropist are somewhat out of the ordinary, they reflect a very important aspect of human personality. A complex, interdependent, urbanized society such as ours could not continue to exist if most of its citizens failed to abide by social norms and refused to be generally cooperative and helpful toward one another.

A sociologist's definition of *norms*, by the way, is that they are the values by which behavior is regulated. *Roles* are behavior patterns (such as good parenting) which are defined by norms. A person's norms are internalized values and cannot be directly observed by others unless the person chooses to discuss his or her belief system. A person's enactment of role behaviors, however, can be observed and evaluated by others, who may then use this information to infer the person's norms.

In the case of the ghetto philanthropist and the student whose honesty he sought to reward, it is of interest to ask how they acquired the moral norms which seem to have guided their behavior. Beyond this, it is also of interest to ask why, when people are motivated to act on their beliefs, their role behaviors follow a particular course.

Why did the philanthropist decide to send $1000 to a high school student who first came to his attention by way of a newspaper article when there were undoubtedly equally needy people just around the corner? Why did the philanthropist feel it was so important to reward the student's honest act, and, perhaps more intriguingly, why did some of the student's classmates ridicule it?

This chapter will initially be concerned with how prosocial norms are internalized. The European psychoanalytic tradition views such beliefs either as an outcome of a child's identification with the nurturant aspects of a parent's character during the Oedipal stage of development or as an ego defense employed for the purposes of coping with neurotic anxiety and concealing sexual or aggressive impulses of a very unhelpful nature. The American personological tradition links moral development to a maturational process that progresses in stages which parallel the growth of a child's capacity to engage in representational thought. As always, psychologists in the behaviorist tradition treat moral development like any other behavior which is shaped and maintained by the reinforcement contingencies in a person's environment.

When we consider the role aspects of helping behavior, it is mainly the dispositional and behavioral viewpoints which must be contrasted with one another. The former maintains that individuals develop helpful prosocial personalities which will find expression in an appropriate behavior more or less independently of the reinforcement contingencies operating in an immediate situation. Surprisingly, there is a biological variation on this theme which proposes that humans and other animal species are inherently motivated to engage in certain kinds of helpful acts. The behavioral viewpoint, by contrast, simply states that prosocial behaviors will be engaged in when either reward or stimuli which have in the past been associated with reward (such as social approval) are perceived to be forthcoming. Both the dispositional and the behavioral approaches are supported by an impressive body of research evidence, as will be demonstrated further on in this chapter.

INTERNALIZATION OF MORAL NORMS

As was mentioned above, there are psychoanalytic, personological, and environmental explanations for the development of moral norms. Research bearing on each of these traditions will be discussed in turn.

Psychoanalytic Explanations for Moral Norms

It will be recalled from Chapter 2 that Freud (1925) related a child's acquisition of a capacity for moral judgment to the emergence of the superego at around 5 years of age, when the child tries to resolve conflicting feelings of Oedipal love and hate for his or her parents. Fear of either physical attack or withdrawal of love by the parent of the same sex causes the child to identify with the value system of this parent and to give up the erotic desire for the parent of the opposite sex. A fear of castration by the father causes boys to identify with him. Awareness of their already-castrated condition leads to a desire on the part of girls to acquire a penis through an erotic attachment to the father. Recognizing the futility of this approach, girls develop the sublimated goal of giving birth to a baby and, consequently, identify with the mother and internalize her value system. Despite the early resolution of the Oedipus complex, residues of the suppressed anxieties and the erotic feelings for the parent of the opposite sex remain in the child's personality and are likely to reemerge in some disguised form during adolescence.

Friedman (1950, 1952) tried to test some of these ideas by asking twenty-six male and twenty-six female children in each of six age groups (5, 7, 9, 11, 13, and 15 years) to complete fragmentary "fables" begun by the researcher or to tell stories in response to pictures. One fable described a child who entered a playroom and discovered that a favorite toy, an elephant, was broken. The subjects were asked to indicate what might be wrong with the elephant. It was found that 5-year-old and 13-year-old boys, in particular, avoided referring in their stories to broken or cut protuberances. This was interpreted as a defense against thinking about castration-related themes at times in their lives when such thoughts would arouse particularly strong anxieties. One of the pictures was of father and son (for boys) or a father and daughter (for girls) standing by a stairway with a toy. Here it was discovered that girls were significantly more likely than were boys to imagine that the father climbed the stairs and entered a room at the top. Because the usual psychoanalytic interpretation of dream symbols regards mounting stairs as a representation of sexual intercourse and rooms as womblike spaces, Friedman argued that the girls were revealing repressed penis envy.

Somewhat similar findings were obtained by Hall and Van de Castle (1963), who asked 120 college students to record the contents of their dreams. Castration anxiety was attributed to a dream if it contained an actual or threatened injury to the dreamer's body or to an animal belonging to the dreamer, an inability of the dreamer to use a phallic object such as a gun or spear, or (for men only) a transformation of the dreamer into a woman. Penis envy was attributed to a dream if the dreamer acquired a phallic object, envied a man's physical characteristics, or (for women only) was transformed into a man. Men were more likely than were women to have dreams revealing castration anxiety, while women were more likely than were men to dream about themes relating to penis envy. Eysenck and Wilson (1973) criticized this study on the grounds that some categories of dream content could be scored for one sex only, but Kline (1972) believes it provides "impressive support" for psychoanalytic theory.

Whether the foregoing support is impressive or

not, it is by no means clear that the contents of the superego are related to psychosexual anxieties and complexes. Argyle (1964) reported that children's moral attitudes tend to be more similar to those of their same-sex than their opposite-sex parent. These relationships are rather weak, however, and Kline (1972) does not place much faith in them.

Dispositional Explanations for Moral Norms

Piaget (1932) discovered that children pass through at least two discrete stages in their moral development, much as they seem to pass through stages in their general intellectual development (see Chapter 9). Until about 8 years of age, a child, according to Piaget, has a _heteronomous morality,_ which means, literally, "morality subject to another's law." *Rightness* or *wrongness* is defined in terms of the things that adult authority figures are likely to reward or punish. Simple criteria—such as objective damages—are used to infer the probable reactions of adults to a given situation. After the age of 8, however, a child's cognitive skills have matured sufficiently to permit the development of an _autonomous morality,_ which employs general principles derived from events experienced during the earlier stage but which now includes the concepts of intention, mitigating circumstances, and the relativistic nature of rules of conduct. Piaget's research on this topic consisted of presenting children with stories describing varying degrees of misbehavior which produced varying degrees of damages. The results suggested that a fully autonomous morality is not usually attained until early adolescence.

After completing his doctorate at the University of Chicago, Lawrence Kohlberg traveled to Switzerland to study with Piaget. Kohlberg accepted the idea of stages of moral development, but he believed that there are six stages rather than two. He also felt that while physical and mental maturation push the individual through

the sequence of stages, it is also possible for a person to become fixated at an early stage and never progress any further. To estimate an individual's stage of moral development, Kohlberg, like Piaget, asked subjects to respond to stories which he called *moral dilemmas.* Here is a frequently quoted example (Kohlberg, 1963, pp. 18–19):

In Europe, a woman was near death from a special kind of cancer. There was one drug that the doctors thought might save her. It was a form of radium that a druggist in the same town had recently discovered. The drug was expensive to make, but the druggist was charging ten times what the drug cost him to make. He paid $200 for the radium and charged $2,000 for a small dose of the drug. The sick woman's husband, Heinz, went to everyone he knew to borrow money, but he could only get together about $1,000 which is half of what it cost. He told the druggist that his wife was dying, and asked him to sell it cheaper or let him pay later. But the druggist said, "No, I discovered the drug and I'm going to make money from it." So Heinz got desperate and broke into the man's store to steal the drug for his wife. Should the husband have done that? Why?

Most readers of this dilemma reply that Heinz did the right thing in stealing the drug. Kohlberg was not particularly interested, though, in whether his subjects thought Heinz was right or wrong; what he wanted to examine was the *reasoning* behind each subject's overall moral evaluation. Assuming that the response to the dilemma is always supportive of Heinz, let us see how several different avenues of moral reasoning might be traveled in arriving at this common destination.

Stages 1 and 2 make up what Kohlberg calls the *preconventional level of moral development* and are most representative of the thinking of children, though more than a few adults can be found at this level also. Stage 1, called the *punishment-*

and-obedience orientation by Kohlberg, corresponds closely to Piaget's heteronomous morality. A person in stage 1 might say that Heinz was right to steal the drug because his wife's friends and relatives, or perhaps some supernatural force, would take vengeance on him if he failed to act. Stage 2 is called *instrumental hedonism* and would be reflected in an answer which, like stage 1, is phrased primarily in terms of Heinz's self-interest. The difference here is that some consideration is also given to the conflicting interests of other parties and an effort is made to strike a balance. Someone at stage 2 might say that the druggist is entitled to a profit, but Heinz is entitled to the services of his wife as a loving companion and helpmate; since Heinz's self-interest is the greater of the two, his needs should take precedence over those of the druggist.

The second level of moral development, comprising stages 3 and 4, is called *conventional* by Kohlberg because it is the level at which most adults may be found. Answers at this level tend to subordinate self-interested motives to a desire to live up to the expectations of others. Stage 3, the *"good boy, good girl" orientation*, stresses the importance of being regarded as a "nice" person (e.g., "What would people think of Heinz if he just let his wife die?"). Stage 4, the *law-and-order approach*, stresses the importance of obeying social rules to the letter. An answer at this stage might be that, yes, stealing is against the law, but Heinz and his wife entered into a socially recognized contractual arrangement when they were married. Since Heinz and his wife agreed to do everything they could to help one another ("'til death them do part"), Heinz is caught between conflicting legal obligations. He has to break one contractual commitment in order to uphold the other, a stage-4 person might say, and while I support his decision to save his wife, he should expect to be punished for breaking laws against theft.

The third, *postconventional, level* (stages 5 and 6) is comparable to Piaget's autonomous morality, but Kohlberg, unlike Piaget, believes that relatively few people ever attain it. Stage 5 is called the *social-contract orientation*; it recognizes that rules are necessary in any society but includes the notion that no set of rules can fully define the specific behavior that is most important for the maintenance of social institutions. Rules are thus regarded as flexible enough to be adapted to special circumstances, as potentially modifiable by some legal process, and as relativistic rather than absolute guides for human behavior. A stage-5 answer might be that laws against theft are important for the maintenance of society, but the preservation of trust in close personal relationships such as the institution of marriage is of greater importance. Preservation of faith in the marital bond is more crucial to the stability of society than is the enforcement of laws against simple theft, this subject might reason. Since Heinz's action upheld the higher of two social institutions which, in that particular case, were in conflict with one another, he was justified in stealing the drug. At stage 6, self-chosen universal ethical principles are supposed to replace this intricate, relativistic balancing of individual and group interests. Kohlberg states that such principles must meet at least three requirements; they must be (1) universally applied (others must act on them as well as oneself or one's friends), (2) logically consistent (which "principles" like breaking promises allegedly cannot be), and (3) comprehensive in their applicability to as many moral dilemmas as possible. A stage-6 answer to Heinz's moral problem could be that human life always has priority over property; hence, Heinz was right to steal the drug in order to save his wife's life. To be scored at stage 6, though, this answer must also include the notions that Heinz should be willing to do the same thing to save *anyone's* life, not just that of a close relative, and that if saving a life requires that he part with some of his property, he should willingly do so.

While all the foregoing sample answers have been written in support of Heinz's theft, it is theoretically possible to generate arguments against Heinz's actions at each of the foregoing

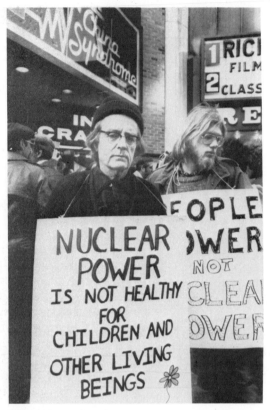

Individuals scoring at a postconventional level on Kohlberg's scale of moral development have been found to be more likely than their more conventional counterparts to engage in "principled" activities such as political protest demonstrations. Individuals at the postconventional level are at an advanced level of moral reasoning. Not all participants at protest demonstrations are at this advanced stage, however. Many have been found to be opportunistic, "stage 2" preconventional types. (United Press International Photo)

six stages. Admittedly, it is difficult to write a stage-5 or stage-6 argument to the effect that it is better for Heinz's wife to die than for the drug to be stolen, but the dilemma could be adjusted slightly so such arguments would be easier to create. (Suppose, for instance, that Heinz had shot and killed the druggist during the theft.) Kohlberg maintains that moral development is both "pushed" by a child's maturational proc-

esses and "pulled" by the dilemmas and higher-level moral reasoning the child encounters in his or her social interactions. If the environment does not provide sufficiently profound moral dilemmas or any examples of high-level moral reasoning, the individual may never progress to his or her full potential. Between ages 7 and 16, the percentage or moral judgments falling at the preconventional level drops from about 95 percent to about 20 percent, while the proportion at the conventional level increases from 5 percent to 55 percent and those at the postconventional level increase from 0 percent to 25 percent (Kohlberg, 1963). This pattern held for middle-class urban boys in the United States and Taiwan, but the majority of 16-year-old boys from economically backward and socially isolated villages in Turkey and Mexico remained fixated at the preconventional rather than at the conventional level (Kohlberg & Gilligan, 1971).

In support of Kohlberg's view that social interaction can "pull" moral development are results obtained by Maitland and Goldman (1974). In this study, a group of four adolescents participated in a discussion of Kohlberg's moral dilemmas and arrived at a unanimous consensus regarding the resolution of each dilemma. This group showed a preconventional to postconventional increase in level of moral reasoning which was not achieved by adolescents who did not participate in discussions or who participated in discussions which failed to reach a consensus.

Much as Kohlberg would predict, individuals scoring at a postconventional level on his scales have been found to be more likely than their more conventional counterparts to engage in "principled" activities. For example, individuals at stages 5 and 6 were relatively overrepresented at a sit-in by advocates of the Free Speech Movement at the University of California in 1964 (Fishkin, Keniston, & MacKinnon, 1973). The parents of these and other postconventional students (e.g., Peace Corps volunteers) appear to have offered models of principled moral reasoning for their children and to have been more active in political affairs—primarily those with a liberal or leftist orientation—than were parents of conventional students (Haan, Smith, & Block, 1968). Haan et al. administered a Q sort to the students in their sample (see Chapter 3 for more information on Q sorts) to see how young adults at various stages of moral development would describe their own personalities. Appropriately enough, students at the conventional levels were the most likely to apply the adjective "conventional" to themselves, while students at the postconventional level were the most likely to describe themselves as "idealistic." In addition, postconventional males were more likely to report that their parents had "expected a lot" from them, while postconventional females tended to believe that their parents were disappointed in them. For both males and females, a postconventional level of moral development was associated with abandonment of traditional religious beliefs and adherence to a leftist political ideology. Fontana and Noel (1973) also found that leftist students are less likely to be at a conventional level and more likely to be at a postconventional level than are middle-of-the-road or rightist students, but these differences are not very large.

One implication of relating moral development to maturational processes is that the stages should fall into a fixed chronological sequence, with young children beginning at stage 1 and adults whose development has not been hindered by some personal or environmental obstacle finally arriving at stage 6. Kohlberg (1969) goes further to insist that regression is impossible. In other words, once a child understands and accepts the moral reasoning of stage 3, he or she can never again be a stage 1. Similarly, a person who arrives at stage 5 or 6 will not, in the future, be found at stage 3 or 4. The higher stages are more comprehensive than the lower, which are supplanted as the individual's reasoning skills progress.

Kurtines and Greif (1974) strongly objected to Piaget's and Kohlberg's account of the origins of moral reasoning. These critics pointed to evidence of children's imitation of a model's regressive moral judgments in studies using Piaget's two-stage approach to moral reasoning which called into question Kohlberg's assumption that stages follow one another in a nonreversible sequence (see Bandura & McDonald, 1963; Cowan et al., 1969; Dorr & Fey, 1974). On the other hand, studies which provided progressive as well as regressive models did find that advancement from the heteronomous to the autonomous level was more easily and permanently induced than was regression from the latter to the former (Schleifer & Douglas, 1973; Sternlieb & Youniss, 1975).

Another objection raised by Kurtines and Greif to evidence cited in support of Kohlberg's theory was that in many of the political-activism studies, stage-2 preconventional types were almost as likely as were their more principled postconventional counterparts to be found at protest demonstrations (Haan et al., 1968). Fishkin et al. (1973) suggested that the stage 2s at these demonstrations were acting out opportunistic, aggressive impulses, as indicated by their endorsement of violent radical slogans like "Kill the pigs." The stage 5s and 6s, though, showed little tendency to endorse such slogans and, instead, distinguished themselves from lower stages by the extent to which they rejected conservative slogans like "America: Love it or leave it." Fontana and Noel (1973) similarly found that while stage 6s make up a higher proportion of leftist than of middle-of-the-road or rightist students, so do stage 2s. Stage-2 reasoning tends to be associated with high scores on Machiavellianism, a scale which measures the extent to which a person has an opportunistic, exploitive attitude toward others.

Apart from the suggestion that the presence of stage-2 types at protest demonstrations may be a result of opportunism rather than commitment to principle, Kohlberg and Kramer (1969) discovered what is perhaps a general tendency for people of college age to display a style of moral reasoning which superficially appears quite similar to stage-2 hedonism but which, in fact, represents a transition from stages 4 to 5. Kohlberg (1976) called this transitional period *stage 4-B* in order to salvage his theoretical assumption that a person's progress toward higher levels of moral development can never reverse itself. Critics like Kurtines and Greif would probably object that Kohlberg was simply adjusting his perception of disconfirming data so they would fit his theory. An alternative method of handling objections such as these would be to discard the assumption that moral development progresses in a nonreversible maturational sequence. Such a method would, however, be more compatible with an environmentalist perspective than with Kohlberg's dispositional viewpoint.

Research on Environmentalist Explanations for Moral Norms

We have already encountered among the studies critical of the cognitive-developmental approach several which demonstrate that peer or adult models can influence a child's level of moral reasoning. These studies—particularly the ones which found that moral reasoning can regress as well as advance within the cognitive-developmental sequence—lend support to the social-learning theorists who argue that moral reasoning, like any other mental or physical behavior, is controlled by a person's anticipation of reward (i.e., praise from the model) in the immediate situation (Bandura & McDonald, 1963; Cowan et al., 1969; Dorr & Fey, 1975). More will be said further on in this chapter about the specific types of learning experiences and situational pressures which serve to influence prosocial behavior. For now, we will examine an environmentally oriented theory of moral development which is every bit as elaborate as Kohlberg's dispositional theory.

The two most fundamental dimensions in Hogan's (1973) model for moral-decision making are socialization and empathy. *Socialization* refers simply to the number of cultural norms an individual has learned and accepted as personally mandatory during the course of growing up. *Empathy* refers to an ability to put oneself in another person's shoes and feel what they are feeling. Hogan believes that children's capacity for empathy may be stunted if they are either overindulged or consistently rejected by their parents; apparently children need to see a range of spontaneously occurring moods in their caretakers and to learn the circumstances which cause those moods to change. Actually, Hogan might object to my assignment of his theory to a section concerned with environmentalist explanations, since he seems to believe that the capacity for empathy has some inherent components in addition to those provided by social learning. For the most part, however, an individual's placement on Hogan's dimensions of moral-decision making would be determined by environmental experience rather than built-in dispositions.

Complete moral maturity, for Hogan, cannot exist unless both socialization and empathy are highly developed, but two additional dimensions are also needed to round out his theoretical model. One, *autonomy*, is the ability of the individual to make and defend moral decisions independently of the social pressures being exerted by others. The second dimension is a belief system which either emphasizes adherence to the legal code as it is set down in official documents and law books or accepts the existence of a *higher*, or natural, law that cannot be comprehensively written down on paper and must be discovered intuitively in the search for principles which protect the rights of the individual and promote the general welfare of society. Endorsers of the first system, the *ethics of responsibility*, tend to believe that the morality of a given act is determined by what the legal system says is right, while endorsers of the second system, the *ethics of conscience*, believe that what is right is whatever they personally *feel* to be right, regardless of the precepts of the legal code. Hogan (1973, p. 125) notes that scores on such assessment devices as the California Psychological Inventory (see Chapter 6) reveal that each of these belief systems is associated with both negative and positive traits. Endorsers of the ethics of responsibility are reasonable, helpful, and dependable but may also be overly conventional and resistant to change. Endorsers of the ethics of conscience, on the other hand, are "independent, innovative, and form creating; however, they also tend to be impulsive, opportunistic, and irresponsible." One might, perhaps, see some similarity between the latter individuals and Maslow's self-actualized personality type.

In Table 11-1, I have indicated how these four dimensions might combine with one another to produce at least sixteen distinctively different moral types. While some of these types appear descriptively similar to some of Kohlberg's stages, Hogan does not assume that change in an individual's character occurs in a fixed, maturational sequence. While it seems plausible to assume (as psychologists always have) that infants begin life as self-centered creatures, lacking in both the socialization and empathy that most parents painstakingly strive to encourage, the exact route by which a child travels from the bottom row of Table 11-1 to one of the higher ones depends very much on his or her life

TABLE 11-1 Character types derivable from Hogan's model for moral judgment

		Ethics of Responsibility (Legalistic)		Ethics of Conscience (Intuitive)	
		Low Autonomy	High Autonomy	High Autonomy	Low Autonomy
High Socialization	High Empathy (morally mature)	"Official" morality of the U.S. government	[Kohlberg's stage 5]	Independently morally mature [Kohlberg's stage 6]	Morally mature in the presence of moral models
	Low Empathy (moral realists)	"Stuffy rule mongers"		"Colorful autocrats"	
		Faceless bureaucrat	Petty tyrant	Melville's Captain Ahab	Ahab's first mate
		Follower Types	Leader Types	Leader Types	Follower Types
Low Socialization	High Empathy (chic types)	"Mild Sociopaths" People who cannot be relied upon to do the right thing but who "mean well"		"Moderate Sociopaths" People who will do whatever feels good for them but whose self-centeredness is restrained by a concern for others	
	Low Empathy (delinquents)	"Moderate Delinquents" People who follow what few rules they have internalized but without much concern for others		"Extreme Delinquents" Character of Alex in Stanley Kubrick's film, A Clockwork Orange	Members of Alex's gang

Ideal Type: High Socialization, High Empathy, High Autonomy

The "official" morality of the United States government, as interpreted by the justices of the Supreme Court, has sometimes been described as comparable to Kohlberg's stage 5, "social contract" orientation. Stage 5 morality tries to balance the rights of the individual and the needs of society so as to arrive at "justice tempered with mercy." (Robert A. Isaacs/Photo Researchers)

experiences. Furthermore, an adult's moral type can either progress or regress depending on life experiences which change his or her orientation toward one or more of the four basic dimensions of moral judgment.

If Hogan has an "ideal type" in his system (and it is not certain that he does), it must lie between the stage-5 and stage-6 characters at some point of moderation on the ethics-of-responsibility– ethics-of-conscience dimension (Hogan, 1973, p. 226). He describes the attributes of this "ideal type" as follows: (a) concern for the sanctity of the individual, (b) judgments based on the spirit rather than the letter of the law, (c) concern for the welfare of society as a whole, (d) capacity to see both sides of an issue, and (e) ability to defend one's decisions in the face of criticism.

DETERMINANTS OF PROSOCIAL BEHAVIOR

Prosocial behavior, often called *helping behavior,* can be defined as behavior whose intent is to change the physical or psychological state of the recipient in such a way that the helper will perceive the recipient to be healthier or more materially or psychologically satisfied. Unfortunately, use of the word "intent" in a definition of this sort poses some problems when one seeks to apply it to real-life situations. We cannot directly observe a person's intentions any more than we can observe his or her internalized norms. Instead, we must infer intentions from observable behavior. People could volunteer to reveal their intentions and beliefs to us, but we would still want to observe their behavior so as to be sure the self-reports were accurate.

One way that psychologists infer intent is to see whether a behavior is repeated in the event that it fails to achieve its assumed goal. To take an example close to the present topic, suppose a boy drops a bit of food which the family dog would thoroughly enjoy finding and eating. The dog does not notice the food, however. If the boy intends to help the dog, he will repeat the act of dropping the food, or he will find some other way of attracting the dog's attention. If the dropping of the food was an accident, unnoticed by both boy and dog, then the boy will simply walk away from the scene; even if the dog eventually finds and eats the food, the boy's actions will still not be regarded as helpful according to the above definition. Ironically, if the boy did intend to help the dog, succeeded in calling the dog's attention to the food, and observed the dog's expressions of satisfaction while eating, he will perceive himself as having helped the animal even if (unknown to the boy) the food later caused the dog to become sick. While most helping behavior does result in some benefit to the recipient, such benefits are technically irrelevant to our definition. The crucial components of helping behavior are its *intent* to benefit the recipient and the helper's *perception* that those benefits have been provided. Even if a recipient is ultimately hurt by such behavior, it remains prosocial by our definition so long as the hurtful outcome was not foreseen by the helper.

In the sections which follow, we will first examine explanations for helping which are cast in terms of internal motives or personality traits—essentially the dispositional viewpoint. We will then consider research on the situational determinants of helping, which is derived from the environmentalist tradition.

Dispositional Explanations for Prosocial Behavior

"Altruism" is a term reserved for helping behavior motivated solely by the desire to make some other person or organism "feel better," with the actions of the altruist being characterized by self-sacrifice and not at all by self-interest. Not all helping behavior is altruistic, according to our definition, but all altruistic actions are helpful. Given these considerations, you may be surprised to learn that there is a well-established contemporary school of thought which argues that even animals sometimes display exalted, altruistic behavior and that, consequently, altruistic motives may, to some extent, be innate. We will begin our treatment of dispositional explanations for helping at this biological level and then move on to the more familiar ground of personality traits.

Biological dispositions for helping In his ground-breaking book *Sociobiology,* Wilson (1975) put forward what is probably the most controversial hypothesis regarding the origins of helping behavior. Scientists who study animals have long been aware that individual members of a species will sometimes risk or even sacrifice their own lives for the apparent purpose of rescuing or furthering the interests of other individuals or the species as a whole. Social insects like ants or termites provide the most dramatic examples of this behavior. Individual members of a colony will work long and hard primarily to benefit the group and (if they belong to the "soldier" castes) will rush into battle when the colony is attacked and place themselves in great danger of dying. It seems reasonably clear that such behavior patterns among social insects are innate rather than learned, so there must be some gene or combination of genes which programs these animals for altruism. The inferred existence of genes which code for helping behavior in social insects caused sociobiologists to speculate on the possible genetic determinants of altruistic motives in higher animals, including human beings.

One instance of mammalian behavior said to be altruistic occurs when an antelope flashes a patch of white hair on its rump or jumps in an awkward fashion (called *stotting*) to signal to other members of the herd that a predator is near. While such signals benefit the herd as a whole, they are also likely to handicap and call attention to the animal that sounded the alarm, thus causing an increase in the odds that it will be the target of the predator's attack (Wilson, 1975, pp. 123–124). Chimpanzees provide another example of helping behavior when they signal to other members of the group that they have discovered a food source. By signaling, the chimp may expose itself to danger; in any event, it will now have to share the food.

According to evolutionary theory, the frequency of a genetically determined trait can rise above the level of random mutation only if it provides a reproductive (hence, survival) advantage to its possessors. As Williams (1966) pointed out, helping behavior seems to have little evolutionary survival value because the altruist's actions benefit everyone in the group, including those members who lack the "altruistic gene." Because of the risks run or the resources lost, the altruistic animal reduces its own likelihood of survival while other species members enjoy the benefits provided by its helpfulness while avoiding the costs. Altruism as a genetically determined trait should, therefore, be maladaptive and thus never appear with greater-than-chance frequency in populations of higher animals. Ants or termites may be exceptions to this rule because all individuals within a given species of social insects are brothers and sisters, hatched from eggs laid by one queen.

In reply to Williams' pessimism regarding the survival value of altruistic traits, Wilson and other sociobiologists suggested that kin selection may confer an evolutionary adaptability to characteristics which are disadvantageous for the individual. If the animal who warns of the approach of a predator, for example, succeeds in rescuing several of its close relatives, even at the cost of its own life, the net contribution of its genes to succeeding generations may still be positive because relatives share certain genes by common descent above and beyond those genes shared by any two members of a species. In particular, siblings share half of their genes by common descent, so if a self-sacrificing altruist rescues at least two of its siblings, or quadruples the number of offspring left by one surviving sibling, altruism as a genetically determined trait could have evolutionary adaptive value for the species as a whole.

It has also been argued that helping behavior is adaptive even at the individual level if it is reciprocal (Trivers, 1971). Thus, if one person dives into a river to rescue another unrelated individual who is drowning, the act is temporarily risky for the altruist and beneficial for the drowning man. If the rescued individual becomes thereby motivated to reciprocate, however, the ultimate benefit to the altruist could outweigh the risks. How is it guaranteed that those individuals who are helped will later reciprocate rather than simply walk away with their benefits? Among higher animals, it is claimed, individuals become identifiable and held accountable for their acts by other members of the group, who will become angry if they perceive "cheating" to have occurred. Such a complex social arrangement, based on genetically activated motives for engaging in reciprocal altruism and punishing "cheaters," would be highly interdependent and ultimately beneficial both for the individual and the species as a whole.

Washburn (1978) strongly objected to this willingness of sociobiologists to propose genes to account for diverse features of animal and human behavior. In addition to genes for aggression, altruism, and opposition to "cheating," Wilson and others hypothesized the existence of genes for conformity, behavioral flexibility, and various cultural differences. The mere fact that a behavior exists, Washburn noted, does not necessarily mean that a gene has programmed its emergence.

A possible middle-ground position was taken by Campbell (1975), who proposed that among humans, because of the capacity for language, social evolution is a more potent determinant of behavior than biological evolution. Humans develop norms of social responsibility which, transmitted by preaching and "setting a good example" from one generation to the next, counteract the biologically evolved predispositions toward selfishness and aggression that threaten to disrupt communal life. Campbell went on to warn against contemporary philosophies in psychology and in the culture at large which urge the pursuit of individual goals and a weakening of laws and moral codes that place restrictions on self-gratification. He cautioned that such a course may forfeit the cultural benefits of a million years of social evolution and abandon us to our biologically based greedy and hostile impulses. Campbell's position, too, provoked a great deal of controversy (Wispé & Thompson, 1976).

While acknowledging the ingenuity of many of their deductions, it is not necessary to endorse the more extreme views of some sociobiologists regarding the genetic origins of specific and

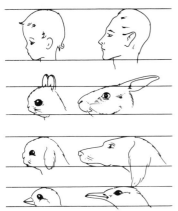

FIGURE 11-1

(Left) Konrad Lorenz believes that humans have a built-in affectional response to animals having "cute" juvenile features. The pictures in the left column show that the young of many species have large eyes, bulging craniums, and retreating chins. Animals with more adultlike features such as those shown in the right column (smaller eyes, longer snouts, and receding foreheads) do not arouse the same degree of affection. *(Above)* Mickey Mouse has passed through at least three developmental stages in his appearance since 1928 which have resulted in his becoming "cuter" and more youthful. Accompanying this change in appearance was his progress toward a more sociable, affection-eliciting personality. (The figures at the left are from Lorenz, 1971, and those above from Gould, 1979.)

diverse behaviors like conformity, punishing "cheaters," altruism, and so forth. As in the case of the angry feelings which motivate much of our aggression (see Chapter 12), it is conceivable that altruism is activated by emotions which result from states of internal arousal. Possibly, the distress of other species members—communicated by facial expression, cries of pain, begging for food, and so forth—evokes feelings of empathy which, if not counteracted by learning or situational constraints, motivate helping behavior. There is evidence for such empathetically motivated helping behavior in rats (Lavery & Foley, 1970), monkeys (Masserman, Wechkin, & Terris, 1964), and human beings (Weiss et al., 1973). Murray (1979) reviewed many studies on animals and especially human beings which point to the conclusion that an infant's cry of distress activates a built-in motivational system which produces a desire to help. Helping the infant also tends to shut off the aversive cry, so it

is not entirely clear that these efforts are altruistic. In any event, while altruism may not be genetically *determined*—among higher animals at least—we may be *predisposed* to respond to distress cues by experiencing emotional states which activate an urge to help.

Konrad Lorenz (1971), a theorist whose views will be examined in some detail in Chapter 12, suggested that humans (and perhaps other species as well) are genetically predisposed to feel affection for animals and humans with *juvenile features*. These features include large eyes, a retreating chin, and a bulging cranium which causes the head as a whole to appear large in proportion to body length. On the other hand, small eyes, a protruding chin or long snout, and a head which constitutes no more than 15 to 20 percent of body length confer a more adultlike appearance which does not excite the same affectionate response (see Figure 11-1). Gould (1979) applied these concepts to an analysis of changes in the cartoon character Mickey Mouse from his debut in 1928 to the present day. Originally, Mickey had a longer snout, smaller eyes, and a shorter head; he was also rather mischievous and occasionally downright mean. Today, Mickey's features are somewhat more juvenile, and he has a more lovable all-around character.

Personality traits and helping Some time ago, Berkowitz hypothesized the existence of a *social-responsibility norm* which, he said, requires people to give resources to anyone whom they perceive as being in need of assistance (Berkowitz & Daniels, 1963, 1964).

Schwartz (1970a) suggested, however, that a motivation to help required not only an awareness of moral norms but also a sense of personal responsibility for acting in accordance with these norms and a consciousness of the consequences which the help (or failure to help) will have for the welfare of others. He designed personality scales to measure these last two traits and found that subjects who rank high on feelings of responsibility and awareness of consequences are perceived by their peers as behaving in a manner that is generally consistent with moral norms. Subjects who score low on both dimensions are not perceived by their peers as living up to their expressed moral norms.

An experimental procedure for eliciting aggression provided Tilker (1970) with an opportunity to investigate the impact of awareness of consequences and feelings of personal responsibility on subjects' willingness to rescue someone else from punishment. In this procedure, the subject and a partner were ordered by the experimenter to deliver electric shocks as punishment for errors made by someone working at a learning task; the shocks increased in intensity following each successive error. Subjects were given either both auditory and visual feedback, auditory feedback only, or no feedback regarding the pain that the learner was experiencing as a result of receiving shock; in addition, subjects were led to believe either that they personally were responsible for the welfare of the learner, that they shared the responsibility with their partners, or that the experimenter was completely responsible for the learner's well-being. As expected, subjects who received the most feedback regarding the hurtful consequences of their actions and who were made to feel personally responsible for the welfare of the learner were the ones most likely to protest to the experimenter that the study was inhumane and to demand that it be stopped. Since it was an experimental study, Tilker's research suggests that tendencies toward helpful behavior may be socialized in children by providing them with explanatory feedback regarding the pleasurable or unpleasurable consequences their actions have for others and making it clear that they will be held personally accountable for such consequences.

Aside from the variables identified by Schwartz and Tilker, there is one other important limitation on Berkowitz's social-responsibility norm. In stating that people should be helped in direct proportion to their needs, the norm implies that a *just world* would be one of strict equality of individual circumstances. An alternative norm, also widely shared, is that the good or bad things in life should be distributed on the basis of contributions rather than needs. This norm is often called *distributive justice*, or *equity* (Adams, 1965; Homans, 1974).

A few examples should clarify the difference between the equity and equality norms. Suppose you and a friend agree to make candles to sell for a profit at a flea market. You are very industrious and have 100 candles ready on the appointed day, but your friend has only 20. The candles are a popular item at the flea market, and all 120 are sold for a total of $360. Now you and your friend must split this amount. The equality rule would call for $180 each, but equity says that your greater contributions to the manufacture of the candles entitles you to a larger share of the reward. Specifically, since your contributions were five times larger than your partner's you should receive $300 and she or he only $60. Effort and ability are the most legitimate and probably the most common types of contributions which are evaluated in decisions regarding the equitable distribution of resources, but people often include superficial and somewhat irrelevant characteristics such as age, physical appearance, or socioeconomic status in their assessment of contributions.

The relevance of the equity norm to helping is that we are inclined to help only those whom we perceive to be deserving of our assistance, where deservedness consists of the sum total of an individual's contributions. The operation of an equity norm seems to be reflected in the results of a simple field study organized by Latané and Darley (1970). College students asked hundreds of pedestrians in New York City to give them a dime. If the student appeared to be simply a panhandler, only 34 percent of those approached would hand over a dime. If, on the other hand, the student gave a reason for needing a dime which made him or her appear to be more deserving of a favor, the likelihood of receiving help increased. For instance, if the student said the dime was needed to make a phone call because his or her wallet had been stolen, 74 percent of passersby provided a dime.

Norms of deservedness serve a useful function in directing our help where it will do the most long-term good. There is a danger, though, that the belief that everyone should get what she or he deserves may be distorted into a conviction that everyone must be perceived as deserving whatever she or he has received (Lerner, Miller, & Holmes, 1976). Research has turned up evidence of this tendency to overrate the deservedness of the recipients of good fortune and to devalue the contributions of the victims of misfortune (Lerner, 1965; Lerner & Simmons, 1966; Samuel, 1975, pp. 138–146). To paraphrase Lerner, a truly *just world* is one in which the good are rewarded and the wicked are punished, but we must guard against misapplying this belief system so as to construe reward as proof of goodness and punishment as proof of wickedness.

At an early age, we learn that equity and equality norms often place us in a state of conflict. Children who contributed three times as much effort to the completion of a task as their partners, when placed in charge of distributing the rewards, did give themselves larger shares than their partners—but not the full three-times-larger shares permitted by the equity norm (Lerner, 1974). If the child and his or her partner had been encouraged to think of themselves as a "team," an equal sharing of the rewards was observed, regardless of the partner's contribution. It has even been shown that children will approve another child's "Robin Hood" style theft of undeserved rewards from a "wealthy" third party, but only if the "Robin Hood" passes the loot along to a "poor" fourth party, thus making the distribution of rewards more equal (Brickman & Bryan, 1975).

In a long series of studies of a trait called *delay of gratification*, children were asked to choose between small rewards which they could have immediately or larger rewards which they could obtain only by waiting (e.g., a small candy bar today or a much larger one a week from now). A decision to wait for the larger reward indicated a willingness to delay gratification. Mischel (1974) maintains that this willingness to defer self-gratification is a component of a child's motivation to achieve and is based on early learning experiences which teach the child that delayed rewards will actually materialize. In research on equity and helping, it was observed that if children perceive themselves to have been the recipients of an undeserved reward, they are more likely to contribute to a charity for orphans than if they believe their contributions make them fully deserving of the reward (Long & Lerner, 1974). This effect was found only among children high in the ability to delay gratification, however. Mischel (1974) relates a child's willingness to defer gratification to his or her degree of trust in other people, and Lerner regards this developing reliance on other people to honor their commitments as the basis for a belief in *distributive justice*, or equity.

As adults, if we have inflicted undeserved harm on another person, we are likely to feel guilt over having violated norms of distributive justice. This guilt should, and does, increase our motivation to help both the particular person harmed and third parties (Freedman et al., 1967; Konečni, 1972; Regan et al., 1972).

Environmentalist Explanations for Prosocial Behavior

To Aronfreed (1970, 1976), the crucial distinction between true altruism and mere helping behavior is that altruism is motivated solely by the desire to make someone else "feel better" while helping behavior may be primarily self-interested even when it serves to benefit another individual. Working within the behaviorist tradition, Aronfreed assumes that altruistic motives develop through some sort of conditioning process. In particular, his research pursued the hypothesis that empathy has its origins in situations in which others transmitted cues regarding an emotional state—such as smiles and laughter or grimaces and exclamations of pain—which happened to coincide with the emotional state of the child at that moment. This might happen quite often, as when both parent and child experience joy over the sight of a birthday cake or fear over impending danger. Anyway, through associative learning, the overt emotional cues transmitted by others become eliciting stimuli for a comparable emotional state in the child. The next step in the progression from empathy to altruism occurs when the child is reinforced for making the parent happy rather than unhappy (and what parent fails to do this?). Finally, provision of extrinsic rewards (candy, hugs and kisses) for helping behavior is eventually replaced by cognitive self-reinforcers ("I am a good boy," and so on) as the child grows older. When self-reinforcement rather than extrinsic reinforcement motivates the desire to make others happy, the child is intrinsically motivated. Helping behavior is, at that point, engaged in "for its own sake," and the child is, according to Aronfreed, truly altruistic.

In a field study of the development of altruism in children, Hoffman (1975) related parental characteristics to ratings of their children made by the children's peers (e.g., "Which three boys or girls in your class are most likely to stick up for some kid that the other kids are making fun of or calling names?"). Parental discipline which emphasized the feelings of the victims of a child's hurtful behavior and which demanded that the child make adequate restitution of damages was found to be quite strongly related to the child's altruistic behavior at school (r's were around 0.5). Interestingly, though, it seemed that the parent who was opposite in sex to the child was most effective in using this socialization technique. In addition, the most altruistic children had at least one parent (usually the father) who "modeled" altruistic values and was willing to go to some trouble to help others.

However it is socialized, empathy is clearly an important component of the motivation to help. Weiss, Boyer, Lombardo, and Stich (1973) exposed college-age subjects to an accomplice of the experimenter's who feigned great pain and emotional stress while allegedly enduring electric shock as a distractor on a radarlike tracking task. The subjects were told to monitor the accomplice's reactions by pressing buttons which activated a recording apparatus. In the experimental group, pressing the sixth button allegedly placed the apparatus into a "report" mode which gave the accomplice ten seconds of relief from the painful shock. In a control group, the accomplice continued to emit pain cues and allegedly continued to receive shock throughout the report period. Weiss et al. discovered that in the experimental group only, the speed with which the buttons were depressed by the subjects steadily increased over trials, indicating that this behavior was reinforced by its helpful consequences for the suffering accomplice.

While direct conditioning of empathic reactions probably is important for the learning of altruistic motives, a review of the literature on this topic suggests that "modeling" processes have an even stronger and more durable impact

Parental discipline which emphasizes the feelings of the victims of a child's hurtful behavior and which demands that the child make adequate restitution of damages has been found to be quite strongly related to the child's altruistic behavior at school. Discipline which merely emphasizes physical punishment has not been found to promote altruistic behavior. (Christy Park/Monkmeyer)

on helping behavior (Rushton, 1976). One of the primary means by which parents encourage children to develop a repertory of helpful behaviors is by setting a "good example." Among children in laboratory settings, the increase in helping behavior which resulted from exposure to a helpful model was found to persist for at least two to four months following the exposure and to generalize to a new experimenter asking subjects to respond in a novel situation (Rice & Grusec, 1975; Rush-

ton, 1975). Television programs with prosocial contents (e.g., "Mister Rogers' Neighborhood") may also provide "modeling" experiences which increase cooperativeness with and interest in others on the part of child viewers (Friedrich & Stein, 1973; Contes et al., 1976).

Darley and Latané (1970) have been somewhat critical of dispositionally oriented researchers who maintain that prosocial behavior is guided by norms and other personality traits. They note that norms are often stated in vague and contradictory ways. We are encouraged to help others, for instance, but we are simultaneously urged to be self-reliant and to avoid receiving help from others. So what does society value more, helping or self-reliance? Furthermore, norms of helping and intervention sometimes conflict with norms of privacy and the recommendation to "mind your own business." Finally, they say, there is little evidence that people actually think about norms when responding to an immediate situation. The presence of helping models and other stimulus characteristics of the situation, rather than the individual's normative belief system, seem to be the strongest determinants of helping behavior. Some of these determinants are briefly outlined below.

Liking for the recipient   The role of empathy in facilitating helping is apparently somewhat influenced by our feelings of attraction to the recipient. We find it easier to empathize with the feelings of those who share our beliefs, and we are more likely to extend help to these "similar others" (Krebs, 1975; Sole et al., 1975).

Diffusion of responsibility   As a result of a real-life incident in which a woman named Kitty Genovese was attacked at night on a New York street and stabbed and killed while at least thirty-eight of her neighbors watched from their apartment windows without bothering to call the police, Darley and Latané (1968) conducted a pioneering laboratory experiment in helping behavior. The subject, isolated in a small cubicle, listened over headphones as a male partner in his or her discussion group simulated an epileptic seizure and called for help. Subjects were led to believe that varying numbers of *witnesses* (members of the discussion group) also heard the call for help. It was found that when subjects believed they were alone with the victim, 85 percent left their cubicles to report the emergency and did so within 1 minute of the onset of the seizure. When subjects assumed one other witness was present

besides themselves, 62 percent left their cubicles within about 1.5 minutes, and when four other witnesses were assumed to be present, only 31 percent emerged from the cubicles, taking an average of nearly 3 minutes to do so. Actually, subjects were alone in all conditions; the other members of their discussion group were merely tape-recorded voices controlled by an elaborate switching device. Darley and Latané concluded from these data that one factor contributing to the lack of responsiveness to Kitty Genovese's cries for help was the ability of witnesses to see one another at their windows while being unable to communicate among themselves. Consequently, each witness felt less personally responsible for taking action and may have assumed that someone else would surely do so; they called the phenomenon *diffusion of responsibility*.

Subsequent research has often supported the notion that people are more likely to intervene in an emergency when alone than when in the presence of one or more other bystanders, even when the bystanders can see and talk to one another (Latané & Rodin, 1969; Schwartz & Gottlieb, 1976). When the emergencies were unambiguous and relatively nonthreatening to the helper, however, as when a man suddenly collapsed in a subway car or a worker received a powerful electric shock within sight and sound of bystanders (Piliavin, Rodin, & Piliavin, 1969; Clark & Word, 1974), the victims received help on more than 90 percent of trials, regardless of the number of witnesses present.

Another factor which seems to influence whether or not diffusion occurs is the type of emotional cues transmitted by other bystanders. If they act unconcerned by the emergency, they constitute models for not "blowing one's cool," and a particular witness to the event will be less likely to intervene than he or she would be if there were no other bystanders. Latané and Rodin (1969), for example, found that pairs of friends are somewhat more likely than are pairs of strangers to try to help a woman who has apparently fallen and hurt herself in an adjoining room. Presumably friends are less inhibited about expressing their emotional reactions to one another, and so they are able to act on the basis of their shared feelings of concern. Even strangers, though, are less inhibited and more likely to help than are subjects who hear the emergency while in the presence of an impassive accomplice of the experimenter's.

Anticipated costs Even if helping norms have been aroused and a bystander does not diffuse responsibility, he or she may still not intervene if the anticipated costs are excessive. *Costs* could be expenditure of time and resources, risk of physical harm, and so forth. In another subway study, Allen demonstrated that commuters are much less likely to intervene to correct erroneous directions supplied by one accomplice (the "misinformer") to another (the "questioner") if they must interrupt an ongoing conversation between the two accomplices or if they have reason to feel physically threatened by the "misinformer" (Darley & Latané, 1970, pp. 93–96). The effect of a physical threat on attitudes toward helping seems to be demonstrated by the results of an interview study of people who received awards under California's Good Samaritan law. This law provides anyone who intervenes to prevent a crime or to apprehend a criminal with reimbursement for any injuries suffered in the attempt. Most of the "Samaritans" interviewed said that they had intervened impulsively, that their intervention and the resulting suffering from their injuries had not been sufficiently appreciated, and that they regretted their impulsiveness and would probably not get involved in similar situations in the future (Huston et al., 1976).

Mood Research data demonstrate fairly consistently that people are more helpful toward others when they have just experienced a success, received a reward, or are, for some other reason, in an exceptionally good mood (Isen et al., 1978). Some investigators go further to suggest that being in an exceptionally bad mood depresses

helping (Rosenhan et al., 1974). Weyant (1978) reported that a negative mood depresses helping when anticipated costs are high and potential recipients do not appear particularly deserving of assistance.

CONCLUSION

If we think once again about the ghetto philanthropist mentioned at the beginning of this chapter, we can probably make some educated guesses regarding the motivations underlying his behavior. Apparently he found it exceptionally easy to empathize with the plight of others in need of assistance and felt an exceptionally strong degree of personal responsibility for acting in accordance with this empathy. He himself was not deterred by the expenditure of his meager resources, and this may have made him particularly sympathetic toward the boy who turned in $40 found on a school bus. Upon hearing that the boy was jeered for engaging in an act of helping that his classmates perceived as foolishly costly, the philanthropist was perhaps eager to set an example of upholding helping norms and, at the same time, to reaffirm the validity of his own life-style. Self-interested motives could have been operating as well, of course, such as a desire to achieve personal recognition through a public display of generosity.

Much as psychoanalytic theorists would predict, there is considerable evidence that helping norms are strongly influenced by a child's identification with the prosocial values of his or her parents or other adults who serve as parental substitutes. Two field studies not mentioned earlier in this chapter explored the backgrounds of Christian Europeans who risked their lives to rescue Jews from the Nazis during World War II (London, 1970) and young Americans who actively participated in the Freedom Rides which dramatized and ultimately brought to an end racially segregated public facilities in the South (Rosenhan, 1970). While a spirit of adventure seemed to be one of the motivations underlying these altruistic acts, a common biographical element appeared to be an intense identification with the moral values of one or both parents. Perhaps the ghetto philanthropist was unconsciously trying to assume a parental role in the minds of the honest high school student and his cynical friends and to demonstrate that identification with the prosocial aspects of this role can be very rewarding.

In contradiction to psychoanalytic accounts of the origin of the superego, however, there is no consistent support for the proposition that one's moral values are more closely related to those of one's same-sex than to those of one's opposite-sex parent. While parental models do appear to be important for the internalization of prosocial norms, it seems that social-learning theory provides a more defensible and useful account of the mechanics of this process than does Freud's notion of the resolution of the Oedipus complex.

Psychologists have themselves been working to resolve the "complex" which exists within their own profession regarding the determinants of helping and other behaviors. I am referring here to the dispute between those who call attention to dispositional person variables and those who prefer environmental situation variables as explanations for human thought and action. Staub (1978) regards helping as the outcome of an interaction between internal feelings and beliefs and the external features of a particular setting. Much the same position was advocated by Batson, Darley, and Coke (1978, p. 119):

> External determinant models such as the one developed by Latané and Darley are simply not sufficient to explain why a person helps. While these models have proven quite successful in explaining when a person will help and when he will not, they cannot explain why a person helps at all. The notion of diffusion of responsibility, for example, assumes that there is a sense of responsibility to diffuse. Individuals apparently are concerned that others' distress

be reduced. Where does this sense of responsibility come from, and how does it operate? Is it a function of some individual difference variable? Of some norm? Or, could it stem from some aspect of the psyche not considered previously?

Batson et al. believe that the concept of empathy may be a theme which can bring some unity to these diverse perspectives on helping behavior. Progress toward the higher stages of Kohlberg's model of moral development, for instance, requires an increasing concern for the needs and feelings of ever-larger numbers of people, culminating in the development of universal ethical principles. In Hogan's model, a high degree of socialization does not lead to moral maturity unless it is accompanied by a correspondingly high degree of empathy. Empathy is assumed by Batson et al. to produce a state of emotional arousal in an individual who witnesses the distress of others. The preferred response to this arousal state is the initiation of actions which reduce others' distress; this in turn discharges the arousal and restores the internal state of the helper to a more comfortable baseline level. If empathic emotions do have a physiological component which is activated by distress cues from other individuals, this could provide the basis for a sociobiological predisposition toward altruism.

On the other hand, we are all too aware of the fact that, in humans at least, any such predispositions and any internalized prosocial norms can be overridden if situational contingencies provide no rewards, or even threaten punishments, for helpful acts. Furthermore, if people believe they have been abused or mistreated by others in the past, they may apply a norm of equity in the present and conclude that others are not particularly deserving of their assistance—as the classmates of the boy who found $40 on the bus may have done. Other deterrents to norm- or empathy-induced helping are anticipated costs, being in a bad mood, or the opportunity to diffuse responsibility.

Despite all the constraints identified by psychologists, helping continues to occur in the real world. Schwartz (1970b) discovered that a high percentage of people who understood they were the one person in 1000 who could donate bone marrow to a young mother dying of leukemia volunteered for what they knew to be a somewhat painful surgical procedure. The persistence of tendencies among humans (and occasionally among lower animals as well) to sacrifice their own interests in order to help others provides some grounds for optimism regarding "human nature." In Chapter 12, though, we will examine the less reassuring aspects of human nature as we consider the origins of antisocial and aggressive behavior.

SUMMARY

1   Prosocial behavior can be studied either at the level of internalized norms and other dispositions or at the level of environmental contingencies which influence the enactment of role behavior. Freud believed that internalized norms originate with the emergence of the superego at around 5 years of age, when the child resolves his or her Oedipus complex through identification with the parent of the same sex.

2   Piaget and Kohlberg regard the internalization of moral norms as a cognitive-developmental process. This process is dispositional in that a child is pushed by biological maturation through a graded sequence of stages and, at any particular time, shows moral reasoning which is fairly consistent with his or her present stage. The process is a social one in that most children must be exposed to examples of higher-stage reasoning in order to progress in their moral development. Critics questioned Kohlberg's assumption that moral development progresses in a fixed sequence of stages which can never reverse itself.

3   Hogan provided an elaborate theory of moral development based primarily on social learning rather than dispositional processes. Complete *moral maturity*, for Hogan, combines a high degree of socialization, empathy, and autonomy with a moderate position on the dimension identified as "ethics of responsibility" vs. "ethics of conscience."

4   *Prosocial*, or helping, *behavior* is defined as behavior whose intent is to change the physical or psychological state of the recipient in such a way that the helper will perceive the recipient to be healthier or more materially or psychologically satisfied. The crucial components of helping behavior are its *intent* to benefit the recipient and the helper's *perception* that those benefits have been provided. Even if a recipient is ultimately hurt by such behavior, it remains prosocial so long as the hurtful outcome was not foreseen by the helper.

5 The more extreme proponents of a biological disposition for helping argue that animals and humans possess genes which activate this behavior in appropriate situations. Genes have also been proposed for other traits, such as aggression, conformity, and opposition to "cheating." The less extreme position is that in humans and other higher mammals, distress cues from other species members generate a state of emotional arousal in the potential helper. This arousal may be discharged through efforts to alleviate another's distress. Lorenz maintains that the "cute" facial features characteristic of juvenile animals and humans may also activate this built-in emotional response.

6 *Social-responsibility norms* require us to help all others who appear to be in need of assistance. Whether we act on these norms depends on the extent to which we feel personally responsible for doing so and can foresee the consequences of failing to help. Furthermore, social-responsibility norms are often qualified by equity norms, which tell us to extend help only to those whom we perceive to be deserving of assistance. For a person who has internalized the equity norm, the consequences of inflicting undeserved harm on another person are guilt and a desire to make restitution. Guilt has been shown to be a reliable elicitor of helping in many studies.

7 A behavioral account of the origins of empathy is that it arises from situations in which others (e.g., parents) transmit cues regarding an emotional state which happens to coincide with the emotional state of the child at that moment. Eventually, cues from others reliably elicit comparable emotional reactions in the child. The step from empathy to altruism occurs when the child is rewarded for making others happy, which eventually causes the child to feel happy, too. Making others happy could now be said to be a behavior engaged in "for its own sake." On the other hand, straightforward modeling of prosocial behavior has also been found to increase its frequency among children, independently of any conditioning of empathic reactions. Environmentally oriented psychologists regard helping behavior as either encouraged or suppressed by the contingencies present in the immediate situation. Some of these contingencies are liking for the recipient, the opportunity to diffuse responsibility, anticipated costs, and mood.

8 Parental modeling appears to have a very strong influence on the internalization of prosocial norms, but there is no consistent support for the psychoanalytic proposition that one's moral values are more closely related to those of one's same-sex than to those of one's opposite-sex parent. Many psychologists regard prosocial behavior as the outcome of an interaction between internal feelings and beliefs and the external features of a particular setting. Empathy seems to be

a characteristic which <u>has both dispositional and behavioral origins.</u> As such, it may provide a common focus around which conflicting theoretical perspectives could be unified.

TERMS TO KNOW

norms and roles
autonomous morality
stages of moral development
empathy
ethics of conscience

sociobiology
social responsibility norm
altruism
equity norm

12

CAUSES OF AGGRESSION AND ANTISOCIAL BEHAVIOR

1   Why is it so difficult to state a definition of aggression that is both precise and psychologically meaningful?
2   What sorts of biological factors and environmental conditions are likely to trigger aggressive outbursts?
3   How can social-learning theory and research on child development account for the existence of aggressive personalities?

A 33-year-old computer programmer, complaining that he was passed over for promotion at work and that he is annoyed by such things as "kids' revving their motorcycles while I'm trying to sleep" and "the guy who parks in two parking places," barricades himself and seven hostages inside the clubhouse of his apartment complex in Indianapolis, Indiana. Firing bursts of shots from a semiautomatic weapon, he holds police at bay for thirteen hours before surrendering. Fortunately, no one is injured (Associated Press, May 7, 1978).

Though the above incident had a fairly happy ending, we are all familiar with other, similar ones which ended disastrously. Indeed, it sometimes seems as if the price of civilized existence is continual exposure via the news media to the consequences of violent acts which horrify us and lead us to ask ourselves what causes them, what can be done to forestall them, and what hope there is of rehabilitating their perpetrators. Psychoanalytic theory tells us that aggression is motivated by a death instinct that is represented within all persons by an automatically accumulating urge to attack and destroy. This urge may be sublimated, or it may be repressed and neurotically defended against, but it is always there. When the increasing tension bursts the restraints set upon it by the ego and superego, the result is an explosion of violence.

One reason why this explanation fails to satisfy dispositional and behavioral theorists is that it does not tell us why, when people are motivated to aggress, their behavior follows a particular course. It seems clear that the computer-programmer's aggression was activated, in part, by the frustrations and annoyances he was experiencing, but this observation is not, by itself, sufficient to explain his actions. Others, equally or even more provoked, have not reached for a weapon. Also, given that the programmer was motivated to aggress, why did he choose to act out his impulse by taking hostages and barricading himself inside a building? Prior learning experiences and personality traits must have influenced the many choices that he made. Dispositional and environmentalist theorists are more concerned than are psychoanalytic theorists with accounting for such complexities in human aggression.

Each of the foregoing approaches, as well as the various offshoots and subhypotheses that each has spawned, will be explored in this chapter's treatment of aggressive behavior. Before this exploration can begin, though, it is necessary to settle upon a working definition of the behavior to be examined.

What is aggression? Bandura (1973, p. 5) defined it as "behavior that results in personal injury and destruction of property." Baron (1977, p. 7) on the other hand, described aggression as "any form of behavior directed toward the goal of harming or injuring another living being who is motivated to avoid such treatment." As a social-learning theorist in the American tradition, Bandura wishes to de-emphasize unobservable psychological states, such as intentions, in defining his terms. If intentions are totally ignored, though, we will be unable to distinguish behavior which produces accidental damage from that which is premeditatedly destructive. Use of the word "injury" raises similar problems. Does injury mean only observable physical damage, or does it include psychological damage as well?

Baron, in referring to goals, makes it clear that an act is aggressive if and only if the actor intended it to be injurious, and the act, because of the destructive intentions which motivated it, is aggressive even if it misses the mark and fails to inflict injury. Baron deals with the problem of how to define injury by turning, as in the case of intentions, to internal psychological processes; namely, the feelings of the target of the hurtful behavior. If the target wants to terminate or escape from the treatment, then it must be causing some degree of psychological (and perhaps physical) injury. In order to use this definition of injury, however, Baron must exclude damage to inanimate objects from the concept of aggression—a step which Bandura need not take.

It should be acknowledged that Bandura, like Baron, wrestles with each of the foregoing problems and concludes that intentions and psychological injury must be considered when particular actions are to be judged aggressive or not. In order to proceed with the business of the present chapter, it is necessary either to adopt one of the foregoing definitions or to suggest a third possibility. For now, we will adopt as our working definition of aggression a synthesis of the concepts put forward by Bandura and by Baron: _Aggression_ is behavior whose intent is either to cause physical or psychological injury to a person or other living thing or to cause physical damage to an object. The terms "injury" and "damage" are defined as a change in the state of the target of the behavior which is perceived _by the aggressor_ to be less healthy or satisfied, in the case of living organisms, or generally less whole or intact.

This working definition no doubt has a few loopholes of its own, which this chapter will, it is hoped, make some progress toward patching up. One omission that is immediately apparent is that the definition makes no mention of the emotional states, particularly anger, often associated with aggressive intentions. Another problem (which the lay reader is likely to see in _all_ psychologists' definitions of aggressive behavior) is that it makes no distinction between this behavior and self-defense. The word "aggression" is loaded with negative connotations, and we usually prefer that it be applied to our enemies while our own hurtful actions be labeled _self-defense_. Psychologists, though, resist making such distinctions and prefer to create definitions that apply to all hurtful acts, regardless of whether or not a given act would be perceived as justified either by its perpetrator or by outside observers. It would perhaps make matters easier if psychologists used a less negatively weighted term in place of "aggression." Calling the phenomenon _agonistic behavior_ might make it easier to treat the topic objectively, but then the discussion might become so academic that the public would lose interest in whatever psychologists had to say on the subject.

It should be easier to appreciate the importance and complexity of each of the foregoing issues once a common ground of basic information has been provided and discussed. Consequently, we will tentatively adopt the working definition of aggression with the understanding that this discussion will be resumed at the conclusion of this chapter.

PSYCHOANALYTIC EXPLANATIONS FOR AGGRESSION

In Chapter 2 it was mentioned that after World War I, Freud revised his theory of personality to give death instincts a status equal to the instincts which promote life. You will also recall that Adler's "drive for power" and Jung's "shadow archetype" were conceptually similar to Freud's aggressive instinct. Freud (1920) argued, however, that aggression was an indirect rather than a direct expression of the instinctual impulse. Strictly speaking, the death instincts (_Thanatos_) work toward the individual's _self_-destruction and are expressed biologically in the breakdown of cells and metabolic processes which accompanies advancing age. They are opposed by the life instincts (_Eros_) which seek to deflect them away from the self and outward toward the world. The accumulating urge to attack and destroy others is thus due to a redirection of the urge to destroy oneself. In response to a question posed by Albert Einstein regarding what might be done to prevent war, Freud (1932) essentially said "not much." He argued that the best hope for handling humanity's aggressive tendencies was to provide harmless displacement activities, such as organized sports, which might drain off the instinctual energy motivating more hurtful forms of behavior.

In a sense, the notion of an aggressive instinct can be neither proved nor disproved. On the one hand, the record of human history is so replete with tales of cruelty and slaughter that the existence of instinctual impulses certainly seems plausible (Storr, 1968). Even in human prehistory, the earliest known remains of Homo sapiens as well as those of more ancient human precursors like Neanderthal man, Peking man, and the australopithecines, often show evidence of injury, murder, and even cannibalism (Leakey & Ardrey, 1972). On the other hand, human beings have always been social animals, with ample opportunity to learn violent behavior from a few demented individuals who succeed in accomplishing their goals by attacking others.

Distinguishing instinct (assuming it exists) from social learning in human behavior would appear to be a hopelessly complex task. The task is somewhat simpler when one studies animal behavior, and the scientists who do so are called *ethologists*. One prominent ethologist, Konrad Lorenz (1966) accepted the existence of an aggressive instinct. His evidence is based primarily on observations of behavior in animals that appears to be instinctual; he then generalizes these observations to the motivations underlying similar human behavior. For example, Lorenz (Carthy & Ebling, 1964, p. 46) noted that a male cichlid ("fighting fish") will attack, bite, and eventually kill his mate if he has no other male with whom to fight. If another male-female pair is placed in the aquarium, separated from the first couple by a pane of glass, the two males will engage in ritualized combat on opposite sides of the pane, displaying their brightly colored fins, beating water with their tails, and assuming various threat postures. When given this outlet for aggressive energy, the males will not abuse their female partners. If algal growth clouds the glass, however, the males, unable to see each other, will turn once again to attacking their mates. Two features of within-species aggression are illustrated by this cichlid example: (1) it is much more likely to be exhibited by males than by females and (2) it tends to consist mainly of ritualized display so that mortal injuries are infrequent.

Ritualized, within-species aggression serves a useful purpose. In territorial animals, it ensures spacing between breeding pairs sufficient to permit adequate forage for the pair and their offspring (Lorenz, 1966). In animals that group together in troops, herds, or flocks, ritualized aggression typically creates a *dominance hierarchy* (which gives priority to the most dominant males) that provides a simple system for sharing resources such as food or mates without the danger of murderous fights. In the case of both territoriality and dominance, the ritualized aggression that maintains the system serves the beneficial evolutionary purpose of maximizing the likelihood of species survival; species that did not evolve such a system for dividing up resources would probably have an extraordinarily large number of killed and wounded animals, the latter being vulnerable to predators or disease. The species with the most potent natural weapons, such as horns, claws, and sharp teeth or fangs, are the ones for whom a ritualization of aggression is most imperative. The human tragedy, says Lorenz, is that we have little in the way of natural weapons and so have evolved relatively few biological restraints on the discharge of our aggressive impulses against other human beings. Relatively recently (on an evolutionary time scale) humans have also used their large brains to develop weapons of incredible destructive force, with the result that our survival as a species is now threatened by having both extremely potent weapons and relatively few natural restraints against using them on one another.

The hypothesis that an automatically accumulating urge to aggress exists in human beings is difficult, if not impossible, to disprove conclusively. Demonstrating that hurtful behavior can be increased or diminished in frequency by learning experiences does not, in and of itself, rule out the possibility that the motivation to engage in this behavior has an instinctual origin. The fact that we can locate apparently nonaggressive aboriginal societies, such as the Tasaday in the Philippines or the Fore in New Guinea, might imply that humans do not have an urge to engage in physical aggression that will overpower all socially learned restraints, but it cannot be taken as final proof that humans have no inherent aggressive impulses.

Furthermore, there are structures in the human brain, joined together in the limbic system, whose activity is known to be strongly related to our subjective sensation of emotion (see Chapter 7). We share these structures with other animal species, and perhaps we share some of their motivations as well. According to Wilson (1975, p. 3), one of the charter members of a new field known as *sociobiology*, emotions are the key to the genetic transmission of behavioral traits.

The biologist, who is concerned with questions of physiology and evolutionary history, realizes that self-knowledge is constrained and shaped by the emotional control centers in the hypothalamus and limbic system of the brain. These centers flood our consciousness with all the emotions—hate, love, fear, and others—that are consulted by ethical philosophers who wish to intuit the standards of good and evil. What, we are then compelled to ask, made the hypothalamus and limbic system? They evolved by natural selection.

If the emotion of anger is likely to motivate aggressive behavior, and if the individuals within a given species who are most easily angered are also the ones who, because of their aggressiveness, have the greatest success in passing their genes on to future generations through reproduction, then the genes which contribute to a propensity to anger will increase in frequency across generations, while "pacifist genes" will drop out. Such a process could provide the biological basis for the so-called aggressive instinct.

The behavioral and dispositional traditions would, to a greater or lesser extent, dispute the existence of an inherent aggressive drive. In the sections which follow, I am going to reverse the order in which these traditions have customarily been presented in previous chapters. The behavioral viewpoint will be considered first, followed by the dispositional one. At the end of the chapter, I will offer my own model for aggressive behavior, which attempts to integrate material from all three theoretical traditions.

BEHAVIORAL EXPLANATIONS FOR AGGRESSION

The prevailing view in American psychology is that aggression is a behavior which, in human beings and higher animals at least, is governed by the same principles of conditioning which regulate all forms of learning. Theorists in the behavioral tradition are divided, however, in their emphasis on one or another of the processes by which learning may occur. The most fundamental difference of opinion exists between those who believe that hurtful behavior is governed by simple-conditioning processes and those who go beyond trial-and-error learning to include a concept of vicarious reinforcement (see Chapter 4 for an explanation of this term).

Simple Conditioning Approaches

In what is today regarded as a classic demonstration of the conditioning of aggressive behavior in animals, Ginsberg and Allee (1942) staged one-to-one contests between unevenly matched pairs of male mice from different strains. When subsequently paired with animals from their own strain, the mice which had been victorious in the cross-strain contests were found to be more aggressive than mice who had not had this previous experience. Conversely, mice which had been defeated in the cross-strain contests were found to have had their subsequent aggressiveness sharply reduced.

There are data which indicate that initially submissive nursery school children may learn to become more aggressive in much the same way as do young mice (Patterson et al., 1967). Children who experienced success in their counter aggression against others who attempted to bully them became increasingly likely to engage in counter aggression in future interactions. Children who could not successfully resist being bullied became increasingly passive in future interactions. It might be pointed out that the results of this study raise the issue of "aggression" vs. "self-defense" which was mentioned earlier. Even though resistance to bullies is likely to be regarded as a justifiable act of self-defense, it is still classified as *aggression* under any general psychological definition of this term.

Cowan and Walters (1963) found a dramatic increase in the frequency of punching a padded target protruding from the stomach area of a painted picture of a clown when young boys were rewarded with marbles for making this response. Extending the latter finding, Walters and Brown (1963) reported that children who were rewarded for their hitting responses on the clown apparatus, particularly if the reward was delivered on a fixed-ratio schedule, showed greater aggressive behavior in a subsequent rough-and-tumble game than did children who were never rewarded for hitting the clown.

Adults as well as children may show an increase in hurtful behavior in response to a monetary reward or social approval (Borden, 1975; Buss, 1971; Geen & Pigg, 1970). Bandura (1973, pp. 92–101) makes the obvious points that in real life, as in the foregoing laboratory studies, (1) aggressors often succeed in achieving desirable goals by coercing others and (2) families and various social groups often provide approval for physical violence directed against members of other families or other groups. The idea that aggressive behavior is, to some degree, developed and maintained by rewarding consequences is both congruent with our commonsense observations and supported by empirical data. Many in the environmentalist tradition, however, question whether simple-conditioning processes can entirely account for this phenomenon and argue that the notion of vicarious learning must be included in a complete behavioral analysis.

Social-Learning Approaches

One of the earliest laboratory demonstrations of the considerable extent to which children will imitate modeled aggression was conducted by Bandura, Ross, and Ross (1963). Boys and girls (3 to 6 years of age) who witnessed an adult punching, kicking, and verbally abusing ("Sock him in the nose," and so on) an inflated "Bobo the Clown" doll were themselves far more inclined to attack the doll when left alone in a room full of toys than were children in a control group who had seen the model playing peacefully in the presence of the doll or who had seen no model at all. A group which had been exposed to the model's aggressive actions via a television monitor behaved almost as aggressively toward the doll as did a group which had seen a live model. Liebert and Baron (1972) obtained similar results in a study which exposed children to a brief televised sequence from either a violent crime program or a nonviolent but exciting track race.

Comparable findings have been obtained for adult subjects (Diener et al., 1975). In one experiment, college students watched a peer model who selected either weak or strong shocks as punishment for a partner's errors on a learning task (Baron & Kepner, 1970). When it was their turn to punish the learner, the students who had witnessed a punitive model gave stronger shocks than did those who had witnessed a lenient model. Disturbingly, in both groups of subjects, there was a significant tendency for the level of punishment to increase over trials. Perhaps those who deliver painful stimulation become models for their own punitiveness, and this is why the intensity of punishment tends to escalate. Alternatively, the subjects may have become familiar with and desensitized to the painful consequences of their actions. Either or both of these possibilities could account for Wolfe and Baron's (1971) finding that prisoners incarcerated for violent crimes consistently select higher shock levels in situations like the foregoing than do college students, regardless of the presence or absence of a punitive model.

More optimistically, Baron (1972) has shown that at least among college students, if a punitive model receives criticism from another accomplice, an observing-subject's tendency to imitate the model is considerably diminished. Bandura and Walters (1965, p. 82) similarly reported that children are not inclined to copy the aggressive

In a classic study by Bandura, Ross, and Ross (1963), children first observed an adult model who hit, threw, and kicked an inflated "Bobo the clown" doll (top row of photos). The children were then left alone in a playroom and were observed by a hidden camera. Both boys and girls showed a strong tendency to imitate the aggressive behavior they previously witnessed. (Albert Bandura)

behavior of a model whom they have seen punished.

Studies demonstrating an effect of modeled aggression on the imitative aggressive acts of witnesses have obvious implications for the question whether or not the violence shown on television affects the personality and behavior of its viewers.

Bandura (1973, pp. 101–107) has compiled an impressive set of accounts from newspapers and other sources of the effects of the modeling of hurtful behavior on television viewers. Airline hijackings and sensational murders, according to Bandura, have especially visible modeling effects. When one occurs, there is likely to be a flurry of obviously imitative others spread out over the following few days or weeks.

While accounts of specific real-life incidents always have a dramatic impact and raise a good deal of justifiable concern, they cannot, in the end, substitute for systematic investigation. While some individuals seem unquestionably to have been influenced by what they saw on TV, how many millions of other children or adults have watched the same types of programs and shown no tendency to imitate what they saw? Indeed, is it possible that some individuals are so repulsed by the violence shown on television that they become *less* inclined to engage in personal acts of violence than they would be otherwise? An individual's self-restraint is much less likely to be reported in the newspapers than his or her acts of violence. Perhaps our perception of a link between TV violence and aggressive acts is created by the selective coverage of individuals who were motivated to commit aggression anyway and who happened to pick an act they had seen on television as their specific means for acting out their impulses.

Laboratory studies clearly imply a cause-effect relationship between modeled and imitative aggression, and the superficial aspects of TV programming would appear to implicate this medium as an instigator of some of the hurtful behavior so prevalent in American society. Baker and Ball (1969) reported that 60 percent of the major characters in dramatic programs engage in violence, Gerbner (1972) found that violent incidents occur at a rate of about eight per hour during prime time, and Barcus (1971) described children's Saturday-morning shows as "saturated" with violence, 71 percent of them containing at least one aggressive incident enacted with or without the use of weapons.

Despite this impressive chain of evidence and logic—extending from laboratory research and anecdotes indicating that modeling of aggression occurs in real life to a demonstration of the high level of violence which appears on television—field studies which have examined the spontaneous behavior of people watching television in somewhat natural settings have not convincingly shown an impact of televised violence on aggressive behavior.

In one of these studies, Eron et al. (1972) ascertained the aggressiveness of each of 875 third-graders in a semirural area of upstate New York by asking them to nominate one another. The children were asked questions like "Who starts a fight over nothing?" The television preferences of each of the children were then determined by interviewing their mothers. All of this happened in 1960. Ten years later, when the participants in the study were graduating from high school, they were once again asked to make peer nominations for aggressiveness and were interviewed regarding their TV preferences.

For both males and females, peer-rated aggressiveness in the third grade was significantly positively correlated with aggressiveness ten years later. Thus, aggressiveness as a behavioral

trait had considerable durability over time. For males only, a preference for violent TV in the third grade was positively correlated with aggressiveness in the third grade as well as with aggressiveness ten years later. For females (who constituted slightly more than half the total sample), these correlations were close to zero, or even slightly negative. One problem encountered by the investigators was a high rate of subject loss over the ten-year period. Only 427 remained out of the original population of 875.

To summarize the results of this field study, support was found for the predicted relationship between early exposure to violent TV and both current and future aggressive behavior. These relationships were not strong ones, however (the correlations were 0.21 and 0.31, respectively), and they were found only among male subjects. Since the study was correlational in nature, it is difficult to ascertain whether viewing violent TV caused higher levels of aggressive behavior or whether kids who are more aggressive to begin with seek out displays of violence wherever they can find them, including the TV screen. The researchers went to great statistical lengths in attempting to demonstrate that the former causal relationship was more likely to be correct. Still, given the weakness of the major findings, the problems with subject loss, and the difficulties in interpreting correlational results, one can only conclude that this study suggests the possibility of a causal link between violent TV and aggressive behavior; it by no means conclusively demonstrates that such a link exists.

Using an experimental rather than a correlational method, Stein, Freidrich, and Vondracek (1972) exposed children in a preschool to either violent (e.g., "Batman," "Superman"), neutral (travelogues), or nonviolent ("Mister Rogers' Neighborhood") TV over a four-week period. No overall change in aggressive behavior from before to after the TV "diet" was found for children watching violent programs, but when the subjects were categorized on the basis of their initial level of aggressiveness, it was discovered that the most aggressive ones did, indeed, have their hurtful physical and verbal behavior facilitated by a diet of violent programs. On the other hand, Feshbach and Singer (1971) exposed a sample of 395 boys in either private schools or orphanages to a minimum of six hours per day of either violent or neutral television, extending over a six-week period. Many of their findings were not significant, but it appeared that a diet of violent TV had, if anything, caused the boys to become *less* aggressive than they had been before the experiment began and less aggressive than the boys in the group who watched neutral programs. These results were statistically significant for boys in the orphanage sample, where it appeared that the children with the highest initial levels of aggressiveness showed the greatest reduction in their hurtful behavior after exposure to a diet of violent programs.

Bandura (1973, pp. 140–142) sharply criticized Feshbach and Singer's research on several methodological grounds, but the fact remains that the results of field studies of the effects of violent TV on children in natural settings do not present a very strong or even very consistent case for a deleterious effect. Furthermore, it could be (and has been) claimed by the television industry that since antisocial behavior is always portrayed as undesirable, and since the industry's production code requires that its perpetrators always receive their just deserts by the end of the program, the effect of television should be to *reduce* the likelihood of similar behavior on the part of viewers. (Recall that Bandura, Ross, and Ross as well as Baron and Kepner discovered that aggressors who were punished or reprimanded were not imitated by child or adult observers.) Bandura would perhaps reply that the violent acts committed by the "good guys" in their pursuit of the "bad guys" are portrayed as justifiable and socially approved; moreover, even the "bad guys" often prosper from their dastardly deeds all the way up to the end of the show, and some observers might conclude that they could get away with such behavior themselves if only they could avoid making the television-character's fatal mistake. In any case, because of ambiguities and controversies such as these (and, perhaps, because of political considerations) a report of the Surgeon General (1972, p. 10) concerning the impact of television violence on children reached the following, somewhat equivocal, conclusion:

> Thus, there is a convergence of the fairly substantial experimental evidence for *short-run* causation of aggression among some children by viewing violence on the screen and the much less certain evidence from field studies that extensive violence precedes some *long-run* manifestations of aggressive behavior.

Because the question whether television shapes personality and behavior—particularly in the area of aggression—is such an important one in our media-oriented society, we will return to it further on in this chapter. Berkowitz (1962) expounded and researched a theory of aggressive behavior which might account for some of the inconsistency observed in the foregoing studies. Before his theory can be appreciated, however, we must first consider the frustration-aggression hypothesis.

DISPOSITIONAL EXPLANATIONS FOR AGGRESSION

On the question of aggressive behavior, the trait-dispositional and social-learning viewpoints show considerable overlap. The primary distinction between them is, as always, the emphasis that dispositional theorists place on the internal processes, such as emotions or personality traits, that guide an individual's response to a given situation.

Frustration-Aggression Hypothesis

In 1939, an interdisciplinary group of psychologists, sociologists, and social anthropologists at

Yale University put forward a hypothesis concerning the origins of aggressive behavior that has been a focus of interest and controversy ever since (Dollard, Doob, Miller, Mowrer, & Sears, 1939). Defining *frustration* as "that condition which exists when a goal-response suffers interference," the Yale researchers proposed that (1) all aggression is preceded by some form of frustration and (2) frustration always leads to some form of aggression. This hypothesis is dispositional in that it describes the foregoing events in terms highly compatible with the notion that the frustration-aggression sequence is a built-in reflex. Even so, Dollard et al. declined to take a position as to whether the pattern was instinctual or learned.

An example of a frustration-aggression sequence that I usually mention in my classes is the experience of looking for a vacant space in a crowded parking lot when you have some important appointment (i.e., a "goal") that you must get to on time. After driving around the lot for fifteen minutes and becoming increasingly worried that you will miss your appointment, you see someone walking toward a parked vehicle. You stop and wait for this person to leave so you can claim the space, and yours is the only car waiting. After fumbling around arranging belongings and looking for the car keys (and increasing your worries about being on time), the driver finally starts the car and backs out, but in such a way that you cannot enter the space until she or he

Gasoline shortages in the United States have caused a great deal of frustration and seem to have provoked aggression as well. Here, service station operators are pouring battery acid over the red, yellow, and green flags they were required to fly by law as signals of gasoline availability. They are protesting a requirement that they not give preferential treatment to long-term customers. (United Press International Photo)

drives away. As the car slowly moves off, you breathe a sigh of relief and prepare to drive forward. Suddenly, a sports car darts around the corner and into the space you have been waiting for. How do you feel? Angry. What are you motivated to do? Get out of your car and give the sports-car owner a tongue-lashing or even a punch in the nose? Perhaps you will settle for shouting obscenities out of your window, muttering them under your breath, honking your horn, or convulsively jabbing your gas pedal and roaring off. This is what is meant by frustration-induced aggression.

Early studies of the frustration-aggression relationship which were described by Dollard et al. showed that young conservation-corps workers who had been prevented from attending a movie they wanted to see expressed more unfavorable attitudes toward ethnic minorities than they had indicated prior to the frustration (p. 43) and that when the economy of the Deep South was depressed because of low cotton prices, the frequency of lynchings increased (p. 31). These findings suggest that frustration-induced aggression may sometimes not be directed against the immediate source of frustration but instead displaced against a substitute target. The same phenomenon has been observed in animals. For example, hungry pigeons, frustrated in their attempts to obtain food, were observed to turn and spontaneously attack a restrained and helpless target bird in the apparatus with them. The target bird had been attacked only infrequently prior to the frustration (Azrin, Hutchinson, & Hake, 1966).

Miller (1948) accounted for displacement by explaining that while the most satisfying target for aggression would be the source of the frustration—mainly because a successful attack might remove the obstacle preventing us from reaching our "goal"—the source of frustration is often either so powerful, so remote, or so ambiguous that a direct attack might be either dangerous or just simply infeasible. In such situations, aggression is likely to be displaced. The most satisfying target would be one that is most like

the source of frustration and least likely to retaliate. Hence, a little boy who is told by his mother that he cannot have a quarter to buy an ice-cream cone may be motivated to knock her down and take the quarter, but he is restrained from acting on this impulse by the knowledge that his mother has a great deal of retaliatory power. He may then storm away to attack his sister, kick the family dog, or just chop up a piece of wood with an ax. Presumably, the sister would be the most satisfying displacement, since she shares the most characteristics in common with the "frustrating" mother. Sisters may fight back, however, so the dog might be chosen as the target instead. If the dog is a big and menacing one, though, the frustrated little boy may have to settle for chopping up the wood.

One of the early objections to the frustration-aggression hypothesis was that for human beings, at least, the response to frustration depends heavily on whether it is perceived as arbitrary or unintentional. If a bus passes you by and leaves you at the stop, thus frustrating you in your efforts to get where you want to go, it makes a great deal of difference whether you perceived it was the right bus and the driver intentionally roared past or whether you saw a sign on the vehicle saying "Out of service. Garage" (Pastore, 1952). Burnstein and Worchel (1962) studied this idea experimentally and found that groups of people who were prevented by the incessant interruption of a confederate from reaching a unanimous decision within a given time limit were far more likely to vote to remove the confederate from the group if the interruptions appeared arbitrary than if they appeared to be caused by a hearing problem. Social inhibitions against the overt rejection of even an arbitrary "frustrater," however, were quite strong; only 29 percent of the subjects voted to remove the interrupter if they had to do so publicly, while *all* voted for the removal on a secret ballot.

Another, more basic objection to the frustration-aggression hypothesis has been that in several experiments, frustration did not cause

In a long series of studies using the same basic design, Berkowitz arranged for subjects to be either insulted or treated politely by a partner and then to watch a film clip showing either a nonviolent track race or a fight sequence from a film like *Rocky II* (the source of this still photo). In general, as predicted by Berkowitz's theory, viewing the fight film served to increase aggressiveness only among subjects who had previously been insulted. (Bettmann Archive)

subjects to increase the level of shock being administered to a partner working at a learning task (Buss, 1966; Taylor & Pisano, 1971). Baron (1977, p. 87) explained these contrary findings by noting that the frustrations used in these studies may not have been sufficiently arbitrary or intense to overcome social inhibitions against engaging in overtly aggressive behavior. With regard to the latter possibility, Harris (1974) demonstrated that people waiting in line to get to cash registers, bank tellers, or airline check-in counters responded with much less verbal or physical aggression when someone cut in ahead of them if they were twelfth in line (i.e., distant from their goal) than they did if they were third in line. Other studies, too, have found that when frustration is relatively mild, it does not elicit a strong, overtly aggressive response.

With certain qualifications, the frustration-aggression hypothesis has been generally accepted by psychologists. If frustration is both intense and arbitrary, it is very likely to instigate aggressive behavior. Psychologists also generally acknowledge that other events besides frustration (e.g., reward or exposure to successful, aggressive models) can initiate hurtful behavior. Frustrations and other stress-inducing experiences are, though, still usually regarded as powerful instigators of much of the aggression we see around us, and these experiences play a central role in Berkowitz's theory of aggressive behavior.

According to Berkowitz (1962, pp. 32–33), an important omission from the frustration-aggression hypothesis is its failure to specify or examine the internal states which are aroused by frustration and which motivate aggression. Foremost among these internal mediators is the emotion we call *anger*. Berkowitz also believes, however, that even a frustrated, angry person will probably behave aggressively only if there are appropriate releasing cues available in the immediate environment. *Releasing cues are stimuli which, in the past, have been associated with the discharge of aggressive impulses.* An example should serve to illustrate how they function.

Berkowitz and LePage (1967) paired college-age subjects with partners and arranged for the subjects to be angered (or not angered) by a partner's unfavorable (or favorable) evaluation of their creative work. The subjects were then permitted to evaluate their partners' work by sending them some electric shocks. One shock meant a highly favorable evaluation; more shocks meant increasingly unfavorable evaluations. Some of the subjects delivered these shocks in the presence of releasing cues (a shotgun and a revolver were near the shock key); for others, no such cues were available. The results showed that more shocks were administered when weapons were present than when they were not, but only if the subjects themselves had been previously angered. If the subjects were not angry, the presence or absence of weapons had no effect on their behavior.

While the results of this study provided support for Berkowitz's notion that releasing cues can "pull" aggression out of an angry subject, there have been several notable failures to reproduce these findings (Buss, Booker, & Buss, 1972; Page & Scheidt, 1971). Despite occasional duplications of Berkowitz's "weapons effect" (Turner et al., 1975), Baron has urged caution in trying to apply these data too literally to such issues as gun-control legislation. It has even been argued that

Berkowitz's subjects may have guessed his hypotheses and so may have simply given him the data he seemed to want (Baron, 1977, p. 166).

Berkowitz has applied his model for aggressive behavior to the television-violence controversy discussed earlier. In a long series of studies using the same basic design, subjects were insulted (or not insulted) by a partner and were then shown a film clip from a nonviolent track race or the film clip from the movie *Champion* in which Kirk Douglas is badly beaten up by an opponent named Dunne. In general, as predicted by Berkowitz's theory, viewing the violent film increased aggressiveness only in subjects who had previously been insulted. Aggression was further increased for these subjects by the presence of additional aggressive cues, cues such as a perceived similarity between the disliked partner and the battered Kirk Douglas, or identification with Douglas's opponent, or a perception that the violence directed against Douglas was somewhat justified (Berkowitz & Geen, 1967; Geen & Berkowitz, 1967; Turner & Berkowitz, 1972).

In an elaborate field study which combined both Berkowitz's and Bandura's hypotheses regarding the origins of aggressive behavior, Milgram and Shotland (1973) tried, once again, to demonstrate an impact of television violence on aggression in a real-life setting. Subjects were recruited off the streets of New York City with promises of transistor radios in exchange for previewing a show from the popular series, "Medical Center." For one group, the show was a nonviolent romance; for two other groups, it was a depiction of a series of robberies (smashing plastic banks containing money for the hospital's charity drive) by a disgruntled employee. One of the latter versions ended with the arrest and punishment of the employee; the other version ended with the employee escaping to Mexico, being joined by his wife, and apparently living happily ever after off his ill-gotten gains.

Subjects were informed that they would have to pick up their radios at a later date, and an intricate scheduling procedure guaranteed that nearly all would be alone when they did so. When each subject arrived, he or she found the office empty. There was a notice taped to the desk which either brusquely stated that the office was closed and no further radios would be distributed or politely informed the subject that the office was temporarily closed due to illness and that the radio could be picked up downstairs. A Project Hope charity bank on the wall gave subjects in the two aggressive-program conditions an opportunity to imitate what they had seen. Bandura's theory would predict that viewers of the rewarded-aggression program would be more likely to rob the charity bank than would either viewers of the punished-aggression program or subjects in the control condition. Berkowitz might add that this effect should be observed only when subjects had been frustrated by the rude notice.

It was found that the type of program the subjects had watched a few days before had no reliable effect on their behavior, but the frustrating or nonfrustrating content of the notice had a considerable impact. Only 2.9 percent of the 210 people exposed to the polite note committed an antisocial act while in the office, but 18.7 percent of the 278 people who saw the rude notice committed such an act (usually robbing the charity bank). The study had certain methodological problems, one of which was the fact that a considerable period of time had passed between the viewing of the program and the subjects' appearance at the office. Since the frustrating notice was present in the office with them, it is perhaps not surprising that the latter stimulus had a stronger influence on their behavior. All subjects, incidentally, eventually received their transistor radios.

Despite its flaws, the fact remains that yet another field study has failed to support predictions for the impact of violent TV on aggressive behavior that seem plausibly derivable from either Bandura's social-learning theory or Berkowitz's aggressive-cue hypothesis. One additional effort was somewhat more successful, however

(Leyens, Camino, Parke, & Berkowitz, 1975). In this study, boys in two dormitories of a Belgian institution for delinquent adolescents were exposed to a week of violent movies, while boys in two other dormitories were exposed to nonviolent, romantic movies. Within this period, the frequency of aggressive behavior increased dramatically among the former group and declined slightly among the latter. Unfortunately, there was no difference in aggressive behavior between the two groups during the following week. The transient nature of the effect raises the possibility that the boys shown the violent movies saw through the experimenters' not-very-subtle hypothesis and so acted out the behavior that was expected of them; when the films ended, they reverted to "normal." It is difficult, if not impossible, to do a field study in this area for which some plausible alternative explanation cannot be offered.

The Search for Aggressive Personalities

Perhaps there are simply aggressive and nonaggressive personality types who will behave in a more or less characteristic way regardless of the content of the television programs or motion pictures in their environment. This possibility will be explored in the subsections which follow.

Studies of obedience to malevolent authority In what is perhaps the most widely known series of experiments in psychology, Milgram (1963, 1964, 1965a, 1965b) recruited male subjects off the streets of New Haven, Connecticut, for a study of teaching and learning. Forty subjects, representing a cross section of age and occupational categories, were run individually through each experimental condition. The experimenter said that the research was designed to discover the effect of punishment on learning. A rigged drawing of lots guaranteed that the subject, in each case, would be the teacher on the learning task, while an experimental accomplice, a 50-year-old man who mentioned to the subject that he had a

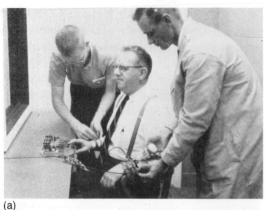
(a)

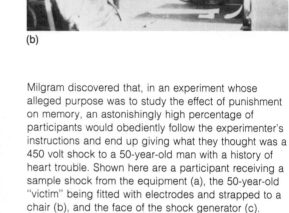
Milgram discovered that, in an experiment whose alleged purpose was to study the effect of punishment on memory, an astonishingly high percentage of participants would obediently follow the experimenter's instructions and end up giving what they thought was a 450 volt shock to a 50-year-old man with a history of heart trouble. Shown here are a participant receiving a sample shock from the equipment (a), the 50-year-old "victim" being fitted with electrodes and strapped to a chair (b), and the face of the shock generator (c). (Stanley Milgram from the film *Obedience*, New York University)

(b)

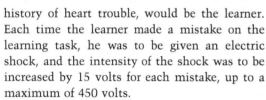
(c)

history of heart trouble, would be the learner. Each time the learner made a mistake on the learning task, he was to be given an electric shock, and the intensity of the shock was to be increased by 15 volts for each mistake, up to a maximum of 450 volts.

Milgram discovered that an astonishingly high percentage of subjects would, in fact, follow the experimenter's instructions to the letter and give the full 450 volts to the accomplice. If the accomplice made no protest other than jerking convulsively when a shock was ostensibly being delivered (actually, a secret switch on the apparatus protected him from receiving any shocks), virtually all of the subjects progressed to 450 volts. If the accomplice made verbal protests from an adjoining room, about 60 percent of the subjects were still fully obedient; but if he was in

the same room as the subject while being shocked, the percentage of obedient subjects dropped to 40. If the subject had previously witnessed two other subjects defy the experimenter and refuse to continue after the accomplice protested, only 10 percent reached the 450-volt level before similarly defying the experimenter. The subjects showed many signs of distress in this experiment and it was clear that they did not enjoy hurting the learner. In one condition, the experimenter gave the instructions for the task and then left the laboratory; under these circumstances, only one subject out of 40 was fully obedient to the experimenter's directions. It should perhaps be added here that the true purposes of the study were explained to the participants before they left the laboratory, and Milgram went to great lengths to allay any lingering symptoms of distress. Even so, these studies have been and continue to be a focus of ethical controversy (Baumrind, 1964).

Elms and Milgram (1966) conducted extensive interviews with selected subjects who had been either obedient or defiant in the experimental situation. In general, subjects' personalities and belief systems did not reliably discriminate the "obedients" from the "defiants," with one exception. Scores on the California F Scale, also called the *authoritarianism scale*, did discriminate between the two groups: "Obedients" scored higher. Authoritarianism is a trait which, from the superficial content of many of the scale items, would appear to reflect a willingness to inflict corporal punishment on others who do not think or behave as one wants (see Table 12-1). This makes its relationship with the level of obedient aggression shown in the Milgram experiments intriguing, to say the least. The originators of the F scale regarded the classic-authoritarian syndrome as incorporating slavish obedience to superiors and harsh treatment of subordinates. The F in their designation for the scale stood for "potentiality for fascism" (Adorno et al., 1950).

Aggressiveness and child development Social-learning theorists like Bandura maintain that parents who use physical punishment as the primary means of socializing their offspring are providing a model for the child to imitate. Such children may learn to suppress physical aggressiveness within the home environment but may be highly assaultive in their interactions outside the home. In a study of 201 males thirty years after their home environments had been evaluated by psychologist observers, it was found that degree of parental fighting, aggression against the child, and lack of supervision were all reliably related to the child's frequency of convictions for crimes against persons as an adult. Childrearing practices had a stronger relationship with adult criminality than did another well-known predisposing factor, socioeconomic status (McCord, 1979). Adorno et al. (1950) related parental reliance on physical punishment to the development of an authoritarian personality. The parents of nonassaultive children, by contrast, appeared to use physical punishment only as a last resort and employed reason, guilt, and encouragement of empathy as their primary socialization techniques (Johnson, 1972, pp. 124ff).

Three basic styles of parenting have been discerned by Baumrind (1966, 1971).

1 The authoritarian style, based on Puritan values, stresses the curbing of self-will and self-indulgence as the proper path toward personal salvation and places heavy emphasis on physical punishment.
2 The permissive style grew out of psychologists' and pediatricians' (e.g., Dr. Spock's) concern that suppression of individual impulses would produce neurotic anxiety. This style was a conscious reaction to the excesses of the authoritarian one.

TABLE 12-1 Items from the Berkeley authoritarianism scale (California F Scale)

Obedience and respect for authority are the most important virtues children should learn.

Young people sometimes get rebellious ideas, but as they grow up they ought to get over them and settle down.

Sex crimes, such as rape and attacks on children, deserve more than mere imprisonment; such criminals ought to be publicly whipped, or worse.

If people would talk less and work more, everybody would be better off.

People can be divided into two distinct classes: the weak and the strong.

Homosexuality is a particularly rotten form of delinquency and ought to be severely punished.

Too many people today are living in an unnatural, soft way; we should return to the fundamentals, to a more red-blooded, active way of life.

What this country needs is fewer laws and agencies, and more courageous, tireless, devoted leaders whom the people can put their faith in.

Note: A response indicating agreement with any item was scored in the authoritarian direction.

3 The third style, called *authoritative* by Baumrind, combines the firm enforcement of reasonable standards of behavior with a willingness to discuss the rationale behind the rules and provide an opportunity for argument from the child. Baumrind believes it is this style which is most likely to produce self-reliance combined with a concern for the feelings and legitimate rights of others.

The highly punitive style of authoritarian parents, Baumrind believes, is associated with hostile withdrawal (sulking), aggressive "acting out," and lowered school achievement on the part of the child. She maintains, however, that permissive parenting, which abandons the child to his or her own devices, can also lead to hostility and aggressiveness, even though it may cultivate some capacity for innovation and rebelliousness. Instead she concludes from research on this topic that mild punishment, delivered for just cause in a consistent manner by a loved and respected authoritative parent, has beneficial rather than negative effects on personality. Generally, the offspring of authoritative parents do better in school, feel more socially and intellectually secure, and are more optimistic about the future than are the children of permissive parents.

However it gets started, aggressiveness and antisocial, delinquent behavior seems to be a fairly stable personality trait. Eron et al. (1972) found this to be true for both males and females in their longitudinal study of the effects of TV violence on aggression. Similarly, the antisocial tendencies of delinquent adolescents have been observed to be somewhat consistent across different situations (Koretzky, Kohn, & Jeger, 1978). In a study of 3475 adolescents in Philadelphia, all of whom had had at least one recorded contact with police, it was discovered that only 18 percent had been charged with five or more offenses. These chronic offenders accounted for 71 percent of the homicides, 77 percent of the rapes, 70 percent of the robberies, and 69 percent of the aggravated assaults committed by the entire sample (Wolfgang, Figlio, & Sellin, 1972). Discharged mental patients with no records of previous arrests are less likely to commit crimes than are members of the general public, but patients with prior-arrest records are far more likely than are members of the general public to commit crimes following their release (Rabkin, 1979). As the number of patients with arrest records has increased in recent years, the problems posed by these chronically antisocial types have become more serious.

People at a preconventional level of moral development on the Kohlberg scale described in Chapter 11 are much more likely than are those at a conventional or postconventional level to exercise a "zap" (or "hurt") option which damages their partners monetarily in a game which makes such aggression *maladaptive* (i.e., the zapper will lose more than the partner). Mental patients are more likely to zap than are college students, and mental patients with some college are less willing to engage in maladaptive aggression than are patients with no college (Anchor & Cross, 1974). One effect of college on students is to reduce their authoritarianism and, presumably, enhance their moral development (Feldman & Newcomb, 1969). Scores on self-report measures of assertiveness and aggressiveness have been found to be negatively correlated with education and occupation (Bakker, Bakker-Rabdau, & Breit, 1978), and those who have committed violent crimes score lower on the Wechsler IQ scales—particularly on the similarities subtest—than do those who have committed only nonviolent crimes (Kunce, Ryan, & Eckelman, 1976). These findings suggest that blocked or delayed moral and intellectual development contribute to a propensity toward aggressive behavior.

Observations of children suggest that at young ages, most aggression is object-oriented and provoked simply by frustration of the child's effort to gain access to desired toys, foods, or other goals. As children grow older, threats to their self-

Is aggressive and antisocial, delinquent behavior a stable personality trait? Prisoners rioted at the Attica State Correctional Facility in New York in 1971 and threatened forty-nine hostages (mostly prison guards) with death if a list of demands was not agreed to by state authorities. In this photo, rebellious prisoners talk with a news reporter in an Attica corridor. After several days of negotiations, police stormed the prison; twenty-nine prisoners and ten hostages were killed in the fighting which followed. (United Press International Photo)

esteem become the predominant elicitors of aggression, which is then more likely to consist of an effort to injure the person who instigates such a threat (Hartup, 1974). These and the foregoing findings fit reasonably well with conclusions drawn by Toch (1969) regarding the personalities of seventy-seven convicted violent offenders. The reasons given by the majority of these men for their violent acts were that they had to defend themselves against threats to their self-esteem or their physical or social well-being which were (or which they imagined to be) posed by others. They used assaultive means for meeting these threats partly because they had never learned that alternative methods might also be effective and partly because their families or subcultural environments did not explicitly disapprove of the use of physical violence to settle disputes.

Aggressiveness and the psychopathic personality In Chapter 11 it was emphasized that the capacity for empathy is an important contributor to the motivation to help others. Conversely, a lack of empathy may contribute to someone's willingness to hurt others. One particular form of mental disorder, the *psychopathic personality*, manifests itself in a profound lack of empathy for the feelings of others and a lack of a sense of guilt for behavior which inflicts injury on them; this disorder was once, in fact, referred to as *moral insanity* (McCord & McCord, 1964). Psychopaths are often fully knowledgeable regarding social norms and can be quite adept at exploiting this knowledge so as to create a public facade of normality and even engaging charm (Cleckley, 1941). They are equally capable, however, of violating those same norms when it is to their advantage to do so and of feeling no remorse for their transgressions, even for a crime like murder. The term "sociopath"—which means, literally, "one who has a disturbed relationship with society"—is often used somewhat interchangeably with "psychopath."

It has traditionally been believed that the psychopath fails to respond internally to events which produce autonomic arousal in "normal" people and which thus provide the basis for learning a wide range of emotional reactions. Lykken (1957) devised a questionnaire consisting of thirty-three pairs of items, each item describing an undesirable activity or event. The items in each pair were matched for unpleasantness, but one always described something that was merely distasteful or tedious (e.g., cleaning up a broken bottle of catsup) while the other was embarrassing or anxiety-arousing (e.g., being seen naked by a neighbor). The subject was asked to check which alternative seemed to him or her to be the lesser of the two evils. Lykken found that subjects nominated by clinicians as manifesting sociopathic tendencies picked the anxious alternatives more often than did their "normal" counterparts. Lykken interpreted this as meaning that the sociopaths, who were lacking in emotionality, were more willing to endure embarrassing or frightening experiences than were people who customarily had a strong autonomic reaction to such events.

Schachter and his associates, however, discovered that male subjects showing a sociopathic profile on Lykken's questionnaire were actually *more* internally responsive (in terms of galvanic skin response and heart rate) than were their presumably more emotional "normal" counterparts across a wide range of experimental situations, including exposure to electric shock or

pictures of nude females (Schachter & Latané, 1964; Valins, 1967a, 1967b). The subject populations from which sociopathic types were drawn included prisoners incarcerated for violent crimes as well as college undergraduates. Schachter and Latané concluded that the sociopathic individual does react autonomically to environmental events but does not attach an emotional label to his or her internal state (see Chapter 10 for a discussion of Schachter's theory of emotion). Thus, the sociopath appears to possess the physiological component of emotional experience but suffers a deficit in his or her cognitive ability to attach an emotional label to events which "normal" people have learned to regard as anxiety-arousing or guilt-inducing.

The psychopathic-deviate type on the MMPI (see Chapter 6) has been associated with hyperaggressiveness. Wilkins, Scharff, and Schlottman (1974) reported that college students scoring high on the Pd subscale may, in fact, be more habitually aggressive than "normals" in administering shock to their partners on a learning task, but "normals" are equally aggressive if provoked by insults from their partners. In other laboratory studies involving such tasks, it was found that the stronger a "normal" person's fear of social disapproval or guilt over inflicting physical harm on others, the milder the shocks that he or she administers (Dengerink, 1971; Taylor, 1970; Knott, Lasater, & Shuman, 1974). Sociopathic children have been found to score significantly lower than their "normal" counterparts on Kohlberg's scale for moral development and on the verbal portion of the Wechsler IQ scales (Campagna & Harter, 1975). An unintended demonstration of the lack of social concern exhibited by sociopathic types was observed by Valins (1967b), who found that only 3 percent of thirty-three normally anxious individuals failed to keep a scheduled appointment whereas 37 percent of thirty-five sociopathic types were no-shows.

On the other hand, Megargee (1971) found evidence that some of the most dramatically violent assaultive acts are committed, not by psychopathic deviates or Toch's "under-controlled aggressors," but by individuals who suffer from *overcontrolled hostility*. This is the kind of person who, for years, appears to be meekly accepting of frustration, insult, and outright provocation from others and then one day explodes in an outburst of seemingly senseless violence (bringing a rifle to work and randomly shooting anyone who happens to be there, for example). The existence of such types, whose behavior seems incongruent with the principles of social learning, has suggested to many that we must look beyond strict environmentalism if we want to achieve a comprehensive understanding of the phenomenon of hurtful behavior.

AGGRESSION—AN INTEGRATED VIEWPOINT

Recall our discussion of Schachter's theory of emotion in Chapter 10. For human beings, emotions involve attaching a cognitive label to an undifferentiated state of internal arousal produced by discharge of the sympathetic nervous system. In animals, who lack the language capacity provided by a highly developed cerebral cortex, the labeling is probably much more reflexive and automatic.

For example, if someone steps on your foot and causes you pain, some discharge of your sympathetic system is likely to take place, thus putting you in an aroused state. Your emotional experience, though, will probably be modified by your interpretation of the situation. If the other person stepped on your foot accidentally and promptly apologizes, you are much less likely to label your arousal *anger* and behave aggressively toward this person than you would if he or she had obviously, maliciously, and deliberately stepped on your foot. Among animals, though, fighting erupts almost reflexively in response to sudden and extreme pain. Conceivably, it was adaptive over the course of evolution for organisms feeling sudden pain to launch an automatic attack on the nearest living thing that appeared to be the source of discomfort. The researchers who have studied reflexive fighting believe it to be an unlearned aggressive behavior (Azrin, 1967; Azrin, Hutchinson, & Sallery, 1964; Ulrich, Hutchinson, & Azrin, 1965).

Crowding is another environmental stressor which may increase the level of aggressive behavior in animal populations (Calhoun, 1962). Although its effects on humans have been found to be somewhat variable, it appears that for males at least, crowding may intensify hostile feelings (Freedman, Heshka, & Levy, 1975; Freedman, Klevansky, & Ehrlich, 1971; Freedman et al., 1972). It seems plausible that crowding places the organism in a state of internal arousal (Worchel & Teddlie, 1976). If this arousal is interpreted as being due to invasions of personal space by others, the individual is likely to become irritated and aggressive. If, instead, arousal is attributed to the influence of various distracting stimuli in the environment, hostile feelings and behavior are less likely to emerge.

Heat, under some conditions, may produce a similar increase in hostile feelings and aggressive behavior (Bell & Baron, 1976; Griffitt & Veitch, 1971). The relationship between aggression and heat is even more complex and inconsistent than the relationship between aggression and crowding, however (Baron, 1977, pp. 137–149). Even so, it is noteworthy that studies of the reasons for the eruption of riots in ghetto areas of major American cities in the 1960s and early 1970s mentioned crowding and a "long, hot summer" as conditions which, combined with long-standing frustration and perceived injustice, may have triggered the outbursts (U.S. Riot Commission, 1968; Carlsmith & Anderson, 1979).

My own conception of the origins of aggressive behavior, which borrows from each of the theorists considered thus far, is shown in Figure 12-1. Stress is assumed to be the triggering mechanism which causes the sympathetic nervous system to discharge and places the individual in a state of heightened arousal. Frustration is one type of

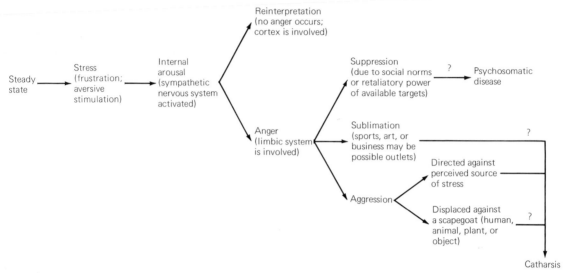

FIGURE 12-1
Theoretical model for stress-induced aggression.

stressor that we know about; the others can be put into the general category of aversive environmental stimulation (pain, crowding, heat, loud noise, and so forth). This arousal is very likely to produce the emotional state of anger unless reinterpretation occurs—as, for example, when you decide that the person who stepped on your toe did so accidentally and is sincerely sorry for causing you pain. Zillmann and Cantor (1976) found direct evidence that reinterpretation can reduce the arousal state. Much of what we call *socialization* involves teaching children to discriminate between situations in which anger is appropriate and situations in which it is not; and this is the decision point at which conditioning, modeling, and other social-learning experiences have a powerful impact on the outcome.

If anger is aroused, it implies that the brain's limbic system has been activated and aggression is likely to follow (see Chapter 7). The most satisfying form of aggression is against the perceived source of stress, but displacement of the aggression onto an alternative target may occur for reasons discussed earlier in this chapter. There is evidence that aggression against the perceived source of stress (say, someone who has insulted us) not only serves to reduce our hostile feelings toward that person (Bramel, Taub, & Blum, 1968; Doob & Wood, 1972; Konečni, 1975) but may also reduce our level of internal arousal (Hokanson & Burgess, 1962; Hokanson, Burgess, & Cohen, 1963). In other words, such attacks may provide an emotional catharsis and a return of arousal to baseline levels. There is also some evidence that even stress-induced aggression displaced against an innocent scapegoat may be cathartic (Konečni & Doob, 1972; Gambaro & Rabin, 1969), but this evidence is contradicted by other studies (Hokanson et al., 1963; Geen, Stonner, & Shope, 1975).

The issue of catharsis is a controversial one because the producers of violent television programs sometimes claim that vicarious participation in fantasy aggression on the part of viewers provides them with cathartic relief from any hostile feelings they may be experiencing and so *decreases* their motivation to commit real acts of aggression. Regardless of their theoretical stand on the existence or nonexistence of catharsis, however, all academic reviewers of the relevant literature appear to agree that fantasy displays of violence are far more likely to facilitate viewer aggression through modeling than they are to provide a cathartic reduction in hostile feelings (Berkowitz, 1962; Bramel, 1969; Bandura, 1973).

It is even conceivable that exposure to fantasy displays of violence may produce *both* cathartic and modeling effects simultaneously, with the net outcome depending on which of these opposing forces has a stronger impact on a particular individual at a particular time. Such instability may contribute to the inconsistent results obtained in studies of the effects of exposure to violent television on aggressive behavior. One effect of such programs which seems fairly clear-cut and which may prove to be consistently replicable is the densensitization of viewers to the occurrence of real-life violence (Cline, Croft, & Courrier, 1973; Thomas et al., 1977). Since, as was seen in the preceding chapter, our capacity to empathize with the pain and suffering of victims is an important contributor to our willingness to help them, desensitization effects could, by themselves, provide sufficient justification for efforts directed toward limiting the public's exposure to displays of gratuitous violence.

To summarize, then, it appears that a catharsis of the arousal state which energizes angry feelings and aggressive behavior may occur as a result of inflicting or witnessing injury being inflicted upon a perceived source of stress. In the parking-lot example mentioned earlier, for example, where you were asked to imagine that a sports-car driver arbitrarily zoomed into a space you had been patiently waiting for, your anger might have been somewhat lessened if, as the frustrater zoomed into the space, you saw that he had misjudged the turn and scraped the fender of his shiny new sports car against the massive bumper of an old truck parked in an adjoining space. There is very little evidence, however, that your angry feelings would have been reduced by simply driving off to a movie theater and watching *Bonnie and Clyde*. On the contrary, such a movie seems more likely to facilitate a desire for re-

venge against a frustrater and to serve as a desensitizer to the painful consequences of a hurtful act.

Returning to Figure 12-1, another possible outlet for angry feelings is, to use a traditional psychoanalytic term, "sublimation." *Sublimated aggression* is behavior that supposedly reduces arousal in a socially acceptable way. Artistic expression, sports, and business competition have often been mentioned as possible sublimations. Whether such activities really succeed in producing catharsis remains an open question, however (Konečni, 1975; Zillmann et al., 1972).

Finally, if there are strong social norms which prohibit overt aggression, or if all available targets are too threatening, aggressive impulses may simply be suppressed. The psychoanalytic viewpoint has traditionally assumed that suppression of a strong impulse will produce a neurosis or cause a psychosomatic disease such as a peptic ulcer. The involvement of the digestive tract in states of internal arousal provides some logical basis for this proposition, but social-learning theorists strongly disagree. Both Bandura (1973) and Berkowitz (1974) believe the best way to handle angry feelings is to suppress them. In any event, it is clear that an individual's social-learning experiences will have a considerable influence on the direction his or her behavior takes when the time comes to choose between suppression, sublimation, or direct or displaced aggression in Figure 12-1.

While an individual's response to stress can thus be considerably modified by his or her social environment, it remains conceivable that there is a built-in "natural" pathway which predisposes us all to respond to stress by becoming angry and motivated to aggress. This certainly seems to be the sequence commonly followed by animals. One implication of this line of reasoning would be that it is easier to teach children to respond to frustration with aggression than it is to show them how to reinterpret frustration-induced arousal in a nonhostile way or to channel their angry feelings into constructive rather than hurtful behavior. Berkowitz (1969, pp. 3–4) made much the same point in commenting that the "frustration-aggression relationship may be *learnable* without being entirely *learned.*" It is to be hoped, of course, that any innate patterning in human aggression reflects predispositions which can be modified by learning rather than some automatically accumulating urge to attack and destroy. Much as we would like to rule out the possibility that humans are afflicted with a death instinct, however, the question remains an open one and cannot, in the light of present knowledge, be firmly and finally pushed aside.

It should be noted that besides the anger-motivated aggression described in Figure 12-1, there is also _instrumental aggression, aggression motivated primarily by the expectation of reward_. The aggression of prizefighters, for example, is primarily instrumental. They probably would not fight if they were not offered a substantial amount of cash to do so. Similarly, the robber who holds you up is probably not particularly aroused and angry; he just wants your money. While instrumental aggression can undeniably be very hurtful, angry aggression is, to me, the more extreme and genuine of the two forms because all of the individual's physiological, cognitive, and behavioral systems are involved in its expression. For this reason, I would like to modify my earlier definition of _aggressive behavior_ to read "_Aggression is a behavior which, in its purest form, is motivated by anger and whose intent is either to cause physical or psychological injury to a person or other living being or to cause physical damage to some object._"

Thus, one feature which distinguishes aggression from other behavior is the emotional state which accompanies the aggressive act. Chopping down a tree to clear some land is probably not a very aggressive act, even though its intent is to do damage to the tree. When the person chopping down the tree does so in the heat of anger, however, the act begins to acquire more aggressive content. A psychoanalytic observer might even be inclined to ask whether the tree might not, for that angry individual, symbolize a particularly disliked person.

CONCLUSION

To return to the real-life example with which this chapter began, we might ask once again why the computer programmer behaved as he did. One immediate set of causes seems to be that he was stressed by frustrations at work and aversive environmental stimulation (uncontrollable noise) at home. This may have made him angry, but why didn't he suppress his motivation to aggress? Maybe he had been suppressing these motivations for a long time, and a short-term accumulation of stressors overwhelmed his suppressive capacity. Alternatively, maybe he had been inadequately socialized in how to restrain himself. Then why didn't he try to sublimate his anger by throwing himself into his work? Maybe he did, but his failure to win a promotion made this sublimation appear ineffective and added the "final straw" to his escalating levels of stress and angry feelings. Why did he reach for a weapon instead of complaining to his apartment manager and his boss at work? Maybe he had complained, but his complaints were ineffective in changing the circumstances which were causing him stress. Furthermore, as Berkowitz might point out, the fact that a gun was available to him provided a cue for this method of "acting out" his feelings. Why did he seize hostages and demand that his boss come to the apartment complex to talk with him? Perhaps here we have a real-life example of the effect of television on aggressive behavior. Nowadays it seems that many people who have demands to make think that threatening harm to innocent bystanders is a way to get others to give them what they want, and the programmer would have had ample opportunities to observe such behavior on television.

These are just speculative guesses because the

personality of the programmer is revealed to us only by the sketchy outline provided in a news report. Even if we had a complete biography of this person, though, it might turn out that his life history was not very different from the life histories of many other people who underwent comparable stress and did *not* take hostages or barricade themselves against the police. Individual differences in behavior can arise from many sources. There may be differences in the ability to tolerate stress, some of which are related to the biological properties of our nervous systems. In addition, there are obvious differences in social learning which make it easier for some to look philosophically upon life's stresses and frustrations and so reinterpret their arousal states in a nonhostile way. Finally, temperament and life experiences may interact in such a way as to produce one or more personality types which habitually respond to even moderate levels of stress with overt aggression.

The possibility remains that the triggering of some aggressive acts may result from internally accumulating drives or emotional mechanisms which are genetically programmed to respond to certain types of stimuli. Capable scholars have argued persuasively that the existence of such instincts in humans is at least conceivable. Needless to say, the issue of aggressive instincts in human beings is a very controversial one. We will touch upon this topic once again in Chapter 13.

SUMMARY

1. *Aggression* may be defined as behavior whose intent is either to cause physical or psychological injury to a person or other living thing or to cause physical damage to an object. The terms "injury" and "damage" are defined as a change in the state of the target of the behavior which is perceived *by the aggressor* to be less healthy or satisfied, in the case of living organisms, or generally less whole or intact.

2. Psychoanalytic explanations for aggression assume the existence of an instinctual drive which motivates this behavior. Disentangling socially learned from biologically based motives in humans is an extremely complex task, but animals show evidence of built-in aggressive drives. These are often ritualized into harmless displays for the purpose of defending territories or maintaining dominance hierarchies. If, within a given species, the most aggressive individuals are the ones most likely to pass on their genes to future generations, then aggressiveness as a trait could be somewhat instinctual.

3. Behavioral explanations for aggression have considered simple conditioning and vicarious learning as possible origins of this behavior. Television, because it provides so many violent models to viewers, has long been attacked by psychologists as an instigator of aggression. Laboratory research has, for the most part, confirmed the fears of

these psychologists, but the evidence from field studies is far less clear-cut.

4   The frustration-aggression hypothesis is classified as a dispositional approach because it strongly implies that the frustration-aggression sequence is innate. Some qualifications to the hypothesis are that frustration may not produce aggression when it is perceived as appropriate, temporary, or easily tolerated. Berkowitz's *aggressive-cue hypothesis* states that frustration produces the emotion of anger, which will erupt into aggression only if there are appropriate releasing cues in the immediate environment. Violent television programs can, according to Berkowitz, serve as releasing cues for frustrated and angry persons.

5   The search for aggression-associated traits within the Milgram obedience paradigm has turned up largely negative results, with the notable exception of authoritarianism. Parents who use physical punishment as the primary means of socializing their offspring tend to foster both authoritarianism and a high degree of aggressiveness in children. Baumrind maintains that an authoritative style of parenting is superior to both authoritarian and permissive styles in raising children who are low in hostility and aggressiveness and high in self-esteem and scholastic motivation. Antisocial behavior is a personality trait with considerable stability across time and different situations. It appears to be related to a child's moral and intellectual development. Psychopathic personalities show a lack of empathy for the feelings of others and a lack of guilt for inflicting injury upon them; psychopathic types seem to be more habitually aggressive than "normals."

6   The frustration-aggression sequence may be more comprehensively elaborated into a stress-arousal-anger-aggression sequence. Sudden pain, crowding, and heat are examples of stimuli other than frustration which can induce an arousal state that could be labeled *anger* and so lead to aggressive action. Modeling and social learning influence the labeling process and the final form that aggression takes. Aggression against the perceived source of frustration has, in several studies, been found to be cathartic, but fantasy displays of violence do not appear to have the same effect. When motivated by anger, aggression is a behavior which probably has unlearned as well as learned components. Even if this proposition is accepted as true, however, it need not imply acceptance of Freud's notion of a death instinct. Aside from anger-induced aggression, which is the most complete expression of this behavior, there also exists instrumental aggression, which is motivated primarily by the expectation of reward.

TERMS TO KNOW

dominance hierarchy
imitative aggression
frustration-aggression hypothesis
displacement
aggressive cue hypothesis

authoritarianism
psychopathic personality
reflexive fighting
catharsis
instrumental aggression

13

SEX DIFFERENCES IN PERSONALITY AND BEHAVIOR

ISSUES TO CONSIDER

1 Do physiological differences between boys and girls cause them to prefer different types of activities and to develop different personality styles as a result?
2 How important are the socialization practices of parents in determining the direction and degree of sex-typing of their child?
3 What sex differences in personality seem to be "real" ones in contemporary American culture, and what differences appear to be myths?

In this chapter we deal with issues that are at least as controversial as any raised thus far. The chapter title could itself be controversial, since it implies that real differences in personality between the sexes could exist. In recent years, we have all become sensitized to the fact that such real or imagined differences have, in the past, been put to the purpose of justifying the inferior social status and unequal career opportunities which male-dominated societies have imposed on women. Since the resurgence of feminism in the United States during the 1960s, women have been especially critical of the role that psychoanalytic conceptions of sex differences have played in supporting sexist beliefs and social customs (Janeway, 1974.)

We will see that, while it is easily possible to apply psychoanalytic concepts in a manner that justifies female subordination, such an application does not necessarily follow from Freud's theories. One feminist author noted this fact and argued that a blind rejection of psychoanalysis is unwise: "However it may have been used, psychoanalysis is not a recommendation *for* a patriarchal society, but an analysis *of* one. If we are interested in challenging the oppression of women, we cannot afford to neglect it" (Mitchell, 1974, p. xiii). To say that Freud's ideas merit one's attention is, furthermore, by no means to say that all or even most of those ideas have been supported by research conducted in the years since they were first put forward.

Objective evaluation of research results is easier to recommend than to accomplish, of course. In a landmark book that will frequently be cited in this chapter, Maccoby and Jacklin (1974) reviewed more than 1600 studies of sex differences in personality and behavior in the hope of clearly distinguishing the differences that are real from those that are myths. Their overall conclusion was that most popular conceptions of sex differences are myths, though there are a few traits on which the sexes seem to differ significantly. This conclusion was challenged by Block (1976), who noted a tendency for Maccoby and

Jacklin to show a preference for studies finding no sex differences when compling the tables on which they based their final evaluation of the data. (All three participants in this debate, incidentally, are women). Furthermore, Block said, studies of preadolescent children were heavily overrepresented in Maccoby and Jacklin's sample, and this inadvertently caused their summary tables to be biased against revealing any sex differences that emerge during the biologically active period of adolescence. Block believes that many of the differences dismissed as myths by Maccoby and Jacklin could, in fact, be real but she also cautions against drawing any firm conclusions given the problems in interpreting research findings that frequently conflict with one another.

When traits on which males and females reliably differ have been identified, the next question is whether such phenomena reflect inherent dispositions or are simply the product of social learning. The "nature-nurture" controversy is as alive in this area as it is anywhere in the field of psychology. Like many other personality characteristics, sex-linked traits appear to emerge from an interaction between person variables (including biological ones) and situation variables. Though this interactionist position is widely accepted, theorists differ in their emphasis on internal or external factors in accounting for the existence of sex differences. In other words, there is plenty of room for controversy within an interactionist perspective.

This chapter begins by examining the psychoanalytic position on sex differences and then undertakes a detailed study of both dispositional and environmental factors which contribute to the frequently observed tendency for males to be more physically aggressive than females. Studies of other aspects of personality also have revealed sex differences which sometimes favor males and sometimes favor females. These aspects include empathy and nonverbal communication, the helping response, conformity and field dependence, self-esteem, moral judgment, and cognitive abilities. Dispositional and behavioral approaches are examined within each of these contexts. Finally, we consider (1) the impact of parental styles of socializing their children on the development of sex-typed behavior and (2) an alternative to the sex-typed personality called *androgyny*.

PSYCHOANALYTIC EXPLANATIONS FOR SEX DIFFERENCES

Freud admitted that he was more confident of his theory of psychosexual development when discussing the male than when discussing the female personality. He hoped that women psychoanalysts would be able to add the details missing in his outline of feminine psychology, and he regarded many of his ideas on this subject as hypotheses to be confirmed or refuted by future research. This tentativeness notwithstanding, Freud (1933) made a number of observations on the psychology of women.

Freud conceived of human beings as fundamentally bisexual in that the genitalia of each sex has structural counterparts in the genitalia of the other. The life and death instincts are also represented in both sexes, and Freud believed that girls and boys pass through the first two stages of psychosexual development in much the same way. Little girls, he thought, may be less instinctually disposed toward aggressiveness and self-sufficiency and have a greater need for affection than little boys, but events occurring during the phallic stage of development have greater importance for the differentiation of male and female personalities than do these few predispositions.

At the phallic stage, you will recall, the boy gives up his erotic attachment to his mother because he fears castration by his father. By identifying with his father, he reduces still further the threat of castration, and in this internalization of his father's values lies the origin of his superego. The stronger the perceived threat of castration, the stronger this identification (and the resulting masculinity) of male child. The phallic character type that emerges from this process typically displays aggressiveness, self-confidence, and courage bordering on recklessness. Conversely, the weaker the perceived threat of castration and the weaker the boy's identification with his father, the more he retains his mother as a love object, identifies with her values, and develops a feminine character. For girls, identification with the mother does not occur because of the threat of castration but because it is assumed to have already occurred. The child's resulting envy for her lost penis leads to an erotic attraction to the father, an attraction she gives up only because (1) her father will not cooperate, (2) she risks losing the love of her mother, with whom she is in hostile competition for her father, and (3) the best way to attain her substitute goal of having a baby is to identify with her mother and prepare for an eventual marriage. Allegedly, the substitute goal of pregnancy and childbirth is never entirely satisfactory to the girl. Some desire for her father remains, along with some hostility toward her mother.

Since the resolution of the Oedipus complex was supposed to be less complete in women than in men, Freud believed that women are less certain of their internalized values and possess weaker, less trustworthy superegos than men. For similar reasons, women are also more emotionally unstable than men. Because society's expectations for women include a suppression of aggressiveness, Freud felt there is a turning inward of this instinct and a resulting tendency toward masochism. Masochism in males was presumed to be a sign of inadequate identification with the father and a tendency toward feminine character traits. He assumed that penis envy in women is never entirely abandoned and provides the basis for lifelong traits of enviousness and low self-esteem. Feminine vanity is a compensation for feelings of sexual inferiority, and feminine modesty developed originally from childhood attempts to hide the perceived deficiency in the female genitalia.

Freud even maintained that the little girl gains sexual pleasure from her own active stimulation of her penislike clitoris, but when she accepts the vaginal stimulation of intercourse as a more practical means of satisfying her penis envy she becomes more passive in her overall personality and behavior. Female homosexuality is assumed to be caused by a fixation at the pre-Oedipal, clitoral stage of psychosexual development and a weak identification with the mother. Many doubt that infants really engage in sexual self-stimulation, so Galenson and Roiphe (1974) repeatedly observed mothers engaged in diapering and tending their children over several months. There were fifty-three infants in the sample, equally divided by sex and ranging in age up to 23 months. Boys were observed to begin genital play at the age of 6 or 7 months and girls at the age of 10 or 11 months. Boys began actually masturbating as early as 15 to 16 months, but girls were more variable in this behavior and often used indirect methods, such as riding a rocking horse.

A test of some of Freud's ideas was conducted by Erikson (1968), who asked 300 boys and girls, 10 to 12 years of age, to construct tabletop scenes from imaginary motion pictures, using a wide variety of building blocks, dolls, and toys. The children, participants in a long-term study conducted by the University of California, were then asked to describe the scenes and to identify the major characters. Erikson discovered that the boys' structures usually had towers or other protrusions, often topped by cannons. Boys' constructions were predominantly exterior scenes in which people or animals were mobile and active. The boys often described their high towers as being in danger of collapsing into ruin, and this possibility was, in fact, acted out by some of them. Girls, by contrast, created interior scenes of houses or enclosures with people or animals sitting or standing inside. Through an elaborate doorway, wild animals or dangerous people might occasionally intrude. Erikson (p. 271) concluded that a child's preferred constructions reflect the physical features of his or her genitalia: "in the

male, an external organ, erectable and intrusive in character, serving the channelization of mobile sperm cells; in the female, internal organs, with vestibular access, leading to statically expectant ova." Thus the anatomy of boys and girls leads the former toward aggression and activity and the latter toward submission and passivity.

Strong criticisms were made of Erikson's procedures and conclusions, as well as the psychoanalytic theorizing on which they were based (Weisstein, 1971). It was said that no one has demonstrated any direct connection between biological sex differences on the one hand and sex differences in personality on the other. Furthermore, the age of the children in Erikson's study makes it especially likely that the differences he claimed to have observed (which were not quantified in a rigorous statistical manner) develop from the different expectations placed on the play behavior of boys and girls. Boys engage in aggressive tower building and girls in the decoration of dollhouses because that is what they are rewarded for doing, not because of the biological ground plans of their bodies. Erikson (1975) acknowledged that learned social expectations probably contribute to sex differences in play constructions, but he insisted that those social expectations are themselves to some extent based on biological distinctions between the sexes. He added that his harshest critics were showing the same defensive reaction to psychoanalytic insights that Freud had encountered among Viennese Victorians around the turn of the century.

Needless to say, the foregoing controversy is far from settled. What should be kept in mind, though, is that neither Freud nor Erikson was necessarily advocating a patriarchal society which places a positive value on active, intrusive masculinity and a negative value on passive, yielding feminity. Freud regarded the aggressive instinct as the great scourge of human existence. He did not believe it should simply be suppressed, as society demands of women, since he felt this has detrimental effects on personality. Rather, he felt that better sublimations should be found for it. The physical safety and mental health of both men and women would benefit if childhood socialization practices changed in the direction of encouraging greater insight into the compromises we must make with the instincts that motivate our behavior. Freud sought to describe personality dynamics as they operate within a particular cultural context—not as he thought they should operate.

For those who remain committed to the view that psychoanalysis and feminism are mutually incompatible, it might be recalled from Chapter 2 that Karen Horney was able to reinterpret Freud's concept of penis envy and still remain a leading psychoanalyst. Penis envy, she said, is not a literal desire for a male sex organ but a resentment on the part of girls and women over the special prerogatives of boys and men in patriarchal societies. When girls express hostility toward their mothers, it is often over their mothers' acceptance of unjust treatment by males and their attempt to enforce patriarchal values on their daughters.

Philosophical arguments between theorists and their critics are seldom finally resolved. It may be a relief at this point to shift our attention to the more empirical research conducted within the dispositional and behavioral traditions.

AGGRESSION: A CASE STUDY IN SEX DIFFERENCES

In the Harlow studies described in the overview to this unit, infant monkeys were raised in isolation from other animals and provided with either bare-wire or cloth-covered "surrogate mothers." These monkeys showed severe abnormalities in behavior when placed in a peer group as juveniles, but in one important respect they were fairly typical: Isolate-reared males were more aggressive and less passive than isolate-reared females, and this difference appeared as early as 2 months of age (Harlow, 1962, 1965). Among conventionally reared monkeys, too,

males are much more likely than are females to engage in threat posturing (staring, baring their teeth, and so forth) and rough-and-tumble play; and these differences are obvious even when they are very young and even when the males and the females are nearly equal in size. Harlow concludes from these studies that males must be predisposed to be more aggressive and less passive than females because isolate-reared monkeys have no early social experiences from which they might have learned sex-typed behavior patterns. Harlow believes these findings must generalize to some extent to human beings.

What do you think? Generalizing animal motivations and behaviors in an effort to account for apparently similar behavior in humans can be interesting and informative, but it can also be somewhat misleading. The reasons why the males are more aggressive and less passive than the females in one species could be entirely different from the reasons underlying analogous behavior in another species.

Despite these cautions, it is noteworthy that in humans, as in Harlow's monkeys, males have been found to be more physically aggressive than females from the age of 2 onward; and this sex difference appears to be virtually universal across diverse cultures (Maccoby & Jacklin, 1974).

To be sure, in laboratory studies in which aggression amounts to pushing a button which delivers a shock to a partner, females, especially since 1970, have not been found to be less aggressive than males (Baron, 1977, pp. 218–219; Frodi et al., 1977). Also, in situations in which aggression is primarily verbal, women may be as aggressive as or even more agressive than men (Feshbach & Feshbach, 1973; Harris, 1974; Shope et al., 1978). When aggression involves the direct application of physical force to another human being, however, males have consistently been found to be more violent than females, even at very young ages. Violent crime in our society is committed five times more frequently by males than by females (Mulvihill & Tumin, 1969).

Maccoby and Jacklin regard this sex difference

as a real one which cannot be dismissed as a myth. As with most traits, there is considerable individual variation in aggressiveness. Some females are certainly more violent than most males. Despite such individual variability, however, the fact remains that males, as a group, are much more likely than are females to display physical aggressiveness. The next question to be asked is, Why? As usual, dispositionally and behaviorally oriented researchers each have their own preferred answers to this question.

Dispositional Explanations for Sex Differences in Aggressiveness

Among monkeys, it appears that the greater aggressiveness exhibited by males is largely due to the action of *testosterone*, a sex hormone which predominates in males. Young et al. (1964) administered testosterone to pregnant female monkeys and discovered that the female offspring of these animals were masculinized. When placed with two "normal" female peers at around 2 months of age, the monkeys whose mothers had been treated with testosterone behaved in a characteristically masculine way: They threatened their cage mates and initiated rough-and-tumble play. Conversely, male chimps who had their natural supply of testosterone drastically reduced through castration typically became less aggressive and more passive in their interactions with other males. If given injections of testosterone, however, their aggressiveness was restored (Clark & Birch, 1945).

Money and Ehrhardt (1972) believed that in humans as well as animals the sex hormones—of which testosterone (predominating in males) and estrogen (predominating in females) are especially important—may influence the development of certain neural structures in the brain. The limbic structures of a brain "masculinized" by testosterone may, in contrast to a "feminized" brain, be more easily stimulated by stressors such as frustration, aversive stimulation, or even the mere physical presence of a potential opponent.

Evidence for an effect of sex hormones on the substrates of behavior has been found, in mice, by Barkley and Goldman (1977). They noted that male mice, under natural conditions, are far more aggressive than females, but the aggressiveness of the males is sharply reduced by castration (which greatly diminishes their testosterone levels). A small dose of testosterone will restore aggressive behavior to these castrated males, but it has no effect on the behavior of females whose ovaries have been removed. A very large dose of testosterone will induce aggressive behavior even in castrated females, however, and, following such treatment, the females seemed to become sensitized so that only a small dose was required to maintain their aggressiveness.

Among human females, there is a large premenstrual decrease in the level of *progesterone* (another important sex hormone) in the blood. During this period, women are also more likely than they are at other times during their monthly cycle to display wide fluctuations in mood, report feelings of hostility, and engage in aggressive acts, including even crimes of violence (Moyer, 1974). Whether it is the decrease in concentration of the female sex hormones which triggers these emotional reactions is unclear. Furthermore, there is wide individual variation among females in the expression of this premenstrual syndrome (Williams, 1977, pp. 114–115).

Some writers sum up the weight of clinical and experimental evidence by concluding that "primarily owing to prenatal genic and hormonal influences, human beings are definitely predisposed at birth to a male or female gender orientation" (Diamond, 1965, p. 167). For girls, these predispositions are expressed in a style of play that is low on physical aggression (playing with dolls), pronounced tendencies toward nurturance and dependence, and, during adolescence, typically feminine erotic fantasies (seeing oneself in the role of the passive partner, for example). Diamond of course acknowledges the importance of the child's social environment in encouraging and maintaining his or her sex-typed behavior

Boys as well as young male chimpanzees and monkeys engage in a lot of rough and tumble play. Some research suggests that the motivation to engage in this behavior is stimulated by testosterone, a sex hormone which predominates in males. (David Strickler/Monkmeyer)

percent heavier, 10 percent taller, and as much as 50 percent stronger than adult females (Terman & Tyler, 1954). These differences may, to some extent, be due to the greater societal emphasis on athletic training for boys, but they probably also reflect the action of genetic and hormonal factors. Consequently, males may have an inherent advantage in any activities requiring strength and vigorous exertion (Garai & Scheinfeld, 1968). Popularizers of anthropology such as Morris (1967) have written that these traits made prehistoric males better suited for the roles of hunting and group defense. Since the evolving brain of human precursors long ago reached a size requiring the bulk of its growth to take place after birth, someone had to assume the role of nurturing and protecting the infant during his or her prolonged period of mental and physical immaturity; this lot fell to women, the nonhunters. If such a division of labor tended to promote the survival of the primate species who adopted it, it could, over the course of millennia, have become a part of our evolutionary inheritance. Morris infers that males may be predisposed by their genes and hormones to be active, aggressive hunters while females are predisposed to want to have babies and engage in more passive, nurturant, and dependent activities.

The influence of hormones on human behavior is not so straightforward, however. Females produce some testosterone (also called *androgen*) in the cortex of their adrenal glands. Sometimes these glands produce an excess of androgen in a female fetus prior to her birth. While the internal organs of these girls are normal, the external genitalia are enlarged to a point where they have a decidedly masculine appearance.

Although corrective surgery can produce normal-looking genitalia, these "androgenized" females are likely to engage in more rough-and-tumble play and to exhibit more masculine interests than a control group of normal females matched for IQ, socioeconomic status, and race (Money & Ehrhardt, 1972). Money and Ehrhardt

and recognizes that there is usually considerable room for individual variability within the sex role defined by the culture. Thus it is normal for most males to exhibit some stereotypically feminine behavior and for most females to have some masculine character traits. Even so, Diamond and others (Beach, 1965) believe that genetic and hormonal factors predispose young boys and girls toward learning the divergent behavior patterns that lead to reliably different sex roles in adulthood.

Among the more obvious differences between the sexes are those relating to size and strength. While some women are taller or stronger than most men, mature males are, on the average, 20 also reported, however, that these girls think of themselves as female, have typically feminine sexual fantasies during adolescence, and have no desire to change their sex. Alternatively, corrective surgery on androgenized females sometimes results in construction of a functional penis instead of a vagina. In such cases, the child is raised as a boy and shows typically masculine interests and behavior. Finally, these authors describe the case of a boy whose penis was accidentally burned off at the age of 7 months during a routine circumcision. After considerable psychological torment, the parents decided, when the boy was 17 months old, to have his genitals surgically transformed into those of a girl. As fate would have it, this child had an identical twin brother, who was raised as a boy while his sibling was raised as a girl. Despite the fact that the latter child was prenatally exposed only to androgens and had the same genes as her twin brother, she easily identified with the feminine sex role. She learned to wear dresses, have her hair set, and be neat, polite, and relatively quiet. Her brother wore pants and was sloppy, disheveled, noisy, and active. Money and Ehrhardt (pp. 144–145) decided that hormones do have an influence on sex-role behavior but sex-typed "patterns of rearing have extraordinary influence on shaping a child's psychosexual differentiation and the ultimate outcome of a female or male gender identity." Social-learning theorists would be relatively pleased with this conclusion. So, incidentally, would Freud, who believed that human beings were inherently bisexual and could identify with either sex role.

Among the 23 pairs of chromosomes which provide the biological code by which each individual develops, there is one pair which determines a person's sex. One member of this pair is provided by the egg of the mother, and all eggs carry the sex chromosome called X. The other member of the pair is provided by the sperm of the father; some sperm carry an X chromosome, while others carry another sex chromosome

called Y. If an egg is fertilized by an X-carrying sperm the baby's pair of sex chromosomes will be XX, and she will be a female. If, instead, the egg is fertilized by a Y-carrying sperm the baby's sex chromosomes will be XY, and he will be a male. Clearly it is the Y chromosome which determines maleness.

About 13 of every 10,000 males babies born have an extra Y chromosome and so are XYY rather than XY. If all males are biologically disposed toward physical aggressiveness, and if the Y chromosome determines maleness, then a male with an extra Y chromosome might be "supermale" and hence hyperaggressive. In a review of twenty-five studies in which the sex chromosomes of more than 5000 male prison inmates were identified, it was found that the frequency of XYYs was 190 per 10,000 inmates, a rate fifteen times higher than that among all newborn male infants (Jarvik et al., 1973). Since chromosome abnormalities like XYY are often associated with mental retardation, it is possible that XYYs are overrepresented in prison populations not because they are hyperaggressive but because their limited intelligence causes them to experience difficulties in coping with a complex social world. There is, however, another chromosome abnormality which also appears in about 13 of every 10,000 male babies and which is also frequently associated with retardation. It consists of the presence of an extra X chromosome, making the individual XXY. These individuals are also overrepresented in prison populations (90 per 10,000 males), but significantly less so than XYYs. It appears, then, that an extra Y chromosome contributes something to antisocial behavior beyond the simple effects of mental retardation. Perhaps that something is a disposition toward aggressiveness.

An alternative explanation is offered by the fact that XYY males tend to be taller than XYs, the former averaging over 6 feet. The XYY prototype is a tall, acne-scarred man who has a reputation for being a "loner" and has chronic difficulties with heterosexual relationships. Daniel Hugon, a murderer of French prostitutes and an XYY, unsuccessfully used his chromosome abnormality as evidence of diminished capacity at his trial.

Perhaps the greater height of XYYs causes society to expect greater aggressiveness from them, and this expectation becomes a self-fulfilling prophecy. In a large-scale study conducted in Copenhagen, Witkin et al. (1976) contacted the tallest 16 percent of males born in the years 1944 to 1947 so as to determine their chromosomal types and whether they had ever been convicted of a crime. The sample consisted of 4139 persons, 12 of whom were XYYs and 16 of whom were XXYs. Of the normal XYs, 9.3 percent had been convicted of a criminal offense (the fact that relatively minor offenses were counted tended to inflate this percentage above what would normally be expected). A slightly larger proportion (18.8 percent) of XXYs had been convicted. Among the XYYs, however, fully 41.7 percent had been convicted. Individual height seemed to have little effect upon the conviction rate. While the average height of XYYs was slightly greater than the average height of XYs, it was found that within each group, those with convictions were generally *shorter* than their law-abiding counterparts. On the other hand, the crimes for which XYYs had been convicted showed no tendency to be more violent than the crimes of XYs, so a connection could not be clearly drawn between the extra Y chromosome and aggressiveness. On standardized tests of mental ability, XYYs were found to score lower than XYs, and convicted criminals scored lower than males with no convictions. Witkin et al. concluded that it was the lower intelligence of the XYYs, rather than any disposition toward hyperaggressiveness, which caused them to be overrepresented in criminal populations.

It seems that there is some evidence for a dispositional explanation of sex differences in aggressiveness in terms of the hormones and genes associated with the male sex type. At the same time, there is also evidence that the social environment interacts with any such dispositions so as to suppress or encourage the emergence of aggressive behavior. What are these environmental experiences?

Behavioral Explanations For Sex Differences in Aggressiveness

The learning of sex roles begins immediately after birth, and a child's parents are generally the earliest teachers. Rubin et al. (1974) interviewed thirty sets of parents within 24 hours after the birth of their first child. Boys and girls were equally represented among the thirty infants in the study, and all of them had been routinely examined by the hospital staff for muscle tone, color, reflexes, size, and weight; there were no significant sex differences. Yet both the fathers and the mothers of daughters rated them as softer, more finely featured, more inattentive, and smaller than did the parents of sons. Fathers of sons went even further in rating their offspring hardier, stronger, and better coordinated than did the fathers of daughters. Given these perceptions, it is not unlikely that the first time a father lifts his baby, he might give the infant a little jostling if it is a boy but be more inclined to cuddle it gently if it is a girl. As Chafetz (1974, chap. 3) pointed out, it is not difficult to imagine how this expectation that boys are tougher than girls could become a self-fulfilling prophecy through exposure of the sexes to different experiences during socialization.

What are these experiences? From the time they are carried home from the hospital in pink or blue blankets, girls and boys are encouraged to associate themselves with different physical objects and environments and to develop different behavioral styles. Mothers are inclined to feed boys more on the first day and to dress their male and female offspring in different styles and colors of clothing (Lewis, 1975). As they grow older, boys encounter more parental approval if they

The examples of "masculine" and "feminine" behaviors shown on television probably have a strong influence on the sex-typing of child viewers. Research indicates that the degree to which children exhibit sex-typed attitudes and behaviors is directly related to the number of hours they have spent watching television. (Vivienne/Photo Researchers)

play with building blocks than if they play with dolls, and parents try harder to keep their daughters cleaner and neater than their sons. After children become more active and mobile, any rough-and-tumble play on the part of boys may be tolerated or even encouraged, while girls may be told to avoid any activity that would reveal the underpants beneath their dresses.

It has long been suspected that television is a major socializing agent in various areas of behavior, including aggression and sex roles. According to McGhee (1977), television programs portray men and women in roles that are highly sex-typed and which communicate very effectively the prevailing standards for masculinity and femininity in our society. Females are portrayed as attractive, warm, sociable, fair, and peaceful, while males are portrayed as rational, smart, violent, powerful, and stable. In an investigation of the sex-role attitudes of eighty children in kindergarten and grades 2, 4, and 6, McGhee discovered that sex typing increases with age as well as with the number of hours a week that a child spends watching television.

Such social-learning experiences no doubt contribute to the stereotyped view of males as vigorous, muscular, tough, strong, aggressive, and domineering and females as soft, delicate, tender, helpless, and submissive (Bryson & Corey, 1977). Once established, such learned expectations can easily be translated into behavior.

A MEDLEY OF SEX DIFFERENCES AND DISPOSITIONAL AND BEHAVIORAL EXPLANATIONS

Males and females have been observed to differ on a number of traits other than aggression. Some, but not all, of these traits are examined in the following subsections.

Dependence and Conformity

Evidence exists that even at ages as young as 13 months, girls are more dependent than boys on the presence and reassurance of others (Tyler, 1965). In a typical study, young girls and boys were placed on the floor of a playroom by their mothers, who then returned to their seats. It was found that the girls looked back at their mothers more often and returned to make physical contact with their mothers more quickly than did the boys. When prevented by a flimsy barrier from reaching their mothers, the little girls were likely to break into tears, while the little boys tried to push the barrier aside (Goldberg & Lewis, 1969).

In their review of the literature on this topic, Maccoby and Jacklin (1974) concluded that no consistent sex differences in dependency had been demonstrated, but Block (1976) disputed their conclusion on the grounds that at least eight studies indicating a greater dependency among females on help and reassurance from others had been overlooked in Maccoby and Jacklin's review.

Research on conformity Before sex differences in conformity can be discussed meaningfully, we must examine the procedures used to research this trait. The classic investigations in this area were conducted by Asch (1958) and Sherif (1937). Asch studied compliance by placing a naive subject in a group of seven accomplices of the experimenter. It was arranged that the subject would always be seated in the seventh of a row of eight chairs. The task for the group was to judge which of a set of three lines was the same length as a standard line shown on a display card. The correct answer was obvious in each case, but the accomplices were unanimous in agreeing on an incorrect response on twelve out of eighteen trials. It was found that the subjects were induced to make errors in order to agree with the accomplices on an average of four of the twelve critical trials. Subjects who viewed the lines alone in a control group made virtually no errors. The size of the group had some effect on compliance. In other variations on the procedure, subjects were found to be very little affected by the erroneous judgments of only one or two accomplices.

The process studied by Asch has been called *compliance* by social psychologists because the subjects were aware that the judgments of the group were erroneous; they simply succumbed to the pressure to report something other than what they were actually seeing.

The word "conformity" is usually reserved to describe movement toward a group which occurs unconsciously rather than consciously. The research situation created by Sherif seems to have studied conformity rather than compliance. Sherif exposed subjects to a tiny point of light emitted by a source about 15 feet away from them in a totally darkened room. Subjects were told that the light would come on and go off periodically and that when it was on, it would start to move. Subjects were asked to call out their estimates of the distance the light had moved on a given trial. The light was, in fact, stationary and only appeared to move because of a little-known optical illusion called *autokinesis*. Subjects in the Sherif situation usually perceived the light to be moving about 4 to 5 inches. This was an average estimate, however, and individual subjects developed highly personal norms of movement after exposure to the light for one or more blocks of thirty trials. Subjects were found to settle on perceived median estimates of movement of anywhere between 1 and 10 inches.

In other studies, it was found that if three subjects with well-established personal norms of, say, 1, 3, and 8 inches of movement are placed together in the judgment situation, their median estimates tend to converge over trial blocks. After several trial blocks comprising many judgments, each of the three subjects may, for example, have a median estimate of movement of about 4 inches. It seems the group compromises its differences; that is, the 8-inch person becomes more moderate, and the other two become more extreme in judging the light's range of movement. Yet in postexperimental reports, the majority of subjects in such studies indicate little awareness that their perceptions were altered by the judgments of others. Instead, they maintain

that they had privately made their own estimates *before the others spoke.* The influence process, then, appears to be a rather subtle phenomenon which may occur on an unconscious level.

Sherif and Sherif (1969) summarized many years of research with this procedure by noting that partners who are well-liked, have high status, are considered competent on the judgment task, or merely exude self-confidence when announcing their estimates are all especially effective in influencing other subjects' personal norms of movement. Furthermore, subjects lacking in self-confidence—who are anxious about the accuracy of their estimates—are more easily influenced than are subjects led to believe that their judgments are probably correct.

Using the Asch procedure, Allen and Newtson (1972) found that the tendency of children to comply with the judgments of peers and adults on perceptual and opinion items declined steadily

Some studies indicate that females are more likely to conform to group styles of appearance and behavior than are males. What do you think? (Sybil Shelton/Monkmeyer)

from the first to the seventh grades but increased slightly as they entered high school. Costanzo (1970) similarly found an increase in compliance as children approached high school and a decline after they graduated and assumed a fully adult status. Perhaps the increase in the tendency to comply which seems to occur during early adolescence can be interpreted as reflecting Erikson's concept of the identity crisis (see Chapter 2). Adults were presumably less compliant than adolescents because, by age 21, they have developed more strongly internalized value systems, and so their judgments are less influenced by group pressures exerted in the immediate situation.

Some studies using these methods found females to be more compliant or conforming than males, but the magnitude and even the direction of this sex difference depends on such things as the race and birth order of the subjects (Hollander & Marcia, 1970; Iscoe et al., 1964; Sampson & Hancock, 1967). Furthermore, while females have often been found to be more conforming on opinion items related to stereotypically "masculine" interests such as auto mechanics, the tables may be turned when items are drawn from areas of "feminine" expertise such as cooking (Sistrunk & McDavid, 1971). Thus, either males or females may be the more conforming sex depending on who is on unfamiliar ground in a given situation. Such inconsistent results led Maccoby and Jacklin (1974) to conclude that there is no overall sex difference in suggestibility or conformity. Even so, Cooper (1979, p. 141) reexamined the literature on this topic and reopened the issue by saying that, "Taken as a whole, the body of evidence supports the conclusion that more females conform than males."

If there is any reliable tendency for females to be more conforming, social-learning theorists would attribute it to socialization pressures on females to be particularly "nice" and responsive to the needs and wishes of others while rebelliousness and inconsiderateness are more likely to be indulged in males. It is important, more-over, to avoid attaching any evaluative significance to such a sex difference. Psychologists have often treated conformity versus nonconformity as being at the undesirable or desirable extremes, respectively, of a bipolar trait, but Hollander and Willis (1967) regard this view as overly simplistic and stress that both conformity and nonconformity can be either desirable or undesirable, depending on the situation.

Research on field dependence In the early 1950s, Witkin identified a perceptual skill which seems to reflect an underlying personality dimension that contributes to a person's mode of expression of a variety of different psychological traits. The perceptual skill is measured by the rod-and-frame test, which asks the subject to adjust the orientation of a rod within a tilted square frame so that the rod will be vertical with respect to gravity. The rod and frame are illuminated, and the test is conducted in a darkened room so that there will be no landmarks other than the frame to provide clues as to the true orientation of the rod. Some people are strongly influenced by the tilt of the frame in their efforts to adjust the rod to an upright orientation. These subjects are called *field-dependent*. Others are more able to disregard the misleading information provided by the frame and orient the rod very close to a true perpendicular; they are called *field-independent*.

Witkin and Goodenough (1977) maintain that the basic personality dimension underlying a tendency toward field dependence is a general reliance on the external world to provide information which will validate or invalidate one's personal perceptions. Field independence, by contrast, is presumed to reflect a greater attentiveness to subjective feelings and sensations in evaluating one's perceptions. This trait distinction is reminiscent of Jung's extraversion-introversion dichotomy, which was later studied by Eysenck (see Chapter 2). Relative to their field-independent counterparts, field-dependent subjects have been found to be more influenced by an accomplice's judgments in a Sherif autokinetic situation (Linton, 1955), more accepting of persuasive communications attributed to an authoritative source (Brillhart, 1970), and more willing to agree with a majority in making various kinds of social judgments (Solar et al., 1969). In short, field-dependent types appear to attend to outside influences more often than do field-independent types in trying to interpret their perceptions and beliefs; consequently, the field-dependent types are more susceptible to social pressures toward compliance or conformity.

A large number of studies have indicated that females may be more field-dependent than males (Waber, 1977). Witkin and his associates noted that the sex difference is not universally found across cultures and proposed that socialization practices in the most westernized cultures (where the field dependence of females is most different from that of males) might cause females to become more dependent on the opinions of others for validation of their beliefs (Witkin et al., 1962).

Suprisingly, there exists a body of correlational data which suggests that spatial abilities of the type studied on tests of field dependence may be influenced by a sex-linked major gene (Bock & Kolakowski, 1973). The Y chromosome may be regarded as an X chromosome with its lower right-hand leg missing. According to the sex-linkage hypothesis, the gene for strong spatial ability (s) is recessive and carried on this leg of the X chromosome. You may recall from Chapter 7 that a recessive gene will only be expressed as a trait if it is paired with another recessive gene *or* if its effects are not canceled by a dominant gene. In the case of spatial ability, the dominant gene for weak ability (S) will be expressed in three out of every four females. In males, the dominant gene for weak ability and the recessive gene for strong ability will each be expressed about half the time (see Figure 13-1). Much as this theory predicts, the proportion of field-independent males has been found to be about twice that of

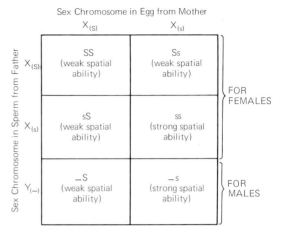

FIGURE 13-1
Hypothetical diagram of the inheritance of strong spatial ability, a sex-linked trait carried by a recessive gene (s) on the X chromosome. If the recessive gene is paired with a dominant gene for weak spatial ability (S), only the dominant trait will be expressed. Consequently, just 25 percent of all females should show strong spatial ability, while 50 percent of all males (who can receive no S gene from their father) should show strong spatial ability.

field-independent females. Also as the theory predicts, the field independence of females correlates more highly with that of their fathers than with that of their mothers (since the trait can be expressed only if the X chromosome contributed by the father carried the s gene and, if it does, the father must also express the trait). Males, on the other hand, correlate more highly with their mothers than with their fathers in field independence, since whether a male expresses the trait depends entirely on whether the X chromosome contributed by his mother carried the recessive gene (Hartlage, 1970).

Waber prefers an alternative explanation for sex differences in field dependence. She argues that field independence is a trait associated with early maturation among males as well as females. Since the rate of maturation is set by the endocrine system and the hormones it secretes (particularly the sex hormones, androgen and estrogen) it seems probable to Waber that these hormones, secreted in especially large quantities during early adolescence, may channel the growth and differentiation of the central nervous system in a direction which favors field dependence. The activity of the endocrine system is partly under genetic control, which makes it appear that there are genes for spatial ability when in fact, according to Waber, it is the hormones which contribute to individual differences on this trait dimension. Since females generally mature earlier than males, a greater proportion of the former are disposed toward field dependence.

Sex differences in field dependence may, therefore, have a biological basis which is unrelated to personality traits like conformity that Witkin has shown to have a weak but statistically significant association with this perceptual ability. Let me quickly add, however, a cautionary comment to the effect that the biological basis of field dependence is still more a speculative idea than an established fact. Sherman (1978) reviewed more recent large-scale studies which failed to find the father-daughter, mother-son correlations in spatial ability predicted by the hypothesis that strong spatial ability is a sex-linked genetic trait. She feels that research conducted by herself and others has raised serious doubts about the validity of the sex-linkage hypothesis and comments that, "The ease with which these hypotheses were accepted should serve as a reminder of the readiness of society to accept biological explanations that serve to justify the status quo" (Sherman & Fennema, 1978, p. 166). Both Sherman and Witkin believe that field dependence-independence is a trait which develops from social learning and that sex differences on this dimension are culturally rather than biologically induced.

Empathy and Nonverbal Communication

Careful reviews of the relevant literature have arrived at the conclusion that females are more adept than males in decoding the nonverbal cues which reveal others' emotional states and that females are more empathically responsive to the emotional states of others (Hall, 1978; Hoffman, 1977). These sex differences could conceivably originate in the differential treatment of boys and girls by their mothers. Lewis (1975) reported that mothers are likely to discourage their sons from touching them but to be more tolerant of being touched by their daughters. Girls may therefore end up feeling freer about touching others, and perhaps these and similar experiences lay the foundation for their greater accuracy in decoding nonverbal communications of emotion.

Moral Judgment

Kohlberg and Kramer (1969) found indications in their data that males achieve a higher level of moral development than do females, much as Freud would have predicted. Kurtines and Greif (1974) pointed out, however, that this phenomenon could, in some way, be related to the fact that the main characters in Kohlberg's "moral dilemmas" are male.

Indeed, a conclusion contrary to Freud's could be drawn from the overrepresentation of males in prison populations. Perhaps males are more vulnerable than females to a loss of the capacity for empathy and the development of psychopathic disorder.

Helping Behavior

A very special form of helping behavior consists of the extraordinary effort expended by females of many species to feed and care for their offspring; these efforts may even include feigning injury so as to distract predators and draw them away from the nest (Wilson, 1975, pp. 122–123). The fact that, in nature, paternal behaviors do not generally approach this same degree of altruism has led to some speculation that there could be sex differences in the motivation to help. Among

There is evidence that women have lower self-esteem than men and that many may actually be motivated to avoid success. These self-defeating attitudes can be counteracted by esteem-building experiences, such as receiving praise for mastering a difficult task. (Peter Vandermark/Stock, Boston)

humans, it is conceivable that there is some biologically based attachment between mothers and their offspring which is, during infancy at least, stronger than the bond between the male parent and his child. Primate studies conducted by Harlow and others certainly suggest the possibility of this special maternal attachment in humans.

Outside of the maternal context, however, in laboratory research of the type emphasized in Chapter 11, no sex differences are generally observed when a helping response consists of reporting or otherwise calling attention to an emergency (see, e.g., Darley & Latané, 1968). When an act of helping requires physical strength, mechanical expertise, or accepting some risk of bodily harm, males are more likely to intervene than females (see, e. g., West, Whitney & Schnedler, 1975). These sex differences as well as the differences in the care of and attachment to infants could, of course, arise from the process of learning sex-typed social roles.

Self-esteem

Several investigators have compared males and females on various components of self-esteem, and the general finding has been that females tend to score lower (see, e.g., Janis & Field, 1959). Maccoby and Jacklin disputed this assessment on the grounds that more recent research has not found such a sex difference. Other lines of evidence, however, do provide some support for the original conclusion. By high school age, females are more oriented toward externality on the I-E scale (see Chapter 10), indicating that they perceive themselves to be less able to control major events in their lives (Samuel, 1980). Females also appear to have a lower opinion of their own abilities, as indicated by a preference for games of luck over those of skill—the opposite of the preference expressed by most males (Deaux et al., 1975). Assuming there is a genuine sex difference in self-esteem, it could contribute to the sex differences in conformity that were mentioned earlier.

Cognitive Abilities

Practically every survey of sex differences, Maccoby and Jacklin's included, has noted that females excel on verbal tasks relative to males. Males excel on mathematical and spatial tasks, the latter including such things as mazes or visualizing a three-dimensional figure which could be constructed by folding a two-dimensional cutout. You will recall from Chapter 6 that the Wechsler intelligence scales contain subtests that are primarily verbal, mathematical, or perceptual-motor in content. Females score higher than males on the verbal subtests, but males generally outscore females on the other subtests. This counterbalancing of sex differences in performance causes the overall IQs of males and females to be equivalent. The differences in cognitive abilities become most clearly observable during adolescence, and it is not known whether they are entirely the result of social learning or influenced by underlying dispositional factors (e.g., the possible biological aspects of language development or field dependence).

SOCIALIZATION INTO SEX ROLES

An extreme dispositional explanation for the origins of sex-typed behavior patterns is that they reflect the action of the genes and hormones which differentiate between male and female human beings. Evidence bearing on this hypothesis was examined earlier in this chapter. While it appears that biological processes might well contribute to some sex differences—aggressiveness in particular—research also indicates that social learning can greatly modify the extent to which these differences appear and perhaps even cancel them out.

The social-learning viewpoint assumes that "acquisition and performance of sex-typed behaviors can be described by the same learning principles used to analyze any other aspect of an individual's behavior" (Mischel, 1966, p. 56). Parents, for instance, are likely to directly reinforce sex-typed toy preferences and clothing styles and to decorate their children's rooms accordingly: Boys get action toys and sports equipment while girls get dolls and floral furnishings (Rheingold & Cook, 1975).

Because of their own sex-typed socialization history, parents also provide models of masculine and feminine behavior for their offspring to imitate. A question immediately arises with regard to modeling of sex roles, however: namely, why would boys tend to model only the behavior of their fathers or other males while girls tend to model their mothers or other females? Both girls and boys witness the behavior of models of the opposite sex, and both see the models reinforced for their behavior, so why would they select to imitate only the behavior of models of the same sex? Presumably, vicarious learning does occur, but children receive approval from the socializing community only when they "act out" behavior adopted from models of the same sex (Mischel, 1966, p. 59). In other words, boys know how to wear dresses and girls know how to play in a rough-and-tumble fashion, but peers as well as parents probably discourage the overt expression of these behaviors.

Kohlberg (1966) adopts something of a middle ground between the dispositional and social-learning positions with his cognitive-developmental analysis of sex-role identification. Kohlberg notes that Money and his associates found evidence of a critical period during which sex typing is fairly flexible (see, e.g., Money et al., 1957). Before the age of 3 or 4, children can be imprinted into either masculine or feminine sex roles regardless of their genetic sexes or initial sex-role assignments. It is easier for a child to accept an identity consistent with the appearance of his or her external genitalia, but irrespective of the genitalia, it is very difficult for a child to accept a sex-role reassignment after the age of 4. From this, Kohlberg infers that the cognitive categorization of oneself as a boy or girl is the major determinant of sex-role identification. This categorization occurs early in development, and because it is normally consistent with gender identity it has a biological basis. Once made, however, it is relatively irreversible, even if the self-categorization is incongruent with the individual's biological makeup.

Once a stable self-categorization has been made, it causes the child to value those physical and social attributes which are perceived to be consistent with his or her sex role. Kohlberg believes that sex roles come to be fixed and inflexible in a child's mind at about the same time that he or she develops perceptual constancies in other areas of mental life. Between the ages of 4 and 7, for example, children become increasingly aware that the quantity of matter in a ball of clay is not altered by rolling it into a sausage (see Chapter 10). The salience of gender role for a child may be influenced by the sexual composition of his or her household. In unstructured interviews, boys from households in which women were in the majority, and girls from households in which men were in the majority, were observed to be more likely to mention their genders spontaneously than were children from households with equal numbers of males and females (McGuire et al., 1979). Apparently children develop a sense of sexual identity by comparing themselves with what they are not as well as with what they are.

The cognitive-developmental approach assumes the self-categorization of gender causes a child to want to do those things believed to be consistent with his or her sex. If the males in the environment are perceived as aggressive, athletic, and socially dominant, while the females are perceived as passive, dependent, and nurturant, a male child will tend to adopt the former behavior and a female child the latter. Kohlberg also entertains the possibility that young girls and boys are inherently predisposed to imitate some of the behaviors that are culturally defined as feminine or masculine, respectively. This could account for cross-cultural similarities in sex-role attitudes (Kohlberg, 1966, p. 82).

Parental Involvement in Sex-Role Identification

Although past practices regarding the parental division of labor in child care may be changing, the most recent studies of this topic confirm the continued existence of old traditions. It is mothers who care for infants and young children; fathers interact with newborns as little as thirty-seven seconds per day, on the average, and with older infants about fifteen minutes per day (Lewis, 1975). During and after a child's second year, the father interacts with him or her more and more frequently, but the behavior can, for the most part, be described as playing with rather than tending. Consequently, it is the mother who introduces the child to the social world, and children of both sexes become highly dependent on her nurturance and affection. The later involvement of the father in the socialization of the child, according to Johnson (1975), reduces the intensity of this psychological dependence on the mother, exposes the child to the values of the world outside the family, and facilitates the progress of children of both sexes toward independent identities. Johnson believes that the father plays a crucial role in the development of sex-appropriate heterosexual behavior in the female, whereas the mother has a somewhat weaker influence on the heterosexual sex typing of her son.

Older brothers and other male relatives can, says Johnson, assume the role of a missing father, but if no males are available as substitutes, children from homes without a father are likely to maintain a lifelong dependence on the nurturance and approval of others. The father can also be "absent" psychologically rather than physically if he is being uncaring and aloof.

Sex Typing and Achievement Motivation

As will be recalled from Chapter 5, McClelland devised a method of scoring a person's need for achievement (n-Ach) on the basis of stories told in response to pictures selected from Murray's Thematic Apperception Test (see McClelland et al., 1953). According to McClelland, a high n-Ach grows out of successful problem solving at a young age, when the child learns to walk, talk, and read. Children with this trait are likely to have been required to perform more tasks on their own at earlier ages than children low in n-Ach. They are also more likely to have had experience with comparing their performances against standards of excellence that, when met, are associated with expressions of positive emotional approval on the part of others. These hypotheses have been supported by research, but there is some indication that the early experiences which develop a high n-Ach also foster fear of failure in children (Rosen & D'Andrade, 1959; Winterbottom, 1958; Teevan & McGhee, 1972).

Most of the research in the achievement literature has used male subjects, and it is males who show the strongest relationships between n-Ach and actual achievement striving in day-to-day life. According to Horner (1970), this is hardly surprising because in our culture it is primarily males who are given the early training in self-reliance and mastery of skills so fundamental to n-Ach. In Horner's research, responses to story cues designed to arouse conflict in females were scored for fear-of-success imagery, that is, fear of social rejection as a result of success, concern about one's normality following success, or denial that success has really occurred. One of the cues described a women named Anne who unexpectedly finds herself at the top of her first-year class in medical school (for men, the person in the story was named John). Success-avoiding stories written to this cue included stories in which Anne drops out of school to avoid antagonizing her boyfriend and stories in which she discovers that the class standings were in error and she is not really at the top after all.

Horner discovered that 65 percent of the women in her sample wrote stories high in fear-of-success imagery, while only 9 percent of the men did so. Women high in the motive to avoid success performed better in noncompetitive than in competitive achievement conditions, while women low in this motive performed better in competition. Later research has found that boys and men are just as likely as girls and women to reveal a motive to avoid success but that the *themes* in the success-avoiding stories differed between the sexes. Females are more likely than males to mention a loss of love and affiliative support as a consequence of high achievement whereas males are more likely to mention a tragic accident befalling the high achiever or cynically to deny the worth of the success. Women high in fear of success do, as Horner said, appear to have difficulty performing well in a competitive situation, and they are likely to take a pessimistic view of heterosexual relationships, emphasizing the dangers of being emotionally hurt rather than (as low-fear women do) the pleasures offered by such relationships (Romer, 1977; Schnitzer, 1977). The motive to avoid success has been observed to be negatively correlated with n-Ach for women but not for men (Karabenick, 1977).

Since research on the motive to avoid success

began, there has been a change in the types of story cues used as well as a change in the scoring procedure. Many studies have turned up contradictory results, and one of Horner's early collaborators felt compelled by this disorderliness in the data to consider seriously whether fear of success is really an important factor in women's strivings for achievement (Tresemer, 1979). Despite such complications, women's achievement motivation will remain an important area of research and social concern. Women enter college and graduate school with grades and test scores equal to or even higher than men's but are more likely either to drop out before completing a degree or to set lower vocational goals for themselves upon graduating. Lenney (1977) has suggested that this phenomenon may be due to a lack of self-confidence among women. In reviewing the literature on sex differences in self-confidence, however, Lenney noted that girls and women may be as confident as boys and men when a task is presented as relevant to "feminine" rather than "masculine" goals, when performance feedback is clear and unambiguous, when the task may be completed privately, or when a nonprivate social setting is made explicitly noncompetitive. Conversely, women's self-confidence is lowest when they must perform a masculine sex-typed task under public, competitive conditions which provide ambiguous feedback as to the quality of their achievement. Obviously, the latter conditions are most prevalent in the work situations and academic settings where women have encountered the greatest difficulty in attaining goals commensurate with their abilities. Fortunately, there are indications that, as a career orientation among women becomes more socially accepted, sex differences in achievement-related motives and behaviors will diminish and perhaps dissappear altogether (Hoffman, 1977).

The Androgynous Sex-Role Orientation

In a frequently cited study, clinical psychologists in three groups were given a list of 122 traits and were asked to indicate which traits would be expressed by a mature, socially competent, all-around healthy *male*, a healthy *female*, or a healthy *adult* (sex unspecified), respectively. It was discovered that similar traits were attributed to the healthy male and the healthy adult, but both of these persons were perceived as different from the healthy female. She was supposed to be more submissive, conforming, excitable, and conceited and less independent, adventurous, aggressive, competitive, and objective than the healthy adult (Broverman et al., 1970). Clearly, these clinicians' concepts of mental health were applied in a peculiar way when they were referring to women rather than men.

Bem (1974) sought to remedy this problem with traditional sex roles by pointing out that both masculine and feminine sex types contain desirable as well as undesirable traits and that the ideal healthy personality represents a blend of the positive qualities of both sex types. Bem developed a scale which lists sixty traits and asks the subject to indicate the degree to which each is characteristic of him or her. Surveys of college students had previously indicated that twenty of the traits (e.g., understanding, sensitive to the needs of others) reflected a feminine sex type, twenty reflected a masculine sex type (self-reliant, willing to take risks), and twenty were neutral "fillers" (truthful, happy). Subjects scoring above the median for masculinity but below the median for femininity set by Bem's standardization sample are classified as having a male sex-type. Similarly, those above the median for femininity and below the median for masculinity have a female sex-type. Those below the median on both dimensions are placed in an ambiguous category called "undifferentiated," while those above the median on both represent what, for Bem, is an ideal state of sex-role flexibility known as *androgyny*. Androgynous people constituted about a third of a sample of Stanford students given the sex role inventory (Bem, 1975, 1977). These individuals were found to be generally affectionate and helpful in most situations, but were also strong and self-willed when the circumstances called for it. Some data suggest that sex-typed children may be more psychologically rigid and less creative than their more androgynous counterparts (Lott, 1978).

Contrary to Bem's expectations, however, the androgynous type has not always been found to be more psychologically "healthy" than the male sex-type. It is the female sex-type which most consistently appears deficient in terms of self-esteem and self-rated adjustment (Silvern & Ryan, 1979; Spence et al., 1975; Summers, 1979). One study found that androgynous women had a lower fear of success than either the sex-reversed (i.e., masculine), the feminine sex-typed, or the undifferentiated, but both the androgynous and the sex-reversed had higher achievement motivation and showed stronger performance on a problem-solving task than the sex-typed or undifferentiated (Major, 1979). These observations may be due to the fact that nearly half of the traits assigned to the female sex-type on Bem's scale have negative connotations (e.g., "gullible," "childlike") while nearly all the masculine traits exemplify the positively valued attributes of assertiveness and competence. Even when they have positive connotations, the feminine traits reflect sociability rather than task competence (Pedhazur & Tetenbaum, 1979). Consequently, the association of androgyny with healthy adjustment seems to be mainly due to the masculine traits it incorporates rather than the feminine ones. The association of femininity with social adjustment does increase, however, if negatively valued items are dropped fom this scale (Silvern & Ryan, 1979).

Bem's notion of androgyny has been criticized on the grounds that it is too loosely defined in both a statistical and a psychological sense (Locksley & Colten, 1979). Androgyny, it is said, should not be blindly assumed to represent mental health for all people in all situations (Lenney, 1979). A coequal presence of masculine and feminine traits could, in some cases, indicate a chaotically disorganized personality rather than a well-adjusted one, and a problem for therapists has been how to encourage both sex-role flexibility and situationally appropriate behavior simultaneously (Kaplan. 1979).

CONCLUSION

Evidence supportive of the malleability of sex-role identification was reported long ago by anthropologist Margaret Mead in her 1935 classic work, *Sex and Temperament in Three Primitive Societies.* On the island of New Guinea she found three native cultures, each of which had a different conception of the temperament considered appropriate for males and females. She contrasted these cultures with American culture which, as both she and we have noted, favors an active, aggressive temperament for males and a passive, nonaggressive temperament for females. The Tchambuli culture appeared to reverse the American definition of sex roles: There, an emotionally dependent, artistic, and sensitive temperament was exhibited by males, while females were aggressive and domineering. Another tribe, the Arapesh, preferred a passive, gentle temperament for *both* sexes. Finally, the Mundugmor expected both sexes to be hostile and aggressive. Despite the undeniable plasticity of human temperament, however, there appeared to be some limits to these socialization processes. Even among the role-reversed Tchambuli, for instance, it was the men who engaged in warfare.

Those who insist that sex-role identification is entirely the product of social learning must eventually deal with those aspects of sex roles which appear with considerable regularity in cultures widely separated by geography, language, and technological sophistication. Did these regularities appear by accident, or are they the behavioral manifestation of certain universal differences in the biological makeup of female and male members of our species? Obviously, social learning is of very great importance in the shaping of sex-typed behavior, but can we really be certain that biology plays no part in developing this fundamental aspect of human temperament? Even if we could account for every sex-typed behavior in contemporary culture by means of social learning, we would still have to explain why distinct sex roles evolved in the first place. Many of these distinctions could simply be due to the greater physical power of males: Since males had this power, they used it long ago to force females into a dependent role. But then one must go back a further step to ask why, in the course of evolution, it was adaptive for males to have greater physical strength than females and why some of our primate relatives exhibit analogously sex-typed traits.

Our present state of knowledge does not allow definitive answers to questions like the ones above. While the material in this section has clearly demonstrated the impact of cultural values and social-learning processes on the development and maintenance of sex-role attitudes and behavior, it would be inappropriate to infer that biological processes play no part in this phenomenon. To admit to the possibility of biological determinants of sex-role identification is not, to be sure, to say that any such predisposing factors cannot be considerably influenced (if not indeed overridden altogether) by social learning. Certainly we should expect to see a dominance of learning over biology in technological societies where those who "bring home the bacon," so to speak, need no longer be brawny male hunters and where child care need no longer be the exclusive concern of females.

It may be important at this point for us all to remind ourselves that personality differences do not necessarily imply deficits. In the case of sex typing, there is a sorry history of ideologically biased research masquerading as science which, first, gathered questionable evidence of such things as human maternal instincts and sex differences in brain configuration and, next, advocated a denial of voting rights and higher education to women on the grounds that nature had not equipped them to handle anything outside the home environment (Gould, 1978; Shields, 1975). Such misguided applications of scientific methods and the patriarchal stereotypes they supported understandably provoked a strong reaction among those attuned to the socially learned aspects of many sex differences and the political arrangements which contributed to the maintenance of sexist ideologies. Whether socially learned or biologically based, though, the differentiating traits discussed in this chapter do not imply an overall inferiority of either sex relative to the other. If, for instance, women are less physically aggressive than men, that would be a plus rather than a minus for membership in a civilized community. If females are more empathic or more helpful than males, these, too, are positive qualities.

Furthermore, on all sex-typed traits, there is wide individual variability within each group so that some women express more masculine characteristics than some men, and conversely. As people become freer to actualize all aspects of their personalities in a society which is progressing further and further in the direction of providing truly equal opportunities for all its citizens, we can expect to see this individual variability increase, thereby diminishing, or perhaps even eliminating, many sex differences. Need for achievement seems to be moving in this direction already, and as more and more women act out their achievement orientation we should expect to observe a corresponding increase in their self-esteem and perhaps also a reduction in susceptibility to social influence in traditionally masculine content areas.

Looking back over the chapter, one cannot help but be impressed by the accuracy with which Freud delineated sex differences that later found research support. Despite his perceptive insights into human behavior, it seems fair to say that Freud underestimated the extent to which changes in social and economic conditions, as well as changes in people's perceptions of their goals in life, could alter personality characteristics that he felt were cultural universals, engraved on one's character in early childhood. The impact of social forces on personality and its capacity for change in middle and late adulthood are central themes of Chapter 14.

SUMMARY

1 The study of sex differences in personality is controversial because real or imagined differences have, in the past, been put to the purpose of justifying the inferior social status and unequal career opportunities which male-dominated societies have imposed on women. Even psychologists disagree on what interpretations can be made of objectively gathered data bearing on this topic.

2 Freud conceived of human beings as fundamentally bisexual and capable of assuming a variety of sex-role orientations depending on their resolutions of the Oedipus conflict in childhood. In the usual case, however, in which the boy identifies with his father and the girl with her mother, the female personality is distinguished from the male in being more envious, less stable in terms of emotions and moral values, lower in self-esteem, more masochistic, more vain, more modest, less active, and more passive. Erikson found evidence of sex differences on the latter two traits in a study of the play constructions of preadolescent boys and girls. Both Freud and Erikson have been sharply criticized by feminist writers, but their work is most appropriately thought of as an *analysis of* patriarchal society rather than a *recommendation for* one.

3 Physical aggressiveness is a trait on which all reviewers agree males exceed females. In monkeys, and, as far as can be known, in humans, the sex hormones have a significant effect on sex differences in aggressiveness. At the same time, early training in the opposite sex type seems to be capable of overriding the sex type to which a child is disposed by his or her genes and hormones. It is the Y chromosome which determines maleness. If maleness is associated with dispositions toward antisocial aggression, one would expect that a male with an extra Y chromosome would be "supermale" and hence hyperaggressive. These XYY males have been found to be overrepresented in male prison populations relative to their frequency among newborn male infants, but it may be a tendency toward mental retardation among the XYYs which accounts for this phenomenon rather than any hyperaggressiveness.

4 The environmentalist explanation for sex differences in aggression takes note of the fact that parents perceive sex differences in their newborn infants which do not, in fact, exist. This and other parental perceptions and behaviors become self-fulfilling prophecies in which girls come to see themselves as less active and aggressive than boys and behave accordingly. Television provides models of male aggression and female passivity from which children also learn sex-typed behavior patterns.

5   Another frequently observed sex difference is the greater dependence of females on the presence and reassurance of others, which may contribute to the tendency for females to be more conforming than males. Females also are more dependent on cues in the external environment in making perceptual judgments, whereas males are more attentive to cues inside themselves. The stronger spatial ability of males could even conceivably be a trait carried by a sex-linked recessive gene, but the inventor of one widely used task which measures spatial ability believes that sex differences are produced primarily by differential social learning.

6   Females have been found to be generally more empathic and attentive to nonverbal cues of others' emotions than are males. Males tend to score higher in moral judgment on the Kohlberg scale, but it has been pointed out that this phenomenon could be related to the fact that the major characters in Kohlberg's "moral dilemmas" are males. The sexes have been shown to be equal in their willingness to report emergencies or extend aid to others (so long as there is no risk of bodily harm), but females seem to have lower self-esteem. Females excel at cognitive tasks with a great deal of verbal content, while males excel at mathematical and spatial tasks.

7   Parents provide models of masculine and feminine behavior for their children to follow. The children witness the behavior appropriate to the opposite sex but do not "act out" this behavior for fear of punishment or disapproval. Kohlberg believes it is the child's self-categorization of gender which causes him or her to value male things if he is a boy or female things if she is a girl. Recent theories of sex typing argue that children of both sexes become highly dependent on the nurturance and affection of their mothers. The father's function is to reduce the intensity of this dependence by exposing his child to the values and expectations of the world outside the family. The father may play a crucial role in the development of sex-appropriate heterosexual behavior in the female.

8   Need for achievement is a trait which is nurtured by requiring children to perform more tasks on their own at earlier ages and providing positive approval when their performances meet some standard of excellence. Need for achievement in females has not generally been found to be related to actual achievement striving, and this may be due to a lack of social encouragement for such behavior. Many females (as well as many males) may be afflicted with an outright fear of success. For females, the motive to avoid success seems to be related to a fear of social rejection as a consequence of individual achievement.

9   Bem argued that neither the masculine nor the feminine sex type can be regarded as psychologically healthy. The optimum sex-role orientation, she says, is one which combines the positive qualities of

traditional masculinity and femininity. Such a person is psychologically flexible rather than rigid—able to express a feminine tenderness but also a masculine toughness when the situation calls for it.

10 Those who insist that sex-role identification is entirely the product of social learning must eventually deal with those aspects of sex roles which appear with considerable regularity in cultures widely separated by geography, language, and technological sophistication. At the same time, it must be acknowledged that humans may have the cognitive capacity to override any biological forces disposing them toward different sex types. Furthermore, any differences which may reliably be demonstrated do not, in the light of contemporary knowledge, imply an overall superiority of either sex.

TERMS TO KNOW

identification	sex-linked genetic traits
sex-typing	nonverbal communication
testosterone	sex roles
XYY chromosome abnormality	motive to avoid success
field dependence	androgyny

14

PERSONALITY DEVELOPMENT IN MIDDLE AND LATE ADULTHOOD

ISSUES TO CONSIDER

1 What types of life-styles promote "successful aging" or the greatest degree of life satisfaction among the elderly?

2 To what extent can age-related declines in physical and psychological health be attributed to lowered expectations regarding the stamina and competence of the elderly rather than to degenerative biological processes?

3 Are there distinct "stages" of personality development in adulthood, separated by transition points or "passages" of particular psychological turmoil?

The Abkhasian Republic is located in an area of the Soviet Union where the Caucasus mountains come down almost to the coast of the Black Sea. There are about 100,000 Abkhasians, most of whom tend flocks or grow tea and tobacco in the foothills and mountain valleys. They have attracted the attention of researchers interested in aging because an extraordinarily large proportion of them live to the age of 90 and beyond. The people are remarkable not only for their longevity but for their generally good physical and mental health. It is not unusual to find individuals more than a century old working steadily in the fields, walking at least 2 miles a day, and taking recreational swims in cold mountain streams. Their vision, hearing, and memory may show some impairment, but the degree is mild compared with the degree of impairment shown by most elderly people in the Soviet Union or, for that matter, the United States. In a nine-year study of 123 Abkhasians over the age of 100, no cases of either cancer or mental illness were found (Benet, 1976).

What accounts for the long life and good health of the Abkhasians? Diet is one possibility. They eat meat only about twice a week. Chicken, beef, young goat, or pork is strongly preferred to fish, which is seldom served. The meat is freshly slaughtered, minimally cooked, and eaten the same day; since Abkhasians will not eat leftovers, even the poorest families immediately dispose of table scraps by feeding them to the animals. Some cheese and a couple of glasses of buttermilk are consumed daily, along with generous quantities of fresh fruits and vegetables. The Abkhasian diet results in a relatively high intake of vitamin C and a low intake of sugar. Food is always eaten in small bites and savored slowly. Small amounts of red wine are typically consumed at lunch and dinner, and vodka is used to celebrate special occasions. Though they supply tobacco to other Soviet citizens, the Abkhasians themselves rarely smoke. Medical authorities have speculated that the buttermilk, wine, and pickled vegetables may destroy bacteria detrimental to health, and the low intake of saturated fats may benefit the cardiovascular system. The Abkhasians regard overeating and obesity as a sign of illness. Social pressure encourages people of all ages to remain slender.

Slenderness is valued by the Abkhasians because they are descended from a fierce nomadic people for whom light but muscular horsemen were the first line of defense. This warlike history suggests a possible hereditarian explanation for their longevity. Perhaps those who were genetically disposed toward lesser physical fitness and mental alertness were selectively weeded out by hand-to-hand combat and so were less likely to reproduce and pass on their genetic weaknesses to future generations.

The Abkhasians themselves offer a reason for their lifelong vigor which would be music to the ears of a psychoanalytically oriented psychologist. They give a good deal of credit to their sexual habits. Marriage and regular sexual relations traditionally do not commence until the age of 30, and there is absolute insistence that the young bride be a virgin. If she is not, she is rejected by her husband, and there is likely to be a blood feud between her family and that of the man accused of deflowering her. While normal sexual intercourse is delayed by the threat of such dire consequences, the span of sexual activity following marriage is long. Most men continue to be sexually potent after the age of 70, and nearly 14 percent of women are still menstruating at the age of 55. It is not uncommon for babies to be born to couples who are, by our standards, too "old" for childbearing. Despite its regulation by strong customs and taboos even after marriage, sex is regarded as one of the healthy appetites of life, much like food and wine, to be thoroughly satisfied at the proper time and place but not overindulged. There is, consequently, an absence of neurotic guilt concerning sexual matters.

Finally, one explanation for the Abkhasians' longevity is especially compatible with behavior-

The Abkhasians and others who live to advanced ages demonstrate that the years after 70 need not be ones of infirmity and psychological decline. Shown here is a German couple who were married on the groom's one hundredth birthday; the bride was 77. (United Press International Photo)

al psychology. The people in this society simply *expect* to live a long time, so they do. There is no retirement at 65 and no perception that a person is "old" until, perhaps, she or he passes the age of 100 and sharply reduces her or his schedule of daily activities. A carefully defined and regulated kinship system creates a tightly knit extended family in which the oldest members receive the greatest respect. In effect, people are rewarded for being old rather than being psychologically punished, as so often happens in a youth-oriented society like our own.

Clearly, there are many nutritional, hereditary, biological, and social forces at work in the Abkhasian community, any or all of which could promote long life and good health. In the literature pertaining to the growth of personality through early, middle, and late adulthood in our own culture, we also see evidence for characterological, personological, and behavioral influences. No single theoretical tradition seems to offer a complete account of this development, but each has provided valuable insights into the forces which promote either change or stability in one's identity throughout the adult life span.

Chapter 14 is not exclusively concerned with events occurring during old age, though that is the ultimate end point of the processes we will be considering. We will briefly examine that fuzzy stage where adolescence blends into adulthood, as well as the eras which succeed it. We will see indications of the continuity of personality traits through these many years of life, but we will also see that personality can often show abrupt changes in response to the crises of adulthood.

Turning, as we must all do eventually, to the forces impinging upon personality in old age, we find that psychodynamic, dispositional, and environmental factors are as relevant here as they are in any other stage of human life. A primary concern of those who study human aging (called *gerontologists*) has been to identify strategies of successful aging—i.e., life-styles which promote the greatest degree of satisfaction among the elderly. Two strategies in particular have been contrasted with one another. *Disengagement theory* proposes that as older people perceive their physical abilities to be declining, they achieve the best psychological adjustment to the inevitability of death by withdrawing from the activities and social obligations of the workaday world, reminiscing about the past, and putting together a personal philosophy which will bring a greater sense of cohesiveness and meaning to the greater and lesser triumphs and disasters of their preceding years (Cumming & Henry, 1961). *Activity theory*, on the other hand, argues that successful aging requires continued involvement with the world of work and social relationships. Withdrawal from the mainstream of life, say these theorists, leads to feelings of worthlessness, loss of self-esteem, depression, and a premature and dissatisfied death (Havighurst & Albrecht, 1953).

The example of the Abkhasians seems to support activity theory more than disengagement theory, but it would be inappropriate to name either of these approaches to old age as the best for all people in all circumstances. It may be that some are most satisfied when they disengage and others when they remain active. Perhaps the optimum approach would be some type of com-

promise between these extremes. Suffice it to say that here, as always, a number of theoretical viewpoints are defensible, and each receives some measure of empirical support.

THE LIFE CYCLE IN THE EUROPEAN TRADITION

You will recall from Chapter 2 that Freud did not extend his psychoanalytic theory of personality development much beyond adolescence. It was others in the European tradition—notably Jung and Erikson—who undertook this effort.

Jung's Stages of Adulthood

Jung (1931) placed the stage called *youth* immediately after adolescence and described its major theme as the replacement of childhood aspirations with more realistically attainable goals. In this process, the individual begins to stabilize his or her self-esteem at a relatively high or low level and confronts the role demands created by adult sexuality. Jung identified a midlife transition period, around 35 to 40 years of age, in which repressed characteristics seek expression. This may lead to a change in interests or reemergence of thoughts and behavior associated with childhood. Some stability and even rigidity is reestablished by age 50, but after age 60 the individual again becomes open to the expression of repressed characteristics. It is the fear of impending death which causes individuals to look within themselves for interests, abilities, and personal styles which they have never before expressed. This progress toward self-realization can sometimes be accomplished by the individual alone, but usually she or he is helped along by a "spiritual guide." The guide could be a psychotherapist, an older person who has already gone through these changes, or a religious figure. Jung (1933) noted that religions have traditionally played an almost psychotherapeutic role by providing rituals which dramatize and facilitate the major psychological transitions in a person's life: birth, pubertal initiation into adulthood, marriage, death, and so forth.

In one research study, 200 people in their seventies, eighties, and nineties were administered the Rorschach inkblot test. It was found that many of them, irrespective of age, gave responses comparable to the responses of normal younger adults, but some did show signs of deviance in that their responses reflected psychological immaturity. The investigators concluded that while many people retain essentially normal patterns of cognitive functioning into their nineties others (whom the researchers called *presenile* or *senile*) show indications in their inkblot-test responses of becoming psychologically similar to children 10 years or less in age (Ames et al., 1973). These results could be considered evidence of Jung's hypothesized reemergence of the thoughts and feelings of childhood among the elderly, but it seems more likely that the deviant group was experiencing special physical or mental health problems which caused them to differ from their "normal" counterparts. More relevant to Jung's ideas may be the observation that when the inkblot tests were completed, most of the participants seized the opportunity to talk to a psychologically trained researcher by beginning long conversations filled with reminiscences of family and former friends and expressions of concern regarding the approach of death, the nature of the Deity, and the extent to which life has meaning or purpose.

The Final Crises in Erikson's Life Cycle

You may recall from our discussion of Erikson's theory of personality development in Chapter 2 that the first task of adolescence is to establish a sense of identity and chart a course away from dependence on one's parents and toward self-sufficiency. Next to emerge is a sense of intimacy; that is, an empathic concern for others which

is expressed most intensely within an intimate sexual relationship based on mutual affection and respect. Failure to achieve intimacy results in isolation and a desire to reject or even destroy those perceived as happier than oneself or as threats to one's self-esteem.

The first stage specifically associated with adulthood in Erikson's life cycle involves making a decision as to whether one should make some contribution to the lives of future generations, either by raising a family or by engaging in productive work, especially work of the type that requires self-sacrifice for the good of others. A failure to choose this generativity may result in a stagnation of one's personality development at a level of superficial intimacy with others and narcissistic self-indulgence. The generative choice is future-oriented and strives toward goals which transcend the self.

At the terminal stage of adulthood, by contrast, the individual becomes past-oriented as she or he reviews her or his life cycle and comes to accept its disappointments along with its satisfactions as significant and inevitable events in one's psychological development. A sense of ego integrity and an acceptance of approaching death emerges from the realization that whatever its ups and downs, one's life has been a significant contribution to the history of human existence; this realization is easier to attain if one has previously exercised a generative choice. The alternative to ego integrity is bitterness and cynicism regarding the meaning of life and a psychologically oppressive feeling of despair and disgust.

Because of his analytic orientation, Erikson has not been particularly interested in gathering empirical data to support his stage theory. Instead, he offers insights such as his analysis of the symbolism in the film *Wild Strawberries*, directed by Ingmar Bergman (Erikson, 1978). The main character is a 76-year-old Swedish physician who has spent his life furthering his professional career (mostly as a university-based researcher)

In Ingmar Bergman's film *Wild Strawberries*, the main character is a 76-year-old Swedish physician named Borg. Borg has spent his life furthering his professional career at the expense of remaining psychologically isolated and failing to develop a sense of intimacy even with members of his immediate family. The film is a symbolic journey through Borg's past and shows his growing realization of the unfulfilled aspects of his personality, his determination to change in the years remaining to him, and his acceptance of the faults along with the strengths in his character. (Culver Pictures)

and striving to enhance his feelings of self-esteem and competence. Dr. Borg's generativity in his creative work and raising a family, however, has never included a sense of intimacy. Psychologically, he has remained an isolated fortress all his life ("borg" in Swedish means "fortress").

Dr. Borg must journey to another city to accept an award for his distinguished research and, following a disturbing dream, decides to travel by car instead of flying. He is accompanied on his trip by his daughter-in-law, Marianne, a beautiful young woman about 30 years of age.

In his dream, Borg was taking his morning stroll along strangely deserted streets and stopped by a watchmaker's shop to set his own timepiece, but his watch, as well as the watchmaker's clock, had no hands. Holding his watch to one ear, Borg hears, instead of ticking, the sound of his own heart beating wildly. He then sees a solitary figure, dressed like himself, standing on the sidewalk facing away from him. Upon being tapped on the shoulder by Borg, the figure turns to reveal a face with eyelids and lips tightly closed. The figure collapses and turns into a heap of clothes oozing some liquid. The horrified Borg is then further startled by a horse-drawn hearse, which catches its wheel on a lamp post near him and, after some eerie creaking sounds resembling the cry of a baby, discharges a coffin, which splinters on the ground. From the coffin, a corpse reaches out for the doctor, who sees that it bears his own face.

To Erikson, the solitary figure in the dream represents Borg's own unfeeling, closed-up, anal-retentive personality. The manner in which the coffin appears on the scene suggests the end points of the life cycle itself, starting with the birth cry and stopping with death. The oozing fluid and the clocks without hands symbolize the universal human anxiety regarding when the mysterious biological processes going on inside of us will suddenly quit.

Marianne, Borg's partner on the automobile trip, is pregnant by Borg's son, Evald. The young couple is struggling with the crisis of generativity, both in terms of their forthcoming child and in terms of Evald's efforts to launch a productive career. Marianne has come to Borg for financial help, and Borg is resisting because even at his advanced age, he worries that Evald may not be able to repay the loan.

The journey becomes a symbolic trip through the stages of Borg's life cycle. It reveals a childhood identification with an aloof father (whose watch, an heirloom, has no hands) and a traumatic rejection by his adolescent first love in a strawberry patch near the family's summer house by the sea. It also reveals Borg's withdrawal from the interpersonal intimacy required in his early career as a general practitioner in favor of the relative seclusion of a career as a researcher and his sexual unresponsiveness to his wife, which drove her into extramarital affairs and the breakup of their marriage.

By the end of this journey, and the film, Borg has understood his failure to achieve intimacy in his life, mourned the negative consequences of this character defect but accepted their inevitability, and resolved to become a more complete person in the time remaining to him. The award ceremony itself is an anticlimax which no longer holds any great personal significance for Borg. The real climax to the film is Borg's decision to relieve the financial crisis which threatens to destroy the marriage of Evald and Marianne and to become emotionally involved in the lives of succeeding generations. Borg no longer fears death because of his active participation in a process which transcends his own life.

Empirical studies have also found some support for Erikson's description of the life cycle. For example, a high school sophomore's sense of self-esteem correlates moderately well with educational attainment by the age of 23 (Bachman et al., 1978). Self-esteem is a fairly stable trait which shows moderate to strong positive correlations in repeated measurements taken across a span of two, four, six, or eight years, and the educational attainments associated with high self-esteem are positively correlated with the status of the job which one strives for and attains. Perhaps reflected in these findings is the adolescent search for identity which, if it leads to a positive self-perception, provides a foundation on which subsequent generativity can build. Those with lower educational attainment and lower self-esteem are more likely to engage in interpersonal aggression; more likely to use alcohol, drugs, and cigarettes;

and more likely to be unemployed by the age of 23 than are their better-educated counterparts. While more likely to establish intimacy in adolescence through an early marriage, the less well educated are also more likely to see their marriages fall apart when they are in their 20s (Troll, 1975).

A number of long-term studies of adult personality development have found evidence of an Erikson-type generativity crisis in the years 35 to 40. At this pivotal point of midlife, many people seem to make major decisions regarding the meaningfulness of their commitments to their families and careers. Increased devotion to or a dramatic change in the content of either of these generative outlets is likely to occur during the midlife crisis. We will postpone discussion of these studies until the next section.

Finally, at the last stage in Erikson's life cycle, a contemplative review of the major events in one's life is supposed to bring a sense of purpose out of what, in previous years, seemed like a chaotic jumble of joys and sorrows. This sense of purpose is called *ego integrity* by Erikson, and its attainment prepares the individual to accept death as an event which, like all the events which preceded it, is a necessary and important part of a complete, meaningful life. Using personality scales to measure the extent to which a sample of forty-one elderly males had achieved intimacy, generativity, and ego integrity, Boylin et al. (1976) found that frequency of self-reported reminiscences is positively correlated with ego integrity. Also as Erikson would predict, reminiscing is associated with ego integrity even when the memories evoke negative rather than positive emotional reactions. In a nationwide survey of nearly 1400 persons, Rokeach (1973) asked respondents to rank thirty-six values in order of personal importance. When the participants were grouped by age into those in their twenties, thirties, forties, fifties, sixties, and seventies, it was found that values such as ambition and family security clearly decline in importance with advancing age, while values like a world at peace, a comfortable life, broadmindedness, and salvation become increasingly important.

DISPOSITIONAL PERSPECTIVES ON PERSONALITY DEVELOPMENT IN ADULTHOOD

In general, the European theorists perceive the adult personality as moving away from extraverted, achievement-oriented action and toward introverted, somewhat philosophical contemplativeness with advancing age. This perspective seems most compatible with the disengagement theory of successful aging discussed in the introduction. Thus, personality development appears to parallel the age-related decline in the ability to engage in strenuous physical and mental effort which is discussed below. On the other hand, research has indicated that biological processes may not decline as steadily as some have supposed and that, in any event, there are wide individual variations in biological aging. There are also wide variations in terms of what style of aging is most compatible with an individual's personality. Some people experience great changes in their life-styles at various time periods, while others hold to a more or less steady course. For some, disengagement is most conducive to satisfaction in old age, while others must continue their participation in the mainstream of human activity in order to remain happy.

Before we can discuss research concerning age-related changes in biological functioning and personality processes, a methodological issue must be confronted. Many studies use a large sample of persons at a particular time period and divide the sample into age groups, or *cohorts*, which are then compared with one another on biological or personality dimensions. A major problem with this cross-sectional procedure is that any observed differences between two groups might be a result of aging but might also be due to the fact that the people in the two groups were born in different historical epochs. We know that health care and the availability and quality of education have varied greatly from one decade to another since the turn of the century, and these variations could be the reason for any observed physiological or psychological differences between cohorts. An alternative strategy is the longitudinal study, in which the same group of persons is studied periodically from young adulthood through old age. While this approach handles the problem of cohort differences in past experience, it also introduces new problems. Participants inevitably drop out of longitudinal studies, either because of death or, more usually, because their whereabouts cannot be traced and they have become uninterested in the project. Consequently, the people who remain in a longitudinal study come to represent an increasingly select sample. We may observe changes in their biological and personality functioning over time, but these changes could be due not to aging but to the fact that the sample we are currently studying is not representative of the larger group with which we began. These methodological problems do not invalidate the research to be discussed below, but they do counsel some degree of caution in interpreting its results.

Biology and Aging

Beginning in the decade of the twenties, there are gradual declines in the sensitivity of most people's perceptual systems. In vision, there is a steady progression toward farsightedness (which may actually be beneficial for the nearsighted) and, beginning in the late forties, a reduction in the amount of light which reaches the retina (due to changes in the lens and its focusing system). People may require a third more brightness in order to match the visual acuity they possessed in their twenties and thirties. Hearing shows declines in sensitivity on the order of 10 percent in the higher frequencies from the twenties to the forties. Taste and smell show noticeable reductions in sensitivity somewhat later, especially during the fifties. Muscular coordination and reaction time begin to diminish during the thirties, but the most noticeable declines occur after age 60 (Hunt & Hunt, 1974).

All of the foregoing observations are generalizations based on average tendencies. Individuals show wide variations around these averages, based partly on the types of environmental conditions they have been exposed to in their lives and partly on their inherited biological characteristics. Hearing loss, for example, is accelerated by living in a noisy environment, and the age of onset of respiratory and cardiovascular problems may be advanced by smoking cigarettes. Furthermore, many age-related changes in physiology are so gradual and so small in magnitude that the average person hardly notices them until after the age of 50. Only for trained athletes, who place severe demands on their bodies, will these changes be perceptible at a young age. Finally, declines in sensory acuity and reaction time are often more than compensated for by increases in experience and foresight. Because of their generally greater caution and good judgment, middle-aged automobile drivers and workers suffer fewer accidents and disabling injuries than do their younger counterparts (Hunt & Hunt, 1974).

Among women, there is a sharp decrease during the late forties (the median age being 49) in the production of estrogen, a decrease which is associated with the end of ovulation, menstruation, and the ability to bear children. Sensations of sudden heat coursing through the body (*hot flashes*) are also likely to occur during this time of *menopause*. Mood may become unstable, fluctuating through wide and seemingly unpredictable extremes but often settling on depression. There is also likely to be a thinning of the vaginal lining, which can make sexual intercourse painful. The administration of estrogen, which can alleviate these symptoms, appears to increase the risk of uterine cancer and so is becoming less popular as

a therapeutic intervention. Though the menopause itself may be a difficult time to get through—both physiologically and psychologically—many women feel healthier when it is over because they no longer suffer from the aches and pains associated with menstruation (Olds, 1970). Men do not experience sudden hormonal changes like the menopause and retain the ability to father children until they are in their seventies or eighties. They do, however, undergo a gradual decrease in their rate of testosterone production, which results in decreased fertility and frequency of orgasm and so may cause psychological distress.

Probably the most frequently mentioned personality change attributed to the biological processes associated with aging is a deterioration in mental functioning; specifically, lapses of short-term memory, a decline in tested intelligence, and periods of overall mental confusion.

In the 1920s and 1930s, shortly after the Stanford-Binet intelligence test had been developed, studies were conducted which appeared to demonstrate that IQ reaches a maximum in early adulthood and then declines steadily for the remainder of one's life. These early studies all used the cross-sectional method described at the beginning of this section and so tended to confound the effects of aging with the effects of the different types of environmental experience (e.g., times of war, prosperity, or depression) encountered by people born in different historical periods. *Longitudinal studies*, in which the same individuals are tested repeatedly at successively older ages, have, for the most part, not found an overall decline. Scores on subtests measuring vocabulary, verbal comprehension, and general information actually increase as persons grow older, while scores on other tests show little change until after the age of 60 (Riley et al., 1968). On the other hand, longitudinal studies may underestimate any tendency toward intellectual decline because the less intelligent members of the original cohort are less likely to be available for retesting than are the more intelligent members. In addition, those who remain in the study from beginning to end may become familiar with the testing materials and show improvements in score simply as a result of practice.

Schaie and his associates tried to deal with these problems by combining the two research methods in a single study. In the most complete of these studies, cohorts spaced seven years apart and starting at age 25 (i.e., there were groups 25, 32, 39, 46, 53, 60, 67, 74, and 81 years of age) were first sampled in 1956. Two retests were conducted at seven-year intervals, in 1963 and 1970, to provide longitudinal data for each cohort. In addition, new subjects, drawn from each of the age categories used in 1956, joined the study in 1963 and again in 1970. The overall findings were that differences between cohorts were somewhat larger and more indicative of an age-related decline in mental ability than were differences in the test-retest scores of the same individuals studied longitudinally over a fourteen-year time span. These results suggest that the early cross-sectional studies had, indeed, overestimated the extent of intellectual decline by confounding the effects of aging with those of being born within a particular historical period. Furthermore, the abilities for which *both* cross-sectional and longitudinal data seemed to suggest an age-related decline were those measured by timed tests, in which a quick response is necessary to obtain a high score (Schaie & Labouvie-Vief, 1974). Schaie (1974) concluded that apparent declines in intellectual ability with age are primarily a result of a slowing down of the reflexes and a consequent difficulty with timed tests rather than to a significant loss in reasoning power.

Schaie's conclusions were questioned by Horn and Donaldson (1976), who noted that only a third of the original sample of 490 persons were available for retesting fourteen years later. The possibility that more intelligent people were selectively overrepresented in the retesting, plus the likelihood of improvement on the tasks as a result of repeated exposure, made these critics skeptical of Schaie's dismissal of age-related declines in mental ability as a myth. When all the data from Schaie's study were considered, there appeared to be a clear downward trend in ability, particularly after the age of 50. Baltes and Schaie (1976) replied that some mental abilities might, indeed, deteriorate with age, but not all do. Their data, they said, refuted the myth of a *general* intellectual decline.

Cross-sectional studies have found disturbing tendencies toward a loss of short-term memory and Piagetian abilities (see Chapter 9) among persons past middle age (Inglis et al., 1968; Papalia, 1972). As regards memory loss, Hultsch (1971) reported that the elderly do as well as younger persons in recognizing previously learned material but show evidence of a deficit when asked to retrieve learned material entirely from memory. As regards Piagetian abilities, the evidence indicates a regression among many persons over 65 toward the preoperational thinking characteristic of children under 8 (perceiving that changing the shape of a ball of clay might change the amount of matter it contains, for example).

The foregoing studies used cross-sectional designs and so are vulnerable to cohort effects. Even so, a biological explanation for these and other, comparable findings cannot be ruled out. In laboratory experiments on rats, it has been found that a reduction in the number of nerve cells in the cerebral cortex occurs with advancing age, and this loss of cells has been found to be associated with impairment of short-term memory (Hsu & Peng, 1978; Ordy et al., 1978). In humans, it is known that brain weight declines by about 8 percent between the ages of 30 and 75. Moreover, a loss in the elasticity of the blood vessels (*hardening of the arteries*), plus the partial blockage of some vessels by fat deposits, create circulatory problems in the brain which eventually interfere with the supply of oxygen to nerve cells and increase susceptibility to strokes (Leaf, 1973). It is conceivable that these biological events have a detrimental effect on short-term

While some research suggests that a person's abilities steadily decline with advancing age, other studies have found that this general statement does not apply to either all persons or all abilities. Particularly when allowed to work at their own rate, the elderly can perform well at tasks requiring a high degree of alertness and skill. (*Left:* United Press International Photo; *right:* United Nations/John Isaac)

memory and other mental abilities in humans as well as animals.

It has been argued that there is an absolute natural limit on the length of human life, a limit which is set by the number of times cells are capable of doubling before they become worn out. Hayflick (1980) calculates this number to be fifty and infers that the upper limit of age is 110 years. He therefore doubts the scientific accuracy of reports of persons older than this among the Abkhasians, who were discussed at the outset of this chapter. Longevity is also related to the ability of DNA to repair itself after damage from injury, infection, or other stressors (Sacher, 1978).

Problems with the repair of DNA could be related to the chromosome loss which has been associated with advancing age (Jarvik, 1975). Chromosome loss, in turn, seems to be associated with impairment of mental abilities and increased susceptibility to disease (Bromley, 1974).

The above observations could be related to the phenomenon of _terminal drop_, a sudden decline in a person's IQ score within the five years immediately preceding his or her death (Riegel, 1971; Riegel & Reigel, 1972). Terminal drop is an especially reliable predictor of imminent death among persons younger than 65, including even persons classified as _young adults_. The sudden decline in IQ could be related to a general physiological deterioration, or it could be related to an attitude of hopelessness and depression. Riegel found that those most likely to be experiencing terminal drop were overrepresented among people who refused to be retested in a longitudinal study. Consequently, such studies may, as was suggested earlier, selectively exclude persons showing the greatest intellectual decline. In cross-sectional studies, an increasing number of people experiencing terminal drop with increasing age may be the main cause of age-related declines in ability. That is, those who have not yet experienced terminal drop show little intellectual impairment over time, whereas the increasing proportion of their age-mates who suffer this condition creates a misleading impression of a universal, gradual decline in mental ability with advancing age.

To some extent, the biological clocks which tick away inside of us have a genetic mainspring. Twin studies appear to have demonstrated that longevity is partly an inherited trait (Jarvik et al., 1960). On the other hand, it is also partly related to a person's physical and social environment and to his or her psychological state. In longitudinal studies of aging twins, it was found that if one member of the pair continued regular physical exercise, mental activity, and emotional involvement with the mainstream of life while the other twin did not, the former outlived the latter (Jarvik, 1975,). Jarvik also pointed out that attitudes of hopelessness and depression serve to accelerate intellectual decline, physiological deterioration, and the imminence of death. This observation is reminiscent of our discussion of learned helplessness in Chapter 10.

The present discussion of biological processes in aging may have been more than a little depressing, but old age and death are no less a part of the life cycle than are youth and vigor. To be forewarned of the potential for intellectual and physical decline is to be psychologically forearmed against the possibility of being overwhelmed by these changes.

It is also important to be aware that some persons remain stable in their mental functioning and show a surprising amount of physical stamina even after the age of 80, while others who are younger show precipitous declines. The aging process has an uneven impact on different individuals, and some are more susceptible to its detrimental aspects than others because of biological, environmental, and psychological predisposing factors (Birren, 1968). The phenomenon of terminal drop may be as much a psychological giving up in the face of environmental stress as it is a reflection of changes in one's physiology. Today, the average male life expectancy is 69 years, while for females it is six years longer. Some of this difference is thought to be due to the greater exposure of males to the psychological stress of competitive achievement striving in the work place (Kalish, 1975). It is also due to the fact that men are more likely than women to die early as a result of accident, homicide, and suicide as well as from cardiovascular and respiratory diseases for which environmental causes have been implicated (Riley et al., 1968). The point here is that one's life-style interacts with the biological aspects of aging and can either advance or delay the onset of physical and mental decline.

Personality and Aging

Dispositional theories of personality assume the existence of traits which are characteristic of a person and which endure across time and diverse situations. Theories of attitude structure in social psychology would predict this stability in personality from the assumption that people often adjust their perception of new information about themselves or their environment so as to maintain an overall consistency in self-perceptions and beliefs (see, e.g., Festinger, 1957). The humanistic or phenomenological theorists within the personological tradition (along with Jung and the existentialists in the European tradition) anticipate great changes in the superficial aspects of someone's personality in the event that he or she perceives an incongruity between his or her social self and the "true self" underneath. As we see below, there is evidence for both stability and sudden change in the adult personality.

The case for personality stability In the course of his longitudinal studies on aging and changes in mental abilities, Schaie also examined the stability of personality traits, using Cattell's 16 Personality Factor Questionnaire (see Chapter 6). While some traits appeared to be affected by sociocultural changes occurring at various stages in the lifetimes of different generations, the overall impression conveyed by the data was one of long-term stability in personality (Schaie & Parham, 1976). In research discussed earlier in this chapter, Bachman et al. (1978) observed considerable stability in the self-concept, value orientations, and behavior patterns of young men as they progressed from adolescence through early adulthood. As was noted in Chapter 1, Block observed a similar stability in personality from junior high school to adulthood and concluded that "the unity or consistency of personality is compellingly apparent in these data and is manifest in so many and so diverse ways as perhaps to establish the unity principle once and for all" (Block, 1971, p. 268).

People seem to adopt the particular styles of aging most consistent with the central characteristics of their adult personalities. A large-scale study of 159 men and women between 50 and 90 years of age was conducted over a six-year period in Kansas City, beginning in 1956. It identified eight major personality types and the patterns associated with them (Neugarten, Havighurst, & Tobin, 1968). The first four patterns were associated with a high degree of life satisfaction for the persons who chose them.

1 The *reorganizers* are very busy people who continually substitute new activities for those which have become difficult (e.g., shuffleboard for tennis).

One style of aging which seems to produce a reasonably high degree of life satisfaction is called "successful disengagement." The elderly persons who adopt this style seem content to withdraw from activities and social commitments and to look out at the world from their rocking chairs. (Max and Kit Hunn/Photo Researchers)

2 The *focused* are moderately active but concentrate on one or two things in which they are particularly interested.

3 The *successful disengaged* take the opposite approach, content to withdraw from activities and social commitments and look out at the world from their rocking chairs, so to speak.

4 The *holding-on* maintain, as long as possible, the behavior patterns and social relationships of middle age, including a strong achievement orientation and a scheduled life.

5 The *constricted* are similar to the focused, but their limited activities are primarily a distraction from thinking about growing old and

offer only a moderate amount of meaning and satisfaction.

6 The *succorance seeking* succeed in inducing others to provide them with emotional and material support and so maintain a medium level of social involvement and a moderate amount of life satisfaction.

7 The *apathetic* seem to care little about what happens to them and are relatively low on self-initiated activity.

8 The *unintegrated* show clear symptoms of mental disorganization and loss of emotional control and are barely able to maintain themselves in the community at a low level of life satisfaction.

Reichard et al. (1962) identified a smaller but similar-sounding number of life-styles among eighty-seven men aged 55 to 84. They did include two categories not on Neugarten et al.'s list, however: the angry and the self-haters. These men blamed others for causing them to fail to achieve their goals and were especially hostile toward the young. Some turned their hostility inward and were extremely cynical, bitter, and depressed.

The failure of one's life-style to provide satisfaction is stressful for anyone and especially for the aged, who are likely to perceive their alternatives to be rather limited. Life changes like the death of a spouse or close relatives and friends, or the necessity of moving from one living situation to another, may be especially detrimental to the physical and mental health of older persons (Lawton, 1974). One reaction to such stresses may be the emergence of neurotic or psychotic symptoms, especially severe depression (Savage et al., 1977, p. 33). The majority of new cases of psychopathology diagnosed within any given year consists of persons aged 65 and older. There is an implication in this finding that stability—both within oneself and within one's environment—strengthens the individual's capacity to withstand the shocks that one inevitably encounters while traveling through the life cycle.

The case for personality change In an eloquent paragraph, a popularizer of psychological literature on personality development in adulthood has described the feelings likely to accompany significant change.

It is frightening to step off onto the treacherous footbridge leading to the second half of life. We can't take everything with us on this journey through uncertainty . . . There is grieving to be done because an old self is dying. By taking in our suppressed and even unwanted parts, we prepare at the gut level for the reintegration of an identity that is ours and ours alone—not some artificial form put together to please the culture or our mates. It is a dark passage at the beginning. But by disassembling ourselves, we can glimpse the light and gather our parts into a renewal. (Sheehy, 1977, p. 44)

In the early 1930s, an Austrian clinical psychologist named Charlotte Bühler outlined five stages of personality development, three of which spanned the years of adulthood. Her theory provided inspiration for Erikson's original conception of the life cycle. Bühler updated her outline in the 1960s after she had emigrated to the United States (Bühler, 1968). Since this pioneering work, there have been several other efforts to identify the crisis points in adult personality development.

One such effort is called the *Grant study*, after a philanthropist who, in 1938, donated funds to Harvard University for the purpose of conducting longitudinal research on the lives of a socioeconomically privileged group of male college graduates. A sample of 268 men was drawn from the Harvard classes of 1942, 1943, and 1944, interviewed, given a battery of personality tests, and periodically reinterviewed at various times extending to the present day. When the men were around 50 years old, the psychiatrist who had inherited the role of project director decided to identify the thirty best and thirty worst outcomes in terms of life satisfaction from among ninety-five cases which had received particularly close scrutiny over the years (Vaillant, 1977).

It turned out that when evaluated as college undergraduates, none of the "best outcomes" had their personality integration placed in the bottom fifth of the sample by the original investigators. A stable marriage had been achieved by 93 percent of the "best outcomes" before the age of 30 but not before the age of 23, and they were still married at the age of 50. By contrast, 37 percent of the "worst outcomes" had failed to marry by age 30, and most who had married were divorced by the age of 50. None of the "best outcomes," but 40 percent of the "worst outcomes," were perceived by Vaillant to be dominated by their mothers as adults. The majority of the "worst outcomes" could count few friends at the age of 50, and nearly all held jobs with little supervisory responsibility. As for life crises, the men seemed to focus on establishing intimacy while they were in their twenties, usually through marriage and family but also through close friendships.

Vaillant regards the emotional disorders to which young adults are particularly susceptible (schizophrenia, mania, impulsive delinquency, suicide) as reactions to a failure to attain intimacy. In the decade of the thirties, concerns with achieving success in one's career supersede and may even begin to erode the intimacy established in the twenties. Often this career orientation is facilitated by an older person, a master craftsman of the trade, who introduces the young aspirant to the ins and outs of his chosen field; Vaillant calls this person the *mentor*. After 40, however, the aspirant has consolidated his status as a member of his profession, and the mentor is no longer needed.

It was at this stage that the men in the Grant study began asking themselves about the meaning of all the hustle and bustle of the preceding two decades. This is the midlife crisis, and the soul searching which accompanies it may result in the abandonment of a marriage perceived as unfulfilling or a change in one's career toward something which permits more self-expression or which is perceived as contributing more to the public good. The capacity to play—to indulge childhood fantasies of recreation or adventure which may have been suppressed during the thirties—is likely to reemerge after age 40. The "best outcomes" in Vaillant's sample viewed the ages 35 to 40 as their happiest and 21 to 35 as their unhappiest. The "worst outcomes," who had failed to achieve satisfaction with their lives by age 50, yearned nostalgically for the years of early adulthood, before they were required to cope with the crises discussed above.

Vaillant's theoretical assumption is that each stage of adult development requires the temporary suppression of certain aspects of one's personality so that others can be actualized. In the twenties, one's career gets off to a slow start as intimacy is established. In the 30s, intimacy and playfulness are suppressed as one's career is consolidated. Psychological defenses are erected against the motives suppressed at any particular time, but these defenses weaken as the dominant motives are satisfied. The result is a series of transition points, where several seemingly incompatible motives are in one's mind simultaneously. The conflict and stress this generates are reduced by making a choice which again suppresses some motives to allow the expression of others. The good news in all this is that after the age of 40, it seems psychologically possible to actualize several motives at once and to attain a more healthy, less neurotic personality.

Bühler, too, made the drive toward self-fulfillment a cornerstone of her stage theory of personality, and studies similar to Vaillant's have found evidence of similar times of crisis in adult personality development (Gould, 1972; Levinson, et al., 1974).

Women and racial minorities are greatly underrepresented in these studies, in which the bulk of the participants are socioeconomically advantaged white males. This naturally limits the extent to which the researchers' conclusions can be generalized. Sheehy (1977) attempted to extend the notion of life crisis to female personality development and argued, for example, that the midlife crisis occurs about five years sooner in women than in men. For women, the most powerful conflicting motives are likely to be childrearing and pursuit of a career.

BEHAVIORAL PERSPECTIVES ON PERSONALITY CHANGE IN ADULTHOOD

Behavioral psychologists prefer to search for the causes of personality change in forces influencing the person from the outside rather than in biological processes or the action of repressed motives. If we wish to understand the psychology of the aged, a social-learning theorist might say, we must examine the expectations society holds for the behavior of the elderly and the rewarding or punishing consequences of major events in their lives. Through vicarious learning or direct reinforcement, these experiences may shape the perceptions that old people have of themselves and channel their behavior accordingly.

Young adults and the middle-aged express more feelings of dislike for the life circumstances commonly associated with old age (poor health, financial insecurity, social isolation, and old age itself) than do elderly persons (Collette-Pratt, 1976). Adolescents and adults aged 35 to 40 also overestimate the degree of psychological dependence among the elderly. They perceive older persons as placing a lower value on autonomy and achievement and a higher value on nurturance than they actually do (Ahammer & Baltes, 1972; Labouvie-Vief & Baltes, 1976). College students and adults tend to regard themselves as more intellectually astute than older persons; when explaining the rules of a game to an elderly person, the students use simpler, shorter sentences than they use with peers or middle-aged adults (Rubin & Brown, 1975).

To the extent that old persons learn the negative expectations attached to their social roles, they may act them out and so appear less competent than they actually are. If mental ability appears to decline with age, therefore, it could be because the elderly have learned to hold their abilities in low esteem and so may show a deterioration of performance due to anxiety over being tested (Carey, 1958; Schaie & Gribbin, 1975). Furthermore, older persons are somewhat more cautious in their decision making, either because they have learned to doubt their ability to make wise choices or because experience has taught them to "look before they leap" (Botwinnick, 1978, Chaps. 8 & 9). If two persons are equal in mental ability but differ in cautiousness, it will be the cautious one who scores lower on a timed test. Thus the trait of <u>cautiousness could cause old people to appear less able</u> than they actually are. When the elderly are allowed as much time as they need to complete a test, their performances show a significant improvement over their performances under timed conditions (Bromley, 1974; Horn & Cattell, 1966).

If older persons feel less competent and less successful in controlling their lives, this may bring about the motivational deficit called *learned helplessness* in Chapter 10. Such a decline in motivation could cause the elderly to score low on tests of mental ability and to reduce their levels of activity in areas of their lives in which they do have a considerable degree of potential control. The result can be apathy, social isolation, and an acceleration of mental and physical decline.

In one study, the administrator of a highly rated nursing home gave a talk to ninety-one ambulatory patients (aged 65 to 90) housed on two separate floors. For the patients on one floor, the talk emphasized the control patients had over the arrangement of furniture, social activities, the scheduling of entertainment, and so forth; at the end of the talk, each was given the opportunity to select a small plant which he or she might care for. For those on the other floor, the talk emphasized the concern the staff had for the patients' welfare, as manifested in the furnishings, social acitivities, and entertainment that the staff had selected for them; at the end of the talk, each patient was presented with a plant and

Some nursing homes develop a custodial atmosphere in which the elderly become increasingly dependent and passive as time goes by (*left*). Other homes, however, encourage the elderly to remain socially active and to develop new skills (*right*). Research indicates that inhabitants of the latter type of home are happier and more likely to live longer than those of the former. (*Left:* United Nations/G. Palmer; *right:* Miriam Reinhart/Photo Researchers)

told that the staff would water and care for it. These messages might be summarized by saying that in the former, responsibility-inducing treatment, the emphasis was on "what you can do for yourself," while in the latter, comparison treatment, the emphasis was on "what we can do for you." It was found that the people hearing the responsibility-inducing message became happier and more socially active over the next three weeks. They were also rated as more alert and "improved" by interviewers and the nursing staff (Langer & Rodin, 1976). In a follow-up study, these changes were found to have persisted for eighteen months. Especially dramatic was the finding that while seven of the forty-seven persons (i.e., 15 percent) exposed to the responsibility-inducing treatment had died during this 18-month period, thirteen of the forty-four persons (30 percent) in the comparison group had died (Rodin & Langer, 1977).

Because the facilities of many nursing homes and other institutions for the elderly fall far short of those in the excellent home in which Rodin and Langer conducted their study, serious attention must be paid to the effects of institutionalization on physical and mental health (Kosberg, 1973). In the care of the aged, as in the treatment of those designated mentally ill, behavioral psychologists have advocated de-institutionalization wherever feasible (see Chapter 8 for a fuller discussion of this issue). Siegel and Lasker (1978) found that forty-four of sixty-one elderly persons discharged from a rest home after receiving training in social-interaction skills were able to maintain themselves more or less independently in the community over a follow-up period of several months. The fact that most of these patients had been diagnosed as suffering from organic brain disorder suggested to the investigators that emotional disturbance—depression, in particular—may, in many cases, be the true cause of symptoms that appear to have a biological basis. Some have argued that even when organic pathology exists, physical and social isolation cause changes in mental and emotional status which aggravate the biologically based symptoms. For the organically as well as for the emotionally afflicted, then, treatment which counteracts isolation should produce an alleviation of symptoms (Ernst et al., 1978).

Behavioral psychologists would clearly endorse the activity theory over the disengagement theory of successful aging and agree with such statements as "You're as old as you feel." Old persons who are actively involved in the mainstream of social life have been shown, in several studies, to have higher morale than those who have become disengaged. "Morale" was defined, in these studies, as an absence of regret over missed opportunities and feelings of present happiness and optimism for the future (Lipman & Smith, 1968). A personal commitment to maintain one's activities has been found to be positively correlated with self-ratings of happiness, health, and pleasure derived from family and social relationships among persons over 65, while reduced activities were associated with decreased life satisfaction (Palmore, 1968; Schonfield, 1973). In addition, older persons who remain active are viewed more favorably by both peers and younger persons than are those who become disengaged (Sherman et al., 1978).

Some studies do not show strong relationships between social activity and life satisfaction, and others report that physical as well as mental health are more positively correlated with the continuation of *cognitive* than of recreational activities among the elderly (DeCarlo, 1974; Lemon et al., 1972). The weight of the evidence, however, provides more support for the activity theory than for the disengagement theory of successful aging. Even when the aged isolate themselves in retirement communities, the result may not be a withdrawal from the affairs of the wider world but a concentration of forces for the purposes of political activism and "senior power" (Anderson & Anderson, 1978). Elderly people who take action to cope with stressful life events have a more positive self-concept and are happier with their lives than those who respond passively to such events (Gutmann, 1978). Disengagement, when it occurs, may be an act of psychological self-preservation in response to repeated life stresses in the areas of interpersonal relations, finances, or health rather than the inevitable result of aging itself (Tallmer & Kutner, 1969). In several of the foregoing studies, it was noted that the affluent elderly are more likely to remain actively involved with life than are the less financially secure.

As was mentioned earlier, life stress and a failure to initiate effective coping or other cognitive activity may contribute to mental deterioration in older persons (Amster & Krauss, 1974; Jarvik, 1975). Life stresses and physical inactivity may undermine health and jeopardize one's capacity for independent living (Bassey, 1978; Lawton, 1974).

Because of their physiological orientation, medical doctors may be inclined to attribute poor task performance, depression, or even the routine physical complaints of the elderly to some internal disease or other biological malfunction rather than to possible environmental causes. The physician might then prescribe a drug rather than recommend changes in social activities, diet, or exercise which might actually be more effective in combating the patient's problems. This process can all too easily become a vicious circle because most drugs disturb the normal functioning of the autonomic nervous system and produce side effects which, in turn, may be mistakenly attributed to the aging process (Mouat, 1978). Physicians must take care in diagnosing the symptoms of older persons and, in particular, avoid the blanket assumption that all such symptoms have an organic basis (Gfeller, 1978).

Behavioral psychologists can also offer their own explanation for the life crises which dispositional theorists have associated with different stages of personality development in adulthood. The environmentalist position is that the way in which we perceive ourselves and the course of action we "ought" to pursue depends upon the rewards or punishments we receive for our immediate behavior and the consequences we antici-

The stages and transition points which have been observed in the adult life cycle may be caused by age-related changes in social expectations for behavior. After a period of adolescent rebelliousness, people in their twenties are expected to search for a stable, intimate relationship. This typically means entering marriage and beginning a family. (David Strickler/Monkmeyer)

pate for the same or different behavior in the future. Over a seven-week period, college students' favorable or unfavorable perceptions of their own personalities were found to fluctuate depending on the pleasant or unpleasant consequences of important events in their lives (Allen & Potkay, 1977). If people tend to search for intimacy when they are in their twenties, it is because that is what society expects them to do and rewards them for doing. If there is a conflict at age 30 between intimacy-oriented and career-oriented behavior, it is because the social or material rewards offered for the latter are, at that time of life, roughly equivalent to those offered for the former. A resolution of this approach-approach conflict in favor of career-oriented be-

havior means that the rewards anticipated for such a course were, ultimately, more powerful incentives for the individual. The "mentor" who often appears on the scene at this time would be regarded by a social-learning theorist as a role model who communicated, through vicarious learning, the rewarding consequences of a career orientation. The crises in later stages of adult development would be explained in analogous terms.

Behaviorally oriented psychologists might also note that the sorts of crises faced by succeeding generations are likely to be influenced by environmental factors such as changes in social values and customs. One study found that people 65 or older today, when recalling themselves at age 20, made self-ratings of their likelihood of engaging in self-disclosure, physical contact, and overall social interaction which were consistently lower than comparable self-ratings made by contemporary 20-year-olds (Rands & Levinger, 1979). Forty years from now, the youth exposed to contemporary values of self-expression and openness will probably be very different from today's elderly.

CONCLUSION

At the age of 56, Leonardo da Vinci painted the *Mona Lisa*, and at 57 Handel composed his *Messiah*. College presidents and Presidents of the United States are customarily in their fifties or older, members of Congress in their sixties, Supreme Court Justices in their seventies, and Popes in their eighties (Lehman, 1953). What conclusion can be drawn from observations like these? That "you're as old as you feel" or "life begins at 80"? Well, yes, and at the same time, no. There is abundant evidence that life stress, negative self-perceptions, and an attitude of giving up and disengagement from the wider social world are likely to produce symptoms of psychological disturbance at any age and contribute to unsuccessful aging. At the same time, it would be foolish to view the aging process as a purely psychological phenomenon. Physiological change takes place in all persons and, to a greater or lesser extent, affects their physical and mental functioning as well as their perceptions of themselves. As has been repeatedly mentioned in many contexts in this book, what we observe as personality develops during middle and late adulthood through an interaction of person variables with situation variables.

In our own culture, couples are most likely to have children during the years when biological fertility coincides with a stable relationship and financial independence—the twenties to the mid-thirties. Having children changes the parents' perceptions of themselves and the expectations others hold for their behavior. Children grow up, which is in large part a biological process, and leave home. This makes a profound change in the parents' physical and social environment. Meanwhile, the parents have noticed certain biologically based changes in their bodies which remind them that life is finite and that they, too, are mortal. This change in self-perception is accompanied by changes in social expectations regarding their behavior, first, as middle-aged persons and, later, as senior citizens. In this abbreviated description of the adult life span, one sees the extent to which biology, situational events, social expectations, and self-perceptions interact with one another to influence personality development.

The most optimistic view of the aging process is that it does not consist of a universal gradual decline in abilities, but, instead, reflects the increasing likelihood that an individual will drop from a plateau of ability reached in the mid-thirties. Those who drop from the plateau early may have taken inadequate precautions to guard their health through diet and exercise, may have experienced environmental stresses which fostered a pessimistic outlook on life and a willingness to give up, may have succumbed to disease through misfortune or biological susceptibility, or may be genetically disposed to pass through the aging process more rapidly than others. Those who remain at the plateau until very late in life may be resistant to the entire aging process, may have dispositional strengths in one area which counterbalance weaknesses in another, or may have learned how to acquire strengths or at least how to avoid exposing their weaknesses. For instance, extremely careful attention to one's diet and one's exposure to social or environmental stress may, to some extent, compensate for a biological susceptibility to disease. It is even conceivable that becoming more positive in one's self-perceptions or outlook on life can cause beneficial changes in one's physiology.

There are indications that people maintain a fair amount of stability in their personality traits as they pass through the stages and crises of adult development and that these traits may be carried forward into a preferred style for coping with the onset of old age. Most of the styles which appear to promote life satisfaction, or *successful aging,* are those which involve the maintenance of social relationships with family and friends as well as work, hobbies, or other interests. This support for activity theory notwithstanding, it appears that there are some persons for whom withdrawal from a busy schedule and the stresses of life's mainstream is most conducive to satisfaction. The latter types provide support for disengagement theory.

Ultimately, no matter how much activity is pursued and no matter how fortunate one is in prolonging one's time on the plateau of ability, one must face the prospect of decline. Changing our expectations or our perceptions of old age cannot stop the biological clock. Regardless of one's past personality or the conditions of one's present existence, each of us, to some extent, becomes a philosopher when asked to think about this stark reality. Toward the end of a normal life span, there is plenty of time to deliberate the existential issues described by Jung and Erikson. Perhaps the elderly reminisce because they have learned that this behavior is expected of them, but to call their soul-searching a conditioned *behavior* is to understate its significance. Here it is the European theorists who seem (to me, anyway) to be closest to the truth when they explain this introspection as an effort to interpret the meaning of one's life and attain self-realization, ego integrity, or some feeling of self-acceptance and psychological calm.

In any event, with the end of the human life cycle we arrive also at the end of this book on personality. I hope that Chapter 14, along with the others which precede it, succeeds in conveying my main message, which is that the study of human personality can be meaningfully approached from a variety of theoretical viewpoints and using a variety of methods of assessment and research. Each of these approaches contributes its own insights and information, and none can be said to be in possession of the whole truth. Sometimes there is a direct contradiction between the propositions advanced or the types of evidence presented by different theorists. Despite such contradictions and the tremendous practical problems one encounters in conducting research on something as complex as human personality, our knowledge of this subject is enhanced rather than diminished by giving due consideration to all approaches and striving toward a unified view.

SUMMARY

1 In trying to account for the exceptional longevity of the Abkhasians, one must consider diet, heredity, and social expectations for the abilities of the elderly as possible contributing factors. Gerontologists have debated the relative merits of two alternative life-styles ("activity" v. "disengagement") in terms of their capacity to promote life satisfaction, or *successful aging.*

2 Jung believed there are stages of adult personality development, including a period of midlife transition and a time after age 60 when people look inside themselves for personality characteristics they have repressed during their lifetimes. This process of self-realization is often assisted by a "spiritual guide." In Erikson's stages of personality development, the search for intimacy which characterizes

late adolescence and early adulthood is followed by a stage at which the adult must decide whether or not to pursue *generativity*, in the sense of contributing to the lives of future generations through raising a family or through doing some productive work. At the last stage, which is associated with old age, the individual becomes past- rather than future-oriented as she or he reviews her or his life cycle in order to appreciate the significance of its pain and failure along with its joy and success. Completion of this review provides a sense of ego integrity and an acceptance of one's own mortality. Erikson illustrates the issues raised at various stages of the life cycle by referring to the film *Wild Strawberries*, directed by Ingmar Bergman.

3 Research concerning age-related changes in biological functioning and personality processes has adopted one of two basic designs. The *cross-sectional design* takes a large sample of persons at a single point in time and divides it into age groups. The problem with this design is that the members of different age groups, or *cohorts*, were born at different historical periods, and the effects of aging can be confounded with the differences between cohorts which are due to the different social and physical environments to which they were exposed as children and young adults. The *longitudinal design* follows the same group of persons from young adulthood through old age. This eliminates the cohort problem, but many people drop out of the original group of participants as a longitudinal study wears on. Here, the effects of aging can be confounded with the tendency for the sample to become an increasingly select group of people over time or for repeated measurement of the same individuals to have some sequential effect on the characteristics being assessed.

4 Speaking in general terms, visual perception, hearing, taste and smell, muscular coordination, and reaction time all begin a gradual decline following the decade of the twenties. This decline becomes most noticeable after the age of 60. There is wide individual variation around this average tendency, however, and many people will not show evidence of much decline in these abilities until relatively late in life. Decreases in the production of sex hormones in the decade of the 40s bring about the female menopause and, in males, a decreased fertility and frequency of orgasm. Many studies using cross-sectional designs have suggested that mental ability and short-term memory decline with age, partly because of such biological changes as the progressive loss of nerve cells from the brain. Longitudinal studies have tended to refute this evidence of a universal gradual decline. Instead, it appears that some persons may remain on a plateau of ability they attained during their thirties over a long period extending even to their sixties and beyond. The increasing proportion of persons who have dropped from this plateau in older age groups produces what may be a false impression of universal decline. Among those persons showing sudden declines in mental ability, death is likely to occur within five years (the phenomenon of *terminal drop*).

5 There is evidence which indicates that personality traits remain fairly stable from adolescence through adulthood and into old age. The style of aging that a person selects (e.g., "active" v. "disengaged") seems to be an outgrowth of traits which have been characteristic of that person throughout his or her adulthood. The failure of a style of aging to produce life satisfaction is likely to be stressful to the person and to produce symptoms of psychopathology.

6 There is also evidence which indicates that personality may undergo abrupt changes in adulthood as the individual is confronted with age-related developmental crises. Career goals are often suppressed in the twenties as a person seeks to establish intimacy, while in the thirties, it may be intimacy which is suppressed as the individual seeks to establish a secure position in his or her career. When the midlife crisis occurs at around the age of 40, the person asks himself or herself what important aspects of identity may have been sacrificed in the search for intimacy and security and what might be done in the years ahead to actualize all aspects of his or her self simultaneously.

7 From the behavioral viewpoint, the main causes of personality change in adulthood are changes in the environmental contingencies to which people are exposed. If people are expected to raise families in their twenties and receive social approval for doing so, they are likely to engage in this behavior. If, in the decade of the thirties the contingencies change so that a person receives and anticipates greater rewards for a career than for a family orientation, then his or her self-perceptions and behavior patterns are likely to change accordingly. If society negatively evaluates the abilities and personality characteristics of the elderly, and if these negative evaluations are learned and accepted by the latter, the aged are likely to have low self-esteem and behave in ways to fulfill the prophecy of progressively decreasing competence. Older persons who remain active or who have been induced to perceive that they have personal control over their lives display higher morale and greater social competence than do those who become inactive or have not been induced to perceive that major events in their lives are, in fact, under their control. A failure to cope effectively with life stresses may undermine health and contribute to mental deterioration in older persons, and a reduction in stress or the initiation of effective coping may alleviate these symptoms.

TERMS TO KNOW

gerontology

disengagement theory

activity theory

self-realization

ego integrity

longitudinal studies

terminal drop

styles of aging

life crises

EPILOGUE: FURTHER THOUGHTS ON THE PERSONALITY OF ERNEST HEMINGWAY

In the introduction to Unit One, we considered the diverse interpretations which might be made of Ernest Hemingway's biography by psychologists having different theoretical orientations toward the study of personality. At the end of the introduction it was asked whether each of these approaches might provide us with its own unique and valuable insights into the character of Hemingway, a man widely regarded as the greatest novelist of the twentieth century. Now that you have arrived at the end of this textbook in personality psychology and are better informed about the promises and problems of the field, let us take another look at Ernest Hemingway and the "person" and "situation" variables which appear to have motivated him.

The most detailed and authoritative biography of Hemingway noted that the facts of his life clearly revealed long-term continuities in his character development:

To a remarkable degree, the child was father to the man: many traits of Ernest's boyish character held on with only slight modifications well into his adult life. "Afraid of nothing"—the maxim he had first uttered at the age of three—was an ideal of behavior in the face of adversity long after he had discovered that many things and events might legitimately arouse fear. All his life he sought scrupulously to uphold the code of physical courage and endurance which his father, and sometimes his mother, had early impressed upon him. The love of nature, of hunting and fishing, of the freedom to be found in the woods or on the water, stayed solidly with him to the end of his life. . . . Like his father he was never able to carry a tune quite on key, nor was he ever to be so fully at home in the realms of music as his mother would have wished. But he soon moved far past her in the judgment and appreciation of the graphic arts, particularly oil painting, while the impulse to creativity, which he clearly owed to her both by inheritance and youthful training, took directions in his own life that she could neither understand nor approve.

. . . He shared his father's determination to do things "properly" (a favorite adverb in both their vocabularies), whether building a fire, rigging a rod, baiting a hook, casting a fly, handling a gun, or roasting a duck or a haunch of venison. . . . In later life he shared the tendency of both his parents to take on weight, and it may even be that the luxuriant beards he grew in adulthood were motivated partly by the fact that he had never known his father to be without one. (Baker, 1969, pp. 16–17)

Despite our interest in such facts, the real issue we must consider, as students of personality, is not whether Hemingway's (or anyone else's) life showed evidence of continuity or discontinuity but *why* a particular individual's life followed the course that it did.

Those who lean toward a psychoanalytic viewpoint would no doubt be most impressed by events in Ernest's childhood suggestive of the Oedipal crisis. Grace Hemingway wrote in her diary that, at the age of 5, "My darling boy was *so* delighted when he came into my bed one morning . . . and I told him the happy secret that God was going to give us another little baby." A few months later, Grace's father died, and the family moved from his house, where they had lived since before Ernest was born, to a spacious new dwelling in Oak Park. Many years later, Ernest could still vividly recall a curious detail of this transition—the disposal of his grandfather's snake collection: "Many things that were not to be moved were burned in the back-yard and I remember those jars from the attic being thrown in the fire, and how they popped in the heat and the fire flamed up from the alcohol. I remember the snakes burning in the fire in the back-yard." Was young Ernest sexually attracted to his mother? Did he resent his father as a rival with whose personality he nonetheless identified because of a fear of castration? The fact that Dr. Hemingway maintained an office in the home which contained jars of pickled human organs, a skeleton, and stuffed and mounted animals could have reinforced any castration anxieties lurking in his son's vivid imagination. So could the doctor's choice of a razor strap as the preferred device for administering punishment (see Baker, 1969, pp. 6–7).

Ernest Hemingway had a lifelong fear of snakes, a pronounced insecurity in the face of any real or imagined challenge to his masculinity and sexual potency, and a fascination with and fear of death. Though the latter trait was evident in his character long before his father's suicide, this traumatic event served to intensify it. Ernest had always perceived his father to be excessively dominated by his mother, exploited to the point of doing the cooking and housework (when the hired help resigned, as they frequently did) while at the same time working to provide the family income. Ernest despised these signs of "weakness" in his father's character and blamed his mother for having driven her husband to suicide.

Pulling together all these threads of evidence, a psychoanalytic interpretation of Hemingway's character might be that he suffered from an incomplete resolution of the Oedipus complex. Superficially, he might appear to be a perfect example of the recklessly aggressive phallic character, but the extremity of his behavior suggests that he was also motivated by a reaction formation against the feminine aspects of his personality. As Jung would put it, the more the animus is expressed in a man's persona, the stronger his repressed anima must be. Adler would use a

c (Springer/Bettmann Film Archive)

a (Mary Hemingway)

b (Mary Hemingway)

Scenes from the life of Ernest Hemingway: (a) The first three Hemingway children, with Ernest in the center, are held by their parents for a family portrait. Ernest, an active 4-year-old when this photo was taken in 1903, insisted he was "'fraid 'a nothin'." (b) Ernest began doing some serious fishing at the age of 5, using a basket to hold his catch that could almost have held him as well. (c) Ernest's early interests in fishing and other activities stayed with him his entire life. Here, he poses with an 800-pound swordfish caught during the filming of his famous novel *The Old Man and the Sea*. (d) Finally, Hemingway's stamina deteriorated under the strain of various physical ailments, psychological stresses, and the onset of old age. Partly because he could not accept his progressively increasing debilitation, he chose to commit suicide on July 2, 1961.

d (The Bettmann Archive, Inc.)

different terminology, noting that Hemingway must have had strong feelings of inferiority arising from social insecurities, genuine or imaginary physical defects, or his status as a second-born child who throughout his school years was always coming along behind an older sister. As a way of dealing with these inferiority feelings, Hemingway developed an overcompensatory superiority complex. For Freud, a key factor in Hemingway's personality would be the failure of the ego fully to redirect the death instinct outward from the self, leading to a lifetime tendency toward masochistic self-destructiveness—a typically "feminine" personality trait. For Erikson, on the other hand, Hemingway's aggressiveness and ultimate suicide might be viewed as the products of a failure to establish genuine intimacy in young adulthood. Hemingway was married four times, was reputed (by himself as well as others) to have had numerous affairs, and never seemed to know what it was he was seeking in a female partner. Like Dr. Borg in *Wild Strawberries*, he was vulnerable to despair in later life as a result of his unsuccessful passage through an earlier psychosocial crisis point.

What about the trait-dispositional viewpoint of American personology? Can it shed any additional light on the psychology of Ernest Hemingway? Obviously, Baker's comment that "the child was father to the man" is consistent with trait theory. Allport would say that the behavior patterns and interests established early in life by parental encouragement later became functionally autonomous motives which caused Hemingway to set goals for himself—for example, his love of hunting and good art—which were pursued for their own sake. Murray would add that the needs peculiar to Hemingway's personality caused his life to show certain thematic dispositions as he sought out the kinds of activities and acquaintances which would permit his needs to be expressed. Foremost among Hemingway's needs would presumably have been those in the ascendance cluster (n-Aggression, n-Dominance, n-Exhibition) and those relating to sensual expression (n-Exhibition, n-Play, n-Sentience, n-Sex). One suspects, too, that Dr. and Mrs. Hemingway did not socialize their son in a way that provided him with a secure sense of self-esteem. Though he became skillful at many tasks, Ernest, even after he achieved fame as a novelist, acted like a man who was very unsure of himself and especially of others' affection for him. This may have been due to his lasting uncertainties regarding the depth of his parents' love for him and the ambivalence of his feelings toward them. As for his moral development, the heavy reliance on physical punishment and the enforcement of inflexible religious standards by Papa and Grace Hemingway could be expected to hold their offspring's moral reasoning at the "dog eat dog" stages 1 and 2 of Kohlberg's scale. In general, Hemingway does appear to have operated at this level for most of his life and to have upheld it as an ideal in his novels.

The personological tradition has a biological side, too, as has often been noted in this book. Hemingway's love of action and physical combat could possibly be a characteristic which to some degree was inherited from his similarly disposed father. Extraversion and aggressiveness, in other words, are traits which show some evidence of heritability, as do depressive disorders and tendencies toward emotional instability. Grace Hemingway was very unstable emotionally and frequently lapsed into fits of depression. In addition, one must consider the possibility that physical damage to Hemingway's brain from frequent injuries and excessive drinking could have had disruptive effects on his personality which stimulated hyperaggressiveness and depression. Particularly during the 1950s, such factors could have contributed to his increasing difficulties with his private and professional lives and the final, severe bout of depression which ended in suicide.

What insights can humanistic psychology contribute to our understanding of Ernest Hemingway? Was he a self-actualized person? I think we would have to say that he was not. According to

Maslow's hierarchy of needs, Hemingway's unsatisfied longings for security, love, and esteem held him back from self-actualization, though he certainly seems to have been responsive to peak experiences in developing his talents as a writer. Hemingway also appears to have had difficulty trusting others and disclosing his true feelings to them. He concealed his core of identity behind a facade of exaggerated masculinity. Rogers would perceive these aspects of Hemingway's character to have posed serious obstacles to his self-actualization. On a less humanistic and more existential level, it must be acknowledged that Hemingway did have a philosophy of life which incorporated the idea that each individual is ultimately responsible for the choices that he or she makes. This philosophy was stated many times in Hemingway's books, a notable example being *For Whom the Bell Tolls*. The hero of this novel is Robert Jordan, an American scholar fighting on the side of the Republicans in the Spanish Civil War and a character clearly patterned after Hemingway himself. Jordan even has a cowardly father who was bullied by a domineering wife and who shot himself to death with a treasured antique revolver. At the end of the novel, a wounded Jordan chooses to commit suicide indirectly as he prepares for single-handed combat with a force of Fascist troops in an obviously hopeless situation.

Last, but by no means least, we can examine Hemingway's personality from the standpoint of behavioral psychology and social learning theory. Some relevant theorists here would be Dollard and Miller, Skinner, and Bandura and Walters. They might note that, as a child, Ernest received numerous rewards for behaving in an exhibitionistic manner. The family carefully documented the parties hosted by the Hemingway children for their schoolmates, the plays and pageants in which they participated, and the honors they received. Grace Hemingway provided a model for self-expressiveness with such activities as musical performances from her miniature concert stage in the family home. At the same time, both parents would have encouraged in their son behaviors appropriate to a masculine sex-type, so it is not surprising that Ernest also adopted many of the traits and interests of his father. Furthermore, it was noted in the introduction to Unit One that the contents of the stories Hemingway wrote as an adult may have been as much due to what society was eager to hear (and pay for) as to any deep-seated aspects of the author's personality. After World War II and the unpopular conflict in Korea, Americans became less interested in the rough-and-tumble adventurism of Hemingway's novels. Finding it difficult for himself to develop new styles of writing and behaving, Hemingway became frustrated and depressed.

Hemingway's depression and even his suicide could be interpreted in terms of the phenomenon of learned helplessness. Physically unable to participate in his favorite strenuous pastimes and distressed by the death of several persons close to him, Hemingway in his fifties may have felt that life no longer offered sufficient rewards to be worth living. In addition, he was increasingly cast into a "sick patient" role in which things he had previously done for himself were now done for him by others. Such a state of dependency could have augmented Hemingway's feelings of helplessness and depression.

Once again, let me ask which approach seems to you to offer the clearest, most complete insight into the mind of Ernest Hemingway: psychoanalytic, trait-dispositional, humanistic-existential, or behaviorist? Regardless of your answer, I think we all would agree that each of these viewpoints has its own perspective on the character of this famous author and that each to a greater or lesser extent rings true. Hemingway's biography tells us what clinical psychologists and psychiatrists have known for a long time—that the same case can be interpreted in a variety of ways. It does not seem very likely to me that just one interpretation is in possession of the truth with all the others being in error. It instead seems more reasonable to conclude that the personality of each and every human being, famous or not, is a highly complex phenomenon which cannot be fully comprehended using just one theory, one assessment technique, and one style of research.

It could be said that the greatest single discoveries of the psychoanalytic, dispositional, and environmentalist traditions were, respectively, the unconscious mind, the stability of traits, and the power of the immediate situation to shape behavior. I believe there is no necessary incompatibility among these contributions and that the field of psychology should, and must, pay serious attention to each if it is to break the endless circle of bickering among rival schools speaking from polarized positions and move on to its next major advance toward becoming a comprehensive science of social and mental life. If, after reading this book, you are inclined to agree with the foregoing statement, then our mutual efforts have succeeded in establishing a higher-level communication between us than can be achieved by a mere citation of studies or description of theories. If you are not inclined to agree with my conclusion but if reading this book has exposed you to some new ideas regarding the past, present, and possible future of personality psychology which you are at least willing to mull over, then that is the most that I or any author can legitimately ask for.

REFERENCES

ABC News. "Mission: Mind control." American Broadcasting Company telecast, January 30, 1979.

Abramson, L. Y., Seligman, M. E. P., & Teasdale, J. D. Learned helplessness in humans: Critique and reformulation. *Journal of Abnormal Psychology*, 1978, *87*, 49–74.

Adams, H. E., Doster, J. A., & Calhoun, K. S. A psychologically based system of response classification. In A. R. Ciminero, K. S. Calhoun, & H. E. Adams (Eds.), *Handbook of behavioral assessment*. New York: Wiley, 1977.

Adams, J. S. Inequity in social exchange. In L. Berkowitz (Ed.), *Advances in experimental social psychology*, (Vol. 2). New York: Academic, 1965.

Ader, R., & Conklin, P. M. Handling of pregnant rats: Effects on emotionality of their offspring. *Science*, 1963, *142*, 411–412.

Adler, A. *The science of living*. London: G. Allen, 1929.

Adorno, T. W., Frenkel-Brunswik, E., Levinson, D. J., & Sanford, R. N. *The authoritarian personality*. New York: Harper, 1950.

Ahammer, I. M., & Baltes, P. B. Objective versus perceived differences in personality: How do adolescents, adults, and older people view themselves and each other? *Journal of Gerontology*, 1972, *27*, 46–51.

Ahrens, R. Beitrag zur entwicklung des physiognomie und mimikerkennens. *Zeitschrift für Experimentelle und Angewandte Psychologie*, 1953, *2*, 412–454.

Ainsworth, M. D. Patterns of attachment behavior shown by the infant in interaction with his mother. *Merrill-Palmer Quarterly*, 1964, *10*, 51–58.

Akiskal, H. S., & McKinney, W. T. Depressive disorders: Toward a unified hypothesis. *Science*, 1973, *182*, 20–29.

Allen, B. P., & Potkay, C. R. The relationship between AGT self-description and significant life events: A longitudinal study. *Journal of Personality*, 1977, *45*, 207–219.

Allen, E. K., Hart, B. M., Buell, J. S., Harris, F. R., & Wolf, M. M. Effects of social reinforcement on isolate behavior of a nursery school child. *Child Development*, 1964, *35*, 511–518.

Allen, V. L., & Newtson, D. Development of conformity and independence. *Journal of Personality and Social Psychology*, 1972, *22*, 18–30.

Allport, G. W. *Personality: A psychological interpretation*. New York: Holt, 1937.

Allport, G. W. European and American theories of personality. In H. P. David & H. von Bracken (Eds.), *Perspectives in personality theory*. New York: Basic Books, 1957.

Allport, G. W. *Pattern and growth in personality*. New York: Holt, 1961.

Allport, G. W., & Cantril, H. Judging personality from voice. *Journal of Social Psychology*, 1934, *5*, 37–55.

Allport, G. W., & Odbert, H. S. Trait-names: A psycho-lexical study. *Psychological Monographs*, 1936, *47* (Whole No. 211), 1–171.

Allport, G. W., & Vernon, P. E. *A study of values*. Boston: Houghton Mifflin, 1931.

Allport, G. W., & Vernon, P. E. *Studies in expressive movement*. New York: Macmillan, 1933.

Allport, G. W., Vernon, P. E., & Lindzey, G. *A study of values* (2nd ed.). Boston: Houghton Mifflin, 1951.

Altman, I., & Taylor, D. A. Social penetration: *The development of interpersonal relations*. New York: Holt, 1973.

Amacher, P. Freud's neurological education and its influence on psychoanalytic theory. *Psychological Issues*, 1965, *4*(4), 1–93.

Ambrose, J. A. The development of the smiling response in early infancy. In B. M. Foss (Ed.), *Determinants of infant behavior*. London: Methuen, 1959.

American Psychiatric Association. *Diagnostic and statistical manual of mental disorders* (2nd ed.). Washington: Author, 1968.

American Psychiatric Association. *Diagnostic and statistical manual of mental disorders* (3rd ed.). Washington: Author, 1978. (Available in draft form from Publications Sales, American Psychiatric Association, 1700 18th Street, N.W., Washington, D.C. 20009.)

American Psychological Association. *Ethical principles in the conduct of research with human participants*. Washington: Author, 1973.

American Psychological Association. *Standards for educational and psychological tests and manuals*. Washington: Author, 1966.

Ames, L. B. Metraux, R. W., Rodell, J. L., & Walker, R. N. *Rorschach responses in old age*. New York: Brunner, 1973.

Amster, L. E., & Krauss, H. H. Life crises and mental deterioration. *International Journal of Aging and Human Development*, 1974, *5*, 51–55.

Amsterdam, B. Mirror self-image reactions before age two. *Developmental Psychobiology*, 1972, *5*, 297–305.

Anastasi, A. *Psychological testing* (2nd ed.). New York: Macmillan, 1961.

Anastasi, A. *Psychological testing* (4th ed.). New York: Macmillan, 1976.

Anchor, K. N., & Cross, H. J. Maladaptive aggression, moral perspective, and the socialization process. *Journal of Personality and Social Psychology*, 1974, *30*, 163–168.

Anderson, N. H. Likableness ratings of 555 personality-trait words. *Journal of Personality and Social Psychology*, 1968, *9*, 272–279.

Anderson, W. A., & Anderson, N. D. The politics of age exclusion: The adults only movement in Arizona. *Gerontologist*, 1978, *18*, 6–12.

Andrews, J. M. Neuromuscular re-education of the hemiplegic with the aid of the electromyograph. *Archives of Physical Medicine and Rehabilitation*, 1964, *45*, 530–532.

Anrep, G. V. Pitch discrimination in the dog. *Journal of Physiology*, 1920, *53*, 367–395.

Ansbacher, H., & Ansbacher, R. *The individual psychology of Alfred Adler*. New York: Basic Books, 1956.

Argyle, M. Introjection: A form of social learning. *British Journal of Psychology*, 1964, *55*, 391–401.

Arlin, M. Causal priority of social desirability over self-concept: A cross-lagged correlation analysis. *Journal of Personality and Social Psychology*, 1976, *33*, 267–272.

Aronfreed, J. The socialization of altruistic and sympathetic behavior: Some theoretical and experimental analyses. In J. Macaulay & L. Berkowitz (Eds.), *Altruism and helping behavior*. New York: Academic, 1970.

Aronfreed, J. Moral development from the standpoint of a general psychological theory. In T. Lickona (Ed.), *Moral development and behavior*. New York: Holt, Rinehart & Winston, 1976.

Aronowitz, A. G., & Hamill, P. *Ernest Hemingway: The life and death of a man*. New York: Lancer, 1961.

Asch, S. E. Forming impressions of personality. *Journal of Abnormal and Social Psychology*, 1946, *41*, 258–290.

Aserinsky, E., & Kleitman, N. Regularly occurring periods of eye motility, and concomitant phenomena, during sleep. *Science*, 1953, *118*, 273–274.

Associated Press. Mailman stays poor so that others may benefit. In the *Los Angeles Times*, November 26, 1976, Pt 1, p. 1.

Associated Press. Mirror image . . . Twin meets "dead" brother. In the *Sacramento Bee*, February 20, 1979, p. A-3.

Associated Press, Siege in Indiana ends as gunman surrenders. In the *Sacramento Bee*, May 7, 1978, p. A-24.

Atkinson, J. W. (Ed.). *Motives in fantasy, action, and society*. Princeton, N.J.: Van Nostrand, 1958.

Ax, A. F. The physiological differentiation of fear and anger in humans. *Psychosomatic Medicine*, 1953, *15*, 433–442.

Axelrod, J. Neurotransmitters. *Scientific American*, 1974, *230*, 58–71.

Ayllon, T., & Azrin, N. The measurement and reinforcement of behavior of psychotics. *Journal of the Experimental Analysis of Behavior*, 1965, *8*, 357–383.

Azrin, N. H. Pain and aggression. *Psychology Today*, January 1967, 27–33.

Azrin, N. H., Hutchinson, R. R., & Hake, D. F. Extinction-induced aggression. *Journal of the Experimental Analysis of Behavior*, 1966, *9*, 191–204.

Azrin, N. H., Hutchinson, R. R., & Sallery, R. D. Pain-aggression toward inanimate objects. *Journal of the Experimental Analysis of Behavior*, 1964, *7*, 223–228.

Bachman, J. G., & O'Malley, P. M. Self-esteem in young men: A longitudinal analysis of the impact of educational and occupational attainment. *Journal of Personality and Social Psychology*, 1977, *35*, 365–380.

Bachman, J. G., O'Malley, P. M., & Johnston, J. *Youth in transition* (Vol. 6). Ann Arbor, Mich.: Institute for Social Research, 1978.

Back, K. W. (Ed.). *In search for community: Encounter groups and social change*. Boulder, Colo.: Westview, 1978.

Baker, C. *Ernest Hemingway: A life story*. New York: Scribner, 1969.

Baker, R. K., & Ball, S. J. *Mass media and violence: Staff report to the National Commission on the Causes and Prevention of Violence* (Vol. 9). Washington: U.S. Government Printing Office, 1969.

Baker, S. *Ernest Hemingway: An introduction and interpretation*. New York: Holt, 1967.

Bakker, C. B., Bakker-Rabdau, M. K., & Breit, S. The measurement of assertiveness and aggressiveness. *Journal of Personality Assessment*, 1978, *42*, 277–284.

Baltes, P. B., & Schaie, K. W. On the plasticity of intelligence in adulthood and old age. *American Psychologist*, 1976, *31*, 720–725.

Bandura, A. Vicarious processes: A case of no-trial learning. In L. Berkowitz (Ed.), *Advances in experimental social psychology* (Vol. 2). New York: Academic, 1965.

Bandura, A. Behavioral psychotherapy. *Scientific American*, 1967, *216*(3), 78–86.

Bandura, A. *Principles of behavior modification.* New York: Holt, 1969.

Bandura, A. Analysis of modeling processes. In A. Bandura (Ed.), *Psychological modeling: Conflicting theories.* Chicago: Aldine-Atherton, 1971.

Bandura, A. *Aggression.* Englewood Cliffs, N.J.: Prentice-Hall, 1973.

Bandura, A. Behavior theory and the models of man. *American Psychologist*, 1974, *29*, 859–869.

Bandura, A. *Social learning theory.* Englewood Cliffs, N.J.: Prentice-Hall, 1977.

Bandura, A., Blanchard, E. G., & Ritter, B. The relative efficacy of desensitization and modeling approaches for inducing behavioral, affective, and attitudinal changes. *Journal of Personality and Social Psychology*, 1969, *13*, 173–199.

Bandura, A., & McDonald, F. J. Influence of social reinforcement and the behavior of models in shaping children's moral judgments. *Journal of Abnormal and Social Psychology*, 1963, *67*, 274–281.

Bandura, A., Ross, D., & Ross, S. A. Imitation of film-mediated aggressive models. *Journal of Abnormal and Social Psychology*, 1963, *66*, 3–11 (a).

Bandura, A., Ross, D., & Ross, S. A. A comparative test of the status, envy, social power, and secondary reinforcement theories of identificatory learning. *Journal of Abnormal and Social Psychology*, 1963, *67*, 527–534 (b).

Bandura, A., & Walters, R. H. *Social learning and personality development.* New York: Holt, 1965.

Bannister, D. (Ed.). *New perspectives in personal construct theory.* London: Academic, 1977.

Bannister, D., & Mair, J. M. M. *The evaluation of personal constructs.* London: Academic, 1968.

Bannister, D., Salmon, P., & Lieberman, D. M. Diagnosis-treatment relationships in psychiatry: A statistical analysis. *British Journal of Psychiatry*, 1964, *110*, 726–732.

Barcus, F. E. *Saturday children's television: A report of TV programming and advertising on Boston commercial television.* Boston: Action for Children's Television, 1971.

Barkley, M. S., & Goldman, B. D. Testosterone induced aggression in adult female mice. *Hormones and Behavior*, 1977, *9*, 76–84.

Baron, R. A. Reducing the influence of an aggressive model: The restraining effects of peer censure. *Journal of Experimental Social Psychology*, 1972, *8*, 197–206.

Baron R. A. *Human aggression.* New York: Plenum, 1977.

Baron, R. A., & Kepner, C. R. Model's behavior and attraction toward the model as determinants of adult aggressive behavior. *Journal of Personality and Social Psychology*, 1970, *14*, 335–344.

Bassey, J. E. Age, inactivity and some physiological responses to exercise. *Gerontology*, 1978, *24*, 66–77.

Bassuk, E. L., & Gerson, S. Deinstitutionalization and mental health services. *Scientific American*, 1978, *238*(2), 46–53.

Bateson, G. *Steps to an ecology of mind.* New York: Ballantine Books, 1972.

Batson, C. D., Darley, J. M., & Coke, J. S. Altruism and human kindness: Internal and external determinants of helping behavior. In L. A. Pervin & M. Lewis (Eds.), *Perspectives in interactional psychology.* New York: Plenum, 1978.

Bauer, R. A. *The new man in Soviet psychology.* Cambridge, Mass.: Harvard, 1952.

Baumrind, D. Some thoughts on the ethics of research: After reading Milgram's "Behavioral study of obedience." *American Psychologist*, 1964, *19*, 421–423.

Baumrind, D. Effects of authoritative parental control on child behavior. *Child Development*, 1966, *37*, 887–907.

Baumrind, D. Current patterns of parental authority. *Developmental Psychology*, 1971, *4*(1), Pt. 2.

Bayley, N. Mental growth during the first three years. *Genetic Psychology Monographs*, 1933, *14*, 1–89.

Beach, F. Retrospect and prospect. In F. Beach (Ed.), *Sex and behavior*. New York: Wiley, 1965.

Becker, H. S. Becoming a marijuana user. *American Journal of Sociology*, 1953, *59*, 235–242.

Bell, P. A., & Baron, R. A. Aggression and heat: The mediating role of negative affect. *Journal of Applied Social Psychology*, 1976, *6*, 18–30.

Bell, R. Q. A reinterpretation of the direction of effects in studies of socialization. *Psychological Review*, 1968, *75*, 81–95.

Bell, R. Q. Contributions of human infants to caregiving and social interaction. In M. Lewis & L. Rosenblum (Eds.), *The effect of an infant on its caregiver*. New York: Wiley, 1974.

Bellack, A., Hersen, M., & Turner, S. Generalization effects of social skills training in chronic schizophrenics: An experimental analysis. Unpublished manuscript, University of Pittsburgh, 1976. Cited in D. Meichenbaum. *Cognitive-behavior modification*. New York: Plenum, 1977, p. 76.

Bellak, L. *The Thematic Apperception Test and the Children's Apperception Test in clinical use* (1st ed.). New York: Grune & Stratton, 1954.

Bellak, L. *The Thematic Apperception Test and the Children's Apperception Test in clinical use* (2nd ed.). New York: Grune & Stratton, 1971.

Bellugi, U., & Brown, R. The acquisition of learning. *Monographs of the Society for Research in Child Development*, 1964, *29* (No. 92), 107–114.

Beloff, H. The structure and origin of the anal character. *Genetic Psychology Monographs*, 1957, *55*, 141–172.

Bem, D. J., & Allen, A. On predicting some of the people some of the time: The search for cross-situational consistencies in behavior. *Psychological Review*, 1974, *81*, 506–520.

Bem, S. L. The measurement of psychological androgyny. *Journal of Consulting and Clinical Psychology*, 1974, *42*, 155–162.

Bem, S. L. Androgyny vs. the tight little lives of fluffy women and chesty men. *Psychology Today*, September 1975, pp. 58 ff.

Bem, S. L. On the utility of alternative procedures for assessing psychological androgyny. *Journal of Consulting and Clinical Psychology*, 1977, *45*, 196–205.

Benet, S. Why they live to be 100, or even older, in Abkhasia. *New York Times Magazine*, December 26, 1971. Reprinted in C. S. Kart & B. B. Manard (Eds.), *Aging in America*. Sherman Oaks, Calif.: Alfred, 1976.

Benson, H., Beary, J., & Carol, M. The relaxation response. *Psychiatry*, 1974, *37*, 37–46.

Benson, H., Kotch, J. B., Crassweller, K. D., & Greenwood, M. M. Historical and clinical considerations of the relaxation response. *American Scientist*, 1977, *65*, 441–445.

Bergin, A. E. The evaluation of therapeutic outcomes. In A. Bergin & S. Garfield (Eds.), *Handbook of psychotherapy and behavior change*. New York: Wiley, 1971.

Berkowitz, L. *Aggression*. New York: McGraw-Hill, 1962.

Berkowitz, L. *Roots of aggression*. New York: Atherton, 1969.

Berkowitz, L. The case for bottling up rage. *Psychology Today*, July 1973, 24–31.

Berkowitz, L., & Daniels, L. R. Responsibility and dependency. *Journal of Abnormal and Social Psychology*, 1963, *63*, 429–436.

Berkowitz, L., & Daniels, L. R. Affecting the salience of the social responsibility norm: Effects of past help on response to dependency relationships. *Journal of Abnormal and Social Psychology*, 1964, *68*, 275–281.

Berkowitz, L., & Geen, R. G. Stimulus qualities of the target of aggression: A further study. *Journal of Personality and Social Psychology*, 1967, *5*, 364–368.

Berkowitz, L., & LePage, A. Weapons as aggression-eliciting stimuli. *Journal of Personality and Social Psychology*, 1967, *7*, 202–207.

Bettelheim, B. *The empty fortress.* New York: Free Press, 1967.

Bieliauskas, V. J. Mental health care in the USSR. *American Psychologist*, 1977, *32*, 376–379.

Bijou, S. J. Experimental studies of child behavior, normal and deviant. In L. Krasner & L. P. Ullmann (Eds.), *Research in behavior modification.* New York: Holt, 1965.

Bijou, S. W., & Baer, D. M. *Child development, II* New York: Appleton Century Crofts, 1965.

Bijou, S. W., & Peterson, R. F. Functional analysis in the assessment of children. In P. McReynolds (Ed.), *Advances in behavioral assessment* (Vol. 2). Palo Alto, Calif.: Science and Behavior Books, 1971.

Binswanger, L. The case of Ellen West: An anthropological-clinical study. In R. May, E. Angel, & H. F. Ellenberg (Eds.), *Existence.* New York: Basic Books, 1958.

Birren, J. E. Psychological aspects of aging: intellectual functioning. *Gerontologist*, 1968, *8*, 16–19.

Bleuler, M. The long-term course of schizophrenic psychoses. In L. C. Wynne, R. L. Cromwell, & S. Matthysse (Eds.), *The nature of schizophrenia.* New York: Wiley, 1978.

Block, J. *Lives through time.* Berkeley, Calif.: Bancroft, 1971.

Block, J. H. Issues, problems, and pitfalls in assessing sex differences: A critical review of *The psychology of sex differences. Merrill-Palmer Quarterly*, 1976, *22*, 283–308.

Blum, G. S. *The Blacky Pictures: Manual of instructions.* New York: Psychological Corp., 1950.

Blum, G. S., & Miller, D. R. Exploring the psychoanalytic theory of the "oral character." *Journal of Personality*, 1952, *20*, 287–304.

Bock, R. D., & Kolakowski, D. Further evidence of a sex-linked major gene influence on human spatial visualizing ability. *American Journal of Human Genetics*, 1973, *25*, 1–14.

Borden, R. J. Witnessed aggression: Influence of an observer's sex and values on aggressive responding. *Journal of Personality and Social Psychology*, 1975, *31*, 567–573.

Borkovec, T. D., & Craighead, W. E. The comparison of two methods of assessing fear and avoidance behavior. *Behavior Research and Therapy*, 1971, *9*, 285–291.

Bornstein, P., & Quevillon, R. The effects of a self-instructional package on overactive preschool boys. *Journal of Applied Behavior Analysis*, 1976, *9*, 179–188.

Boss, M. *Psychoanalysis and Daseinsanalysis.* New York: Basic Books, 1963.

Bottome, P. *Alfred Adler: A portrait from life.* New York: Vanguard, 1957.

Botwinnick, J. *Aging and behavior.* New York: Springer, 1978.

Boulton, D. *The making of Tania Hearst.* London: New English Library, 1975.

Bower, T. G. R. *Development in infancy.* San Francisco: Freeman, 1974.

Bower, T. G. R. Repetitive processes in child development. *Scientific American*, 1976, *235*(5), 38–47.

Bowers, K. S. Situationism in psychology: An analysis and a critique. *Psychological Review*, 1973, *80*, 307–336.

Bowlby, J. Review of evidence on effects of deprivation. In *Maternal care and mental health.* World Health Organization, Geneva Monograph Series, 1952 (No. 2).

Bowlby, J. Grief and mourning in infancy and early childhood. *Psychoanalytic Study of the Child*, 1960, *16*, 9–52.

Bowlby, J. *Attachment and loss* (Vol. 1: *Attachment*). New York: Basic Books, 1969.

Bowlby, J. *Attachment and Loss* (Vol. 2: *Separation*). New York: Basic Books, 1973.

Boylin, W., Gordon, S. K., & Nehrke, M. F. Reminiscing and ego integrity. *Gerontologist*, 1976, *16*, 118–124.

Bramel, D. A dissonance theory approach to defensive projection. *Journal of Abnormal and Social Psychology*, 1962, *64*, 121–129.

Bramel, D. The arousal and reduction of hostility. In J. Mills (Ed.), *Experimental social psychology*. Toronto: Macmillan, 1969, chap. 2.

Bramel, D., Taub, B., & Blum, B. An observer's reaction to the suffering of his enemy. *Journal of Personality and Social Psychology*, 1968, *8*, 384–392.

Breuer, J. & Freud, S. Studies on hysteria. In J. Strachey (Ed.), *Standard ed., Complete psychological works* (Vol. 2). London: Hogarth, 1953. (Originally published 1895.)

Brickman, P., & Bryan, J. H. Moral judgment of theft, charity, and third-party transfers that increase or decrease equality. *Journal of Personality and Social Psychology*, 1975, *31*, 156–161.

Brillhart, B. L. Relationships of speaker-message perception to perceptual field-independence. *Journal of Communication*, 1970, *20*, 153–166.

Brockner, J. The effects of self-esteem, success-failure, and self-consciousness on task performance. *Journal of Personality and Social Psychology*, 1979, *37*, 1732–1741.

Brody, E. B., & Brody, N. *Intelligence: Nature, determinants, and consequences*. New York: Academic, 1976.

Bromley, D. B. *The psychology of human aging* (2nd ed.). Harmondsworth, England: Penguin, 1974.

Broverman, I. K., Broverman, D. M., Clarkson, F. E., Rosenkrantz, P. S., & Vogel, S. R. Sex-role stereotypes and clinical judgments of mental health. *Journal of Consulting and Clinical Psychology*, 1970, *34*, 1–7.

Brown, R. Development of the first language in the human species. *American Psychologist*, 1973, *28*, 97–106. (a)

Brown, R. *A first language: The early stages*. Cambridge, Mass.: Harvard, 1973. (b)

Brožek, J. Spectrum of Soviet psychology: 1968 model. *American Psychologist*, 1969, *24*, 944–946.

Brožek, J., & Slobin, D. I. (Eds.). *Psychology in the USSR: An historical perspective*. New York: International Arts and Sciences Press, 1972.

Bruner, J. S. *Processes of cognitive growth in infancy*. Heinz Werner Memorial Lectures, Clark University, December, 1967.

Bruner, J. S. Nature and uses of immaturity. *American Psychologist*, 1972, *27*, 687–708.

Bruner, J. S. From communication to language: A psychological perspective. *Cognition*, 1975, *3*, 255–287.

Bruner, J. S., Oliver, R. R., & Greenfield, P. M. *Studies in cognitive growth*. New York: Wiley, 1966.

Bryson, J. R., & Corey, D. M. Sex-diagnosticity in 100 personality trait adjectives. *Personality and Social Psychology Bulletin*, 1977, *3*, 301–304.

Buchwald, A. Odd way to stay on even keel. *Sacramento Bee*, September 16, 1979, p. F-3. (Syndicated column).

Bühler, C. The course of human life as a psychological problem. *Human Development*, 1968, *11*, 184–200.

Burkhart, B. R., Christian, W. L., & Gynther, M. D. Item subtlety and faking on the MMPI: A paradoxical relationship. *Journal of Personality Assessment*, 1978, *42*, 76–80.

Burnstein, E., & Worchel, P. Arbitrariness of frustration and its consequences for aggression in a social situation. *Journal of Personality*, 1962, *30*, 528–540.

Burt, C. The inheritance of mental ability. *American Psychologist*, 1958, *13*, 1–15.

Burt, C. Is intelligence distributed normally? *British Journal of Statistical Psychology*, 1963, *16*, 175–190.

Burt, C., & Howard, M. The multifactorial theory of inheritance and its application to intelligence. *British Journal of Statistical Psychology*, 1956, *9*, 95–131.

Burton, R. V. Generality of honesty revisited. *Psychological Review*, 1963, *70*, 481–499.

Buss, A. H. Instrumentality of aggression, feedback, and frustration as determinants of physical aggression. *Journal of Personality and Social Psychology*, 1966, *3*, 153–162.

Buss, A. H. Aggression pays. In J. L. Singer (Ed.),

The control of aggression and violence. New York: Academic, 1971.

Buss, A. H., Booker, A., & Buss, E. Firing a weapon and aggression. *Journal of Personality and Social Psychology,* 1972, *22,* 196–302.

Butcher, J. N. (Ed.). *Objective personality assessment.* New York: Academic, 1972.

Butler, J. M., & Haigh, G. V. Changes in the relation between self-concepts and ideal concepts consequent upon client-centered counseling. In C. R. Rogers & Rosalind F. Dymond (Eds.), *Psychotherapy and personality change: Co-ordinated studies in the client-centered approach.* Chicago: Univ. of Chicago Press, 1954.

Byrne, D. Assessing personality variables and their alteration. In P. Worchel & D. Byrne (Eds.), *Personality change.* New York: Wiley, 1964.

Calhoun, J. B. Population density and social pathology. *Scientific American,* 1962, *206*(2), 139–146.

Callaway, E. *Brain electrical potentials and individual psychological differences.* New York: Grune & Stratton, 1975.

Campagna, A. F., & Harter, S. Moral judgment in sociopathic and normal children. *Journal of Personality and Social Psychology,* 1975, *31,* 199–205.

Campbell, D. P. The practical problems of revising an established psychological test. In J. N. Butcher (Ed.), *Objective personality assessment.* New York: Academic, 1972.

Campbell, D. P. *Manual for the Strong-Campbell Interest Inventory.* Stanford, Calif.: Stanford Univ. Press, 1974.

Campbell, D. T. On the conflicts between biological and social evolution and between psychology and moral tradition. *American Psychologist,* 1975, *30,* 1103–1126.

Cannon, W. B. The James-Lange theory of emotion; a critical examination and an alternative theory. *American Journal of Psychology,* 1927, *39,* 106–124.

Carey, G. Sex differences in problem-solving performance as a function of attitude differenc-es. *Journal of Abnormal and Social Psychology,* 1958, *56,* 156–160.

Carlsmith, J. M., & Anderson, C. A. Ambient temperature and the occurrence of collective violence: A new analysis. *Journal of Personality and Social Psychology,* 1979, *37,* 337–344.

Carthy, J. D., & Ebling, F. J. (Eds.). *The natural history of aggression.* Institute of Biology Symposia (No. 13). New York: Academic, 1964.

Carver, C. S. A cybernetic model of self-attention processes. *Journal of Personality and Social Psychology,* 1979, *37,* 1251–1281.

Cattell, R. B. A culture-free intelligence test. I. *Journal of Educational Psychology,* 1940, *31*(3).

Cattell, R. B. *Personality and motivation structure and measurement.* Yonkers: New World, 1957.

Cattell, R. B. *The scientific analysis of personality.* Baltimore: Penguin, 1965.

Cattell, R. B. *Personality and mood by questionnaire.* San Francisco: Jossey-Bass, 1973.

Cattell, R. B., & Warburton, F. W. *Objective personality and motivation tests.* Urbana: Univ. of Illinois Press, 1967.

Cautela, J. R., & Kastenbaum, R. A. A Reinforcement Survey Schedule for use in therapy, training, and research. *Psychological Reports,* 1967, *20,* 1115–1130.

Chafetz, J. S. *Masculine/feminine or human?* Itasca, Ill.: Peacock, 1974.

Chapman, L. J., & Chapman, J. P. Genesis of popular but erroneous psychodiagnostic observations. *Journal of Abnormal Psychology,* 1967, *72,* 193–204.

Chapman, L. J., & Chapman, J. P. Illusory correlation as an obstacle to the use of valid psychodiagnostic signs, *Journal of Abnormal Psychology,* 1969, *74,* 271–280.

Charlesworth, W. R., & Kreutzer, M. A. Facial expressions of infants and children. In P. Ekman (Ed.), *Darwin and facial expression.* New York: Academic, 1973.

Chomsky, N. *Language and mind.* New York: Harcourt, Brace & World, 1968.

Chorover, S. L. Big brother and psychotechnology

II: The pacification of the brain. *Psychology Today*, May 1974, pp. 59 ff.

Ciminero, A. R., Nelson, R. O., & Lipinski, D. P. Self-monitoring procedures. In A. R. Ciminero, K. S. Calhoun, & H. E. Adams (Eds.), *Handbook of behavioral assessment*. New York: Wiley, 1978.

Clark, D. F. Fetishism treated by negative conditioning. *British Journal of Psychiatry*, 1963, *109*, 404–407.

Clark, G., & Birch, H. G. Hormonal modification of social behavior. The effect of sex-hormone administration on the social status of a male castrate chimpanzee. *Psychosomatic Medicine*, 1945, *7*, 321–329.

Clark, R. D., & Word, L. E. Where is the apathetic bystander? Situational characteristics of the emergency. *Journal of Personality and Social Psychology*, 1974, *29*, 279–287.

Cleckley, H. *The mask of sanity*. St. Louis: Mosby, 1941.

Cline, V. B., Croft, R. G., & Courrier, S. Desensitization of children to television violence. *Journal of Personality and Social Psychology*, 1973, *27*, 360–365.

Collette-Pratt, C. Attitudinal predictors of devaluation of old age in a multigenerational sample. *Journal of Gerontology*, 1976, *31*, 193–197.

Comrey, A. L. *A first course in factor analysis*. New York: Academic, 1973.

Contes, B., Pusser, H. E., & Goodman, I. The influence of "Sesame Street" and "Mister Rogers' Neighborhood" on children's social behavior in the preschool. *Child Development*, 1976, *47*, 138–144.

Cooper, H. M. Statistically combining independent studies: A meta-analysis of sex differences in conformity research. *Journal of Personality and Social Psychology*, 1979, *37*, 131–146.

Coopersmith, S. *The antecedents of self-esteem*. San Francisco: Freeman, 1967.

Coopersmith, S. Studies in self-esteem. *Scientific American*, 1968, *218*(2), 96–106.

Cortes, J. B., & Gatti, F. M. *Delinquency and crime: A biopsychosocial approach*. New York: Seminar Press, 1972.

Costanzo, P. R. Conformity development as a function of self-blame. *Journal of Personality and Social Psychology*, 1970, *14*, 366–374.

Cowan, E. L., & Beier, E. G. Threat-expectancy, word frequencies, and perceptual prerecognition hypotheses. *Journal of Abnormal and Social Psychology*, 1954, *49*, 178–182.

Cowan, P. A., Langer, J., Heavenrich, J., & Nathanson, M. Social learning and Piaget's cognitive theory of moral development. *Journal of Personality and Social Psychology*, 1969, *11*, 261–274.

Cowan, P. A., & Walters, R. H. Studies of reinforcement of aggression: I. Effects of scheduling. *Child Development*, 1963, *34*, 543–552.

Cox, R. H. Psychologists and drugs: II. Psychopharmacology and the nonmedical practitioner. *Professional Psychology*, 1975, *6*, 169–171.

Cozby, P. C. Self-disclosure: A literature review. *Psychological Bulletin*, 1973, *79*, 73–91.

Crano, W. D., Kenny, D. A., & Campbell, D. T. Does intelligence cause achievement? A cross-lagged panel analysis. *Journal of Educational Psychology*, 1972, *63*, 258–275.

Cressen, R. Artistic quality of drawings and judges' evaluation of the DAP. *Journal of Personality Assessment*, 1975, *39*, 132–137.

Cross, D. T., Barclay, A., & Burger, G. K. Differential effects of ethnic membership, sex, and occupation on the California Psychological Inventory. *Journal of Personality Assessment*, 1978, *42*, 597–603.

Crowne, D. P., & Marlowe, D. A new scale of social desirability independent of psychopathology, *Journal of Consulting Psychology*, 1960, *24*, 349–354.

Cummings, E. M., & Henry, W. *Growing old*. New York: Basic Books, 1961.

Dahlstrom, W. G., & Welsh, G. S. *An MMPI handbook: A guide to use in clinical practice and research*. Minneapolis: Univ. of Minnesota Press, 1960.

Dahlstrom, W. G., Welsh, G. S., & Dahlstrom, L. E. *An MMPI handbook. Vol. I: Clinical interpretation*. Minneapolis: Univ. of Minnesota Press, 1970.

Dahlstrom, W. G., Welsh, G. S., & Dahlstrom, L. E. *An MMPI handbook. Vol. II: Research applications.* Minneapolis: Univ. of Minnesota Press, 1975.

Darley, J. M., & Latané, B. Bystander intervention in emergencies. *Journal of Personality and Social Psychology,* 1968, *3,* 377–383.

Darley, J. M., & Latané, B. Norms and normative behavior. In J. R. Macaulay & L. Berkowitz (Eds.), *Altruism and helping behavior.* New York: Academic, 1970.

Darwin, C. *The expression of the emotions in man and animals.* London: Murray, 1872.

Dashiell, J. F. *Fundamentals of general psychology* (3rd ed.). Boston: Houghton Mifflin, 1949.

Davidson, M. A., McInnes, R. G., & Parnell, R. W. The distribution of personality traits in seven-year-old children: A combined psychological, psychiatric, and somatotype study. *British Journal of Educational Psychology,* 1957, *27,* 48–61.

Davies, J. D. *Phrenology: Fad and science.* New Haven, Conn.: Yale, 1955.

Davison, G., & Wilson, G. Attitudes of behavior therapists toward homosexuality. *Behavior Therapy,* 1973, *4,* 686–696.

Deaux, K., White, L., & Farris, E. Skill versus luck: Field and laboratory studies of male and female preferences. *Journal of Personality and Social Psychology,* 1975, *32,* 629–636.

DeCarlo, T. J. Recreation participation patterns and successful aging. *Journal of Gerontology,* 1974, *29,* 416–422.

de Charms, R., & Moeller, G. H. Values expressed in American children's readers: 1800–1950. *Journal of Abnormal and Social Psychology,* 1962, *64,* 135–142.

Deci, E. L. *Intrinsic motivation.* New York: Plenum, 1975.

Dement, W. C. *Some must watch while some must sleep.* San Francisco: Freeman, 1972.

Denenberg, V. H., Garbanati, J., Sherman, G., Yutzey, D. A., & Kaplan, R. Infantile stimulation induces brain lateralization in rats. *Science,* 1978, *201,* 1150–1152.

Denenberg, V. H., Hudgens, G. A., & Zarrow, M. X. Mice reared with rats: Modification of behavior by early experience with another species. *Science,* 1964, *143,* 380–381.

Denenberg, V. H., Rosenberg, K. M., Haltmeyer, G., & Whimbey, A. E. Programming life histories: Effects of stress in ontogeny upon emotional reactivity. *Merrill-Palmer Quarterly of Behavior and Development,* 1970, *16,* 109–116.

Dengerink, H. A. Aggression, anxiety, and physiological arousal. *Journal of Experimental Research in Personality,* 1971, *5,* 223–232.

de Villiers, J. G., & de Villiers, P. A. A cross-sectional study of the acquisition of grammatical morphemes in child speech. *Journal of Psycholinguistic Research,* 1973, *2,* 267–278. (a)

de Villiers, J. G., & de Villiers, P. A. Development of the use of word order in comprehension. *Journal of Psycholinguistic Research,* 1973, *2,* 331–342. (b)

Diamond, M. A critical evaluation of the ontogeny of human sexual behavior. *Quarterly Review of Biology,* 1965, *40,* 147–175.

DiCara, L. V. Learning in the autonomic nervous system. In T. J. Teyler (Ed.), *Altered states of awareness.* San Francisco: Freeman, 1973.

Diener, E., Dineen, J., Endresen, K., Beaman, A. L., & Fraser, S. C. Effects of altered responsibility, cognitive set, and modeling on physical aggression and deindividuation. *Journal of Personality and Social Psychology,* 1975, *31,* 328–337.

Dinitz, S., Reckless, W. C., & Kay, B. A self-gradient among potential delinquents. *Journal of Criminal Law, Criminology, and Police Science,* 1958, *49,* 230–233.

Dinitz, S., Scarpitti, F. R., & Reckless, W. C. Delinquency vulnerability: A cross group and longitudinal analysis. *American Sociological Review,* 1962, *27,* 515–517.

Dixon, N. F. Apparent changes in the visual threshold as a function of subliminal stimulation. *Quarterly Journal of Experimental Psychology,* 1958, *10,* 211–215.

Dixon, N. F., & Haider, M. Changes in the visual threshold as a function of subception. *Quarterly Journal of Experimental Psychology*, 1961, *13*, 229–235.

Dollard, J., Doob, L., Miller, N., Mowrer, O. H., & Sears, R. R. *Frustration and aggression.* New Haven, Conn.: Yale, 1939.

Dollard, J., & Miller, N. *Personality and psychotherapy.* New York: McGraw-Hill, 1950.

Doob, A. N., & Wood, L. Catharsis and aggression: The effects of annoyance and retaliation on aggressive behavior. *Journal of Personality and Social Psychology*, 1972, *22*, 156–162.

Dorfman, D. D. The Cyril Burt question: New findings. *Science*, 1978, *201*, 1177–1186.

Dorr, D., & Fey, S. Relative power of symbolic adult and peer models in the modification of children's moral choice behavior. *Journal of Personality and Social Psychology*, 1974, *29*, 335–341.

Dowling, J. F., & Graham, J. R. Illusory correlation and the MMPI. *Journal of Personality Assessment*, 1976, *40*, 531–538.

Duffy, E. The psychological significance of the concept of "arousal" or "activation." *Psychological Review*, 1957, *64*, 265–275.

Duval, S., & Wicklund, R. A. *A theory of objective self-awareness.* New York: Academic, 1972.

Edwards, A. L. *Edwards Personal Preference Schedule.* New York: Psychological Corp., 1959.

Edwards, A. L. Social desirability and performance on the MMPI. *Psychometrika*, 1964, *29*, 295–308.

Ekman, P. Cross-cultural studies of facial expression. In P. Ekman (Ed.), *Darwin and facial expression.* New York: Academic, 1973.

Elms, A. C., & Milgram, S. Personality characteristics associated with obedience and definace toward authoritative command. *Journal of Experimental Research in Personality*, 1966, *1*, 282–289.

Engel, B. T., & Shapiro, D. The use of biofeedback training in enabling patients to control autonomic functions. In J. Segal (Ed.), Mental health program reports—5. Washington: U.S. Government Printing Office, 1971.

Ennis, B. Civil liberties and mental illness. *Criminal Law Bulletin*, 1971, *7*, 101, 122–123.

Erdmann, G., & Janke, W. Interaction between physiological and cognitive determinants of emotions: Experimental studies on Schachter's theory of emotions. *Biological Psychology*, 1978, *6*, 61–74.

Eriksen, D. A., & Eriksen, C. W. *Perception and personality*, Morristown, N.J.: General Learning Press, 1972.

Eriksen, C. W., & Pierce, J. Defence mechanisms. In E. F. Borgatta and W. W. Lambert (Eds.), *Handbook of personality theory and research.* Chicago: Rand McNally, 1968.

Erikson, E. H. *Childhood and society.* New York: Norton, 1950.

Erikson, E. H. *Identity and the life cycle: Selected papers* (Monograph No. 1, Vol. 1). New York: Internat. Univ. Press, 1959.

Erikson, E. H. Womanhood and the inner space. In E. H. Erikson (Ed.), *Identity: Youth and crisis.* New York: Norton, 1968.

Erikson, E. H. *Life history and the historical moment.* New York: Norton, 1975.

Erikson, E. H. Dr. Borg's life cycle. In E. H. Erikson (Ed.), *Adulthood.* New York: Norton, 1978.

Erlenmeyer-Kimling, L., & Jarvik, L. F. Genetics and intelligence: A review. *Science*, 1963, *142*, 1477–1479.

Ernst, P., Beran, B., Safford, F., & Kleinhauz, M. Isolation and the symptoms of chronic brain syndrome. *Gerontologist*, 1978, *18*, 468–474.

Eron, L. D. A normative study of the Thematic Apperception Test. *Psychological Monographs*, 1950, *64* (Whole No. 9).

Eron, L. D., Huesmann, L. R., Lefkowitz, M. M., & Walder, L. O. Does television violence cause aggression? *American Psychologist*, 1972, *27*, 253–263.

Estes, W. K. An experimental study of punishment. *Psychological Monographs*, 1944, 57(No. 263).

Etzioni, A. Deinstitutionalization . . . A vastly oversold good idea. *Columbia*, 1978, 3(4), 14–17.

Evans, I. M., & Nelson, R. O. Assessment of child behavior problems. In A. R. Ciminero, K. S. Calhoun, & H. E. Adams (Eds.), *Handbook of behavioral assessment*. New York: Wiley, 1977.

Evans, R. I. *B. F. Skinner: The man and his ideas*. New York: Macmillan, 1969.

Exner, J. E. *The Rorschach: A comprehensive system*. New York: Wiley, 1974.

Eysenck, H. J. *Dimensions of personality*. London: Routledge, 1947.

Eysenck, H. J. The effects of psychotherapy: An evaluation. *Journal of Consulting Psychology*, 1952, 16, 319–324.

Eysenck, H. J. Principles and methods of personality description, classification, and analysis. *British Journal of Psychology*, 1964, 55, 284–294.

Eysenck, H. J. *The biological basis of personality*. Springfield, Ill.: Charles C Thomas, 1967.

Eysenck, H. J. *Behavior therapy and the neuroses*. Oxford: Pergamon, 1970.

Eysenck, H. J. *Eysenck on extraversion*. New York: Wiley, 1973.

Eysenck, H. J., & Wilson, G. D. *The experimental study of Freudian theories*. London: Methuen, 1973.

Fairweather, G. W. (Ed.). *Social psychology in treating mental illness: An experimental approach*. New York: Wiley, 1964.

Fairweather, G. W., Sanders, D. H., Cressler, D. L., & Maynard, H. *Community life for the mentally ill: An alternative to institutional care*. Chicago: Aldine, 1969.

Falconer, W. *A dissertation on the influence of the passions upon disorders of the body*. London: Dilly, 1796.

Fantz, R. L. Pattern vision in newborn infants. *Science*, 1963, 140, 296–297.

Feldman, K. A., & Newcomb, T. M. *The impact of college on students*. San Francisco: Jossey-Bass, 1969.

Fernandez, J. W. Passage to community: Encounter in evolutionary perspective. In Back, op. cit., 1978.

Feshbach, S., & Feshbach, N. The young aggressors. *Psychology Today*, April 1973, pp. 90 ff.

Feshbach, S., & Singer, R. D. *Television and aggression: An experimental field study*. San Francisco: Jossey-Bass, 1971.

Festinger, L. *A theory of cognitive dissonance*. Stanford, Calif.: Stanford, 1957.

Filskov, S. B., & Goldstein, S. G. Diagnostic validity of the Halstead-Reitan neuropsychological battery. *Journal of Consulting and Clinical Psychology*, 1974, 42, 382–388.

Fisher, C., Gross, J., & Zuch, J. Cycle of penile erection synchronous with dreaming (REM) sleep. *Archives of General Psychiatry*, 1965, 12, 29–45.

Fisher, L. E., & Kotses, M. Race differences and experimenter race effect in galvanic skin response. *Psychophysiology*, 1973, 10, 578–582.

Fishkin, J., Keniston, K., & MacKinnon, C. Moral reasoning and political ideology. *Journal of Personality and Social Psychology*, 1973, 27, 109–119.

Fitzgerald, H. E., & Brackbill, Y. Classical conditioning in infancy: Development and constraints. *Psychological Bulletin*, 1976, 83, 353–376.

Fontana, A. F., & Noel, B. Moral reasoning in the university. *Journal of Personality and Social Psychology*, 1973, 27, 419–429.

Forer, B. R. The fallacy of personal validation: A classroom demonstration of gullibility. *Journal of Abnormal and Clinical Psychology*, 1949, 44, 118–123.

Forsyth, R. P., & Fairweather, G. W. Psychotherapeutic and other hospital treatment criteria: The dilemma. *Journal of Abnormal and Social Psychology*, 1961, 62, 598–604.

Fouts, R. S. Language: Origins, definitions, and chimpanzees. *Journal of Human Evolution*, 1974, 3, 475–482.

Frank, L. K. Projective methods for the study of personality. *Journal of Psychology*, 1939, 8, 389–413.

Franklin, B. Autobiography. In Spearks, J. (Ed.), *The works of Benjamin Franklin* (Vol. 1). Boston: Hilliard Gray and Company, 1840, chap. 6.

Fransella, F. The self and the stereotype. In D. Bannister (Ed.), *New perspectives in personal construct theory*. London: Academic, 1977.

Freedman, D. G. The social capacities of infants. In D. G. Freedman (Ed.), *Human infancy: An evolutionary perspective*. New York: Wiley, 1974.

Freedman, D. G., & Keller, B. Inheritance of behavior in infants. *Science*, 1963, *140*, 196–198.

Freedman, J. L., Heshka, S., & Levy, A. Population density and pathology: Is there a relationship? *Journal of Experimental Social Psychology*, 1975, *11*, 539–552.

Freedman, J. L., Klevansky, S., & Ehrlich, P. R. The effect of crowding on human task performance. *Journal of Applied Social Psychology*, 1971, *1*, 7–25.

Freedman, J. L., Levy, A. S., Buchanan, R. W., & Price, J. Crowding and human aggressiveness. *Journal of Experimental Social Psychology*, 1972, *8*, 528–548.

Freedman, J. L., Wallington, S., & Bless, E. Compliance without pressure: The effect of guilt. *Journal of Personality and Social Psychology*, 1967, *7*, 117–124.

Freud, A. *The ego and the mechanisms of defense.* New York: Internat. Univ. Press, 1966. (Originally published 1936.)

Freud S. On the general effects of cocaine. *Medizinischchirurgisches Central-Blatt*, 1885, *20* (August), 374–375. Reprinted in *Drug Dependence*, 1970, *5*, 15.

Freud, S. The interpretation of dreams. In J. Strachey (Ed.), *Standard ed., Complete psychological works* (Vols. 4 & 5). London: Hogarth, 1953. (Originally published 1900.)

Freud, S. The psychopathology of everyday life. In Strachey (Ed.) (Vol. 6). (Originally published 1901.)

Freud, S. Fragment of an analysis of a case of hysteria. In Strachey (Ed.) (Vol. 7). (Originally published 1905.)

Freud, S. Three essays on sexuality. In Strachey (Ed.) (Vol. 7). (Originally published 1905.)

Freud, S. Jokes and their relation to the unconscious. In Strachey (Ed.) (Vol. 8). London: Hogarth, 1960. (Originally published 1905.)

Freud, S. The history of the psychoanalytic movement. In Strachey (Ed.) (Vol. 14). (Originally published 1914.)

Freud, S. Mourning and melancholia. In E. Jones (Ed.), *The collected papers of Sigmund Freud* (Vol. 4). London: Hogarth, 1956. (Originally published 1917.)

Freud, S. Beyond the pleasure principle. In Strachey (Ed.) (Vol. 18). (Originally published 1920.)

Freud, S. Psychoanalysis. In Strachey (Ed.) (Vol. 20). (Originally published 1922.)

Freud, S. The ego and the id. In Strachey (Ed.) (Vol. 19). (Originally published 1923.)

Freud, S. Some psychical consequences of the anatomical distinction between the sexes. In Strachey (Ed.) (Vol. 19). (Originally published 1925.)

Freud, S. Inhibitions, symptoms and anxiety. In Strachey (Ed.) (Vol. 20). (Originally published 1926.)

Freud, S. Why war? In E. Jones (Ed.), *The collected papers of Sigmund Freud* (Vol. 5). London: Hogarth, 1956. (Originally published 1932.)

Freud, S. New Introductory lectures. In Strachey (Ed.) (Vol. 22). (Originally published 1933.)

Freud, S. The psychology of women. In W. J. H. Sprott (trans.), *New introductory lectures on psychoanalysis* (Lecture 33). New York: Norton, 1933.

Freud, S. *An outline of psychoanalysis.* (J. Strachey, trans.) New York: Norton, 1949. (Originally published 1940.)

Freund, K. Some problems in the treatment of homosexuality. In H. J. Eysenck (Ed.), *Behavior therapy and the neuroses.* Elmsford, N.Y.: Pergamon, 1960.

Frick, W. B. (Ed.). *Humanistic psychology: Interviews with Maslow, Murphy and Rogers.* Columbus, Ohio: Merrill, 1971.

Friedman, S. M. An empirical study of the Oedipus complex. *American Psychologist,* 1950, *5,* 304.

Friedman, S. M. An empirical study of the castration and Oedipus complexes. *Genetic Psychology Monographs,* 1952, *46,* 61–130.

Friedrich, L. K., & Stein, A. H. Aggressive and prosocial television programs and the natural behavior of preschool children. *Monographs of the Society for Research in Child Development,* 1973, *38* (4, Serial No. 151).

Frodi, A., Macaulay, J., & Thorne, P. R. Are women always less aggressive than men? A review of the experimental literature. *Psychological Bulletin,* 1977, *84,* 634–660.

Furtmuller, C. Alfred Adler: A biographical essay. In H. L. Ansbacher & R. R. Ansbacher (Eds.), *Superiority and social interest.* New York: Viking, 1973.

Gaddes, W. H. Prevalence estimates and the need for definition of learning disabilities. In R. M. Knights & D. J. Bakker (Eds.), *The neuropsychology of learning disorders.* Baltimore: University Park Press, 1976.

Galenson, E., & Roiphe, H. The emergence of genital awareness during the second year of life. In R. C. Friedman, R. M. Richart, & R. L. Vande Wiele (Eds.), *Sex differences in behavior.* New York: Wiley, 1974.

Gallagher, C. E. Opening remarks. Testimony before House Special Subcommittee on Invasion of Privacy of the Committee on Government Operations. *American Psychologist,* 1965, *20,* 955–988.

Gallup, G. G. Chimpanzees: Self-recognition. *Science,* 1970, *167,* 86–87.

Gallup, G. G. Self-recognition in primates. *American Psychologist,* 1977, *32,* 329–338.

Gallup, G. G., McClure, M. K., Hill, S. D., & Bundy, R. A. Capacity for self-recognition in differentially reared rhesus monkeys. *The Psychological Record,* 1971, *21,* 69–74.

Gambaro, S., & Rabin, A. K. Diastolic blood pressure responses following direct and displaced aggression after anger arousal in high- and low-guilt subjects. *Journal of Personality and Social Psychology,* 1969, *12,* 87–94.

Garai, J. E., & Scheinfeld, A. Sex differences in mental and behavioral traits. *Genetic Psychology Monographs,* 1968, *77,* 169–299.

Garcia, J. IQ: The conspiracy. *Psychology Today,* September 1972, pp. 40 ff.

Gardner, B. T., & Gardner, R. A. Comparing the early utterances of child and chimpanzee. In A. Pick (Ed.), *Minnesota Symposium in Child Psychology* (Vol. 8). Minneapolis: Univ. of Minnesota Press, 1974.

Garmezy, N. Observations on high-risk research and premorbid development in schizophrenia. In L. C. Wynne, R. L. Cromwell, & S. Matthysse (Eds.), *The nature of schizophrenia.* New York: Wiley, 1978. (a)

Garmezy, N. Current status of a sample of other high-risk research programs. In Wynne et al. (Eds.), *The nature of schizophrenia.* New York: Wiley, 1978. (b)

Gazzaniga, M. S., Bogen, J. E., & Sperry, R. W. Some functional effects of sectioning the cerebral commissures in man. *Proceedings of the National Academy of Sciences of the United States of America,* 1962, *48,* 1765–1769.

Gazzaniga, M. S., Bogen, J. E., & Sperry, R. W. Laterality effects in somasthesis following cerebral commissurotomy in man. *Neuropsychologia,* 1963, *1,* 209–215.

Geen, R. G., & Berkowitz, L. Some conditions facilitating the occurrence of aggression after the observation of violence. *Journal of Personality,* 1967, *35,* 666–676.

Geen, R. G., & Pigg, R. Acquisition of an aggressive response and its generalization to verbal behavior. *Journal of Personality and Social Psychology,* 1970, *15,* 165–170.

Geen, R. G., Stonner, D., & Shope, G. L. The facilitation of aggression by aggression: Evidence against the catharsis hypothesis. *Journal of Personality and Social Psychology*, 1975, *31*, 721–726.

Gelder, M. G., & Marks. I. M. Aversion treatment in transvestism and transsexualism. In R. Green (Ed.), *Transsexualism and sex reassignment*. Baltimore: Johns Hopkins, 1969.

Gerbner, G. Violence in television drama: Trends and symbolic functions. In G. A. Comstock & E. A. Rubinstein (Eds.), *Television and social behavior* (Vol. 1). Washington: U.S. Government Printing Office, 1972.

Geschwind, N. Anatomy and the higher functions of the brain. *Boston Studies in the Philosophy of Science*, 1969, *4*, 98–136.

Getter, H., & Weiss, S. D. The Rotter Incomplete Sentences Blank Adjustment Score as an indicator of somatic complaint frequency. *Journal of Projective Techniques and Personality Assessment*, 1968, *32*, 266.

Gfeller, E. Pinpointing the cause of disturbed behavior in the elderly. *Geriatrics*, 1978, *33*, 26–30.

Giebink, J., Stover, D., & Fahl, M. Teaching adaptive responses to frustration to emotionally disturbed boys. *Journal of Consulting and Clinical Psychology*, 1968, *32*, 366–368.

Ginsburg, B., & Allee, W. C. Some effects of conditioning on social dominance and subordination in inbred strains of mice. *Physiological Zoology*, 1942, *15*, 485–506.

Ginsburg, B. E. Genetic parameters in behavioral research. In J. Hirsch (Ed.), *Behavior-genetic analysis*. New York: McGraw-Hill, 1967.

Glenn, R. N., & Janda, L. H. Self-ideal discrepancy and acceptance of false personality interpretations. *Journal of Personality Assessment*, 1977, *41*, 311–316.

Glueck, S., & Glueck, E. *Physique and delinquency*. New York: Harper, 1956.

Goffman, E. *The presentation of self in everyday life*. Garden City, N.Y.: Doubleday, 1959.

Goffman, E. *Frame analysis*. New York: Harper & Row, 1974.

Goldberg, P. A review of sentence completion methods in personality assessment. *Journal of Projective Techniques and Personality Assessment*, 1965, *29*, 12–45.

Goldberg, S., & Lewis, M. Play behavior in the year-old infant: Early sex differences. *Child Development*, 1969, *40*, 21–31.

Goldfarb, W. Psychological privation in infancy and subsequent adjustment. *American Journal of Orthopsychiatry*, 1945, *15*, 247–255.

Goldfried, M. R., & Sprafkin, J. N. *Behavioral personality assessment*. Morristown, N.J.: General Learning Press, 1974.

Goldman-Eisler, F. The problem of "orality" and its origin in early childhood. *Journal of Mental Science*, 1951, *97*, 765–782.

Goodman, E. The game of "malparenting." *Sacramento Bee*, June 9, 1978, p. B-7 (Syndicated column).

Gormly, J., & Edelberg, W. Validity in personality trait attribution. *American Psychologist*, 1974, *29*, 189–193.

Gottesman, I. I. Schizophrenia and genetics: Where are we: Are you sure? In L. C. Wynne, R. L. Cromwell, & S. Matthysse (Eds.), *The nature of schizophrenia*. New York: Wiley, 1978.

Gottesman, I. I., & Shields, J. *Schizophrenia and genetics: A twin study vantage point*. New York: Academic, 1972.

Gough, H. G. A Leadership Index on the California Psychological Inventory. *Journal of Counseling Psychology*, 1969, *16*, 283–289. (a)

Gough, H. G. *Manual for the California Psychological Inventory* (Rev. ed.). Palo Alto, Calif.: Consulting Psychologists Press, 1969. (b)

Gould, R. The phases of adult life: A study in developmental psychology. *American Journal of Psychiatry*. 1972, *129*, 521–531.

Gould, S. J. Women's brains. *Natural History*, 1978, *87*(8), 44–50.

Gould, S. J. Mickey Mouse meets Konrad Lorenz. *Natural History*, 1979, *88*, 30–36.

Gregory, R. J., & Morris, L. M. Adjective correlates for women on the CPI scales: A replication. *Journal of Personality Assessment*, 1978, *42*, 258–264.

Grieser, C., Greenberg, R., & Harrison, R. H. The adaptive function of sleep: The differential effects of sleep and dreaming on recall. *Journal of Abnormal Psychology*, 1972, *80*, 280–286.

Griffitt, W., & Veitch, R. Hot and crowded: Influence of population density and temperature on interpersonal affective behavior. *Journal of Personality and Social Psychology*, 1971, *17*, 92–98.

Gross, M. L. *The brain watchers.* New York: Random House, 1962.

Gross, M. L. Testimony before House Special Subcommittee on Invasion of Privacy of the Committee on Government Operations. *American Psychologist*, 1965, *20*, 958–960.

Grotevant, H. D., Scarr, S., & Weinberg, R. A. Patterns of interest similarity in adoptive and biological families. *Journal of Personality and Social Psychology*, 1977, *35*, 667–676.

Guilford, J. P. *The nature of human intelligence.* New York: McGraw-Hill, 1967.

Guillemin, R. Peptides in the brain: The new endocrinology of the neuron. *Science*, 1978, *202*, 390–402.

Gutmann, D. Life events and decision making by older adults. *Gerontologist*, 1978, *18*, 462–467.

Gynther, M. D. White norms and black MMPIs: A prescription for discrimination? *Psychological Bulletin*, 1972, *5*, 386–403.

Haan, N., Smith, M. B., & Block, J. Moral reasoning of young adults: Political-social behavior, family background, and personality correlates. *Journal of Personality and Social Psychology*, 1968, *10*, 183–201.

Hall, C. S. *A primer of Freudian psychology.* New York: World, 1954.

Hall, C. S., & Lindzey, G. *Theories of personality* (2nd ed.). New York: Wiley, 1970.

Hall, C. S., & Lindzey, G. *Theories of personality* (3rd ed.). New York: Wiley, 1978.

Hall, C. S., & Van de Castle, R. L. An empirical investigation of the castration complex in dreams. *Journal of Personality*, 1963, *33*, 20–29.

Hall, J. A. Gender effects in decoding nonverbal cues. *Psychological Bulletin*, 1978, *85*, 845–857.

Halstead, W. C. *Brain and intelligence: A quantitative study of the frontal lobes.* Chicago: Univ. of Chicago Press, 1947.

Harlow, H. F. The heterosexual affectional system in monkeys. *American Psychologist*, 1962, *17*, 1–9.

Harlow, H. F. Sexual behavior in the rhesus monkey. In F. A. Beach (Ed.), *Sex and behavior.* New York: Wiley, 1965.

Harlow, H. F., & Harlow, M. K. Social deprivation in monkeys. *Scientific American*, 1962, *207*(5), 136–146.

Haronian, R., & Saunders, D. R. Some intellectual correlates of physique: A review and a study. *Journal of Psychological Studies*, 1967, *15*, 57–105.

Harris, B. Whatever happened to little Albert? *American Psychologist*, 1979, *34*, 151–160.

Harris, M. B. Mediators between frustration and aggression in a field experiment. *Journal of Experimental Social Psychology*, 1974, *10*, 561–571.

Harrower, M. Rorschach records of the Nazi war criminals: An experimental study after thirty years. *Journal of Personality Assessment*, 1976, *40*, 341–351.

Hartlage, L. C. Sex-linked inheritance of spatial ability. *Perceptual and Motor Skills*, 1970, *31*, 610.

Hartmann, H., Kris, E., & Loewenstein, R. M. Comments on the formation of psychic structure. In A. Freud et al. (Eds.), *The psychoanalytic study of the child.* New York: Internat. Univ. Press, 1947.

Hartshorne, H., & May, M. A. *Studies in the nature of character.* (Vol. 1: *Studies in deceit*). New York: Macmillan, 1928.

Hartup, W. W. Aggression in childhood: Development perspectives. *American Psychologist*, 1974, *29*, 336–341.

Harvey, M. A., & Sipprelle, C. N. Demand characteristic effects on the subtle and obvious subscales of the MMPI. *Journal of Personality Assessment*, 1976, *40*, 539–544.

Hathaway, S. R. MMPI: Professional use by professional people. *American Psychologist*, 1964, *19*, 204–210.

Hathaway, S. R., & McKinley, J. C. A multiphasic personality schedule (Minnesota): I. Construction of the schedule. *Journal of Psychology*, 1940, *10*, 249–254.

Havighurst, R. J., & Albrecht, R. *Older people.* New York: Longmans, 1953.

Hayes, K. J., & Hayes, C. The intellectual development of a home raised chimpanzee. *Proceedings of the American Philosophical Society*, 1951, *95*, 105–109.

Hayflick, L. The cell biology of human aging. *Scientific American,* 1980, *242*(1), 58–65.

Haynes, H., White, B. L., & Held, R. Development of visual accommodation. *Science*, 1965, *148*, 528–530.

Heaton, R. K., Baade, L. E., & Johnson, K. L. Neuropsychological test results associated with psychiatric disorders in adults. *Psychological Bulletin*, 1978, *85*, 141–162.

Hebb, D. O. *Organization of behavior.* New York: Wiley, 1949.

Heidegger, M. *Being and time.* New York: Harper & Row, 1962. (Originally published 1927.)

Henry, W. E. *The analysis of fantasy: The Thematic Apperception Technique in the study of personality.* New York: Wiley, 1956.

Henson, D. E., & Rubin, H. B. Voluntary control of eroticism. *Journal of Applied Behavior Analysis*, 1971, *4*, 37–44.

Heron, W. The pathology of boredom. *Scientific American*, 1957, *196*(1), 52–56.

Hilgard, E. R. Psychoanalysis: Experimental studies. In D. L. Sills (Ed.), *International encyclopedia of the social sciences* (Vol. 13). New York: Macmillan and Free Press, 1968, pp. 37–45.

Hiroto, D. S. Learned helplessness, and locus of control. *Journal of Experimental Psychology*, 1974, *102*, 187–193.

Hiroto, D. S., & Seligman, M. E. P. Generality of learned helplessness in man. *Journal of Personality and Social Psychology*, 1975, *31*, 311–327.

Hoffman, L. W. Changes in family roles, socialization, and sex differences. *American Psychologist*, 1977, *32*, 644–658.

Hoffman, M. L. Altruistic behavior and the parent-child relationship. *Journal of Personality and Social Psychology*, 1975, *31*, 937–943.

Hoffman, M. L. Sex differences in empathy and related behaviors. *Psychological Bulletin*, 1977, *84*, 712–722.

Hogan, R. Moral conduct and moral character: A psychological perspective. *Psychological Bulletin*, 1973, *79*, 217–232.

Hogan, R., DeSoto, C. B., & Solano, C. Traits, tests, and personality research. *American Psychologist*, 1977, *32*, 255–264.

Hokanson, J. E., & Burgess, M. The effects of status, type of frustration, and aggression on vascular processes. *Journal of Abnormal and Social Psychology*, 1962, *65*, 232–237.

Hokanson, J. E., Burgess, M., & Cohen, M. E. Effects of displaced aggression on systolic blood pressure. *Journal of Abnormal and Social Psychology*, 1963, *67*, 214–218.

Holden, C. The plight of the "deinstitutionalized" mental patient. *Science*, 1978, *200*, 1366.

Hollander, E. P., & Marcia, J. E. Parental determinants of peer-orientation and self-orientation among preadolescents. *Developmental Psychology*, 1970, *2*, 292–302.

Hollander, E. P., & Willis, R. H. Some current issues in the psychology of conformity and nonconformity, *Psychological Bulletin*, 1967, *68*, 62–76.

Holmes, T., & Masuda, M. Psychosomatic syndrome. *Psychology Today*, April 1972, pp. 71 ff.

Holtzman, W. H. New developments in Holtzman Inkblot Technique. In P. McReynolds (Ed.), *Advances in psychological assessment* (Vol. 3). San Francisco: Jossey-Bass, 1975.

Holtzman, W. H., Thorpe, J. W., Swartz, J. D., & Herron, E. W. *Inkblot perception and personal-*

ity: *Holtzman Inkblot Technique.* Austin: Univ. of Texas Press, 1961.

Homans, G. C. *Social behavior: Its elementary forms* (Rev. ed.). New York: Harcourt Brace Jovanovich, 1974.

Horn, J. L., & Cattell, R. B. Age differences in primary mental ability factors. *Journal of Gerontology*, 1966, *21*, 210–220.

Horn, J. L., & Donaldson, G. On the myth of intellectual decline in adulthood. *American Psychologist*, 1976, *31*, 701–719.

Horner, M. Femininity and successful achievement: A basic inconsistency. In J. M. Bardwick, E. Douvan, M. S. Horner, & D. Gutmann (Eds.), *Feminine personality and conflict.* Monterey, Calif.: Brooks/Cole, 1970.

Horney, K. *New ways in psychoanalysis.* New York: Norton, 1939.

Horney, K. *Our inner conflicts.* New York: Norton, 1945.

Horney, K. *Neurosis and human growth.* New York: Norton, 1950.

Howes, D. H., & Solomon, R. L. A note on McGinnies' "Emotionality and perceptual defense." *Psychological Review*, 1950, *57*, 229–234.

Hsu, H. K., & Peng, M. T. Hypothalamic neuron number of old female rats. *Gerontology*, 1978, *24*, 434–440.

Hughes, J. R. Biochemical and electroencephalographic correlates of learning disabilities. In R. M. Knights & D. J. Bakker (Eds.), *The neuropsychology of learning disorders.* Baltimore: University Park Press, 1976.

Hultsch, D. R. Organization and memory in adulthood. *Human Development*, 1971, *14*, 16–29.

Humphreys, L. G. Characteristics of type concepts with special reference to Sheldon's typology. *Psychological Bulletin*, 1957, *54*, 218–228.

Hunt, B., & Hunt, M. *Prime time.* New York: Stein and Day, 1974.

Husek, T. R. Acquiescence as a response set and as a personality characteristic. *Educational and Psychological Measurement*, 1961, *21*, 295–307.

Huston, T. L., Geis, G., & Wright, R. The angry Samaritans. *Psychology Today*, June 1976, pp. 61 ff.

Hutt, M. L. *The Hutt adaptation of the Bender-gestalt test* (3rd ed.). New York: Grune & Stratton, 1977.

Huxley, A. *Brave new world.* New York: Bantam, 1960. (Originally published 1932.)

Inglis, J., Ankus, M. N., & Sykes, D. H. Age-related differences in learning and short-term memory from childhood to the senium. *Human Development*, 1968, *11*, 42–52.

Inhelder, B., & Piaget, J. *The growth of logical thinking.* New York: Basic Books, 1958.

Iscoe, I., Williams, M., & Harvey, J. Age, intelligence, and sex as variables in the conformity of Negro and white children. *Child Development*, 1964, *35*, 451–460.

Isen, A. M., Shalker, T. E., Clark, M., & Karp, L. Affect, accessibility of material in memory, and behavior: A cognitive loop? *Journal of Personality and Social Psychology*, 1978, *36*, 1–12.

Iverson, L. L. The chemistry of the brain. *Scientific American*, 1979, *241*(3), 134–149.

Jackson, D. N. *Personality Research Form Manual.* Goshen, N.Y.: Research Psychologists Press, 1967.

Jackson, D. N. *Personality Research Form Manual* (Rev. ed.). Port Huron, Mich.: Research Psychologists Press, 1974.

James, W. What is an emotion? *Mind*, 1884, *9*, 188–205.

Janeway, E. On "female sexuality." In J. Strouse (Ed.), *Women and analysis.* New York: Grossman, 1974.

Janis, I. L., & Field, P. B. Sex differences and personality factors related to persuasibility. In I. L. Janis, C. I. Hovland, P. B. Field, H. Linton, E. Graham, A. R. Cohen, D. Rife, R. P. Abelson, G. S. Lesser, & B. T. King (Eds.), *Personality and persuasibility.* New Haven, Conn.: Yale, 1959.

Jarvik, L. F. Thoughts on the psychobiology of aging. *American Psychologist*, 1975, *30*, 576–583.

Jarvik, L. F., Falek, A., Kallman, F. J., & Lorge, I. Survival trends in a senescent twin population. *American Journal of Human Genetics*, 1960, *12*, 170–179.

Jarvik, L. F., Klodin, V., & Matsuyama, S. S. Human aggression and the extra Y chromosome: Fact or fantasy? *American Psychologist*, 1973, *28*, 674–682.

Jencks, C., Smith, M., Acland, H., Bane, M. J., Cohen, D., Gintis, H., Heyns, B., & Michelson, S. *Inequality*. New York: Basic Books, 1972.

Jenkins, C. D., Zyzanski, S. J., & Rosenman, R. H. Progress toward validation of a computer-scored test of the Type A coronary-prone behavior pattern. *Psychosomatic Medicine*, 1971, *33*, 192–212.

Jensen, A. R. How much can we boost IQ and scholastic achievement? *Harvard Educational Review*, 1969, *39*, 1–123.

Jensen, A. R. *Educability and group differences*. New York: Harper & Row, 1973.

Jensen, A. R. Kinship correlations reported by Sir Cyril Burt. *Behavior Genetics*, 1974, *4*, 1–28.

Jensen, A. R. The current status of the· IQ controversy. *Australian Psychologist*, 1978, *13*, 7–27.

Johnson, H. E., & Garton, W. H. Muscle re-education in hemiplegia by use of electromyographic device. *Archives of Physical Medicine and Rehabilitation*, 1973, *54*, 320–325.

Johnson, M. M. Fathers, mothers, and sex-typing. *Sociological Inquiry*, 1975, *45*(1), 15–26.

Johnson, R. N. *Aggression in man and animals*. Philadelphia: Saunders, 1972.

Jones, E. *The life and work of Sigmund Freud*. Edited by L. Trilling & S. Marcus. New York: Basic Books, 1961.

Jones, M. C., Albert, Peter, and John B. Watson, *American Psychologist*, 1974, *29*, 581–583.

Jones, R. R., Reid, J. B., & Patterson, G. R. Naturalistic observation in clinical assessment. In P. McReynolds (Ed.), *Advances in Psychological Assessment* (Vol. 3). San Francisco: Jossey-Bass, 1975.

Jourard, S. M. *The transparent self* (Rev. ed.). New York: Van Nostrand, 1971.

Jourard, S. M. *Healthy personality: An approach from the viewpoint of humanistic psychology*. New York: Macmillan, 1974.

Jung, C. G.· *Collected papers on analytical psychology*. New York: Moffat, Yard, 1917.

Jung, C. G. *Psychological types*. London: Routledge, 1923.

Jung, C. G. The psychological diagnosis of evidence. In H. Read, M. Fordham, & G. Adler (Eds.), *Collected works* (Vol. 2). Princeton: Princeton Univ. Press, 1953. (Originally published 1909.)

Jung, C. G. The stages of life. *Collected works* (Vol. 8). (Originally published 1931.)

Jung, C. G. Archetypes and the collective unconscious. *Collected works* (Vol. 9). (Originally published 1939.)

Jung, C. G. *Modern man in search of a soul*. New York: Harvest Books, 1955. (Originally published 1933.)

Jung, C. G. Two essays on analytical psychology. *In Collected works* (Vol. 9). (Originally published 1951.)

Jung, C. G. *The undiscovered self*. New York: Mentor, 1958.

Jung, C. G. *Memories, dreams, and reflections*. Edited by A. Jaffe. New York: Pantheon, 1961.

Jung, C. G. *Analytical psychology: Its theory and practice*. New York: Pantheon, 1968.

Kagan, J., & Moss, H. *Birth to maturity*. New York: Wiley, 1962.

Kalish, R. A. Late adulthood: Perspectives on human development. Monterey, Calif.: Brooks/Cole, 1975.

Kamin, L. J. *The science and politics of IQ*. Potomac, Md.: Lawrence Erlbaum, 1974.

Kamin, L. J. Comment on Munsinger's review of adoption studies. *Psychological Bulletin*, 1978, *85*, 194–201.

Kanfer, F. H., & Saslow, G. Behavioral diagnosis. In C. M. Franks (Ed.), *Behavior therapy: Ap-*

praisal and status. New York: McGraw-Hill, 1969.

Kaplan, A. G. Clarifying the concept of androgyny: Implications for therapy. *Psychology of Women Quarterly,* 1979, *3,* 223–230.

Kaplan, M. F., & Eron, L. D. Test sophistication and faking in the TAT situation. *Journal of Projective Techniques and Personality Assessment,* 1965, *29,* 493–503.

Karabenick, S. A. Fear of success, achievement and affiliation dispositions, and the performance of men and women under individual and competitive conditions. *Journal of Personality,* 1977, *45,* 117–149.

Kardiner, A., & Ovesey, L. *The mark of oppression.* New York: Norton, 1951.

Karst, T. O., & Groutt, J. W. Inside mystical heads: Shared and personal constructs in a commune with some implications for a personal construct theory social psychology. In D. Bannister (Ed.), *New perspectives in personal construct theory.* London: Academic, 1977.

Kassebaum, G. G., Couch, A. S., & Slater, P. E. The factorial dimensions of the MMPI. *Journal of Consulting Psychology,* 1959, *23,* 226–236.

Keen, E. *Three faces of being: Toward an existential clinical psychology.* New York: Appleton Century Crofts, 1970.

Keleman, G. The anatomical basis of phonation in the chimpanzee. *Journal of Morphology,* 1948, *82,* 229–256.

Kelley, D. M. Preliminary studies of the Rorschach records of the Nazi war criminals. *Rorschach Exchange,* 1946, *10,* 45–48.

Kelley, H. H. The warm-cold variable in first impressions of persons. *Journal of Personality,* 1950, *18,* 431–439.

Kellogg, W. N., & Kellogg, L. A. *The ape and the child: A study of environmental influence upon early behavior.* New York: Hafner, 1967. (Originally published 1933.)

Kelly, G. A. *The psychology of personal constructs.* New York: Norton, 1955.

Kelly, G. A. Man's construction of his alternatives. In G. Lindzey (Ed.), *Assessment of human motives.* New York: Holt, 1958.

Kelly, G. A. The autobiography of a theory. In B. Maher (Ed.), *Clinical psychology and personality: Selected papers of George Kelly.* New York: Wiley, 1963.

Kesey, K. *One flew over the cuckoo's nest.* New York: Viking, 1962.

Kety, S. S., Rosenthal, D., Wender, P. H., Schulsinger, F., & Jacobsen, B. The biologic and adoptive families of adopted individuals who became schizophrenic: Prevalence of mental illness and other characteristics. In L. C. Wynne et al. (Eds.), *The nature of schizophrenia.* New York: Wiley, 1978.

Kleinmuntz, B. *Personality measurement.* Homewood, Ill.: Dorsey, 1967.

Kline, P. Obsessional traits, obsessional symptoms, and anal eroticism. *British Journal of Medical Psychology,* 1968, *41,* 299–305.

Kline, P. The anal character: A cross-cultural study in Ghana. *British Journal of Social and Clinical Psychology,* 1969, *8,* 201–210.

Kline, P. *Fact and fantasy in Freudian personality theory.* London: Methuen, 1972.

Klopfer, B., Ainsworth, M. D., Klopper, W. C., & Holt, R. R. *Developments in the Rorschach technique.* New York: Harcourt, Brace & World, 1954.

Klopfer, B., & Davidson, H. H. *The Rorschach technique: An introductory manual.* New York: Harcourt, Brace & World, 1962.

Knott, P. D., Lasater, L., & Shuman, R. Aggression-guilt and conditionability for aggressiveness. *Journal of Personality,* 1974, *42,* 332–344.

Kobasa, S. C. Stressful life events, personality, and health: An inquiry into hardiness. *Journal of Personality and Social Psychology,* 1979, 37, 1–11.

Kohlberg, L. The development of children's orientations toward a moral order: I. Sequence in the development of moral thought. *Vita humana,* 1963, *6,* 11–33.

Kohlberg, L. A cognitive-developmental analysis of children's sex-role concepts and attitudes. In E. E. Maccoby (Ed.), *The development of sex differences.* Stanford, Calif.: Stanford, 1966.

Kohlberg, L. Stage and sequence: The cognitive developmental approach to socialization. In D. A. Goslin (Ed.), *Handbook of socialization theory and research.* Chicago: Rand McNally, 1969.

Kohlberg, L. Moral stages and moralization. In T. Lickona (Ed.), *Moral development and behavior.* New York: Holt, 1976.

Kohlberg, L., & Gilligan, C. The adolescent as a philosopher: The discovery of the self in a post-conventional world. *Daedalus,* 1971, *100,* 1050–1086.

Kohlberg, L., & Kramer, R. Continuities and discontinuities in childhood and adult moral development. *Human Development,* 1969, *12,* 93–120.

Kolata, G. B. Mental disorders: A new approach to treatment. *Science,* 1979, *203,* 36–38.

Konečni, V. J. Some effects of guilt on compliance: A field replication. *Journal of Personality and Social Psychology,* 1972, *23,* 30–32.

Konečni, V. J. Annoyance, type and duration of postannoyance activity, and aggression: The "cathartic effect." *Journal of Experimental Psychology: General,* 1975, *104,* 76–102.

Konečni, V. J., & Doob, A. N. Catharsis through displacement of aggression. *Journal of Personality and Social Psychology,* 1972, *23,* 379–387.

Koretzky, M. B., Kohn, M., & Jeger, A. M. Cross-situational consistency among problem adolescents: An application of the two-factor model. *Journal of Personality and Social Psychology,* 1978, *36,* 1054–1059.

Kosberg, J. I. Differences in proprietary institutions caring for affluent and nonaffluent elderly. *Gerontologist,* 1973, *13,* 299–304.

Kraepelin, E. Clinical psychiatry. New York: Macmillan, 1923 (Abstracted from the 7th German edition by A. R. Diefendorf).

Krantz, D. S., Glass, D. C., & Snyder, M. L. Helplessness, stress level, and the coronary-prone behavior pattern. *Journal of Experimental and Social Psychology,* 1974, *10,* 284–300.

Krebs, D. Empathy and altruism. *Journal of Personality and Social Psychology,* 1975, *32,* 1134–1146.

Kretschmer, E. *Physique and character.* Translated by W. J. H. Sprott. New York: Harcourt, 1925. (Originally published 1921.)

Kripke, D., & Sonneschein, D. A 90-minute daydream cycle. *Proceedings of the Association for the Psychophysiological Study of Sleep,* 1973, *2,* 1977.

Kunce, J. T., Ryan, J. J., & Eckelman, C. C. Violent behavior and differential WAIS characteristics. *Journal of Consulting and Clinical Psychology,* 1976, *44,* 42–45.

Kurtines, W., & Greif, E. B. The development of moral thought: Review and evaluation of Kohlberg's approach. *Psychological Bulletin,* 1974, *81,* 453–470.

Labouvie-Vief, G., & Baltes, P. B. Reduction of adolescent misperceptions of the aged. *Journal of Gerontology,* 1976, *31,* 68–71.

Laing, R. D. The divided self: A study of sanity and madness. Chicago: Quadrangle, 1960.

Lambert, M. J. Spontaneous remission in adult neurotic disorders: A revision and summary. *Psychological Bulletin,* 1976, *83,* 107–119.

Langer, E. J., & Abelson, R. P. A patient by any other name . . .: Clinician group difference in labeling bias. *Journal of Consulting and Clinical Psychology,* 1974, *42,* 4–9.

Langer, E. J., & Rodin, J. The effects of choice and enhanced personal responsibility for the aged: A field experiment in an institutional setting. *Journal of Personality and Social Psychology,* 1976, *34,* 191–198.

Lanyon, R. I. *A handbook of MMPI profiles.* Minneapolis: Univ. of Minnesota Press, 1968.

Lanyon, R. I., & Goodstein, L. D. *Personality assessment.* New York: Wiley, 1971.

Latané, B., & Darley, J. *The unresponsive bystander: Why doesn't he help?* Englewood Cliffs, N. J.: Prentice-Hall, 1970.

Latané, B., & Rodin, J. A lady in distress: Inhibiting effects of friends and strangers on bystander intervention. *Journal of Experimental Social Psychology,* 1969, *5,* 189–202.

Lavery, J. J., & Foley, P. J. Altruism or arousal in the rat? *Science,* 1963, *140,* 172–173.

Lawton, M. P. Social ecology and the health of

older people. *American Journal of Public Health*, 1974, *64*, 257–260.

Lazarus, A. A. New methods in psychotherapy: A case study. *South African Medical Journal*, 1958, *32*, 660–664.

Lazarus, A. A. *Behavior therapy and beyond*. New York: McGraw-Hill, 1971.

Lazarus, A. A. Has behavior therapy outlived its usefulness. *American Psychologist*, 1977, *32*, 550–554.

Lazarus, R. S., Averill, J. R., & Opton, E. M. Towards a cognitive theory of emotion. In M. B. Arnold (Ed.), *Feelings and emotions*. New York: Academic, 1970.

Lazarus, R. S., & McCleary, R. A. Autonomic discrimination without awareness: A study of subception. *Psychological Review*, 1951, *58*, 113–122.

Leaf, A. Getting old. *Scientific American*, 1973, *229*(3), 45–52.

Leakey, L. S. B., & Ardrey, R. Man the killer—a dialogue. *Psychology Today*, September 1972, pp. 73 ff.

Lehman, H. C. *Age and achievement*. Princeton, N.J.: Princeton, 1953.

Lemere, F., & Voegtlin, W. An evaluation of the aversion treatment of alcoholism. *Quarterly Journal for the Study of Alcoholism*, 1950, *11*, 199–204.

Lemon, B. W., Bengtson, V. L., & Peterson, J. A. An exploration of the activity theory of aging: Activity types and life satisfaction among in-movers to a retirement community. *Journal of Gerontology*, 1972, *27*, 511–523.

Lenneberg, E. H. A biological perspective of language. In E. Lenneberg (Ed.), *New directions in the study of language*. Cambridge, Mass.: M.I.T., 1964. (a)

Lenneberg, E. H. Language disorders in childhood. *Harvard Educational Review*, 1964, *34*, 152–177. (b)

Lenneberg, E. H., Rebelsky, F. G., & Nichols, I. A. The vocalization of infants born to deaf and hearing parents. *Human Development*, 1965, *8*, 23–37.

Lenney, E. Women's self-confidence in achieve-ment settings. *Psychological Bulletin*, 1977, *84*, 1–13.

Lenney, E. Androgyny: Some audacious assertions toward its coming of age. *Sex Roles*, 1979, *5*, 703–719.

Lepper, M. R., Greene, D., & Nisbett, R. E. Undermining children's intrinsic interest with extrinsic reward: A test of the "overjustification" hypothesis. *Journal of Personality and Social Psychology*, 1973, *28*, 129–137.

Lerner, M. J. Evaluation of performance as a function of performer's reward and attractiveness. *Journal of Personality and Social Psychology*, 1965, *1*, 355–360.

Lerner, M. J. The justice motive: "Equity" and "parity" among children. *Journal of Personality and Social Psychology*, 1974, *29*, 539–550.

Lerner, M. J., Miller, D. T., & Holmes, J. G. Deserving and the emergence of forms of justice. In L. Berkowitz & E. Walster (Eds.), *Equity theory: Toward a general theory of social interaction. Advances in experimental social psychology* (Vol. 9). New York: Academic, 1976.

Lerner, M. J., & Simmons, C. H. Observers' reaction to the "innocent victim": Compassion or rejection? *Journal of Personality and Social Psychology*, 1966, *4*, 203–210.

Levinson, D., Darrow, C., Klein, E., Levinson, M., & McKee, B. The psychosocial development of men in early adulthood and the midlife transition. In D. F. Ricks, A. Thomas, & M. Roff (Eds.), *Life history research in psychopathology*. Minneapolis: Univ. of Minnesota Press, 1974.

Lewis, M. M. *Infant speech* (2nd ed.). New York: Humanities Press, 1951.

Lewis, M. M. *Language, thought, and personality in infancy and childhood*. New York: Basic Books, 1963.

Lewis, M. Early sex differences in the human: Studies of socioemotional development. *Archives of Sexual Behavior*, 1975, *4*, 329–335.

Lewis, M. & Brooks-Gunn, J. Self, other, and fear: The reaction of infants to people. Paper presented at the meeting of the Eastern Psychological Association, Boston, April 1972. Reprinted in E. M. Hetherington & R. D. Parke (Eds.), *Contemporary readings in child psychology.* New York: McGraw-Hill, 1977.

Leyens, J. P., Camino, L., Parke, R. D., & Berkowitz, L. Effects of movie violence on aggression in a field setting as a function of group dominance and cohesion. *Journal of Personality and Social Psychology*, 1975, *32*, 346–360.

Lieberman, P. D., Klatt, H., & Wilson, W. Vocal tract limitations of the vocal repertoires of rhesus monkeys and other non-human primates. *Science*, 1969, *164*, 1185–1187.

Liebert, R. M., & Baron, R. A. Some immediate effects of televised violence on children's behavior. *Developmental Psychology*, 1972, *6*, 469–475.

Limber, J. Language in child and chimp? *American Psychologist*, 1977, *32*, 280–295.

Linton, H. B. Dependence on external influence. Correlates in perception, attitudes, and judgment. *Journal of Abnormal and Social Psychology*, 1955, *51*, 502–507.

Lipman, A., & Smith, K. J. Functionality of disengagement in old age. *Journal of Gerontology*, 1968, *23*, 517–521.

Lipsitz, L. *The test score decline: Meanings and issues.* Englewood Cliffs, N.J.: Educational Technology Publications, 1977.

Lockhart, R. A., & Siegel, B. A Jungian approach to the Rorschach: An exploration of differing patterns of aggression. *Journal of Personality Assessment*, 1976, *40*, 234–247.

Locksley, A., & Colten, M. E. Psychological androgyny: A case of mistaken identity? *Journal of Personality and Social Psychology*, 1979, *37*, 1017–1031.

Loehlin, J. C., Lindzey, G., & Spuhler, J. N. *Race differences in intelligence.* San Francisco: Freeman, 1975.

Loehlin, J. C., & Nichols, R. C. *Heredity, environment, and personality.* Austin: Univ. of Texas Press, 1976.

Loevinger, J. *Ego development.* San Francisco: Jossey-Bass, 1976.

Loevinger, J., & Wessler, R. *Measuring ego development* (Vol. 1). San Francisco: Jossey-Bass, 1970.

London, P. The rescuers: Motivational hypotheses about Christians who saved Jews from the Nazis. In J. Macaulay & L. Berkowitz (Eds.), *Altruism and helping behavior.* New York: Academic, 1970.

Long, G. T., & Lerner, M. J. Deserving, the "personal contract," and altruistic behavior by children. *Journal of Personality and Social Psychology*, 1974, *29*, 551–556.

Lorenz, K. *On aggression.* New York: Harcourt, Brace & World, 1966.

Lorenz, K. *Studies in animal and human behavior* (Vol. 2). Cambridge, Mass.: Harvard, 1971.

Lott, B. Behavioral concordance with sex role ideology related to play areas, creativity, and parental sex typing of children. *Journal of Personality and Social Psychology*, 1978, *36*, 1087–1100.

Lovaas, O. I., Freitag, G., Gold, V. J., & Kassorla, I. C. Experimental studies in childhood schizophrenia: I. Analysis of self-destructive behavior. *Journal of Experimental Child Psychology*, 1965, *2*, 67–84.

Lovell, V. R. The human use of personality tests: A dissenting view. *American Psychologist*, 1967, *22*, 383–393.

Lovibond, S. H., & Caddy, G. Discriminated aversive control in the moderation of alcoholics' drinking behavior. *Behavior Therapy*, 1970, *1*, 437–444.

Lucas, G. *Star wars.* New York: Ballantine, 1976.

Lykken, D. T. A study of anxiety in the sociopathic personality. *Journal of Abnormal and Social Psychology.* 1957, *55*, 6–10.

Maccoby, E. E., & Jacklin, C. N. *The psychology of sex differences.* Stanford, Calif.: Stanford, 1974.

Machover, K. *Personality projection in the drawing of the human figure.* Springfield, Ill.: Charles C Thomas, 1948.

Machover, K. Drawing of the human figure: A method of personality investigation. In H. H. Anderson & G. L. Anderson (Eds.), *An intro-*

duction to projective techniques. Englewood Cliffs, N.J.: Prentice-Hall, 1951.

MacLean, P. D. The limbic brain in relation to the psychoses. In P. Black (Ed.), *Physiological correlates of emotion*. New York: Academic, 1970.

Maddi, S. R., & Costa, P. T. *Humanism in personology*. Chicago: Aldine, 1972.

Mahoney, T. A., Jerdee, T. H., & Nash, A. N. *The identification of management potential: A research approach to management development*. Dubuque, Iowa: Wm. C. Brown, 1961.

Maitland, K. A., & Goldman, J. R. Moral judgment as a function of peer group interaction. *Journal of Personality and Social Psychology*, 1974, *30*, 699–704.

Major, B. Sex-role orientation and fear of success: Clarifying an unclear relationship. *Sex Roles*, 1979, *5*, 63–70.

Malmo, R. B. Activation: A neuropsychological dimension. *Psychological Review*, 1959, *66*, 367–386.

Mancuso, J. C. Current motivational models in the elaboration of personal construct theory. *Nebraska Symposium on Motivation*, 1976, *24*, 43–97.

Mandler, G. Emotion. In R. Brown, E. Galanter, E. H. Hess, & G. Mandler (Eds.), *New directions in psychology*. New York: Holt, 1962.

Mann, L. The effects of emotional role playing on desire to modify smoking habits. *Journal of Experimental Social Psychology*, 1967, *3*, 334–348.

Markowitz, I. Relevance of psychoanalysis to education. In J. Masserman (Ed.), *Science and psychoanalysis* (Vol. 21). New York: Grune and Stratton, 1972.

Marshall, G. D., & Zimbardo, P. G. Affective consequences of inadequately explained physiological arousal. *Journal of Personality and Social Psychology*, 1979, *37*, 970–988.

Maslow, A. H. The role of dominance in the social and sexual behavior of infra-human primates: I. Observations at Vilas Park Zoo. In R. J. Lowry (Ed.), *Dominance self-esteem, self-actualization: Germinal papers of A. H. Maslow*. Belmont, Calif.: Wadsworth, 1973. (Originally published 1936.)

Maslow, A. H. Dominance-feeling, behavior and status. In Lowry (Ed.). (Originally published 1937.)

Maslow, A. H. Dominance, personality, and social behavior in women. In Lowry (Ed.). (Originally published 1939.)

Maslow, A. H. Self-esteem (dominance-feeling) and sexuality in women. In Lowry (Ed.). (Originally published 1942.)

Maslow, A. H. A theory of human motivation. In Lowry (Ed.). (Originally published 1943.)

Maslow, A. H. Self-actualizing people: A study of psychological health. In Lowry (Ed.). (Originally published 1950.)

Maslow, A. H. *Motivation and personality* (2nd ed.). New York: Harper & Row, 1970.

Maslow, A. H. *The farther reaches of human nature*. New York: Viking, 1971.

Maslow, A. H., & Flanzbaum, S. The role of dominance in the social and sexual behavior of infra-human primates: II. An experimental determination of the behavior syndrome of dominance. In Lowry (Ed.). (Originally published 1936.)

Mason, E. P. Cross-validation study of personality characteristics of junior high school students from American Indian, Mexican, and Caucasian ethnic backgrounds. *Journal of Social Psychology*, 1969, *77*, 15–24.

Masserman, J. H., Wechkin, S., & Terris, W. "Altruistic" behavior in rhesus monkeys. *American Journal of Psychiatry*, 1964, *121*, 584–585.

May, R. Contributions of existential psychotherapy. In R. May, E. E. Angel, & H. F. Ellenberger (Eds.), *Existence: A new dimension in psychiatry and psychology*. New York: Basic Books, 1958.

May, R. (Ed.). *Existential psychology*. New York: Random House, 1961.

McClelland, D. C. *The achieving society*. Princeton, N.J.: Van Nostrand, 1961.

McClelland, D. C. Achieving man: To know why men do what they do. *Psychology Today*, January 1971, pp. 35 ff.

McClelland, D. C. Love and power: The psychological signals of war. *Psychology Today*, January 1975, 44–48.

McClelland, D. C., Atkinson, J. W., Clark, R. A., & Lowell, E. L. *The achievement motive.* New York: Appleton-Century, 1953.

McCord, J. Some child-rearing antecedents of criminal behavior in adult men. *Journal of Personality and Social Psychology*, 1979, *37*, 1477–1486.

McCord, W., & McCord, J. *The psychopath: An essay on the criminal mind.* Princeton, N.J.: Van Nostrand, 1964.

McCrew, W. C. *An ethological study of children's behavior.* New York: Academic, 1972.

McCullough, J. P., Huntsinger, G. W., & Nay, W. R. Self-control treatment of aggression in a 16-year-old male. *Journal of Consulting and Clinical Psychology*, 1977, *45*, 322–331.

McDonald, R. L., & Gynther, M. D. MMPI difference associated with sex, race, and social class in two adolescent samples. *Journal of Consulting Psychology*, 1963, *27*, 112–116.

McGhee, P. E. Television as a source of learning sex-role stereotypes. In S. Cohen & T. J. Comiskey (Eds.), *Child Development.* Itasca, Ill.: Peacock, 1977.

McGinnies, E. Emotionality and perceptual defense. *Psychological Review*, 1949, *56*, 244–251.

McGuire, W. (Ed.). *The Freud/Jung letters: The correspondence between Sigmund Freud and C. G. Jung.* (R. Manheim & R. F. C. Hull, Trans.) Bollingen Series XCIV. Princeton, N.J.: Princeton, 1974.

McGuire, W. J., McGuire, C. V., & Winton, W. Effects of household sex composition on the salience of one's gender in the spontaneous self-concept. *Journal of Experimental Social Psychology*, 1979, *15*, 77–90.

McReynolds, P. Historical antecedents of personality assessment. In P. McReynolds (Ed.), *Advances in Psychological Assessment* (Vol. 3). San Francisco: Jossey-Bass, 1975.

Mead, M. *Sex and temperament in three primitive societies.* New York: Morrow, 1935.

Meehl, P. E. A comparison of clinicians with five statistical methods of identifying psychotic MMPI profiles. *Journal of Counseling Psychology*, 1959, *6*, 102–109.

Meehl, P. E. Reactions, reflections, projections. In J. N. Butcher (Ed.), *Objective personality assessment.* New York: Academic, 1972.

Meehl, P. E., & Rosen, A. Antecedent probability and the efficiency of psychometric signs, patterns, or cutting scores. *Psychological Bulletin*, 1955, *52*, 194–216.

Megargee, E. I. The role of inhibition in the assessment and understanding of violence. In J. L. Singer (Ed.), *The control of aggression and violence.* New York: Academic, 1971.

Megargee, E. I. *The California Psychological Inventory Handbook.* San Francisco: Jossey-Bass, 1972.

Meichenbaum, D. *Cognitive-behavior modification.* New York: Plenum, 1977.

Meichenbaum, D., & Cameron, R. Training schizophrenics to talk to themselves: A means of developing attentional controls. *Behavior Therapy*, 1973, *5*, 515–534.

Meichenbaum, D., & Goodman, J. Training impulsive children to talk to themselves: A means of developing self-control. *Journal of Abnormal Psychology*, 1971, *77*, 115–126.

Mendel, W. M., & Rapport, S. Determinants of the decision for psychiatric hospitalization. *Archives of General Psychiatry*, 1969, *20*, 321–328.

Merbaum, M. The modification of self-destructive behavior by a mother-therapist using aversive stimulation. *Behavior Therapy*, 1973, *4*, 442–447.

Meyer, V., Liddell, A., & Lyons, M. Behavioral interviews. In A. R. Ciminero, K. S. Calhoun, & H. E. Adams (Eds.), *Handbook of behavioral assessment.* New York: Wiley, 1978.

Meyers, A., Mercatoris, M., & Sirota, A. Use of

covert self-instruction for the elimination of psychotic speech. *Journal of Consulting and Clinical Psychology,* 1976, *44,* 480–483.

Miale, F., & Selzer, M. *The Nuremberg mind: The psychology of the Nazi leaders.* New York: McGraw-Hill, 1975.

Milgram, S. Behavioral study of obedience. *Journal of Abnormal and Social Psychology,* 1963, *67,* 371–378.

Milgram, S. Group pressure and action against a person. *Journal of Abnormal and Social Psychology,* 1964, *69,* 137–143.

Milgram, S. Liberating effects of group pressure. *Journal of Personality and Social Psychology,* 1965, *1,* 127–134. (a)

Milgram, S. Some conditions of obedience and disobedience to authority. *Human Relations,* 1965, *18,* 57–76. (b)

Milgram, S., & Shotland, R. L. *Television and antisocial behavior: Field experiments.* New York: Academic, 1973.

Miller, G. A. *Psychology: The science of mental life.* New York: Harper & Row, 1962.

Miller, N. E. Theory and experiment relating psychoanalytic displacement to stimulus-response generalization. *Journal of Abnormal and Social Psychology,* 1948, *43,* 155–178.

Miller, N. E., & Banuazizi, A. Instrumental learning by curarized rats of a specific visceral response, intestinal or cardiac. *Journal of Comparative and Physiological Psychology,* 1968, *65,* 1–7.

Miller, R. E., Caul, W. F., & Mirsky, I. A. Communication of affects between feral and socially isolated monkeys. *Journal of Personality and Social Psychology,* 1967, *7,* 231–239.

Mills, G., & Campbell, M. A critique of Gellhorn and Kiely's mystical states of consciousness. *Journal of Nervous and Mental Disease,* 1974, *159,* 191–195.

Milton, G. A., & Lipetz, M. E. The factor structure of needs as measured by the EPPS. *Multivariate Behavioral Research,* 1968, *3,* 37–46.

Mineka, S., & Suomi, S. J. Social separation in monkeys. *Psychological Bulletin,* 1978, *85,* 1376–1400.

Mischel, W. A social-learning view of sex differences in behavior. In E. E. Maccoby (Ed.), *The development of sex differences.* Stanford, Calif.: Stanford, 1966.

Mischel, W. *Personality and assessment.* New York: Wiley, 1968.

Mischel, W. Toward a cognitive social learning reconceptualization of personality. *Psychological Review,* 1973, *80,* 252–283.

Mischel, W. Cognitive appraisals and transformations in self-control. In B. Weiner (Ed.), *Cognitive views of human motivation.* New York: Academic, 1974.

Mischel, W. Processes in delay of gratification. In L. Berkowitz (Ed.), *Advances in experimental social psychology* (Vol. 7). New York: Academic, 1974.

Mischel, W. *Introduction to personality* (2nd ed.). New York: Holt, 1976.

Mischel, W. On the future of personality measurement. *American Psychologist,* 1977, *32,* 246–254.

Mitchell, J. *Psychoanalysis and feminism.* New York: Vintage, 1974.

Money, J., & Ehrhardt, A. H. *Man and woman, boy and girl.* Baltimore: Johns Hopkins, 1972.

Money, J., Hampson, J., & Hampson, J. Imprinting and the establishment of gender role. *Archives of Neurological Psychiatry,* 1957, *77,* 333–336.

Morgan, C. D., & Murray, H. A. A method for investigating fantasies: The Thematic Apperception Test. *Archives of Neurology and Psychiatry,* 1935, *34,* 289–306.

Morris, D. *The naked ape.* London: Cape, 1967.

Moscovitch, M., Scullion, D., & Christie, D. Early versus late stages of processing and their relation to functional hemispheric asymmetries in face recognition. *Journal of Experimental Psychology. Human Perception and Performance,* 1976, *2,* 401–416.

Mouat, D. Evaluating dysfunction of the autonomic nervous system. *Geriatrics,* 1978, *33,* 83–93.

Mowrer, O. H. Speech development in the young child. I. The autism theory of speech development and some clinical applications. *Journal of Speech and Hearing Disorders*, 1952, *17*, 263–268.

Moyer, K. E. Sex differences in aggression. In R. C. Friedman, R. M. Richart, & R. L. Vande Wiele (Eds.), *Sex differences in behavior.* New York: Wiley, 1974.

Mulvihill, D. J., & Tumin, M. M. (Dirs.). *Crimes of violence: Staff report to the National Commission on the Causes and Prevention of Violence* (Vol. 2). Washington: U.S. Government Printing Office, 1969.

Munsinger, H. Reply to Kamin. *Psychological Bulletin*, 1978, *85*, 202–206.

Murphy, G., and Murphy, L. B. (Eds.). *Asian psychology.* New York: Basic Books, 1968.

Murray, A. D. Infant crying as an elicitor of parental behavior: An examination of two models. *Psychological Bulletin*, 1979, *86*, 191–215.

Murray, H. A. Explorations in personality: *A clinical and experimental study of fifty men of college age.* New York: Oxford, 1938.

Murray, H. A. *Thematic Apperception Test manual.* Cambridge, Mass.: Harvard, 1943.

Murray, H. A. Preparations for the scaffold of a comprehensive system. In S. Koch (Ed.), *Psychology: A study of a science* (Vol. 3). New York: McGraw-Hill, 1959.

Murray, H. A. Autobiography. In E. G. Boring & G. Lindzey (Eds.), *History of psychology in autobiography* (Vol. 5). New York: Appleton Century Crofts, 1967.

Nathan, P. E., Andberg, M. M., Behan, P. O., & Patch, V. D. Thirty-two observers and one patient: A study of diagnostic reliability. *Journal of Clinical Psychology*, 1969, *25*, 9–15.

National Institute of Mental Health. *Schizophrenia Bulletin* (No. 11). Washington: U.S. Government Printing Office, 1974.

Nay, W. Comprehensive behavioral treatment in a training school for delinquents. In K. Calhoun, H. Adams, & K. Mitchell (Eds.), *Innovative treatment methods in psychopathology.* New York: Wiley, 1974.

Nay, W. R. *Behavioral intervention.* New York: Gardner Press, 1976.

Nebes, R. D. Hemispheric specialization in commissurotomized man. *Psychological Bulletin*, 1974, *81*, 1–14.

Neugarten, B., Havighurst, R., & Tobin, S. Personality and patterns of aging. In B. Neugarten (Ed.), *Middle age and aging.* Chicago: Univ. of Chicago Press, 1968.

Newmark, C. S., Gentry, L., Simpson, M., & Jones, T. MMPI criteria for diagnosing schizophrenia. *Journal of Personality Assessment*, 1978, *42*, 366–373.

O'Connor, R. D. Relative efficacy of modeling, shaping, and the combined procedures for modification of social withdrawal. *Journal of Abnormal Psychology*, 1972, *79*, 327–334.

Office of Strategic Services Assessment Staff. *Assessment of men.* New York: Holt, 1948.

Ohman, A., & Dimberg, V. Facial expressions as conditioned stimuli for electrodermal responses: A case of "preparedness"? *Journal of Personality and Social Psychology*, 1978, *36*, 1251–1258.

Olds, S. W. Menopause: Something to look forward to? *Today's Health*, May 1970, pp. 48 ff.

Ordy, J. M., Brizzee, K. R., Kaack, B., & Hansche, J. Age differences in short-term memory and cell loss in the cortex of the rat. *Gerontology*, 1978, *24*, 276–285.

Ornstein, R. *The psychology of consciousness.* New York: Viking, 1973.

Ottinger, D. R., & Simmons, J. E. Behavior of human neonates and prenatal maternal anxiety. *Psychological Reports*, 1964, *14*, 391–394.

Page, M. P., & Scheidt, R. J. The elusive weapons effect: Demand awareness, evaluation apprehension, and slightly sophisticated subjects. *Journal of Personality and Social Psychology*, 1971, *20*, 304–318.

Palmore, E. B. The effects of aging on activities and attitudes. *Gerontologist*, 1968, *8*, 259–263.

Papalia, D. The status of several conservation abilities across the life span. *Human Development*, 1972, *15*, 229–243.

Pastore, N. The role of arbitrariness in the frustration-aggression hypothesis. *Journal of Abnormal and Social Psychology*, 1952, *47*, 728–731.

Patterson, C., & Mischel, W. Effects of temptation-inhibiting and task-facilitating plans on self-control. *Journal of Personality and Social Psychology*, 1976, *33*, 209–217.

Patterson, G. R., Littman, R. A., & Bricker, W. Assertive behavior in children: A step toward a theory of aggression. *Monographs of the Society for Research in Child Development*, 1967, *32* (5, Serial No. 113).

Paul, G. *Insight versus desensitization in psychotherapy: An experiment in anxiety reduction.* Stanford, Calif.: Stanford, 1966.

Pavlov, I. P. *Selected works.* Moscow: Foreign Languages Publishing House, 1955. (Originally published 1934.)

Pederson, P. B. Asian personality theory. In R. J. Corsini (Ed.), *Current personality theories.* Itasca, Ill.: Peacock, 1977.

Pedhazur, E. J., & Tetenbaum, T. J. Bem Sex Role Inventory: A theoretical and methodological critique. *Journal of Personality and Social Psychology*, 1979, *37*, 996–1016.

Perry, H. S. Introduction. In H. S. Sullivan, *The fusion of psychiatry and social science.* New York: Norton, 1964.

Peterson, D. R. *The clinical study of social behavior.* New York: Appleton Century Crofts, 1968.

Pettigrew, T. F. Introduction. In R. I. Evans, *Gordon Allport: The man and his ideas.* New York: Dutton, 1970.

Phares, E. J., Ritchie, E. D., & Davis, W. L. Internal-external control and reaction to threat. *Journal of Personality and Social Psychology*, 1968, *10*, 402–405.

Piaget, J. *The moral judgment of the child.* New York: Harcourt, Brace, 1932.

Piaget, J. *The origins of intelligence in children.* New York: Internat. Univ. Press, 1952. (Originally published 1936.)

Piaget, J. *The construction of reality in the child.* New York: Basic Books, 1954. (Originally published 1937.)

Piaget, J. *The language and thought of the child.* New York: Meridian, 1955. (Originally published 1923.)

Piaget, J. Biology and cognition. In B. Inhelder and H. H. Chipman (Eds.), *Piaget and his school.* New York: Springer-Verlag, 1976. (a)

Piaget, J. Identity and conservation. In B. Inhelder and H. H. Chipman (Eds.), *Piaget and his school.* New York: Springer-Verlag, 1976. (b)

Piliavin, I. M., Rodin, J., & Piliavin, J. A. Good samaritanism: An underground phenomenon? *Journal of Personality and Social Psychology*, 1969, *13*, 289–299.

Pilkonis, P. A. Shyness, public and private, and its relationship to other measures of social behavior. *Journal of Personality*, 1977, *45*, 585–595.

Pollak, J. M. Obsessive-compulsive personality: A review. *Psychological Bulletin*, 1979, *86*, 225–241.

Postman, L., Bruner, J. S., & McGinnies, E. Personal values as selective factors in perception. *Journal of Abnormal and Social Psychology*, 1948, *43*, 142–154.

Premack, A. J., & Premack, D. Teaching language to an ape. *Scientific American*, 1972, *227*(4), 92–99.

Premack, D. *Chimpanzee: Trivial language in a non-trivial mind.* Invited address, meeting of the Western Psychological Association, San Diego, 1979.

Prigatano, G. P., & Parsons, O. A. Relationship of age and education to Halstead test performance in different patient populations. *Journal of Consulting and Clinical Psychology*, 1976, *44*, 527–533.

Provence, S., & Lipton, R. *Infants in institutions.* New York: Internat. Univ. Press, 1962.

Rabin, A. I. Enduring sentiments: The continuity of personality over time. *Journal of Personality Assessment*, 1977, *41*, 564–572.

Rabkin, J. G. Criminal behavior of discharged mental patients: A critical appraisal of the research. *Psychological Bulletin*, 1979, *86*, 1–27.

Rachman, S. The role of muscular relaxation in

desensitizing therapy. *Behavior Research and Therapy*, 1968, *6*, 159–166.

Rachman, S. J. *The effects of psychotherapy.* Oxford: Pergamon, 1973.

Rands, M., & Levinger, G. Implicit theories of relationship: An intergenerational study. *Journal of Personality and Social Psychology*, 1979, *37*, 645–662.

Rathus, S. A. A 30-item schedule for assessing assertive behavior. *Behavior Therapy*, 1973, *4*, 398–406.

Rawls, D. J., & Rawls, J. R. Personality characteristics and personal history data of successful and less successful executives. *Psychological Reports*, 1968, *23*, 1032–1034.

Reckless, W. C., Dinitz, S., & Kay, B. The self component in potential delinquency and potential nondelinquency. *American Sociological Review*, 1957, *22*, 566–570.

Rees, L. Constitutional factors and abnormal behavior. In H. J. Eysenck (Ed.), *Handbook of abnormal psychology.* San Diego, Calif.: Knapp, 1973.

Regan, D. T., Williams, M., & Sparling, S. Voluntary expiation of guilt: A field experiment. *Journal of Personality and Social Psychology*, 1972, *24*, 42–45.

Reichard, S., Levson, F., & Peterson, P. *Aging and personality: A study of 87 older men.* New York: Wiley, 1962.

Reitan, R. M. Assessment of brain-behavior relationships. In P. McReynolds (Ed.), *Advances in psychological assessment* (Vol. 3). San Francisco: Jossey-Bass, 1975.

Reitan, R. M., & Davidson, L. A. *Clinical neuropsychology: Current status and applications.* New York: Winston-Wiley, 1974.

Reynolds, N. J., & Risley, T. R. The role of social and material reinforcers in increasing talking of a disadvantaged preschool child. *Journal of Applied Behavior Analysis*, 1968, *1*, 253–262.

Reynolds, V. *The biology of human action.* San Francisco: Freeman, 1976.

Rheingold, H. L. Exploration in a strange environment. In B. Foss (Ed.), *Determinants of infant behavior* (Vol. 4). London: Methuen, 1969.

Rheingold, H. L., & Cook, K. V. The contents of boys' and girls' rooms as an index of parents' behavior. *Child Development*, 1975, *46*, 459–463.

Rheingold, H. L., Gewirtz, J. L., & Ross, H. Social conditioning of vocalization in the infant. *Journal of Comparative and Physiological Psychology*, 1959, *52*, 68–73.

Rice, M. E., & Grusec, J. E. Saying and doing: Effects on observer performance. *Journal of Personality and Social Psychology*, 1975, *32*, 584–593.

Richards, M. P. M. First steps in becoming social. In M. Richards (Ed.), *The integration of a child into a social world.* London: Cambridge, 1974.

Rickers-Ovsiankina, M. A. Psychological premises underlying the Rorschach. In M. A. Rickers-Ovsiankina (Ed.), *Rorschach psychology.* New York: Wiley, 1960, pp. 3–24.

Riegel, K. F. The prediction of death and longevity in longitudinal research. In E. Palmore & F. C. Jeffers (Eds.), *Prediction of life span.* Lexington, Mass.: Heath, 1971.

Riegel, K. F., & Riegel, R. M. Development, drop, and death. *Developmental Psychology*, 1972, *6*, 306–319.

Riley, M. et al. *Aging and society* (Vol. 1). New York: Russell Sage, 1968.

Ring, K., Lipinski, C. E., & Braginsky, D. The relationship of birth order to self-evaluation, anxiety reduction, and susceptibility to emotional contagion. *Psychological Monographs*, 1965, *79* (whole No. 603).

Ritzler, B. The Nuremberg mind revisited: A quantitative approach to Nazi Rorschachs. *Journal of Personality Assessment*, 1978, *42*, 344–353.

Roback, H. B., Langevin, R., & Zajac, Y. Sex of free choice figure drawings by homosexual and heterosexual subjects. *Journal of Personality Assessment*, 1974, *38*, 154–155.

Robin, A., Armel, S., & O'Leary, D. The effects of self-instruction on writing deficiencies. *Behavior Therapy*, 1975, *6*, 178–187.

Robson, K. S. The role of eye-to-eye contact in

maternal-infant attachment. *Journal of Child Psychology and Psychiatry*, 1967, 8, 13–25.

Rodin, J., & Langer, E. J. Long-term effects of a control-relevant intervention with the institutionalized aged. *Journal of Personality and Social Psychology*, 1977, 35, 897–902.

Rogers, C. R. *Clinical treatment of the problem child*. Boston: Houghton Mifflin, 1939.

Rogers, C. R. *Counseling and psychotherapy*. Boston: Houghton Mifflin, 1942.

Rogers, C. R. A theory of therapy, personality, and interpersonal relationships, as developed in the client-centered framework. In S. Koch (Ed.), *Psychology: A study of a science* (Vol. 3). New York: McGraw-Hill, 1959.

Rogers, C. R. *On becoming a person*. Boston: Houghton Mifflin, 1961.

Rogers, C. R. In retrospect: Forty-six years. Address to the meeting of the American Psychological Association, Montreal, Canada, 1973. In R. I. Evans (Ed.), *Carl Rogers: The man and his ideas*. New York: Dutton, 1975.

Rogers, C. R., & Dymond, F. R. (Eds.). *Psychotherapy and personality change; co-ordinated studies in the client-centered approach*. Chicago: Univ. of Chicago Press, 1954.

Rokeach, M. *The nature of human values*. New York: Free Press, 1973.

Romer, N. Sex-related differences in the motive to avoid success, sex role identity, and performance in competitive and noncompetitive conditions. *Psychology of Women Quarterly*, 1977, 3, 260–272.

Rorschach, H. Psychodiagnostics: A diagnostic test based on perception (4th ed.). New York: Grune & Stratton, 1942. (Originally published 1921.)

Rose, S. D. *Treating children in groups*. San Francisco: Jossey-Bass, 1972.

Rosen, A. Detection of suicidal patients: An example of some limitations in the prediction of infrequent events. *Journal of Consulting Psychology*, 1954, 18, 397–403.

Rosen, B. C., & D'Andrade, R. G. The psychoso-cial origin of achievement motivation. *Sociometry*, 1959, 22, 185–218.

Rosenhan, D. L. The natural socialization of altruistic autonomy. In J. Macaulay & L. Berkowitz (Eds.), *Altruism and helping behavior*. New York: Academic, 1970.

Rosenhan, D. L. On being sane in insane places. *Science*, 1973, 179, 250–258.

Rosenhan, D. L., Underwood, B., & Moore, B. Affect moderates self-gratification and altruism. *Journal of Personality and Social Psychology*, 1974, 30, 546–552.

Rosenthal, B. Encounter groups: Some empirical issues, explanations, and values. In Back, op. cit., 1978.

Rosenthal, D. *Genetics of psychopathology*. New York: McGraw-Hill, 1971.

Rosenthal, R. *Experimenter effects in behavioral research*. New York: Appleton Century Crofts, 1966.

Rosenthal, R. Interpersonal expectations: Effects of the experimenter's hypothesis. In R. Rosenthal & R. L. Rosnow (Eds.), *Artifact in behavioral research*. New York: Academic, 1969.

Rosenthal, R., & Jacobsen, L. *Pygmalion in the classroom*. New York: Holt, 1968.

Rosenthal, T., & Bandura, A. Psychological modeling: Theory and practice. In S. L. Garfield & A. E. Bergin (eds.), *Handbook of psychotherapy and behavior change* (2nd ed.). New York: Wiley, 1978.

Roszack, T. *The making of a counter-culture*. Garden City, N.Y.: Doubleday, 1969.

Rotter, J. B. Generalized expectancies for internal versus external control of reinforcement. *Psychological Monographs*, 1966, 80 (Whole No. 609), 1–28.

Rotter, J. B., & Rafferty, J. E. *The Rotter Incomplete Sentences Test*. New York: Psychological Corp., 1950.

Roueche, B. Annals of medicine. As empty as Eve. *New Yorker*, September 9, 1974, pp. 84 ff.

Rourke, B. P. Brain-behavior relationships in

children with learning disabilities. *American Psychologist*, 1975, *30*, 911–920.

Rubin, J. Z., Provenzano, F. J., & Luria, Z. The eye of the beholder: Parents' views on sex of newborns. *American Journal of Orthopsychiatry*, 1974, *44*, 512–519.

Rubin, K. H., & Brown, I. D. R. A life-span look at person perception and its relationship to communicative interaction. *Journal of Gerontology*, 1975, *30*, 461–468.

Ruitenbeek, H. M. *Psychoanalysis and existential philosophy*. New York: Dutton, 1962.

Runyan, W. M. The life course as a theoretical orientation: Sequences of person-situation interaction. *Journal of Personality*, 1978, *46*, 569–593.

Rushton, J. P. Generosity in children: Immediate and long-term effects of modeling, preaching, and moral judgment. *Journal of Personality and Social Psychology*, 1975, *31*, 459–466.

Rushton, J. P. Socialization and the altruistic behavior of children. *Psychological Bulletin*, 1976, *83*, 898–913.

Ruskin, R., & Maley, R. Item preference in a token economy ward store. *Journal of Applied Behavior Analysis*, 1972, *5*, 373–378.

Sacher, G. A. Longevity, aging, and death: An evolutionary perspective. *Gerontologist*, 1978, *18*, 112–119.

Sackeim, H. A., Gur, R. C., & Saucy, M. C. Emotions are expressed more intensely on the left side of the face. *Science*, 1978, *202*, 434–436.

Sackett, G. P., Porter, M., & Holmes, H. Choice behavior in rhesus monkeys: Effects of stimulation during the first month of life. *Science*, 1965, *147*, 304–306.

Sampson, E. E. The study of ordinal position: Antecedents and outcomes. In B. A. Maher (Ed.), *Progress in experimental personality research* (Vol. 1). New York: Academic, 1965.

Sampson, E. E., & Hancock, T. An examination of the relationship between ordinal position, personality, and conformity: An extension, replication, and partial verification. *Journal of Personality and Social Psychology*, 1967, *5*, 398–407.

Samuel, W. *Contemporary social psychology: An introduction*. Englewood Cliffs, N. J.: Prentice-Hall, 1975.

Samuel, W. Observed IQ as a function of test atmosphere, tester expectation, and race of tester: A replication for female subjects. *Journal of Educational Psychology*, 1977, *69*, 593–604.

Samuel, W. Mood and personality correlates of IQ by race and sex of subject. *Journal of Personality and Social Psychology*, 1980, *38*, 993–1004.

Samuel, W., Baynes, K., & Sabeh, C. Effects of intial success or failure in a stressful or relaxed environment on subsequent task performance. *Journal of Experimental and Social Psychology*, 1978, *14*, 205–216.

Samuel, W., Soto, D., Parks, M., Ngissah, P., & Jones, B. Motivation, race, social class, and IQ. *Journal of Educational Psychology*, 1976, *68*, 273–285.

Santogrossi, D., O'Leary, K., Romanczyk, R., & Kaufman, K. Self-evaluation by adolescents in a psychiatric hospital school token program. *Journal of Applied Behavior Analysis*, 1973, *6*, 277–287.

Sarason, I. G. Test anxiety, general anxiety, and intellectual performance. *Journal of Consulting Psychology*, 1957, *21*, 435–490.

Sarason, I. G. Test anxiety, attention, and the general problem of anxiety. In C. D. Spielberger & I. G. Sarason (Eds.), *Stress and anxiety*. New York: Wiley, 1975.

Sarbin, T. R. On the futility of the proposition that some people can be labeled "mentally ill." *Journal of Consulting Psychology*, 1967, *31*, 447–453.

Sarbin, T. R. Contextualism: A world view for modern psychology. *Nebraska Symposium on Motivation*, 1976, *24*, 1–41.

Sato, K. Zen from a personological viewpoint. *Psychologia*, 1968, *11*, 3–24.

Satz, P., Finnell, E., & Reilly, C. Predictive validity of six neurodiagnostic tests: A decision theory analysis. *Journal of Consulting and Clinical Psychology*, 1970, *34*, 375–381.

Saunders, T. R. Toward a distinctive role for the psychologist in neurodiagnostic decision making. *Professional Psychology*, 1975, *6*, 161–167.

Savage, R. D., Gaber, L. B., Britton, P. G., Bolton, N., & Cooper, A. *Personality and adjustment in the aged.* New York: Academic, 1977.

Savage-Rumbaugh, E. S., & Rumbaugh, D. *The state of the apes in the language debate.* Invited address, meeting of the Western Psychological Association, San Diego, 1979.

Sawyer, J. Measurement and prediction, clinical and statistical. *Psychological Bulletin*, 1966, *66*, 178–200.

Scarpitti, F. R., Murray, E., Dinitz, S., & Reckless, W. C. The "good boy" in a high delinquency area: Four years later. *American Sociological Review*, 1960, *25*, 555–558.

Scarr, S., & Weinberg, R. A. Intellectual similarities within families of both adopted and biological children. *Intelligence*, 1977, *1*, 170–191.

Schacht, T., & Nathan, P. E. But is it good for psychologists? Appraisal and status of DSM III. *American Psychologist*, 1977, *32*, 1017–1025.

Schachter, S. Pain, fear and anger in hypertensives and a psychophysiologic study. *Psychosomatic Medicine*, 1957, *19*, 17–29.

Schachter, S. *The psychology of affiliation: Experimental studies of the sources of gregariousness.* Stanford, Calif.: Stanford, 1959.

Schachter, S. Birth order, eminence, and higher education. *American Sociological Review*, 1963, *28*, 757–767.

Schachter, S. Birth order and sociometric choice. *Journal of Abnormal and Social Psychology*, 1964, *68*, 453–456.

Schachter, S. The interaction of cognitive and physiological determinants of emotional state. In L. Berkowitz (Ed.), *Advances in experimental social psychology* (Vol. 1). New York: Academic, 1964.

Schachter, S., & Latané, B. Crime, cognition, and the autonomic nervous system. In D. Levine (Ed.), *Nebraska symposium on motivation.* Lincoln: Univ. of Nebraska Press, 1964.

Schachter, S., & Singer, J. E. Cognitive and physiological determinants of emotional state. *Psychological Review*, 1962, *69*, 379–399.

Schachter, S., & Singer, J. E. Comments on the Maslach and Marshall-Zimbardo experiments. *Journal of Personality and Social Psychology.* 1979, *37*, 989–995.

Schaie, K. W. Translations in gerontology—from lab to life: Intellectual functioning. *American Psychologist*, 1974, *29*, 802–807.

Schaie, K. W., & Gribben, K. Adult development and aging. In M. Rosenzweig & L. Porter (Eds.), *Annual review of psychology* (Vol. 26). Palo Alto, Calif.: Annual Reviews, 1975.

Schaie, K. W., & Labouvie-Vief, G. Generational versus ontogenetic components of change in adult cognitive behavior: A fourteen-year cross-sequential study. *Developmental Psychology*, 1974, *10*, 105–320.

Schaie, K. W., & Parham, I. A. Stability of adult personality traits: Fact or fable? *Journal of Personality and Social Psychology*, 1976, *34*, 146–158.

Schleifer, M., & Douglas, V. I. Effects of training on the moral judgment of young children. *Journal of Personality and Social Psychology*, 1973, *28*, 62–68.

Schnitzer, P. K. The motive to avoid success: Exploring the nature of the fear. *Psychology of Women Quarterly*, 1977, *3*, 273–282.

Schonfield, D. Future commitments and successful aging: I. The random sample. *Journal of Gerontology*, 1973, *28*, 189–196.

Schooler, C. Birth order effects: Not here, not now! *Psychological Bulletin*, 1972, *78*, 161–175.

Schulman, A. H., & Kaplowitz, C. Mirror-image responses during the first two years of life. *Developmental Psychobiology*, 1977, *10*, 133–142.

Schwartz, G. E. Biofeedback as therapy. *American Psychologist*, 1973, *28*(8), 666–673.

Schwartz, S. H. Moral decision making and behavior. In J. Macaulay & L. Berkowitz (Eds.), *Altruism and helping behavior*. New York: Academic 1970. (a)

Schwartz, S. H. Elicitation of moral obligation and self-sacrificing behavior: An experimental study of volunteering to be a bone marrow donor. *Journal of Personality and Social Psychology*, 1970, *15*, 283–293. (b)

Schwartz, S. H., & Gottlieb, A. Bystander reactions to a violent theft: Crime in Jerusalem. *Journal of Personality and Social Psychology*, 1976, *34*, 1188–1199.

Searleman, A. A review of right hemisphere linguistic capabilities. *Psychological Bulletin*, 1977, *84*, 503–528.

Sechrest, L. Incremental validity: A recommendation. *Educational and Psychological Measurement*, 1963, *23*, 153–158.

Sechrest, L. Personal constructs theory. In R. J. Corsini (Ed.), *Current personality theories*. Itasca, Ill.: Peacock, 1977.

Segal, B. M. Involuntary hospitalization in the USSR. In S. A. Corson & C. O. Corson (Eds.), *Psychiatry and psychology in the USSR*. New York: Plenum, 1976.

Seligman, M. E. P. Phobias and preparedness. *Behavior Therapy*, 1971, *2*, 307–320.

Seligman, M. E. P. *Helplessness*. San Francisco: Freeman, 1975.

Selye, H. *The stress of life* (Rev. ed.). New York: McGraw-Hill, 1976.

Sheehy, G. *Passages*. New York: Bantam, 1977.

Sheldon, W. H. *The varieties of temperament: A psychology of constitutional differences*. New York: Harper, 1942.

Sheldon, W. H. *Atlas of men: A guide for somatotyping the adult male at all ages*. New York: Harper, 1954.

Sheldon, W. H., Lewis, N. C. C., & Tenney, A. M. Psychotic patterns and physical constitution: A thirty-year follow-up of thirty-eight hundred psychiatric patients in New York State. In C. V. Siva Sandar (Ed.), *Schizophrenia: Current concepts and research*. New York: PJD Publications, 1969.

Sherif, M. An experimental approach to the study of attitudes. *Sociometry*, 1937, *1*, 90–98.

Sherif, M. & Sherif, C. W. *Social psychology*. New York: Harper & Row, 1969.

Sherman, J. A. *Sex-related differences in cognition: An essay in theory and evidence*. Springfield, Ill.: Charles C Thomas, 1978.

Sherman, J. A., & Fennema, E. Distribution of spatial visualization and mathematical problem-solving scores: A test of Stafford's X-linked hypothesis. *Psychology of Women Quarterly*, 1978, *3*, 157–167.

Sherman, N. C., Gold, J. A., & Sherman, M. F. Attribution theory and evaluations of older men among college students, their parents, and grandparents. *Personality and Social Psychology Bulletin*, 1978, *4*, 440–442.

Shields, S. A. Functionalism, Darwinism, and the psychology of women. *American Psychologist*, 1975, *30*, 739–754.

Shoben, E., Jr. The therapeutic object: Men or machines? *Journal of Counseling Psychology*, 1963, *10*, 264–268.

Shope, G. L., Hedrick, T. E., & Geen, R. G. Physical/verbal aggression: Sex differences in style. *Journal of Personality*, 1978, *46*, 23–42.

Shurcliff, A. Judged humor, arousal, and the relief theory. *Journal of Personality and Social Psychology*, 1968, *8*, 360–363.

Siegel, B., & Lasker, J. Deinstitutionalizing elderly patients: A program of resocialization. *Gerontologist*, 1978, *18*, 293–300.

Silverman, L. H. Psychoanalytic theory: "The reports of my death are greatly exaggerated." *American Psychologist*, 1976, *31*, 621–637.

Silvern, L. E., & Ryan, V. L. Self-rated adjustment and sex-typing on the Bem Sex-Role Inventory: Is masculinity the primary predictor of adjustment? *Sex Roles*, 1979, *5*, 739–763.

Silverstein, S. J., Nathan, P. E., & Taylor, H. A.

Blood alcohol level estimation and controlled drinking by chronic alcoholics. *Behavior Therapy*, 1974, *5*, 1–15.

Singer, J. L. Navigating the stream of consciousness. *American Psychologist*, 1975, *30*, 727–738.

Sistrunk, F., & McDavid, J. W. Sex variables in conforming behavior. *Journal of Personality and Social Psychology*, 1971, *17*, 200–207.

Skinner, B. F. *The behavior of organisms*. New York: Appleton Century Crofts, 1938.

Skinner, B. F. *Science and human behavior*. New York: Macmillan, 1953.

Skinner, B. F. *Verbal behavior*. New York: Appleton Century Crofts, 1957.

Skinner, B. F. *Walden Two*. New York: Macmillan, 1962.

Skinner, B. F. *Beyond freedom and dignity*. New York: Knopf, 1971.

Skinner, B. F. Why I am not a cognitive psychologist. *Behaviorism*, 1977. *5*, 1–10.

Slobin, D. I. Developmental psycholinguistics. In W. O. Dingwall (Ed.), *A survey of linguistic science*. College Park, Maryland: W. O. Dingwall, Linguistics Program, University of Maryland, 1971.

Smith, M. B. Encounter groups and humanistic psychology. In Back, op. cit., 1978.

Snibbe, J. R. Psychologists and drugs. I. Psychopharmacology and the need to know. *Professional Psychology*, 1975, *6*, 167–169.

Snow, B. Level of aspiration of coronary prone and noncoronary prone adults. *Personality and Social Psychology Bulletin*, 1978, *4*, 416–419.

Snyder, S. H. *Madness and the brain*. New York: McGraw-Hill, 1974.

Sokolov, A. N. *Inner speech and thought*. New York: Plenum, 1972.

Solar, D., Davenport, G., & Bruehl, D. Social compliance as a function of field dependence. *Perceptual and Motor Skills*, 1969, *29*, 299–306.

Sole, K., Marton, J., & Hornstein, H. A. Opinion similarity and helping: Three field experiments investigating the bases of promotive tension. *Journal of Experimental Social Psychology*. 1975, *11*, 1–13.

Solomon, R. L. Punishment. *American Psychologist*, 1964, *19*, 239–253.

Spence, J. T., Helmreich, R., & Stapp, J. Ratings of self and peers on sex-role attributes and their relation to self-esteem and conceptions of masculinity and femininity. *Journal of Personality and Social Psychology*, 1975, *32*, 29–39.

Spence, J. T., & Spence, K. M. The motivational components of manifest anxiety: Drive and drive stimuli. In C. D. Spielberger (Ed.), *Anxiety and behavior*. New York: Academic, 1966.

Sperry, R. W. Changing concepts of consciousness and free will. *Perspectives in Biology and Medicine*, 1976, *20*, 9–19.

Spitz, R., & Wolf, K. M. Anaclitic depression. *The Psychoanalytic Study of the Child*, 1946, *2*, 313–342.

Stampfl, T., & Levis, D. Essentials of implosive therapy: A learning theory-based psychodynamic behavioral therapy. *Journal of Abnormal Psychology*, 1967, *72*, 496–503.

Staub, E. Predicting prosocial behavior: A model for predicting the nature of personality-situation interaction. In L. A. Pervin & M. Lewis (Eds.), *Internal and external determinants of behavior*. New York: Plenum, 1978.

Stein, A. H., Friedrich, L. K., & Vondracek, F. Television content and young children's behavior. In J. P. Murray, E. A. Rubinstein, & G. A. Comstock (Eds.), *Television and social behavior* (Vol. 2). *Television and social learning*. Washington: U.S. Government Printing Office, 1972, pp. 202–317.

Sternlieb, J. L., & Youniss, J. Moral judgments one year after intentional or consequence modeling. *Journal of Personality and Social Psychology*, 1975, *31*, 895–897.

Stolz, L. M. *Ethical issues in behavior modification*. San Francisco: Jossey-Bass, 1977.

Storr, A. *Human aggression*. New York: Atheneum, 1968.

Stricker, L. J. Review of the EPPS. In O. K. Buros (Ed.), *The sixth mental measurements yearbook*. Highland Park, N. J.: Gryphon, 1965.

Strong, E. K. *Vocational interests of men and women*. Stanford, Calif.: Stanford, 1943.

Stuart, R. B., & Stuart, F. *Marital Pre-counseling Inventory*. Champaign, Ill.: Research Press, 1972.

Sullivan, H. S. *Conceptions of modern psychiatry*. Washington: William Alanson White Psychiatric Foundation, 1947.

Summers, J. *Psychological androgyny: Self-esteem and anxiety correlates*. Unpublished master's thesis, California State University, Sacramento, 1979.

Sundberg, N. D. *Assessment of persons*. Englewood Cliffs, N.J.: Prentice-Hall, 1977.

Surgeon General's Scientific Advisory Committee on Television and Social Behavior. *Television and growing up: The impact of televised violence*. Washington: U.S. Government Printing Office, 1972.

Sweet, W. H., Ervin, R., & Mark, V. H. The relationship of violent behavior to focal cerebral disease. In S. Garattini & E. Sigg (Eds.), *Aggressive behavior*. New York: Wiley, 1969.

Szasz, T. S. The psychiatric classification of behavior: A strategy of personal constraint. In L. D. Eron (Ed.), *The classification of behavior disorders*. Chicago: Aldine, 1966.

Szasz, T. S. *The manufacture of madness*. New York: Dell, 1970.

Tallmer, M., & Kutner, B. Disengagement and the stresses of aging. *Journal of Gerontology*, 1969, *24*, 70–75.

Taylor, D. A., Altman, I., & Sorrentino, R. Interpersonal exchange as a function of rewards and costs and situational factors: Expectancy confirmation-disconfirmation. *Journal of Experimental Social Psychology*, 1969, *5*, 324–339.

Taylor, J. A. A personality scale of manifest anxiety. *Journal of Abnormal and Social Psychology*, 1953, *48*, 285–290.

Taylor, S. P. Aggressive behavior as a function of approval motivation and physical attack. *Psychonomic Science*, 1970, *18*, 195–196.

Taylor, S. P., & Pisano, R. Physical aggression as a function of frustration and physical attack. *Journal of Social Psychology*, 1971, *84*, 261–267.

Teevan, R. C., & McGhee, P. E. Childhood development of fear of failure motivation. *Journal of Personality and Social Psychology*, 1972, *21*, 345–348.

Terman, L. M., & Tyler, L. E. Psychological sex differences. In L. Carmichael (Ed.), *Manual of child psychology* (2nd ed.). New York: Wiley, 1954.

Terrace, H. S., Petitto, L. A., Sanders, R. J., & Bever, T. G. Can an ape create a sentence? *Science*, 1979, *206*, 891–902.

Thomas, A., Chess, S., & Birch, H. G. The origin of personality. *Scientific American*, 1970, *223*(2), 102–109.

Thomas, M. H., Horton, R. W., Lippencott, E. C., & Drabman, R. S. Desensitization to portrayals of real-life aggression as a function of exposure to television violence. *Journal of Personality and Social Psychology*, 1977, *35*, 450–458.

Thompson, W. R. Influence of prenatal maternal anxiety on emotionality in young rats. *Science*, 1957, *126*, 73–74.

Thoresen, C., & Mahoney, M. *Self-control*. New York: Holt, 1974.

Thorndike, E. L. Animal intelligence: An experimental study of the associative processes in animals. *Psychological Review Monograph Supplement*, 1898 (No. 8).

Thorndike, E. L. *The elements of psychology*. New York: A. G. Seiler, 1905.

Thorndike, E. L. Reward and punishment in animal learning. *Comprehensive Psychological Monographs*, 1932, *8* (No. 39).

Tilker, H. A. Socially responsible behavior as a function of observer responsibility and victim feedback. *Journal of Personality and Social Psychology*, 1970, *14*, 95–100.

Toch, H. *Violent men.* Chicago: Aldine, 1969.

Tresemer, D. W. *Fear of success.* New York: Plenum, 1979.

Trivers, R. L. The evolution of reciprocal altruism. *Quarterly Review of Biology,* 1971, 46(4), 35–57.

Troll, L. *Early and middle adulthood.* Monterey, Calif.: Brooks/Cole, 1975.

Tuddenham, R. D. The constancy of personality ratings over two decades. *Genetic Psychology Monographs,* 1959, 60, 5–29.

Tuke, D. H. *Illustrations of the influence of the mind upon the body in health and disease, designed to elucidate the action of the imagination.* London: Churchill, 1872.

Turner, C. W., & Berkowitz, L. Identification with film aggressor (covert role taking) and reactions to film violence. *Journal of Personality and Social Psychology,* 1972, 21, 256–263.

Turner, C. W., Layton, J. F., & Simons, L. S. Naturalistic studies of aggressive behavior: Aggressive stimuli, victim visibility, and horn honking. *Journal of Personality and Social Psychology,* 1975, 31, 1098–1107.

Tyler, L. E. *The psychology of human differences.* New York: Appleton Century Crofts, 1965.

Ullmann, L. P., & Krasner, L. *A psychological approach to abnormal behavior.* Englewood Cliffs, N.J.: Prentice-Hall, 1969.

Ulrich, R. E., Huchinson, R. R., & Azrin, N. H. Pain-elicited aggression, *Psychological Record,* 1965, 15, 111–126.

Ulrich, R. E., Stachnik, T. J., & Stainton, N. R. Student acceptance of generalized personality interpretations. *Psychological Reports,* 1963, 13, 831–834.

U.S. Riot Commission. *Report of the National Advisory Commission on Civil Disorders.* New York: Bantam, 1968.

Vaillant, G. E. *Adaptation to life.* Boston: Little, Brown, 1977.

Valenstein, E. *Brain control.* New York: Wiley, 1974.

Valins, S. Emotionality and autonomic reactivity. *Journal of Experimental Research in Personality,* 1967, 2, 41–48. (a)

Valins, S. Emotionality and information concerning internal reactions. *Journal of Personality and Social Psychology,* 1967, 6, 458–463. (b)

Valins, S. The perception and labeling of bodily changes as determinants of emotional behavior. In P. Black (Ed.), *Physiological correlates of emotion.* New York: Academic, 1970.

Vandenberg, B. Play and development from an ethological perspective. *American Psychologist,* 1978, 33, 724–738.

Vandenberg, S. G. What do we know today about the inheritance of intelligence and how do we know it? In R. Cancro (Ed.), *Intelligence: Genetic and environmental influences.* New York: Grune & Stratton, 1971.

Van Praag, H. M. *Depression and schizophrenia: A contribution on their chemical pathologies.* New York: Spectrum, 1977.

Vygotsky, L. *Thought and language.* New York: Wiley, 1962.

Waber, D. P. Biological substrates of field dependence: Implications of the sex difference. *Psychological Bulletin,* 1977, 84, 1076–1087.

Wade, T. C., Baker, T. B., Morton, T. L., & Baker, L. J. The status of psychological testing in clinical psychology: Relationships between test use and professional activities and orientations. *Journal of Personality Assessment,* 1978, 42, 3–10.

Wallace, R. K. The physiology of meditation. In T. J. Teyler (Ed.), *Altered states of awareness.* San Francisco: Freeman, 1973.

Walters, R. H., & Brown, M. Studies of reinforcement of aggression: III. Transfer of response to an interpersonal situation. *Child Development,* 1963, 34, 563–572.

Washburn, S. L. Human behavior and the behavior of other animals. *American Psychologist,* 1978, 33, 405–418.

Watson, J. B. Psychology as the behaviorist views it. *Psychological Review,* 1913, 20, 158–177.

Watson, J. B. *Behavior: An introduction to comparative psychology.* New York: Holt, 1914.

Watson, J. B. *Psychology from the standpoint of a behaviorist.* Philadelphia: Lippincott, 1919.

Watson, J. B. *Behaviorism.* New York: People's Institute Publishing Company, 1924.

Watson, J. B., & Rayner, R. Conditioned emotional reactions. *Journal of Experimental Psychology,* 1920, *3,* 1–14.

Watson, J. B., & Watson, R. R. Studies in infant psychology. *Scientific Monthly,* 1921, *13,* 493–515.

Webb, W. B. *Sleep: The gentle tyrant.* Englewood Cliffs, N.J.: Prentice-Hall, 1975.

Wechsler, D. *Wechsler Intelligence Scale for Children manual.* New York: Psychological Corp., 1949.

Wechsler, D. *Manual for the Wechsler Adult Intelligence Scale.* New York: Psychological Corp., 1955.

Wechsler, D. *The measurement and appraisal of adult intelligence.* Baltimore: Williams & Wilkins, 1958.

Wechsler, D. *Manual: Wechsler Intelligence Scale for Children—Revised.* New York: Psychological Corp., 1974.

Weiner, B., Frieze, I., Kukla, A., Reed, L., Rest, S., & Rosenbaum, R. M. Perceiving the causes of success and failure. In E. E. Jones, D. E. Kanouse, H. H. Kelley, R. E. Nisbett, S. Valins, & B. Weiner (Eds.), *Attribution: Perceiving the causes of behavior.* Morristown, N.J.: General Learning Press, 1971.

Weiner, I. B., & Exner, J. E. Rorschach indices of disordered thinking in patient and nonpatient adolescents and adults. *Journal of Personality Assessment,* 1978, *42,* 339–343.

Weisler, A., & McCall, R. B. Exploration and play: Résumé and redirection. *American Psychologist, 1976, 31,* 492–508.

Weiss, R., Boyer, J. L., Lombardo, J. P., & Stich, M. H. Altruistic drive and altruistic reinforcement. *Journal of Personality and Social Psychology,* 1973, *25,* 390–400.

Weisstein, N. Psychology constructs the female, or the fantasy life of the male psychologist (with some attention to the fantasies of his friends, the male biologist and the male anthropologist). In I. Cohen (Ed.), *Perspectives on psychology.* New York: Praeger, 1971.

Wenger, D. L., & Fletcher, C. R. The effects of legal counsel on admissions to a state hospital: A confrontation of professions. *Journal of Health and Human Behavior,* 1969, *10,* 66–72.

Werner, C., & Latané, B. Interaction motivates attraction: Rats are fond of fondling. *Journal of Personality and Social Psychology,* 1974, *29,* 328–334.

West, S. G., Whitney, G., & Schnedler, R. Helping a motorist in distress: The effects of sex, race, and neighborhood. *Journal of Personality and Social Psychology,* 1975, *31,* 691–698.

Weyant, J. M. Effects of mood states, costs, and benefits on helping. *Journal of Personality and Social Psychology,* 1978, *36,* 1169–1176.

White, B. L. *Human infants.* Englewood Cliffs, N.J.: Prentice-Hall, 1971.

White, B. L. Critical influences in the origins of competence. *Merrill-Palmer Quarterly,* 1975, 21(4), 243–266.

White, B. L. Exploring the origins of human competence. *APA Monitor,* 1976, 7(4), 4–5.

White, R. W. Motivation reconsidered: The concept of competence. *Psychological Review,* 1959, *66,* 297–333.

Whybrow, P., & Mendels, J. Toward a biology of depression: Some suggestions from neurophysiology. *American Journal of Psychiatry,* 1969, *125,* 1491–1500.

Wickelgreen, L. W. Development of convergence. *Journal of Experimental Child Psychology,* 1967, *5,* 74–85.

Wilkins, J. L., Scharff, W. H., & Schlottman, R. S. Personality type, reports of violence, and aggressive behavior. *Journal of Personality and Social Psychology,* 1974, *30,* 243–247.

Williams, G. C. *Adaptation and natural selection.* Princeton, N.J.: Princeton, 1966.

Williams, J. H. *Psychology of women.* New York: Norton, 1977.

Williams, R. J. The biological approach to the study of personality. In T. Millon (Ed.), *Theo-*

ries of psychopathology. Philadelphia: Saunders, 1967.

Wilson, C. *New pathways in psychology: Maslow and the post-Freudian revolution.* New York: Taplinger, 1972.

Wilson, E. O. *Sociobiology.* Cambridge, Mass.: Harvard, 1975.

Wilson, R. S. Twins: Early mental development. *Science,* 1972, *175,* 914–917.

Wine, J. Test anxiety and the direction of attention. *Psychological Bulletin,* 1971, *76,* 92–104.

Wing, J. K. Social influences on the course of schizophrenia. In L. C. Wynne et al. (Eds.), *The nature of schizophrenia.* New York: Wiley, 1978.

Winterbotton, M. R. The relation of need for achievement to learning experiences in independence and mastery. In J. W. Atkinson (Ed.), *Motives in fantasy, action, and society.* Princeton, N.J.: Van Nostrand, 1958.

Wishner, J. Reanalysis of "Impressions of personality." *Psychological Review,* 1960, *67,* 96–112.

Wispé, L. G., & Thompson, J. N. The war between the words: Biological versus social evolution and some related issues. *American Psychologist,* 1976, *31,* 341–380.

Witkin, H. A. Psychological differentiation and forms of pathology. *Journal of Abnormal Psychology,* 1965, *70,* 317–336.

Witkin, H. A., & Goodenough, D. R. Field dependence and interpersonal behavior. *Psychological Bulletin,* 1977, *84,* 661–689.

Witkin, H. A., Kyk, R. B., Faterson, H. F., Goodenough, D. R., & Karp, S. A. *Psychological differentiation.* New York: Wiley, 1962.

Witkin, H. A., Mednick, S. A., Schulsinger, F., Bakkestrom, E., Christiansen, K. O., Goodenough, D. R., Hirschhorn, K., Cundsteen, C., Owen, D. R., Philip, J., Rubin, D. B., & Stocking, M. Criminality in XYY and XXY men. *Science,* 1976, *196,* 547–555.

Wolfe, B. M., & Baron, R. A. Laboratory aggression related to aggression in naturalistic social situations: Effects of an aggressive model on the behavior of college student and prisoner observers. *Psychonomic Science,* 1971, *24,* 193–194.

Wolff, P. H. The natural history of crying and other vocalizations in early infancy. In B. M. Foss (Ed.), *Determinants of infant behavior* (Vol. 4). London: Methuen, 1969.

Wolfgang, M. E., Figlio, R. M., & Sellin, T. *Delinquency in a birth cohort.* Chicago: Univ. of Chicago Press, 1972.

Wolpe, J. *Psychotherapy by reciprocal inhibition.* Stanford, Calif.: Stanford, 1958.

Wolpe, J. Cognition and causation in human behavior and its therapy. *American Psychologist,* 1978, *33,* 437–446.

Wolpe, J., & Lang, P. J. *Fear Survey Schedule.* San Diego, Calif.: Educational and Industrial Testing Service, 1969.

Woodworth, R. S. *Personal data sheet.* Chicago: Stoelting, 1920.

Worchel, S., & Teddlie, C. The experience of crowding: A two-factor theory. *Journal of Personality and Social Psychology,* 1976, *34,* 30–40.

World Health Organization. *Manual of the international statistical classification of diseases, injuries, and causes of death.* Geneva: Author, 1977.

Wynne, L. C., Cromwell, R. L., & Matthysse, S. (Eds.), *The nature of schizophrenia.* New York: Wiley, 1978.

Yerkes, R. M., & Dodson, J. D. The relation of strength of stimulus to rapidity of habit formation. *Journal of Comparative Neurological Psychology,* 1908, *18,* 459–482.

Young, W. C., Goy, R., & Phoenix, C. Hormones and sexual behavior. *Science,* 1964, *143,* 212–218.

Zajonc, R. B., Markus, H. & Markus, G. B. The birth order puzzle. *Journal of Personality and Social Psychology,* 1979, *37,* 1325–1341.

Zeigarnik, B. V. Personality and the pathology of activity. *Soviet Psychology,* 1972–73, *11(2),* 4–89.

Ziferstein, I. Psychotherapy in the USSR. In S. A.

Corson & E. O. Corson (Eds.), *Psychiatry and psychology in the USSR*. New York: Plenum, 1976.

Zigler, E., & Phillips. L. Psychiatric diagnosis and symptomatology. *Journal of Abnormal and Social Psychology*, 1961, *63*, 69–75.

Zigler, E., & Trickett, P. IQ, social competence, and evaluation of early childhood intervention programs. *American Psychologist*, 1978, *33*, 789–798.

Zillmann, D., & Cantor, J. R. Effect of timing information about mitigating circumstances on emotional responses to provocation and retaliatory behavior. *Journal of Experimental Social Psychology*, 1976, *12*, 38–55.

Zillmann, D., Katcher, A. H., & Milavsky, B. Excitation transfer from physical exercise to subsequent aggressive behavior. *Journal of Experimental Social Psychology*, 1972, *8*, 247–259.

Zubin, J., Eron, L. D., & Schumer, F. *An experimental approach to projective techniques.* New York: Wiley, 1965.

Zubin, L. Classification of the behavior disorders. *Annual Review of Psychology*, 1967, *18*, 377–406.

GLOSSARY

Activity theory The hypothesis that an aging person is most successful in maintaining his or her physical and psychological health through continued involvement with the world of work and social relationships.

Aggressive cue hypothesis The hypothesis that even a frustrated, angry person will probably behave aggressively only if there are appropriate "releasing stimuli" (i.e., cues) in the immediate environment which have in the past been associated with aggressive impulses.

Altrusim Helping that is in no way self-interested and is motivated solely by the desire to make someone else feel better.

Anaclitic depression Feelings of hopelessness and self-contempt which emerge following a traumatic separation from a loved person.

Anal retentive character A personality type distinguished by orderliness, obstinacy, and thrift. Supposedly produced by toilet training that involves *either* excessive punishment or praise.

Androgyny According to Bem, an ideal state of sex role flexibility in which an individual feels free to behave in either a "masculine" or a "feminine" way depending on what seems appropriate for a given situation. (See also *Sex roles.*)

Approach-avoidance conflict A situation in which an organism is simultaneously motivated to engage in a behavior because some stimuli in the environment indicate a reward may be forthcoming but at the same time to refrain from the behavior because other stimuli indicate a punishment may follow.

Authoritarianism A set of personality traits

which incorporates slavish obedience to superiors, inconsiderate treatment of subordinates or outgroups, and a willingness to inflict severe punishment on others who do not think or behave as one wants.

Autonomous morality According to Piaget, a type of moral reasoning which appears after about 8 years of age and which includes the concepts of intentions, mitigating circumstances, and the relativistic nature of rules of conduct.

Aversion therapy A therapeutic procedure which relies on respondent conditioning to build in a fear of some stimulus which previously has elicited an unwanted attraction (e.g., of a male fetishist for women's undergarments).

Barnum effect In personality assessment, the tendency of clients to accept uncritically an examiner's description of their character, even when the examiner has not based these descriptions on any analysis of test data.

Basic anxiety According to Horney, a built-in fear of finding oneself alone and helpless in a threatening environment. Various styles of personality development represent different ways of coping with this fear.

Behavior diary A record kept by a client of the time and day of occurrence as well as the events which immediately preceded or followed the enactment of a target behavior.

Biofeedback A technique for teaching an individual how to control his or her own physiological functioning by attaching the subject to devices which translate biological activity into a clearly perceptible stimulus, such as a tone or a flashing light. When the subject succeeds in altering his or her physiological activity, the tone or light signals the change.

Birth order The position in chronological order among siblings of a particular child in a family group.

Catharsis An emotional discharge which is assumed to occur following an aggressive act and to reduce the likelihood that the aggressive act

will be immediately repeated. Some investigators have maintained that catharsis can also be induced by watching violent movies and television programs, but the available evidence contradicts this hypothesis.

Central traits Five to ten personality characteristics that have a frequent and consistent influence on the behavior of a particular individual.

Cerebral cortex The portion of the brain which reached its greatest evolutionary development in human beings and which provides the capacity for language and abstract thought. It is divided into two halves, or "hemispheres."

Client-centered therapy A procedure devised by Rogers in which the therapist simply reflects back to the client what the client has just said, while at the same time maintaining a warm and accepting atmosphere.

Clinical judgment A therapist's subjective, often diagnostic, evaluation of the verbal and nonverbal content of an interview.

Closed interview An interview in which the client responds with a short answer or a choice to a series of questions posed by the therapist.

Cognitive behaviorism A variant on behavioral psychology which maintains that ideas, expectations, and memories are as much a part of behavior as actions and speech. It is assumed that these cognitive or covert behaviors follow the same laws of conditioning as the more active or overt ones, however.

Cognitive behavior modification A therapeutic technique which seeks to promote adaptive changes in the client's behavior by having him or her recite the proper sequence of steps to follow in acting out a new behavior and/or having the client witness the actions of a successful model.

Collective unconscious In Jung's analytical psychology, the accumulation of cultural symbols resulting from their frequent and consistent use extending across many generations.

Comprehensive system An alternative means of scoring the Rorschach inkblots devised by

Exner. Includes categories of "deviant verbalization," "autistic logic," and so forth.

Consciousness   That aspect of the mind which we call self-awareness or identity and which seems to us to be able to plan ahead and make spontaneous choices among alternative possibilities for behavior.

Coronary-prone personality   Also called *Type A* and characterized by very strong competitiveness, time-urgency, and needs for environmental control. This personality type appears to be especially susceptible to cardiovascular disease.

Correlational research   A research approach which involves taking various measurements on a group of people and seeing how scores on each measurement relate to scores on all the other measurements.

CPI   The California Psychological Inventory, a paper-and-pencil test used to determine the most salient traits in the personalities of "normal" individuals.

Criterion keying   Selection of items for a personality test in a way that includes those which are answered differently by members of a particular "criterion" group as compared with some control group (e.g., mental patients versus "normals").

Death instincts   Biological processes and urges which work toward an individual's self-destruction. The motivation to aggress against others results from a turning-outward of the death instincts.

Deinstitutionalization   An innovation in mental health care whereby patients are removed from custodial institutions as quickly as possible and returned to the wider community where they will be exposed to more "normal" reinforcement contingencies.

Disengagement theory   The hypothesis that as older people perceive their physical abilities to be declining they achieve the best psychological adjustment to the inevitability of death by withdrawing from the activities and social obligations of the workaday world.

Displacement   The redirection of frustration-induced aggression away from the frustrating agent and toward a substitute target. (See also *Frustration-aggression hypothesis.*)

Dizygotic twins   Twins who develop from the simultaneous fertilization of separate eggs and, though they share a common prenatal environment in the mother's womb, are genetically no more alike than any two siblings would be. Also called fraternal twins.

Dominance hierarchy   Among social animals, a pecking order which specifies who will be able to enforce compliance on whom in terms of gaining access to valued resources such as food or mates.

Early self   According to Allport, a sense of identity which develops by the age of 3 and includes an awareness of one's bodily capacities and limitations, the feeling states and evaluations that can be attached to one's personal name, and the perception that one's relationships with other people or even objects are important components of one's identity.

Ego   The conscious portion of the mind whose primary purpose is to devise plans for satisfying id impulses while at the same time protecting the individual's physical and psychological security.

Ego defenses   Mechanisms other than simple repression or denial by which the ego can remain unaware of unacceptable thoughts or wishes.

Ego integrity   The last of Erikson's psychosocial stages of personality development, at which the individual comes to accept his or her impending death along with the fact that his or her life has made its own significant contribution to the history of human existence. (See also *Psychosocial stages.*)

Electroencephalogram   A chart which records the electrial activity of the brain at various locations. The lines on the chart are sometimes referred to as "brain waves."

Empathy   The ability to feel another's feelings and to look at a situation from another's point of view.

Encounter group   A group organized for the

purpose of engaging in a candid exchange of feelings among participants, who are encouraged by a permissive setting to reveal thoughts and desires that they would normally conceal from others in their daily lives.

Epinephrine A substance naturally secreted by the adrenal gland whose effects on the body are to place it in a condition of "arousal" or readiness to fight or flee. Schachter argues that epinephrine-induced arousal underlies all strongly felt emotional states.

Equity norm A hypothesized cultural value which states that people should be rewarded in direct proportion to their deservingness.

Erotogenic zones Areas of the body which, when stimulated, produce feelings of sexual pleasure (especially the mouth, anus, and genitals).

Ethics of conscience In Hogan's model of moral development, the belief that right conduct consists in whatever one intuitively *feels* to be right, regardless of the precepts of the legal code.

Existentialism A philosophy which states that the individual exists simply by virtue of acting in the world and that the world exists because there are individual minds which perceive its existence. The special capacity of human beings is the ability to choose how they will perceive themselves and the world of which they are aware.

Experimental neurosis An emotional disturbance created by presenting an organism with an ambiguous stimulus that is similar in some respects to each of two conditioned stimuli which elicit incompatible responses.

Experimental research A research approach which seeks to cause a temporary change in the personality of one group (the experimental group) while leaving another group (the control group) unaffected. Differences in personality and behavior between the experimental and control group are attributed to whatever procedures were applied to the former but were not applied to the latter.

Experimenter bias Occurs when the researcher, who knows the hypothesis, unintentionally influences subjects' behavior so as to generate results which will confirm the researcher's expectations.

Extraversion A personality trait which consists of an interest in events and objects in the world outside oneself. Extraverts are likely to be active and sensation-seeking in their interactions with the world.

Face validity The degree to which items on a personality test have an obvious relationship to the trait that is being measured.

Factor analysis A mathematical technique for simplifying a complex array of information about a person which has been scored on a number of different dimensions. Dimensions whose scores are strongly correlated with one another are combined to form factors.

Field dependence A personality trait which reflects a tendency to be considerably influenced by the surrounding environment in making perceptual judgments. Also appears to be related to susceptibility to conformity pressures.

Fixed role therapy A procedure devised by Kelly in which a client is asked to act out behaviors which contradict his or her present role behaviors. This procedure has much in common with the technique of *psychodrama*.

Free association A procedure used in psychoanalysis in which the patient agrees to verbalize every idea that floats spontaneously into consciousness.

Frustration-aggression hypothesis The hypothesis that a block to a goal response (i.e., frustration) always produces a motive to aggress and that all aggression is preceded by frustration.

Functional analysis An attempt to discover the major environmental contingencies which are maintaining an individual's behavior. A behavior therapist would then seek to alter those contingencies so as to modify a problem behavior.

Functional autonomy The selection of goals to pursue not on the basis of immediate rewards or punishments but on the basis of what activities are most congruent with one's sense of selfhood or identity.

Genes Biologically active elements carried on the chromosomes which determine the expression of hereditary characteristics.

Gerontology The scientific study of human aging.

Halstead-Reitan Neuropsychological Test Battery A test consisting of various subtests of verbal and performance skills which is designed to assess the extent and location of any damage to the brain.

Heritability The extent to which the expression of a personal characteristic can be attributed to genetic factors.

Holtzman Inkblot Technique An assessment device which uses a large number of inkblots not in Rorschach's original set. Examinees are restricted to one response per card, and responses are scored on twenty-two well-defined variables.

Id In psychoanalytic theory, the source of energy for the mind, with which each infant is endowed in the form of instincts.

Identification Acceptance of the normative beliefs and role behaviors of another person out of a desire to be as much like that other person as possible. (See also *Norms* and *Roles*.)

Identity crisis A concern common among adolescents regarding whether or not the development of their interests is moving in a direction congruous with some social role.

Illusory correlation The tendency in clinical assessment to perceive statistical links between certain types of test data (e.g., inkblot descriptions) and various symptoms of personality disorder when there is in fact only a random association between test responses and symptoms.

Imitation The tendency for an observer to repeat the behaviors of another individual (the *model*). Imitation is especially likely to occur when an observer has witnessed the model being rewarded for his or her behavior.

Inferiority complex An individual's self-perception of being so physically or socially inferi-

or that it leads to self-defeating behaviors, such as depression, apathy, or even suicide.

Insight In psychoanalysis, the sudden breakthrough into conscious awareness of repressed wishes or memories which have caused neurotic anxiety.

Instrumental aggression Aggression which is primarily motivated by the expectation of reward but not by anger or any other strong emotion.

Internal control Belief that one is able to exert considerable influence over the outcome of major events in one's life.

Introversion A personality trait which consists of an interest in events occurring within oneself. Introverts are likely to be passive and sensation-avoiding in their interactions with the world.

IQ The intelligence quotient, or a measure of a person's abstract reasoning ability in comparison with other persons of the same age. On the most reliable tests, the IQ represents a combined score from ten to twelve diverse subtests.

Learned helplessness A condition in which an organism is unmotivated to respond because past learning has taught it that no behaviors will be successful in providing access to reward or relief from punishment.

Life crises Transition points in the development of adult personality at which sudden changes in interests and activities may be expected. These transitions are generally associated with movement from one age decade to another (teens to twenties, twenties to thirties, for example).

Life instincts Instincts which motivate behavior that promotes individual pleasure or survival (e.g., needs for food or water or the sexual urge).

Limbic system A set of relatively old (in evolutionary terms) structures in the brain which form the inner border of the cerebral cortex. These structures seem to be heavily involved in motivational and emotional states.

Lobotomy A surgical operation in which the part of the cerebral cortex that is located near the front of the head is detached from the rest of the brain. It was intended to be a technique for calming highly excitable mental patients.

Longitudinal study A strategy of conducting research on age-related characteristics in which the same group of persons is studied periodically from childhood through young adulthood and perhaps on into old age.

Mean Length of Utterance (MLU) A count of the average number of morphemes contained in a distinct grouping (i.e., an "utterance"). This count is used as one objective measure of a child's progress in learning a language.

Medical model A view which regards mental illness as analogous to infections and other physical ailments.

Mental age An age (in years and months) corresponding to how an "average" examinee would perform on an IQ test.

MMPI The Minnesota Multiphasic Personality Inventory, a paper-and-pencil test used to match a client's self-description of beliefs and feelings against those of mental patients in various diagnostic categories.

Monozygotic twins Twins who develop from the cleavage of a single fertilized egg and so share all of their genes in common. Also called identical twins.

Moral anxiety A fear on the part of the ego that it may be punished by the superego for imagining or acting out some socially unacceptable impulse.

Morpheme The smallest unit of meaning of a language (i.e., single words).

Motive to avoid success Reflected in fear of social rejection as a result of success, concern about one's normality following success, or denial that success has really occurred.

Need for achievement A motive to strive for success in setting and accomplishing important goals whose strength can be measured using scoring procedures applied by McClelland to people's responses to TAT pictures.

Neonatal abilities Abilities which appear so early in infancy that they seem to be primarily innate rather than learned (e.g., primitive imitative capacities or depth perception).

Neurons Cells in the brain and nervous system which transmit information from one location to another through an electrical and chemical process.

Neurotic anxiety Fear on the part of the ego that it will be unable to maintain the barriers it has erected to prevent conscious awareness and expression of socially unacceptable impulses.

Neurotic triad The Hypochondriasis, Depression, and Hysteria subscales of the MMPI; elevated scores on Hypochondriasis and Hysteria combined with a lower score on Depression are said to be characteristic of the anxiety neurotic.

Neurotransmitter A chemical messenger which is released by an activated neuron into the space separating it from another neuron. The neurotransmitter causes the receiving neuron to become activated.

Nonverbal communication Cues which reveal one's emotional state and which are transmitted by means of eye contact, posture, gestures, and so on.

Norms Socially accepted values which are supposed to regulate a person's overt behavior.

Oedipus complex Feelings of sexual attraction toward the opposite-sex parent and hostility toward the same-sex parent by the 4- to 5-year-old child. These feelings are finally resolved by an internalization of the values of the same-sex parent and the formation of the superego.

Open interview An interview in which the client defines the content and direction of the dialogue, except for an occasional probing question by the therapist.

Operant conditioning A type of learning in which a previously neutral stimulus (e.g., sight of a lever) comes to elicit a novel response (e.g., lever-pressing) as a result of the response being followed either by a reward (e.g., a food pellet) or relief from punishment (e.g., termination of shock).

Operational definition In therapy, a clear description of the problem behaviors which constitute the presenting complaint and which are targets for treatment.

Oral optimist A personality type distinguished by generosity, sociability, openness to new ideas, and a belief in better days to come. Supposedly a result of liberal nursing and late weaning as an infant.

Overcompensation Excessive striving to overcome perceived physical and social deficits.

Peak experience According to Maslow, a mystical or spiritual state in which a person feels he or she has attained insight into a great truth.

Personal constructs The categories used by an individual to summarize the complex social world and to predict others' behavior. This term is very close in meaning to *stereotype*.

Person-situation interaction The idea that both person variables and situation variables influence personality and that any theory of personality must take account of each of these sources of influence.

Person variables Causes of behavior which lie inside the individual, such as desires, habits, expectations, biological processes, and so forth.

Preoperational reasoning According to Piaget, this is the first major step in the cognitive development of a child after the period of infancy. Characterized by a belief in the permanency of objects that are outside of one's immediate sphere of action and capacities for delayed imitation and representational play.

Psychopathic personality A personality type characterized by a profound lack of empathy for the feelings of others and a lack of guilt for behaviors which have inflicted injury on others.

Psychosocial stages In Erikson's theory of personality development, eight periods in which the conflicts to be resolved are primarily social rather than sexual in content.

Radical behaviorism A school of psychological thought which holds that the goal of psychology is to understand the laws by which observable stimuli come to elicit observable responses and not to understand the working of inner mental processes and physiological events.

Reality testing The means by which the ego (conscious mind) evaluates the safety and practicality of its plans for satisfying the needs of the id.

Reflexive fighting In many species, violent behavior which is apparently an automatic response to sudden and extreme pain.

Reliability A statistical measure of the stability of a trait whose strength is purportedly being assessed by a personality test.

Repression Erection of a psychological barrier by the ego which prevents some personally threatening or socially unacceptable thought or wish from becoming conscious.

Respondent conditioning A type of learning in which a previously neutral stimulus (e.g., a bell) comes to elicit a preexisting response (e.g., salivation) as a result of frequent pairing with another stimulus which naturally elicits the response (e.g., sight of food).

Roles Patterns of behavior which are specified by norms; for example, the role of being a good parent. (See *Norms.*)

Schizophrenia A broad category of severe (psychotic) mental disorders characterized by emotional detachment from others, inappropriate and sometimes extreme emotional reactions, illogical thinking, delusions, and hallucinations.

Self A person's inner core of identity.

Self-actualization Development of interests, skills, and behavior in a way that is congruent with the individual's sense of self.

Self-concept The sense of personal identity. Some researchers have inferred that self-concept must exist in organisms which effectively use mirrors to gain information about parts of their bodies that are hidden from direct view.

Self-disclosure Revealing personal desires, fears, embarrassments, and so forth to at least one intimate other. Humanistic psychologists believe that self-disclosure is necessary for maintaining mental health.

Self-esteem Feelings of competence and pride which are established by early experiences of success in setting and accomplishing one's goals.

Self-realization According to Jung, an increasing openness to the expression of repressed desires, interests, abilities, and styles of thinking and behaving. This openness often occurs after the age of 60, when individuals have more leisure time available for self-examination.

Sex-linked genetic traits Traits whose expression is influenced by genes carried on the X or Y sex chromosomes and thus differ in their frequency of expression between females and males.

Sex roles Patterns of behavior which are expected to differ between socially "well-adjusted" men and women. (See also *Roles.*)

Sex-typing The development of interests and behaviors in boys and girls that are congruent with cultural expectations regarding "masculine" and "feminine" styles of thinking and acting.

Shaping The use of operant conditioning to develop behaviors which successively approximate some particular pattern desired by the trainer.

Situation variables Causes of behavior which lie outside the individual, such as the pressures and learning experiences provided by the physical and social environment.

Sixteen Personality Factor Questionnaire A paper-and-pencil test designed to place the individual on each of sixteen personality dimensions which emerged as independent factors in earlier research. (See also *Factor analysis.*)

Social responsibility norm A hypothesized cultural value which requires people to give resources to anyone whom they perceive as being in need of assistance.

Sociobiology A field of scientific study which seeks to investigate the possibility that altruism and other traits may have a genetic basis because of their evolutionary survival value.

Somatotype A measurement of physique devised by Sheldon which he believed to be related to various personality traits.

Split brain The result of a surgical operation in which a band of tissue connecting the two halves of the cerebral cortex is severed, thus preventing direct communication between the left and right hemispheres of the brain. Studies of patients who have undergone this operation reveal that each hemisphere has certain specialized abilities.

Stages of moral development According to Piaget and Kohlberg, distinct time periods in a child's social and maturational development at which his or her moral reasoning is at a stage-characteristic level of complexity.

Stimulus generalization The ability of other stimuli which are similar to a conditioned stimulus to elicit the conditioned response, though usually to a lesser degree.

Strong Vocational Interest Blank A paper-and-pencil test which measures the extent to which an examinee's interests and hobbies match those of members of various occupational groups. Used in vocational counseling.

Styles of aging Broadly distinguishable patterns of activities, interests, and social relationships by which people cope with advancing age. These patterns range from a quiet, "rocking chair" strategy to the continual substitution of new activities for those which have become difficult to maintain.

Subliminal perception Showing reactions to stimuli which are too weak to register in one's conscious awareness.

Subvocal speech Speech which was originally conditioned on an overt, vocal level but which later became a silent, internalized pattern of tiny muscle movements in the larynx. Behavioral psychologists have long held that what we call "thinking" consists of subvocal speech.

Superego An internal representation of the moral judgments of parents, teachers, and peers which rewards or punishes the thoughts and deeds of the ego.

Synapse The junction of two neurons. The space between them is called the synaptic cleft.

Systematic desensitization A procedure for removing internal anxiety or fear reactions which motivate unwanted tendencies to avoid certain people, animals, objects, or situations. The feared stimulus is vividly imagined while the client tries simultaneously to maintain a state of deep relaxation.

Temperament Emotional reactions and cognitive and behavioral aptitudes which are to some extent the product of a person's biological inheritance.

Terminal drop A sudden decline in a person's IQ score within the five years immediately preceding his or her death. It is an especially reliable predictor of imminent death among persons younger than 65 years of age.

Testosterone The sex hormone which predominates in males (though females manufacture some of it) and appears to be related to the motivation to engage in physical aggression.

Thematic Apperception Test An assessment device which presents clients with pictures of people in real-life settings. They are asked to make up a story which describes who the people are in the picture and what they are doing.

Thematic dispositions The tendency of people to seek out other persons and situations which are likely to activate as well as satisfy their most important needs.

Token economy A therapeutic procedure which relies on operant conditioning to teach new behaviors which are more adaptive than those currently in the client's repertory (e.g., coins might be given to inmates of a mental hospital for tasks like sweeping the floor and keeping their beds neat).

Traits Consistencies in beliefs, values, and behavior patterns across situations and across time.

Transference A patient's expression of strong emotions of love or hate for his or her analyst, in which the analyst is really a symbol for the true object of the patient's emotions.

Types Traits which are categorized in an either-or fashion; for example, honest vs. dishonest, warm vs. cold, and so on.

Unconscious mind A portion of the mind dominated by instincts, desires, and memories of which the individual does not want to be consciously aware. Unconscious impulses often find expression in dreams or Freudian slips.

Validity A statistical measure of the extent to which scores on a personality test relate to beliefs or behavior in a way that one would expect.

Vicarious learning Learning how to initiate new behaviors simply by watching other people being rewarded for engaging in them.

Word Association test An assessment technique in which the examinee is presented with a word or phrase and is asked to complete the thought suggested by this verbal stimulus.

XYY chromosome abnormality An addition of an extra Y chromosome to the XY pair which is present in every male child. Since it is the Y chromosome which determines maleness, research has been conducted to determine whether males having the extra chromosome are any more aggressive than normal XYs.

Yerkes-Dodson Law The proposition that peak performance on a task will be observed when internal arousal is neither too low nor too high but rather at some optimal moderate level.

INDEXES

NAME INDEX

Buell, J. S., 225
Buhler, C., 386
Bundy, R. A., 281
Burgess, M., 342
Burkhart, B. R., 180
Burnstein, E., 332
Burt, C., 177, 196
Burton, R. V., 9
Buss, A. H., 327, 333, 334
Buss, E., 334
Butcher, J. N., 168
Butler, J. M., 93
Byrne, D., 277

Caddy, G., 227
Calhoun, J. B., 341
Calhoun, K. S., 233, 240
Callaway, E., 203
Cameron, R., 230
Camino, L., 335
Campagna, A. F., 340
Campbell, D. P., 162
Campbell, D. T., 311
Campbell, M., 95
Cannon, W. B., 286, 288
Cantor, J. R., 342
Cantril, H., 79
Carey, G., 388
Carlsmith, J. M., 341
Carol, M., 95
Carthy, J. D., 325
Carver, C. S., 292
Cattell, R. B., 59, 173–175, 178, 249, 388
Caul, W. F., 257, 282
Cautela, J. R., 218
Chapman, J. P., 155
Chapman, L. J., 155
Charlesworth, W. R., 257, 258
Chess, S., 248, 250
Chomsky, N., 261, 263
Chorover, S. L., 210
Ciminero, A. R., 218
Clark, D. F., 224
Clark, G., 353
Clark, R. D., 316
Cleckley, H., 340
Cline, V. B., 343
Cohen, M. E., 342
Coke, J. S., 318

Collette-Pratt, C., 388
Colten, M. E., 368
Comrey, A. L., 171
Conklin, P. M., 251
Contes, B., 315
Cook, K. V., 364
Cooper, H. M., 360
Coopersmith, S., 283
Corey, D. M., 358
Cortes, J. B., 192
Costa, P. T., 73, 101
Costanzo, P. R., 360
Courrier, S., 343
Cowan, E. L., 278
Cowan, P. A., 305, 306, 327
Cox, R. H., 210
Cozby, P. C., 284
Craighead, W. E., 218
Crano, W. D., 179
Crassweller, K. D., 228
Croft, R. G., 343
Cross, D. T., 183
Cross, H. J., 338
Crowne, D. P., 283
Cumming, E. M., 376

Dahlstrom, L. E., 167, 175
Dahlstrom, W. G., 167
D'Andrade, R. G., 366
Daniels, L. R., 312
Darley, J., 313, 315–318, 363
Darwin, C., 258
Dashiell, J. F., 107
Davidson, H. H., 139
Davidson, L. A., 200
Davidson, M. A., 192
Davies, J. D., 189
Davis, W. L., 293
Davison, G., 238
Deaux, K., 364
DeCarlo, T. J., 390
DeCharms, R., 146
Deci, E. L., 293
Dement, W. C., 42, 43, 44
Denenberg, V. H., 254, 269
Dengerink, H. A., 340
DeSoto, C. B., 237
deVilliers, J. G., 263
deVilliers, P. A., 263

Garmezy, N., 199, 200
Garton, W. H., 228
Gatti, F. M., 192
Gazzaniga, M. S., 268
Geen, R. G., 327, 334
Gelder, M. G., 224
Gerbner, G., 329
Gerson, S., 236
Geschwind, N., 262
Getter, H., 147
Gewirtz, J. L., 253
Gfeller, E., 390
Giebink, J., 231
Gilligan, C., 304
Ginsberg, B. E., 205, 326
Glenn, R. N., 181
Glueck, E., 192
Glueck, S., 192
Goffman, E., 87
Gold, V. J., 225
Goldberg, P., 147
Goldberg, S., 358
Goldfarb, W., 278
Goldfried, M. R., 219
Goldman, B. D., 353
Goldman, J. R., 304
Goldman-Eisler, F., 249
Goldstein, S. G., 201
Goodenough, D. R., 360
Goodman, E., 2
Goodman, J., 231
Goodstein, L. D., 138, 143, 175
Gormly, J., 17, 18
Gottesman, I. I., 199
Gottlieb, A., 316
Gough, H., 169, 171
Gould, R., 387
Gould, S. J., 311, 369
Graham, J. R., 181
Greenberg, R., 44
Greene, D., 293
Greenfield, P. M., 266
Greenwood, M. M., 228
Gregory, R. J., 171
Greif, E. B., 305, 362
Gribben, K., 388
Grieser, C., 44
Griffitt, W., 341
Gross, J., 43

Gross, M. L., 182
Grotevant, H. D., 252
Groutt, J. W., 85
Grusec, J. E., 315
Guilford, J. P., 197
Guillemin, R., 206
Gur, R. C., 268
Gutmann, D., 390
Gynther, M. D., 183

Haan, N., 305
Haider, M., 277
Haigh, G. V., 93
Hake, D. F., 332
Hall, C. S., 36, 50, 94–96, 98, 301
Hall, J. A., 137, 362
Halstead, W. C., 200
Hamill, P., 30, 31
Hancock, T., 274, 360
Harlow, H. F., 244, 279, 282, 352
Harlow, M. K., 244, 279, 282
Haronian, R., 192
Harris, B., 109
Harris, F. R., 225
Harris, M. B., 333, 352
Harrison, R. H., 44
Harrower, M., 151
Hart, B. M., 225
Harter, S., 340
Hartlage, L. C., 361
Hartmann, H., 64
Hartshorne, H., 9
Hartup, W. W., 339
Harvey, M. A., 180
Hathaway, S. R., 162, 163, 182
Havighurst, R. J., 376, 385
Hayes, C., 261
Hayes, K. J., 261
Hayflick, L., 383
Haynes, H., 254
Heaton, R. K., 202
Hebb, D. O., 254
Heidegger, M., 65
Held, R., 254
Henry, W., 376
Henry, W. E., 143
Henson, D. E., 228
Heron, W., 281

Oliver, R. R., 266
O'Malley, P. M., 283
Ordy, J. M., 382
Ornstein, R., 268
Ottinger, D. R., 251
Ovesey, L., 183

Page, M. P., 334
Palmore, E. B., 390
Papalia, D., 382
Parham, I. A., 385
Parke, R. D., 335
Parnell, R. W., 192
Parsons, O. A., 202
Pastore, N., 332
Patterson, C., 237
Patterson, G. R., 219, 326
Paul, G., 222
Pavlov, I. P., 4, 105–108
Pedersen, P. B., 94, 97, 98
Pedhazur, E. J., 368
Peng, M. T., 382
Perry, H. S., 73
Peterson, D. R., 9
Peterson, R. F., 217, 234
Pettigrew, T.F., 76
Phares, E. J., 293
Phillips, L., 231
Piaget, J., 264, 265, 267, 302
Pierce, J., 277, 278
Pigg, R., 327
Piliavin, I. M., 316
Piliavin, J. A., 316
Pilkonis, P. A., 284
Pisano, R., 333
Pollak, J. M., 249
Postman, L., 277
Potkay, C. R., 391
Premack, A. J., 261
Premack, D., 261, 262
Prigatano, G. P., 202
Provence, S., 257

Quevillon, R., 231

Rabin, A. I., 9
Rabin, A. K., 342

Rabkin, J. G., 338
Rachman, S. J., 155, 223
Rafferty, J. E., 147
Rands, M., 392
Rapport, S., 233
Rathus, S. A., 218
Rawls, D. J., 170
Rawls, J. R., 170
Rayner, R., 109
Rebelsky, F. G., 260
Reckless, W. C., 170
Rees, L., 192
Regan, D. T., 314
Reichard, S., 386
Reid, J. B., 219
Reitan, R. M., 200–202
Reynolds, N. J., 221, 258, 262
Rheingold, H. L., 253, 258, 364
Rice, M. E., 315
Richards, M. P. M., 257, 261
Rickers-Ovsiankina, M. A., 151
Riegel, K. F., 383
Riegel, R. M., 383
Riley, M., 381–384
Ring, K., 275
Risley, T. R., 114, 221
Ritchie, E. D., 293
Ritter, B., 229
Ritzler, B., 151
Roback, H. B., 148
Robin, A., 231
Robson, K. S., 258
Rodin, J., 316, 389
Rogers, C. R., 91–100, 159
Roiphe, H., 351
Rokeach, M., 379
Romanczyk, R., 226
Romer, N., 366
Rorschach, H., 139
Rose, S. D., 220
Rosen, A., 180
Rosen, B. C., 366
Rosenhan, D. L., 153, 236, 317
Rosenman, R. H., 290
Rosenthal, B., 100
Rosenthal, D., 198, 199, 292
Rosenthal, R., 22, 183
Rosenthal, T., 120
Ross, D., 119, 327
Ross, H., 253

Sokolov, A. N., 230
Solano, C., 237
Solar, D., 361
Sole, K., 316
Solomon, R. L., 112, 278
Sonneschein, D., 43
Spence, J. T., 289, 368
Spence, K. M., 289
Sperry, R. W., 237, 268
Spitz, R., 257, 278
Sprafkin, J. N., 219
Spuhler, J. N., 197
Stachnik, T. J., 181
Stainton, N. R., 181
Stampfl, T., 223
Staub, E., 318
Stein, A. H., 315, 329
Sternlieb, J. L., 305
Stich, M., 314
Stolz, L. M., 238
Stonner, D., 342
Storr, A., 324
Stover, D., 231
Stricker, L. J., 75
Strong, E. K., 161
Stuart, F., 218
Stuart, R. B., 218
Sullivan, H. S., 72, 73
Summers, J., 368
Sundberg, N. D., 136, 137, 141, 169, 180, 192, 207, 234
Suomi, S. J., 279
Sweet, W. H., 204, 210
Szasz, T., 215, 233

Tallmer, M., 390
Taub, B, 342
Taylor, D. A., 284
Taylor, H. A., 228
Taylor, J. A., 289
Taylor, S. P., 333, 340
Teasdale, J. D., 295
Teddlie, C., 341
Teevan, R. C., 366
Tenney, A. M., 191
Terman, L. M., 354
Terrace, H. S., 262
Terris, W., 311

Tetenbaum, T. J., 368
Thomas, A., 248, 250, 251, 270
Thomas, M. H., 343
Thompson, J. N., 310
Thompson, W. R., 251
Thoresen, C., 238
Thorndike, E. L., 4, 108
Tilker, H. A., 312
Tobin, S., 385
Toch, H., 339
Tresemer, D. W., 367
Trickett, P., 184
Trivers, R. L., 310
Troll, L., 379
Tuddenham, R. D., 9
Tuke, D. H., 227
Tumin, M. M., 352
Turner, C. W., 334
Turner, S., 231
Tyler, L. E., 354, 358

Ullmann, L. P., 233
Ulrich, R. E., 181, 341

Vaillant, G. E., 387
Valenstein, E., 208, 209
Valins, S., 289, 340
Van de Castle, R. L., 301
Vandenberg, B., 282
Vandenberg, S. G., 193, 197
Van Praag, H. M., 207
Veitch, R., 341
Vernon, P. E., 77, 80
Voegtlin, W., 223
Vondracek, F., 329
Vygotsky, L. S., 126, 230

Waber, D. P., 361
Wade, T. C., 141
Wallace, R. K., 95
Walters, R. H., 118–119, 327
Warburton, F. W., 173
Washburn, S. L., 310
Watson, J. B., 4, 108–109
Watson, R. R., 109
Webb, W. B., 43

SUBJECT INDEX

Hereditary factors in personality:
    depression, 292
    extraversion, 198
    genes and chromosomes, 192
    IQ, 195–198, 208
    phenylketonuria (PKU), 193
    recessive traits, 192–193
    schizophrenia, 198–200
    twin studies, 193–194
Holtzman inkblot techniques, 142
Horney, Karen:
    biography, 64
    theory of personality, 64–65
Hull, Clark L., 116
Human nature:
    in behavioral psychology, 5, 109–110
    in humanistic psychology, 98–99
    in psychoanalysis, 40
Humanistic psychology, 91, 100
    phenomenology in, 92, 283–284
    repression in, 92–93
    therapeutic approaches in, 93, 137
Humor and psychoanalysis, 50–51
Hysteria, 38, 47

Id, 40
Identity crisis, 62–64
Illusory correlation, 153–154, 181
Implosion (flooding) technique, 223
Individual psychology:
    birth order, 52, 273–275
    inferiority complex, 52
    overcompensation, 52
    repression in, 92–93
    self (ego) in, 273–275
    social interest, 52
    striving for superiority, 52
    style of life, 52
    therapeutic approaches, 53, 136
Infant abilities:
    conditioning of, 252–253
    emotional expression, 257–258
    perceptual and motor, 254–257
    recognition of faces, 255
    self-recognition, 280–281
Infants, stages of development, 256–257
Inferiority complex, 52
Inhibition, reciprocal, 222
Innate grammar, 261

Intelligence (IQ) tests:
    aging and, 381–384
    birth order and, 275
    Burt controversy, 177–178, 196–197
    distribution of scores, 177–178
    g factor, 178–179
    measurement of, 175–176
    mental age vs. chronological age, 176–177
    national decline in scores, 184
    racial differences in scores, 183–184, 207–208
    reliability and validity, 179
    Stanford-Binet, 175
    subscales of WISC, 177
    use in diagnosing learning disorders, 203–204
    Wechsler scales (WAIS and WISC), 176–177
Internal vs. external control of reinforcement:
    assessment of belief in, 293
    and depression, 295
Interviews:
    closed, 136
    open, 136
Introversion (see Extraversion vs. introversion)

Jung, Carl Gustav, 53–55
    (See also Analytical psychology)
Just world hypothesis, 313
Justice, distributive, 312–313

Karma, 97
Kelly, George A.:
    biography, 80
    fixed-role therapy, 85–86
    Role Construct Repertory (Rep) Test, 83–85
    theory of personality: fundamental postulate, 82
        personal constructs, 81–82
Kirkegaard, Søren, 65

Language development:
    in apes, 261–262
    behavioral explanation for, 260–261
    dispositional explanation for, 261
    relevance to personality, 263
    stages of, 263–264
    and thinking: behavioral explanations for, 264
        dispositional explanations for, 264–265
Latency period, 49
Law of effect, 108, 110

Personality disorders (*Cont.*):
  psychosomatic ailments, 227, 343
  schizophrenia, 198–200
  in young adults, 387
Personality traits (*see* Traits)
Personality type, definition of, 8
Personology, definition of, 5, 73
Phallic character, 49, 249, 301
Phenomenology:
  in Asian psychologies, 94
  in existential psychology, 66
  in humanistic psychology, 92, 283–284
Phenylketonuria (PKU), 193
Phoneme, 260
Phrenology, 189–190
Press vs. needs in Murray's theory of personality, 74
Piaget, Jean (*see* Stages of development)
Play, 281–282
Pleasure principle, 40
Power, need for, 147
Primary process, 41
Prisoner-of-war syndrome, 295
Projection, 47
Projective tests (*see* Assessment techniques, projective tests)
Proprium, Allport's concept of, 76
Prosocial behavior:
  altruism and, 309
  criticisms of normative explanations, 315–316
  and cultural evolution, 310–311
  definition of, 308–309
  field studies of rescuers, 317–318
  internal arousal and, 318
  juvenile features as elicitor, 311
  personality traits and, 312–314
  sex differences in, 362–363
  situational determinants: anticipated costs, 317
    conditioning of empathic responses, 314
    diffusion of responsibility, 316–317
    liking for recipient, 316
    modeling and imitation, 314–315
    mood, 317
  sociobiological explanations for, 309–312
Psychoanalysis:
  aggression in, 40, 48, 324
  anaclitic depression, 278–279
  anxiety: castration, 49, 301, 397
    moral, 45, 276
    neurotic, 46, 276
    realistic, 47

Psychoanalysis (*Cont.*):
  cathexis, 40
  components of personality: ego (self), 41
    id, 40
    superego, 41, 301
  death instincts, 40, 48
  displacement, 40, 46
  dreams and, 41, 42, 311
  ego defenses, 47, 275–277
  free association, 39, 136
  humor and, 50–51
  identification, 49
  influence of, 50–51
  inner conflict, 45
  insight in, 39
  life instincts (libido), 40, 48
  masochism, 41, 350, 400
  narcissism, 41
  neurotic symptoms: compulsions, 47
    "Freudian slips," 46–47
    hysteria, 38, 47
  Oedipus complex, 49, 249, 301, 350–351
  origins of, 38–40
  penis envy, 49, 64–65, 301, 350, 352
  pleasure principle, 40
  primary process, 41
  psychosexual stages: anal, 48–49, 249
    genital, 50
    latency period, 49
    oral, 48, 249
    phallic, 49, 249, 301
    reality principle, 41
    repression, 46, 275–277
    secondary process, 41
    sublimation, 46
    synthesis, 46
    therapeutic approaches, 39, 136
    transference, 39
    unconscious mind, 39, 48
    wish fulfillment, 41
Psychological Response Classification System (PRCS), 233
Psychosexual stages (*see* Psychoanalysis, psychosexual stages)
Psychosocial stages of Erik Erikson, 61–63, 376–380
Psychosomatic ailments, 227, 343
Psychosurgery, 204, 209–210

Q-sort technique, 93